Y0-CLH-814

Officers of the Society
1962–1963

(Term of office expires March 1 of the year indicated.)

WALTER W. COOK
(1965)
University of Minnesota, Minneapolis, Minnesota

EDGAR DALE
(1964)
Ohio State University, Columbus, Ohio

LAURENCE D. HASKEW
(1963)
University of Texas, Austin, Texas

ROBERT J. HAVIGHURST
(1963)
University of Chicago, Chicago, Illinois

HERMAN G. RICHEY
(1965) (Ex-officio)
University of Chicago, Chicago, Illinois

STEPHEN M. COREY
(1964)
Teachers College, Columbia University, New York, New York

RALPH W. TYLER
(1965)
Center for Advanced Study in Behavioral Sciences, Stanford, California

Secretary-Treasurer

HERMAN G. RICHEY
5835 Kimbark Avenue, Chicago 37, Illinois

CHILD PSYCHOLOGY

CHILD PSYCHOLOGY

The Sixty-second Yearbook of the National Society for the Study of Education.

PART I

By

THE YEARBOOK COMMITTEE
and
ASSOCIATED CONTRIBUTORS

Edited by

HAROLD W. STEVENSON WITH THE ASSISTANCE OF
JEROME KAGAN AND CHARLES SPIKER

Editors for the Society

NELSON B. HENRY AND HERMAN G. RICHEY

19  63

Distributed by THE UNIVERSITY OF CHICAGO PRESS • CHICAGO, ILLINOIS

The responsibilities of the Board of Directors of the National Society for the Study of Education in the case of yearbooks prepared by the Society's committees are (1) to select the subjects to be investigated, (2) to appoint committees calculated in their personnel to insure consideration of all significant points of view, (3) to provide appropriate subsidies for necessary expenses, (4) to publish and distribute the committees' reports, and (5) to arrange for their discussion at the annual meeting.

The responsibility of the Society's editors is to prepare the submitted manuscripts for publication in accordance with the principles and regulations approved by the Board of Directors.

Neither the Board of Directors, nor the Society's editors, nor the Society is responsible for the conclusions reached or the opinions expressed by the Society's yearbook committees.

Published 1963 by

THE NATIONAL SOCIETY FOR THE STUDY OF EDUCATION

5835 Kimbark Avenue, Chicago 37, Illinois

First printing, 10,000 Copies

Printed in the United States of America

The Society's Committee on Child Psychology

WALTER W. COOK

Dean, College of Education
University of Minnesota
Minneapolis, Minnesota

JEROME KAGAN

Head, Psychology Department
Fels Research Institute for the Study of Human Development
Yellow Springs, Ohio

CHARLES SPIKER

Professor and Acting Director,
Iowa Child Welfare Research Station, State University of Iowa
Iowa City, Iowa

HAROLD W. STEVENSON

(*Chairman*)

Director, Institute of Child Development, University of Minnesota
Minneapolis, Minnesota

Associated Contributors

ALBERT BANDURA

Associate Professor of Psychology, Stanford University
Stanford, California

URIE BRONFENBRENNER

Professor of Psychology and of Child Development and
Family Relationships, Cornell University
Ithaca, New York

JOHN A. CLAUSEN

Director, Institute of Human Development
University of California
Berkeley, California

VAUGHN J. CRANDALL

Senior Research Associate
Fels Research Institute for the Study of Human Development
Yellow Springs, Ohio

DOROTHY H. EICHORN

Administrator, Harold E. Jones Child Study Center, and
Associate Research Psychologist, Institute of Human Development
University of California
Berkeley, California

SUSAN M. ERVIN
Assistant Professor, Speech Department and Center for Human Learning
University of California
Berkeley, California

ELEANOR J. GIBSON
Research Associate, Department of Psychology, Cornell University
Ithaca, New York

WILLARD W. HARTUP
Associate Professor, Iowa Child Welfare Research Station
State University of Iowa
Iowa City, Iowa

LAWRENCE KOHLBERG
Assistant Professor, Department of Psychology
University of Chicago
Chicago, Illinois

WICK R. MILLER
Assistant Research Linguist, Center for Human Learning
University of California
Berkeley, California

BRITTON K. RUEBUSH
Assistant Professor of Child Psychology, Institute of Child Development
and Center for Personality Research, University of Minnesota
Minneapolis, Minnesota

MICHAEL A. WALLACH
Associate Professor of Psychology, Duke University
Durham, North Carolina

RICHARD H. WALTERS
Assistant Professor, Department of Psychology, University of Toronto
Toronto, Ontario

SHELDON H. WHITE
Assistant Professor, Department of Psychology, University of Chicago
Chicago, Illinois

JUDITH R. WILLIAMS
Graduate Research Psychologist, Institute of Human Development
University of California
Berkeley, California

Editors' Preface

The Board of Directors devoted several meetings during 1959 and 1960 to the study and discussion of proposals for a yearbook on child psychology and development. It was agreed that there was urgent need for a yearbook that would present a comprehensive picture of our present knowledge about the behavior and development of normal children. At the October meeting of 1960, the Board scheduled the publication of the yearbook for 1963 and voted to ask Professor Harold W. Stevenson, Director of the Institute of Child Development, University of Minnesota, to accept the chairmanship of a committee to plan and prepare the yearbook. Professor Stevenson, who had advised Professor Ruth Strang and other members of the Board during the preliminary discussions, accepted the chairmanship and, shortly thereafter, nominated as contributing authors a number of outstanding scholars in the field of child psychology and development.

That a new synthesis of research and thought in the field was needed is evidenced by the extensive bibliographies of important and, for the most part, recent studies and, also, by the readily observed changes that have occurred in research interests and emphases —changes so fundamental that the committee felt itself compelled to depart radically from the traditional frameworks that have been used to present child psychology in the past.

It is hoped that this volume will serve students of education and psychology by providing them with a synthesis of the findings of recent research in child psychology and that it will acquaint all persons interested in the field with a better understanding of child behavior. This yearbook makes it clear that an understanding of the child is not easily acquired, but it makes even clearer the importance of achieving the best possible understanding.

HERMAN G. RICHEY and NELSON B. HENRY
Editors for the Society

Table of Contents

Introduction

HAROLD W. STEVENSON

The last decade has been one of the most exciting and productive in the history of child psychology. There has been a growing recognition outside the field that something interesting was happening, but the rapidity with which the field has grown makes it impossible for most people to keep up with current research. The last general review of research in child psychology was the second edition of Carmichael's *Manual of Child Psychology*, published in 1954. Most of the recent studies are available to the interested reader only in professional journals. Books of readings and elementary textbooks in child psychology have tended to present small, detailed reports or to treat the material in a somewhat general fashion. There is no single volume which gives a comprehensive picture of the current status of our knowledge about the behavior and development of normal children. It is especially appropriate, therefore, that the National Society for the Study of Education has chosen child psychology as the subject for one part of its Sixty-second Yearbook.

An exhaustive review of current research would be impossible in other than a manual or handbook. This volume was not intended to be either of these; it does not include all topics of current concern or frequent reference to the vast number of earlier studies which form the background for contemporary child psychology. The volume is nearly twice as long as was originally planned. It could easily have been twice its present length. In organizing the volume, an attempt was made to break away from the traditional frameworks that have been used in presenting child psychology in the past. It would be difficult to incorporate the new trends in research in such frameworks, for the new studies are not determined by age of the child or category of behavior or by modes of conceptualization which were popular earlier. The book concentrates upon an integrated discussion of currently active and representative research areas in child psychology. There is no series of chapters on infancy, preschool children, and the like; developmental changes in behavior are discussed in each chapter whenever possible. The common division into chapters on such subjects as social behavior and emotional behavior has been discarded. Again, no attempt was made to include a discussion of the rapidly growing literature on the deviant or abnormal child. Approximately 2,000 studies, most of them conducted during the past decade, are reviewed, with the goal of providing the reader with a picture of the breadth, vitality, and richness of our current knowledge about children.

We could have attempted to include discussions of the practical application of our knowledge, but have chosen not to be concerned with the application of research studies in educational, family, or other contexts. Field studies, which utilize laboratory research as a basis of problems, hypotheses, and methods, but which translate them from the laboratory to the applied situation are needed before generalizations can be made concerning where and how the results of the more basic research can be meaningfully and confidently applied.

Child psychology of the past decade differs greatly from that of earlier years. Longitudinal studies, observational methods, and a developmental orientation have largely been replaced or supplemented by short-term experimental studies of the effects of particular variables on child behavior. The "variable" approach has played an increasingly significant role in research in general psychology, and its impact on child psychology has been strongly felt during the past decade.

Behavior is governed not only by psychological but also by biological and sociological forces. It is appropriate, therefore, that the volume begins with a discussion of current research on the biological and sociological correlates of behavior. Certain broad behavioral processes, such as learning, thinking, and perceiving, have always been of concern to the child psychologist, and a group of chapters reviews the current status of our knowledge about these processes. There is a group of chapters on more specific aspects of behavior, such as aggression, anxiety, and dependence, which have always been of interest to the child psychologist, but which have received major attention in recent years. The final chapter deals with the theoretical backgrounds of child psychology.

We have been extremely fortunate in getting a group of the most able research persons in child psychology to contribute chapters to this volume. All of the authors are actively engaged in doing research in the areas in which they are writing and can, therefore, bring to the chapters the freshness and thoughtfulness that come from active involvement in the issues being discussed. The volume is heavily documented. The references included with each chapter should be helpful to the individual interested in pursuing research in a particular area, or in reading the studies discussed in greater detail. Each of the chapters could, of course, become a book in itself. In fact, the attempt to condense the material has made it impossible for the authors to elaborate on many of the provocative findings and issues.

We wish to express our appreciation to the authors for the skill and speed with which they have done their work, and to the National Society for the Study of Education for providing the impetus for bringing the material together. It is hoped that the book helps to meet the need that is so clearly present. Research is fruitless unless it is read and unless it has some consequence in everyday life. We have a long way to go before we attain a comprehensive knowledge of child behavior, but if research continues to develop at its current rate we will be closer to such a goal much sooner than anyone would have believed twenty years ago.

CHAPTER I

Biological Correlates of Behavior

DOROTHY H. EICHORN[1]

Human biology encompasses the study of all the structural and functional characteristics of man, from the cellular to the organismic level, and their ontogenesis. Advances in technology have made it possible to extend cytologic and histologic studies to the point where behavioral correlates may be sought even at these levels, and progress in both the biological and physical sciences has resulted in the emergence, within the broader interdisciplinary fields of biochemistry and biophysics, of highly specialized disciplines such as histochemistry and cytochemistry. The topics singled out for discussion here are ones which offer a group of studies with some direct behavioral implications. Each section demonstrates a different way of systematizing the biological data and their potential behavioral correlates.

The first section deals with a major branch of biology, genetics, beginning with a consideration of the ultimate somatic and behavioral consequences of variations at the cytological level. It then moves to biochemical studies, which reveal some of the metabolic steps between gene and trait, and concludes by reviewing newer approaches to the modes of genetic transmission of molar characteristics. Another approach is represented in the second section. Here the embryology, microscopic anatomy, and electrophysiology of a specific tissue (neural) and of a particular functional system (the visual) are considered. The final section exemplifies an approach at the organismic level, examining many behavioral ramifications of rate of maturing. This concept is derived from the observation that, on the average, developmental changes in morphological, physio-

1. The assistance of Francena Hancock, Jane Hunt, and Donald McVarish is gratefully acknowledged.

logical, histological, and biochemical characteristics occur at similar rates. Although indices of physical maturity are often structured in terms of puberal development and have most often been used in studies of adolescents, individual differences in physical maturity exist and can be assessed long before adolescence (**11, 150**). Further, the trend toward reduction in age of the onset of puberty continues (**152**), and ages which were once considered to belong to the period of childhood must now be classified as adolescent, while the behavioral patterns associated with puberal changes appear progressively earlier (**79**).

Genetics

Progress in human genetics has been made at such an accelerated pace during the past decade as to render a comprehensive review of even recent research impracticable. Basic to this rapid advance has been the acquisition of new techniques. As has so often happened in the history of science, real break-throughs have followed improved methodology. It seems most profitable, therefore, to present here some examples, drawn from three branches of genetics, which illustrate the general nature of the theoretical and technical developments.

CYTOGENETICS

One consequence of the rapid rate of gain in our knowledge of human genetics is that statements made with reasonable confidence today may have an historical aura about them tomorrow. This statement is particularly applicable to cytogenetics. Texts in child psychology published as recently as 1957 give the diploid number of chromosomes in man as 48 rather than 46. For it was only in 1956 that the first reports (**51, 156**) appeared of counts made on chromosomes which had been separated well enough to permit accurate enumeration. The techniques used in those studies, and other techniques which have been devised since, hinged upon the development of methods for growing cells *in vitro* and for coping with the tendency of mammalian chromosomes to clump together. Techniques for separating chromosomes include pretreatment of cultures with colchicine to stop meiosis in metaphase, the use of hypotonic saline to swell the cells, and a "squash" method for pressing cells into a single layer (**26**). Some of the smaller chromosomes are difficult to identify even with the methods now available. It has been possible, however, for workers from different laboratories to agree on a common system of nomenclature (**8**).

Application of the new cytological techniques not only established the normal chromosomal complement in man as 46 but also led to the discovery of individuals with abnormal numbers of chromosomes. Not all variations in chromosome number result in overt abnormalities, but the first cases shown to have variant numbers of chromosomes were developmental sex deviants. Prior to 1956, research on human beings with sexual anomalies had depended upon a staining method for the determination of "chromosomal sex." In 1949, Barr and Bertram (**9**) had discovered a small stainable body in the nuclei of nondividing nerve cells of some cats. Further research demonstrated that this material was present in many other tissues, in man as well as in the cat, and was found in the normal female but rarely in the male (**59**). Persons whose cells contained the stainable bodies, now called "sex chromatin," were referred to as "chromosomal females," and those whose cells lacked sex chromatin were called "chromosomal males." These labels became suspect when it was discovered that some infants had cells with the staining properties of one sex, but a somatic constitution more characteristic of the other sex (**115**). Further discrepancies became apparent with cytological identification of the sex chromosomes of developmental sex deviants. Persons with Klinefelter's syndrome usually have an XXY chromosomal sex type (**75**). They are males in most phenotypic respects (although the testes are very small and rarely produce mature sperm), yet one-half to three-fourths are sex-chromatin positive (**165**). In Turner's syndrome the phenotype is, in general, female, but development is rather infantile and there is complete, or almost complete, gonadal agenesis. About 80 per cent of women with this syndrome are "chromosomal males," or sex-chromatin negative (**165**). The sex chromosome complement in most cases is XO, i.e., one sex chromosome is lacking (**53**). There are individuals displaying the stigmata of these syndromes who have chromosomal sex types other than XXY or XO (**10, 27, 167**). Some of these individuals are mosaics. They have, for instance, cells of both the XX type and the XXY type.

A human female with three X chromosomes has been located (**73**). The characteristics of this individual as well as those of persons with Klinefelter's syndrome make it clear that the presence of an extra X chromosome, whether in an XXX or XXY combination, does not result in a "super-female," but rather in a disturbance of sexual development.

The phenotypes of persons with sex chromosome abnormalities also suggest that the theory of sex determination which had been derived from studies of aberrant complements of sex chromosomes in Drosophila may not be generalizable to man. It appears that in man the Y chromosome is male-determining; its presence usually results in a male phenotype. In Drosophila phenotypic sex seems to be a function of the balance between autosomes and the X chromosome complement, such that the combination of a full set of autosomes and one X chromosome results in a normal male phenotype, but the presence of an additional X chromosome produces a phenotypically normal female. Skeletal age studies of children with Klinefelter's and Turner's syndromes (**153**) support the male-determining role of the Y chromosome in man. This research also helps to explain the genesis of the sex difference in rate of development. Children with an XXY chromosomal constitution are equal in skeletal development to normal boys (XY). Those with an XO constitution show the more accelerated maturation typical of normal girls (XX).

In addition to the variations on Klinefelter's and Turner's syndromes, other cases of human sexual anomalies have been described in which the sex chromosome complement was not abnormal. It is impossible to review these here, or to list all of the qualifications which should be made regarding the phenotypic manifestations of sex chromosome aberrations. There are a number of good sources to which the interested reader may refer (**10, 27, 59, 147**). The implications of such reports are, however, of great theoretical importance. The existence of persons with normal sex chromosome constitution but abnormal sexual development indicates that it is possible for other genetic and environmental factors to override the XX-XY mechanism of sex determination and makes it necessary to distinguish between sex determination and sex differentiation.

The psychological aspects of chromosomal and phenotypic sexual aberrations have also been studied (**117, 129**), albeit less thoroughly than the cellular ones. Particularly intriguing to the behavioral scientist have been contrasts between sex of rearing and chromosomal or phenotypic sex (**62, 111, 113**), but the relevant literature ranges from behavioral assessments of children with idiopathic precocious puberty (**63, 112, 131**) to surveys of the concordance of homosexuality in twins (**87**). A review of such investigations can be found in Fuller and Thompson (**55**). The tenor of the conclusions which can be drawn from psychological studies of persons whose genotypic and phenotypic sex are inconsistent has been stated lucidly by Stern: "Psychologically, most of these persons regard themselves as belonging to that sex which they phenotypically represent or approach" (**146:** 241). This generalization emphasizes the importance of the distinction between sex determination and sex differentiation.

Anomalies resulting from variations in chromosome number are not limited to the sex chromosomes. A number of abnormalities associated with autosomic trisomy in man have been reported (**27, 33, 123, 135**). Some of these, however, may actually be additional instances of a third X chromosome. One of the most important break-throughs consequent upon the acquisition of cytological techniques which made it possible to count and classify human chromosomes was the demonstration that mongolism is the result of the presence of an extra autosome (**95**). Mongolism is now often referred to as "Trisomy 21," because the cells of afflicted individuals contain three rather than two of the small autosomes designated as 21 in the standard nomenclature. Cases of mongolism have been reported in which the chromosome number was 46 or 48 (**52, 124**). In the latter instance, the individual also was afflicted with Klinefelter's syndrome, the additional X chromosome making a total of 48. A count of 46 would be obtained if the additional chromosomal material were attached to another chromosome, or if the person had the sex chromosome constitution of Turner's syndrome (lacking one sex chromosome) and the autosomal constitution of mongolism (an extra autosome).

Mongolism also represents an instance in which the chromosomal defect is present in all the cells of the afflicted individual but not necessarily in those of either of his parents. The extra autosome is the result of nondisjunction occurring during parental, probably maternal, gametogenesis. Nondisjunction occurs frequently in overripe eggs of the rat (**166**). It is possible that a gene for nondisjunction occurs in man. The operation of such a mechanism in some cases is suggested by the presence of modified forms of some of the stigmata of mongolism in otherwise normal relatives. Future research can be expected to be concentrated on the causes of this type of nondisjunction and on the nature of the intermediary metabolism in mongolism.

BIOCHEMICAL GENETICS

Advances in human genetics along another front have resulted from the development of new or improved biochemical techniques. Enzymatic methods for tracing the steps in the pathways of intermediary metabolism have made it possible to specify the nature of the metabolic error in a number of genetic disorders (**69, 110**). Both enzymatic and other biochemical methods have been devised which permit the identification of heterozygous "carriers" who cannot otherwise be recognized and the early identification of persons homozygous for genes responsible for metabolic errors (**70, 107, 138**). Detection of carriers is not only of practical importance but also serves to establish the heritability of an abnormality and to clarify the mode of genetic transmission (**139**). A knowledge of the biochemical nature of the metabolic error and early identification of the homozygote mean that in some instances environmental adjustments can be made to prevent the deleterious consequences of the genetic defect. All of these points are illustrated in the work on hereditary galactosemia. The elucidation of the biochemistry of this disease, like that of phenylketonuria, is a classic in the annals of biochemical genetics. Galactosemia is a rare metabolic abnormality which appears early in infancy. It had been known for some time that afflicted individuals were mentally retarded, had a variety of tissue lesions, could not tolerate galactose, and excreted galactose in their urine. A genetic basis had been suspected because of a number of reports of the familial incidence of the disorder. The chapters dealing with the biochemistry of the disease, however, were begun within the last decade, and they have not yet been finished. During the early 1950's, Leloir outlined the steps (**97, 98**) in the metabolism of galactose and predicted (**96**) the existence of the enzyme which has since been shown to be defective in galactosemics (**85**). The first attempt to identify heterozygotes (**66**) revealed that one or both parents of galactosemic children had a lowered tolerance for galactose. Almost simultaneously, two major discoveries were reported. Maxwell and his associates (**105, 106**) succeeded in developing enzymatic techniques for the analysis of the metabolism of galactose. Schwartz *et al.* (**137**) demonstrated that galactose-1-phosphate accumulates in the red blood cells of galactosemics. The next step—a comparison of the enzymatic activity of the erythrocytes of galactosemics, their parents, and normals—led to the definite identification of the defective enzyme in galactosemia (**92, 93**). Subsequent studies revealed the existence of this enzymatic defect in the liver of galactosemics and in the umbilical cord blood of susceptible infants (**7**).

Although galactose is an important constituent of the cellular matrix of the central nervous system, it is not an essential nutrient because it can be produced in the body from glucose or glucose metabolites. Milk, the major item in the diet of most infants, contains galactose. It has been shown (**14**) that if a galactose-free diet is introduced sufficiently early (probably within the first three months of life), susceptible individuals are almost completely insured against the development of the anomalies characteristic of galactosemia. Obviously, early diagnosis is critical. Knowledge of family pedigrees is an aid in identifying parents who may be carriers. If parental tests are positive, restriction of milk in the diet of the mother during pregnancy and testing of the child at birth are definitely indicated.

Continuing efforts are being exerted to devise simple, specific tests for the detection of both heterozygotes and homozygotes and to unravel the exact biochemical basis of the tissue lesions in galactosemia. If the next decade of research is as productive as the last, solutions to these problems may confidently be expected.

BEHAVIORAL GENETICS

In the research reviewed thus far, the traditional methods of human genetics—collating pedigrees in terms of their conformity to Mendelian ratios, estimating heritability from familial correlations, and comparing trait variance in monozygotic and dizygotic twins—have been subordinated to cytological and biochemical methods. Statistical analysis is, however, the only approach open to the behavioral geneticist who deals with human familial data. The effects which he observes are much farther removed from the primary actions of genes, and the physiological steps between genes and traits are largely unknown. Further, most behavioral characteristics are graduated rather than segregated. Continuous distributions imply the cumulative effects of a number of genes and cannot be predicted from simple application of the principles governing single-factor inheritance. Despite these difficulties, there has been a resurgence of interest in behavioral genetics within recent years. The impressive progress in this field, documented in Fuller and Thompson's *Behavior Genetics* (**55**), has been achieved primarily through the efforts of a small corps of investigators engaged in programmatic research with lower animals. They have studied the interaction of genotype and environment and the developmental aspects of this interaction. Investigators who work with animals are able to manipulate genotypes in a way which those who work with human data cannot, but their substantive accomplishments also stem from the development of improved techniques for both the collection of family-line data and the statistical analysis of these data (**49, 104**). The suitability of different selection and breeding procedures for the analyses to be made is better understood. Controls for pre- and postnatal maternal influences have been introduced in the form of transplantation, crossbreeding, and cross-fostering techniques (**16, 60, 61**). Use of the diallel[2] cross has made it possible to obtain in one generation information which otherwise would require several generations of backcrosses. Two methods used to advantage in research with animals are also applicable in human behavioral genetics: reduction of complicated patterns of behavior to their component parts and application of statistical techniques appropriate to the analysis of data from small families of unequal size (**49**).

For the most part, a vigorous, systematic attack has been lacking in the research on man. Exceptions are to be found in a few labora-

2. All possible crosses of the genotypes being studied are obtained. Each parental strain is crossed with every other, and "from each pair of lines involved *two* crosses are made—the cross A x B, and its reciprocal B x A, for example. . . . In addition, there will be mating within the parental lines themselves" (**17:** 75).

tories where multivariate and factor-analytic methods are being used, primarily in the study of the inheritance of personality characteristics (**18, 19, 47, 48**). Multiple test batteries provide a larger number of more molecular psychological measures and a source of intercorrelations for factor analysis. Heritability estimates may be made either from scores on individual tests or from factor scores. Cattell, who has worked with both children and adults, finds that many of his "personality source traits" derived from factor analyses are reasonably persistent across a wide age range. He has proposed a "multiple hypothetical variance analysis method" to be used with factor scores (**18, 19**). "It designates four sources of individual differences in any trait: *between-family environmental* differences; *between-family hereditary* differences; *within-family environmental* differences; and *within-family hereditary* differences" (**19:** 147). Ideally this method requires data from eight groups of subjects, representing four degrees of genetic relationship (identical twins, fraternal twins, siblings, and unrelated persons) and two rearing conditions (raised together or apart from birth). The results of investigations concentrating on a factor analytic approach are encouraging. Reports from different laboratories (**15, 149, 155, 160**) agree in indicating that spatial and verbal (comprehension and fluency) factors are strongly dependent on genotype. Cattell concludes that the value of his multiple-variance model is confirmed by the fact that, "in general, the variance ratios obtained, and the directions of the correlations, fit expectations from the psychological natures of the particular source traits concerned, and are in line with any previously known, independent findings on these traits" (**19:** 158).

An innovation in the traditional correlational method of studying quantitative inheritance has been made possible by the accumulation of longitudinal data. Several studies have appeared which trace the development of parent-child similarities in intelligence from infancy through late childhood or adolescence (**12, 84**). Honzik's paper (**67**) aligning such data from a sample of children reared by their own parents with Skodak and Skeels' data (**141**) from children reared by adoptive parents demonstrates quite strikingly that both the level and the pattern of increase of correlation between children and their biological parents are almost identical despite the difference in circumstances of rearing.

One problem in the interpretation of correlations between scores of parent and child or of sibling and sibling on standard intelligence tests is that test content differs with age level. This difficulty can be circumvented by administering identical tests to both family members at comparable ages. Three investigations in which this method was used have been reported. One is from the Scottish Survey (**108**) and is based on the scores of sets of sibs each of whom was tested at eleven years of age. The other two studies are preliminary reports. The first (**29**) used parent-child test data obtained when each subject was of nursery-school age. The second (**36**) drew on longitudinal tests of both parent and child from early in the first year through the fourth year. Investigations of the latter type also permit inferences about familial resemblances in the *pattern* of intellectual development. The research project from which these data were reported also has data on siblings. Comparison of parent-child and sib-sib correlations at similar ages may provide some insight into environmental influences. When standard intelligence tests are available for parent and child or for pairs of siblings, similarity analysis can be extended by the extraction of factor scores.

Twin studies have long been a primary source of data for human genetics. The discovery of new immunological factors has provided further refinement of similarity diagnosis (**130, 143**). Although the diagnosis of zygosity is now almost completely reliable, other more serious limitations of the twin method have become apparent. It is now known, for example, that the prenatal environments of monozygotic (MZ) twins may differ more than those of dizygotic (DZ) twins. The differences which may result from such environmental variations are illustrated in a case described by von Sydow and Rinne (**151**). A pair of MZ, monochorionic, diamniotic twins differed markedly in weight and hemoglobin values during at least the first ten months of life. Bias may also exist in twin studies unless unselected samples are used, since twins who are similar in appearance are more easily located. Another difficulty is that indices of heritability estimated from comparison of MZ and DZ twins and those derived from familial aggregations may be quite different, as, for example, in mongolism. Concordance is almost invariable between MZ twins but rare for DZ twins, yet the familial incidence of mongolism is not great (**2**). Stern (**146**) gives an excellent summary of the limitations of the twin method, and Price (**126**) has outlined the sources of primary biases in twin studies. Combining the twin and familial resemblance methods, as has been done by Cattell, avoids some of the pitfalls inherent in the twin method. Kallman (**86**) introduced this twin-family method into the study of mental disorders. In the future the twin method can be expected to contribute most to an understanding of the environmental factors responsible for lack of expression, or decreased expressivity, of a known genetic predisposition. A major advance will have been made when psychologists and sociologists are able to specify the nature of the environmental variables which produce such suppression.

Vision

ANATOMICAL DEVELOPMENT OF THE SENSORY SYSTEM

This section will be concerned only with those peripheral and central structural changes which have the most direct implications for function, a knowledge of which can contribute most to the design and interpretation of experiments utilizing visual cues, e.g., studies of perception and discrimination learning.

Several recent texts (**8, 45, 103**) deal comprehensively with the embryology of the eye, but only in Keeney's (**89**) concise tables is the chronology of ophthalmic development extended through to early adulthood. Conel's (**20–25**) work on the microscopic anatomy of the infant cortex provides the major source of new developmental data on the central visual system. Until the publication of his series of volumes, knowledge about the postnatal development of the human cerebral cortex was limited largely to gross changes in size and the progression of myelination.

Retina.–In the "mixed" retina of man, color vision and the more precise discriminations of form and motion are mediated by the photopic, or cone, system. The development of maximal acuity is dependent upon an increase in the number of cones, lengthening and narrowing of cones, and lateral displacement of other cell layers in the macula. This pattern is not established until the seventh fetal month, although outside of the macular region progressive thinning of the bipolar, horizontal, amacrine, ganglion, and nerve fiber layers is concomitant with growth in retinal area. Postnatal development of the fovea and pericentral area is most rapid during the first four months. Mann's (**103**) and Barber's (**8**) statements of this fact have been quoted as meaning that the development of the macula is complete by four to six months, but Keeney's tabulations show gradual changes to adolescence.

In the fovea the ganglion cells decrease to a two-cell depth by the eighth fetal month, and by term both the ganglion cells and bipolar cell layers are reduced to a single row. Even these layers have disappeared by adolescence, except for a few scattered ganglion cells. The cones, which were poorly developed and stubby at birth, are noticeably thinner and better developed by eight weeks, but slight increments in length and decrements in thickness continue through puberty. The concentration of cone nuclei increases from the single-layered state at birth to a triple layer by 16 weeks. Thereafter, the increase in number is slower, the maximum depth of 4 or 5 tiers being achieved by adolescence.

Some of the improvement of visual acuity with age, particularly in the dark, may result from the enlargement of the pupil as well as from changes in the retina. The pupil remains small during the first year, expanding thereafter to a maximum at adolescence (**89**). Keeney also notes that during late childhood the optic axis is displaced laterally so that at puberty it strikes the retina closer to the fovea.

Visual pathways.—Dekaban (**28**) reports that at birth the cell layers of the lateral geniculate bodies are essentially like those of the adult, but the cells are smaller and their nuclei are relatively large in proportion to the amount of cytoplasm. Nissl bodies are found within the cells, although in lesser numbers than at lower levels. Older data indicate that myelination begins centrally at the seventh lunar month and moves distally, progressing into the optic nerve during the last fetal month. Sometimes by term, but more usually by ten weeks, the optic nerve is myelinated as far as the *lamina cribosa,* where medullation ends. Conel (**20**) observes that many fibers in the thalamo-occipital radiations have a fair amount of myelin at birth, and he notes that throughout infancy the vertical exogenous fibers in the core of the gyri immediately subjacent to the primary visual afferent area are more heavily myelinated than fibers within the occipital lobe. Little myelin is added within the cortex during the first month, but a general postnatal acceleration of myelination is apparent subcortically. Although the rate of medullation is slower after infancy, increases in the amount of myelin along nerve tracts have been observed until about the sixtieth year (**171**).

Cerebral cortex.—Conel's descriptions (**20–25**) of the microscopic anatomy of the human cortex at birth and at 1, 3, 15, and 24 postnatal months are based on detailed examinations of a small number of brains at each age. The changes occurring in nine criteria are elaborated for each of the six horizontal laminae and the subdivisions of III, IV, V, and VI in from 34 to 46 cortical areas.

Since little is known about the functional properties of the structures examined, interpretations of the developmental changes are largely speculative. Although it is possible that the type, size, and quantity of neurons are related to function, Conel points out that fiber connections are, in all probability, the most important determiners of function, since the microscopic structure from area to area within the cortex is very similar. In general, the internal cortical laminae are more precocious in their ontogenetic development, and the degree of development of cells is directly related to their size. For example, throughout infancy the extra-large pyramidal cells in V are more advanced, and the small cells in II, least advanced. The innermost cell layers, particularly V, are believed to have efferent functions, whereas lamina IV is considered to receive incoming sensory impulses and is permeated in the primary visual area by fibers from the thalamo-occipital radiations. In IVb and IVc in this area are some peculiarly shaped horizontal cells which are not found elsewhere in the cortex and have been thought to be specifically sensory cells. However, within layer IV in the primary visual area there are also large Meynert cells which seem to be efferent neurons. All sensory areas, but particularly the visual, are characterized by a dense mesh of axons of Golgi type 2 cells in lamina IV. These cells have short processes, establishing contact only with near-by cells. The network of their axons increases noticeably throughout infancy, except from three to six months.

During the first three months, the Cajal-Retzius cells and their processes in lamina I degenerate. Almost none of these cells are found at six months. On the other hand, the terminal branches of apical dendrites ascending to this lamina increase throughout the first two years. These changes are of particular interest because recent work (**128**) suggests that they are related to changes in the characteristics of evoked responses.

Except for statements comparing development of the primary motor area (FAγ) and the primary somesthetic area (PB) the developmental sequences outlined in the discussions below and in Tables 1 to 3 pertain only to the primary visual area (OC). At birth FAγ is the most advanced area in the cortex, followed in order by PB and OC. The rate of postnatal development of OC often exceeds that of FAγ and PB; so that, at least by some criteria, OC becomes as well developed as these other areas at some time during infancy.

Two of Conel's criteria are rather general morphological characteristics: (*a*) *width* of cortical areas and laminae and (*b*) *neuronal density* per unit volume. Total width increases only during the first month and between the third and sixth months, but increases in at least some of the laminae occur throughout infancy (see Table 1). Since neurons do not multiply after birth, an increase in width is usually accompanied by a decrease in density. An inverse relationship is not invariable, however, and there are also reversals in the age trends and variations from area to area and from lamina to lamina. These fluctuations are accounted for, at least in part, by the fact that width and density are affected not only by neural growth but also by other histologic changes, e.g., vascularization and development of supporting cells. Decrease in density is slight during the first month, but marked during the next five months, being greatest in layers IV and VI and least in III and V. Between six and 15 months, density is further reduced in all laminae except III and V. The reduction is at a less accelerated rate, but OC shows greater decreases than PB or FAγ. From 15 to 24 months, decreases are noted only in some cells of V; reduction in density is much less than in PB.

The majority of Conel's measures assess specific components of neural development. Increments in the (*c*) *size of cell bodies* are summarized in Table 1. Dendrites do not become more numerous except on the small cells in II, which even at three months lack the definitive number of basal dendrites. There are, however, definite increases in the (*d*) *length, caliber and compactness of the axons and dendrites* and (*e*) *number of pedunculated bulbs* throughout infancy. The few exceptions, as well as sites of particular increment, are given in Table 1. Arborization of cellular processes enlarges the surface available for the transmission of impulses. The function of the pedunculated bulbs is not known, but they resemble receptor cells, are found only on dendrites, and may serve to extend the receptive area.

Increments in the (*f*) *size and number of tangential, horizontal,* and *vertical exogenous fibers* and of *subcortical association fibers*

TABLE 1

WIDTH OF CORTICAL LAMINAE, CELL BODY SIZE, AND DEVELOPMENT OF CELLULAR PROCESSES*

Age in Months	Width of Laminae	Cell Body Size	Length, Caliber, and Compactness of Cellular Processes; Bulbs and Myelin
1......	Increase in all except III.	Slight increase, except granular and small pyramidal cells in II and IV. Increase more consistent in V than in III and IV.	Increase in bulbs, but little increase in length and caliber. Development in OC greatest in III; elsewhere in cortex is in V. Axons of extra-large pyramidal cells in V have a little myelin.
3......	Increase in all except I and III.	Marked increase, particularly in large cells in V and IIIc.	Increase by all criteria. Axons of many of large cells in V and VI and of Golgi type 2 cells in IV have some myelin. Increase in bulbs particularly great on dendrites of Meynert cells in IV.
6......	Increase in all except V and VI.	Slight increase, except in II and some cells in V.	Increase by all criteria in Meynert cells in IV. Little increase in size of dendrites of even larger cells in III, V, and VI, but myelin on axons of these cells, and more bulbs on dendrites of cells in V and VI. Number of cells whose axons have branches increased, particularly in III.
15......	Increase in all except II and III.	Increase, greatest in II and IV. Some cells in III, V, and VI now as large as comparable cells in PB.	Increase by all criteria. Axons and dendrites about as well developed as those in most advanced region in PB. Number of secondary and tertiary branches of axons of some cells increases.
24......	Only V and VI increase.	Increase only in II, IVa, and V.	Increase by all criteria. Bulbs less numerous than in best-developed region in PB. Meynert cells in IV have about as many bulbs as large ordinary and special pyramid cells in V. In II there has been an increase in bulbs, in apical dendrites and collateral branches, and in terminal branches of pyramidal cells from III.

* Data from Conel (**20–25**).

(see Table 2) add to the volume of the cortex and to the complexity of the neuropil. These fibers are axons from cell bodies located elsewhere than in the laminae in which the fibers are found and must conduct impulses from a distance, but their source is not known. Some of the vertical fibers are undoubtedly projection fibers from subcortical centers. Others are probably efferent fibers to subcortical centers or intralaminal fibers. Vertical fibers ascend to progressively higher levels at each age from one to 24 months. Conel

TABLE 2

DEVELOPMENT OF EXOGENOUS AND SUBCORTICAL ASSOCIATION FIBERS*

Age in Months	Development
1......	Increase in number and size of all except horizontals. Order of quantity still: vertical, tangential, subcortical, horizontal. Some verticals and subcorticals have a little myelin.
3......	Increase in number and size of all fibers. Subcorticals now second in number to verticals. Myelination greatest on verticals. Number of myelinated verticals equal to most-advanced region in PB. Some horizontals in IV, V, and VI have myelin. A very few verticals reach IV.
6......	Increase in number and size of all fibers. Order of quantity now: vertical, subcortical, horizontal, tangential. Verticals in all laminae and horizontals in V equal in number to region in PB where these fibers are most numerous. A few more verticals reach IV.
15......	Number of all fibers and amount of increase in all except horizontal equal to less-advanced regions in FAγ and slightly greater than best-developed region in PB. Percentage increase of horizontals in II, III, IV, and about equal to most rapidly developing region in PB and greater than any other region in isocortex. Fiber size equal to best-developed region in PB. Even some small fibers myelinated. Verticals ascend higher than elsewhere in isocortex, most end in IVb, and a few higher.
24......	No increase in number. All fibers increase in size. More fibers myelinated except in II and IIIa. Most verticals end in IVb, some in IVa, and a few in IIIc.

* Data from Conel (**20–25**).

suggests that the tangential and horizontal exogenous fibers and the subcortical association fibers may be intracortical connections.

In addition to the increases in the cytoplasm of cells and their processes, (*g*) *myelination* of both endogenous and exogenous axons adds to the size of the cortex. The pattern of myelination of both types of axons is included in the pertinent tables. Myelin is not necessary for function, but it does serve to insulate axons and, at least to some extent, seems to be associated with more mature electrophysiological responses (**71**). Conel's statements that axons are unmyelinated are based on staining methods and should be regarded as relative. Myelin can be visualized with the electron microscope on fibers which do not stain with hematoxylin.

Conel also examines such aspects of differentiation as (*h*) the transformation of *chromophil substance* into Nissl bodies (see Table 3), and (*i*) the development of *neurofibrils* (see Table 3). The protein synthesis which produces growth of nerve cells and their processes seems to be associated with the metabolism of ribonucleic acid (RNA), and Nissl bodies contain high concentrations of RNA. There is considerable evidence to indicate that variations in visual stimulation affect the concentration of RNA and the quantity and dispersion of Nissl bodies (**133**). In addition to changes in the form of the chromophil substance, its quantity in the cytoplasm of the cell body and among the dendrites gradually increases. The function of the neurofibrils is unknown. They appear in the axons and dendrites earlier than in the cell bodies and differentiate more slowly than the Nissl bodies.

The histologic development of OC at two years does not yet equal that of the adult. As can be noted from Table 3, the differentiation of Nissl bodies and neurofibrils is not complete in all cells. There will be further increments in the length and caliber of nerve fibers and in the thickness of the myelin sheaths. A comparison of Conel's data on widths with other data for the adult (**171**) indicates that between the end of infancy and adulthood laminae I, II, and III decrease while IV, V, and VI widen. There are also some slight further reductions in neuronal density, particularly in lamina V (**17, 171**).

ELECTROPHYSIOLOGICAL RESPONSES TO VISUAL STIMULATION

Retinal.—The electroretinogram (ERG) is probably generated in the inner segments of the receptor cells and the outer region of the bipolar cells (**134**). The former may contribute more to the negative a-wave, and the latter to the positive b-potential. Neither the ganglion cells nor the optic nerve seems to contribute to the ERG. Only two components of the ERG, the initial a-wave and the larger b-wave which follows, have been studied developmentally.

The majority of investigations of the ERG of the human infant have been conducted by Zetterström, who used healthy infants with normal fundi and media free of opacities as subjects. In her original study (**173**) records were obtained from 35 newborn infants, 14 of whom were re-examined every two or three months for about one

TABLE 3

DIFFERENTIATION OF CHROMOPHIL SUBSTANCE AND NEUROFIBRILS*

Age in Months	Chromophil	Neurofibrils
1......	Little change. Even in largest cells is in form of peripheral agglutinations and granules in nuclei of cell bodies.	No evidence of differentiation.
3......	Many extra-large pyramidal cells in V have small, well-formed Nissl bodies in cell body and a few in proximal end of apical dendrites. These cells more advanced than those in less well-developed regions in PB. Larger cells in IV contain very small dark clumps of chromophil and a few Nissl bodies, but large amorphous clumps more numerous than in V. No small cells contain Nissl bodies.	Largest cells in V have rows of granules.
6......	Small clumps of chromophil and Nissl bodies more numerous in all large cells in IV, V, and VI, and extend into dendrites in larger numbers and for greater distances.	Largest cells in V have granules connected by small strands, but no beaded structure. Giant stellate cells of Meynert in IVb second only to extra-large pyramidal cells in V in differentiation; most granules arranged in longitudinal rows, but a few dendrites have strands of granules.
15......	All cells contain a few small, well-formed Nissl bodies. Small clumps and Nissl bodies more numerous in proportion to large clumps and extend farther along apical and basal dendrites. Quantity and differentiation in large stellate cells of Meynert in IV about equal to extra-large pyramidal cells in V, but stain less darkly and have more large clumps.	Marked advance over six months. Neurofibrils more numerous than longitudinal rows of granules in extra-large pyramidal cells in V; are still some scattered granules within cell bodies, but axons and dendrites have only rows of granules or neurofibrils. These cells better developed than comparable cells in most advanced regions in PB. Meynert cells in IVb have neurofibrils, but less numerous than extra-large cells in V.
24......	Some of larger cells in IV, V, and VI have only Nissl bodies, but no small cells contain only Nissl bodies. Cells in IIIc, IV, V, and VI as well differentiated as those in FAγ and PB, and some contain more chromophil in proportion to size of nucleus than in PB.	Large cells in IV as well differentiated as largest cells in V; dendrites contain only neurofibrils, are a few scattered granules in cell bodies. Differentiation in III less advanced than IV and V, but these three laminae about as well developed as most-advanced regions in PB.

* Data from Conel (**20–25**).

year. Illuminances of 20 to 80 meter-candles (m.c.) were used with all subjects. Neonates who did not respond to the higher intensity were also tested with a stimulus of about 1600 m.c. Stimuli of these intensities elicited either no response or only a slight rise in the base line until the infants were two or three days old. At this age a low voltage b-potential of longer latency and duration than that of the adult was detectable in all records. There was no a-wave, and at the end of the first year an a-wave was present in the ERGs of only three of the 13 infants tested. By this time the latency and duration of the b-wave had decreased to the adult mean, and the amplitude had increased to the lower limits of the adult range. Two findings of this first study—the absence of an ERG during the first few days of life and the late appearance of the a-wave—are contradicted by later experiments (**68, 175**).

The study of full-term infants was followed by work (**174**) with 30 infants born 1 to 10 weeks before term. Here Zetterström explored the relative influences of maturity and of environmental conditions, such as exposure to light, on the first appearance of the ERG. That both degree of maturity and extra-uterine factors affect the time of appearance is indicated by the fact that although in general the delay in appearance was greater the more premature the infant, the ERG did appear as promptly in infants born only a few weeks before term as in the full-term infant.

Zetterström's third investigation (**175**) was of the flicker ERG in 15 infants aged birth to eight weeks. Flicker responses to stimulating intensities of 50–200 lux were detectable in the records of all infants aged two to three days, and low frequency flicker was occasionally recorded during the first 24 hours at intensities of about 1000 lux. All of these early flicker ERGs were of a scotopic (monophasic) type. Before the end of the first week fusion frequency had increased to about 35 per second, and flicker could be obtained at intensities as low as 5–10 lux. Further, a transition from a scotopic to a photopic (biphasic) type of flicker response could be discerned at high intensities. Among infants aged six to eight weeks flicker could be induced at an intensity of less than 1 lux, and maximum fusion frequency had risen to 50 per second. Definite transition from scotopic to photopic flicker with sharper b-waves was produced by stimulating intensities of more than 10 lux. Scotopic flicker can be evoked in adults with an intensity of .5 lux, and photopic flicker with fusion frequencies as high as 70 per second is obtained with intensities of 10–1000 lux.

Zetterström's results with flicker demonstrate that it is possible to obtain a scotopic ERG during the first 24 hours and a-waves by the end of the first week. The clinical method of Karpe (**88**) used by Zetterström in her first two studies yields an ERG determined primarily by the scotopic elements. Subjects are dark-adapted for only five minutes. Even adult ERGs obtained with this method sometimes lack the a-wave. Flicker electroretinography at flash rates of above 20 cycles per second incorporates several variables (short exposure, light-adaptation, and off-effects) which accentuate the photopic, and reduce the scotopic, components of the ERG. More recently Horsten and Winkleman (**68**) have shown that single flashes of higher intensities than those used by Zetterström evoke both a- and b-waves immediately after birth, even in the premature, if the infant is sufficiently dark-adapted.

Data on the development of the amplitude of the b-potential after infancy were obtained by Zeidler (**172**). She assembled a large series of ERGs from earlier studies on adults aged 20 to 80 years. These she supplemented with her own data on adults and on boys and girls aged five to 20 years. The method was essentially the same as that used by Zetterström in her first two studies. Amplitude rose from a mean of approximately .38 mV. in the 5 to 10 year group to a maximum of approximately .42 mV. at 11 to 20 years. Among males, amplitude declined after 20 years, but among females it remained constant through 50 years, declining thereafter.

Amplitude of the ERG is directly related to intensity of the stimulus and area of stimulation, and, to a considerable extent, the two variables are interchangeable. Enlargement of retinal area with age is one factor producing increasing amplitude. In studies relating the development of the ERG to the differentiation of the receptors in the rabbit, Noell (**121**) found that increments in the amplitude of the b-waves occurred concomitantly with lengthening of the outer segment of the receptors. He infers that growth of the latter is accompanied by increased concentration of rhodopsin.

Cortical.—Cortical responses to both isolated and repetitive flashes of light have been observed in the electroencephalogram (EEG) of the human infant. Such responses can be recorded from electrodes placed over the occipital cortex, but do not appear in simultaneous tracings from electrodes attached elsewhere on the scalp (**35, 38**). We shall consider first the potentials evoked by a single stimulus. The most comprehensive data available are from a recent paper by Ellingson (**38**), extending his earlier observations on full-term newborn infants (**39**) to a detailed report on both full-term and premature neonates. A preliminary account of developmental changes, based on both cross-sectional and longitudinal data, is included.

Bipolar recordings were made on 622 full-term and 71 premature infants, all free from abnormality at the time of recording. Full-term infants were first examined within five days after birth, and premature infants between the first day and the third week. Some full-term infants were retested while still in the hospital. Efforts were made to retest premature infants at one-week intervals until discharged from the hospital. One or more additional longitudinal records were obtained from 107 infants at ages up to about 29 weeks post term. Fourteen adults were also tested. Amplitude and latency comparisons can be made only with adults tested under the same conditions, because these parameters are especially influenced by stimulating conditions.

Research with cats and rabbits (**40, 71**) indicates that, in the course of development, the first response which can be elicited is a surface-negative wave, usually monophasic. Next is a biphasic response in which the negative component is preceded by a brief low-voltage positive wave. With increasing age, the amplitude of the positive phase becomes greater relative to that of the negative component, and some responses may consist of only the positive wave. Among Ellingson's subjects, the primitive, completely negative wave was seen significantly more often in the first or second tests of premature infants (11.1 per cent) than in those of full-term infants (2 per cent). The initially positive biphasic response appeared in subsequent records from babies whose first responses contained only the negative component. The fact that the more mature form of the evoked response was typical of most infants suggests that the visual system of man develops more rapidly than that of other mammals (**40, 71, 128**), except primates (**122**).

The most salient developmental change was a decrease in latency.

A brief report by another investigator (**41**) confirms the observation of longer latencies among premature infants. Ellingson also found a significant decrease in latency occurring within the first few days post term. The number of subjects in each of his age groups beyond two weeks was small, but the plot of latency against age from five to six weeks before term to over 29 weeks after term suggests that the relationship is not monotonic. Latency decreased gradually to three or four weeks post term, then rapidly to seven or eight weeks. Thereafter, the curve leveled off. However, the mean latency for adults was sufficiently shorter than that for the oldest group of infants to indicate that a further reduction takes place sometime after 29 weeks.

Despite developmental changes and considerable inter-individual variation in wave-form, amplitude, and latency, intra-individual consistency in these characteristics of specific evoked responses was pronounced. Individual differences in latency were particularly stable; variations in amplitude within one subject were more common. Amplitude tended to decrease with age. Nevertheless, with the younger subjects it was often necessary to allow a longer interval between stimuli in order to evoke a second response as large as that elicited by the previous stimulus. This phenomenon is termed "fatigability" and is characteristic of other young animals (**71**). Ellingson observed that some neonates gave no response to a second flash unless stimuli were separated by several seconds. For others, a one-second interval was sufficient. At times, however, continued stimulation resulted in increased amplitude or produced a response although the initial stimulation had elicited none.

"Photic driving" of brain waves in response to intermittent photic stimulation (IPS) has been observed in the human adult (**157, 164**) at frequencies of 1 to 60 cycles per second, although the greatest amount of driving occurs between 7 and 20 cycles per second. Experimental work with monkeys suggests that photic driving represents a low level of cortical activity, and is a response only slightly more complex than that occurring in the optic nerve and lateral geniculate body. Generalized anesthesia, bilateral temporal lobectomy, and experimental concussion all enhance driving, while lesions of the retina, optic tracts, and striate cortex impair driving (**162, 169**).

Intermittent photic stimulation is used as an activation technique for the diagnosis of pathology, and a number of clinical studies using IPS with children having overt or suspected disorders have been reported (**64**, **94**). There are, however, only a few developmental studies of photic driving in normal subjects. The first attempt to alter the cortical potentials of infants by repetitive visual stimulation appears to be that of Walter and Walter (**163**). Subjects between the ages of six weeks and 70 years were included in their exploratory study of the central effects of sensory stimulation. Normative data are not given, and the authors mention only that "in most children below the age of six the response is very small compared with the amplitude of the resting rhythms and may not be detected" (pp. 76–77) without the use of a frequency analyzer.

Eichorn (**35**) studied the development of electroencephalographic and autonomic responses to visual and auditory stimulation during early infancy. Only the data on photic driving will be reviewed here. Cross-sectional records were obtained from 38 healthy infants, seven to 81 days after birth. Five of the subjects were born from three to seven weeks before term, but they were assigned to age groups on the basis of postnatal age because their reactions to stimulation corresponded to those of full-term infants of comparable postnatal, rather than gestational, age.

Although the incidence of driving was considerably less than that which has been reported for adults (**157**, **164**), the general characteristics of the response to photic activation among the infants paralleled those of adults: (*a*) driving was recorded only from the occiput; (*b*) there were marked individual differences in the amount of driving, even within one age group; (*c*) the greatest amount of driving was obtained at those frequencies at which an infant had, or soon would have, spontaneous rhythms; (*d*) some driving was induced in a frequency range slightly higher than that of the normally dominant rhythms; and (*e*) harmonic responses occurred. In addition, the records showed more and better-defined activity during rhythmic visual stimulation than during its absence, whether or not driving was elicited. A similar tendency toward more regular activity during the course of repeated visual stimulation has recently been reported (**145**) for infants tested within five days post-partum.

Driving was induced in 33 subjects, the individual percentages for all frequencies combined ranging from .14 to 25.13 with a median of 3.15. These percentages are small but differ significantly [$p < .01$] from the percentage of trains of waves at the same frequencies in the basal records. Both the infrequency with which driving could be elicited and the short duration of the episodes which did occur are manifestations among these older infants of the fatigability noted by Ellingson in neonates. A sharp break in the mean incidence of driving, occurring between the 11–20 day group and the 21–30 day group, is apparent in the figures given in Table 4. The means

TABLE 4

PERCENTAGE OF BRAIN WAVES AT EACH FREQUENCY RANGE WITH AND WITHOUT STIMULATION*

Age in Days	Number	Frequency Range						Total	
		1–3 per Second		4–6 per Second		7–9 per Second			
		With	Without	With	Without	With	Without	With	Without
1–10......	5	0.17	0.00	0.64	0.41	0.05	0.00	0.86	0.41
11–20......	6	0.24	0.00	0.62	0.20	0.00	0.00	0.86	0.20
21–30......	6	0.36	0.05	4.54	0.31	0.14	0.00	5.04	0.36
31–60......	16	2.34	0.25	3.06	0.21	0.06	0.01	5.46	0.47
61–90......	5	2.16	0.21	1.92	0.26	0.03	0.00	4.11	0.47
Total..	38	1.47	0.14	2.47	0.25	0.05	0.01	3.99	0.40

* Data from Eichorn (**35**).

for the two younger groups are almost identical, while the means for the three older groups are very similar. Probably as a function of these facts, the over-all age difference, as tested by the analysis of variance, was not significant. A significant, moderate [.36] rank-difference correlation was found between age and amount of driving. Further, of the five subjects from whom no driving could be elicited four were less than 15 days old, and only one infant under 24 days of age showed driving at any frequency above 6 per second. The driving induced by various stimulus frequencies differed significantly. Frequencies of 4 to 6 per second were optimal, with the 1 to 3 per second range next most effective. Very little driving occurred in the frequency range 7 to 9 per second, and no trains of waves meeting the criteria were found at flicker rates of 10 per second or above.

Dreyfus-Brisac and Blanc (**32**) stated that they were unable to evoke photic driving in infants under three months of age. However, Ellingson's data (**38**) on photic driving, although less complete than those on specific evoked responses, confirm the observations made by Eichorn in almost all respects. Both clinical studies (**64, 94**) and the data of Dreyfus-Brisac and Blanc (**32**) show optimal driving frequencies to be slower than those of adults until adolescence.

Discussion.—Relationships between the anatomical and physiological data are imprecise. Cortical responses of high amplitude can be evoked a few hours after birth even in premature infants, demonstrating that retinal receptors are functional, yet the ERG is difficult to record at this age. On the other hand, once retinal flicker appears it can be obtained at much higher frequencies than can photic driving throughout infancy and childhood. Summation at successive synapses may partially explain both this paradox and the fact that the b-potential is greater than the a-wave. The curves for the ERG and the cortical responses to both single and intermittent stimuli show breaks at about the same time, i.e., at about the end of the first month. All three curves may be a function of rapid differentiation of the retina. The greater length of time required for the complete development of the cortical responses parallels the slower maturation of neural pathways beyond the receptors.

Only 20 to 30 per cent of the delay in the cortical responses of the neonate can be attributed to the longer latency of the ERG. Monnier's analysis (**114**) of retino-cortical response time in adults suggests that the greater part of the delay is subcortical. The conduction velocity of nerve fibers is known to increase with age (**102, 154, 161**). Degree of myelination has often been assumed to be a major determinant of this increase, but Hunt and Goldring (**71**), working with the rabbit, report that acceleration of myelination and conduction velocity do not coincide. Purpura *et al.* (**128**) note a prolonged absolute refractory period in the excitability cycle of superficial cortical responses (SCRs) in the perinatal kitten and cite evidence indicating that it is unlikely that the long delay results from the failure of transmitter substances to produce an electrogenic effect in the apical dendrites. They comment that the changes in excitability over time suggest, instead, acceleration of biochemical processes, and postulate that prolonged latencies during the neonatal period are the result of "delayed synthesis of transmitter(s) coupled with refractoriness in the presynaptic conductile pathways" (p. 343).

The studies on the rabbit and the cat cited above also provide data on histologic changes which may be associated with the development of the positive phase of the cortical potential. The stage of rapid myelination does coincide with the appearance of the positive wave in the rabbit. Examination of cortical tissue from the neonatal kittens showed that Cajal-Retzius cells of lamina I were still numerous at ages when only a negative wave was present. Assuming that "synaptic activity generated in the cortical depths at this stage is relatively weak" (p. 345), the authors propose that it is obscured by summated potentials developed by the Cajal-Retzius cells and apical dendrites. Dondey and Brazier's recordings (**30**) from various laminae in the cat support this interpretation. The initial positive phase seems to result from the arrival of the afferent volley in layer IV, and the following negative wave, from potentials in the most dense dendritic structures.

DEVELOPMENT OF VISUAL ACUITY

Method.—Performance on clinical tests of visual acuity, e.g., the Snellen charts, is affected by other variables in addition to acuity, but such tests do offer a reasonably objective basis for developmental comparisons over a considerable age span. However, testing the acuity of children younger than five or six years with the clinical methods used for adults confounds the measurement of acuity with the ability to identify letters or numbers. For preschool children the testing method has usually involved either the illiterate E or a picture test. Allen's new picture test (**3**) overcomes a number of limitations of other procedures. The objects are familiar but interesting, the probability of chance success is reduced by using a larger number of pictures, and the relative proportions of black and white in the designs have been carefully controlled to prevent blurring. The assessment of acuity is, of course, even more difficult in the nonverbal infant. Within recent years Schwarting (**136**) and Gorman *et al.* (**57, 58, 132**) have devised instruments for measuring visual acuity which capitalize on the optokinetic reflex. Any optokinetic method introduces the complication of motion. Although it is possible to specify the visual angle subtended by a line of any size at any distance and to convert this angle to the corresponding Snellen notation, the acuities so derived are those which would obtain if perfect fixation, with no change in speed, were maintained throughout the tracking period. Although the velocity which Gorman *et al.* use would have little effect on adult acuities (**101**), the reduction might be greater in infants with poorer muscular control.

Normative Data.—In their initial study Gorman *et al.* (**57**) tested 100 neonates, approximately 20 at each age from one to five days, with two line patterns. An additional 100 infants, all under four days of age, were examined in their second study (**58**), using a larger number of test patterns. Schwarting's and Allen's papers were primarily methodological, and sample sizes are not reported. Each, however, gives approximate norms. Behavioral aspects of visual development are comprehensively illustrated in the volume of Gesell *et al.* (**56**), but normative data on acuity are fragmentary. "Naked acuities" for five- and seven-year-olds are mentioned. Keeney (**89**) lists acuity estimates for several ages from four months through four years, but does not cite his source. A monumental set of normative data has been accumulated by Slataper (**142**) for both refraction and acuity over a wide age span (2–87 years). Generalization from these standards is limited by the fact that they were obtained in clinical practice. It is highly likely that persons consulting an ophthalmologist are a biased sample.

Only Schwarting and Slataper mention correcting for refractive errors. Although such correction may be necessary for an occasional infant or child, and must be considered in norms based on clinical populations, it is probably not an important factor in standards derived from normal samples. The majority of infants and young children are hypermetropic (**142, 144**), but the range of accommodation is so great that failure to correct systematically for refractive errors should not introduce any appreciable bias.

Table 5 is a collation of the data from the sources cited above. All acuities which were reported in other than the Snellen 20-foot notation have been converted to this system to facilitate inter-age comparisons. Combining the data from these several sources provides a reasonable approximation of the developmental trend in acuity. The relatively slight discrepancies from study to study probably reflect differences in technique or sample. Slataper's patient population, for example, yields slightly poorer acuities at five to seven years than the figures given by Gesell, whereas Allen's estimates for normal

TABLE 5

DEVELOPMENT OF VISUAL ACUITY

Age	Source of Data					
	Schwarting	Allen	Gorman *et al.*	Keeney*	Gesell *et al.*	Slataper*
Newborn	....	....	20/350–20/450	....	....	....
4 Months	....	....	....	20/235–20/335	....	....
6 Months	20/400	....	....	....	....	....
9 Months	....	....	....	20/235	....	....
1 Year	20/200	....	....	20/200	....	20/140 (Estimate)
2 Years	20/100	....	....	20/40	....	20/48
3 Years	20/50	20/40–20/50	....	20/30	....	20/42
4 Years	....	....	....	20/20	....	20/40
5 Years	....	20/30–20/35	....	....	20/25–20/30	20/33
6 Years	....	....	....	....	....	20/27
7 Years	....	....	....	....	20/20	20/26
8 Years	....	....	....	....	....	20/24
9 Years	....	....	....	....	....	20/23
10 Years	....	....	....	....	....	20/22
11–13 Years	....	....	....	....	....	20/20
14–15 Years	....	....	....	....	....	20/19
16–18 Years	....	....	....	....	....	20/18
19–54 Years	....	....	....	....	....	20/18

* Data from these two studies have been converted to the 20-ft. notation.

children aged three to four years fit in well with Gesell's estimates for children five to seven years from what is probably a reasonably comparable sample. It will also be noted that Slataper's two-year mean, based on only seven cases, is about the same as Allen's figure for three years. Schwarting's method is less refined than that of Gorman *et al.*, and his approximate norms for children under three differ most from those of other investigators. Nevertheless, his data, and to an even greater extent those of Gorman *et al.*, indicate considerably better acuity for the young infant than had been suggested by older studies (**170**).

Improvement in acuity is most rapid during the first two years, but not all of it can be accounted for at the retinal level. A marked increase in acuity occurs in the second year, yet differentiation of the macula is most accelerated during the first four months. Both enlargement of the pupil, beginning at about one year, and cortical maturation throughout infancy may be important variables. Conel notes that during most of infancy the region within the occipital lobe which receives a larger proportion of its fibers from the macula is less well developed in all respects than regions receiving fibers primarily from the periphery of the retina. At two years, however, these regions are of about equal development by a few criteria, e.g., the development of neurofibrils and the degree of myelination of exogenous fibers. The slight continuing improvement in acuity throughout adolescence in individuals without anomalies, apparent in Slataper's data, is consistent with the anatomical and electrophysiological data. Both the ERG and the EEG involve mass responses and are not measures of acuity. The only study in which the postnatal development of the retina, the ERG, evoked cortical responses, and visual acuity have been traced in the same subjects was conducted with the rhesus monkey (**122**). Those data also indicated only approximate relationships among the anatomical, physiological, and behavioral variables, the latter measures indicating better function than would be predicted from the morphological development of the retina.

Rate of Maturing

It is now axiomatic among students of development that, over the period from conception to adolescence, chronological age becomes a progressively poorer predictor of an individual's physical size and many other characteristics. Evidence for this maxim is provided by a large body of research conducted during the first half of this century. A variety of measures were devised for grouping children on the basis of their physical or "physiological" maturity. Despite the fact that some of these indices are only partially objective and not strictly quantitative, the intercorrelations among them are high

(**120**). In particular, the close parallels between skeletal maturation, the sequence of appearance of secondary sexual characteristics, and the adolescent growth spurt in height have been well documented. The concept of rates of maturing is a corollary of the principle of developmental age. Increasing differences in status imply differences in the velocity at which developmental changes occur. Thus, from status groupings of developmental age have been derived classifications of individuals in terms of rate of maturing. During the past decade or so a growing literature has accumulated attesting to the ubiquitous behavioral correlates of rate of physical maturing.

MALES

The series of papers analyzing the social and psychological concomitants of rate of maturing among boys began with a paper by Jones and Bayley (**82**). Since the behavioral measures on which early- and late-maturing boys were compared in that study have also been used in similar studies of girls and in adult follow-ups, discussion of the findings from several investigations will be facilitated if we first describe these devices. Two types of ratings were made independently by at least three adult observers. "ICW ratings" (Institute of Child Welfare, University of California) were done each semester from Grades H6–L7 (High 6–Low 7) through H9–L10 and annually in Grades H10–L11 and H11–L12, a total of nine ratings over a six-year period. The observations on which these ratings depend were made while the youngsters were in small, same-sex, free-play groups on the playground or in the waiting room before their physical examinations. Behavior exhibited in a wider range of informal and formal situations involving small and large, same- and mixed-sex groups provided the basis for the second set of ratings. These are referred to as "clubhouse ratings" because a large part of the observations were made in the clubhouse set up by the Oakland Growth Study near the school playground. They include, however, observations made during dances, excursions, and other social activities. Six annual ratings were derived by averaging the observations obtained during the course of each year. Rater-reliability for the clubhouse ratings, while adequate [.74], was lower than that for the ICW ratings [.87]. Reputation scores derived from a "guess-who" test administered to peers once or twice a year furnished a third source of data. The nature of the traits assessed by the rating scales and peer nominations is illustrated in Table 6, which summarizes the characteristics found to be significantly related to rate of maturing in both sexes.

TABLE 6

BEHAVIORAL CHARACTERISTICS SIGNIFICANTLY RELATED TO RATE OF MATURING IN BOTH SEXES*

	Boys		Girls	
	Early-maturing	Late-maturing	Early-maturing	Late-maturing
ICW ratings				
Individual traits:†				
Eager-listless	=	+	−	+
Peppy-indifferent	=	+	−	+
Animated-stolid	=	+	−	+
Active-stationary	=	+	−	+
Busy-idle	=	+	−	+
Talkative-silent	=	+	−	+
Uninhibited-inhibited	=	+	−	+
Initiative–at a loss	=	+	−	+
Composite traits:				
Expressive-inexpressive	=	+	−	+
Sociable-unsociable	=	+	=	+
"Guess-who" nominations				
Bossy-submissive	−	+	=	+
Avoids center of attention–attention-getting	=	−	+	−
Restless-quiet	−	+	−	=

* Data from Jones and Bayley (**82**) and Everett (**46**).

† The signs (+), (=), and (−) refer to "above," "equal to," and "below" the group mean, respectively.

Selection of subjects for the Jones and Bayley study was made according to the method used in almost all of the work done thus far at the University of California on the physical, physiological, and behavioral correlates of rate of maturing. From the total sample, two groups were drawn, comprised of the 16 boys who were most accelerated (EM, early-maturing) and the 16 who were most retarded (LM, late-maturing), and most consistently so, in rate of skeletal development during adolescence. It should be noted that these are not pathological cases but simply the extremes of the continuum in a sample of 90 normal, public school boys.

The statistical significance of the differences in ratings and reputation scores of the two extreme groups of boys was assessed by binomial tests of the consistency of the mean differences over the nine semesters. In all of the data analyses to be cited, standard, rather than raw, scores were used.

Adult ratings of attractiveness of physique produced the greatest separation of mean scores found for any single trait, with the EM consistently rated as above average, and the LM as below average, over almost the entire six years. A pattern of above-average ratings for the EM and below-average ratings for the LM was also maintained over most of the period on the clubhouse ratings of interest in the opposite sex. Reference to Table 6 will make it obvious, however, that the majority of characteristics which significantly differentiated these boys were those relating to expressiveness or physical and social activity. On these traits the group differences are largely a function of the high ratings of the LM; the EM usually ranked at about the mean. Jones and Bayley suggest that this pattern of high scores among the late-maturing may reflect both continuation of a "little-boy" type of activity and compensation for physical inferiority, the LM resorting to the techniques most readily available to them for securing attention. This interpretation is supported by the direction of the differences on several other variables. On the trait "relaxed *vs.* tense," the ratings significantly and consistently placed the EM above the mean; the LM were usually below the mean. The tendency for the LM to be rated as more attention-seeking approached significance, while the EM were consistently above average on the ratings of the contributory traits "matter-of-fact *vs.* show-off" and "unaffected *vs.* affected."

By the end of senior high school, adult observers tended to contrast the two groups less sharply. The LM were judged to be closer to the mean on traits associated with expressiveness and attention-seeking, and the EM were scored as high as or higher than the L on activity and social interest.

"Guess-who" scores differentiated the extreme groups less clearly than did the adult ratings, probably as a function of the fact that such scales "tend to identify outstanding individuals, but may fail to distribute the middle range of cases, who receive few or no mentions from their classmates" (**82:** 144). Nevertheless, peer responses were consonant with the staff ratings in showing the LM to be chosen more often than the EM as those who were restless, talkative, "bossy," attention-seeking, less good-looking, less grown-up, and less likely to have older friends.

It is important to note that neither adults nor peers distinguished between the extreme groups on some socially important characteristics. Judging from behavior in small, same-sex groups, adults did not see the groups as differing in popularity, leadership, prestige, poise, assurance, cheerfulness or social effect on the group. Peer choices for popular, leader, friendly, daring, active in games, and having humor about self did not differentiate the early- and late-maturing until the latter part of junior high school. At this time the reputational status of the LM tended to deteriorate.

Although scores based on behavior in the clubhouse and at the Institute over the entire six-year period did not distinguish the extreme groups on popularity, prestige, or leadership, other data indicate that in senior high school the peer culture did discriminate between them. Over half of the EM acquired either the distinction associated with outstanding athletic performance or were elected to important student offices. The late-maturing group included only one recognized athlete and one student officer. A subsequent study (**81**) revealed that four of the 12 senior high school boys receiving the highest number of mentions in the school paper came from the group of 16 early-maturers. None of the LM appeared in the high-mention category. Rather, this fifth of the total sample accounted for five of the nine boys who, in 540 issues of the school paper published during a three-year period, were never even casually mentioned. Only one early-maturing boy remained so inconspicuous.

Evidence that the influence of rate of maturing among boys is not confined to the extreme groups is provided by two analyses involving a larger proportion of the total sample. Fifty-six of the boys in the Oakland Growth Study sample attended the high school from which the material for the study of "newsworthiness" was drawn. For this group, a highly significant correlation of .42 was found between rank order of mention in the school paper and the ratio of skeletal age to chronological age. At age 15, the mean skeletal age of the high-mention group was 16.43; of the no-mention group, 15.46. Table 7 presents a set of correlations between rate of skeletal maturing during adolescence and a number of behavioral measures described earlier, based on about 40 study members of each sex. The investigation in which these correlations were obtained (**4**) was primarily concerned with the prediction of adult social behavior and is reviewed below. That section should be consulted for a description of this subsample and the method of scoring skeletal maturity. The

TABLE 7

CORRELATIONS OF SKELETAL MATURATION RATE DURING ADOLESCENCE WITH ADOLESCENT MEASURES OF SOCIAL BEHAVIOR*

	Males	Females
ICW social prestige	.06	....
Clubhouse leadership	.05	....
Opinion test leader	.09	....
ICW sociability	.39†	.05
Clubhouse popularity	.24	−.05
Opinion test popularity	.37†	−.39†

* Data from Ames (**4**).

† Significant at the .05 level.

correlations computed for the group of 40 boys support the analysis of the extreme groups in showing no relationship between rate of maturing and scores on leadership and prestige based on behavior outside of school. Conclusions about popularity and sociability are, however, contradicted. In the extreme groups there were no significant differences in popularity scores, and the LM tended to score higher on several traits related to sociability. Across the larger sample, both popularity and sociability were positively correlated with rate of maturing. These relationships are more consistent with the data on election to offices and mentions in the school paper. Further, the tendency for the EM to score higher on sociability is more compatible with the results from other groups of adolescents (**91, 116**) and adult differences between extreme maturing groups (**5, 80, 91**) cited below.

Other studies (**34, 42–44, 71, 78, 140**) demonstrated that the early- and late-maturing differed in many physical and physiological attributes, e.g., height, weight, body build, secondary sexual characteristics, athletic ability, and basal metabolic rate. Most of the physical discrepancies increased to a maximum at 14 to 15 years and diminished after that age. We have seen that, in social situations, the EM were viewed by both adults and peers as behaving more like adult males and that they were increasingly chosen to fill roles of responsibility and leadership within the student community. For a time the LM's activity and energy secured a reasonable amount of social recognition, particularly in small, same-sex groups. But this childish pattern became increasingly different from the modal behavior, and the social rewards given to boys who displayed it decreased. Once the distinctions had been established it appears that a shift by the LM toward greater maturity of physical appearance and behavioral traits did not necessarily produce a concomitant change in their reputation and status within the peer culture.

The obvious physical disparities between the early- and late-maturing and the different social climates in which they lived led Mussen and Jones to suspect that there might also be dissimilarities in the boys' motivations and their perceptions of themselves and others. They examined the TAT protocols (**119**) obtained when the boys were 17 years old and a set of drive ratings (**118**) made about a year after the groups were graduated from senior high school. The LM told significantly more stories in which the hero was described in negative terms (inadequate, stupid, weak), was rejected by his parents, left or defied his parents, was nurtured by someone other than the parents, in which he established heterosexual affiliations (the LM showed little *overt* interest in girls), and fewer stories in which he was aggressive, particularly in a physical, asocial way. They also produced suggestively, but not significantly, more themes of being dominated by the parent, desiring succorance, and achieving friendly relations with others. In anticipation of some of the adult differences between the early- and late-maturing groups, it is of interest that the LM tended less frequently to state that the pictures aroused no ideas or feelings. It is also noteworthy that there were no differences between the groups on inferred needs for achievement, recognition, or affiliation with parents.

Staff members who observed the boys throughout their adolescence in a wide variety of situations independently made standardized ratings of the strength of nine drives. They judged, not behavior per se, but what they inferred to be the motivations for the behavior. Of the nine ratings, only two were differentiating. Late-maturers were rated significantly higher on drives for social ties and aggression. The former score is consistent with their needs for affiliation and nurturance inferred from the TAT data, but the aggression scores are contradictory. A possible reconciliation of this discrepancy is suggested by Mussen and Jones (**118**). They hypothesize that in this middle-class sample, "the early-maturers, having identified with a mature male role," have internalized the cultural restrictions on the direct expression of aggression and "are more likely to express their aggressive motivations in fantasy. On the other hand, the late-maturers, being defiant of authority, may not accept the middle-class standards of behavior so readily. Consequently, the may express aggression more freely and overtly and, therefore, may reveal less aggressive motivation in their fantasy productions" (p. 66).

A report from the University of Chicago (**116**) in part confirms, and in part contradicts, the findings for the California sample. The generalizations from this study are limited by the small size of the sample, the basis of selection of subjects, and the limitations of the data used to determine age at puberty. The 16 boys and 17 girls who constitute the subsample for the analyses were originally selected at *age 10*, not on the basis of developmental age but, rather, as the best adjusted and most maladjusted of the total population of 149 youngsters, as judged by multiple test and rating criteria. Age at puberty for boys was estimated from maximum growth rate and pubic and axillary hair ratings. Physical measurements were made about every four months from age 11 to 15 and again at approximately 16 and 17 years, thus making the determination of age at puberty of the LM less exact. Judging from More's tabulations, there were 5 early-maturing, 3 to 5 late-maturing, and 6 to 8 average-maturing boys. The social data examined were "guess-who" instruments, filled out by peers when the group was about 11, 13, 14, and 16 years old, and ratings by an eight-member clinical case conference which drew on all the social and psychological material available. The psychological data included a Rorschach, three TAT's, a sentence-completion test, a lengthy set of essays, and a set of conference ratings of emotional reactivity, autonomy, internal consistency of values, guilt about inner impulses, accuracy of self-perception, empathy, and inner acceptance of appropriate sex role. Because the sociometric instruments varied from year to year, five summary categories—warmth, participation, dominance, activity, and emotional stability—were used, rather than individual items. Conference ratings on developmental tasks were made at 10, 13, and 16 years, but ratings of peer-group interaction and emotional stability in social relationships were available only for age 16.

For boys, the correlations between peer ratings and physical maturing were negligible at ages 11 and 13, but rose to the order of .3 to .4 at ages 14 and 16, indicating greater warmth, participation, dominance, activity, and emotional stability for the early-maturing. Relationships to staff ratings of social interactions at age 16 were all very low. Low positive correlations [.2 to .3] were obtained between physical maturity and staff ratings of autonomy, accuracy of self-perception, empathy, and inner acceptance of appropriate sex role. Staff ratings on overt manifestations of learning an appropriate sex role and achieving emotional independence, done for ages 10, 13, and 16, yielded correlations of about the same magnitude. These data are reasonably consistent within themselves and with those previously cited. The early-maturing were seen as more likeable and friendly, forceful, sociable, co-operative, hard workers on teams and in clubs, good at sports, well-groomed, calm, and as not being attention-demanding, argumentative, or restless. The psychological data also suggest that they exert more independent control over their own behavior, and, to a greater degree, have assimilated cultural restraints and role models. More's data differ from those for the California sample chiefly in showing lower correlations between behavioral variables and rate of maturing for boys than for girls, fewer relationships with adult ratings than with peer ratings, and in the tendency for activity and sociability to be positively rather than negatively related to rate of maturing as early as 14 years.

It is possible that the estimates of age at puberty were poorer for the boys than for the girls, being based on two rather than four criteria. Further, one of the two criteria was hair ratings. The development of pubic and axillary hair, while usually paralleling skeletal maturation and increase in height, is under adrenal rather than gonadal control, and is a more fallible index of puberty. The summary categories derived from the "guess-who" test combine items which were found in the California studies to distinguish the early- and late-maturers. For example, the activity classification includes games among same-sex groups as well as team sports, and the social participation category is heavily weighted with mixed-group activities, such as dances. Adult ratings seem to have been made largely from secondary sources rather than from direct observations by the raters.

The data of Kinsey *et al.* (**91:** chap. ix) corroborate a number of the traits which have been ascribed to accelerated- and retarded-maturers and, in addition, furnish evidence of divergent behavior in another sphere of social interaction. Age at onset of adolescence was defined chiefly by age at first ejaculation, first appearance of pubic hair, and onset of rapid growth. In the analyses, five categories of age at onset were used: 8–11 years (N = 395), 12 years (N = 1013), 13 years (N = 1481), 14 years (N = 1175), and 15 years and over (N = 292). Despite the fact that, except for the younger boys, dating of puberty was done from anamnesic data, relationships were found between age at onset of adolescence and most of the aspects of sexual behavior assessed. There were, for example, differences in the sources of first ejaculation, amount of sexual activity, and in age at which regular activity began. The latter coincided with age at onset among the EM, but for the LM, who were four to five years older at onset, regular activity usually did not begin for some time thereafter. Within the Caucasian sample, the rate of activity between onset and age 15 was greater for the EM than for any other category of single males, of any age, in any classification.

As was the case with the behavior ratings used in the Oakland Growth Study, personality notations in the Kinsey survey were made before the investigators became aware of the possible importance of rate of maturing. Over half of the EM, but only one-third of the LM, were described on the original histories as socially extroverted and/or aggressive, alert, energetic, vivacious, spontaneous, and physically active. Conversely, less than one-third of the EM, but over half of the LM, were characterized as introverted and/or socially inept, slow, quiet, mild in manner, without force, reserved, timid, and taciturn. Most of these distinctions tally well with those which characterized the California groups. The inconsistencies can probably be accounted for by two factors. First, the Kinsey descriptions do not distinguish the "little-boy" pattern of activity of the LM from the more mature forms of directed energy of the EM. Second, the Kinsey data are heavily weighted by descriptions of the adult rather than the adolescent and correspond more closely to the adult picture of the California group (**5, 80**) subsequently presented.

The developmental psychologist is concerned not only with the characteristics of various age groups but also with predicting later behavior from earlier and with tracing the evolution of patterns of adult behavior and personality. Some preliminary answers to questions about the persistence of social and psychological differences between the early- and late-maturing come from a follow-up study of the California sample, undertaken when the subjects were in their early thirties. At the time when the two reports to be reviewed in this chapter were prepared, data were available for only about 40 males, 11 of whom were from the early-maturing group and 9 from the late-maturing.

By the end of adolescence, the physical disparities between the early- and late-maturers had been markedly reduced, and in young adulthood there were no longer any significant differences in height, weight, or body build. As adolescents they had not differed in intelligence, grade placement, or social status, and as adults they did not differ significantly in educational level, socioeconomic rating of home and neighborhood, incidence of marriage,[3] or number of children. There were, however, definite differences in personality characteristics, social behavior, and occupational level.

Adult personality differences, as reflected in responses to the California Personality Inventory and the Edwards Personality Preference Schedule, were examined by Jones (**80**). On the former test, the EM scored significantly higher on the scales for good impression and responsibility. They also tended to make responses indicative of

3. Rate of maturing has been shown to be related to educational level, socioeconomic status, and incidence of marriage in larger and more continuous samples (**1, 4, 91, 152**).

greater socialization, dominance, and self-control. On the Edwards Schedule, the EM again scored significantly higher on the dominance scale; the LM on the succorance scale. Correlations between scale scores and skeletal maturity at age 15, computed for the total group of about 40 men who took tests, reinforced the findings for the extreme groups. Significant relationships were found for the CPI scales of good impression [.50], socialization [.40], impulsivity [—.31], and responsibility [.35] and for the Edwards scales for dominance [.40] and succorance [—.48]. The descriptive phrases for these various scales point to the men who matured early as persons whose advice is sought, who are interested in and capable of making a good impression, co-operative, enterprising, persistent, goal-directed, sociable, warm, conforming, and, perhaps, overcontrolled. The late-maturers give responses characteristic of those who, while more insightful and flexible, are impulsive, rebellious, touchy, self-assertive, and indulgent and who seek the aid and encouragement of others. These adjectives are highly reminiscent of the traits assigned to these subjects during adolescence.

The second study (**4, 5**) analyzed the relationships between a number of measures taken during adolescence, e.g., rate of maturing, sociability, popularity, and adult measures of social participation, for approximately 40 subjects of each sex. An index of skeletal maturation was derived by averaging the ratios of skeletal age to chronological age over the 14th to 17th years. From standardized, semi-structured, open-ended interviews, two judges made independent ratings of three types of adult social participation–informal, formal, and occupational. Informal participation involved "the frequency with which the subjects entertained, or were entertained by, friends, relatives, casual acquaintances, etc." (**5:** 3), as well as participation in sports and hobbies of a relatively social nature. Formal social participation referred to active rather than simply nominal membership in clubs and other structured organizations. The occupational–social participation rating was based not only on the relative amount of social contact ordinarily required in a given occupation but also on the men's reports of the degree to which their specific positions demanded social contact. These three ratings were combined to yield a total social participation score. Two additional variables examined were occupational status, ranked by the Warner Scale and supplemented by interview data on the subject's position within his particular occupation, and organizational leadership. The latter measure was treated as a dichotomy because officership in formal organizations was not continuously distributed.

When the total sample was divided into early-, average-, and late-maturers on the basis of standard scores on skeletal maturity of above 50.0, 50.0, and below 50.0, respectively, it was found that only one late-maturer scored above the mean on total social participation. Of the 15 men whose occupational positions required that they supervise the work of others, only three were late-maturers. A highly significant biserial correlation of .51 was obtained between skeletal maturation rate and supervision (directors *vs.* nondirectors). None of the eight subjects who held offices in organized groups was a late-maturer. The mean standard score for maturation rate of nonleaders was 47.9; of leaders, 58.1.

It is striking that the single, best predictor of adult male social participation was rate of skeletal development during adolescence. This variable correlated .52 with total participation score, .47 with occupational status, .48 with informal social participation, .44 with formal social participation, and .35 with occupational social participation. All of these correlations are significant. In contrast, only one statistically significant relationship was found between a category of adolescent social behavior and an adult measure of social participation (.39 between clubhouse popularity and informal social participation). Although a correlation of .52 accounts for only 25 per cent of the variance, probably the only other instances in the literature of a single variable predicting even this much of the variability in any nonphysical, human, personal characteristic are the relationships among I.Q., education, occupational level, and income.

Kinsey's statistics on adult sexual activity (**91**) reveal other behavioral differences between the early- and late-maturing which continue long past adolescence. Rates of activity were highest among the EM, regardless of marital status or educational level, to the oldest ages at which the data permitted analysis of the maturity variable, i.e., about 30 to 35 for single males and 36 to 40 for married males. The EM married earlier and, in contrast to the findings in the Oakland Growth Study, a larger proportion of the LM were still single at 35 years. Further, almost 20 per cent of the LM had had no heterosexual experience by this age. Although Kinsey *et al.* phrase most of their discussion in terms of contrasts between the extreme groups, the relationship between age at onset of adolescence and many of their variables is reasonably linear.

FEMALES

The first investigation of the behavioral correlates of rate of maturing among girls (**46**) involved comparisons of 16 EM and 16 LM on the ICW ratings and "guess-who" scores, but the method of analysis differed in some important respects from that used for boys. Although mean scores from nine ratings over the six-year period were reported, in most instances tests of significance were computed only for the data from Grades H7–L8 through H10–L11. Further, the groups were compared on the basis of means computed from the average score for each case over the four-year period rather than by binomial tests for the consistency of mean differences from year to year.

Like the boys, the extreme groups of girls did not differ in C.A., I.Q., grade placement, or socioeconomic status. Of course, both the timing and the pattern of contrasts in physical size were different from those of boys. The early-maturing were taller than the total sample of 87 girls until about 13.5 years; the late-maturing were shorter until about 15 years. For both groups the differences were maximal from about 11.5 to 13 years. The accelerated group was not only markedly heavier than the other two groups during early adolescence but continued to have somewhat more weight for height throughout the period, while the retarded group remained slightly below the group mean even at 17 years.

It is evident from Table 6 that on the ICW ratings the direction of the differences between the EM and the LM were in the same direction as those for the boys, but in general they were more clear cut. The girls were differentiated on a larger number of traits, but, as with the boys, the greatest discrepancies between the two groups were on characteristics having to do with expressiveness and activity. Among girls, the LM not only were scored above average but the EM, rather than being about average, were rated definitely below the group mean. Traits associated with sociability and prominence in the group were also more frequently attributed to late-maturing girls. In addition, differences on traits related to attention-seeking were in the same direction as those for boys but failed to reach significance. The means for the last year show an even more pronounced tendency for the the late-maturing girls to have higher ratings on these behaviors. Had these scores been used, or the consistency of the differences tested, the differences for girls would probably also have been significant. By the H10th to L12th grades the EM were also rated as cheerful and as sociable as the LM and more good-natured, popular, and relaxed. Two characteristics on which the boys were very dissimilar—attractiveness of physique and relaxation—did not differentiate the girls, but, as just noted, the EM were considered to be more relaxed during the later observations.

Although reputation scores for the extreme groups did not support staff ratings of greater popularity for the late-maturing girls, Ames (**4**) found a significant correlation of —.39 (see Table 7) between rate of maturing and peer nominations for popularity among his 40 subjects. Further support for the staff observations is found in the analysis of mentions in the school paper (**81**). The pattern of mentions and no-mentions is the reverse of that for boys. The early- and late-maturing group each constitutes 20 per cent of the sample of girls, but the LM account for 42 per cent of the high-mentions and only 8 per cent of the low-mentions, while the EM contribute 33 per cent of those who were never mentioned and 11 per cent of the high-mention girls. For the 52 girls on whom skeletal ages and newspaper data were available, the correlation between the ratio of skeletal to chronological age and rank order of mention was —.42. At 15 years, the mean skeletal age of the high-mention group was .5 years younger than that of the low-mention group.

Despite her relative lack of social prestige, the early-maturing girl's psychological adjustment, as expressed in TAT responses, was good (**83**). Early- and late-maturing girls differed significantly on only two variables, negative characteristics and need for recognition, and in each case it was the LM, not the EM, who scored higher. The protocols of the LM girls resembled those of the LM boys in several respects. They not only characterized the hero in negative terms but also tended to produce more themes in which the hero was dominated by the parents, rejected by the parents, in need of help, or helped by someone other than the parent. In addition to the significant difference on need for recognition, two other deviations from the trends among boys were found, although neither was significant. Need for achievement was somewhat higher among late-maturing girls; boys did not differ on either this or the recognition variable. Whereas late-maturing boys produced significantly more themes of romantic love, such stories were more common among the early-maturing girls. This trend is consistent with Harrison's finding (**54**) of a higher incidence of these themes among post-puberal than among puberal or prepuberal girls.

An early study of the girls' responses on a self-report inventory (**159**), while not consistent in all respects, substantiates the more favorable psychological picture of the EM on the TAT. On that inventory the EM tended to score more favorably than the LM on total adjustment, family adjustment, and feelings of personal adequacy.

Contradictory data on emotional adjustment come from another longitudinal study at the University of California (**100**). Behavior problems of children from the age of 21 months to 14 years, as reported by their mothers, were classified and analyzed with respect to a number of variables. The age cut-off point in data collection precluded assessment of the influence of maturity in boys. The earlier age of puberty in girls made it possible to evaluate this variable for the 43 girls who were followed through to 14 years. From age 9 to 14 the seven girls who matured before 11.9 years had a higher total number of problems than did all the other girls. The 15 girls maturing at age 13 or later presented the least number of problems at all ages. Girls maturing before 11.9 and those maturing between 12 and 12.9 each had their peak incidence of total problems a year before menarche. There was no relation between age and problem incidence among girls maturing at 13 years or later. Of course, there is the distinct possibility that had information for later years been available, such a relationship and a higher incidence of problems might have been found for the late-maturers.

In More's small midwestern sample (**116**), both social and psychological data indicate a more favorable status for the early-maturing girl. At age 11, correlations ranging from .2 to .5 were found between physical maturity (as judged by reported menarcheal age, breast development, and growth in height and hip width) and all the social interaction variables derived from peer choices. However, only the correlation with participation was significant. The level of most of these correlations dropped at ages 13 and 14, then rose again at 16 years. At that age all the correlations were .4 to .5 and significant, except the correlation of .30 with activity. Of the adult ratings of peer group interaction, only the relationship to "same sex overt behavior" [.40] was significant. Correlations between physical maturity and staff ratings of emotional maturity at age 16 were also of the order of .4 to .5, except for the very low correlation for "inner acceptance of an appropriate sex role." Positive relationships [.4 to .5] were also obtained with staff ratings of developmental tasks at ages 10, 13, and 16, with the exception of a drop to the level of .2 for the 16-year ratings on "learning an appropriate sex role in outer behavior" and "getting along with age mates." It seems likely that most of the girls had reached sufficiently high levels on these variables by this age to curtail the range and thus reduce the correlation. In general, the most consistently high and significant relationships were found for measures assessing various aspects of emotional independence.

Two factors may explain the variance of some of More's results from those of the California group. First, none of the girls in his sample could really be classified as an early-maturer. The group is composed of three girls who seem quite clearly to be late-maturers, two who are marginal, and 12 average-maturers. Within this restricted range, representing the modal group plus a few decidedly late-maturers, positive relationships might reasonably be expected. Second, the Oakland Growth Study sample was drawn from a large urban community. The majority attended a high school with a sizeable student body and one in which participation in extracurricular activities was stressed. The University of Chicago study group came from a smaller community, and it is quite possible that the school which they attended placed fewer demands for a high level of organized social activity upon them. Smaller schools also usually afford more opportunity for association with students from other grades, so that the developmentally deviant girl may find it easier to find a compatible social group.

A recent paper by Faust (**50**) is of considerable help in reconciling conflicting data for girls. Subjects for her study were 731 girls in the sixth through ninth grades of suburban schools. Girls in Grades VII–IX were enrolled in the same junior high school; the sixth-graders attended various elementary schools in the same district. In each grade the girls were classified as prepuberal, puberal, postpuberal, or late adolescent on the basis of menarcheal ages reported in health or physical education classes. The "guess-who" test used in the Oakland Growth Study, plus two additional items dealing with prestige, was administered. The only items on which the developmental groups deviated significantly were "grown-up" and "older friends." These items did not differentiate the Oakland Growth Study sample of girls, but they were discriminating for boys. Of much greater import, however, is the shift in the groups to which favorable scores on prestige-lending traits were attributed. The traits which were related to prestige were approximately the same for all grades, but in each grade one developmental group was credited with a significantly larger number of these characteristics. For the sixth grade it was the least mature group. The average girl in this grade was prepuberal, and belonging to this modal group was an asset. In the junior high school it was the most mature group in the class which was thus favored. The average seventh-grader was puberal, yet the prestige traits were ascribed to the postpuberal, the most mature group in that grade. In the eighth and ninth grades, the average girl was postpuberal, but again prestige was accorded to the most mature group, now the late adolescents. Faust summarizes the implications of her results by stating, "This discontinuity suggests that for girls neither physical acceleration nor physical retardation is consistently advantageous" (p. 181). In her sample, early-maturing became an advantage in junior high school. In the Oakland sample it did not, but the shift in popularity ratings in Grades H11–L12 suggests that it might have become so in late senior high. Faust's data were collected about 20 years later than those of the University of California. Secular trends in age at puberty (**152**) and in acceptance of interests and attitudes characteristic of adolescent girls (**79**) would lead one to expect the discontinuity in developmental advantage to occur earlier.

Fewer long-term predictive data are available for girls, but such as there are stand in marked contrast to those for boys. Rate of maturing was not related to adult social participation in Ames' sample (**4**) of 40 girls from the Oakland Growth Study. Girls who had obtained high ratings on clubhouse and reputation-test popularity were more active in structured organizations as adults (r's =.40 and .37), but no other adolescent measure of social participation predicted their adult social behavior. The best single predictor of both informal and formal social activity for females was husbands' occupational status. These correlations were .39 and .58, respectively. There were also intricate interrelationships among educational level, parental socioeconomic status, husbands' occupational status, and social participation.

Kinsey *et al.* (**90**) report little differentiation among females during either adolescence or adulthood on the basis of age at onset of adolescence. There were a few low-level relationships for single women, particularly at the younger ages, among several variables having to do with incidence of sexual activity. An analysis of age at marriage was not made, but the data are clear in indicating that in married females this form of social behavior, like that in the wider community, is better predicted from their husbands' characteristics than from their own.

DISCUSSION

The data for boys from various climes and times indicate that, over a rather prolonged period, early-maturing males enjoy social and psychological advantages. Is it simply that they are destined to come into the world "trailing clouds of glory?" Although rate of maturing is to some extent genetically determined (**65**), it seems unlikely that the metabolic variables, e.g., endocrinological, through which the skeletal and somatic effects are mediated have much direct influence on personality characteristics. Pre- and postpuberal youngsters differ in interests and behavior, and maturational differences in hormonal levels or thresholds for some classes of stimuli may be involved. However, even sexual behavior in man and other primates appears to be more dependent on experiential than on somatic factors. Many of the behavioral differences between early- and late-maturers may reasonably be interpreted as functions of differential experience. The early- and late-maturing differ not only in superficial characteristics but also in actual physical abilities. In some cases these differences have existed for a number of years—some individuals who will arrive at puberty late or early can be identified in infancy or early childhood (**11, 150**). Adults and peers may react first to the physical appearance of the early-maturer and give him tasks and privileges ordinarily reserved for older individuals. Often he is able to meet the challenge, and in so doing he confirms their impression, increases his own skill, and derives personal satisfaction. If he was also larger than his age-mates before puberty, this circular process may have been recurring for some time.

Conversely, the LM's feelings of inferiority and dependency have a realistic basis for many years. He is less able physically and has greater need for succorance from others. If he feels resentment at the childish status and treatment, he may express it in rebellious, impulsive behavior. Much of the exuberance and impulsivity of the late-maturer, however, may simply be that which is characteristic of most young animals. This assertion is supported by the fact that the same traits are associated with late-maturing among girls. Unfortunately, these patterns and attitudes, while perhaps appropriate and successful coping devices during childhood and early adolescence, may be maintained when they are no longer adaptive. Attitudes and behavior which were once a function of ability and status have become habitual and now reduce performance and status. In most respects these arguments can be generalized to girls, granting that the sequence and pattern of cultural demands and reinforcements differ from those for boys.

Although the results of a considerable portion of the studies summarized here are congruent, the inferences which have been drawn from them by the writer and by the original investigators must be regarded as tentative. There are still many questions to which we have no answers or only preliminary and partial answers. The relationships demonstrated are group trends and negative instances exist, as exemplified in case histories from the sample from which the group data were derived (**99, 148**). Environmental factors, such as nutrition and disease (**1, 31, 152**), are known to affect rate of maturing, but the specific nature of even these physical variables has not been determined. The psychological and social factors which relieve or exaggerate the group trends have hardly been explored, but studies of traits valued by adolescent groups of differing socioeconomic status (**6, 125**), as well as some of the data reviewed here, suggest that the behavioral correlates of rate of maturing would not be the same in all school and community settings, nor in all social strata within them.

Study of the behavioral correlates of rate of maturing has been carried forward from adolescence; it must also be pushed backward. The hypothesis that persistence of overt and covert personality characteristics is attributable in large part to experience and acquired reaction patterns requires such studies for substantiation. Further, behavioral data at different ages on individuals of known maturational rates offer a means of testing theories of personality development which assume that certain periods of time are required before puberty for achieving successive phases of emotional integration. We do not know whether or not all the prepuberal stages are proportionately foreshortened, but early puberty does not necessarily imply that the duration of childhood, or "latency," is less. It may be infancy or early childhood which is cut short. In fact, the physical growth data suggest the latter (**11, 109, 150**).

Despite the reservations which have been outlined, the material reviewed in this section leads full circle to a conclusion reached in connection with genetic data on sex determination and differentiation: that much of human behavior is a function, not of structure per se, but of the environmental supports, outlets, expectations, and reactions relative to that structure.

BIBLIOGRAPHY

1. Acheson, R. M. "Effects of Nutrition and Disease on Human Growth," in *Human Growth*, pp. 73–92. Edited by J. M. Tanner. Symposium of the Society for the Study of Biology, Vol. III. Oxford: Pergamon Press, 1960.
2. Allen, G., and Baroff, G. S. "Mongoloid Twins and Their Siblings," *Acta Genet.*, V (1955), 295–326.
3. Allen, H. F. "Testing of Visual Acuity in Preschool Children: Norms, Variables and a New Picture Test," *Pediatrics,* XIX (1957), 1093–1100.
4. Ames, R. "A Longitudinal Study of Social Participation." Unpublished Doctor's dissertation, University of California, 1956.
5. ———. "Physical Maturing among Boys as Related to Adult Social Behavior," *Calif. J. Educ. Res.*, VIII (1957), 69–75.
6. Anastasi, Anne, and Miller, Shirley. "Adolescent 'Prestige Factors' in

Relation to Scholastic and Socioeconomic Variables," *J. Soc. Psychol.*, XXIX (1949), 43–50.

7. ANDERSON, E. P.; KALCKAR, H. M.; and ISSELBACHER, K. J. "Defect in Uptake of Galactose-1-Phosphate into Liver Nucleotides in Congenital Galactosemia," *Science*, CXXV (1957), 113–14.
8. BARBER, AELETA N. *Embryology of the Human Eye*. St. Louis: C. V. Mosby, 1955.
9. BARR, M. L., and BERTRAM, E. G. "A Morphological Distinction between Neurons of the Male and Female, and the Behavior of the Nucleolar Satellite during Accelerated Nucleoprotein Synthesis," *Nature*, CLXIII (1949), 676–77.
10. BARR, M. L., and CARR, D. H. "Sex Chromatin, Sex Chromosomes, and Sex Anomalies," *Canadian Med. Assn. J.*, LXXXIII (1960), 979–86.
11. BAYLEY, NANCY. "The Accurate Prediction of Growth and Adult Height," *Mod. Probl. Paediat.*, VII (1962), 234–55.
12. ———. "Some Increasing Parent-Child Similarities during the Growth of Children," *J. Educ. Psychol.*, XLV (1954), 1–21.
13. ———. "Some Psychological Correlates of Somatic Androgyny," *Child Develpm.*, XXII (1951), 47–60.
14. BENNETT, C. E. "Congenital Galactosemia," *U.S. Armed Forces Med. J.*, IX (1958), 112–19.
15. BLEWETT, D. B. "Experimental Study of the Inheritance of Intelligence," *J. Ment. Sci.*, C (1954), 922–33.
16. BROADHURST, P. L. "Part One: Experiments in Psychogenetics," in *Experiments in Personality*, pp. 3–102. Edited by H. J. Eysenck. New York: Humanities Press, 1960.
17. BRODY, H. "Organization of Cerebral Cortex: Study of Aging in Human Cerebral Cortex," *J. Comp. Neurol.*, CII (1955), 511–56.
18. CATTELL, R. B. "The Multiple Abstract Variance Analysis Equations and Solutions: For Nature-Nurture Research on Continuous Variables," *Psychol. Rev.*, LXVII (1960), 353–72.
19. CATTELL, R. B.; STICE, G. F.; and KRISTY, N. F. "A First Approximation to Nature-Nurture Ratios for Eleven Primary Personality Factors in Objective Tests," *J. Abnorm. Soc. Psychol.*, LIV (1957), 143–59.
20. CONEL, J. L. *The Postnatal Development of the Human Cerebral Cortex. I. Cortex of the Newborn*. Cambridge, Massachusetts: Harvard University Press, 1939.
21. ———. *Ibid. II. Cortex of the One-month Infant*. Cambridge, Massachusetts: Harvard University Press, 1941.
22. ———. *Ibid. III. Cortex of the Three-month Infant*. Cambridge, Massachusetts: Harvard University Press, 1941.
23. ———. *Ibid. IV. Cortex of the Six-month Infant*. Cambridge, Massachusetts: Harvard University Press, 1955.
24. ———. *Ibid. V. Cortex of the Fifteen-month Infant*. Cambridge, Massachusetts: Harvard University Press, 1955.
25. ———. *Ibid. VI. Cortex of the Twenty-four-month Infant*. Cambridge, Massachusetts: Harvard University Press, 1959.
26. DARLINGTON, C. D., and LA COUR, L. F. *The Handling of Chromosomes*. London: George Allen & Unwin, 1960 (third edition).

27. Davidson, W. M., and Smith, D. R. *Human Chromosomal Abnormalities.* London: Staples Press, 1961.

28. Dekaban, A. "Human Thalamus. An Anatomical, Developmental and Pathological Study. II. Development of the Human Thalamic Nuclei," *J. Comp. Neurol.*, C (1954), 63–98.

29. Deno, Evelyn. "Parent-Child Resemblances in Intellectual Development," *Amer. Psychologist,* XII (1957), 364.

30. Dondey, M., and Brazier, Mary A. B. "Remarks concerning the Recording of Primary Visual Responses from Diffierent Cortical Layers in a Lightly Anaesthetized Cat," *EEG Clin. Neurophysiol.*, X (1958), 761.

31. Dreizen, S.; Snodgrasse, R. M.; and Associates. "The Retarding Effect of Protracted Undernutrition on the Appearance of the Postnatal Ossification Centers in the Hand and Wrist," *Hum. Biol.*, XXX (1958), 253–64.

32. Dreyfus-Brisac, C., and Blanc, C. "Electro-encephalogramme et Maturation Cerebrale," *L'encephale*, XLV (1956), 205–41.

33. Edwards, J. H.; Harnden, D. G.; and Associates. "A New Trisomic Syndrome," *Lancet,* I (1960), 787–90.

34. Eichorn, Dorothy. "A Comparison of Laboratoy Determinations and Wetzel Grid Estimates of Basal Metabolism among Adolescents," *J. Pediat.*, XLVI (1955), 146–54.

35. ———. "Electrocortical and Autonomic Response in Infants to Visual and Auditory Stimuli." Unpublished Doctor's dissertation, Northwestern University, 1951.

36. Eichorn, Dorothy, and Bandy, Marcia. "A Preliminary Report on a Longitudinal Study of the Relationship between Parent's and Child's Mental Test Scores." Paper read at Western Psychol. Assn., Monterey, California, May, 1957.

37. Eichorn, Dorothy, and Jones, H. E. "Maturation and Behavior," in *Current Psychological Issues,* pp. 211–48. Edited by Georgene H. Seward and J. P. Seward. New York: Henry Holt & Co., 1958.

38. Ellingson, R. J. "Cortical Electrical Responses to Visual Stimulation in the Human Infant," *Neurophysiol.*, XII (1960), 663–77.

39. ———. "Electroencephalograms of Normal, Full-term Newborns Immediately after Birth with Observations on Arousal and Visual Evoked Responses," *EEG Clin. Neurophysiol.*, X (1958), 31–50.

40. Ellingson, R. J., and Wilcott, R. C. "Development of Evoked Responses in Visual and Auditory Cortices of Kittens," *J. Neurophysiol.*, XXIII (1960), 363–75.

41. Engle, R. "Evaluation of Newborn EEG Tracings," *EEG Clin. Neurophysiol.*, XIII (1961), 497.

42. Espenschade, Anna. "Dynamic Balance in Adolescent Boys," *Res. Quar.*, XXIV (1953), 270–75.

43. ———. "Motor Performance in Adolescence," *Monogr. Soc. Res. Child Develpm.*, V (1940), No. 1.

44. ———. "Physiological Maturity as a Factor in the Qualification of Boys for Physical Activity," *Res. Quar.*, XV (1944), 113–15.

45. *Eugene Wolff's Anatomy of the Eye and Orbit.* Revised by R. J. Last. Philadelphia: W. B. Saunders & Co., 1961 (fifth edition).

46. Everett, Evalyn G. "Behavioral Characteristics of Early- and Late-maturing Girls." Unpublished Master's thesis, University of California, 1943.

47. EYSENCK, H. J. "The Inheritance of Extraversion-Introversion," *Acta Psychologica*, XII (1956), 95–110.
48. EYSENCK, H. J., and PRELL, D. B. "The Inheritance of Neuroticism: An Experimental Study," *J. Ment. Sci.*, XC (1951), 429–32.
49. FALCONER, D. S. "Quantitative Inheritance," in *Methodology in Mammalian Genetics*. Edited by W. J. Burdette. San Francisco: Holden Day (in press).
50. FAUST, MARGARET S. "Developmental Maturity as a Determinant in Prestige of Adolescent Girls," *Child Develpm.*, XXXI (1960), 173–84.
51. FORD, C. E., and HAMMERTON, J. E. "The Chromosomes of Man," *Nature*, CLXXVIII (1956), 1020–23.
52. FORD, C. E.; JONES, K. W.; and ASSOCIATES. "The Chromosomes in a Patient Showing Both Mongolism and the Klinefelter Syndrome," *Lancet*, I (1959), 709–10.
53. ———. "A Sex-Chromosome Anomaly in a Case of Gonadal Dysgenesis (Turner's Syndrome)," *Lancet*, I (1959), 711–13.
54. FRANK, L. K.; HARRISON, R.; and ASSOCIATES. "Personality Development in Adolescent Girls," *Monogr. Soc. Res. Child Develpm.*, XVI (1951), Serial No. 53.
55. FULLER, J. L., and THOMPSON, W. R. *Behavior Genetics*. New York: John Wiley & Sons, 1960.
56. GESELL, A.; ILG, FRANCES L.; and BULLIS, GLENNA E. *Vision, Its Development in Infant and Child*. New York: Paul P. Hoeber, Inc., 1949.
57. GORMAN, J. J.; COGAN, D. G.; and GELLIS, S. S. "An Apparatus for Grading the Visual Acuity of Infants on the Basis of Optikokinetic Nystagmus," *Pediatrics*, XIX (1957), 1088–92.
58. ———. "A Device for Testing Visual Acuity in Infants," *Sight Saving Rev.*, XXIX (1959), 80–84.
59. GRUMBACH, M. M., and BARR, M. L. "Cytologic Tests of Chromosomal Sex in Relation to Sexual Anomalies in Man," *Recent Progr. Hormone Res.*, XIV (1958), 324–35.
60. HALL, C. S. "Genetic Differences in Fatal Audiogenic Seizures between Inbred Strains of House Mice," *J. Hered.*, XXXVIII (1947), 3–6.
61. ———. "The Genetics of Behavior," in *Handbook of Experimental Psychology*, pp. 304–29. Edited by S. S. Stevens. New York: John Wiley & Sons, 1951.
62. HAMPSON, J. L.; HAMPSON, JOAN G.; and MONEY, J. "The Syndrome of Gonadal Agenesis (Ovarian Agenesis) and Male Chromosomal Pattern in Girls and Women: Psychological Studies," *Bull. Johns Hopk. Hosp.*, XCVII (1955), 207–26.
63. HAMPSON, JOAN G., and MONEY, J. "Idiopathic Sexual Precocity in the Female: Report of Three Cases," *Psychosom. Med.*, XVII (1955), 16–35.
64. HERRLIN, K. M. "EEG with Photic Stimulation: A Study of Children with Manifest or Suspected Epilepsy," *EEG Clin. Neurophysiol.*, VI (1960), 573–98.
65. HEWITT, D. "Some Familial Correlations in Height, Weight, and Skeletal Maturity," *Ann. Hum. Genet.*, XXII (1957), 26–35.
66. HOLZEL, A., and KOMROWER, G. M. "Study of Genetics of Galactosaemia," *Arch. Dis. Childh.*, XXX (1955), 155–59.
67. HONZIK, MARJORIE P. "Developmental Studies of Parent-Child Resemblance in Intelligence," *Child Develpm.*, XXVIII (1957), 216–77.

68. Horsten, G. P. M., and Winkelman, J. E. "Development of the ERG in Relation to Histologic Differentiation of the Retina in Man and Animals," *Arch. Ophth.*, LXIII (1960), 232–42.

69. Hsia, D. Y.-Y. "Medical Genetics," *New Eng. J. Med.*, CCLXII (1960), 1172–77, 1222–27, 1273–77, 1318–22.

70. ———. "Recent Advances in Bio-chemical Detection of Heterozygous Carriers in Hereditary Diseases," *Metabolism*, IX (1960), 301–15.

71. Hunt, W. E., and Goldring, S. "Maturation of Evoked Responses of the Visual Cortex in Postnatal Rabbits," *EEG Clin. Neurophysiol.*, III (1951), 465–71.

72. Isselbacher, K. J.; Anderson, E. P.; and Associates. "Congenital Galactosaemia: A Single Enzymatic Block in Galactose Metabolism," *Science*, CXXIII (1956), 635–36.

73. Jacobs, P. A.; Baikie, A. G.; and Associates. "Evidence for the Existence of the Human 'Super Female,'" *Lancet*, II (1959), 423–25.

74. ———. "The Somatic Chromosomes in Mongolism," *Lancet*, I (1959), 710.

75. Jacobs, P. A., and Strong, J. A. "A Case of Human Intersexuality Having a Possible XXY Sex-Determining Mechanism," *Nature*, CLXXX (1959), 302–3.

76. Jones, H. E. "Adolescence in our Society," in *The Family in a Democratic Society*, pp. 70–82. New York: Anniversary Papers at the Community Service Society of New York, 1949.

77. ———. *Motor Performance and Growth*. Berkeley: University of California Press, 1949.

78. ———. "Skeletal Maturing as Related to Strength," *Child Develpm.*, XVII (1946), 173–85.

79. Jones, Mary C. "A Comparison of the Attitudes and Interests of Ninth-grade Students over Two Decades," *J. Educ. Psychol.*, LI (1960), 175–86.

80. ———. "The Later Careers of Boys Who Were Early- or Late-maturing," *Child Develpm.*, XXVIII (1957), 113–28.

81. ———. "A Study of Socialization Patterns at the High-School Level," *J. Genet. Psychol.*, XC (1958), 87–111.

82. Jones, Mary C., and Bayley, Nancy. "Physical Maturing among Boys as Related to Behavior," *J. Educ. Psychol.*, XLI (1950), 129–48.

83. Jones, Mary C., and Mussen, P. H. "Self-conceptions, Motivations, and Interpersonal Attitudes of Early- and Late-maturing Girls," *Child Develpm.*, XXIX (1958), 492–500.

84. Kagan, J., and Moss, H. A. "Parental Correlates of Child's I.Q. and Height: A Cross-validation of the Berkeley Growth Study Results," *Child Develpm.*, XXX (1959), 325–32.

85. Kalckar, H. M.; Anderson, E. P.; and Isselbacher, K. J. "Galactosemia, a Congenital Defect in a Nucleotide Transferase," *Biochem. Biophys. Acta*, XX (1956), 262–68.

86. Kallman, F. J. "The Genetic Theory of Schizophrenia," *Amer. J. Psychiat.*, CIII (1946), 309–22.

87. ———. "Twin and Sibship Study of Overt Male Homosexuality," *Amer. J. Hum. Genet.*, IV (1952), 136–46.

88. Karpe, G. "Apparatus and Method for Clinical Recording of the Electroretinogram," *Doc. Ophth.*, II (1948), 268–76.

89. Keeney, A. H. *Chronology of Ophthalmic Development.* Springfield, Illinois: C. C. Thomas, 1951.
90. Kinsey, A. C.; Pomeroy, W. R.; and Associates. *Sexual Behavior in the Human Female.* Philadelphia: W. B. Saunders & Co., 1953.
91. ———. *Sexual Behavior in the Human Male.* Philadelphia: W. B. Saunders & Co., 1948.
92. Kirkman, H. N., and Bynum, E. "Enzymic Evidence of a Galactosemic Trait in Parents of Galactosemic Children," *Ann. Hum. Genet.*, XXIII (1959), 117–26.
93. Kirkman, H. N., and Kalckar, H. M. "Enzymatic Deficiency in Congenital Galactosemia and Its Heterozygous Carriers," *Ann. N.Y. Acad. Sci.*, LXXV (1958), 274–78.
94. Laget, P., and Humbert, R. "Facteurs Influencant la Response Electroencephalographique à la Photostimulation chez l'Enfant," *EEG Clin. Neurophysiol.*, VI (1954), 591–97.
95. Lejeune, J.; Turpin, R.; and Gautier, M. "Le Mongolisme, Premier Exemple d'Aberration Autosomique Humaine," *Ann. Genet.*, I (1959), 41–49.
96. Leloir, L. F. "The Enzymatic Transformation of Uridine Diphosphate Glucose into a Galactose Derivative," *Arch. Biochem. Biophys.*, XXXIII (1951), 186–90.
97. ———. "The Metabolism of Hexosephosphates," in *Phosphorous Metabolism,* pp. 67–93. Edited by W. D. McElroy and B. Glass. Baltimore: Johns Hopkins Press, 1951.
98. ———. "The Uridine Coenzymes," in *Proc. Third Int. Cong. of Biochem., Brussels, 1955,* pp. 154–62. New York: Academic Press, 1956.
99. Macfarlane, Jean W. "The Significance of Early or Late Maturation," in *Physical and Behavioral Growth,* pp. 69–78. Report of the Twenty-sixth Ross Pediatric Research Conference. Columbus, Ohio: Ross Laboratories, 1958.
100. Macfarlane, Jean W.; Allen, Lucille; and Honzik, Marjorie P. *A Developmental Study of the Behavior Problems of Normal Children between Twenty-one Months and Fourteen Years.* Berkeley: University of California Press, 1954.
101. Mackworth, N. H., and Kaplan, I. T. "Visual Acuity When Eyes Are Pursuing Moving Targets," *Science,* CXXXVI (1962), 387–88.
102. Magladery, J. W.; Teasdall, R. D.; and Associates. "Cutaneous Reflex Changes in Development and Aging," *Arch. Neurol.*, III (1960), 23–31.
103. Mann, Ida C. *The Development of the Human Eye.* New York: Grune & Stratton, Inc., 1950 (second edition).
104. Mather, K. *Biometrical Genetics: The Study of Continuous Variation.* London: Methuen & Co., Ltd., 1949.
105. Maxwell, E. S. "The Enzymic Interconversion of Uridine Diphosphogalactose and Uridine Diphosphoglucose," *J. Biol. Chem.*, CCXXIX (1957), 139–51.
106. Maxwell, E. S.; Kalckar, H. M.; and Burton, R. M. "Galacto-Waldenase and the Enzymic Incorporation of Galactose-1-Phosphate in Mammalian Tissues," *Biochem. Biophys. Acta,* XVIII (1955), 444–45.
107. Maxwell, E. S.; Kalckar, H. M.; and Bynum, E. "A Specific Enzymatic Assay for the Diagnosis of Congenital Galactosemia. I. The Consumption Test," *J. Lab. Clin. Med.*, L (1957), 469–77.

108. MAXWELL, J., and PILLINER, A. E. G. "The Intellectual Resemblance between Sibs," *Ann. Hum. Genet.*, XXIV (1960), 23–32.

109. MEREDITH, H. V., and MEREDITH, E. MATILDA. "Concomitant Variation of Measures of Body Size on Boys 5 Years of Age and Measures of Growth Rate for the Ensuing Sexenium," *Growth*, XXII (1958), 1–8.

110. *Molecular Genetics and Human Disease*. Edited by L. I. Garden. Springfield, Illinois: C. C. Thomas, 1961.

111. MONEY, J. "Hermaphroditism, Gender and Precocity in Hyperadrenocorticism: Psychologic Findings," *Bull. Johns Hopk. Hosp.*, XCVI (1955), 253–64.

112. MONEY, J., and HAMPSON, JOAN G. "Idiopathic Sexual Precocity in the Male: Management; Report of a Case," *Psychosom. Med.*, XVII (1955), 1–15.

113. MONEY, J.; HAMPSON, JOAN G.; and HAMPSON, J. L. "An Examination of Some Basic Sexual Concepts: The Evidence of Human Hermaphroditism," *Bull. Johns Hopk. Hosp.*, XCVII (1955), 301–19.

114. MONNIER, M. "Retinal, Cortical, and Motor Responses to Photic Stimulation in Man. Retino-cortical Time and Opto-motor Integration Time," *J. Neurophysiol.*, XV (1952), 469–86.

115. MOORE, K. L. "Sex Reversal in Newborn Babies," *Lancet*, I (1959), 217–19.

116. MORE, D. M. "Developmental Concordance and Discordance during Puberty and Early Adolescence," *Monogr. Soc. Res. Child Develpm.*, XVIII (1953), No. 1.

117. MOSIER, H. D.; SCOTT, W.; and DINGMAN, H. F. "Sexually Deviant Behavior in Klinefelter's Syndrome," *J. Pediat.*, LVII (1960), 479–83.

118. MUSSEN, P. H., and JONES, MARY C. "The Behavior-inferred Motivations of Late- and Early-maturing Boys," *Child Develpm.*, XXIX (1958), 61–67.

119. ———. "Self-conceptions, Motivations, and Interpersonal Attitudes of Late- and Early-maturing Boys," *Child Develpm.*, XXVIII (1957), 243–56.

120. NICOLSON, ARLINE B., and HANLEY, C. "Indices of Physiological Maturity: Derivation and Interrelationships," *Child Develpm.*, XXIV (1953), 3–38.

121. NOELL, W. K. "Differentiation, Metabolic Organization, and Viability of the Visual Cell," *Arch. Ophth.*, LX (1958), 702–33.

122. ORDY, J. M.; MASSOPUST, L. C., JR.; and WOLIN, L. R. "Postnatal Development of the Retina, Electroretinogram, and Acuity in the Rhesus Monkey," *Exp. Neurol.*, V (1962), 364–82.

123. PATAU, K.; SMITH, D. W.; and ASSOCIATES. "Multiple Congenital Anomaly Caused by an Extra Autosome," *Lancet*, I (1960), 790–93.

124. POLANI, P. E.; BRIGGS, J. H.; and ASSOCIATES. "A Mongol Girl with 46 Chromosomes," *Lancet*, I (1960), 721–24.

125. POPE, B. "Socioeconomic Contrasts in Children's Peer Culture Prestige Values," *Genet. Psychol. Monogr.*, XLVIII (1953), 157–220.

126. PRICE, B. "Primary Biases in Twin Studies. A Review of Prenatal and Natal Difference-producing Factors in Monozygotic Pairs," *Amer. J. Hum. Genet.*, II (1950), 293–352.

127. "A Proposed Standard System of Nomenclature of Human Mitotic Chromosomes (Denver, Colorado)." Editorial Comment, *Ann. Hum. Genet.*, XXIV (1960), 319–25.

128. PURPURA, D. P.; CARMICHAEL, M. W.; and HOUSEPIAN, E. M. "Physio-

logical and Anatomical Studies of Development of Superficial Axodentritic Synaptic Pathways in Neocortex," *Exp. Neurol.*, II (1960), 324–47.

129. RABOCH, J., and NEDOMA, KAREL. "Sex Chromatin and Sexual Behavior: A Study of 36 Men with Female Nuclear Pattern and of 194 Homosexuals," *Psychosom. Med.*, XX (1958), 55–59.

130. RACE, R. R., and SANGER, R. *Blood Groups in Man.* Springfield, Illinois: C. C. Thomas, 1959 (third edition).

131. RAFFERY, F. T., and STEIN, ELEANOR S. "A Study of the Relationship of Early Menarche to Ego Development," *Amer. J. Orthopsychiat.*, XXVIII (1958), 170–79.

132. REINECKE, R. D., and COGAN, D. G. "Standardization of Objective Visual Acuity Measurements," *Arch. Ophth.*, LX (1958), 418–21.

133. RIESEN, A. H. "Brain and Behavior: Session I, Symposium, 1959. 4. Effects of Stimulus Deprivation on the Development and Atrophy of the Visual Sensory System," *Amer. J. Orthopsychiat.*, XXX (1960), 23–36.

134. RIGGS, L. "The Human Electroretinogram," *Arch. Ophth.*, LX (1960), 739–54.

135. SANBERG, A. A.; CROSSWHITE, LOIS H.; and GORDY, E. "Trisomy of a Large Chromosome," *J. Amer. Med. Assn.*, CLXXIV (1960), 221–25.

136. SCHWARTING, B. H. "Testing Infants' Vision: An Apparatus for Estimating the Visual Acuity of Infants and Young Children," *Amer. J. Ophth.*, XXXVIII (1954), 714–15.

137. SCHWARZ, V.; GOLDBERG, L.; and ASSOCIATES. "Some Disturbances of Erythrocyte Metabolism in Galactosaemia," *Biochem. J.* LXII (1956), 34–40.

138. SCHWARZ, V.; HOLZEL, A.; and KOMROWER, G. M. "Laboratory Diagnosis of Congenital Galactosemia at Birth," *Lancet*, I (1958), 24–25.

139. SCHWARZ, V.; WELLS, AGNES R.; and ASSOCIATES. "A Study of the Genetics of Galactosemia," *Ann. Hum. Genet.*, XXV (1961), 179–88.

140. SHOCK, N. W. "Basal Blood Pressure and Pulse Rate in Adolescents," *Amer. J. Dis. Child.*, LXVIII (1944), 16–22.

141. SKODAK, MARIE, and SKEELS, H. M. "A Final Follow-up Study of One Hundred Adopted Children," *J. Genet. Psychol.*, LXXV (1949), 85–125.

142. SLATAPER, F. J. "Age Norms of Refraction and Vision," *Arch. Ophth.*, XLIII (1950), 466–79.

143. SMITH, SHEILA M., and PENROSE, L. S. "Monozygotic and Dizygotic Twin Diagnosis," *Ann. Hum. Genet.*, XIX (1955), 273–89.

144. SORSBY, A.; BENJAMIN, B.; and SHERIDAN, M. "Refraction and Its Components during the Growth of the Eye from the Age of Three." Privy Council Medical Research Council Special Report Series No. 301. London: Her Majesty's Stationery Office, 1961.

145. STECHLER, G.; GALLANT, D.; and BERRY, T. "Some Aspects of the Sleeping EEG in the Human Newborn," *EEG Clin. Neurophysiol.*, XIII (1961), 305.

146. STERN, C. *Principles of Human Genetics.* San Francisco: W. H. Freeman & Co., 1960 (second edition).

147. STEWART, J. S. S. "Genetic Factors in Intersexes," *Proc. Royal Soc. Med.*, LII (1959), 817–18.

148. STOLZ, H. H., and STOLZ, LOIS M. *Somatic Development of Adolescent Boys.* New York: Macmillan & Co., 1951.

149. Strandskov, H. H. "A Twin Study Pertaining to the Genetics of Intelligence," *Caryologia Suppl., Att. 9th Int. Cong. Genet.*, 1954, 811–13.

150. Stuart, H. C.; Reed, R. B.; and Associates. "Longitudinal Studies of Child Health and Development, Series II," *Pediatrics*, XXIV (1959), Suppl. No. 5, Part II, 875–974.

151. Sydow, von, G., and Rinne, A. "Very Unequal 'Identical' Twins," *Acta Pediat.*, LXVII (1958), 163–71.

152. Tanner, J. M. *Growth at Adolescence.* Springfield, Illinois: C. C. Thomas, 1955.

153. Tanner, J. M.; Prader, A.; and Associates. "Genes on the Y Chromosome Influencing Rate of Maturation in Man," *Lancet*, II (1959), 141–44.

154. Thomas, J. E., and Lambert, E. H. "Ulnar Nerve Conduction Velocity and H-Reflex in Infants and Children," *J. Appl. Physiol.*, XV (1960), 1–9.

155. Thurstone, Thelma G.; Thurstone, L. L.; and Strandskov, H. H. *A Psychological Study of Twins.* Chapel Hill: University of North Carolina, Psychometric Laboratory, No. 4, 1953.

156. Tjio, J. H., and Levan, A. "The Chromosome Number of Man," *Hereditas*, XLII (1956), 1–6.

157. Toman, J. "Flicker Potentials and the Alpha Rhythm in Man," *J. Neurophysiol.*, IV (1941), 51–61.

158. Tompkins, W. T., and Wiehl, D. G. "Epiphyseal Maturation in the Newborn as Related to Maternal Nutritional Status," *Amer. J. Obstet. Gynecol.*, LVIII (1954), 1366–76.

159. Tryon, Caroline M. *Adjustment Inventory I: Social and Emotional Adjustment.* Berkeley: University of California Press, 1939.

160. Vandenberg, S. G. "The Hereditary Abilities Study," *Eugen. Quar.*, III (1956), 94–99.

161. Wagman, I. H. "Reflex Time during Growth Considered in Relation to Internodal Length and Conduction Velocity," *J. Neurophysiol.*, XVII (1954), 66–71.

162. Walker, A. E.; Woolf, J. I.; and Associates. "Photic Driving," *Arch. Neurol. Psychiat.*, LII (1944), 117–25.

163. Walter, V. J., and Walter, W. G. "The Central Effects of Rhythmic Sensory Stimulation," *EEG Clin. Neurophysiol.*, I (1949), 57–86.

164. Walter, W. G.; Dovey, V. J.; and Shipton, H. "Analysis of the Electrical Response of the Human Cortex to Photic Stimulation," *Nature*, CLVIII (1946), 540–41.

165. Wiedeman, H.-R. "The Result of Haematological Determination of the Genetic Sex in Disturbances of Sexual Development," in *Symposium on Nuclear Sex*, pp. 102–11. Edited by D. R. Smith and W. M. Davidson. London: William S. Heinemann, 1958.

166. Witschi, E. "Genetic and Postgenetic Sex Determination," *Experientia*, XVI (1960), 274–78.

167. ———. "Sex Reversals in Animals and Man," *Amer. Scientist*, XLVIII (1960), 399–414.

168. Witschi, E.; Nelson, W. O.; and Segal, S. J. "Genetic, Developmental and Hormonal Aspects of Gonadal Dysgenesis and Sex Inversion in Man," *J. Clin. Endocr. Metabol.*, XVII (1957), 737–53.

169. WOOLF, J. I.; WALKER, A. E.; and ASSOCIATES. "The Effect of Lesions of the Visual System on Photic Driving," *J. Neuropath. Exp. Neurol.*, IV (1945), 59–67.

170. *Worth's Textbook on Squint.* Edited by F. B. Chavasse. Philadelphia: Blakiston Co., 1939.

171. YAKOVLEV, P. I. "Morphological Criteria of Growth and Maturation of the Nervous System in Man," in *Mental Retardation*, pp. 3–46. Edited by L. C. Kolb, R. L. Masland, and R. E. Cooke. Baltimore: Williams & Wilkins Co., 1962.

172. ZEIDLER, INGA. "The Clinical Electroretinogram. IX. The Normal Electroretinogram. Value of the B-Potential in Different Age Groups and Its Differences in Men and Women," *Acta Ophth.*, XXXVII (1959), 294–301.

173. ZETTERSTRÖM, BIRGITTA. "The Clinical Electroretinogram. IV. The Electroretinogram in Children during the First Year of Life," *Acta Ophth.*, XXIX (1951), 295–304.

174. ———. "The Electroretinogram in Prematurely [Born] Children," *Acta Ophth.*, XXX (1952), 405–8.

175. ———. "Flicker Electroretinography in Newborn Infants," *Acta Ophth.*, XXXIII (1955), 157–66.

CHAPTER II

Sociological Correlates of Child Behavior

JOHN A. CLAUSEN
and
JUDITH R. WILLIAMS

Introduction

The child develops within a social matrix. The nature of that matrix influences what he learns and how he feels about it, even though the processes by which learning takes place may be the same in all societies. Each culture and, to a lesser extent, each group to which the individual belongs provides patternings of expectations and relationships which influence the development of the child's behaviors, skills, and attitudes. More generally, it is only by becoming a participant in society that the child becomes fully human, acquiring a sense of self and realizing his potentialities for symbolic thought.

By the expression, "sociological correlates of child behavior," we may designate the effects of social arrangements, relationships, and expectations, which are not primarily reflections of unique personality constellations surrounding the child but which influence the probability of occurrence of particular types of behavior opportunities and outcomes. The content of behavior is, of course, very largely provided by the culture and subcultures in which one participates. In contemporary urban society, the child has access to a wide range of behavioral alternatives, especially after he has begun to move outside the family and neighborhood environment. The expectations that he comes to share with others are, to a large extent, forged in the process of interaction itself. Nevertheless, they are shaped by the opportunities and constraints of culture and social organization.

Most of the studies which we shall review relate to the broad area of inquiry that sociologists, anthropologists, and psychologists designate as *socialization.* This term refers both to a process and to a set of institutional structures and practices. Through the process of socialization, the biological individual becomes a member of society, endowed with the attitudes and behaviors that are appropriate to his particular society and place in society. In this process, he must learn, at appropriate times, to control impulses, to communicate effectively with others (to interpret their behavior with some accuracy), and to master the interpersonal and technical skills which are required by a person of a given sex, age, and social position. Much that the child must learn will be mastered without formal instruction; all that is needed is incorporation in relationships with others who manifest the behaviors. But nurturance and protection must be provided, limits for the child's behavior must be defined, commentaries on performance must be available and, in addition, some technical knowledge and some lore will require that formal instruction be given by a specialist. These matters are not left to chance, and thus society has its institutional arrangements and preferred ways of accomplishing the socialization of the child. These arrangements vary greatly from society to society, but everywhere one finds some degree of explicit formulation of the aims to be served, designation of agents charged with the responsibility for child care and tutelage, favored techniques of motivating and controlling the child, and rough timetables for the achievement of given phases of the process.

Much of the research on socialization carried out by sociologists and anthropologists has been concerned primarily with describing the patterning of socialization arrangements in a given society, with showing the relationship between particular arrangements and other aspects of social organization and culture, or with delineating variations in child-rearing practices among cultures or within contemporary society. Most often such research has not proceeded to the next step of ascertaining the influence of socialization practices upon child behavior or personality. On the other hand, much of the research reviewed elsewhere in this volume has selected specific behavioral outcomes and has then attempted to identify antecedents in socialization practice which have influenced these outcomes. We shall draw on each of these types of studies, but, in general, the question with which we shall be concerned is: "To what extent are particular types of social arrangements associated with significant differences in the child's socialization experience and in his behavior and personality?"

We shall begin with consideration of the most general features of social organization and culture which have some bearing upon socialization, then narrow the focus somewhat to examine variations associated with social class, ethnic background, and other bases of social differentiation, and finally proceed to the examination of influences deriving from such specific features of socialization arrangements as family size, sibling order, and maternal employment. The progression is thus not only from broad to specific but also from remote to immediate in impact upon the child. To attempt to trace the ways in which features of the economy are translated into child-rearing is to follow a more circuitous and less discernible pathway than that which can be followed for sibling order or father-absence. But whether the features to be discussed are global and remote or specific and immediate, the underlying assumption is that these features have consequences for the child, affecting what and how he is taught and what he learns.

While we shall touch here and there upon the direct interplay of child behavior and the social environment, the amount of research upon which we have to draw in this area is meager in comparison with that on child-rearing practices. Sociologists and anthropologists have devoted surprisingly little study to child behavior as such. Perhaps the greatest interests of sociologists in this area have been in characterizing the general process wherein the child incorporates the responses of others to achieve a social self, and in analyzing the general social conditions and processes that give rise to social conformity on the one hand or various types of deviant behavior on the other. While we shall touch somewhat upon work in these areas, the nature of our assignment—to examine sociological *correlates* of behavior rather than sociological *perspectives* on behavior—directs us more largely to those sociological and anthropological studies which have been concerned with behavioral variations rather than general processes.

Culture and Socialization

To begin with cultural features as the broadest determinant of what happens to the child is also to begin with the most massive and diffuse body of data. There is little in either the substance or theory of cross-cultural literature that is not in some ways pertinent to a review of the impact of culture on the child. Anthropology has not only documented the range and variation of practices but has, by providing a "laboratory of cross-cultural comparison," made it possible to sift out what is culture-bound from what relates to human behavior in general (e.g., see **23, 124**).

If only a few fragments of the cross-cultural literature are covered here, it is not merely a matter of feasibility. Anthropology is essentially concerned with how societies function and how personalities maintain the social order. Child-rearing has most often been viewed as cause and antecedent of personality and of certain features of culture. As Aberle has observed: "In this version, antecedent and consequent pursue each other in a small circle forever, and the answer as to why the socialization pattern is as it is can only be because the socializers were reared as they were" (**1**: 382). Selected for review here are a few contributions which have in part, at least, assumed the inverse and considered aspects of child-rearing as product or consequent of certain aspects of culture.

In a cross-cultural correlational study by Barry, Child, and Bacon (**7**), for instance, child-rearing was related to features of the economy. Over one hundred primarily nonliterate societies were classified as to accumulation of food resources. Rearing practices were rated on a seven-point scale and ranked so as to ascertain the relative stress a society placed on various aspects of socialization. High emphasis on responsibility and obedience were positively correlated with accumulation of food resources; achievement, self-reliance, and independence were negatively correlated with accumulation. A combined, more generalized variable—compliance *vs.* assertion—gave more significant results than any single measure. Societies with low accumulation of food resources almost always had predominant pressure toward assertion. The magnitude of the correlation (.93) leads the authors to conclude that from knowledge of the economy alone, one can predict with accuracy whether a society will, in the rearing of its children, emphasize compliance or assertion.

Another correlational study by Barry and his associates (**6**) narrows the focus on the problem of sex differences in rearing practices and deals with the question of the universality of differential treatment of boys and girls. Again drawing on ethnographic data from over a hundred nonliterate societies, ratings were made on child-rearing practices. For the infancy period, the majority of societies made no sex differentiation and treated their boy and girl children alike. For later childhood, however, differences were common and, in general, consistent with certain universal tendencies in the differentiation of adult sex roles: girls experienced greater pressure toward nurturance, obedience, and responsibility; boys toward self-reliance and achievement-striving. There was, however, by no means perfect uniformity. A careful analysis of the variations, suggested the two following broad generalizations: Large sex differences in the rearing of children are associated (*a*) with an economy that is dependent on superior strength and motor skills requiring strength and (*b*) with societies characterized by large family groups with high co-operative interaction.

Not only sweeping features of culture but such fragmentary aspects as household composition, residence patterns, sleeping arrangements, and the specifics of kinship relationships can affect the timing, techniques, and emphases of child-rearing, as Whiting and his associates (**124**) have demonstrated. The ways in which parents deal with aggression, for instance, are affected by household composition. Children's aggression is most closely but indirectly controlled in extended-family households. When large families share a single dwelling, not only hostilities must be controlled but the methods of control as well must be subdued and unobtrusive. Physical punishment, on the other hand, occurs most frequently in societies where mothers live alone with their children.

Child-rearing also tends to be related to aspects of the cultural belief system. In a study of the correlates of supernatural beliefs, societies with aggressive gods and spirits were found to have relatively rigid, nonpermissive practices, while more indulgent treatment was related to beliefs in benevolent deities. Children's behavior also related to the characteristics attributed to the supernatural; where gods were viewed as aggressive, children were more self-reliant, more independent, and less nurturant than where gods were considered benevolent (**71**).

The emotional fabric of the culture will also shape the child-rearing context. The typical ways in which people in the society relate to each other are manifest within the family (**8, 11, 44**). Javanese society, for example, is marked by extremely pervasive status differentiations and exaggerated formal behavior toward superiors. These patterns are rehearsed within the nuclear family, where the father occupies a paramount position. The respect and deference that must be shown by the child to the father are reflections of and preparations for the ways in which all social relationships are structured among Javanese (**44**).

The Israeli collective settlements (*kibbutzim*) provide an extreme illustration of child-rearing as shaped by ideology and values (**37, 112**). The eastern European settlers were rebels against their origins and came to Israel to establish a society rooted in the land, dedicated to work, a society which would abolish the patriarchal family structure and emancipate its women from their traditional social impediments. The system of child care and education they evolved reflects their ideological rejection of the past and their attempt to fashion a new present and future. The child is reared communally and socialized within and by the peer group. The parents are divested of the authoritarian, disciplinary aspects of their role, and deliberately cast as primarily nurturant, affectional figures. They are neither socializers nor providers, for the *kibbutz* wants its children unencumbered by emotional ambivalence toward parents as well as free of economic dependence upon them. While the collective system of child-rearing is functional and utilitarian for the *kibbutz*, its antecedents must be sought in the ideological convictions and value system of the founding generation.

Social Differentiation and Socialization

SOCIAL CLASS

Linton has pointed out that "no one individual is ever familiar with the total culture of his society, still less required to express all its manifold patterns in his overt behavior. However, the participation of any given individual in the culture of his society is not a matter of chance. It is determined primarily and almost completely as far as the overt culture is concerned, by his place in the society and by the training he has received in anticipation of his occupying this place" (**72:** 55). For the complex industrial society of the

United States, social class—the way people are ranked in the hierarchy of prestige and power—is but one way of defining the individual's place. It has been assumed that the training the child receives is markedly influenced by the position his parents occupy in the hierarchy, that this position provides a distinctive context and distinctive experiences for the child, and that these have an irreversible, or at least enduring, effect. These assumptions, by no means always explicitly stated, have produced a voluminous but often contradictory literature on the relationship of social class to child-rearing and child behavior. Perhaps the very failure to state some of these assumptions explicitly and the failure to conceptualize as to what it is about social class that is relevant and makes the difference for the child account for some of the confusion in findings. There have been several attempts to set the house in order, most notably by Bronfenbrenner (**17**) and Sewell (**109**).

The bulk of the class-linked literature has dwelled on specific infant- and child-care practices, an aspect of child-rearing that has been shown to be least stable (**65**) and least relevant to personality outcome in modern society (**92, 108**). It is also these studies, often remarkably innocent of theory, focusing on specific practices and routines, without any reference to context, that have been most inconsistent and contradictory in their findings (**18, 110**).

The picture is not nearly so chaotic when the focus shifts from these specifics to an assessment of class differences in the less manifest and more enduring dimensions, such as quality of family relationships, patterns of affection and authority, conceptions of parenthood, and expectations for the child. In these studies an attempt is made—either explicitly or implicitly, by the choice of variables—to translate the behavioral requirements and dominant value orientations of a given social class into what impinges on the child. What is consequential for the child is traced to the objective realities of class and the subjective definitions that meaningful adults give to these realities. It is primarily these studies—recent and all too few—that will be drawn upon for an overview of class-linked differences in child-rearing and child behavior.

To begin with the somewhat elusive area of attitudes, it has been shown that, regardless of social status, parents are future-oriented in the qualities they stress and value for their children. The solutions they seek are neither random nor capricious. Middle- and working-class parents,[1] alike, accord high priority to those values that seem both problematic (difficult of achievement) and important (failure to achieve would affect the child's future) (**67**). Their concerns revolve around traits which are deemed to insure success in the role that is anticipated for the child (**3, 85**). Yet what is a matter of concern and stress at the present, as well as the envisioned "end product," reflect the differences in ideology and behavioral requirements for each class. Middle-class parents emphasize internalized standards of conduct: honesty and self-control, curiosity for boys, considerateness for girls. For the working class, what is important and problematic revolves around qualities that assure respectability: obedience, neatness, and cleanliness (**67**).

Conceptions of "good parenthood" parallel the polarized conceptions of the "good child." Working-class mothers were found to conceive of their role as primarily eliciting specific behavioral conformities from the child. Middle-class mothers' expectations were more often in terms of growth and development, affection and satisfaction for themselves and the child (**39**).

In the exercise of authority, parents reflect the differential class patterns of expectations and values. Working-class parents are more likely to respond in terms of the immediate consequences of the child's actions and to focus on the act itself; middle-class parents respond in terms of their interpretations of the child's intent and take into account the child's motives and feelings (**68**). The classes differ, then, in what is punished and what is overlooked. As for the "how" of punishment, the findings are not entirely clear-cut. Bronfenbrenner's summary of evidence over a twenty-five-year span shows that there is consistently more use of physical punishment by working-class parents. Middle-class parents more often resort to "love-oriented" techniques, such as reasoning, isolation, and appeals to guilt—techniques which, while more lenient, are also more compelling and effective (**106**). However, the divergence between classes was less marked in more recent studies. Bronfenbrenner suggests a reduction in the cultural "lag" among working-class parents,

1. "Working class" in this discussion denotes persons who labor or are engaged in less "prestigeful" occupations than those in which the "middle class" generally engage.

a lag which in Kohn's very current data seems to have been wiped out altogether. Kohn (**68**) found that, in dealing with children aged ten or eleven, both working-class and middle-class parents used physical punishment rarely and reserved it for extreme situations only. Definitions of what is extreme, however, varied with class.

The lower-class-family system has been described as rigid, geared toward the maintenance of order, and hierarchical not only in the parent-child relationship but in the parent-parent relationship as well. The child is, therefore, once removed from direct communication with one parent (**75**). Middle-class parents have more acceptant, equalitarian relationships with their children and with each other, and both are more accessible to the child than parents in the working class (**18, 75**). Parental roles in the middle class are less differentiated and less rigidly defined (**20**). Such differentiation as there is, is likely to take the form of each parent assuming more responsibility for support of the child of his own sex. In an inquiry as to the relative importance of support and constraint in child-rearing and their allocation between parents, middle-class mothers were found to emphasize the father's supportive role to the same extent that they emphasized their own. The working-class mothers expected their husbands to be more directive and to play a major role in the imposition of constraints (**69**).

The father who is available and accessible both as instrumental companion and authority figure, especially for the son, is much more of a middle-class than working-class phenomenon (**17, 53**). And in this dual role of companion and authority figure, there seems to be a gradual shift toward emphasis of the former and decline of the latter (**20**). The middle-class mother is taking over some of the authoritative functions the father is abdicating and so, perhaps, closing yet another gap between classes: in the past, the working-class mother has more often been the dominant authority figure in the family (**17, 20**). While the working-class mother has had the longer tradition as authority figure, it is her middle-class counterpart who is more articulate and clear as to her rearing practices and who also tends to assume more personal responsibility for the behavior of her children (**63**).

The nebulous, ill-defined dimension of parental "permissiveness" has been a vigorously debated subject in the class-linked literature.

It is not the intent here to get enmeshed in yet another attempt to unravel the apparent inconsistencies, beyond suggesting that the issue seems to be less one of degree of permissiveness than of kind and timing. The evidence is now preponderantly on the side of greater permissiveness among middle-class parents toward the infant and young child, particularly in respect to his needs and impulses (**9, 18, 106**). As the child grows older, however, and into adolescence, it is the working class that grants greater freedom from parental control and supervision (**75, 96**). Whether freedom from parental control and supervision can be classified in the rubric of "permissiveness" is perhaps questionable. On the other hand, to suggest that it implies parental rejection and neglect does not seem warranted either (**75**). Middle-class and working-class parents do not seem to differ in their amount of involvement and concern for their children but rather in the way they manifest such involvement and concern (**19, 69**).

While there is now greater permissiveness on the part of middle-class parents in respect to the child's needs, there is no relenting in their greater pressures toward ultimate performance. More often for the middle-class than the working-class child, there is greater emphasis on independence in early childhood, and there are more demands and expectations associated with school performance in later years (**101**). "Associated with the stress on scholastic achievement are other achievement oriented values that are more characteristic of the middle than lower class . . . middle-class children are more likely to be taught not only to believe in success, but also to be willing to take those steps that make achievement possible" (**101:** 211). The details of class differences in achievement motivation and achievement values are dealt with elsewhere (see chap. xi).

The enduring effects of social class on personality remain a controversial area with, as yet, far too little substantial evidence to justify even controversy. Much of the data remains inferential. From relationships that have been established between socioeconomic status and rearing practices, assumptions have frequently been made about child personality without any independent assessment of the latter. Rich and textured class personality profiles have been drawn which, while largely unsubstantiated, have resulted in some remarkably tenacious and persistent stereotypes (**34, 48**). In general, these impressionistic approaches attribute better adjustment to the working-class child, who is seen free of the guilt, repressed hostility, and driving anxiety of his middle-class counterpart. For this contention, one can cite no substantial corroboration. Quite to the contrary, several large-scale correlational studies of socioeconomic level and personality favor the middle-class child in "adjustment" (**22, 110**).

A review of the inconclusive literature led Sewell to suggest that future explorations confine themselves "to aspects of personality which are more likely to be directly influenced by the position of the child's family in the social stratification system, such as attitudes, values and aspirations, rather than with deeper personality characteristics" (**109:** 352). If, however, there are class differences in the affective environment, interpersonal patternings, degrees of parental involvement, the family authority structure—and the foregoing review suggests that these do indeed exist—there is no reason to assume that "deeper personality characteristics" remain unscathed.

Recent attempts to define the child-rearing context more precisely have been paralleled by similar attempts at the level of personality outcome. Circumscribed, precisely defined, but not necessarily peripheral, personality variables have been substituted for such global and undefined dimensions as "adjustment" and related to the more consequential and relevant child-rearing antecedents.

Exemplifying this approach is Miller and Swanson's report (**86**) of a series of empirical studies designed to test the hypothesis that differences in children's ways of resolving conflict (defenses) reflect the contrasting experiences of social class. Social class was here, as elsewhere, found to be associated with certain methods of child-rearing. The studies focus on conflicts between aggression and moral needs, and between ambition and fear of failure. In the most general way, the preference for certain kinds of defenses was, indeed, related to the postulated antecedents, with middle-class children favoring defense mechanisms which require many skills, involve minimal distortion, are specific to a situation, and which result in socially acceptable behavior. The working-class children, on the other hand, were predisposed toward defenses that require little previous experience, involve maximum distortion, and that create social difficulties.

Other research attempts have been less ambitious but no less substantial. There is now considerable evidence on the relationship between social class and children's conscience development, aggression, and, particularly, achievement motivation. These findings are reviewed in other chapters.

Identification, as it relates to class, remains as yet little explored, perhaps because it has generally proved to be a precarious and elusive variable. Differences in this respect for working- and middle-class children have been postulated due to different patterns of parental role allocation in the two classes (**69**). Role imitation and role-taking—aspects of identification—are now being studied in relation to early child-rearing practices, and class-linked differences may well emerge (**52, 77**). At least one study has dealt with sex-role identification and has documented the clearer and earlier awareness of sex-role patterns among working-class children (**97**).

More manifest personality dimensions have been related to social class. The degree of conformity and attitudes toward authority, for instance, bear some relationship. Lower middle-class boys are more conforming and acceptant of authority than boys of the upper middle-class, who are reared for greater independence and rebelliousness (**120**). Preliminary findings on adolescent leadership and responsibility, as rated by teachers, suggest that both traits are more pronounced at higher socioeconomic levels. The parental correlates for both leadership and responsibility vary with the sex of the child as well as with social class (**19**).

"INTEGRATION SETTINGS" AND OCCUPATIONAL EXPERIENCE

Social class is but one of the ways of locating the individual in the social structure and is but one of the facets of the over-all cultural fabric that parents reflect in the rearing of their children.

A study by Miller and Swanson (**85**) confirmed many of the class-related trends outlined above and then, cutting across class lines, viewed child-rearing patterns in terms of "integration settings," the ways in which people are integrated with others in the occupational order. Two such settings are delineated: the "individuated-entrepreneurial," now on the decline, and the rapidly emergent "welfare-bureaucratic." The entrepreneurial setting, small in size and with a simple division of labor, values risk-taking and competition. Its participants lack close and continuing contact with each other. Bureaucratic settings are large and employ many different kinds of specialists. Here, neither risk-taking nor competition is relevant, since mobility and income are achieved through specialized training for a particular job. A bureaucratic organization provides support and security to its participants. The child-rearing patterns were expected to be disparate, with entrepreneurial families emphasizing self-control and self-reliance for their children and encouraging an active, manipulative approach to life. Bureaucratic families were expected to stress skills that require getting along with people, to favor accommodative and passive ways, and to allow children spontaneous expression of impulses. While the results fell short of predictions, the relationships found did suggest that occupational settings add a promising dimension to the definition of an individual's place in the society.

A somewhat more circumscribed exploration by Aberle and Naegele (**3**) probed the connection between the father's job situation and his behavior at home. There was a clear-cut though nonspecific relationship between the father's experience in the middle-class occupational role, his future expectations for his children and his evaluation of their conduct. For their sons, the traits which were a matter of concern to the fathers were those which might interfere with success in middle-class occupational life: initiative, achievement, responsibility, appropriate aggressiveness. Far fewer concerns were expressed regarding their daughters, both in terms of their present behavior as well as their future. Marriage was envisioned as the chief goal for girls, and the possibility of a career was most often frowned upon.

Another contribution to the same end is McKinley's study of the relationship between a father's experience of supervision on the job and the closeness with which he supervised his own son (**82**). Fathers who were closely supervised on the job tended either to supervise their sons closely (if they felt content with close supervision) or to neglect them (if they resented the close supervision they themselves received). This resultant takes on additional significance in the light of Maccoby's finding that boys whose parents were restrictive tended to act as rule enforcers with their peers (**77**).

ETHNIC AND MINORITY STATUS

Ethnic group membership—based on race or nationality—is another major basis of social differentiation in American society whose bearing on parental and child behavior has been explored. Here we shall deal with a single ethnic subculture—the Negro—in order to illustrate the meaning to the child of membership in a devalued minority. While devaluation may not be specific to the Negro, it is for him most consistent and relentless.

The Negro child, like all other children, is affected by his family's participation in the culture of the larger society. The characteristic class patternings delineated above, for instance, are largely recapitulated within the Negro subculture (**35, 42, 43**). They are modified but not obliterated by the structural peculiarities of the Negro family, whose historical origins in the slave system have made for a mother-centered, relatively unstable and disorganized family unit (**26, 42**). Simultaneously, however, the Negro child's participation in a devalued group demands additional solutions that take precedence over all others. For the Negro child the life space soon becomes structured in terms of black and white (**98**). He must learn that he has a racial identity that is different from the dominant group and that this identity relegates him to a lower caste status. The adaptations to the lower, devalued status have been shown to vary with historical period, with geographic area, and with socio-economic position (**26, 43, 95**). The learning itself, however, is shared by and common to all Negro children and is accomplished early and well. It begins with the self-recognition as Negro but soon encompasses the perception of social inequalities and the development of compensatory devices and defensive mechanisms—all the psychological by-products that come with devalued position.

The developmental sequence of ethnic learning, which culminates in self-devaluation for the Negro and a well-integrated discriminatory pattern for the white child, has been fairly well documented. It begins at the early preschool level with the simple ability to note similarities and differences (**27, 47, 114**). In response to the variety of pictorial and play stimuli that have been used, most children between the ages of three and five can tell "white" from "colored." These earliest responses are purely perceptual discriminations, and they emerge at a younger age in response to test materials than they do to the self or other people. Self-discriminations occur later and at a differential rate for the Negro and white child. The white child recognizes himself correctly much more often than the Negro, and the discrepancy between the two groups increases with age, with the Negro's confusion persisting much longer and well into the first years of school. The dark Negro child sees himself as a Negro more consistently and at an earlier age than does the lighter one (**27**). Whether for the Negro child there is a genuine lag in racial self-awareness or whether subtle factors of denial are already operative has not as yet been established. While self-recognition is less rapid for the Negro than the white child, the preference for the white doll, face, or puzzle—whatever the experimental stimulus material happens to be—emerges for both Negro and white children as early as the age of three. Again, it is somewhat less marked among the dark and southern Negro children.

While racial preference is clear-cut, it is, at the preschool level at least, phrased simply and concretely and is free of the hostility that comes with age (**47**). Very quickly, however, it becomes embedded in a context of social implications (**98**). Between the ages of five and eight, as the Negro child begins to prefer the doll of his own color, he becomes increasingly aware of its social devaluation. With play materials that afford the opportunity to create unequal situations, the white child will consistently and directly create these for the Negro. For the Negro child, awareness of social inequalities is as high but much more indirect. Denial, avoidance, and ambivalence as well as retaliatory responses are apparent. With the perception of the Negro in the inferior social role, the white child develops not only patterns of exclusion but also a set of interpretations and rationalizations for his excluding behavior—in other words, a philosophy of prejudice. For the Negro child there is an increase in defensive reactions, in negative self-feelings, and in conflicts concerning group belongingness (**99**).

If later ethnic learning has been less extensively explored than the events of the early years, it may be that for both the Negro and the white child so much is "accomplished" by the age of ten. Ethnic learning has been described as a composite of three phases or functions: differentiation, identification, and evaluation. Long before adolescence, children of the white majority and the Negro minority have mastered all three. The ultimate effects for the Negro of the negative self-concepts that emerge so very early have been extensively documented and explored (**33, 38, 64, 90**).

SOCIAL CHANGE AND CHILD BEHAVIOR

The effects of social change upon child behavior are to be sought both in changing socialization practices and in the modification of the child's environment. As Aberle and Naegele (**3**), and others, have pointed out, socialization is to a substantial degree future-oriented. That is, parents and other agents of socialization endeavor to prepare the child for participation in the kind of society that they envision, rather than simply passing on the emphases under which they were raised.

We have already noted the way in which ideology and an image of the society to be established led to the communal system of child care in the *kibbutzim*. To convert barren desert to agricultural use required heavy physical toil, of a sort not previously valued highly by many of the European migrants to Israel. A new set of values had to be infused in the youth who would complete the task, even at the cost of profound alienation between generations. A similar if less dramatic change in values governing child-rearing has been documented by Inkeles for parents in pre- and postrevolutionary Russia (**60**).

As yet, systematic data on changes in socialization practices in the United States are meager, but there are abundant data which reflect changes in ideology and in advice to parents as conveyed by the mass media and other cultural materials. Sunley (**118**), Stendler (**113**), Wolfenstein (**126**), Vincent (**121**), and Miller and Swanson (**85**) have delineated the changing emphases in the literature on child care as these reflect conceptions of human nature, theories of psychological development, current fads in pediatric regimes, and the meaning of parenthood.

In the nineteenth century, the United States was characterized by industrialization, urbanization, expanding commerce, and the growth of a middle class. The literature relating to the family and to child-rearing was predominantly addressed to the rising middle class. The alarms that were sounded may have reflected real changes within the family, or they may merely have reflected an increasingly articulate awareness of problems in a rapidly changing society.

Several conceptions of the child's nature vied for attention. The most prevalent was the Calvinist emphasis on the child's depravity and on the parents' responsibility to break the child's will and free him of his evil nature. At least a few voices, harking back to Locke and Rousseau, stressed the importance of bringing out manly virtues through early "hardening" of the child. A third school viewed the child as inherently innocent, advocated gentle treatment, and emphasized the parents' role in fulfilling and encouraging the child's potentialities and needs (**118**). The last conception gained increasing acceptance with time and with it came the ever stronger advocacy of what are now referred to as love-oriented techniques of discipline, support, and affection—all very much discouraged in the early part of the nineteenth century.

Sunley (**118**), whose analysis covers the period from 1820 to 1860, comments on the emphasis on activity, exploration, and independence, combined, however, with early institution of disciplines, routines, and regularity. The emphasis on activity and independence never waned, but the extreme concern with rigid routines did, prior to its vigorous resurgence following the first World War.

In the latter part of the 1800's the controversy of breast *vs.* bottle took up the bulk of the space in the, by then, very popular advice columns. The bottle, at first seen as the earmark of the wanton woman, became acceptable by the end of the century, although at no time preferable to nursing. The early emphasis on nursing was entirely in terms of its physical benefits; the assertion of psychological benefits did not emerge until the twentieth century (**121**).

Despite changes in conceptions and routines, a number of beliefs have persisted with remarkable tenacity from well before the nineteenth century until well into the twentieth: the emphasis on and concern with early cleanliness and training; the advocacy of early weaning; concern with the evils and dire consequences of masturbation; the desirability of activity and opportunities for the child to explore.

The changing patterns of the last sixty years are more substantially and subtly documented. Stendler (**113**) and Vincent (**121**), whose analyses of child-training literature extend beyond World War II, both conclude that emphasis on rigid disciplines, regimentation, and scheduling reached their peak in the 1920's, then went into gradual decline. Stendler sees this peak as reflecting the impact of Watsonianism as well as the growth of the public health movement, which viewed regimentation and scheduling as one of the antidotes to infant mortality rates and childhood illness. Escalona (**41**) relates the rigidity, scheduling, and careful rationing of manifest affection of the 1920's and 1930's to a sociocultural milieu, whose stability and cohesiveness rested on a sense of technical mastery. Their subsequent upheaval she attributes to a generalized feeling of uncertainty and the absence of a stable value system.

A variant interpretation of the abating rigidity and increasing leniency is given in Wolfenstein's analysis (**126**) of the successive editions of the *Infant Care Bulletin* (1914–1951). She relates the changing conceptions of the infant's nature and the changing trends in handling the child's impulses to a wider range of attitudes in American culture about fun and play. These she sees as gradually having become divested of their puritanical associations with wickedness. Play and fun have assumed an obligatory quality in adult life, and there has been a shift from goodness morality to fun morality. Concomitantly, the infant's impulses, formerly perceived as strong, dangerous, and possibly permanently damaging, have gradually been transformed into harmlessness. The dichotomy between what is pleasant and what is good has been overcome for adult and child alike. Play, which in 1914 was seen as harmful, had by 1945 become a safe and healthful activity.

If dominant ideologies relating to child-rearing, especially in the middle class, can be traced with some confidence for the past half-century, and in a more fragmentary way for a century before that, minimally adequate data on parental practices go back only a little more than two decades. They derive primarily from longitudinal studies of child development and from studies of class differences in child-rearing practices. Bronfenbrenner's review of research on child-rearing practices (**18**) concludes that over the past twenty-five years there have been appreciable changes in parental attitudes and behavior, paralleling to a remarkable degree the changed emphases in expert advice on child care. Although Bronfenbrenner is inclined to regard this correspondence as reflecting the influence of expert advice, as transmitted through the mass media, one may as readily ascribe both the fashions in expert advice and the acceptance of such advice by parents to much more pervasive changes in value orientations. This is not to say that basic value orientations are uninfluenced by developments in science, including psychological science. But far more than the transmission of expert advice is required to change child-rearing patterns. For example, pediatricians and other experts have continually emphasized the desirability of breast-feeding the young infant, yet breast-feeding appears to have declined rather than increased since the beginning of the twentieth century.

In any event, both expert advice and parental socialization practices, especially among the middle class from the 1920's well into the 1950's, do seem to have become more flexible, more permissive of the child's expression of impulses and needs. There is just a suggestion that this trend may have been halted in recent years, and that there has now begun a swing away from extreme permissiveness. The pressure upon colleges now puts a premium on academic excellence that is being transmitted to the child at an ever earlier age. The fun morality which characterizes American childhood is being increasingly challenged by the evidence of greater responsibility, superior physical fitness, and superior intellectual training of children in other countries. This challenge does not necessarily threaten the gains in flexibility and permissiveness in infant care but may do so by bringing about changes in educational emphases which will, in turn, call for anticipatory adjustments on the part of parents.

A recent study by DeCharms and Moeller (**36**) traces changing values through content analysis of public school readers of the fourth-grade level by twenty-year periods from 1800 to 1950. Pages allocated to moral teaching declined over the entire period. Achievement imagery increased from 1800 to 1890, then held constant till the 1930's, then decreased rather markedly in succeeding decades. Affiliation imagery, on the other hand, increased rather steadily until the 1920's and 1930's, then dropped somewhat in succeeding decades. These trends give at least partial support to the thesis advanced by Riesman (**100**) of a trend from child-rearing appropriate to production of inner-directed character types, requiring self-reliance and achievement-orientation, to that which will produce "other-directed" characters, oriented toward winning approval in a society in which one must be able to adapt readily to others. The interpretation of the apparent decline in both achievement and affiliation imagery since the decades centered in 1930 is not clear. If the challenge presented by other educational systems and other value orientations becomes sufficiently strong, however, one might anticipate an increase both in moral teaching and in achievement imagery in educational materials produced in the near future.

Social Contexts and Behavior Settings

The nature and organization of the physical and social environment place a variety of constraints on the child's behavior. He must learn to differentiate among behavior settings and social situations in expressing his behavioral repertoire. At the most obvious level, language and actions appropriate to the boys' clubhouse are often inappropriate to the classroom or even the schoolyard. Proper demeanor in the church service is vastly different from that at the church social. These facts are obvious enough to a preadolescent child, but there has been relatively little systematic study of how the child learns to differentiate appropriate behaviors and of how the variety of behavior settings and personnel available in them influence his participation with others and his feelings about the nature of self and society.

Until quite recently, characterization of the nature of the environment within which the child develops and behaves has been largely limited to somewhat impressionistic descriptions by anthropologists or by sociologists engaged in community studies. The psychological ecology of Roger Barker and his associates, based upon intensive, focused observation and recording, has added data of greater precision than any hitherto available (**5**). Working primarily in small communities, Barker has ascertained the behavior settings in which social interaction takes place and has established the frequency with which various categories of community members participate in these settings. For example, in comparing a small midwestern village ("Midwest") with a slightly larger town in Yorkshire, England ("Yoredale"), Barker notes several significant differences in the distribution by age levels of participants in behavior settings and activities. In Midwest, there was much less segregation by age: inhabitants of all ages were found in 52 per cent of Midwest's behavior settings but in only 23 per cent of Yoredale's. Again, organized recreational activities were predominantly for adults in Yoredale and predominantly for children and adolescents in Midwest. Thus, children growing up in these two communities received very different exposures to adults and perhaps quite different conceptions of how to relate to older persons. While the enduring effects of such situational contexts upon behavior and personality have not yet been assessed, such studies of psychological ecology can be expected to produce more reliable and systematic data on significant patternings of the environment.

The school itself affords a series of behavior settings and definitions of appropriate and inappropriate behaviors and attitudes which have been described in general terms but little studied. Those behavioral scientists who have attempted to characterize the culture and social structure of the school have most often examined urban schools and have been especially struck by the discrepancies between the values and expectations of middle-class teachers and those of lower-class students. To the early studies by Warner, Davis, Havighurst, and their associates (among others, **122**) have been added analyses by Becker (**10**), Hollingshead (**59**), Mayer (**80**), and many others. In general, these studies have found that the most economically and socially deprived segments of the population send to school many children who are (*a*) unmotivated toward educational opportunities, (*b*) disadvantaged in vocabulary and in acquaintance with the phenomena that make up the bulk of the substantive materials presented to the child in the classroom, and (*c*) disapproved of by their teachers because of the offensiveness of much of their speech and deportment to middle-class morality. The school culture is, in general, easily learned by middle-class children. Their parents have prepared them to accept the precepts of the school and provide them with constant reinforcement of the values of the school. For the more deprived members of the working-class population, early school experiences are likely to have been unrewarding for parents, and not much is expected of the school except that it will keep the child for a portion of the day. Under these circumstances, the child enters school triply disadvantaged.

The child's position in the social structure of the classroom is dependent both on personal qualities–intelligence, social skills, talents, appearance–and on his social background (**49**). Children perceived more favorably by their peers are likely to be perceived favorably by their teachers as well. Lippitt and Gold (**73**) found that teachers more often paid attention to the social behavior rather than the performance of children having low power and popularity and were more critical and less supportive of low-power than of high-power boys. In response to their reception by peers and teachers, the self-appraisals of children having low power and prestige among their peers were significantly lower than those of children with high power.

The relationship between self-attitudes and the climate of high-school peer groups has been documented by Coleman (**32**). In general, the high-school culture tends to be dominated by emphases on competitive athletics and social skills, but Coleman found considerable variation among schools in the extent to which other values, such as academic ability, were significant criteria for admission to local elites. Further, degree of expressed satisfaction with self tended to vary according to the extent to which the individual's dominant strengths were those valued in the local student body.

Very similar findings on the importance of the immediate social context in childhood for the individual's performance, aspirations, and self-feelings have recently been reported by Wilson (**125**) and by Rosenberg (**103**). Wilson found that both school performance and aspirations to attend college among high-school boys were markedly influenced by the occupational and educational level of the population served by the school, holding constant the occupational and educational level of the boys' own parents. That is, boys from working-class families tended to achieve higher grades and more often planned to go on to college if they attended schools which served a population predominantly of higher status. It would appear that the greater valuing of educational attainment in such schools was transmitted with sufficient impact to make a difference in the individual's motivations. Rosenberg assessed high-school students' reports of self-esteem and of symptoms frequently associated with psychoneurotic tendencies, as related to the consonance or dissonance between the individual's religious affiliation and the dominant religious group in the neighborhood in which the subjects lived longest. For Catholics, Protestants, and Jews, those reared in neighborhoods in which half or more of the population was of the subject's own faith reported higher self-esteem and fewer psychosomatic symptoms than those reared in dissonant contexts.

The large body of sociological research relating to juvenile delinquency also documents the importance of neighborhood and of the subcultures which thrive in certain urban areas. Even before statistical studies of urban ecology had mapped the distribution of indices of social disorganization, it was apparent that some areas in any large city contain inordinately large amounts of social and personal pathology. Children growing up in such areas are markedly disadvantaged in a wide variety of ways: economic hardship; crowded, dilapidated housing; status deprivation; cultural deprivation; lack of educational and recreational opportunities. Perhaps the greatest disadvantagement of these children comes from the pervasiveness of values and attitudes which, while adaptive to deprivation, tend to neutralize those of the larger society.

The cluster of values prevailing in delinquent groups in urban areas has been well described by Cohen (**30**), Miller (**87**), Matza and Sykes (**79**), and others. It includes the search for excitement or "kicks," disdain for school and work, manipulation and exploitation of others, and an emphasis on aggressive masculinity. Delinquent subcultures take variant forms, such as the criminal, the retreatist, and the conflict types described by Cloward and Ohlin (**29**). Despite some disagreement as to the psychological processes underlying the origins and sustaining the maintenance of such subcultures, there seems little question but that the availability of norms of delinquency and of a social framework within which these norms are transmitted and sanctioned is a psychological fact of tremendous significance to children growing up in many areas of urban America.

The values, social contacts, and social controls to which the child is subject in an urban slum are grossly different from those which surround the middle-class, surburban child. The range of free activity and the heterogeneity of the social context for the child growing up in a disorganized community are likely to confront the child with sharp conflicts as to what constitutes acceptable behavior. How these conflicts are resolved will depend in large part on the degree of satisfaction and reward that can be achieved through available alternatives. It would be difficult to imagine a sharper contrast in environments for the developing child than that between an urban slum in the United States and the small French village that Wylie has described in his *Village in the Vaucluse* (**128**). Here family, school, and other community agents reinforce a single image of the good, the inevitable course of development. At the age of four the child enters school and quickly learns the school routines which will comprise the most important part of his life for the next ten years. Confronted by the unbroken social pressure of parents, teachers, and friends, he learns that there are aspects of life that must be faced, definitions that must be memorized and accepted as they are.

Age and Sex-Role Differentiation

It may seem strange to include categories that are essentially biological along with social class, ethnic status, and situational contexts as bases for social structural differentiation, but age and sex obviously give rise to social as well as biological differentiation. Indeed, as Linton has observed, "the division of the society's members into age-sex categories is, perhaps, the feature of greatest importance for establishing participation of the individual in culture" (**72**: 63–64). While there is an extensive literature on age and sex differences in behavior and personality and there have been a number of general discussions of the importance of age and sex categories (**93**), there are surprisingly little systematic data on the nature of the differing influences upon and definitions of behavior by age and sex. Here again, the most illuminating analyses have tended to come from cross-cultural research and from anthropologists who have viewed socialization practices within Western society from a perspective gained through familiarity with very different patterns. Barry's finding that large sex differences in the rearing of children are associated with an economy dependent on physical strength (**6**) has already been noted. It also appears, in general, that the larger the number of adults in the household, the greater the likelihood of sex-role differentiation both among adults and in the rearing of children.

Sex-role identification has, of course, been widely studied, as has the age at which children recognize their sex and correctly identify themselves. One dramatic evidence of the crucial importance of social definitions in the realm of sex identification comes from medical research on infants born with genital anomalies, so that their sex is ambiguous. Frequently the sex initially assigned to the child is contradictory to their chromosomal, gonadic, and (at puberty) hormonal sex. They nevertheless establish a gender role in conformity to the sex assigned them at birth and confirmed in myriad ways in day-to-day interaction with others. Even their erotic orientation is, with rare exceptions, consonant with the sex of rearing. Moreover, in instances where it is decided medically to reassign sex in accordance with the predominant biological orientation, severe problems of psychological reorientation are encountered unless the change is made before the age of two (**89**).

Descriptions of the different patternings of expectation that extend to boys and girls almost inevitably smack of the obvious when they relate to one's own society. The very fact that they are so completely taken for granted means that they are not problematic for most students of the society. From infancy, there are both marked and subtle differences in the way parents and others speak to sons and daughters, the way they are dressed, the toys they are given, the activities they are encouraged or permitted to engage in. A certain level of aggression is not only permitted to boys; it is enjoined. Much less is approved in the case of girls. Techniques of control tend to differ also, with praise and withdrawal of love used more often with girls; physical punishment used relatively more often with boys (**17, 106**). But there is evidence that sex-role differences among children have markedly diminished in recent decades in the United States, just as they have diminished among adults both within and outside the family. Everyday dress has become almost identical for boys and girls in many communities, with feminine frills reserved for "dress-up" occasions. More so than most European countries, we tend to blur sex differences in activities and division of labor.

Coupled with the increasing similarity in the regimes of boys and girls during their preadolescent years is an increasing precocity in heterosexual dating. The trend to earlier interest in relationships with the opposite sex is documented by Jones (**62**), using data secured from students drawn from the same junior high schools over a period of twenty years. Both boys and girls showed significant and substantial increases in attendance at dances and in preoccupation with dating and personal grooming. Moreover, boys and girls appeared more studious, more broadly interested in the contemporary scene, more tolerant in their social attitudes, and more socially sophisticated in the 1950's as compared with the 1930's. Far more girls reported participation and interest in sports in the 1950's—another sign of increased similarity of behavior patterns of the two sexes.

Formal age-grading does not occur to any great extent in contemporary American society except within the educational system and in connection with legal and political status, though privileges and responsibilities for both sexes are loosely linked with age level. To a considerable extent, however, the status of being a student overrides age, as such, in determining what is expected of a child or adolescent. The long period during which this status is occupied, most often without any other major responsibilities, may be contrasted with the gradual or even sudden taking on of adult occupational-role functions in most other societies and, indeed, in the United States until recent decades. Thus, the child comes to think of himself in the student role and to have only a dim conception of himself as filling an occupational role until well along in adolescence. Rather than anticipating his occupational role, it appears that the preadolescent may look forward to participating in the "youth culture" of adolescence, with its relative freedom from adult-imposed restrictions (**13**). It is in adolescence, in the United States and in Western society generally, that the peer group exerts its strongest pull.

Eisenstadt (**40**) has examined the circumstances under which well-defined age groups arise and the functions which they serve. Age groups tend to come into being in those societies where kinship groupings do not adequately facilitate the attainment of full social status by junior members. The age-homogeneous grouping provides both a vehicle for learning and a source of acceptance and support for the individual. The significance of the peer group for the adolescent in American society can be ascribed, at least in part, to the fact that the status of the adolescent is left ambiguous. In Linton's words:

> In societies which recognize adolescents as a distinct category and ascribe to them activities suited to their condition, the period passes with little or no stress and the transition from the roles of childhood to those of adult life is accomplished with little shock to the personality. Societies which choose to ignore the particular qualities of adolescence may elect to deal with the situation in either of two ways. They may extend the child category, with its ascribed attitudes and patterns of

overt behavior, upward to include adolescents, or they may project the adult category downward to include them. In either case the adolescent becomes a problem for himself and for others. . . . Perhaps the one thing worse than either of these methods is to do as we do and leave the social role of adolescents in doubt (**72:** 67–68).

The example of adolescence illustrates an aspect of all socialization: whether or not formal age grades are recognized, the expectations which the child must meet are constantly changing. The changes may be gradual, shading into one another, so that the child's self-expectations keep pace; or they may be abrupt, bringing discontinuities and sudden demands for which the child is quite unprepared. Where statuses are clear, and where transitions are smooth and continuity is preserved, relationships tend to be more tranquil, less subject to turmoil (**12**).

Family Structure and Functioning

The influences of the larger social structure and culture are mediated almost exclusively through the family during infancy and early childhood. Even when the child moves outside the family circle, his initial orientation to school, to ethnic differences, and to other groups and situations has been provided by the family, consonant with its place within the social structure. Apart from the family's role in transmitting the social heritage, but influencing the way transmission is accomplished, are certain family characteristics. It is a group of definable size and composition, with its own division of labor and of power. Each child occupies a unique position within his family, a place that has consequences for his learning and his self-conception. It is such matters with which we shall deal in this final section.

Studies of the family in other cultures have served to point up the gross variations in child-rearing and family functioning associated with differences in family size and structure. In the matrilineal Hopi household, for example, as in most extended families, not one but several women stand in the relation of mother, minister to the child's needs, and are called by the same name as mother.[2] An assessment of cross-cultural data suggests that extended and polygynous fami-

2. A description of the implications of Hopi family structure for the socialization experience of the child is given by Aberle (**2**).

lies where there are more than two adults living in the household tend to be indulgent with their children, while discipline is most harsh in families where the mother is the sole adult (**124**). Unfortunately, relatively few aspects of family structure and functioning have been systematically studied in a large number of societies. In general, then, anthropological data bearing on this topic serve to illustrate the kinds of variations that are found in family structure and patterns of personality development that are associated with them, but the data do not permit the drawing of firm generalizations.

FAMILY SIZE

There have been surprisingly few studies of the effects of family size upon socialization practices and child behavior. In a study based on a pick-up sample of 100 families, Bossard sought to characterize patterns of interaction and of child-rearing in families with six or more children (**14**). The lack of systematic sampling and of a control group of families with a smaller number of children makes generalization perilous, but Bossard's findings do suggest much greater reliance on rules of conduct and procedure to maintain order in the large family, more enforcement of discipline, often with use of physical punishment, high participation in child-rearing by older siblings, and a substantial division of labor and function among siblings.

Within the larger family, responsibility is likely to be valued above individual achievement, and conformity above individualistic self-expression. The small family tends more often to be oriented toward status-striving and upward mobility. Indeed, a prime reason for limitation of family size is to permit the maintenance of a higher standard of living and the provision of greater opportunities and benefits to the children. On the basis of such considerations, Rosen predicted that children from small families would tend to have a higher achievement motivation than those from large families (**102**). His data, in general, confirmed the prediction but also showed substantial interaction effects with social class and ordinal position.

Several other studies have investigated the relationship between family size and social or emotional adjustment as measured by sociometric choice or by psychological tests. The correlations found have been nonsignificant or, at most, slight. Failure to control for differences in socioeconomic status (larger families tending to be of lower status) renders dubious any interpretation except that the effects of family size upon the child's general adjustment are neither great nor consistently predictable.

SIBLING ORDER

Intertwined with the effects of family size are those related to the child's order of birth and the sex and spacing of siblings. The meaning of ordinal position has been a favorite topic of speculation and research for decades, but only within the past decade have research and theory been well enough co-ordinated to produce consistent results with at least partial specification of intervening processes. Koch's carefully designed study of 360 five- and six-year-old children from two-child families has provided a wealth of data demonstrating that for children of this age-level significant differences in abilities and attitudes are associated with ordinal position and with interactions between ordinal position, age differentials, and sex of sibling.[3] The enduring effects of birth order upon affiliative behavior in the face of anxiety-producing situations have been impressively documented by Schachter (**104**), who combined experimental studies with data from a variety of life situations. First-born children appear to be somewhat more fearful and substantially more inclined to seek the company of others when faced by fearful stimuli or situations. Again, consistent differences in interpersonal styles, persisting into adulthood, have been found by MacArthur (**76**), and others, with first-born children tending to be more conscientious, shy, and somewhat constrictive in comparison with later-born.

Attempts to study differences in socialization experience associated with sibling order have been less widespread than attempts to find personality differences. Since several major studies of child-rearing have included classification of sibling order, however, it is possible to draw upon them to delineate some of the ways in which ordinal position makes a difference. The effects of ordinal position, as regards socialization experience, appear to be a consequence of:

1. Parental attitudes and experience—e.g., parents are more insecure and overconcerned with first-born.

3. Of the many publications resulting from this research, reference **66** has been selected as giving a good overview of methods, findings, and references to other papers in the series.

2. Amount and intensity of parent-child interaction—e.g., parents are generally more available to first-born children because of fewer competing demands for time and attention.
3. Availability of child models in learning age- and sex-roles—e.g., boys with older brothers have pace-setters and models for appropriate behaviors.
4. Displacement of older siblings by new arrivals—e.g., there is greater intensity of displacement experience by the eldest child who has had his parents to himself, possibly leading to greater dependency needs.
5. Effects of parental age, apart from those in item 1, above (since first-born children have younger and last-born have older parents).

The significance of each of these effects has been shown by at least one or two studies, but results are seldom wholly consistent from study to study. One explanation is certainly the importance of interaction effects by age difference, sex of sibling, size of family, and social class. Thus, in the previously reported study by Rosen (**102**), oldest children tended to have higher achievement motivation than youngest children in large-sized, middle-class families, but the reverse was true in lower-class families. Only as findings are based on larger, carefully characterized samples and as replications are obtained can the interacting effects be disentangled.

THE PATTERNING OF PARENTAL AUTHORITY AND FAMILY TIES

It is probable that in no other relationship does one possess such unlimited power over another person as a parent possesses over his children. Parental authority is sanctioned as appropriate so long as it is not exercised with brutality, though it appears that the naked use of parental power (with or without physical force) is markedly less in contemporary America than it was a century or more ago (**17**). It also appears, as earlier indicated, that there has been a relative decrease in the authority role of the father and an increase in that of the mother during recent generations (**20**). Quite apart from trends in authority relations, there is evidence that both the degree and expression of parental control and the relative allocation of control and affectional or supportive functions between parents may have significant consequences for the child's behavior.

The degree of parental restrictiveness will, of course, determine the range of behavior settings available to the child, the composition of his peer-group, and the opportunities he has to try out behavioral alternatives on his own. Degree of restrictiveness appears to be related to ethnic background and social status as well as to parental personality. A good example of extreme parental restrictiveness is afforded by the descriptions given by Wolfenstein (**127**) and by Pitts (**94**) of children's play and peer-group relations among bourgeois French families. Here the child does not fully select his playmates but, in general, plays under close supervision with children approved by his parents. Placidity, cleanliness, and avoidance of aggression are rigorously enforced, with the result that, by American standards, the French child appears extraordinarily controlled. When peer-group relationships are established through the school, these tend to be charged with ambivalence and hostility.

Hoffman, Rosen, and Lippitt have examined the school performance and peer acceptance of children subjected to varying combinations of parental coerciveness and autonomy (**58**). It was hypothesized that parental coerciveness toward boys would arouse hostility and needs for self-assertion but that coerciveness coupled with autonomy would contribute to the development of social skills and self-confidence. Those boys with parents who were coercive and who granted high autonomy did, indeed, show higher hostility and self-assertion, higher self-confidence, and superior performance and peer-acceptance than did boys whose parents showed any other combination of autonomy and coerciveness.

More recently, Bronfenbrenner has presented data on correlates of leadership and responsibility in junior high school students suggesting that

> . . . both extremes of either affection or discipline were deleterious for all children, but that the process of socialization entailed somewhat different risks for the two sexes. Girls were especially susceptible to the detrimental influence of overprotection; boys, to the ill effects of insufficient parental discipline and support. Or, to put it in more colloquial terms: Boys suffered more often from too little taming; girls, from too much (**17**: 11).

He further found that boys tend to be more responsible when the father rather than the mother is the principal disciplinarian; but girls are more dependable when the mother is the chief authority figure.

The relationship between the child's perception of parental authority and of personality has been studied by a number of investigators. Henry and his associates (**55**) found an association between overt aggressiveness or self-punitiveness and the patterning of parental authority and affection. In general, when the father was the primary source of authority and the mother the primary source of affection, boys showed higher aggressive responses; where the mother was the primary source of both authority and affection, the boys responded to stress with self-blame and anxiety. In a similar vein, Hoffman (**57**) finds that boys who report their fathers higher on discipline are rated by their teachers as higher on impulsivity, aggressiveness, and the use of physical force as well as on the initiation of friendships. Their peers regard these boys as having high influence. Girls from mother-dominant homes, however, had difficult relations with the opposite sex, were disliked by boys, and showed a pattern of overcontrol of impulses. It is not clear whether Hoffman's and Bronfenbrenner's findings with reference to girls are consonant.

Cross-cutting relative authority patterns and affectional ties between parents and child are a number of other attributes of the marital relationship. There is, first of all, the actual balance of power and influence between the parents vis-à-vis each other as against their relative authority over the child. Relatively few studies have explicitly dealt with the difference between parental power over major decisions and relative parental authority with reference to a given child. Kohn and Clausen have found the two to be related but by no means the same (**70**). Beyond this, there is the matter of approval or disapproval of the spouse that is communicated to the child by each parent. Particularly in working-class families, Kohn found that mothers who reported themselves the chief setters of limits for the child were more likely to make comments critical of their husband's performance as fathers in the course of the interview. If disparagement of the father is coupled with dominance of the mother, one would expect that sons would have difficulty in identifying with the father, and daughters might well tend to devalue males in general. On the other hand, a mother who is chief disciplinarian of the child but who uses her authority to support and enhance the status of her husband would create quite a different male image for the children. Thus, Helper (**54**) found that the tendency of a high-school boy to see himself as similar to his father is significantly related to the mother's approval of the father as a model for the boy.

THE FATHER-ABSENT FAMILY

The importance of the father as a role model for the son, facilitating appropriate sex-role identification, is one of the most basic elements in psychoanalytic theory. Much research has demonstrated that the father's characteristics and availability do make a difference in the son's personality and behavior (e.g., see **91**). In so far as the presence or absence of a stable father figure is influenced by social or cultural factors, then, one would expect to find resultant group differences in personality characteristics.

Several types of father-absence have been investigated: the matriarchal Negro family, in which father-absence reflects the brittleness of the marital tie, with a high incidence of desertion by the male; the recurrent, long-lasting absences of sailor-fathers; and the long-lasting but single-time absences of fathers in military service during wartime. Mischel (**88**), studying the effects of father-absence on delay of gratification among Negro children in Trinidad and Grenada, found that both boys and girls aged 8–9 were more likely to prefer immediate gratification over delayed, larger gratification if they came from father-absent families. This relationship was not found for older subjects, however.

Tiller (**119**) and Lynn and Sawrey (**74**) have studied a sample of families of Norwegian officers of merchant marine or whaling ships, each with a child aged 8–9 years. As Tiller points out, father-absence for the child is husband-absence for the wife, and the wife's responses to this absence may in themselves influence the child's behavior. Thus, sailors' wives were found to participate less actively in the community, to be more overprotective, and more inclined to stress the importance of obedience and politeness for their children in comparison with controls. The children themselves were found to show higher dependence, pseudo-maturity, and idealization of the absent fathers. Lynn and Sawrey found significant sex differences in personality responses, with boys showing greater immaturity, compensatory masculinity, and poorer peer adjustment (as evidenced by mother's report) and girls showing greater dependency.

In study of children aged 6–10 whose fathers had been in the

Armed Forces abroad for from one to three years, and who were still away at the time of the investigation, Bach (**4**) found a tendency toward idealistic fantasies of the father as evidenced in doll-play. Children whose fathers were away showed more affectionate and less aggressive fantasies than controls from intact families. Especially significant was the finding that the child's fantasies about the father were markedly influenced by the emotional tone and evaluative connotations of the mother's references to her husband. Here again is a dimension which shows class and subcultural variability.

The finding of diminished aggressiveness on the part of boys whose fathers were absent was also obtained by Sears, Pintler, and Sears (**107**). Tendencies toward effeminate, nonaggressive behavior were also noted by Stolz (**116**) among boys born during their fathers' wartime absence. Upon return of the fathers, these children showed a great increase in fantasies of aggression, though they continued for a time to be more effeminate than boys whose fathers had been constantly present.

Relative to father-absence is the closeness and intensity of the child's claim upon his mother during infancy and early childhood. Whiting and his associates have examined cross-cultural data on correlates of mother-child sleeping arrangements (**123**). They reasoned that, in instances where the infant has the exclusive attention of the mother at night (father sleeping elsewhere), males will tend to form a primary identification with the mother, leading to sex-identity conflicts in puberty. Such conflicts would be most intense in patrilocal societies (in which the domestic unit consists of a group of males closely related by blood). In nearly all such societies there are elaborate initiation ceremonies for males at puberty. Whiting has argued that such initiation rites serve to overthrow the primary feminine identity and to establish firmly a male identity (**123**). While Young (**131**) has challenged this interpretation and offered an alternative in terms of the significance in these societies of exclusive male organizations, the relationships between mother-infant sleeping arrangements and sex-role identity remain both plausible and significant.

McCord, McCord, and Thurber (**81**) have examined the correlates and apparent consequences of father-absence in a sample of lower-class, relatively deprived families included in the Cambridge-

Somerville Youth Study. They focused upon broken homes, from which the father was absent by virtue of death, desertion, divorce, or long-term incarceration in a prison or mental hospital. Unlike Tiller, they found no differences in maternal overprotection or punitiveness between father-absent and intact families. In this sample, however, deviance of either or both mother and father (prior to departure) was much more frequent in the group of broken families than in intact families. In contrast to findings on younger boys whose fathers were temporarily out of the home, this study found aggressive behavior more prevalent among boys from father-absent families than among controls. Very often, however, it was coupled with signs of feminine identification, a combination found most often in broken homes where the mother was deviant, cold, ambivalent, or rejecting; or, if the mother was warm and nondeviant, only in those instances when the father left the home when the boy was between the ages of 6–12. Two other types of problem behavior—high sex anxiety and adult criminality—were likewise found more often in the broken homes than in intact homes. Rates of these problem behaviors among father-absent families were not, however, higher than rates among intact families characterized by intense conflict. Thus it appears that the effects of father-absence in this sample, and in others which use broken homes as a means of securing father-absent families, are confounded by the parental characteristics which may have given rise to the absence of the father.

MATERNAL EMPLOYMENT

The increasing number of mothers joining the labor force has stimulated a prolific literature on the resultants of maternal employment. In most studies, maternal employment has been treated as a nonvariant, uniform factor, and one can find corroborative evidence for almost any statement about the effects of the mother's work status on the family and child (**116**). More recently, attempts have been made not only to control various correlates of maternal employment which may lead to spurious inferences but also to view the outcome for the family as a whole and for the child in terms of more subtle categories, such as the meaning of work for the mother, her degree of satisfaction in the worker role, the changes in family structure resulting from maternal employment, and the direct effects of the mother's work on the behavior of the child.

Exemplifying research which specifies the meaning of work is a recent study of middle-class mothers subdivided into four groups according to employment status and preference for working or being at home (**130**). While there were no differences in the child-rearing practices of the working and nonworking mothers, there was a relationship between the mother's satisfaction in her nonmother role and the adequacy of her maternal behavior. Of the four groups, the most deficient were those mothers who wanted to work but did not, out of a feeling of duty. They had more difficulty in areas of control, less emotional satisfaction in their relationships with their children, and less confidence in their function as mother. The same study suggested that maternal employment brings different kinds of familial adaptations. College-trained mothers, for example, made a conscious effort to compensate for time spent away from their children; mothers with less education did not.

A study by Hoffman is one of many recent attempts to specify the changes in family structure that stem from maternal employment (**56**). Treating the mother's employment as the independent variable, the study dealt with the effects of the husband's and wife's household participation and the husband-wife power relationship when relevant ideologies as to male and female roles were held constant. Employed mothers were found to participate less and their husbands more in household tasks. Again, employed mothers made fewer decisions about routine household matters than nonworking mothers, while their husbands made more. The mother's employment affected the family power structure only in interaction with the relevant ideologies and the personalities of husband and wife, suggesting that power relationships are more deeply ingrained and less responsive maternal employment alone than the simple division of household labor.

At the third level—namely the direct effect of maternal employment on the behavior of the child—is a carefully controlled study, by Siegel and associates, of dependence and independence among kindergarten children (**111**). A survey of employment status and family characteristics in two suburban communities revealed that working mothers had significantly fewer children, had older children, and less often represented intact homes. When the effects of these confounding variables were eliminated through matching, the five- to six-year-old children of working mothers did not differ in dependence or independence from the same-aged children of nonworking mothers. There was, however, just a suggestion that boys and girls may respond somewhat differently to the employment of their mothers.

The possibility that the working mother is a different stimulus to the development of self-concepts is now being explored by Hartley (**51**). For girl children, at least, self-concepts are expected to be freer and broader as a result of having a mother who is responding to a greater variety of tasks and opportunities. The effects on boys are expected to be less clear cut.

MATERNAL DEPRIVATION AND INSTITUTIONAL REARING

Having discussed recent studies on the importance of the father and on the effects of maternal employment, at least some brief mention is required of the effects of deprivation of a stable mother figure. It is significant that one can speak of the "father-absent family," while the expression "mother-absent family" seems a contradiction in terms. Fathers are much less likely to maintain a home for their children in the absence of the mother than are mothers in the absence of the father. Instead, the father whose wife dies, or deserts him, or is hospitalized for illness of long duration most often places the child with other relatives, in a foster home, or in an institution. When the child is deprived of his mother during the early years, his immediate response is, in general, one of profound disturbance. The long-range effects may not, however, be as devastating as had been feared when the phenomenon of maternal deprivation first received widespread attention.

Two very thorough reviews of the literature relating to maternal deprivation have very recently been published—by Casler (**25**) and by Yarrow (**129**). Yarrow distinguishes four types of deviation from the hypothetical mode of maternal care which have been dealt with in the literature: institutionalization; separation from a mother or mother-substitute; multiple mothering (as when a child passes through a succession of foster homes); and deficits in the quality of mothering. Especially relevant here is his characterization of the psychologically relevant aspects of institutional environments. In general they tend to be lacking in sensory stimulation and in variations in feeling tone; the infant receives much less mothering contact than he would in his own home; the mother-figure is variable; there is minimal opportunity for learning or practicing new skills; and there is little recognition for positive achievements. It appears that intellectual defects and deficits in interpersonal skills are more frequent long-term correlates of institutionalization than is extreme psychopathology, but findings vary considerably from study to study. The excellence of Yarrow's review of the state of knowledge in this area and the inadequate specification of the nature of the environment (one of the weakest aspects of most of this research) preclude further consideration here.

A GENERAL COMMENT ON RESEARCH ON FAMILY STRUCTURE AND SOCIALIZATION

Patterns of family structure, or changes in structure, are clearly not simple dimensions or variables. While family size, birth order, and absence of either parent can and often do have significant consequences for the child's identification, role-learning, and modes of relating to others, the psychological consequences depend upon processes that are influenced by the larger social context, by interaction with other family characteristics, and by the unique constellations of persons (attitudes, adaptations, relationships) involved. Thus, the effects of family size upon achievement motivation appear to differ by social class and by ordinal position; and the effects of father-absence appear to differ according to the timing and duration of the absence, the mother's attitudes toward the father (and perhaps males in general), and the mother's own adequacy and warmth. Moreover, it is only by specification of the intervening processes of control, modeling, and other modes of influence, along with the feelings which they engender, that one can begin to translate the social facts of family structure and functioning into psychological generalizations.

Conclusion

In this chapter we have attempted to give an overview of recent research on the ways in which the sociocultural environment influences the rearing of children and their behavioral repertoire. Growing up entails the acquisition of a series of group memberships, beginning with the one group that is universal in all societies, the family. Both the structure of the family and the norms that govern relationships within it are responsive to broader cultural orientations and have implications for the child's development. As the child's social world widens to include not only relatives but playmates and adults to whom he is not related, he learns to make assessments of others and to guide his behaviors in terms of situational and contextual requirements. Unfortunately, very little research has focused on the nature of the small child's social world and the ways in which its expansion influences his developing skills and self-concept.

At each age level, often differently for each sex, the child is subject to changing expectations, redefinitions of appropriate behavior, new freedoms and new restrictions. Certain definitions of experience and of the nature of the world in which he lives come to be taken completely for granted; others undergo challenge as he moves from the confines of family and neighborhood into the more heterogeneous, larger society. In each group to which he belongs, the norms of the group—definitions of preferred behavior and of unacceptable behavior—influence the direction of the child's striving and shape his image of himself.

BIBLIOGRAPHY

1. Aberle, David F. "Culture and Socialization," in *Psychological Anthropology: Approaches to Culture and Personality*, pp. 381–99. Edited by Francis L. K. Hsu. Homewood, Illinois: Dorsey Press, 1961.
2. ———. *The Psychosocial Analysis of a Hopi Life-History*. Comparative Psychology Monographs, Vol. XXI. Berkeley: University of California Press, 1951.
3. Aberle, David, and Naegele, Kaspar D. "Middle-class Fathers' Occupational Role and Attitudes toward Children," *Amer. J. Orthopsychiat.*, XXII (April, 1952), 366–78.
4. Bach, George R. "Father-Fantasies and Father-typing in Father-separated Children," *Child Develpm.*, XVII (March–June, 1946), 63–80.
5. Barker, Roger, and Wright, Herbert F. *Midwest and Its Children*. Evanston, Illinois: Row, Peterson & Co., 1955.
6. Barry, Herbert A.; Bacon, Margaret K.; and Child, Irwin L. "A Cross-cultural Survey of Some Sex Differences in Socialization," *J. of Abnorm. Soc. Psychol.*, LV (November, 1957), 327–32.
7. Barry, Herbert A.; Child, Irwin L.; and Bacon, Margaret K. "Relation

of Child-training to Subsistence Economy," *Amer. Anthropol.*, LXI (February, 1959), 51–63.

8. BATESON, GREGORY. "Some Systematic Approaches to the Study of Culture and Personality," in *Personal Character and Cultural Milieu*, pp. 131–36. Edited by Douglas Haring. Syracuse, New York: Syracuse University Press, 1956.
9. BAYLEY, NANCY, and SCHAEFFER, EARL S. "Relationships between Socioeconomic Variables and Behavior of Mothers toward Young Children," *J. Genet. Psychol.*, XCVI (March, 1960), 61–77.
10. BECKER, HOWARD S. "Social Class and Teacher-Pupil Relationships," in *Education and the Social Order*, pp. 273–85. Edited by Edwin R. Carr and Blaine E. Mercer. New York: Rinehart & Co., Inc., 1957.
11. BENEDICT, RUTH. "Child Rearing in Certain European Countries," *Amer. J. of Orthopsychiat.*, XIX (April, 1949), 342–50.
12. ———. "Continuities and Discontinuities in Cultural Conditioning," *Psychiatry*, I (May, 1938), 161–67.
13. BERNARD, JESSIE. "Teen-age Culture: An Overview," *Annals Amer. Acad. Pol. Soc. Sci.*, CCCXXXVIII (November, 1961), 1–12.
14. BOSSARD, JAMES H. S., and BOLL, ELEANOR S. *The Large Family System.* Philadelphia: University of Pennsylvania Press, 1956.
15. BRIM, ORVILLE G., JR. "Family Structure and Sex Role Learning by Children," *Sociometry*, XXI (March, 1958), 1–16.
16. ———. "The Parent-Child Relation as a Social System: I, Parent and Child Roles," *Child Develpm.*, XXVIII (September, 1957), 343–64.
17. BRONFENBRENNER, URIE. "The Changing American Child–A Speculative Analysis," *Journal of Soc. Issues*, XVII, No. 1 (1961), 6–18.
18. ———. "Socialization and Social Class through Time and Space," in *Readings in Social Psychology*, pp. 400–425. Edited by Eleanor Maccoby, Theodore Newcomb, and Eugene Hartley. New York: Henry Holt & Co., 1958.
19. ———. "Some Familial Antecedents of Responsibility and Leadership in Adolescence," in *Leadership and Interpersonal Behavior*, pp. 239–71. Edited by Luigi Petrullo and Bernard Bass. New York: Henry Holt & Co., 1961.
20. BRONSON, WANDA C.; KATTEN, EDITH S.; and LIVSON, NORMAN. "Patterns of Authority and Affection in Two Generations," *Journal of Abnorm. Soc. Psychol.*, LVIII (March, 1959), 143–52.
21. BROWN, DANIEL G. "Sex-Role Development in a Changing Culture," *Psychol. Bull.*, LV (July, 1958), 232–42.
22. BURCHINAL, LEE G.; GARDNER, BRUCE; and HAWKES, GLENN R. "Children's Personality Adjustment and the Socioeconomic Status in Their Families," *J. of Genet. Psychol.*, XCII, Second Half (June, 1958), 149–59.
23. CAMPBELL, DONALD T. "The Mutual Methodological Relevance of Anthropology and Psychology," in *Psychological Anthropology: Approaches to Culture and Personality*, pp. 333–52. Edited by Francis L. K. Hsu. Homewood, Illinois: Dorsey Press, 1961.
24. CARR, EDWIN R., and MERCER, BLAINE E. *Education and the Social Order.* New York: Rinehart & Co., Inc., 1957.
25. CASLER, LAWRENCE. *Maternal Deprivation: A Critical Review of the Literature.* Monographs of the Society for Research in Child Development, Vol. XXVI, No. 2, Serial No. 80, 1961.

26. CAYTON, HORACE, and DRAKE, ST. CLAIR. *Black Metropolis.* London: Jonathan Cape, 1946.

27. CLARK, KENNETH B., and CLARK, MAMIE K. "Racial Identification and Preference in Negro Children," in *Readings in Social Psychology*, pp. 169–78. Edited by Guy Swanson, Theodore Newcomb, and Eugene Hartley. New York: Henry Holt & Co., 1947 (second edition).

28. ———. "Skin Color as a Factor in Racial Identification of Negro Pre-school Children," *J. of Soc. Psychol.*, XI, First Half (February, 1940), 159–69.

29. CLOWARD, RICHARD A., and OHLIN, LLOYD E. *Delinquency and Opportunity.* Glencoe, Illinois: Free Press, 1960.

30. COHEN, ALBERT K. *Delinquent Boys.* Glencoe, Illinois: Free Press, 1955.

31. COHEN, YEHUDI. *Social Structure and Personality.* New York: Holt, Rinehart & Winston,, 1961.

32. COLEMAN, JAMES S. *The Adolescent Society.* Glencoe, Illinois: Free Press, 1961.

33. DAI, BINGHAM. "Some Problems of Personality Development among Negro Children," in *Personality in Nature, Society and Culture*, pp. 545–66. Edited by Clyde Kluckhohn, Henry A. Murray, and David Schneider. New York: Alfred A. Knopf, Inc., 1953.

34. DAVIS, ALLISON. "Socialization and Adolescent Personality," in *Adolescence*, pp. 198–216. Edited by Nelson B. Henry. Forty-third Yearbook of the National Society for the Study of Education, Part I, 1944.

35. DAVIS, ALLISON, and HAVIGHURST, ROBERT J. "Social Class and Color Differences in Child Rearing," *Amer. Sociological Rev.*, XI (December, 1946), 698–710.

36. DECHARMS, RICHARD, and MOELLER, GERALD. "Values Expressed in American Children's Readers, 1800–1950," *J. of Abnorm. Soc. Psychol.*, LXIV (February, 1962), 136–42.

37. DIAMOND, STANLEY, "Kibbutz and Shtetl: The History of an Idea," *Social Problems*, V (Fall, 1957).

38. DREGER, RALPH M., and MILLER, KENT S. "Comparative Psychological Studies of Negroes and Whites in the United States," *Psychol. Bull.*, LVII (September, 1960), 361–402.

39. DUVALL, EVELYN M. "Conceptions of Parenthood," *Amer. J. Sociology*, LII (November, 1946), 193–203.

40. EISENSTADT, SAMUEL N. *From Generation to Generation.* Glencoe, Ill.: Free Press, 1956.

41. ESCALONA, SIBYLLE K. "A Commentary upon Some Recent Changes in Child Rearing Practices," *Child Develpm.*, XX (June, 1949), 157–63.

42. FRAZIER, E. FRANKLIN. *The Negro Family in the United States.* New York: Macmillan Co., 1957 (second edition).

43. ———. *Negro Youth at the Crossways: Their Personality Development in the Middle States.* Washington: American Council on Education, 1940.

44. GEERTZ, HILDRED. "The Vocabulary of Emotion: A Study of the Javanese Socialization Processes," *Psychiatry*, XXII (August, 1959), 225–37.

45. GETZELS, JACOB W., and JACKSON, PHILIP W. "Family Environment and Cognitive Style: A Study of the Sources of Highly Intelligent and of Highly Creative Adolescents," *Amer. Sociological Rev.*, XXVI (June, 1961), 351–59.

46. GLIDEWELL, JOHN C. (Editor). *Parental Attitudes and Child Behavior.* Springfield, Illinois: Charles C Thomas, 1961.

47. GOODMAN, MARY E. *Race Awareness in Young Children.* Cambridge, Massachusetts: Addison-Wesley Pub. Co., Inc., 1952.

48. GREEN, ARNOLD W. "The Middle-Class Male Child and Neurosis," *Amer. Sociological Rev.*, XI (February, 1946), 31–41.

49. GRONLUND, NORMAN E. *Sociometry in the Classroom.* New York: Harper & Bros., 1959.

50. HARTLEY, EUGENE L., and HARTLEY, RUTH E. *Fundamentals of Social Psychology.* New York: Alfred A. Knopf, Inc., 1952.

51. HARTLEY, RUTH E. "What Aspects of Child Behavior Should Be Studied in Relation to Maternal Employment?" in *Research Issues Related to the Effects of Maternal Employment on Children,* pp. 41–50. Edited by Alberta E. Siegel. University Park, Pennsylvania: Social Science Research Center, Pennsylvania State University, 1961.

52. HARTUP, WILLARD W. "Some Correlates of Parental Imitation in Young Children," *Child Develpm.*, XXXIII (March, 1962), 85–96.

53. HAVIGHURST, ROBERT J., and DAVIS, ALLISON. "A Comparison of the Chicago and Harvard Studies of Social Class Differences in Child Rearing," *Amer. Sociological Rev.*, XX (August, 1955), 438–42.

54. HELPER, MALCOLM M. "Learning Theory and the Self-Concept," *J. Abnorm. Soc. Psychol.*, LI (September, 1955), 184–94.

55. HENRY, ANDREW. "Sibling Structure and the Perception of the Disciplinary Roles of Parents," *Sociometry,* XX (March, 1957), 67–74.

56. HOFFMAN, LOIS W. "Effects of the Employment of Mothers on Parental Power Relations and the Division of Household Tasks," *Marriage and Family Living,* XXII (February, 1960), 27–35.

57. ———. "The Father's Role in the Family and the Child's Peer-Group Adjustment," *Merrill-Palmer Quar.*, VII (April, 1961), 97–105.

58. HOFFMAN, LOIS W.; ROSEN, SIDNEY; and LIPPITT, RONALD. "Parental Coerciveness, Child Autonomy, and Child's Role at School," *Sociometry,* XXIII (March, 1960), 15–22.

59. HOLLINGSHEAD, AUGUST B. *Elmtown's Youth.* New York: John Wiley & Sons, 1949.

60. INKELES, ALEX. "Social Change and Social Character: The Role of Parental Mediation," *J. of Soc. Issues,* XI, No. 2 (1955), 12–23.

61. INKELES, ALEX, and LEVINSON, DANIEL J. "National Character: The Study of Modal Personality and Socio-Cultural Systems," in *Handbook of Social Psychology,* Vol. II, pp. 977–1020. Edited by Gardner Lindzey. Cambridge, Massachusetts: Addison-Wesley Pub. Co., Inc., 1954.

62. JONES, MARY C. "A Comparison of the Attitudes and Interests of Ninth-grade Students over Two Decades," *J. of Educ. Psychol.*, LI, No. 4 (1960), 175–86.

63. KANTOR, MILDRED B.; GLIDEWELL, JOHN C.; MENSH, IVAN N.; DOMKE, HERBERT R.; and GILDEA, MARGARET C. L. "Socioeconomic Level and Maternal Attitudes toward Parent-Child Relationships," *Human Organization,* XVI (Winter, 1958), 44–48.

64. KARDINER, ABRAM, and OVESEY, LIONEL. *The Mark of Oppression.* New York: W. W. Norton & Co., 1951.

65. KLATSKIN, ETHELYN H. "Shifts in Child Care Practices in Three Social Classes under an Infant Care Program of Flexible Methodology," *Amer. J. Orthopsychiat.*, XXII (January, 1952), 52–61.

66. KOCH, HELEN L. *The Relation of Certain Formal Attributes of Siblings to Attitudes Held toward Each Other and toward Their Parents*, Monographs of the Society for Research in Child Development, Vol. XXV, No. 4, Serial No. 78, 1960.

67. KOHN, MELVIN L. "Social Class and Parental Values," *Amer. J. Sociology*, LXIV (January, 1959), 337–51.

68. ———. "Social Class and the Exercise of Parental Authority," *Amer. Sociological Rev.*, XXIV (June, 1959), 352–66.

69. KOHN, MELVIN L., and CARROLL, ELEANOR E. "Social Class and the Allocation of Parental Responsibilities," *Sociometry*, XXIII (December, 1960), 372–92.

70. KOHN, MELVIN L., and CLAUSEN, JOHN A. "Parental Authority Behavior and Schizophrenia," *Amer. J. Orthopsychiat.*, XXVI (April, 1956), 297–313.

71. LAMBERT, WILLIAM W.; TRIANDIS, LEIGH M.; and WOLF, MARGERY. "Some Correlates of Beliefs in the Malevolence and Benevolence of Supernatural Beings: A Cross-Cultural Study," *J. Abnorm. Soc. Psychol.*, LVIII (March, 1959), 162–69.

72. LINTON, RALPH. *The Cultural Background of Personality*. New York: Appleton-Century-Crofts, 1945.

73. LIPPITT, RONALD, and GOLD, MARTIN. "Classroom Social Structure as a Mental Health Problem," *J. Soc. Issues*, XV, No. 1 (1959), 40–49.

74. LYNN, DAVID B., and SAWREY, WILLIAM L. "The Effects of Father-Absence on Norwegian Boys and Girls," *J. Abnorm. Soc. Psychol.*, LIX (September, 1959), 258–62.

75. MAAS, HENRY S. "Some Social Class Differences in the Family Systems and Group Relations of Pre- and Early Adolescents," *Child Develpm.*, XXII (June, 1951), 145–52.

76. MACARTHUR, CHARLES. "Personalities of First and Second Children," *Psychiatry*, XIX (January, 1956), 47–54.

77. MACCOBY, ELEANOR E. "The Taking of Adult Roles in Middle Childhood," *J. Abnorm. Soc. Psychol.*, LXIII (November, 1961), 493–503.

78. MACCOBY, ELEANOR E., and GIBBS, PATRICIA K. "Methods of Child Rearing in Two Social Classes," in *Readings in Child Development*, pp. 380–96. Edited by William E. Martin and Celia B. Stendler. New York: Harcourt Brace & Co., 1954.

79. MATZA, DAVID, and SYKES, GRESHAM. "Juvenile Delinquency and Subterranean Values," *Amer. Sociological Rev.*, XXVI (October, 1961), 712–19.

80. MAYER, MARTIN. *The Schools*. New York: Harper & Bros., 1961.

81. MCCORD, JOAN; MCCORD, WILLIAM; and THURBER, EMILY. "Some Effects of Paternal Absence on Male Children," *J. Abnorm. Soc. Psychol.*, LXIV (March, 1962), 361–69.

82. MCKINLEY, DONALD G. "Social Status and Parental Roles." Unpublished Ph.D. dissertation, Harvard University, 1960.

83. MEAD, MARGARET. *Male and Female*. New York: Mentor Books, 1955.

84. MEAD, MARGARET, and WOLFENSTEIN, MARTHA (Editors). *Childhood in Contemporary Cultures*. Chicago: University of Chicago Press, 1955.

85. MILLER, DANIEL R., and SWANSON, GUY E. *The Changing American Parent*. New York: John Wiley & Sons, 1958.

86. ———. *Inner Conflict and Defense.* New York: Henry Holt & Co., 1960.
87. MILLER, WALTER. "Lower-Class Culture as a Generating Milieu of Gang Delinquency," *J. Soc. Issues,* XIV, No. 3 (1958), 5–19.
88. MISCHEL, WALTER. "Father-Absence and Delay of Gratification: Cross-Cultural Comparisons," *J. Abnorm. Soc. Psych.,* LXIII (July, 1961), 116–24.
89. MONEY, JOHN; HAMPSON, JOAN G.; and HAMPSON, JOHN L. "Imprinting and the Establishment of Gender Role," *A.M.A. Archives of Neurology and Psychiatry,* LXXVII (March, 1957), 333–36.
90. MUSSEN, PAUL H. "Differences between the TAT Responses of Negro and White Boys," *J. Consult. Psychol.,* XVII, No. 5 (1953), 373–76.
91. ———. "Some Antecedents and Consequents of Masculine Sex-Typing in Adolescent Boys," *Psychol. Monogr.,* Vol. LXXV, No. 2, Whole No. 506, 1961.
92. ORLANSKY, HAROLD. "Infant Care and Personality," *Psychol. Bull.,* XLVI (January, 1949), 1–48.
93. PARSONS, TALCOTT. "Age and Sex in the Social Structure of the United States," *Amer. Sociological Rev.,* VII (October, 1942), 604–16.
94. PITTS, JESSE. "The Family and Peer Groups," in *A Modern Introduction to the Family,* pp. 266–86. Edited by Norman W. Bell and Ezra F. Vogel. Glencoe, Illinois: Free Press, 1960.
95. POWDERMAKER, HORTENSE. "The Channeling of Negro Aggression by the Cultural Process," in *Personality in Nature, Society and Culture,* pp. 597–608. Edited by Clyde Kluckhohn, Henry A. Murray, and David Schneider. New York: Alfred A. Knopf, Inc., 1953.
96. PSATHAS, GEORGE. "Ethnicity, Social Class, and Adolescent Independence from Parental Control," *Amer. Sociological Rev.,* XXII (August, 1957), 415–23.
97. RABBAN, MEYER. "Sex-Role Identification in Young Children in Two Diverse Social Groups," *Genet. Psychol. Monogr.,* XLII, First Half (August, 1950), 81–158.
98. RADKE, MARIAN J., and TRAGER, HELEN. "Children's Perceptions of the Social Roles of Negroes and Whites," *J. Psychol.,* XXIX, First Half (January, 1950), 3–33.
99. RADKE, MARIAN J.; TRAGER, HELEN; and DAVIS, HADASSAH. "Social Perceptions and Attitudes of Children," *Genet. Psychol. Monogr.,* XL, Second Half (November, 1949), 327–447.
100. RIESMAN, DAVID; GLAZER, NATHAN; and DENNEY, REUEL. *The Lonely Crowd.* New Haven: Yale University Press, 1950.
101. ROSEN, BERNARD C. "The Achievement Syndrome: A Psycho-Cultural Dimension of Social Stratification," *Amer. Sociological Rev.,* XXI (April, 1956), 203–11.
102. ———. "Family Structure and Achievement Motivation," *Amer. Sociological Rev.,* XXVI (August, 1961), 574–85.
103. ROSENBERG, MORRIS. "The Dissonant Religious Context and Emotional Disturbance," *Amer. J. Sociology,* LXVIII (July, 1962), 1–10.
104. SCHACHTER, STANLEY. *The Psychology of Affiliation.* Stanford, California: Stanford University Press, 1958.
105. SCHUMAN, HOWARD. "Social Structure and Personality Constriction in a

Total Institution," Unpublished Ph.D. dissertation, Harvard University, 1961.

106. SEARS, ROBERT R.; MACCOBY, ELEANOR E.; and LEVIN, HARRY. *Patterns of Child Rearing.* Evanston, Illinois: Row Patterson & Co., 1957.

107. SEARS, ROBERT R.; PINTLER, MARGARET H.; and SEARS, PAULINE S. "Effect of Father Separation on Preschool Children's Doll Play Aggression," *Child Develpm.*, XVII (December, 1946), 219–43.

108. SEWELL, WILLIAM H. "Infant Training and the Personality of the Child," *Amer. J. Sociology*, LVIII (September, 1952), 150–59.

109. ———. "Social Class and Childhood Personality," *Sociometry*, XXIV (December, 1961), 340–56.

110. SEWELL, WILLIAM H., and HALLER, ARCHIE O. "Social Status and the Personality Adjustment of the Child," *Sociometry*, XIX (June, 1956), 114–25.

111. SIEGEL, ALBERTA E. "Dependence and Independence in the Children of Working Mothers," *Child Develpm.*, XXX (December, 1959) 533–46.

112. SPIRO, MELFORD E. *Children of the Kibbutz.* Cambridge, Massachussets: Harvard University Press, 1958.

113. STENDLER, CELIA B. "Sixty Years of Child Training Practices," *J. Pediatrics*, XXXVI (January, 1950), 122–34.

114. STEVENSON, H. W., and STEWART, E. C. "A Developmental Study of Racial Awareness in Young Children," *Child Develpm.*, XXIX (September, 1958), 399–410.

115. STOLZ, LOIS M. *Father Relationships of War-born Children.* Stanford, California: Stanford University Press, 1954.

116. ———. "Effects of Maternal Employment on Children: Evidence from Research," *Child Develpm.*, XXXI (December, 1960), 749–82.

117. STRODTBECK, FRED L. "Family Interaction, Values and Achievement," in *Talent and Society*, pp. 135–94. Co-authored by David C. McClelland, Alfred L. Baldwin, Urie Bronfenbrenner, and Fred L. Strodtbeck. New York: D. Van Nostrand Co., 1958.

118. SUNLEY, ROBERT. "Early 19th Century American Literature on Child Rearing," in *Childhood in Contemporary Cultures*, pp. 150–67. Edited by Margaret Mead and Martha Wolfenstein. Chicago: University of Chicago Press, 1955.

119. TILLER, PER OLAF. "Father Absence and Personality Development of Children in Sailor Families: A Preliminary Research Report," in *Studies of the Family*, pp. 115–37. Edited by Nels Anderson. Göttingen, Germany: Vanderhoeck & Ruprecht, 1957.

120. TUMA, ELIAS, and LIVSON, NORMAN. "Family Socioeconomic Status and Adolescent Attitudes to Authority," *Child Develpm.*, XXXI (June, 1960), 387–99.

121. VINCENT, CLARK E. "Trends in Infant Care Ideas," *Child Develpm.*, XXII (June, 1951), 199–209.

122. WARNER, WILLIAM L.; HAVIGHURST, ROBERT J.; and LOEB, MARTIN B. *Who Shall Be Educated?* New York: Harper & Bros., 1944.

123. WHITING, JOHN W. M. "Socialization Process and Personality," in *Psychological Anthropology*, chap. xii. Edited by Francis L. K. Hsu. Homewood, Illinois: Dorsey Press, 1961.

124. WHITING, JOHN W. M., and WHITING, BEATRICE B. "Contributions of Anthropology to the Methods of Studying Child Rearing," in *Handbook of Research Methods in Child Development*, pp. 918–44. Edited by Paul H. Mussen. New York: John Wiley & Sons, 1960.

125. WILSON, ALAN B. "Residential Segregation of Social Classes and Aspirations of High School Boys," *Amer. Sociological Rev.*, XXIV (December, 1959), 836–45.

126. WOLFENSTEIN, MARTHA. "The Emergence of Fun Morality," *J. Soc. Issues*, VII (1951), 15–25.

127. ———. "French Parents Take Their Children to the Park," in *Childhood in Contemporary Cultures*. Edited by Margaret Mead and Martha Wolfenstein. Chicago: University of Chicago Press, 1955.

128. WYLIE, LAURENCE. *Village in the Vaucluse*. Cambridge, Massachusetts: Harvard University Press, 1957.

129. YARROW, LEON. "Maternal Deprivation: Toward an Empirical and Conceptual Re-evaluation," *Psychol. Bull.*, LVIII (November, 1961), 459–90.

130. YARROW, MARIAN RADKE; SCOTT, PHYLLIS; DE LEEUW, LOUISE; and HEINIG, CHRISTINE. "Child-rearing in Families of Working and Nonworking Mothers," *Sociometry*, XXV (June, 1962), 122–40.

131. YOUNG, FRANK W. "The Function of Male Initiation Ceremonies: A Cross-cultural Test of an Alternative Hypothesis," *Amer. J. Sociology*, LXVII (January, 1962), 379–91.

CHAPTER III

Language Development

SUSAN M. ERVIN and WICK R. MILLER

During the last thirty-five years, much of the work of American psychologists, influenced to some extent by the functional studies of Piaget, has been directed toward quantitative and normative aspects of child language. This work has been summarized by McCarthy (**69**). Additional foreign research has been summarized by Kainz (**52**) and El'konin (**26**).[1] We will focus our attention on current trends, in particular on work that has been guided by modern structural linguistics.[2]

The most important contribution that modern linguistics has brought to child language studies is its conception of what a language is. A language is a system that can be described internally in terms of two primary parts or levels—the phonological (sound system) and the grammatical. A complete description of a language would include an account of all possible phonological sequences and also a set of rules by which we can predict all the possible sentences in that language.

We can study the child's developing language system from two viewpoints; first, the child's own system—a description of his own sound system and the set of rules he uses to form sentences—and,

1. We gratefully acknowledge the contributions of A. G. Bratoff in finding, translating, and interpreting Soviet research reports. Thanks are due also to Volney Stefflre for many bibliographical suggestions.

The preparation of this chapter has been facilitated by a grant from the Department of Health, Education, and Welfare to the Institute of Human Development, University of California, Berkeley. Facilities have also been provided by the Center for Human Learning under support of the National Science Foundation.

2. A brief account of linguistically oriented studies is given by Carroll (**17**). Brown and Berko (**8**) summarize psycholinguistic methods used in child language studies and, in addition, discuss some of the more important linguistic concepts that are basic to this approach.

second, progress in the mastery of the linguistic system of the model or adult language. Since the advent of linguistically oriented research, more attention necessarily has come to be given to the analysis of individual cases. Among adults of the same language community, differences in the linguistic system are slight. Among young children, who are developing an internal linguistic system, differences are much greater. Cross-individual comparisons of linguistic elements are not appropriate if there is a possibility that the elements may occupy a different structural position in the system. It is necessary, first, to develop techniques and to discover units through the study of individual systems before comparisons between individuals, or group studies, are possible. For this reason, many of the studies herein reported are analyses of the rules of individual systems.

Since these analyses are producing the most significant changes in current views of language among psychologists, this chapter will give attention primarily to the analysis of the internal system of sound and syntax. Considerations of space have led to the omission of systematic treatment of the semantic and functional aspects of language acquisition which a complete discussion would require.

Phonology

PRELINGUISTIC STAGE

All human languages have certain distinctive properties: (*a*) they are learned; (*b*) they include conventional, arbitrary signs for meanings or for referents which may be displaced in time or space; (*c*) they include conventional units and rules for the combination of those units. It is evident that the vocalizing infant does not have a language. Though he may respond to adult language, we cannot begin to analyze the structure of his own language until he has at least two systematically contrasted meaningful words, a point usually reached by the end of the first year (**69**).

Spectrographic studies of sound during the first few months of infancy indicate that vocal behavior is very unstable. The speech organs are employed in breathing, eating, crying, or gurgling. The cortex is immature and the speech-like sounds which do occur show extreme fluctuations and defy analysis by the ordinary phonetic classifications applicable to speech under more stable cortical control (**68, 60**).

The most striking change in the months immediately following is the acquisition of increasing control over volume, pitch, and articulatory position and type, a control manifested by continuity or repetition of these features. The best recent study of this phase of development is by Tischler (**92**). In a study of seventeen children in contrasted social situations, he noted that there was a gradual increase in the frequency of vocalization. It reached its peak at eight or ten months of age, then declined. Between the eighth and the twelfth month, almost all conceivable sounds occur, including some not in the adult language.

An important theory regarding changes during the prelinguistic stage has been offered by Mowrer (**73**). He has suggested that there is secondary reinforcement in hearing one's self speak as the rewarding parent speaks. This suggestion would account for both increasing quantity of sounds and increasing approximation to adult sounds. There are few data to test this theory. The prelinguistic sounds of deaf and hearing children are indistinguishable in the first three months, but there is a gradual decrease in the range of sounds uttered by the deaf after the age of six months (**60**), with each child specializing idiosyncratically. Thus, the hearing of a variety of speech sounds may increase the range of sounds used by the child, but we do not know if the hearing of a particular range of sounds influences the particular range used by the child. A study of children from two different language communities would shed some light on this problem.

Unfortunately, most studies which have been done at this stage and which have used adequate samples (**43, 44, 45, 46**) have two serious defects for our purposes. One is that they have seldom recorded the complete range of infant sounds, providing no record of rounded front vowels (as in French "tu," German "böse"), glottal trills, implosives, or clicks. The other is that they have not separated sounds uttered during babbling or cooing and those constituting variants in systematic language. Linguists have noted marked differences in vocal behavior even when babbling and language occurred at the same age.

PASSIVE CONTROL

It is usually assumed that passive control of phonological features antedates active control, that a child can hear a phonetic contrast, such as that between "s" and "sh," before he can produce it. The reader may have had the common experience of having his imitation of the child's speech rejected; Brown and Berko (**8**) give an example: "That's your fis?" "No, my fis." "That's your fish." "Yes, my fis." Hearing a contrast may be a necessary but not sufficient condition for producing it.

Little is known about the order of learning to hear differences in various aspects of intonation, stress, and quality in voices. The only study on this subject is reported by Shvarchkin (**25**), in which he taught children between 11 and 22 months Russian words differing only in one phoneme at a time. He presented his results as a series of phonemic features that distinguish groups or classes of phonemes. The phonemic features are learned in a given order.[3] By the end of the second year the children could distinguish all the phonemes of Russian. While techniques which could be expected to yield comparable results to those of this important study have been applied in this country, the results have not been presented according to sounds or features (**83, 91**). Information on the actual phonetic cues used by the child could be obtained by using artificially constructed vocalic stimuli. Such studies have been conducted by psychoacousticians on adults, but not on children.

THE SYSTEM OF CONTRASTS

Just before the transition to the use of meaningful words, there is sometimes a period of complete silence or decreased babbling, but often babbling continues into the linguistic stage.

The use of meaningful words marks the onset of an active phonological system replacing unsystematic phonetic preferences. Now for the first time we are dealing with true language, and we may

3. Vowel distinctions are learned first. The order of acquisition for the remaining features is: (*a*) vowels *vs.* consonants; (*b*) sonorants *vs.* articulated obstruants; (*c*) plain *vs.* palatalized consonants; (*d*) nasals *vs.* liquids; (*e*) sonorants *vs.* unarticulated obstruants; (*f*) labials *vs.* linguals (i.e., nonlabials); (*g*) stops *vs.* fricatives; (*h*) front *vs.* back linguals; (*i*) voiceless *vs.* voiced consonants; (*j*) blade *vs.* groove sibilants; (*k*) liquids *vs.* /y/.

examine the systematic structure of the sound contrasts employed by the child to distinguish meaningful words. A few examples from Joan, described by Velten (**93**), will serve as an illustration. At 22 months, Joan had *bat* (bad), *dat* (cut), *bap* (lamb), and *dap* (cup). In these words, [b-] and [d-] can be seen to contrast, in that they signal differences of meanings in otherwise identical words. These four words also illustrate a phenomenon that applied to all of Joan's vocabulary at this time. Four stops were found, [b], [p], [d], and [t]. The voiced stops, [b] and [d], occurred only in initial position, never final, whereas the voiceless stops, [p] and [t], occurred only in final position, never initial. The stops [b] and [p] did not contrast in the same position and therefore were *allophones* of the *phoneme* /p/,[4] and, similarly, [d] and [t] were allophones of /t/.

Jakobson has developed a very influential hypothesis about the development of child language (**49**). His approach is summarized and applied by Velten (**93**) and Leopold (**62**). The hypothesis is that the development of the sound system can be described in terms of successive contrasts between features that are maximally different and which permeate the whole system. Thus, the first distinction is between a vowel and a consonant, since vowels and consonants are more different than any other part of the system. Next, the child might learn to contrast a stop with a nonstop, e.g., /p/ and /m/, or /p/ and /f/. Theoretically, the child could double his stock of consonants with each pair of contrasting features. When Joan, discussed in the preceding paragraph, learned to contrast /p/ and /b/, she also learned to contrast /t/ and /d/. In short, she learned the contrasting voiced-voiceless feature and applied it to all her stop phonemes. Thus, this theory presents an economical process of learning since the number of contrasting features is much smaller than the number of phonemes. Radical changes in the system come at once rather than through the gradual approximation of the adult phonemes one by one.

Are contrasts of features acquired suddenly as Jakobson hypothe-

4. The symbols [. . .] are customarily used for phonetic writing, and /. . ./ for phonemic writing. The choice of the symbols /p/ and /t/ rather than /b/ and /d/ is arbitrary in representing Joan's phonemes. The concept of phonemic analysis is also applicable to adult speech. A fuller discussion is given by Brown (**7**: 27–50) and Hockett (**40**: chaps. ii–xiii).

sizes? Evidence on phonology stems largely from diary reports about single children (**1, 12, 20, 36, 62, 63, 93**). These reports tend to support the notion of acquisition of features.

Jakobson also suggested an order in the acquisition of contrasting features. He suggested that the order reflects the prevalence of the contrasting features among the languages of the world. It is possible that the more common contrasts are both acoustically or visually distinct and easier to articulate. Evidence has been presented for acoustic confusion of /t/ and /k/ by adults (**71**). The contrast of /p/ *vs.* /t/ or /k/ is also acoustically confused, but, in normal situations, a visual cue is provided. There is probably a relation between the visual cue and the fact that children usually develop a contrast between labial (e.g., /p/) and nonlabial (e.g., /t/, /k/) consonants well before they develop a contrast between dental (e.g., /t/) and velar (e.g., /k/) consonants.

Among adults, auditory confusions are more common among phonemes similar in manner of articulation (e.g., /p/ and /t/) than phonemes similar in place of articulation (e.g., /p/ and /b/) (**71**). Children, however, frequently make substitutions that differ in manner of articulation. Stops replace the corresponding fricative (e.g., "thing" may become *ting*), and semivowels or vowels replace liquids (e.g., "rabbit" may become *wabbit;* "bottle" may become *batto*) (**63, 91**). Degree of difficulty in articulation is probably the crucial factor. Thus, stops (e.g., /p/, /t/) are usually acquired earlier than fricatives (e.g., /f/, /th/), probably because a more delicate adjustment of the tongue is necessary for the fricatives. Caution must be exercised in ascribing articulatory difficulty, because no simple measure of articulatory difficulty exists, and judgments are usually made *post hoc* from acquisition problems.

There is adequate evidence from diary reports to warrant an examination of the generalizations which have the widest support. These generalizations, which follow, appear to be the most tenable current hypotheses, but they must be viewed with extreme caution, in view of the small sample and restricted range of languages. (*a*) The vowel-consonant contrast is one of the earliest, if not the earliest, contrast for all the children. (*b*) A stop-continuant contrast is quite early for all children. The continuant is either a fricative (e.g.,

/f/) or a nasal (e.g., /m/). (*c*) When two consonants, differing in place of articulation but identical in manner of articulation exist, the contrast is labial *vs.* dental (e.g., /p/ *vs.* /t/, /m/ *vs.* /n/). (*d*) Contrasts in place of articulation precede voicing contrasts. (*e*) Affricates (ch, j) and liquids (l, r) do not appear in the early systems. (*f*) In the vowels, a contrast between low and high (e.g., /a/ and /i/) precedes front *vs.* back (e.g., /i/ and /u/). (*g*) Consonant clusters such as /st/ and /tr/ are generally late. In regard to contrasts at different positions within the word, certain tendencies are observed. Children normally acquire initial consonants before final or medial consonants, and consonantal contrasts often apply to initial position before other positions. On the basis of evidence from research on convergent *vs.* divergent habits, this order is what we would expect. Templin's report (**91**) of articulation problems in children three years and older supports these positional generalizations as well as the generalizations in order of appearance of contrasts.

In addition to acoustic, visual, and articulation factors, the size of the vocabulary may play a part in the development of contrasts. Velten, in the only thorough study of the problem (**93**), has provided some measures of the maximum possible number of vocabulary items in his daughter's speech. He reported that, at 22 months, she actually used 86 per cent of the words possible, given her word pattern (consonant-vowel or consonant-vowel-consonant) and her available stock of phonemes. Naturally, this meant she had a great many homonyms. She could expand the possibilities either by using disyllabic words or by expanding the phonemic contrasts employed. The correlation of increasing vocabulary and increasing complexity of the system is obvious, but we do not know what induces change. The few descriptions available suggest wide differences between children in the extent to which they maximize vocabulary potential in a given system. There may be certain points where homonyms are so dysfunctional that the system changes.

RULES OF SUBSTITUTION

In addition to describing the sound system of the child as a self-contained system, one can describe the relation between the adult's and child's systems by rules of substitution.[5] If the child has a smaller stock of phonemes than the adult, it is obvious that the child must make certain substitutions; one phoneme must serve for two or more adult phonemes. Ordinarily, these rules reveal remarkable consistency (**2, 63, 93**).

It is an oversimplification to state that one phoneme in the child's system substitutes for several in the adult's system. The reverse is also frequent. Articulatory assimilation is one of several factors that can produce this result (**1, 20, 63**). One can hear similar assimilations in adult speakers—e.g., nightin-gale *vs.* nighting-gale. Templin's results suggest that medial unvoiced consonants tend to be voiced—especially /-t-/, also often voiced by adults—and that final voiced consonants tend to be unvoiced (**91**).

Complex substitution rules are often the result of anticipation. Morris Swadesh[6] observed such a pattern with his son. Final and medial consonants of the adult's words were dropped by the child. The initial consonant was replaced by a nasal if a noninitial nasal was found in the adult's word; a labial was replaced by the labial nasal /m/, and a nonlabial was replaced by /n/: *blanket* /me/, *green* /ni/, *candy* /ne/. Complicated substitutions of this type are not at all uncommon, but they are ordinarily not recognized by the parent.

Adult allophones are frequently allocated to different phonemes by the child (**1, 63, 93**). Thus, the adult's prevocalic /r/ is often represented in the child's system as /w/, but in other positions it often becomes a vowel or is lost. In adult speech, /r/ is formed with rounded lips before vowels, unrounded lips elsewhere; lip-reading research suggests that /r/ and /w/ are visually very similar before vowels (**104**).

Not infrequently an allophonic feature of the adult's language is reinterpreted by the child and becomes phonemic—i.e., it becomes contrastive—because the factors that condition the adult's allophonic feature are not represented in the child's phonological system(**93**). The relation between the adult's and child's phonological system

5. Similar techniques of language comparison are employed in the study of bilingualism and second language learning (**99**).

6. Personal communication.

and pattern of allophones can become extremely complex. Chao (**20**) presented evidence which suggests that the complex patterns found for one child were in part due to different physiological capabilities of the child and the adult—specifically, the difference in relative size of the tongue and mouth cavity.

The child's phonological system is not a static system. Today's substitution rules are not tomorrow's rules. And, yesterday's rules are still to be found with some words today. The results are archaisms, found in almost every child's vocabulary. We have observed a child who learned to distinguish /t/ from /k/. She continued, unless corrected, to use an earlier word /ta/ for *car*. Velten (**93**) and Leopold (**63**) observed this phenomenon and, also, hypercorrections at times of change. We have noticed that new and old forms are sometimes stylistic variants; for example, the earlier form may be used in "baby-talk" or in talking to parents, the new form with outsiders. Archaisms are probably more common among children who have a relatively larger vocabulary and more primitive phonological system. In such a case, a newly acquired contrast must apply to a larger number of vocabulary items. Some vocabulary items are missed, and archaisms result.

The reverse effect of archaisms is also found, but less often. Chao (**20**) reports a case of a Mandarin-speaking child who applied a newly learned contrast to one frequently occurring word but not to other words for which the new contrast would have been appropriate.

By the fourth year, the child's phonological system closely approximates the model, and the remaining deviations are usually corrected by the time the child enters school. Occasionally, earlier substitution patterns persist, and the child is usually described as having speech problems. Applegate (**2**) describes the rules of substitution for such a child.

GRAMMAR

Children display no evidence of systematic grammar when they first begin to use words at about the age of ten months, yet most observers agree that by four years the fundamentals are mastered. The acquisition of grammar is one of the most complicated intellectual achievements of children. How does the child learn the grammatical structure of the language? Before attempting to answer this question, we must understand something of the nature of grammar and specify some of the grammatical devices used by languages. Try to construct a sentence from a string of English words: *house, hat, ski, John, man, drop.* Out of these we can construct, among others, the sentence *the man dropped his skis and hat at John's house.* The most obvious addition is order. Secondly, we have added markers in the form of function words (*and, the, his, at*) and suffixes (*-ed, -s, -'s*). Together, markers and order are employed for any of several functions. They identify classes (*the* identifies a noun), they specify relations (*and* relates *skis* to *hat; 's* relates *John* to *house;* order indicates the subject-object relationship), or they signal meanings (plurality, possession, and tense are signalled by markers). A third device is *prosody,* or characteristic intonation and stress patterns.

The unit for grammatical analysis is the *morpheme,* the smallest element in speech to which meaning can be assigned. A word may be composed of one or more morphemes; *cats* consists of two morphemes, *cat* and the plural suffix. Morphemes, like phonemes, may take various forms. The plural morpheme appears as /-s/, /-z/, /-əz/, /-ən/, or a vowel change in *cats, dogs, bridges, oxen,* and *men.* All of these various forms of the plural morpheme are called *allomorphs.*

Morphemes are divided into classes, and sentences are composed of certain ordered sequences of classes. Morpheme classes are comparable to traditional parts of speech but are identified in terms of substitutions in linguistic contexts rather than in terms of meaning. Thus, the morphemes that fit in the sentence, "The ______ was good," constitute a class. Morpheme classes can be divided into two groups, lexical and function classes. Lexical classes are few in number but have many members. In English these include nouns, verbs, adjectives, and certain adverbs. Function classes constitute a larger number of small, closed classes. In English these include conjunctions, prepositions, auxiliaries, and suffixes such as the plural and past tense morphemes.

More detailed treatment of morphemic and grammatical analysis can be found elsewhere (**8, 31, 40**). In the remainder of this chapter the term "word" will be used in place of "morpheme," except where the distinction between them is necessary.

PASSIVE GRAMMATICAL CONTROL

The child's first word normally appears before the first birthday, but a year may pass before the child forms his first two-word sentence. During this period the child cannot be said to have an active grammatical system, or grammatical rules for forming sentences, because words are not combined into sentences. All his utterances are one-word sentences. At this stage, however, the very young child may have a passive grammatical system, rules for decoding or understanding many adult grammatical patterns, but the appropriate experimental techniques have not yet been applied to study children so young. A few studies with older children have been made that bear on the problem of passive grammatical patterns.

In Russian, as in English, the subject and predicate constitute the largest units of the sentence; these in turn can be subdivided into smaller units. Karpova (**53**) has reported an ingenious study on sentence analysis by Soviet preschool children. They were trained with pictures, then with isolated words, to list, count, and then report which was first, second, and so on. Then sentences were presented. The majority of children five to seven tended to hear two parts, a subject and a predicate. When they heard more, they more often segregated concrete nouns; less often verbs and adjectives; and least often, function words.

Porter (**78**) observed that in identifying verbs in written sentences, children seven to thirteen and adults relied primarily on structure, relatively little on meaning. He asked them to find a word like "jumped" in "the cow jumped the fence." He used both meaningful and nonsense sentences, varying the cues available–meaning, markers, and order. Prosodic cues were not available since the sentences were written. Children tended to select on the basis of position, adults more often on the basis of markers. Thus, in the nonsense sentence, "docib hegof gufed rupan tesor," children more often thought "hegof" was the verb, and adults chose "gufed."

The two forementioned studies were concerned with the identification of units belonging to lexical classes. The understanding of markers or function words can be studied both from a syntactic and semantic standpoint. Sokhin (**87**) studied the understanding of a Russian locative preposition by children 23 to 41 months of age.

He asked the children, for example, to "put the ring on the block" or to "put the block on the block." The youngest children seemed to depend so heavily on situational probabilities that they could not understand these instructions. Eighteen of the children, between 26 and 36 months of age, who understood the difference between "on" and "under," still were unable to put the block on the block; and when told to put the ring on the block did the reverse half the time. Thus, they could discriminate the semantic contrast between different prepositions but could not distinguish the syntactic difference between the object of the verb and the object of the preposition, and the semantic contrast thereby signalled. Fourteen children 26–41 months of age were relatively successful in this task.

Derivational suffixes were studied by Bogoyavlenski (**26**). He contrasted four Russian derivational suffixes, a diminutive, an augmentative, and two suffixes (*-nik*, *-shchik*) that formed agentive nouns from nouns and verbs. The agentive suffixes are like the English suffix *-er* in *farmer* and *worker*. It was found that the children had much more difficulty in understanding words using the agentive suffixes, evidently because there is a more radical semantic change involved.

THE UNMARKED GRAMMATICAL SYSTEM

Our knowledge is relatively well developed regarding children's sound systems and includes elegant and detailed descriptions of particular children's systems, which can be a prelude to generalizations when more children have been studied. The same is not true of children's grammatical systems. For this reason, the treatment in this section must rely largely on a few studies of individual cases now in progress.

Observers have agreed that when true sentences appear, sentences composed of two or more words, they seem to be abbreviated or "telegraphic" versions of adult sentences (**10, 57**). *That's the ball* becomes *that ball; where's the ball* becomes *where ball.* Function words are almost completely lacking at this stage. Recent studies of individual children show that even in these early sentences there are systematic regularities of order (**5, 10, 11, 72**). How seriously are we to take these regularities? There are grave difficulties in defining children's classes and establishing grammatical rules on internal evidence alone, without analogy to the adult system. A linguist studying an adult language can test his generalizations by composing sentences and asking a speaker to correct them. This is not possible with the young children who view adult imitations of their speech as amusing (**11**). Furthermore, adult informants correct inconsistencies and slips, but children's "errors" (that is—inconsistencies) are indistinguishable from shifts in the structure. There is, of course, a point in time when children begin to correct their own inconsistencies, thereby revealing the existence of a norm, which may be the same or different from the adult norm.

In spite of these difficulties, certain regularities of sequence are apparent and have been found independently by different investigators. Braine found them as early as 18 months of age in the first two-word sentences (**5**). It is possible that the regularities in the early sentences merely reflect memorization of sequential probabilities in adult speech. Only novel sentences can show this is not the case. All studies by these investigators have revealed sentences which are systematic by the induced rules of the child's grammar, but "strange" in adult English. Miller and Ervin reported *all-gone puzzle;* and Braine, *all-gone sticky*, *other fix,* and *the up*. Braine points out that the strangeness of an utterance is no criterion of its grammaticality at this age.

We assume that the development of grammar arises from the economy of coding words into classes. It would tax the capacities of any mind immensely to remember the millions of utterances heard; if the words are coded into grammatical classes, it is not necessary to store specific utterances as such. If class probabilities or rules rather than specific sequences are remembered, new sequences can be generated.

There must be an important relation between the frequency of sequences and learning of classes. We suggest that one way grammatical classes are created is through a sequence consisting of a very frequent item and a highly variable item. The frequent item corresponds to what Jenkins and Palermo (**50**) term an *operator*. In an inflected language, the operator may be an inflectional prefix or suffix even if it is invariant in the child's speech. In English, a function word or another high-frequency word is used as the defining frame; e.g., words such as *that*, *where*, *it*, *off*, *on*, *want*, *see*, *all-gone*. In a language in which only equiprobable lexical items existed, classes would be very hard to learn. Jenkins and Palermo have suggested that operators are necessary for the development of word classes. There is no proof that this is the case, but the evidence so far available supports this contention.

The child's first two-word sentences are frequently something like *that truck*, *that baby*, and *where dolly*, *where truck*. If the child has used *that* and *where* as operators for identifying a class, he can generate a new sentence—*where baby*. An operator occurs in a fixed position; i.e., in either first or second position. The remainder of the vocabulary forms a single, undifferentiated class and can occur with any operator (**5**). Very soon, the remainder is divided into classes; certain operators occur exclusively or almost exclusively with certain words. The classes tend to reflect class distinctions of the model language, e.g., some children use *it* as an operator only after words that are transitive verbs in the model language.

The evidence from three studies conducted by Miller and Ervin (**72**), Brown and Fraser (**10**) and Braine (**5**) reveals a high degree of similarity in the existence of such sequences of high-frequency and low-frequency items. Braine observed that children had periods of concentrated use of certain operators with particularly high frequency, using the favorite with a variety of other words, as new vocabulary was acquired.

A second feature in the evolution of classes may be the common semantic properties of referents. Thus, nouns often refer to things and verbs to actions. Brown has observed that children's classes are more semantically consistent than adults'. He has also demonstrated that preschool children select a picture of action when asked to find "sibbing," a picture of a container or simple object when asked to find "a sib," and a picture of confetti-like material when asked to find "some sib." The word "sib" is, of course, nonsense to the children, but they can select the most probable semantic properties of "sib" by the marker which identifies the word class: "–ing" (verb), "a –" (count noun), and "some –" (mass noun) (**6**).

If grammatical rules simply stated allowable sequences of words, it would be necessary to have one set of rules for two-word sentences, a different set of rules for three-word sentences, and so on. In sentences of more than two words, certain words are nested so that it is necessary to deal with only two units at a time. Thus in the sentence *many birds fly*, the first two words are nested and occupy the same structural position as the first word in the sentence *birds fly*. One rule will account for the subject-predicate sequence in both sentences, and another rule will account for the two-word sequence that composes the subject of the first sentence. The principle of nesting (or immediate constituent analysis, as it is termed in linguistics) is described in detail by Hockett (**40**: chap. xvii). Preliminary evidence suggests that nesting is learned early, but the child sometimes develops his own system before learning the system of the adult language (**5, 72**). It is difficult to assess the evidence, however, because nested constructions are usually delineated by markers which are largely lacking in the early grammatical systems.

THE MARKED GRAMMATICAL SYSTEM

Word classes in the early grammatical system are identified primarily in terms of order. As the child starts using more and more function words and suffixes, the classes are also identified by markers. Nouns are words that can occur after *the* and before the plural suffix; verbs are words that can occur after *can* and before *-ing*. At this time it is convenient to describe the child's grammatical system as a simplified version of the model, along with additional grammatical rules to account for features that have no counterpart in the model.

Rapid progress is commonly observed when the child enters this phase of development. Velten (**93**) reported in his daughter's speech from 27 to 30 months a swift development of prepositions, demonstratives, auxiliaries, articles, conjunctions, possessive and personal pronouns, the past-tense suffix, the plural suffix, and the possessive suffix. At first, the use of markers is usually optional and often inconsistent, and only gradually does the child's usage approach that of the adults, with increasing subdivision of classes (**16**).

Most observers have noted that before a contrast occurs consistently, one of the alternate forms is preferred. Gvozdev has added that, in the case of the Russian child, there is free variation observable just prior to mastery (**36**). Comparisons of different studies are difficult because the criteria of mastery are different. The fact that a given child says *toys* and *eyes* does not necessarily indicate that he has mastered the plural suffix. We must know if the use was spontaneous or imitated, if the singular forms *toy* and *eye* are used, if there is a contrast in meaning between the singular and plural forms, and if the formation is productive, i.e., if the plural suffix can be added to new nouns. Berko (**4**) developed a technique which involved asking children to make new formations using nonsense words. The child was told: "This is a wug. Now there are two of them. There are two ____." The appropriate response is, of course, "wugs." Using this technique, Berko found that four- to seven-year-old children knew the rules for forming the plural and possessive for nouns and the past tense and third person singular for verbs. Their greatest difficulties were partly phonological in nature; e.g., they had difficulty in adding the plural suffix "-s" to items that ended in a sibilant, such as "tass," perhaps because such forms were interpreted as already including a plural suffix. Miller and Ervin (**72**) used this technique with younger children in studying the acquisition of the plural. The tests were repeated at monthly intervals, and both meaningful and nonsense items were used. They found that the plural was usually learned before the child was three years old, but there were large individual differences. Learning of the plural for meaningful words almost always preceded that of the plural for nonsense words that had a similar phonological shape, but the interval between the two was surprisingly short.

Mastery of familiar forms precedes their generalization. The patterns are then extended to irregular forms, so that along with the regular pairs like *dog-dogs* or *walk-walked*, regularized pairs are found: *man-mans*, *foot-foots* (or *feet-feets*), *go-goed*, *break-breaked*. Guillaume (**35**) also was struck with his children's tendency to regularize verbs; *battre* became *batter*, *rire* became *rier*. Even very common verbs such as *prendre* and *tenir* were affected. He reported the only statistics suggesting why such regularization occurs; he found that though the French verbs employing a regular pattern were used only 36.2 per cent of the time, they constituted 76 per cent of the different verbs used.

Syntactic contrasts are often added to the less obvious required markers when the contrast is semantically important. In *I talked to him yesterday*, time is marked by both *-ed* and *yesterday*; in *two books*, plurality is marked by both *two* and *-s*. The child will sometimes use the more specific syntactic indicator (*yesterday* and *two*) in place of the less specific suffix (*-ed* and *-s*). A child is probably more apt to use a syntactic device if his phonological system does not allow him to use the suffix. Miller and Ervin (**72**) reported one case in which the child lacked final sibilants and used *one-two* in place of the standard plural: *one-two shoe* meant more than one shoe. Such a child, though she would fail a standardized test of the plural, would fail for phonological, not grammatical, reasons. Grammatically, she did have a plural signal. We do not know if such syntactic indicators are commonly acquired before suffix contrasts for phonological or other reasons. Gvozdev has reported that in the observations he has made in Russia these indicators are acquired at the same time (**36**).

There has been little systematic study of the order of acquisition of contrasts indicated by markers for English-speaking children. Russian linguists have done some work along these lines. Gvozdev (**36**) contends that the order of evolution depends on meaning. Russian gender contrasts appear relatively late because of their lack of strong semantic support, and the conditional mood, which is grammatically quite simple, occurs a year after the past-tense contrast for reasons of semantic difficulty.

An important aspect of language has been raised by Chomsky's transformational analysis (**21**). Transformations are complex derivations from a simple or kernel sentence. Compare the following sets of sentences, each of which contains a kernel sentence and a question, a negative, an emphatic, an elliptical, and a progressive transformation of the kernel:

HE GOES.	HE WENT.	HE'LL GO.
Does he go?	Did he go?	Will he go?
He doesn't go.	He didn't go.	He won't go.
He *does* go.	He *did* go.	He *will* go.
He does.	He did.	He will.
He's going.	He was going.	He will be going.

A number of rules can be formulated which apply to more than one transformation. In the first four transformations, the auxiliary *do* is added if there is no auxiliary. A past tense or third-person-singular suffix is shifted from the main verb to the auxiliary. Additional, nontransformational rules must be applied to account for contractions and irregular forms; e.g., *go* plus *-ed* becomes *went.* The great advantage of a transformational account is that a small number of rules compared to a large number of possible sentences results in an economy of description and a potential economy in learning as well. The transformation theory remains controversial in linguistics; in the field of language acquisition it is an ingenious hypothesis, which deserves testing.

Whether transformations are imitated or productive requires testing with novel sentences. Then one can discover if the sentences represent simply independent, unrelated patterns without effect upon each other. We would expect that, if transformations are acquired as operations, they should appear suddenly and influence much of the language at once, just as morphological regularities do. Miller and Ervin (**72**) present evidence from one child supporting this expectation.

GRAMMATICAL DEVELOPMENT AFTER FOUR YEARS OF AGE

There have been very few structural analyses of language in older children. What material is available (**4, 16, 38**) suggests that by the age of four most children have learned the fundamental structural features of their language and many of the details. There is then a long period of consolidation, a period of overlearning so that grammatical habits become automatic. Some irregular patterns are learned. Other irregular patterns, already learned, still must become firmly established. A six-year-old often uses forms such as *buyed* and *bought,* or *brang* and *brought* interchangeably. When he corrects himself, changes *buyed* to *bought,* he indicates that he knows the adult norm but has not yet developed a firmly established habit. Less frequent patterns, such as the use of *too* with positive sentences and *either* with negative sentences, are yet to be learned. The child must still acquire certain grammatical patterns that are associated with difficult semantic patterns, such as passive transformations and causal patterns with *why* and *because.*

We have pointed out that sentences can be produced by memorizing sequences. The evolution into classes based on substitution in the same contexts is gradual. The process continues over many years and affects many verbal habits, even when children's sentences seem to conform to adult grammar. Thus, during the primary school years, there is a marked increase in the tendency to give free associations that are grammatically similar to the stimulus word. This tendency is earliest and strongest with nouns and adjectives and weakest with function words (**9, 27**). Experimentally, it has been found that such associations derive from occurrence in identical linguistic contexts (**27, 70**), that is, in the same conditions that we have suggested lead to the learning of grammatical classes. In pursuing the link between grammar and association, Brown and Berko (**9**) found that when children were asked to use nonsense words after they had heard them in sentences, they had difficulty. They were most successful with count nouns and adjectives. Their progress in mastery of classes showed the same sequential development found in mastery of word associations.

For diagnostic purposes, it would be useful to have standardized tests for various aspects of grammatical development. While there have been many separate studies of individual features (**69**), no standardization norms are available. The most common quantitative measures employed to assess development in standardization studies, such as Templin's (**91**), have been sentence length—as judged by adult words—and frequency of structural features, such as phrases and subordination. Brown and Fraser (**10**) compared sentence length in two-year-olds with certain other factors, such as presence of specific auxiliary verbs, and found a high correlation. When age is allowed to vary, all of these features tend to be correlated, since all change with age. One important precaution should be observed in finding appropriate measures of grammatical development. Adult usage differs in the various subcultures of any community. A good developmental measure for general use should include only those features common to all adult speech in the presence of children.

LANGUAGE DIFFERENCES

Comparison of acquisition of different languages may provide some clues to the bases of the particular sequences observed. For example, it has been commonly observed in English that the child who does not yet make a contrast in plurality simply uses no marker at all. The plural suffix in adult speech has a double function; it is both a semantic signal and a noun marker. Usually children say *dog* for both adult *dog* and *dogs*. Why this choice? Frequency and ease of articulation may dictate which of the alternative forms is preferred. As for frequency, *toys, eyes, shoes* may occur so often in the plural that this form is preferred by the child. On the other hand, the development of final consonant contrasts and consonant clusters is usually late, so that the singular of words with consonant finals may be preferred. Languages which use prefixes rather than suffixes might show a different pattern, but no evidence is available.

Most contrasts in English consist of a marker *vs.* no marker. By preferring the unmarked form, the child not only fails to signal a semantic contrast but also lacks a class marker. In some languages, on the other hand, the noun must occur with an inflectional suffix. Before they have inflectional contrasts, children have preferences in the form they use. Thus, these forms would be available as class markers to distinguish nouns from verbs when the child begins to form sentences, even before he uses them contrastively.

To what extent do different language structures condition different learning patterns? This is a question that has not yet received study. Kluckhohn suggested that Navaho children, who must learn an extremely complicated language, are more retarded in their language development than English-speaking children (**19**). Leopold (**62**) has stated that syntax (grammatical rules that apply to arrangements between words) comes before morphology (grammatical rules that apply to arrangements of morphemes within words) in the child's grammatical development. Leopold did his work with an English- and German-speaking child, and these are languages in which syntax plays a more important role than morphology. Burling (**12**) describes the development of a child learning Garo, a language in which morphology plays a more important role. He found that morphology and syntax appeared simultaneously and were of equal importance for the child.

Derivational suffixes (as distinct from inflectional suffixes) such as *-ly* in *wiggily*, *-y* in *fussy*, *-er* in *gunner*, play a less important role in English than in some other languages, such as Russian. Berko (**4**) found that American children, ages four to seven, avoided such suffixes, preferring compounds or syntactic constructions. When they were asked, for example, what they would call a very tiny "wug," most children responded with phrases like *baby wug*, *teeny wug*, or *little wug*. A large number of adults responded with *wuglet*, *wuggie*, *wuggette*, or *wugling*. Russian children studied by Bogoyavlenski (**26**) readily formed derivatives using suffixes such as the diminutive.

Language Socialization

Cultures differ markedly in their practices in and attitudes toward language teaching. Baby talk furnishes an example. At one extreme is Comanche with a uniform and formalized baby talk (**19**). Baby talk has also been reported for Arabic, Gilyak, and Nootka cultures (**3, 29, 82**). At the other extreme are the Hidatsa, who claim to use no baby talk at all. They state, "We don't like baby talk. . . . When they talk, we want them to talk just like us, right from the start" (**96**). The Mohave claim newborn children can understand speech (**24**). It is not known whether these differences are related to any differences in the rate of language acquisition. But we can expect that language instruction will be more casual among the Mohave, for example, than among the Hidatsa.

Baby languages in various societies cast some light on adult views of children's language systems. Baby vocabularies frequently bear a systematic relation to adult vocabularies and have three common features: employment of articulatory simplifications, tending to the use of stops and nasals and the elimination of consonant clusters;[7] use of reduplications, such as *byebye* and *mama;* and the use of special suffixes which may be peculiar to baby talk or may also be used as endearments or diminutives, such as the English suffix *-y* in *doggy*, *horsey*, *Billy*, *sweety*. Grammatical simplification is probably also a feature of the baby talk used in speaking to children, though this feature has not often been thus described.

Steward (**90**) compared two cultures that differ radically in their tolerance of the peculiarities of child language. He found stuttering

7. Whether the articulatory changes are actually simplifications is arguable, since the criteria of simplicity are unclear. Pharyngeal fricatives are common in Arabic baby words (**29**), and glottalized consonants are found in Acoma baby words (authors' notes). Both of these sounds are difficult for second-language learners. It may be significant that a number of words in the formalized baby vocabulary of both languages are not systematically related to adult words.

more common in the society that made more rigid demands on the young speaker. This study is novel in its analysis of a variety of socialization practices related to language learning.

Societies may differ greatly in the amount and type of verbal stimulation given children. Irwin (**46**) has shown that speech development may be affected by reading to children. Children of multiple births are known to be retarded in language development (**69**), implying the importance of siblings in the kind of language the child learns. Hockett (**39**) has suggested that older children are the most important environmental force in shaping the younger child's speech habits. If this is the case, we can expect to find differences across cultures that correlate with differences in the amount and kind of contact found among children.

The development of good miniature tape-recorders makes possible the study of the evolving relation between speech forms and social functions, a study neglected even in the analysis of adult language (**42, 88**). There have been occasional comparisons of children's speech in different social conditions (**37, 41, 97**). The study of the nonlinguistic factors that condition the choice of differing linguistic forms offers another point of departure. A nice example is provided by Fischer (**30**) who studied the stylistic alternation of the participial suffix *-ing vs. -in* among children in a New England town. He found the alternation was related to personality (the "good boy" said *-ing*), to situational formality, and to the type of word used (*swimmin, chewin, hittin,* vs. *correcting, reading, visiting*). There was a slight tendency for girls to use *-ing* more than boys. Social class, in this relatively unstratified group, was not a significant factor.

Studies of the functional development of language are dependent on adequate descriptions of the behavior under study, the linguistic system of the child. As knowledge of the significant properties of children's language increases, it seems probable that more attention will be focused on the evolving differentiated usage of children, which results in the complex functional argots of adults, and on the features of the environment, which alter the rate of change in various aspects of the system.

Language and Cognition

There has been a great interest in the past decade in the effects of language or label learning on nonverbal behavior. Soviet research, with a slightly different focus, has been concerned with the relation between the "first and second signal systems." Since the early 1950's, there has been a resurgence of research in this field in the Soviet Union. English summaries are found in Luria (**66**) and the collection edited by Ivanov-Smolenskii (**48**). Because Soviet research is less familiar to us, we will give it somewhat disproportionate attention.

In this country, many of the studies have been done on adults, since the questions have been framed in terms of general behavior theory rather than developmental changes. There appear to be three explanatory frameworks employed in American studies:

(*a*) *Acquired distinctiveness.* Verbal training during the acquisition of labels alters the similarity of stimulus material, even on a single stimulus dimension, affecting discriminability.

(*b*) *Verbal mediation.* Though discriminability might be unaffected, verbal responses permit chaining, bringing to bear any prior reactions learned to the verbal responses themselves. Delay or stimulus complexity increases the effect.

(*c*) *Dimensional salience.* Verbal training may lead to selective attention to certain dimensions of the environment, as revealed in tasks requiring sorting of complex materials.

ACQUIRED DISTINCTIVENESS

It has not been shown that psychophysical discrimination is altered by the acquisition of labels. In a study of speakers from different language communities, with different categories for color names, Lenneberg found that the capacity to discriminate hues was the same, even though the labels were differently distributed on the hue continuum (**59**). The only form of discrimination known to be affected by language is that of speech sounds themselves. Liberman showed the ability of adults to hear differences between sounds which are discreet in articulation but on the same acoustic continuum is clearly improved at phoneme boundaries (**65**). An example is the contrast between *do* and *to*, differing only in one feature on an acoustic continuum. The studies have shown that there is improved discrimination at phoneme boundaries, but no acquired similarity, or decrease in discrimination, within the phoneme. Why is there such a difference between the effects of acquiring labels for colors and sounds? One explanation may be that we make hue discriminations daily, without the use of color names, in our transactions with the physical world–judging contours, distances, and so on. We only discriminate speech sounds when we are listening to speech.

VERBAL MEDIATION

Many investigations which have been called studies of acquired distinctiveness actually seem to involve the occurrence of verbal mediation. In fact, the speech-sound studies, such as Liberman's, may involve comparison not of two heard speech sounds but of two utterances reinterpreted by the listener in terms of his own phonemic system–i.e., response mediation. Verbal mediation involves a response by the subject, and we may group the studies into two categories–those which are concerned with the distinctiveness of the response-produced cues, and those which are concerned with their chaining.

Spiker and his associates are among those who have studied the first of these two problems with children as subjects (**89**). An example is a study by Hayne Reese (**80**), in which children were taught in two stages. First they learned labels for colored lights; then they learned a motor response to the lights. Reese contrasted four different pairs of labels, differing in the distinctiveness of the labels. The most similar was *wug-wog* with phonetically similar vowels, then *zim-zam* with less similar vowels, and the most different were *lev-mib* and *wug-zam*. Reese found that there were differences in both the time it took to learn the labels and the time it took to learn the motor responses for the different groups. The more distinct the labels, the more quickly they were learned, and the more easily the motor response was learned. Evidently the ease in learning the motor response did not reflect merely the distinctiveness of the labels, but rather the mastery of the labeling response which took longer with the similar labels. Whether an alternative type of distinctive response which was nonverbal might have been equally effective is not known. A theoretical discussion of related studies has been presented by Goss (**33**).

Studies on delayed response suggest that verbal mediation is important in a variety of ways. Brown and Lenneberg (**7**) showed that if there was a delay after a color chip was shown, subjects tended to recognize the color, to choose it from among many, not so much in terms of its hue as in terms of its label. Thus, if a pale lavender blue was called "blue" by a subject, he tended to identify it later as bluer than it actually had been. This study has not been repeated with children, but the phenomenon is very striking and predictable in adults.

Spiker has pretrained children with labels for stimuli in a delayed-reaction experiment and thereby improved their performance (**89**). He designed the labels to fit the performance categories. The children remembered the correct response later because they had verbal labels which corresponded.

Oléron (**76**) has noted that deaf children were inferior to hearing children in their ability to solve double alternation problems of the type "left twice–right twice." He later found that the children did not know how to count and assumed that counting might help solve such problems. A study by Carrier with deaf children also suggests the importance of verbal mediation (**15**). He noted that hearing children judged black or dark objects to be heavier than similar light or white objects. Before adolescence, deaf children did not make such judgments. He had to teach these children the terms "heavy" and "light" for concepts they already had. Clearly the deaf children were unlikely to know the double meaning of "light."

Michèle Vincent (**95**) has found differences between deaf and hearing children, less than eight years of age, in sorting tasks. Verbal mediation was assumed to be the critical factor. Two blocks, alike with respect to one dimension, were displayed, and the children were asked to choose the third. Wrong choices were corrected. The deaf were more than a year retarded. In a similar study meaningful categories, such as animals, were employed (**94**). Deaf children of eight behaved like hearing children of six years. When the hearing children were asked to justify their choices, subsequent performance improved. Presumably, this procedure increased the probability of verbal mediation. Studies comparing deaf and hearing children have the hazard that many features of experience are likely to differ and that some organic defects besides deafness may be present.

It has been common to compare children before and after they can verbalize a contrast and to assume that verbalization reflects the availability of verbal mediation. Of course, where the verbal skill has not been taught by the experimenter, the verbalization and the performance may both reflect a third factor. The Kendlers' recent work with reversal shifts seems to solve this difficulty (**55, 56**). Subjects are trained to criterion on a task requiring response to one of two available cues—such as size or color—and then a new rule is made. The new rule may simply be a reversal—if white was correct, now black is correct—or it may involve a shift to the other cue. Children between five and seven years found the two equally difficult, but, if young children were taught to mention the relevant cue, reversal was easier. For the older children, who presumably verbalized spontaneously anyway, the teaching had no effect, except that teaching them to mention the irrelevant cue impaired performance.

These studies assume the occurrence of a covert or implicit response. One way to test the occurrence of such covert responses is to condition a reaction to them. Volkova found that a response conditioned to the word "right" occurred if children were given arithmetic problems that were correctly solved and that a response conditioned to the word "ten" occurred when the stimulus was "five plus five" (**79**).

DIMENSIONAL SALIENCE

The sorting studies of Vincent, mentioned above, suggest the presence of verbal mediation, but it is possible that sorting or grouping tasks might be affected simply by the relative salience of different dimensions. Such salience varies with experience, and dimensions commonly codified by vocabulary or grammar would tend to be noticed more often. Casagrande (**18**), in a study connected with the Southwestern Project in Comparative Psycholinguistics, compared Navaho- and English-dominant Navaho children who lived on the Navaho reservation. The Navaho language includes a set of verbs referring to handling of objects, with a different verb for long rigid objects, mushy objects, flat flexible objects, and so forth. The classification of objects into these categories is similar to the classification of objects into the gender categories of European languages, except that the Navaho categories display marked semantic consistency. Since verbs of handling are prominent in the vocabulary of children, Casagrande believed the children might attend to the pertinent properties of objects earlier if they spoke primarily Navaho. He asked them to choose from two others a block to match a model, allowing matching on either of two dimensions. Between the ages of three and eight, there were marked differences, the Navaho-dominant children choosing the block similar in form, the English-dominant that similar in color.

This study has been concerned with the impact of the learning of language on nonverbal processes. While positive results have been found, in many studies the total effect is relatively slight and only barely statistically significant. It is possible to exaggerate the importance of verbal processes in simple tasks involving objects and motor responses. In studies involving aiming, mechanical puzzles, or various kinds of visuo-motor co-ordination such as that reported by Ervin (**28**), verbal training can interfere with performance. It may distract by supplying an additional task or by drawing disproportionate attention to part of the relevant stimulus complex. In the experiment by Ervin, a verbally trained group was generally inferior but was better on one difficult item where the usual strategies discovered by visuo-motor experience were inappropriate. In the Casagrande study, a control group of Massachusetts city nursery-school children chose the form match as often as the Navaho-dominant Indian children. Perhaps their training with form-boards and other nursery toys had led them to focus on form as more relevant than color. This kind of experience may have had the same effects as the training supplied by speaking Navaho. And even verbal mediation does not, perhaps, have to be verbal. The complex problem-solving of primates on multiple-sign problems, and the level of play involving planning which can be sustained by deaf children before they receive speech training, suggests that alternative representational processes are available.

SOVIET RESEARCH

A central interest of Soviet research has been in the changing relation between verbal and nonverbal processes as children's mastery of language increases and on the evolution of the self-directive role of language. While there is overlap, for example, with American studies of verbal mediation, the experimental questions have been quite different. The focus has been much more developmental, and the labels studied have been labels acquired in natural language learning. Age is usually the variable of chief interest.

At the earliest ages, children do not distinguish vocal from other auditory stimuli. This was found to be the case at seven to eight months of age, but three months later conditioning to words occurs four times faster than to other sound stimuli (**26**). There is considerable evidence from American research that children at first respond to the sound properties of words and only later to meaning. The classic experiment of Riess (**81**) found that, even at the age of eight, children generalized most to homophones, or words that sound like the training word, and that it was only in adolescence that synonyms became predominant. Also, it is known that children give rhyming or alliterative responses on word-association tests much more often than adults, with a sharp decrease in the early school years (**27**).

There have been many studies of stimulus generalization between words and referents. Korbatov (**58**), using a bell or the word "ring" and various verbal and auditory stimuli, tested generalization at various ages and degrees of training. The youngest and least-trained most often responded to all the stimuli. Then there was a stage of reacting only to the bell and "ring" and not to other stimuli, and finally narrowing to the identical stimulus. When the training stimulus was the bell, the reactions tended to be more primitive in these terms than when the training stimulus was the word. Thus, at the lowest level of training, 70 per cent of the 4- to 6-year-olds and 10 per cent of the 15- to 16-year-olds showed diffuse stimulus generalization after training with the bell. At the same stage, 40 per cent of the youngest and none of the oldest gave such reactions when trained to the word. Specific training with a particular stimulus has effects similar to an increase in age. Studies in the generalization of inhibition of responses have given somewhat similar results, but the interpretation of the results is complicated by the tendency of young children to be very reactive, and thus to show little generalization of inhibition (**84**).

In a study on mediated generalization, Naroditskaia (**74**) conditioned a response to a green light and nonresponse to a blue light. It was found that the discrimination generalized not only to *green* and *blue* but to *leaf*, *grass*, *sky*, and *sea*. Some of the children actually said the word *green* when given these secondary verbal stimuli rather than giving a motor response. Since the effect was strongly related to age, the experimenter tried to induce mediation by giving word-association training to the 5-year-old children but failed to increase the amount of mediated generalization.

Another type of mediation training was attempted by Gerasimchuk (**32**). Children sorted and discussed drawings, for instance, of red chicks and yellow buckets. Then they were conditioned discriminatively to a red and a yellow light. Among the 11- to 12-year-olds, there were 13 out of 20 children who reacted to the word *chick*, for example, although with a long latency.

All of these studies display experimentally the increasingly differentiated linkage of word and referent as the child grows older. A somewhat different frame of reference has been used by the psychologists influenced by Vigotsky and Luria. Luria was an associate of Vigotsky in the early thirties at the time of Vigotsky's vigorous and original work on the functions of language in the adaptive behavior of the child (**97, 98**). The recent resurgence of interest in this approach has resulted in the publication of a series of studies, many summarized by Luria in English (**66**). In the most ambitious of these projects, Luria and Yudovich (**67**) separated two speech-retarded twins and gave intensive verbal training to one. They describe vividly the great changes in behavior which accompanied training, particularly changes in the complexity and integration of play.

A series of single experimental studies was concerned with the evolution of self-control in the child through the use, first, of overt and, then, of covert verbal responses. These studies are reported by Luria (**66**). If a child under sixteen months was engaged in on-going activity, or saw a salient stimulus, he was unresponsive to instructions. A child, told several times to put rings on a peg, would begin to do it; but, once the task was under way, instructions to stop merely increased his activity.

A child, trained to press a bulb whenever a light went on, would press it continuously, once he began. He would stop if the light went out or a bell rang; but, in the absence of these stimuli, children under age three would return to continuous pressure. After age three, a self-produced cue would work, consisting either of a second movement after pressure, and *now* or *boo* said when the light appeared. Thus, language helped to demarcate the short time duration when pressure was to be made. When they were silent, children under age four, trained to use the verbal cue, continued pressing too long.

If a child under age four was told to say *press twice*, Tikhomirov (**66**) has shown that he pressed continuously. But if he said *one-two* or *boo-boo* he responded by pressing only twice. Here we see an overt form of the verbal control that Oléron (**76**) found deaf children lacked in double alternation problems.

A similar difficulty developed in efforts to train children to differentiate between a red and a blue light. At age three and a half a child could only discriminate with accompanying verbal instructions; otherwise he generalized his response to both. If the children were taught to say *now* or *press* to the red and *don't* to the blue, an even higher percentage pressed for the blue stimulus than before. Silence for the blue light was the only effective support for discrimination. After the age of four, such supports were not necessary. In general, Luria concludes that after four and a half years words cease merely to generate impulsive responses and become differentiated signals. This point is supported by the evidence of increasing importance of semantic rather than phonetic properties of words.

Although Vigotsky warned against identifying thought with subvocal speech (**9**: 44–45), these studies imply that verbal control of behavior developmentally undergoes two changes: it comes to be semantically distinctive rather than merely a trigger; and it progresses from the utterance of another to overt utterances by the subject to covert responses. The American studies, conducted largely at ages after this development is well under way, have shown the role of language in certain operations involving visible and tangible stimuli. As yet, little is known about the effects of language on cognition of a more complex type, such as the problems in natural science and mathematics investigated by Piaget. Nor has evidence been sought on an even more difficult implication, namely, the suggestion of G. H. Mead that the learning of language is crucial to the ability to categorize one's self and one's acts and hence crucial to social and moral behavior.

BIBLIOGRAPHY

1. Albright, R. W., and Albright, Joy Buck. "Application of Descriptive Linguistics to Child Language," *J. Speech Research*, I (1958), 257–61.
2. Applegate, Joseph R. "Phonological Rules of a Subdialect of English," *Word*, XVII (1961), 186–93.
3. Austerlitz, Robert. "Gilyak Nursery Words," *Word*, XII (1956), 260–79.
4. Berko, Jean. "The Child's Learning of English Morphology," *Word*, XIV (1958), 150–77.
5. Braine, Martin D. S. "The Ontogeny of English Phrase Structure: The First Phase," *Language* (in press).
6. Brown, Roger W. "Linguistic Determinism and the Part of Speech," *J. Abnorm. Soc. Psychol.*, LV (1957), 1–5.
7. ———. *Words and Things*. Glencoe, Illinois: Free Press, 1958.
8. Brown, R. W., and Berko, Jean. "Psycholinguistic Research Methods," in *Handbook of Research Methods in Child Development*, pp. 517–57. Edited by P. H. Mussen. New York: John Wiley & Sons, 1960.
9. ———. "Word Association and the Acquisition of Grammar." *Child Develpm.*, XXXI (1960), 1–14.
10. Brown, Roger, and Fraser, Colin. "The Acquisition of Syntax," *Child Develpm.* (in press).
11. Brown, Roger; Fraser, Colin; and Bellugi, Ursula. "Evaluation Procedures for Grammars Written for the Speech of Children," in *First-Language Acquisition*. Edited by Ursula Bellugi and Roger Brown. In preparation for submission to *Child Development Monographs*.
12. Burling, Robbins. "Language Development of a Garo and English Speaking Child," *Word*, XV (1959), 45–68.
13. Cantor, Gordon N. "Effects of Three Types of Pretraining on Discrimination Learning in Preschool Children," *J. Exp. Psychol.*, XLIX (1955), 339–42.
14. Carey, J. E., and Goss, A. E. "The Role of Mediating Verbal Responses in the Conceptual Sorting Behavior of Children," *J. Genet. Psychol.*, XC (1957), 69–74.
15. Carrier, E. O. "An Investigation of the Influence of Language in the Color-Weight Associations of Deaf and Hearing Children." Unpublished Doctor's dissertation, Harvard School of Education, 1961.
16. Carroll, John B. "Determining and Numerating Adjectives in Children's Speech," *Child Develpm.*, X (1939), 215–29.
17. ———. "Language Development," *Encyclopedia of Educational Research*, (1960), pp. 744–52.
18. Carroll, J. B., and Casagrande, J. B. "The Function of Language Classifications in Behavior," in *Readings in Social Psychology*, pp. 18–31. Edited by E. E. Maccoby, T. M. Newcomb, and E. L. Hartley. New York: Holt, Rinehart, and Winston, 1958.

19. Casagrande, Joseph B. "Comanche Baby Language," *Int. J. Amer. Linguistics*, XIV (1948), 11–14.
20. Chao, Yuen Ren. "The Cantian Idiolect: An Analysis of the Chinese Spoken by a Twenty-eight-months-old Child," *Univ. Calif. Publ. Semitic Philology*, XI (1951), 27–44.
21. Chomsky, Noam. *Syntactic Structures*. 's-Gravenhage, Holland: Mouton & Co., 1957.
22. Church, Joseph. *Language and the Discovery of Reality*. New York: Random House, 1961.
23. Cohen, Marcel. "Sur l'Étude du Langage Enfantin," *Enfance*, V (1952), 181–249.
24. Devereux, George. "Mohave Voice and Speech Mannerisms," *Word*, V (1949), 268–72.
25. El'konin, D. B. *Detskaya Psikhologiia* (Child Psychology). Moscow: Acad. Ped. Sci. Inst. of Psych., 1960.
26. ———. "Nekotorye itogi izucheniia psikhicheskogo razvitiia detei doshkol'nogo vozrasta," *Psikhologicheskaiia nauka v SSSR*. (Some Results of Studying the Mental Development of Preschool Age Children. Psychological Science in the USSR.) Acad. Educ. Sci. RSFSR, Inst. Psych., Moscow, II (1960), 249–61.
27. Ervin, Susan M. "Changes with Age in the Verbal Determinants of Word-Association," *Amer. J. Psychol.*, LXXIV (1961), 361–72.
28. ———. "Transfer Effects of Learning a Verbal Generalization," *Child Develpm.*, XXXI (1960), 537–54.
29. Ferguson, Charles A. "Arabic Baby Talk," in *For Roman Jakobson, Essays on the Occasion of his Sixtieth Birthday*, pp. 121–28. Compiled by Morris Halle. 's-Gravenhage, Holland: Mouton & Co., 1956.
30. Fischer, John L. "Social Influences on the Choice of a Linguistic Variant," *Word*, XIV (1958), 47–56.
31. Fries, Charles Carpenter. *The Structure of English*. New York: Harcourt Brace & Co., 1952.
32. Gerasimchuk, V. A. "Certain New Data on Serial Conditioned Connections in the Cerebral Cortex of a Child," in *Works of the Inst. Higher Nerv. Activity*. Pathophysiological Series, Vol. II, pp. 140–55. Edited by A. G. Ivanov-Smolenskii. Moscow: Academy of Science, U.S.S.R., 1956. Washington: National Science Foundation, 1960.
33. Goss, A. E. "Verbal Mediating Responses and Concept Formation," *Psychol. Rev.*, LXVIII (1961), 248–74.
34. Grégoire, Antoine. *L'apprentissage du Langage*. Paris: Lib. Droz, (2 vol.), 1947.
35. Guillaume, P. "Le Dévelopment des Éléments Formels dans le Langage de l'Enfant," *J. Psychol. Norm. Path.*, XXIV (1927), 203–29.
36. Gvozdev, A. N. *Voprosy izucheniia detskoi rechi* (Problems in the Language Development of the Child). Moscow: Acad. Ped. Sci., 1961.
37. Hahn, E. "Analysis of the Control and Form of the Speech of First Grade Children," *Quar. J. Speech*, CXXXIV (1948), 361–66.
38. Harwood, F. W. "Quantitative Study of the Syntax of the Speech of Australian Children," *Language and Speech*, II (1959), 236–71.

39. HOCKETT, CHARLES F. "Age-Grading and Linguistic Continuity," *Language*, XXVI (1950), 449–57.

40. ———. *A Course in Modern Linguistics.* New York: Macmillan Co., 1958.

41. HORIKAWA, KATSUTARO; OHWAKI, YOSHIKAZU; and WATANÄBE, TÂKEO. "Variation of Verbal Activity through Different Psychological Situations," *Tohoku Psychol. Folia*, XV (1956), 65–90.

42. HYMES, D. H. "The Ethnography of Speaking," in *Anthropology and Behavior.* Edited by Thomas C. Gladwin and William C. Sturtevant. Washington: Anthropological Society of Washington (in press).

43. IRWIN, O. C. "Development of Vowel Sounds," *J. Speech Hearing Disorders*, XIII (1948), 31–34.

44. ———. "Infant Speech: Consonantal Position," *J. Speech Hearing Disorders*, XVI (1951), 159–61.

45. ———. "Infant Speech: Consonantal Sounds According to Place of Articulation," *J. Speech Hearing Disorders*, XII (1947), 397–404.

46. ———. "Language and Communication," in *Handbook of Research Methods in Child Development*, pp. 487–516. Edited by P. H. Mussen. New York: John Wiley & Sons, 1960.

47. IVANOV-SMOLENSKII, A. G. "Developmental Paths of Experimental Research into the Work and Interaction of the First and Second Signalling Systems," in *Works of the Inst. Higher Nerv. Activity.* Pathophysiological Series, Vol. II, pp. 1–31. Edited by A. G. Ivanov-Smolenskii. Moscow: Academy of Science, U.S.S.R., 1956. Washington: National Science Foundation, 1960.

48. IVANOV-SMOLENSKII, A. G. (Editor). "Experimental Research into Higher Nervous Activity, Especially the Interaction of the First and Second Signalling Systems, under Physiological and Pathological Conditions in Children," in *Works of the Inst. of Higher Nerv. Activity.* Pathophysiological Series, Vol. II. Moscow: Academy of Sciences, U.S.S.R., 1956. Washington: National Science Foundation, 1960.

49. JAKOBSON, ROMAN, and HALLE, MORRIS. *Fundamentals of Language.* 's-Gravenhage, Holland: Mouton & Co., 1956.

50. JENKINS, J. J., and PALERMO, D. S. "Mediation Processes and the Acquisition of Linguistic Structure," in *First-Language Acquisition.* Edited by Ursula Bellugi and R. Brown. In preparation for submission to *Child Development Monographs.*

51. KAHANE, HENRY; KAHANE, RENÉE; and SAPORTA, SOL. "Development of Verbal Categories in Child Language," *Int. J. Amer. Linguistics* (Indiana University Research Center in Anthropology, Folklore, and Linguistics), IX (1958).

52. KAINZ, FRIEDRICH. *Psychologie der Sprache*, Vol. II, pp. 1–161. Stuttgart: Ferdinand Enke, 1960.

53. KARPOVA, S. N. "Osoznanie slovesnogo sostava rechi rebyonka doshkolnogo vozrasta," (Awareness of the Word Content of Speech of a Preschool Child), *Vop. Psikhol.*, I (1955), 43–55.

54. KAVERINA, E. K. *O razvitii rechi detei pervykh dvukh let zhizni.* (On the Development of Child Language in the First Two Years of Life.) Moscow: Medgiz, 1950.

55. KENDLER, H. H., and KENDLER, T. S. "The Effect of Verbalization on Reversal Shifts in Children," *Science*, CXXXIV (1961), 1619–20.

56. KENDLER, T. S.; KENDLER, H. H.; and WELLS, D. "Reversal and Nonreversal Shifts in Nursery School Children," *J. Comp. Physiol. Psychol.*, LIII (1960), 83–87.

57. KONISHI, TERUO. "On the Development of Language in Infants," *Jap. J. Child Psychiat.*, I (1960), 62–74.

58. KORBATOV, B. M. "Study of the Dynamic Transmission of a Conditioned Connection from One Cortical Signalling System into the Other," in *Works of the Inst. Higher Nerv. Activity*. Pathophysiological Series, Vol. II, pp. 92–107. Edited by Ivanov-Smolenskii. Moscow: Academy of Science, U.S.S.R., 1956. Washington: National Science Foundation, 1960.

59. LENNEBERG, E. H. "Color Naming, Color Recognition, Color Discrimination: A Reappraisal," *Percept. Mot. Skills*, XII (1961), 375–82.

60. ———. "Speech as a Motor Skill with Special Reference to Nonaphasic Disorders," in *First-Language Acquisition*. Edited by Ursula Bellugi and R. Brown. In preparation for submission to *Child Development Monographs*.

61. LEOPOLD, WERNER F. *Bibliography of Child Language*. Evanston, Illinois: Northwestern University Press, 1952.

62. ———. "Patterning in Children's Language Learning," *Language Learning*, V (1953–54), 1–14.

63. ———. *Speech Development of a Bilingual Child: A Linguist's Record* (4 vols.), Northwestern University Studies in the Humanities. Evanston, Illinois: Northwestern University, 1939–49.

64. LEWIS, M. M. *Infant Speech*. New York: Humanities Press, 1951.

65. LIBERMAN, A. M.; HARRIS, KATHERINE S.; KINNEY, JO ANN; and LANE, H. "The Discrimination of Relative Onset-Time of the Components of Certain Speech and Nonspeech Patterns," *J. Exp. Psychol.*, LXI (1961), 379–88.

66. LURIA, A. R. *The Role of Speech in the Regulation of Normal and Abnormal Behavior*. New York: Liveright Pub. Corp., 1961.

67. LURIA, A. R., and YUDOVICH, F. IA. *Speech and the Development of Mental Processes in the Child*. London: Staples Press, 1959.

68. LYNIP, A. W. "The Use of Magnetic Devices in the Collection and Analyses of the Preverbal Utterances of an Infant," *Genet. Psychol. Monogr.*, XLIV (1951), 221–62.

69. MCCARTHY, DOROTHEA A. "Language Development in Children," in *Manual of Child Psychology*, pp. 492–630. Edited by Leonard Carmichael. New York: John Wiley & Sons, 1954.

70. MCNEILL, DAVID. "The Development of Paradigmatic Word-Associations under Experimental Conditions." Unpublished Doctor's dissertation, University of California at Berkeley, 1962.

71. MILLER, G. A., and NICELY, PATRICIA. "An Analysis of Perceptual Confusions among Some English Consonants," *J. Acoustical Soc. Amer.*, XXVII (1955), 338–52.

72. MILLER, WICK, and ERVIN, SUSAN. "The Development of Grammar in Child Language," in *First-Language Acquisition*. Edited by Ursula Bellugi

and R. Brown. In preparation for submission to *Child Development Monographs.*

73. MOWRER, O. H. *Learning Theory and the Symbolic Processes.* New York: John Wiley & Sons, 1960.
74. NARODITSKAIA, G. D. "A Study of the Question of the Phenomenon of the So-called Secondary Excitation in the Cerebral Cortex of Children," in *Works of the Inst. Higher Nerv. Activity.* Pathophysiological Series, Vol. II, pp. 131–39. Edited by Ivanov-Smolenskii. Moscow: Academy of Science, U.S.S.R., 1956. Washington: National Science Foundation, 1960.
75. ———. "Complex Dynamic Structure in Children of Different Ages," in *The Central Nervous System and Behavior,* pp. 670–77. Princeton: Josiah Macy Foundation and National Science Foundation, 1960.
76. OLÉRON, P. "Une Contribution à la Psychopathologie Différentielle: Les Caractéristiques Psychologiques Determinées par la Surdi-mutité," *Biotypologie,* XV (1954), 1–12.
77. PIKE, EVELYN G. "Controlled Infant Intonation," *Language Learning,* II (1949), 21–24.
78. PORTER, DOUGLAS. "Preliminary Analysis of the Grammatical Concept 'Verb.'" Unpublished paper, Harvard Graduate School of Education, 1955.
79. RAZRAN, G. "Soviet Psychology and Psychophysiology," *Behavioral Science,* IV (1959), 35–48.
80. REESE, H. W. "Transfer to a Discrimination Task as a Function of Amount of Stimulus Pretraining and Similarity of Stimulus Names." Unpublished Doctor's dissertation, State University of Iowa, 1958.
81. REISS, B. F. "Genetic Changes in Semantic Conditioning," *J. Exp. Psychol.,* XXXVI (1946), 143–52.
82. SAPIR, EDWARD. "Nootka Baby Words," *Int. J. Amer. Linguistics,* V (1929), 118–19.
83. SCHIEFELBUSCH, R. L., and LINDSEY, MARY JEANNE. "A New Test of Sound Discrimination," *J. Speech and Hearing Disorders,* XXIII (1958), 153–59.
84. SEREDINA, M. I. "Selective Irradiation of Extinguishing Inhibition at Different Age Levels," in *Works of the Inst. Higher Nerv. Activity, op. cit.,* pp. 108–21.
85. SHEPARD, WINIFRED, and SCHAEFFER, MAURICE. "The Effect of Concept Knowledge on Discrimination Learning," *Child Develpm.,* XXVII (1956), 173–78.
86. SMITH, STANLEY L., and GOSS, ALBERT E. "The Role of the Acquired Distinctiveness of Cues in the Acquisition of a Motor Skill in Children," *J. Genet. Psychol.,* LXXXVII (1955), 11–24.
87. SOKHIN, F. A. "O formirovanii iaazykovykh obobshcenii v protsesse rechevogo razvitiia" (On the Formation of Language Generalizations in the Process of Speech Development). *Vop. Psikhol.,* V (1959), 112–23.
88. SOSKIN, W. F., and JOHN, VERA. "The Study of Spontaneous Talk," in *Streams of Behavior.* Edited by Roger Barker (in press).
89. SPIKER, C. C. "Verbal Factors in the Discrimination Learning of Children," in *Basic Cognitive Processes in Children.* Edited by John C. Wright and Jerome Kagan. Monograph of the Society for Research in Child Development (in press).

90. STEWARD, J. L. "The Problem of Stuttering in Certain North American Indian Societies," *J. Speech Hearing Disorders, Mongr. Suppl.*, VI (1960), 1–87.

91. TEMPLIN, MILDRED C. *Certain Language Skills in Children: Their Development and Interrelationships.* Inst. Child Welfare Mongr. Ser. No. 26. Minneapolis: University of Minnesota Press, 1957.

92. TISCHLER, HANS. "Schreien, Lallen und Erstes Sprechen in der Entwicklung des Saüglings," *Z. Psychol.*, CLX (1957), 210–63.

93. VELTEN, H. V. "The Growth of Phonemic and Lexical Patterns in Infant Language," *Language*, XIX (1943), 281–92.

94. VINCENT, MICHÈLE. "Les Classifications d'Objets et leur Formulation Verbale Chez l'Enfant," *Enfance*, XII (1959), 190–204.

95. ———. "Sur le Rôle du Langage á un Niveau Élémentaire de Pensée Abstraite," *Enfance*, X (1957), 443–64.

96. VOEGELIN, C. F., and ROBINETT, FLORENCE. " 'Mother Language' in Hidatsa," *Int. J. Amer. Linguistics*, XX (1954), 65–70.

97. VIGOTSKY, L. S. *Thought and Language.* Cambridge: MIT Press, 1962.

98. ———. "Thought and Speech," *Psychiatry*, II (1939), 29–54.

99. WEINRICH, URIEL. *Languages in Contact.* Special Publications of the Linguistic Circle of New York, 1953.

100. WEIR, M. W., and STEVENSON, H. W. "The Effect of Verbalization in Children's Learning as a Function of Chronological Age," *Child Develpm.*, XXX (1959), 143–49.

101. WERNER, HEINZ, and KAPLAN, EDITH. *The Acquisition of Word Meanings: A Developmental Study.* Monograph of the Society for Research in Child Development, Vol. XV, No. 51, 1952.

102. WHORF, BENJAMIN LEE. *Language, Thought, and Reality.* Edited and with an introduction by John B. Carroll. Cambridge: Technology Press, 1956.

103. WINITZ, H., and IRWIN, O. C. "Syllabic and Phonetic Structure of Infants' Early Words," *J. Speech Research*, I (1958), 250–56.

104. WOODWARD, MARY, and BARBER, C. G. "Phoneme Perception in Lipreading," *J. Speech and Hearing Res.*, III (1960), 212–22.

CHAPTER IV

Perceptual Development

ELEANOR J. GIBSON

The primary purpose of this chapter will be to present a framework for the developmental study of perception and to formulate some important issues. Research in this area has tended to be spotty, opportunistic, and lacking a program (except for that of Piaget's laboratory). As a consequence, there is a real need for a systematically oriented outline which will put current research contributions in their theoretical place, so to speak, and which will reveal areas where research is needed. There will be no attempt, therefore, to cover all the available material.[1] The studies which are presented in detail were selected because they illustrate a point of view important for the framework or because they bring out a theoretical issue which is a current focus of research.

The outline is organized around a classification of stimulus sources.[2] It begins with space—that is, the surfaces and edges and places that make up the environment. From there it goes on to the objects proper in the environment (detachable solids) and progresses from these to two-dimensional representations of objects and, finally, to nonrepresentative and "coded" stimulus-sources, such as writing. The chapter is not concerned exclusively with visual perception, but research on vision has exceeded research on other modes of perceiving.

Perception of the Environment

By perception of the environment, we mean perception of the larger aspects of the world; that is, places, surfaces, floors, walls, and

1. Two recent articles provide very inclusive summaries, one a survey of content by Wohlwill (**49**) and one of methods by Gibson and Olum (**14**).

2. By stimulus sources, we mean the places, things, and events in the world which give rise to stimuli. The word "stimulus" may be used for the sake of brevity, however, when "stimulus source" should properly be used. (See **19.**)

the spaces between things. We could, in fact, speak of "locomotor perception" here, for we are speaking of the world in which the child moves around. A trend in the study of comparative behavior in the last decade has been the emphasis of the ethologists (because of their interest in species-specific behavior) on observing the behavior of an animal in its natural world. Perhaps the developmental psychologist, who is in a sense interested in "age-specific" behavior, should profit from the ethologists' successes and strive to study the young animal in a "natural" situation, that is, a situation which is a valid sample of an infant's normal ecology, or relationship with its environment. Such a situation should have real adaptive significance for the young subjects.

There is, of course, little value in perceptual research which is merely anecdotal, which cannot specify the stimulation or make objective measurements of responses. The ideal compromise, therefore, would seem to be a laboratory situation which *simulates* a normal situation of the "real" world. It should be controllable and describable so that it can be exactly replicated; but it should have "ecological validity."

BEHAVIOR IN RESPONSE TO DEPTH-AT-AN-EDGE

The visual cliff.—Research by two investigators, Gibson and Walk (**13, 46**), on locomotor behavior of infants in response to a drop-off has attempted to follow this prescription. These psychologists were interested in studying perception of depth downward at the earliest possible age in human and other infants. The situation devised for this research has been dubbed the "visual cliff." The apparatus simulates a real drop-off. It is constructed so as to give the subject a choice between a shallow (safe) descent and a deep (dangerous) one. The question was, at how young an age would an infant discriminate between a shallow and a deep drop and choose the safe one? And under exactly what stimulus conditions?

Figure 1 shows a drawing of a visual cliff constructed for human infants. It resembles a large table with a fence around the edges. Bisecting the long sides of the rectangle is a center platform one inch higher than the table surface. The platform is wide enough to hold a baby in creeping position. The real surface of the table is heavy plate glass. Under this glass is placed a patterned material of any desired texture or color. The pattern may be directly under the glass or it may be dropped to different depths below. The standard situation for testing depth discrimination was a very shallow drop (patterned surface immediately under glass) on one side of the center platform and a relatively deep drop (pattern four feet below glass) on the other. The baby, once placed on the platform, could simply stay on it, of course. In order to see whether the baby would avoid crawling off over the deep side but would crawl over the

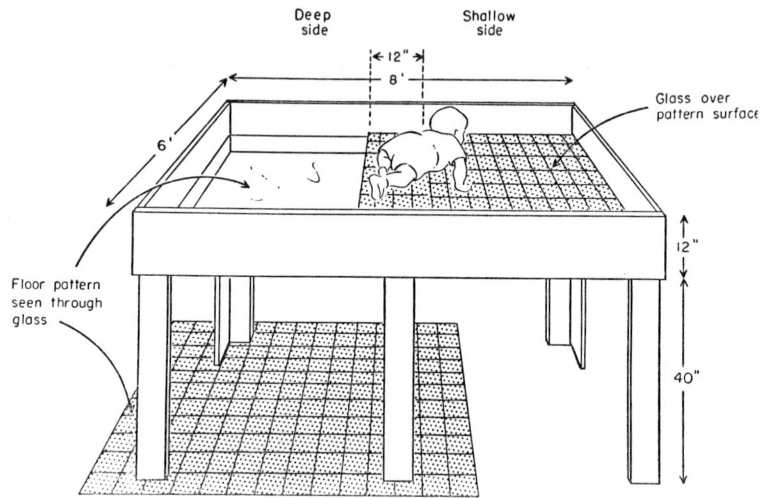

FIG. 1.—Drawing of the visual cliff. The infant is crawling from the center platform toward the shallow side.

shallow side, its mother, twirling a toy (Fig. 4, opp. p. 150), stood alternately at the two sides and called to the baby, urging it to come to her. Each baby was given two minutes to respond before its mother changed sides. In the basic experiment, two trials were given for each side. In this experiment, there were 36 subjects between the ages of 6½ and 14 months. A green and white mottled linoleum was placed directly under the glass on the shallow side. The same linoleum was on the floor four feet below the deep side.

Of the babies tested in this first experiment, one-fourth would not leave the center board (they were probably still unable to crawl adequately). Of the babies who answered their mother's urging and left the board, 24 out of 27, (89 per cent) crawled to her when she stood at the shallow side but refused to come when she called from the deep side. Three babies (11 per cent) went to their mothers over the glass of both sides, deep as well as shallow. No baby went to its mother over the deep side only. From this experiment and later confirming replications, it was concluded that the normal human infant, by the time it locomotes on its own, can perceive a drop-off and that it tends to avoid it.

Relative depth and avoidance behavior.—It has been thus established that infants in the standard "cliff" situation avoid an apparent drop-off, when the floor is 40 inches below. One would like to know also whether differences in the depth of a surface below elicit differential avoidance [as Walk and Gibson (**46**) have shown to be the case for rats]. Walk (**45**) has carried out an experiment which shows that, for human infants, avoidance of a drop-off increases as the deep side, once from the shallow side. As Figure 2 shows, the were tested on a cliff with the "deep" surface at four different depths below the glass: zero inches, 10 inches, 20 inches, and 40 inches. At zero inches, the two sides, deep and shallow, were of course identical except for location in the room. A coarse-checked pattern covered the surface on both sides as well as the starting platform in the center where the baby was placed by its mother. A given baby was tested at only one depth, once with its mother calling the baby to her from the deep side, once from the shallow side. As Figure 3 shows, the percentage of times infants crawled across the glass of the deep side dropped from the high figures of 89 per cent at zero inches to the very low figure of 11 per cent at 40 inches, the greatest drop tested. The tendency to avoid a drop-off increases, therefore, as the depth increases.

There was some evidence that those babies who did cross the deep side were mostly the younger babies. They would cross at the 10-inch depth, but, with a 40-inch drop, nearly all distinguished the difference. It is possible, therefore, that sensitivity to a difference of the kind presented by the cliff situation continues to grow after six months, since practically all the infants avoided the 40-inch drop, but some of the younger ones apparently made no distinction with a smaller difference.

The role of surfaces and texture.—What are the conditions which permit the infant to detect the drop-off in the cliff situation? One of them would certainly seem to be adequate conditions for perceiving a *surface*. We know from the classical experiments of Metzger (see **29:** 111 ff.) that a wall painted so as to have a homogeneous texture does not appear to be a surface at all, if it fills the field of view, but, instead, has an indeterminate location; when the illumination is reduced, such a wall appears as film or fog. What would happen, then, if a plain gray painted surface, nearly textureless, was substituted for the coarsely checked pattern under the glass of the deep side? This experiment was tried with rats by Walk and Gibson (**46**), and the rats' descents significantly decreased with reduction of surface texture. Walk has performed a similar experi-

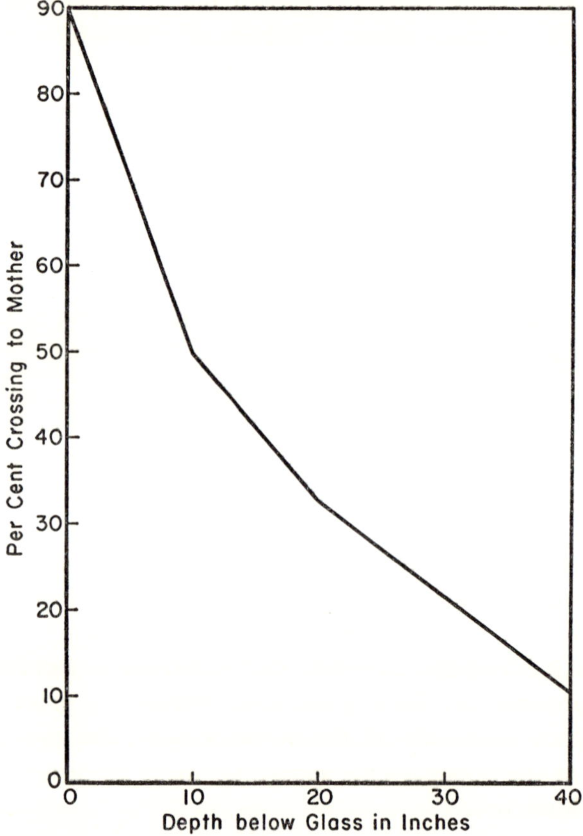

Fig. 2.—Psychometric function showing crossing behavior of infants as related to depth of the surface below the glass.

ment with human infants, comparing percentage of crossings at different depths when the surface was textured (coarsely checked) and when it was relatively textureless (plain gray masonite). In the table below are the results.

When the gray masonite was zero inches below the glass, the babies tended to avoid crossing it, in contrast to the standard situation where the texture (and, therefore, the surface) was highly visible. When the masonite was dropped to 10, then to 20, then to 40 inches, there was no psychometric function such as Walk found with the checked surface. These depth differences with the masonite surface were discriminable from the zero-inch condition, to some babies, but they were not distinguishable from one another. The surface quality of the ground under the infant, therefore, controls its behavior in the cliff situation. If the texture is such that cues to the depth of the surface become ambiguous, crossing behavior is reduced, and the psychometric function disappears. It is possible that relative impoverishment of cues to "surfaceness" affects the younger Ss (subjects) more seriously; that is, that they need more redundant information to perceive a surface as well as do the more mature Ss.

TABLE 1

Depth in Inches	Per Cent Infants Crossing	
	Coarse Texture (Checks)	Fine Texture (Gray Masonite)
0	89	50
10	50	33
20	33	22
40	11	32

As Gibson (**17**: 8) said, "The elementary impressions of a visual world are those of surface and edge." Inhomogeneities of texture are requisite for perception of a surface, and locomotion is controlled by "surfaceness"—in the case described above, the apparent presence of *visual* support.

Analysis of information in the stimulus.—It appears, from these experiments, that an infant will avoid a visual cliff or drop-off even when there is tactual support—an actual solid surface, which can be felt (and nearly all the infants did feel the glass of the deep side by patting it, rubbing it, or even putting their faces to it). It must be, then, that a surface has to *look* safe for locomotion—that is, provide "visual support." What are the cues or stimuli which provide visual support? We know that there must be inhomogeneities or texture; but what does the infant's eye "pick up" from the texture that specifies a drop-off?

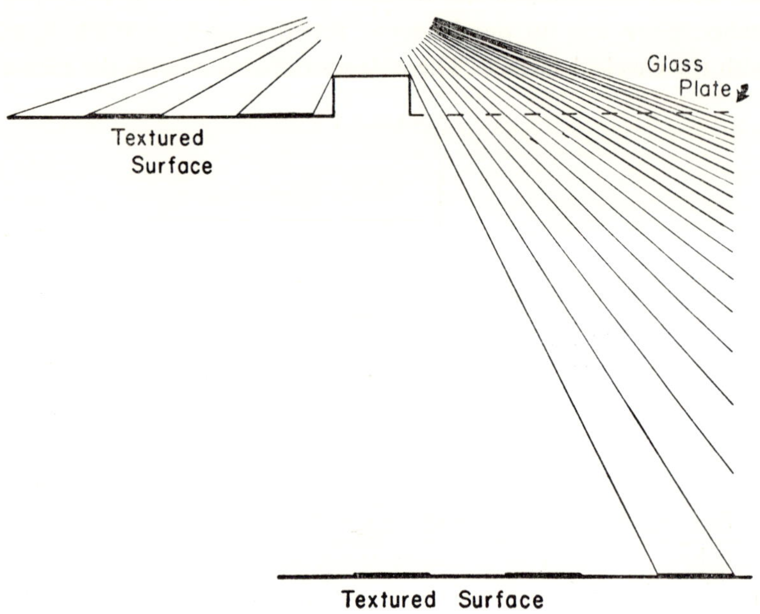

FIG. 3.—Diagram of the cliff showing difference in texture density of light projected from the deep and the shallow sides.

Figure 3 shows a diagram of a cliff with the textured surface dropped lower on one side. When the texture is identical on the two surfaces, the pattern of light rays entering the S's eye from the farther surface will be denser. This is potential information for the differential depth of the two surfaces. Another kind of differential stimulation will be produced if S moves his head as he compares two sides, or better, compares the surface of the board with the surface under the glass. Cues produced by his own motion—velocity differences between the farther and the nearer pattern, or differential motion parallax—will result. For the human infant, binocular parallax

FIG. 4.—A mother urging her baby toward the deep side

may be operating[3] and would, of course, result in a differential for the two sides. Besides these optical differences, accommodation and convergence may provide differential stimulation for the relative depth of the two sides, but we know almost nothing about the actual effectiveness of these processes in infants (or in adults, really). In any case, all of these potential stimuli require a textured surface; the eye must accommodate to *something* and converge on something.

The importance of surface texture is crucial, therefore, in experiments investigating perception of space, especially in infants where redundant stimulation (redundant, at least, for the adult) may be necessary.

BEHAVIOR IN RESPONSE TO IMMINENT COLLISION

The "looming" experiment.—Another kind of "natural" behavior in young animals is the avoidance of collision with solid objects in the environment. They normally avoid moving rapidly into something solid by steering away; or avoid being hit by a rapidly approaching object by ducking. It is possible to study avoidance behavior of this type, as well as avoidance of holes or cliffs, by a simulated situation which duplicates optically the stimulation produced by a rapidly approaching object. Schiff, Caviness, and Gibson (**39**) have studied the behavior of young monkeys in such a situation.

Optical expansion of a closed contour (see **17**) was chosen as specifying approach, and the expansion of an optical form ultimately filling the whole field of view was called "looming." Looming was hypothesized to be a spatio-temporal stimulus, characterizing any case of impending contact with an environmental object. The apparatus was designed to provide such a stimulus, that is, one with the optical properties (but not the physical condition) of a collision. A silhouette (shadow of a ball) on a screen was made to undergo optical magnification. This resulted in a visual impression of a circular object approaching at a high rate of speed. For control stimulation, the shadow was made to contract, or the entire screen was made lighter or darker.

3. Walk has tested a monocular infant of 10 months on the cliff. It behaved precisely as did the normal binocular infants. Binocular parallax is, therefore, not an essential cue.

Twenty-three monkeys (eight infants five to eight months of age and fifteen adolescent and adult animals) were the subjects. The animal's cage faced the screen at a point five feet in front of it. Two hidden observers, unaware of which stimulus was being produced, observed the animal and independently judged its behavior according to categories such as "abrupt retreat."

The four stimulus conditions (expansion, contraction, lightening and darkening) resulted in two distinctly different kinds of response, one avoidant and one not. The majority of both young and older animals withdrew abruptly in response to the looming stimulus, leaping to the rear of the cage. Alarm cries frequently accompanied retreat in the younger animals. The receding stimulus, on the other hand, brought responses which might be characterized as curiosity, but never retreat. The other conditions produced varied responses of curiosity or mild flinching (in the case of darkening) but not retreat. The infants behaved essentially like the adult animals. The avoidance response to looming did not show habituation with repeated trials.

It seems likely from this experiment that optical representation alone of a rapidly approaching object elicits an avoidance response in the young monkey. The experiment is being extended to younger animals and to other species.

Specification of the stimulus.—Comparison of the four conditions of this experiment suggest that it is the expansion component of the stimulus event which evokes the avoidance response. Further research with different ranges of speed and other forms undergoing expansion will shed further light on stimulus conditions which are naturally effective for eliciting avoidance.

JUDGMENTAL STUDIES OF SOME VISUAL SPATIAL VARIABLES

The traditional type of judgmental study of perception can, of course, be carried on developmentally, with comparison of performance under the same stimulus conditions at various age levels. Such studies are, however, restricted to later age ranges, since children younger than four or five cannot understand the task in a typical psychophysical procedure, even if the judgment is simply "same" or "different." Many such experiments have been performed, and the results sometimes seem to be in the greatest contrast with results obtained by a "naturalistic" approach, like the cliff. In addition to the difficulties posed by the complexity of the judgment for younger Ss, these experiments often use "impoverished" set-ups—that is, reduced stimulus information (darkness, untextured substrata, targets which lack solidarity, etc.). These conditions in themselves may be responsible for some of the perplexing disagreements which occur in this area (one of them being the question of developmental changes in constancy of size and shape). The possibility will be considered in discussing the experiments which follow.

A DEVELOPMENTAL STUDY OF DISTANCE JUDGMENTS

Denis-Prinzhorn (**5**) has recently compared the perception of distance ahead in the line of sight for three age groups (five to seven years, nine to ten years, and adults) using a judgment of bisection of a plane surface in front of S. Judgments of size at two distances were taken as well, and size constancy was related to the distance judgment.

The subject sat before a long table (270 × 475 cm.), its surface an unpatterned light beige. His view was limited to the table by screens at the sides and by a back-drop at the end (a large sheet of plain beige paper which filled the field of view). The subject looked at the table through a slit in a screen in front of him. Markers for the distance stretch were black wires (20 cm. long) lying horizontally on the table. A stationary one was placed at the front and at the end of the stretch to be bisected (240 cm. from the near to the far marker). A third wire marker, placed by E (experimenter) somewhere between these two, was variable.

The method of judgment was an adaptation of the constant method, called "Méthode Concentrique Clinique." The variables were presented in a series, in both up and down orders. The variable marker was changed in small steps by E. The S compared the two distance stretches separated by the variable marker, and at each step made a judgment of greater or smaller. The placement of the variable marker for any series of judgments was decided individually for each S, on the basis of preliminary trials. Since judgments varied, depending on whether S judged the *near* stretch with reference to the far or vice versa, the trials were divided so that the subject made half of his judgment with reference to the near stretch as standard, and half with the far stretch as standard. Instructions were given with demonstrations in which the variable was placed so that one stretch was very obviously longer or shorter than the other. The instructions emphasized that the "real" distances were to be compared, not projective distances.

Size comparisons of upright wire sticks at two distances were also taken, to see whether size constancy was related to distance judgments.

The results of the bisection experiment revealed some differences in constant error related to age. The adult Ss had a mean constant error of overestimation of the *farther* stretch. The children, on the other hand, tended to underestimate the farther stretch, the younger group more than the intermediate group. With the farther stretch as a standard, the underestimation was decreased for the children, and the overestimation increased for the adults. The chief difference in the mean point of subjective equality was between the younger children and the adults with standard near (a difference of 15 per cent).

The results for judgment of size of sticks placed near and far showed similar constant errors. The adults tended to overestimate the far stick (mean error of 17 per cent) while the children tended to underestimate it (mean error 8 per cent for youngest group). The adults tended, thus, toward "overconstancy" and the children to slight "underconstancy."

Correlations were run between constant errors of bisection and of size judgment. For adults and older children, none of the correlations was significant, but there was a significant positive correlation for the youngest age group.

Denis-Prinzhorn interprets her results (**5:** 288) as meaning that the infant learns to interpret available "cues" and comes gradually to appreciate the distance and the size of objects in its surroundings. Visual-motor co-ordination, which is extended with age, is thought to play an important role in this learning. It is suggested (**5:** 289) that the young child has fewer cues to distance at his disposal than the adult.

A curious effect of repetition in her experimental set-up was also observed by Denis-Prinzhorn. When a mean constant error curve was constructed for 12 series of judgments, the constant error shifted from underestimation of the far distance toward overestimation of it (or in the case of adults from slight overestimation to great overestimation). The effect was more marked with the adults and the older children when the far stretch was the standard. These results can hardly be interpreted as learning for, in some cases (the adults especially), the later judgments are more and more erroneous. The fact that the developmental shift parallels the shift with repetition makes a learning hypothesis for development rather implausible. One wonders if the difficulty of the judgment under the impoverished conditions of the experiment (no clear texture of the background surface, viewing through a slit) produces an effort at compensation for a suspected error. Comparison with other experimental conditions with greater cue redundancy would be of value in reaching an explanation.

JUDGMENT OF SIZE AND DISTANCE IN PERSPECTIVE DRAWING

A very different stimulus situation has been used by Wohlwill (**50**) for a developmental comparison of size and distance judgments. He used, instead of a real three-dimensional situation (however impoverished), perspective drawings intended to create an illusion of depth. Furthermore, six different stimulus panels (backgrounds) were constructed, of varying degrees of stimulus "information" for depth. All were based on a perspective transformation of a rectangular grid. One panel was the complete grid, one was the outline of the grid with *all* interior lines removed, and the other four were filled in partially so as to create two levels of density (high and low) and two levels of regularity (random and nonrandom). The panels were displayed vertically, and two kinds of judgment obtained. One judgment was distance bisection (deciding when a moving pointer was midway between two points located on a line through the vanishing point). The other was a size match; two rectangles were placed on the panel, one near the bottom and one near the top. One was the standard, and S adjusted the other variable rectangle to match it. The Ss were children from the first, fourth, and eighth grades, and college students.

It was predicted that judgments of apparent distance (bisection) and of size on the perspective surface should be influenced by the perspective as a function of the "information value" of the type of panel filling. This prediction was confirmed for judgments of distance-bisection. The greatest effect of perspective was on the panel displaying the complete grid; the least on the unstriated panel; and the others intermediate, with high density and nonrandom distribution more effective than low density and random distribution. The results for size matches were less consistent.

Age was a factor in the results, in that the perspective was *more* effective in influencing the children's judgments than those of the adults. This finding appears superficially to be the exact contradiction of Denis-Prinzhorn's results. One can only resolve the contradiction by further experimental analysis of the stimulus conditions. Prinzhorn's experimental set-up was three-dimensional, but impoverished as regards surface and background texture, and, therefore, perspective cues. Stimulus information to distance must have come from binocular and motion parallax (though the latter would have been minimal because of the viewing slit). *Neither* of these could operate, of course, in Wohlwill's set-up. Different results, then, are not surprising. However, it seems clear from Wohlwill's results that the underconstancy of the children in the Denis-Prinzhorn experiment is *not* due to incomplete learning of the meaning of perspective-type stimulus information.

Wohlwill's experiment demonstrates strongly the importance of taking into account the *kind* and furthermore the *amount* of information in the stimulus situation when spatial judgments are called for. This finding corresponds well with the fact that infants' discrimination of depth on the cliff is reduced with relative impoverishment.

INTELLIGENCE AND CONSTANCY

In attempting to disentangle the confusion of conflicting evidence for development of perceptual constancy, one of the most perverse facts has been that animals have many times been demonstrated to have good size constancy (Locke, **33**). Why then does the human infant have to progress, as many claim, from no constancy to overconstancy? It has sometimes been claimed that such a progression must be due to the growth of intelligence, which becomes more and more active in "constructing" the perceptual world. Though the animal experiments themselves make this hypothesis fairly implausible, several experimenters have recently put this hypothesis to direct test.

Size constancy in mentally deficient subjects.—An experiment by Jenkin and Feallock (**28**) compared judgments of size as a function of distance in mentally deficient subjects (mean M.A. of 8.2 years, mean C.A. 15.10 years) and in normal subjects of three age groups, children (mean C.A. 8.3), adolescents (mean C.A. 13.7), and adults. The stimulus-objects to be judged for size were white cardboard squares (standard = 4 inches on a side placed 320 inches in front of S) in a raised position (eye-level), viewed against a homogeneous dull green field. The comparison object was of variable size, and a method of limits was used for judging when the squares matched.

The results for the three normal groups of Ss showed small but significant differences, the mean size of the matches increasing from 3.80 inches with the children to 4.47 inches for the adults. Since the standard was a 4-inch square, this is the typical shift to "overconstancy," with the younger Ss being more accurate. The retarded group, who resembled the children in M.A. but the adolescents in C.A., had a mean match of 4.1 inches, the most accurate of any group. Jenkin and Feallock conclude that the progression with age toward larger size-estimates is "not mediated by the kinds of intellectual ability which are measured in a typical intelligence test" (**28**: 272). They believe, instead, that the results indicate a "developing appreciation of depth." But why, then, are the adult Ss least accurate? This experiment, like Denis-Prinzhorn's, employs stimulus conditions which are relatively poor in information for distance, especially since the cards to be judged were raised in the air with no surface between them and S's eyes. Again, one wonders if the results would hold with a textured substratum.

The lack of any difference in size-matching between retarded Ss and normal Ss of approximately the same C.A. has been confirmed in another experiment by Leibowitz (**30**). He compared a group of defective (mean M.A. 8.7 years, mean C.A. 21.3 years) with normal Ss (college undergraduates, mean C.A. 21.2 years). Leibowitz's procedure was also a method of limits. The test-objects were wooden dowels, painted black, 2 to 24 inches in height. They were placed on the floor with the standard at 20 feet down one corridor and the variable at 10 to 120 feet down another corridor at right angles. There was good light and free binocular viewing. Under these conditions, both groups matched correctly the sizes of the test-objects at the various viewing conditions.

Shape constancy and intelligence level.—Developmental studies of shape constancy are rare, perhaps because the judgment involved and the instructions are too complex for very young subjects. Perception of the "real" shape of an object must depend on locating it accurately in its spatial environment, that is, as leaning, tilting, or slanting. Whether veridical perception of a shape under various angles of inclination is primarily an intellectual process related to intelligence level was the subject of an experiment by Leibowitz, Waskow, Loeffler, and Glaser (**31**). There were four groups of Ss, mental defectives, "slow learners" from a public school, normal undergraduate students, and superior undergraduates (recipients of "early admission" fellowships). A white disc (3 cm. in diameter) was shown at seven different angles of inclination and was to be compared with a series of ellipses graded from an axis ratio of .054 to a circle. The S looked into a tachistoscope and compared the disc, which appeared in one of the fields for one second, with the series of ellipses, making a same-different judgment. They were instructed to choose the ellipse which "looks the most like the disc."

Under these instructions, which invite an analytical attitude, the more intelligent Ss tended to produce a geometrical match. The mental defectives, on the other hand, produced matches closest to shape constancy. The authors conclude that their results indicate that with increasing intelligence level, shape matching exhibits a decreasing tendency toward shape constancy.

It seems clear from the foregoing experiments that results of developmental studies of size, distance, and shape, judgments are highly dependent on background conditions, the complexity of the judgment, and the S's attitude. Future experiments in this area should aim at clarification of the role of stimulus and judgmental variables and their possible interaction with age. Observation of constancy in less artificial situations and avoidance of instructions which produce a diversity of sets should lead to less ambiguous results.

SEPARATION OF TWO SURFACES BY DIFFERENTIAL MOTION

Developmental observations on the role of motion parallax in depth perception have recently been made by Smith and Smith (**40**). The apparatus was one designed for the study of two-velocity motion parallax by Gibson, Gibson, Smith, and Flock (**12**). A shadow-casting device presented the stimuli, which were produced by two plastic panels dusted with talcum, placed between a point source of light and a screen. The plastic panels were mounted parallel to the screen on a carriage which moved back and forth on tracks parallel to the screen. Since the panels were at different distances from the point source, the movement produced two sets of shadows which moved with differential velocity. Gibson, Gibson, Smith, and Flock found that when the panels were not in motion all Ss saw only one plane surface. But when the carriage moved, two surfaces appeared, separated in depth. The extent of separation (space between the surfaces) was indeterminate, leading to the conclusion that a two-velocity differential is insufficient for producing scaled perceptions of depth. But depth, in the sense of two separated surfaces, was always observed. Is this effect of the differential motion also perceived by children?

In Smith and Smith's experiment (**40**), the apparatus was altered by slanting the two stimulus panels away from the screen and by placing a paper triangle on one screen and two fish cutouts on the other. When the carriage was motionless, a single surface with no depth was perceived. When the carriage moved, two separated surfaces were perceived, with the faster motion correlated with the panel perceived as in front. The Ss were adults and children from five years to thirteen years of age. There was no difference between the observations of the children and the adults.

Although the stimulus conditions in this setup were again insufficient for producing an impression of scaled, continuous distance, it is clear that differential velocity is just as effective in producing an experience of one thing in front of another in five-year-old children as in adults.

To conclude the discussion of spatial perception and its development, one might emphasize again the contrast between a naturalistic setup rich in stimulus information and a relatively impoverished laboratory situation with careful isolation of cues. Both approaches are useful, but, in making interpretations, the distinction must be kept in mind.

Development of Object Perception

TACTUAL RECOGNITION AND DISCRIMINATION

Where should one begin to study the perception of objects in space? Certainly, with the solid objects themselves as the source of stimulation, not with pictures. Curiously enough, perceptual research has concerned itself far more with drawings than with objects. And that notwithstanding the classical bias that it is the solid object, which can be struck and felt, that gives the ultimate meaning to visual percepts. But research has been increasing lately on the perception of solid objects, with both tactual-kinaesthetic and visual stimulation.

Piaget's stages of object perception.—Is touch the "mother of the senses"? Is the visually perceived object a product of visual sensations and interpretation in the light of tactual-kinaesthetic experience? This is a very old-fashioned way of stating a question which nowadays preoccupies developmental psychologists in a somewhat different form. Piaget would not put the question so naïvely, but he has emphasized again and again that perceptual development is an elaboration of sensori-motor activity. "Every movement may be regarded as a transformation of the perceptual field and every perceptual field as a group of relationships determined by movements" (**36:** 15). Piaget does not imply, however, that one sensory modality is prior to another. "Hence we find visual perception itself made up of a system of relationships determined by probable movements of the eyes, and we shall find in the same chapter the exact analogy to these processes in connection with tactile exploration as it occurs in 'haptic' perception" (**36:** 16). Piaget and Inhelder's analysis of stages of development of haptic perception (and "representation") is a forerunner of many recent studies. Children were presented with familiar objects and cardboard cutouts of geometrical shapes of varied complexity with their hands behind a screen. Their exploratory hand movements were observed and their ability to identify the object or cutout noted. Piaget and Inhelder divided the child's developmental progress into stages (**36:** 120 ff.). During Stage I (3½ to 4 years), the child identifies familiar objects, though tactile exploration is "global" and relatively passive. But later in this stage, geometrical shapes which differ topologically by properties, such as closed, open, intertwined, begin to be distinguished and are explored as if they were three-dimensional objects. During Stage II, the child progresses to crude differentiation of linear from curvilinear shapes but does not yet differentiate within these groups; later there is progressive differentiation of shapes according to angles and dimensions, with some tactile search for clues to identity. And in Stage III (six years on), there is methodical exploration and ability to distinguish between complex forms (e.g., stars, crosses, rhombus).

These observations of Piaget's were corroborated by Page (**35**) in 1959; Page reported that, after exploratory handling, common objects were the first which could be selected correctly from a visual display, followed by forms differing by topological transformations, and, last, "Euclidean" forms. He also emphasized the development, with age, of exploratory handling and the search for significant features. Haptic perception, he pointed out, was much later in developing than visual.

For Piaget, the motor activities of exploration are basic to his analysis—"the shape is abstracted from the object by virtue of the actions which the subject performs on it, such as following its contour step by step, surrounding it, traversing it, separating it, and so on . . ." (**36:** 27). It is interesting to compare the description of these stages with some recent Russian studies.

Russian research on development of touching and looking.—A strong trend in the study of perception in the Soviet Union is an interest in active processes of looking and touching.[4] Since tachisto-

4. The writer is indebted to Dr. Herbert Pick for the use of his extensive notes in summarizing the Russian experiments which follow. The references to these experiments are Zinchenko, V. P.; Lomov, B. F.; and Ruzskaya, A. G., Scravnitel'nÿĭ analiz osyazaniya i zreniya. Soobschenie I. O tak-nazÿvaemoĭ simul'tannosti vospriyatiya. (Comparative analysis of touch and vision. Communication I. Concerning so-called simultaneous perception), *Dokl. Akad. Ped. Nauk RSFSR,* V (1959), 71–74; Zinchenko, V. P. Sravnitel'nÿĭ . . . Soobschenie II. Osobonesti orientirovochno-issledovatel'skikh dvizhenii glaza u deteĭ'doshkol-'nogo vozrasta. (. . . Communication II. Properties of orienting-investigatory movements of eyes in children of pre-school age), *op. cit.,* II (1960), 53–56; Zinchenko, V. P., and Ruzskaya, A. G., Sravnitel'nÿĭ . . . Soobschenie III. Zritel'no-gapticheskiĭ perenos v doshkol'nom vozrost. (Comparative analysis . . .

scopic experiments with adult subjects show that form recognition is possible without dependence on "tracing" of contours by eye-movements, Soviet research has turned to the ontogenetic study of tactual and visual recognition of form. The hypothesis explored is that instantaneous (really short interval) perception is a final stage which must be preceded by movements of the receptor apparatus, the latter being subsequently reduced. Experiments with young children (about three years of age) have been interpreted as showing that a child can differentiate figures visually only after having learned to follow the contours of a figure manually. Movements of the eyes followed after movements of the hand. That is, movements of the hand along the contour were thought to be replaced by movements of looking, which themselves were reduced with repetition until figure differentiation became instantaneous (**51**). This hypothesis clearly deserves further investigation before accepting as necessary a causal relation between the movements and recognition.

Related experiments by Zinchenko and co-workers have made comparative analyses of touch and vision in preschool children, emphasizing intersensory transfer. Studying the development of visual discrimination, Zinchenko presented to the children two-dimensional forms for matching. The child looked at one for 10 seconds and then selected it from a group of three. Three-year-old children made errors of matching in 50 per cent of the cases, but from five on there were no errors. Eye movements while looking at the standard were recorded for three of the children in each age group. The youngest children (three to four) did not follow around the contours. Their eye movements were saccadic and within the figure. In the four-to-five age groups, eye movements were said to be related to contour, and only similar figures were confused. The older children, who made no errors, not only moved the eyes around the contours but paused on distinctive features of the figures.

Communication III. Visual-haptic transfer at pre-school age), *op. cit.*, III (1960), 95–98; Zinchenko, V. P., and Ruzskaya, A. G., Sravnitel'nyĭ . . . Soobschenie IV. Razvitie osyazatel'noĭ orientirovki i gaptiko-zritel'nyĭ perenos v doshkol'nom vozraste. (Comparative analysis . . . Communication IV. Development of tactual orientation and haptic-visual transfer at pre-school age), *op. cit.*, III (1960), 99–102; Lavrent'eva, T. V., and Ruzskaya, A. G., Sravnitel'nyĭ . . . Soobschenie V. Odnovremennoe intersensornoe sopostovlenie formy̆ v doshkol'nom vozraste. (Comparative analysis . . . Communication V. Simultaneous intersensory comparison of form at pre-school age), *op. cit.*, IV (1960), 73–76.

The same figures were prepared for tactual presentation in a second experiment. The child was given a standard to explore tactually and then chose the figure from a group of three by tactual search. The task was too hard for the three-year-olds to perform at all and was very difficult even for seven-year-olds. The percentage of error decreased from 73 for four- to five-year-olds to 23.2 for six- to seven-year-olds. Exploratory hand movements were slow and clumsy in the four-year-olds and did not trace the contour of the figure. In the older children, contour-tracing became expert, one finger often dominated the exploration, while the hand grasped the whole, and salient features were used as "cues" for comparison. It is interesting that this development, which parallels visual search in some ways, is so much later in maturing. How, this being the case, can the hypothesis persist that touch provides the primitive basis for form perception?

However the question of priority may be settled, there remains the interesting question whether a form explored haptically can be identified visually (and vice versa). Zinchenko allowed children to explore figures tactually first (tactual "acquaintance"), and then they selected the figure from a set, first by touch and afterward visually. Visual recognition was considerably better than tactual, even when the prior exploration was tactual. When the situation was reversed and the child explored the figure visually and then chose tactually, tactual choice was successful to some extent (after four years of age) but was poorer than visual selection after visual exploration or after tactual exploration. Tactual search is simply a harder task, but there is clearly some intersensory equivalence of pattern features which permits transfer either way. Acquaintance by one modality does transfer to some extent to recognition by the other.

That whatever transfers is stored as a temporal pattern is suggested by one more experiment of Zinchenko's, in which the child made simultaneous rather than successive comparisons. For the three earlier age groups, the simultaneous method yielded more errors in intersensory transfer. It appeared to be necessary for the child to treat the simultaneous comparison as if it were successive to accomplish the recognition. The older children did this. What, exactly, is it that transfers in intersensory comparison?

Cross-modal transfer.—The explanation of cross-modal transfer is, indeed, the fascinating and focal issue. Piaget's explanation is that a representative schema is built up by systematic exploratory activity and that the schema is a kind of "referent" common to two modalities. For instance, "Thus the whole trend of events appears to suggest that the power to imagine the shapes visually, when they are perceived through the sense of touch alone, is an expression of the sensorimotor schema involved in their perception" (**36:** 41). If it is the schema which makes possible cross-modal transfer, we should find that transfer increases progressively with age, since exploratory and search activities seem to be progressively elaborated. We do not have adequate data, as yet, to say whether this is true, for the studies available have not been set up as developmental transfer studies with suitable control groups. But one experiment with retarded and normal children appears to suggest that skill can increase in one modality without an accompanying increase in transfer. Hermelin and O'Connor (**23**) tested visual recognition after tactual exploration, and vice versa, with a group of normal children (mean C.A., 5 years; mean M.A., 5.4) and a group of retarded children (mean C.A., 12; mean M.A., 5.4). The objects for recognition were ten unfamiliar letter-shapes (from the Greek and Russian alphabets) cut out of $\frac{1}{8}$ in. thick hardboard. Five of these were presented successively for either visual inspection or manual exploration. Afterward there was a recognition test, either visual or manual. In this test, ten shapes were presented; five were the ones previously handled or inspected, and five were new ones. The child made a yes-no judgment, whether he had seen or felt the figure before. There were four experimental conditions so that the test condition could be in the same modality or the other modality after both manual and visual acquaintance. For the normal children, recognition was equally good for same-modality and cross-modality tests; that is, there was no significant difference between any of the four conditions. For the retarded children, three of the conditions were equally good (and not significantly different from the normals), but one condition, manual exploration with manual test, was significantly better than the others.

Since there was no verbal identification of any of the shapes, and all were unfamiliar, cross-modal recognition must have been on some other basis. The authors suggest that the retarded children are impaired in visual discriminative ability but not in stereognosis. A control group of normal 12-year-olds would be useful in interpreting the authors' results. Possibly cross-modal transfer increases with M.A., depending not only on skill developed within the modality but on some central factor as well, such as Piaget's "schema."

Cross-modal transfer has been the subject of several studies with adults, which included a *learning* series as a first stage of the experiment. This technique permits investigation of what *kind* of training yields most transfer and, therefore, might provide, in an encapsulated fashion, a hint of what goes on developmentally. Rudel (**37**) studied the decrement of the Muller-Lyer illusion with repeated exposure, in both the visual and tactual modalities, and measured transfer from one to the other. E moved the center arrowhead until S judged it exactly bisecting the horizontal line with visual presentation, but S moved it himself with haptic presentation. There was initially a significant illusion in both modalities. But a marked decrement developed in both, reaching an asymptote after about 60 trials. There was cross-modal transfer of the decrement both from visual to haptic series, and from haptic to visual. The transfer was slightly greater from haptic to visual. What is changed by repeated exposure to the illusion that can transfer to the other modality? A "schema" in this case is quite implausible as an explanation. But there might be a kind of "education of attention" to direct the judgment toward the comparison of the horizontal extents.

A very recent experiment by Caviness and Gibson (**4**) compared the effect of two kinds of training on cross-modal transfer in adult subjects. They used solid, unfamiliar objects molded from a black plastic material. The objects were easily discriminated visually when presented simultaneously, but hard to discriminate by touch alone. There were two training groups and a control group. The latter had only the final test series, which was haptic presentation of one of the objects (felt but not seen) compared with a visually presented object (seen but not felt). The S made a same-different judgment, going through a long series so that every object could be paired with every other (and of course with a duplicate of itself). One training group was given tactual-visual associative training before the test; that is, S was given an object to feel behind a screen, and its duplicate was shown him for visual inspection at the same time. The other training group was given practice in differentiating by touch only. That is, they felt a pair of unlike objects, presented successively to both hands, and compared them.

The results of this experiment gave striking evidence that skill, acquired by practice in differentiating solid objects by touch, transfers to a visual identification test but that visual-tactual associative pairing, without differential comparison, does not. That is, the tactual-training group performed significantly better on the test than either the control group or the visual-tactual association group. The latter was not superior to the control group. This experiment might be interpreted in terms of learning to notice *distinctive features.* The visual-tactual association should provide a perfectly good opportunity for building a "schema"; what it does not give is the opportunity for discovering in just what ways one object is distinct from another, i.e., is unique. The concept of distinctive features was developed by Jakobsen (**27**) for phoneme description, but we should like to propose now that objects in the world have distinctive features which make them unique and which are perceived in many cases only after a process of discovery or "education of attention."

SOLID AND PLANOMETRIC STIMULI

Object and pattern discrimination.—That touch is primary to vision does not receive much support from the experiments above. But it is quite possible that solid objects, which are haptically distinctive as well as visually distinctive, provide richer stimulus information, because of cross-modal transfer or redundancy, and therefore are discriminable earlier and more easily. It has been known for some time (Harlow, **22**) that monkeys discriminate objects significantly faster than figures painted on cards. Stevenson and McBee (**42**) have compared differences in learning rate with young children when the stimuli for discrimination were solid objects (cubes), planometric objects (comparable to the cardboard cutouts in the experiments above) and patterns (squares painted on pieces of cardboard). There were two groups of children (mean ages, four and six). The children learned to make a size discrimination with three cubes, three cutouts, or three painted patterns. The subjects trained with the solid objects performed significantly better than the other two groups. The planometric figures (cutout squares) were no more effective over-all than the painted patterns. But for the most difficult problem (intermediate size correct), the older children were able to learn with both solid and planometric stimuli, but not at all with painted patterns. (This problem was too difficult for the younger group.)

Why were the solid objects more effective for learning the discrimination? In this experiment they provided considerably more redundancy of stimulus information, since the children handled the stimuli besides looking at them (they picked them up to uncover a reward). The differences should thereby be enhanced. But it is possible that there is an attention factor operating as well.

Early preference for solid over flat stimuli.—Fantz (**7**) has described experiments with a "visual-interest" test, hypothesizing that, if an infant fixes its gaze more often or longer toward one object or pattern than another, it must perceive a difference between them and that the one receiving preferential fixation is more interesting. The infant lies on its back in a "looking chamber." Objects are attached to the ceiling of the chamber and the infant's looking behavior is recorded. The stimulus objects are hung in pairs, and right-left position alternated.

When infants from one to six months old were given paired objects, in this situation a sphere and a circle, the solid shape was consistently preferred. Even though the infants did not handle the objects—in fact, at one month an infant, probably, would never have handled such objects—the solid shape was more attention-getting. The solid shape, from the beginning, is selected for visual inspection over its flat counterpart. Any distinctive features of the solid object would thus come in for inspection and have an opportunity of being differentiated from the total pattern of stimulation.

DISTINCTIVE FEATURES OF OBJECTS

Preference for patterned surfaces.—It was suggested above that objects have distinctive features which distinguish one from another and that selective perceptual activity is important in detecting them. That such activity begins very early is suggested by Fantz's finding that complexity of pattern is a determiner of the infant's looking preference. A bull's-eye was preferred over stripes, a checker-pattern over a plain square, and even a piece of newsprint over plain circles. The infants, in other words, inspected the stimulus objects which offered inhomogeneities of pattern and texture.

Preference for face-like objects.—Are certain patterns intrinsically more interesting than others? If so, perhaps certain object fea-

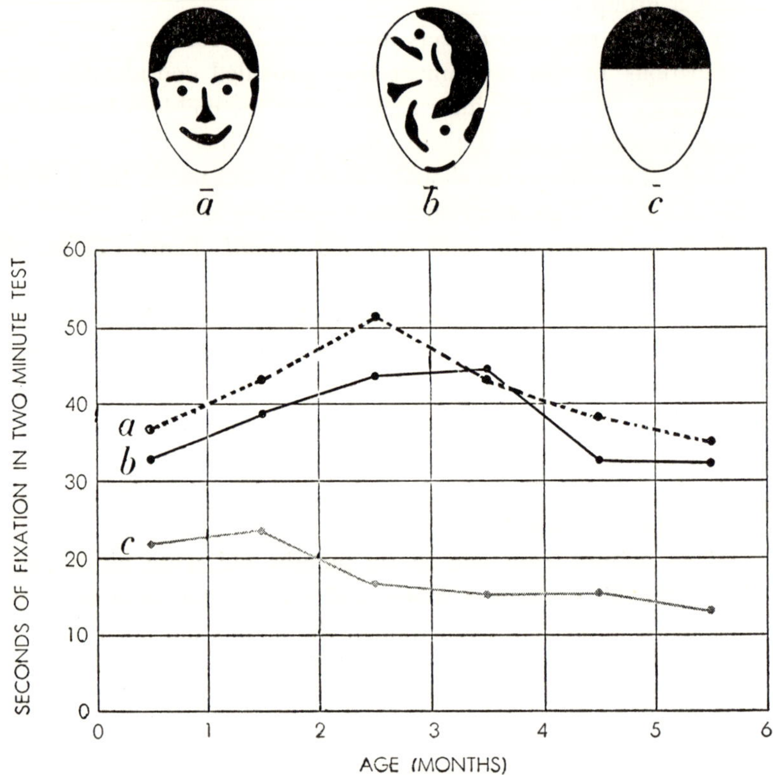

FIG. 5.—Facelike and control patterns shown infants by Fantz

tures are distinctive for the infant almost at once. Fantz investigated this question with face-like patterns, guessing that such a pattern was most likely to bring out selective perception in a very young infant. Three oval-stimulus objects were compared; one a stylized face (black on a pink background), second a rearrangement of the same features in a scrambled pattern, and third, a pink oval with a solid patch of black at one end. The objects were flat, and about the size of a head (see Fig. 5).

The infant subjects ranged from four days to six months old.

Throughout the age range, the infants looked most at the two patterned ovals. There is a suggestion that the face-like shape was preferred over the one with scrambled features, but this is not clear. Perhaps the features are already interesting, even in what seems to the adult a peculiar arrangement. Three dimensional masks, such as Spitz and Wolfe (**41**) used, might have been more effective than the painted face.

Characterization of objects by different perspectives.—There is room for years of research in the developmental study of object perception and a drastic need for some new techniques. An interesting one which could be pushed farther was used by Vurpillot and Brault (**44**) in studying, as they put it, how the schema of an object is built up in childhood. They presented familiar concrete objects (little houses, cups, dolls) on a turntable which was then rotated so that the subject saw the object from all angles. Afterward he was shown eight photographs of the object, in varying orientations and asked to choose the one *most like* the object. The subjects were children five through nine years old.

The children's choices were by no means random, and certain features of the objects played a determining role in the child's selection from the photographs (the cup's handle, the doll's face, windows of the house). There was an age trend, as well. By nine years, three-quarter views (showing more than one side) were chosen over photographs showing only one side. In general, with age, the trend increased to choose the most *informative* picture.

The authors conclude, also, that "class" features play a greater role, with age, as befits their "schema" concept. It seems to this writer that the notion of "distinctive features" would be more useful here. One should consider the set of alternative objects given the child in the experiment and also the set of alternatives in the world. The judgment of "most like" must refer to what is different, as well. The child certainly enlarges his set of alternatives as he grows older. What role the possible comparisons play should be investigated, since choosing the angle which is "most like" implies the one which renders the object unique, with respect to some set of alternatives.

Development of Perception of Pictures and Symbols

Just as research on the perception of solid, three-dimensional objects has been scarce, so has research on the perceptions elicited by realistic pictures of those objects. One sometimes hears anecdotal evidence that people from primitive cultures do not recognize photographs, even photographs of persons or places familiar to them. The assumption seems to be that one must learn that two-dimensional projections of objects are correlated with the objects and represent them, just as one must learn that a sign is correlated with its objective referent. This assumption seems gratuitous when one considers the fact that an accurate projection of a three-dimensional situation should present much of the *same* information as the situation itself. One might ask whether the relative amount of information retained in the representation would be correlated with ease of recognition.

A second question is whether a literal or faithful representation is a better stimulus than an artist's caricature which involves *selection* and *emphasis* of information. Are caricatures easier to recognize than photographs with much detail? If objects are perceived in terms of their distinctive features, a good caricature should be highly perceptible. What, if any, are the facts?

PHOTOGRAPHS AND PICTURES

Picture deprivation.—If a child were raised in an environment without pictures until he was able to speak, could he identify pictured objects? Such a condition is hard to insure in this day of television and advertising, but Hochberg and Brooks (**24**), have approximated it. The rearing condition which they strove to attain was that of allowing a child to develop completely without instruction or training about pictorial meaning or content. The child could not be raised in an environment entirely without pictures (though his exposure to them was greatly reduced), but he was never given names or associations for pictures. His vocabulary was taught solely by means of objects. When the child was 19 months old, the experiment was terminated, and tests of pictorial identifications were made. A set of 21 pictures was prepared on 3 x 5 cards. The pictures included both outline drawings and photographs of objects, such as toys, shoes, spoon, key, car, mother, sister, and so on, all being familiar solid objects. The cards were handed to the subject, one at a time, and all his responses recorded on tape. The tapes were scored by two independent observers who had not been present at the time of testing.

The results of the experiment indicated beyond a doubt that the child recognized pictorial representations of objects, including line drawings. This is strong evidence that ability for pictorial recognition is *not* dependent on association between the picture and the represented object, or association between the picture and a verbal or naming response.

Cross-cultural comparisons provide another approach to the problem. Anecdotal observations are not acceptable as evidence to this writer, but Hudson (**26**) has made some experiments with subjects from different cultural groups in Africa. He was interested specifically in pictorial depth cues, which he refers to as "artistic or graphic conventions." He constructed outline drawings and also used a photograph attempting to isolate the "pictorial depth cues of object size, object superimposition, and perspective." For instance, five of the drawings manipulate a bird and an elephant in a rough series of increasing cue-redundancy. The first picture has a small drawing of an elephant under a large drawing of a bird, with no background detail at all. The next two drawings add overlapping, and the last two perspective lines as well. The subjects were asked "What do you see?" and "Which is nearer, the elephant or bird?" Their responses were classed as "three-dimensional" if they reported as nearer whatever the conventional artistic cue intended.

The test was given to 11 samples, differing in school-attendance or not, black or white, children or adults, and territorial origin (all of African origin, however).

The results of these tests are not easily summarized or interpreted. But it is notable that in all the pictures except one (a very ambiguous one) the objects pictured (man, spear, animals, etc.) were correctly identified, even by subjects from the most primitive subcultures. But lines indicating hills or contours of mountains, or perspective lines presumably representing a road, were misidentified by subjects of some samples. It should be said that the drawing of these contours was extremely simplified and schematic. The lines also served two functions—to represent the hill or road and to signify distance. Correct identification did not "predicate three-dimensional perception."

The main factor associated with three-dimensional responses was school attendance, both on outline drawings and on the photograph, though there were fewer differences among groups with the photograph. Cultural isolation apparently made for lack of depth interpretation, especially in line drawings. Genetic factors played some role. There appeared to be a sort of mental-age "threshold" below which there was no three-dimensional interpretation, but this came out clearly only in the white school population. Of the types of cue used, overlap and size differences were said to be more effective in producing three-dimensional responses than perspective.

Though the import of these results is not too clear, it is probably safe to say that conventionalized pictorial depth cues in schematic line drawings are interpreted in the light of certain educational experiences not available to members of a very isolated culture. This is hardly surprising. But the results also indicate that identifying objects in pictures, even when they are portrayed by simplified line drawings, is culturally universal.

Fidelity or distinctive features?—Is the fidelity of a pictorial representation (see Gibson, **18**) the most effective condition for recognition? There are no developmental experiments on this issue, though one might expect age differences. Ryan and Schwartz (**38**) found with adult subjects that a caricatured representation allowed better discrimination of positional variations than the equivalent high-fidelity photograph. They compared four types of representation: photographs, shaded drawings, line drawings, and cartoons. The objects pictured were a human hand in four different orientations, a group of electrical switches with four combinations of positions (open or closed) of the switch handles, and a cut-away model of the valves of a steam engine at four different stages of the cycle. Slides of the pictures were presented tachistoscopically. The subject's response was identification of the position in which the object was depicted. Line drawings required the longest time for perception, cartoons the least, with photographs and shaded drawings in between. The cartoon would seem to have the advantage of presenting and emphasizing the distinctive features and eliminating the "noisy" or superfluous ones.

A new technique for comparing ease of discrimination of stimuli which vary with respect to distinctive features has been invented by

J. J. Gibson and is presently being tried out with children. It has the advantage of retaining equivalence of nearly all physical features of the stimuli, so that the sets of stimuli compared are commensurate.

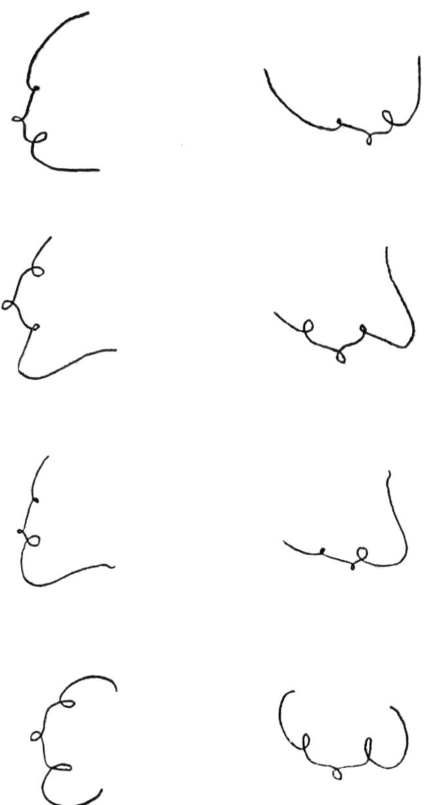

FIG. 6.—Cartoon drawings which resemble profiles of faces in one orientation (left column) but are writing-like in another.

Figure 6 shows examples of the pictures. Those on the left are caricature drawings of profiles. They contain some of the features of a face, and differ from one another with respect to these: the nose, eyes, and chin. The pictures in the right-hand column are the same drawings rotated 90° to the left. They are no longer profiles, but might be characterized as like writing (arabic characters, perhaps). If they constituted a known writing system, they would differ in features distinctive for that system. But they do not—they are nonsense writing. One would expect, therefore, that pairs of these items would be more easily discriminated as different when they are seen in their "profile" orientations than in their "writing" orientation. A first test of this hypothesis with adults gave results in the expected direction, but with children the material selected was too difficult, and no difference was found (scores were near chance). Sets of drawings with somewhat grosser differences (comparable to the ones in the illustration) have been prepared and are being tested with children.

Fraisse and MacMurray (**8**) have obtained threshold values for identifying stimuli of four categories with tachistoscopic exposure and children of three age groups (mean ages 6.9, 8.7, 11.1). The four categories of material were (*a*) photographs (a face, a tricycle, a mitten, a watch), (*b*) simple line-drawn geometric figures (cross, star, circle, square), (*c*) three-letter words (eau, cle, sac, vin) and (*d*) nonsense syllables. The child was shown all the stimuli and asked to name them before beginning the tachistoscopic exposures. He was told that these would be the words and things he would have to recognize. Then the 16 stimuli were presented in the tachistoscope, in random order, for identification. The threshold value was longest, for children of all age groups, for the photographs and shortest for the geometric line drawings, with words and syllables between. Offhand, this outcome may seem surprising, but it must be remembered that the stimulus categories are not equated for simplicity, redundancy, and so on. The geometric forms are extremely simple, symmetrical, and different from one another in very obvious ways. The words can be identified and distinguished from one another by the first letter alone. The names of the objects may even be less "available" than those for the words, which require no mediation. The words, incidentally, were no more quickly recognized than the syllables.

The problem of specifying stimulus differences in experiments such as this one must be given careful consideration. Interesting as the results are, the interpretation is not obvious when the classes of stimuli differ in so many incommensurable ways.

Role of orientation in perception of pictures.—Another issue which needs restatement is the question whether orientation of pictured objects—i.e., right-side-up, upside down, rotated, etc.—has an age-linked role in recognition of the object pictured or in responding equivalently to it. There is more than one issue here. How early can children respond to "form as such" (e.g., respond equivalently to a triangular shape, whatever its orientation)? Is it true that children cannot distinguish between different orientations of a given shape (e.g., that they respond to b and d as if they were the same)? Do children *recognize* a figure upside down, as easily as right-side up (e.g., identify a picture of an animal, tree, etc., equally well upside down)? In fact, *is* there a right side up in pictures for children? And if so, what determines it (for instance, must it be familiar)?

Ghent (**9, 10, 11**) has recently put these questions in a fresh light by asking whether pictures have a right side up for children; if so, what kind of pictures; and also, whether the orientation affects ease of identification. She has used a recognition method, with realistic pictures (e.g., tree, clown) and both a preference and a recognition method for nonrealistic ones (e.g., letter-like figures, squares, lines on squares).

The preference method was used to see whether, for young children, nonrealistic or geometric figures were considered right side up in one orientation, and upside down in another. The children (four to six years old) were shown pairs of pictures on cards, the two members of the pair alike except for position on the card (one was rotated 180° with respect to the other). The child was simply asked to point to the one that was upside down. Some realistic pictures were included, at the beginning and end of the series, to provide a check on the child's comprehension of the instructions. The children did show quite consistent preferences for particular orientations of nonrealistic figures as right side up. These sometimes shifted with age; a V, for instance, was thought upside down by the four-year-olds, but right side up by the six-year-olds. Ghent thought that the determining factor for "right side up" was that the "focal point" of the figure must be in the upper half of the card. She made further experiments with other figures to check this interpretation and felt that it was confirmed. What constitutes a "focal point," however, is not always clear. She says, for instance, "When a simple figure was interrupted by a gap or a line, producing a nonhomogeneous figure, the card was considered upside down when the interrupted portion was in the bottom of the card" (**10:**

184). This was not always true, however, for a circle with a small gap at the top was considered upside down by four-year-olds. This is explained by the statement that the line was focal for the younger group and the gap was focal for the older one. What is focal is, therefore, modifiable. Ghent continues with a Hebbian theory of the development of form perception, suggesting that a form must be scanned, beginning at a focal point, and continuing in a downward direction. Because of the preference for scanning from the top downward, a figure is considered right side up when the focal point is at the top.

Ghent's experiments with a recognition method tested her hypothesis that a picture was recognized and identified more easily, under tachistoscopic presentation, when it is right-side up. Both realistic and nonrealistic pictures were tested, in two experiments (**9, 11**). The method used a multiple-choice array of alternative pictures, projected around the perimeter of a screen. In the center was a dark circle, on which the test picture was projected tachistoscopically. The S had to show which member of the multiple-choice array he had seen. The test figures were presented in different orientations (right-side up, rotated 90° to left, etc.). For the realistic figures, the young children were markedly facilitated in recognition when the object was shown right-side up. There was no difference for the older children.

For the experiment with geometric forms, Ghent selected ones which 80 per cent of the group of four-year-olds had considered right-side up in a given orientation (e.g., Λ). The multiple-choice array was used, as with the realistic pictures. The test figure was shown either right-side up or inverted. The figures in the choice array were presented in both positions as well. The children in this experiment were three to five years old. They recognized the test figure better when it was "right-side up," no matter whether its mate in the multiple-choice array was presented in the same orientation or not. Again the results are interpreted by the hypothesis that recognition is facilitated when scanning can start with a focal point at the top and proceed downward. "In Hebb's terms, a set of cell-assemblies would be more readily aroused when the incoming pattern is such as to arouse the cell-assemblies in the same sequence in which they were organized" (**9:** 255).

Again, the critical question is how the focal point is defined. If this itself can be modified, it does not seem that the hypothesis "explains" form perception. If attention to a focal point can be educated, the form perceived would be modified. We need to know, then, how the locus of a focal point is modified.

GEOMETRIC FORMS

The use of geometric forms as stimuli for studying perceptual development stemmed primarily from interest in Gestalt principles of perception—emphasis on seeing wholes, closure, and the like. There has been a waning of this interest in recent years. However, a study by Graham, Berman, and Ernhart (**21**) analyzed copies of simple forms drawn by children from two-and-a-half to five years old, to see whether characteristics of "primitive organization" were more frequent in the drawings of the younger children. The changes in copying expected in younger children from an organismic view such as Werner's (**48**) include making the figure more closed than the original, simpler, and more symmetrical. The drawings were judged for changes of these three types. They were also judged for accuracy, using the following characteristics; whether the drawing had some form, whether it reproduced open-closedness and curvature-linearity of figures, whether there were the correct number of parts and the correct relationship of parts, whether orientation on the background was correct, whether size relationships of parts were correct, and whether the intersection of parts was correct. The 18 figures were simple line-drawings such as a triangle, circle, broken circle, V, square, and so on.

The results did not show a differential change with age such that "primitive" characteristics were relatively more frequent at the youngest age level and decreased with age. Simplification and closure were more frequent in the drawings of younger than of older children, but so were their opposite characteristics, complication and opening. Accuracy increased with age for all the characteristics chosen as criteria. The relative order of difficulty for the eight characteristics scored was quite different, however, and changed to some extent with age. Form, organization or relationship of parts, open-closedness, and curvature-linearity were the characteristics reproduced with greatest accuracy at all the age levels. Number of parts, orientation in background, size, and intersection fared worst. Correct size and intersection appeared to be especially difficult. Some of the figures were more difficult than others. Number of parts was an important dimension determining difficulty. Orientation of a design did not appear to affect difficulty (there were no consistent trends when figures differing only in orientation were compared). The authors conclude that there may be differences in difficulty with respect to certain dimensions at different age levels, but there are not discrete stages of learning to perceive size or make intersections or identify number of parts, and so on. "Rather, there is a gradual improvement in each of these as a function of age and as a function of the specific stimulus and its difficulty" (p. 357). This conclusion can be compared with the results in the experiment described in the next section, which employs a different method of studying a similar problem.

GRAPHIC SYMBOLS

From the point of view of the stimulus alone, graphic symbols can be classified as line drawings of a geometric rather than a representational type. But their ecological role is obviously very special, since they function in any given culture to symbolize the sounds of its spoken language. How graphic symbols are perceived is a unique question, then, because their correlation with already known speech units may affect the process. It is useful to separate the process into several stages: (*a*) the differentiation of letters from one another; (*b*) the association of graphic symbols with speech units; and (*c*) the perception of graphic units of various sizes when the correlation with speech has entered the picture.

Discrimination of letter-like forms.—A recent study of the discrimination of letter-like forms, by Gibson, Gibson, Pick, and Osser (**16**), traced the development of letter differentiation as related to certain critical features of letters (dimensions of difference which make each letter unique). The aim was not merely quantitative comparison of different age levels but a qualitative developmental study of types of error with respect to these critical features of letters.

The method involved construction of 12 specified transformations for each of a group of 12 standard letter-like forms. The transformations were chosen on an intuitive basis by analyzing the distinctive features of letters as a set. Three types of transformation were selected which were considered critical for discriminating printed letters, and one which was not. The three types considered critical included three transformations of line to curve or curve to line (one, two, or three lines changed for each standard); five transformations of rotation or reversal (45° rotation, 90° rotation, 180° rotation, right-left reversal, up-down reversal); and two topological transfor-

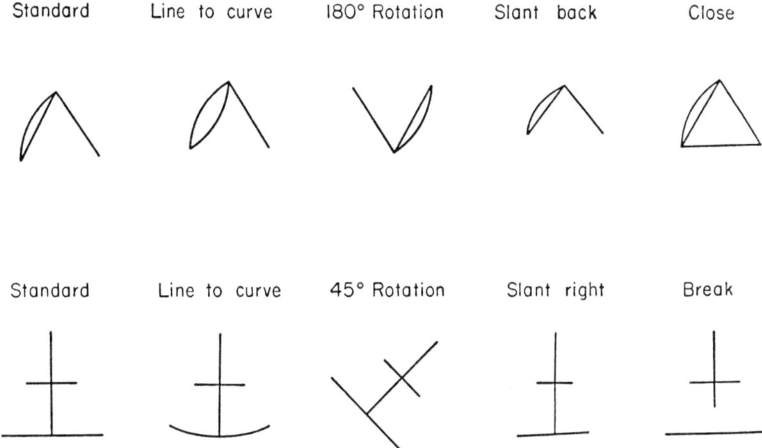

FIG. 7.—Two of the standard letter-like forms and four of the transformations of each one.

mations, a break, and a close.[5] The noncritical transformations chosen were two perspective transformations (a 45° slant right and a 45° slant back). Two of the standards and a sample of each of the four types of transformation are illustrated in Figure 7. The standards and their transformations were prepared from sketches by a draftsman, using tracing and photography to insure that only the changes intended would be introduced. The copies used for the experiment were mounted on 1¼ inch square cards and covered with plastic.

The discrimination task required the subject to match a standard with an identical form. The standard was placed in the center of the

5. Examples of these transformations in letters would be: line to curve, the difference between V and U; rotation and reversal, the difference between d and b or M and W; topological the difference between O and C.

top row of a lectern shaped box. There were four grooved rows below the top one filled with cards. One row contained copies of the standard exhibited above and all 12 of its transformations. The S was shown this row and asked to select and give to the E any form which was exactly like the standard. After he had scanned the row and given E all the forms he considered a match, a new standard was inserted in the top groove and the process repeated, until all 12 standards had been compared with these transformations. The subjects' matches, right or wrong, were filed by E and later classified. Two types of error were possible, omission and confusion. The subjects were children aged from four through eight.

The analysis of errors by transformation type showed that, although confusion errors decreased with age for all transformations, there were significant differences between types not only in number of errors at age four but in rate of error decrease thereafter. The confusion errors with topological transformations were few even at four years and disappeared by eight years. The errors for rotations and reversals were much more frequent at four years, but they, likewise, declined to nearly zero at eight years. For changes of line to curve, mean error varied, of course, with the number of changes. Looking at the composite curve it can be seen that these errors were relatively numerous at four, but, like the first two types, decreased greatly by eight years. By contrast with these three transformation types, the confusion errors with perspective transformations were not only very frequent at four years but they were still frequent at eight years.

Can one generalize these findings to the discrimination of real letters? To check the validity of both the material used and the functioning of the transformations, the same 12 transformations were prepared for 12 real letters (printed capitals), and the experiment was repeated with the kindergarten group. Correlations were obtained between confusion errors with the letter-like forms and with letters for each of the 12 transformations. All the correlations were significant (median $r = +.61$). When the transformations in the two tasks were ordered according to mean number of errors, the rank order correlation was +.87.

Why should the four types of transformation differ in difficulty at four years and why do errors decrease at different rates? We think these differences are best explained by the hypothesis that children learn to detect the distinctive features of objects, both real and pictured. This ability should carry over to letter-like forms, in so far as features which have been critical for objects in the past are present in the set. The topological transformations are a nice exam-

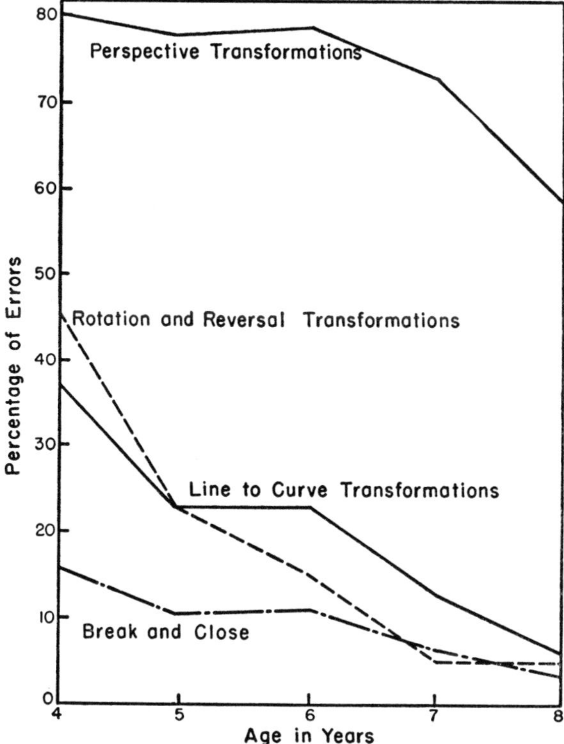

Fig. 8.–Developmental curves showing decrease in errors of confusion for four types of transformation.

ple in point. The early ability of the child to detect topological transformations was discussed in the section on "Development of Object Perception." That this ability is transferred to the discrimination of graphemes seems clear from the few errors of this type, even at four years.

Why are the other three transformation types so much more difficult to detect at four years? Because, I think, they have not been critical for object differentiation. Both perspective transformations and rotation and reversal indicate not a different object but a change in *position* of the *same* object. They must be tolerated in order for size and shape constancy to be possible. Line-to-curve transformations we know are detected later than topological transformations (see p. 180). Perhaps this is because they indicate a change of state (not a different object) in plastic or living objects. Such changes occur in facial expression, for instance. In rigid objects, they would indicate a deformation and are, therefore, ambiguous. The amount of change is important here—three changes of line to curve were easily detected at four years, but one change was not easily detected.

The errors decrease, after four years, depending on whether they are now critical for letter differentiation. The three transformation types which are critical produce scarcely any confusion errors by eight years of age, regardless of how many they produced at four. But perspective transformations which must be tolerated in reading (they are produced by holding a book at different angles, for instance) are still relatively poorly discriminated at eight years of age.

In summary, it seems that transformations of letter-like forms are detected even before school age if the type of transformation has been critical for object differentiation. Types of transformation which have not previously been critical are confused at four years, but, as the child progresses into the early school years, the distinctive features of graphemes are detected and confusions with relevant transformation types drop out. Irrelevant ones do not.

How distinctive features of the set of graphemes are picked up by the child now becomes a focal issue. Are they pointed out to him by the teacher? To some extent, this happens. Teachers spend a good deal of time pointing out reversal errors, for instance. His attention to a certain dimension of difference may thus be deliberately "educated." But the child probably learns a good deal by himself. Distinctive features of phonemes are learned but not taught. It may be that the child detects the critical features of graphemes by selecting the invariants from the flux of inconstant variables over repeated exposures and comparisons. Whether what he learns is essentially a "schema" for each letter or, instead, the critical dimensions of *difference* is the subject of an experiment now in progress.

Perception of higher-order graphic units.—The jump from mere differentiation of letters to the perception (reading) of words, phrases, and sentences is a big one. It passes over an intervening earlier stage of associating graphemes with phonemic units, a process about which we know little. But since this is essentially a learning problem, we shall omit it and consider now the unitary perception of letter-groups. How is it achieved? We know that it exists from the earliest experiments with tachistoscopes; in a fast exposure one can perceive, on the average, four unconnected letters, many more if the letters form a word, and more still if there are words forming a sentence. Is this because the printed word has been associated repeatedly with its spoken counterpart, or with a meaning? Is *familiarity* the unit former?

It has recently been suggested by Gibson, Pick, Osser, and Hammond (**15**) that the units may be structured in quite another way; that is, by the rules of grapheme-phoneme correspondence. Regularities in grapheme-phoneme correspondence (or spelling-to-sound correlations) in the English language have been studied by Hockett (**25**). Such correspondences are complex and "high-order" in the English language, involving position contingencies and clusters. They are analogous, in a crude way, to rules of grammar. It was hypothesized by Gibson, Pick, *et al.*, that these rules are induced, albeit not verbalized, as reading skill increases, that they have generality and transfer value, and that they speed up the perceptual process by organizing units. This hypothesis was tested by comparing tachistoscopic recognition (by adult skilled readers) of pseudo-words which followed the rules and pseudo-words which did not. Results of the experiment, replicated in several ways, clearly supported the prediction that unfamiliar groups of letters (pseudo-words) which follow the correspondence rules are read more accurately under fast exposure than otherwise equivalent ones which do not.

Assuming now that the correspondence rules in skilled readers operate as unit formers and transfer to unfamiliar material (pseudo-words), how have the rules been internalized? They have certainly not been learned as formal statements or, indeed, even verbalized. Does the child learn short whole words, at the beginning, by rote association and, later, begin to analyze words only when he has been given more difficult material? Or do simple rules begin to operate in short-span material as soon as it can be read at all and then increase in complexity as word length increases?

These questions were explored in a further experiment by Gibson,

Pick, and Osser. Children who had just finished first and third grade, respectively, were compared in ability to recognize tachistoscopically familiar 3-letter words, trigrams which followed correspondence rules ("pronounceable" ones) and one which did not, and some longer pseudo-words of both kinds. The three-letter words were taken from the first-grade word list and were anagrams of the two other types of trigrams. The children were run individually with the same tachistoscopic setting.

The results showed both similarities and differences between children of the two grades. All the first-graders and the third-grade boys read the familiar 3-letter words better than non-words. The same children all read pronounceable non-word trigrams (ones which followed the correspondence rules) better than unpronounceable ones. The third-grade girls (like adults) read all 3-letter combinations with equivalent and very high accuracy. From first to third grade, the span had obviously increased, because first-graders could read almost none of the letter-combinations longer than three letters. But the third-graders could, and there was also a significant difference between pronounceable and unpronounceable pseudo-words.

It seems, therefore, that a child generalizes certain simple, consistent predictions of grapheme-phoneme correspondence as soon as he can read 3-letter words. As skill develops, span increases. As span increases, more complex correspondence rules develop, and longer units which these rules could generate are then read more easily than others, even if they are unfamiliar.

It looks to the writer, then, as if a kind of perceptual learning occurs which is inductive in nature. The learning is not verbalized, but it is demonstrated by its transfer to perception of unfamiliar material. Perhaps development of this skill will turn out to be analogous to the acquisition of grammar.

Learning and Motivation in Perception: The Development of Attention

Because this chapter has been organized around a stimulus classification, some readers might suspect an underemphasis on those factors within the organism which influence perception. But if one believes that the problem of perception is *how the individual gets information from his surroundings* (as the writer does) the relationship between perception and the impinging stimulation is of first importance. However, the preceding paragraphs should make clear that other factors influence this relationship. From the developmental point of view, we want to know how the ability to register and process the information in the stimulus changes with age. From this general question, other more specific ones can be separated. Does the amount of stimulus information which can be processed increase with age? Does perception increase in "veridicality" with maturity? Or does it, on the other hand, become more and more influenced by a "private world" of the individual as his experience increases? We do not have the answers to these questions, but some ways of looking at them can be suggested.

PERCEPTUAL LEARNING IN DEVELOPMENT

That perceptual development progresses by both maturation and learning is a truism which has been well documented in this paper. Studies with the visual cliff emphasize the role of maturation. On the other hand, the significance of certain differentiating features in letters may have to be learned. At least three kinds of perceptual learning can be pointed out in developmental studies.

Increase in specificity.—One kind of change which occurs both with practice and with age is an increase in the specificity of correspondence between variables of the physical stimulus and discriminative responses. An experiment by Gibson and Gibson (**20**) illustrates this change. Line drawings which might be described as scribbles were prepared as stimuli. The scribbles varied from the original standard drawing in three dimensions: (*a*) number of coils (three to four), (*b*) degree of compression (three degrees), and (*c*) orientation (two types). Besides these 17 variations prepared from the standard item, 12 easily distinguishable items were constructed. All were printed on cards. The experiment studied the development of a single identifying response. At the outset, the subject was presented with the standard item for five seconds and told to observe it carefully so that he could later identify any other items which were the same. Then the standard was withdrawn, and a pack of cards containing all the variations and the easily distinguished items described above, as well as four duplicates of the standard, was presented item by item. The S simply said whether each item was the same or different from the standard. At the end of a run through the pack S was shown the standard again, told to observe it carefully, and another run followed. Repetitions continued until no incorrect identifications were made.

There were three groups of subjects: adults, older children ($8\frac{1}{2}$ to 11 years), and younger children (6 to 8 years). As one might expect, the class of items responded to incorrectly as "same" on the first run was greatest for the youngest group (46 per cent), less for the older children (27 per cent), and least for the adults (11 per cent). In other words, the specificity of the identifying response is less, the younger the subject. As runs through the pack continued, errors dropped out. The adults achieved an errorless run in an average of 3.1 trials, the older children in 4.7; for those younger children who finished, the mean was 6.7 trials, but most of the younger subjects could not achieve complete specificity. Generalization was reduced to about 10 per cent incorrect recognitions, however.

The class of undifferentiated items was thus reduced for all the Ss with repetition—the specificity of Ss identifying response increased. What the S was learning here, it seemed, was the ways in which the variable items differed from the standard. The S learned to respond, not to an item as such, but to the relation between it and the critical item.

Detection of distinctive features.—This emphasis on *learning to detect differences* is the essence of what we have referred to earlier as a theory of "distinctive features." It has been suggested that the increasing differentiation of the child's world—objects, sounds, pictures—is, at least in part, a result of learning to respond to the distinctive features of objects, of phonemes, of graphemes, and so on.

How might such learning take place? Is external reinforcement necessary, or trial, error, and check? In the scribble experiment just described, the S was never told right or wrong, so that correction from an outside source is certainly not necessary. This would seem to be true also of learning distinctive features of phonemes. However, a kind of feedback and check is possible in the sense that S can compare his own output against another repetition of the standard and other cases of difference in the same dimension.

An alternative to this view of perceptual learning would be the hypothesis that a "schema" is developed; a concept or "image" of the standard which becomes a sort of prototype or absolute for recognition. This would, presumably, be Piaget's view. The notion of schema has appealed to a number of psychologists—Bartlett, Bruner, and Attneave, among others. Attneave's (**1**) discussion of the schema seems to emphasize distinctive features as well. But it may be wisest, in our present state of ignorance, to distinguish between the two views; that is, discovery of dimensions of difference as against the building of a class concept or composite image.

Considering letter discrimination again with respect to this issue, it seems less likely that it is accomplished by developing a concept or image (say, an ideal M and an ideal W) but rather by discovering the ways in which each letter is unique; that is, different from other members of the set.

Development and constant errors.—The kind of perceptual learning described in the scribble experiment, a change toward greater specificity of correspondence between stimulus and perception, does not describe the change that sometimes takes place developmentally in a constant error. An example of such a change was discussed earlier, in connection with constancy experiments. The rather typical finding of a shift from slight underestimation of size at a distance to a greater overestimation of it is a change in constant error. The shift in constant error is accompanied developmentally by a steady decrease in variability or width of threshold. It is paradoxical that the steady increase in precision (a narrowing of the threshold) is an increase in veridicality, but the developmental trend toward overconstancy is not.

A few other judgments show such a shift in constant error away from veridicality. One case is setting a line to the vertical during body tilt in the experiment by Wapner and Werner (**47**). The younger the child, the smaller the constant error. But as age increases, overcorrection for body tilt begins, and the constant error increases. A similar trend toward compensation for displacement was found by Liebert and Rudel (**32**), with auditory localization. The subject was seated in the tilting chair and a sound source emitted clicks over his head. The sound source could be moved in an arc. The S judged when the click was immediately over the midline of his head, when he was upright or tilted to the right or left. The error of displacement of the auditory midline grew from none at age five to a maximum in late adolescence.

Whether these age trends in constant error should be considered learning, is a question. They seem to involve compensation (deliberate or not?) for unusual posture or location of which the S becomes increasingly aware with age. One might guess that this is a phenomenon having to do with attention and its education.

REDUNDANCY AND IMPOVERISHMENT OF STIMULATION AND THEIR INTERACTION WITH DEVELOPMENT

The view is often put forward that the characteristic developmental change in perception is a reduction of "stimulus dependency." The notion seems to be that with increasing experience the individual is able to supply information from some inner store which earlier had to be a result of direct stimulus input. What could this mean? And is there any evidence for it?

It is a fact that perception typically is multiply guaranteed by alternative stimulus inputs. Think of the sensory channels providing information for recognition of a person; visual stimulation from his face and figure, the sound of his voice and footsteps, the smell of tobacco or perfume, the tactual and kinaesthetic cues from a handshake. For simpler percepts, depth for instance, there are multiple channels of informative input, visual, kinaesthetic, and auditory (echolocation).

It is possible, as Wohlwill (**49**) suggests, that this redundancy in stimulation is a requisite for the very young organism but that, progressively, there is a decreasing dependency on multiple cues. A corollary is added, "By the same token, wherever a stimulus permits of several alternative modes of perception, that aspect involving the least amount of information will be the one responded to by the young child" (**49**: 281). Wohlwill cites as evidence for this view the need of a child for more redundancy in a pattern to perceive it correctly, and the constancy experiments where the young child "requires a greater variety of cues than the adult in order to maintain invariance in his perception" (**49**: 267). These latter facts are not too well established; the constancy experiments do indeed make use of impoverished situations, but systematic increase in cue redundancy has rarely been tested experimentally. Walk (**45**) found some tendency for the younger babies to respond to depth less well than older ones in a rather ambiguous situation, although they resembled the older ones with fuller cues. But probably this was due to maturation of acuity.

We would like to suggest here an alternative way of looking at this issue of "reduction of stimulus dependency." Might it be that such reduction, if it exists, is a product of education of attention in the individual; that he has learned to select and enhance for himself the critical features, and to disregard the noisy and redundant ones? The experiment of Ryan and Schwartz, in which cartoon drawings were better stimulus vehicles than high-fidelity photographs, suggests that redundancy under some circumstances is better dispensed with. But we do not know whether learning or development is responsible for this. Certainly eliminating noise from the stimulus can facilitate performance in a perceptual task in children; removal of the camouflaging lines from a Gottschaldt figure improves performance at once—the critical features of the figure to be sought are no longer concealed. So, perhaps, there is not a *need for redundancy* in the young organism but, instead, a need for the education of attention to distinctive features of the world and of things.

ATTENTION AND SPAN

Everyone knows that a young child's span of attention is brief and that, up to a point, it increases developmentally. Mental tests have long made use of memory span as a developmental index. Span of perception ("apprehension") has been little studied developmentally, but two experiments cited earlier provide evidence that it increases. Ghent (**9**) found that it was necessary to use slower exposure durations with a tachistoscope, the younger the child (medians decreased from 100 ms. at three years to 5 ms. at six to seven years). Gibson, Pick, and Osser (**16**) used a constant exposure duration for children of two age groups but found that groups of more than three letters were almost never perceived accurately by children at the end of first grade, whereas four letters and up, depending on the relationship of the letters, could be perceived by children at the end of third grade.

What is responsible for this developmental process? Sheer growth factors, both retinal and neural, may well play a role. But another factor was indicated by the Gibson *et al.* experiment, that is, the formation of larger units for perception. This leads into the whole question of information-processing and its developmental aspect. So far as we know, it has never been studied developmentally. A paper by Miller (**34**) suggests that there is a limit to the number of "bits" that can be processed but that the limit is not absolute because of the possibility of recoding into larger units or "chunks." Words constitute chunks or larger units. But so do pseudo-words which follow the rules of spelling-to-sound correspondence in English.

Here would seem to be one more type of perceptual learning, the formation or registration of higher order units. It was suggested earlier that such units may be generated by "rules" which are progressively induced as samples of written words and their auditory correlates are encountered. The alternative to this notion appears to be a simple frequency or probability theory. To the writer, such an explanation would seem as unacceptable for structuring of letter units as for grammatical ones. But this is clearly an underdeveloped area, and the issue is in need of much thinking and experimentation.

MOTIVATION AND PERCEPTION

The psychologist whose principal interest is in personality and individual differences is undoubtedly concerned to know whether and how motives and personal attitudes interact with age in influencing perception. Some developmental psychologists believe that there is bound to be such an interaction. From Piaget's point of view, for instance, the world and the ego are as yet undifferentiated in the infant, and the child gradually separates his inner feelings from objects and things around him. In that case, the younger the child, the more would perception be influenced by personal and need factors; there would be a developmental function.

Or one might assume that adults are more directed by a "verdicality" urge; as Vernon (**43**) points out in a recent study of personality and perception, marked influences of personality factors on perception are only apparent in clinical situations, and most adults perceive with the aim of knowing their environment. But surely, the average child has tremendous curiosity about his environment, too.

Such discussion is sheer unprofitable speculation, without knowing *how* motives and attitudes operate to affect perception. Here a good theory is needed as a starter. Lack of differentiation of self and environment is insufficient as a theory except for the very young child. Traditional candidates are the "cookie" theory and the perceptual defense theory. By these, I mean *seeing what we want to see and inhibiting what we don't.* These notions are obviously too simple. A child doesn't perceive the carrots as ice cream or perceptually defend himself against seeing the hypodermic needle. It seems far more likely that needs, likes, and dislikes affect perception by directing attention toward relevant aspects of incoming stimulation. Perception is selective; we have seen that learning affects selectivity. Motives may well have a selective function in making *effective* some of the *potential* stimulation.

An example bearing out this notion is an experiment by Dukes and Bevan (**6**) in which children compared the weight of jars visibly filled with candy or with sand. A constant method of judgment was employed so that precision could be compared, as well as tendencies toward over- and underestimation. The children overestimated the candy-filled jars as compared with sand-filled jars. But more interesting, the *precision* of judgment was greater when candy was compared with candy than when candy was compared with sand, or sand with sand. How can the relative improvement in precision be explained except in terms of some attentional concept?

Both the overestimation of the candy jars and the increased precision of comparison are reminiscent of Piaget's "error of the standard," the rather consistent finding that the standard, whatever its nature, tends to be overestimated. An attentional interpretation would demand that a highly disliked substance should be overestimated as well. If Dukes and Bevan had included a third series in which the jars were filled with large, unappetizing pills, what would the results have been?

Actually, an experiment somewhat on this order has been run. Botha (**2, 3**) made colored photographic slides of pairs of test objects of identical size, one of a pair liked and the other disliked (e.g., dry bread and chocolate cake, a bottle of a cold drink and a bottle of castor oil, etc.). The slides were projected one at a time on a ground-glass screen forming one side of a box. The S viewed the picture through a peephole. The projector was mounted on a sliding base so that it could be moved to alter the size of the image.

One of the pair of photographs was presented at a standard size and the S then adjusted the second one to look equal to it. Sometimes the liked object was standard, sometimes the disliked. The subjects were 35 children who had indicated strong likes and dislikes for the objects pictured. Results of these comparisons were that the majority of the subjects adjusted the photograph of the liked object to a larger size than the photograph of the disliked one.

But in a second part of the experiment, the photographs of a pair of objects were presented in rapid succession at the *same* size (life size) and S was asked to report which was larger. The results directly contradicted those with adjustment. The disliked objects were consistently reported as *larger* than the liked ones. The contradiction, according to Botha, disappears, if one interprets the judgments in terms of behavior tendencies. When image-size is adjusted, the object appears to move forward or backward; the S, in making a disliked object smaller, is avoiding, or pushing it away. When the objects are simply compared, Botha infers that the object which would be approached (the liked object) will be perceived as smaller, if the quantity presented is less than S's appetite for it; the object which would be avoided will be perceived as larger if the quantity presented is larger than the amount ordinarily consumed.

This interpretation, in terms of approach and avoidance, is plausible as regards constant errors but does not take care of changes in precision. The selective role of motivation implied in the concept of attention seems worth following through with careful theorizing and experiment.

Attention is sometimes attacked as a vague concept or one implying an antique faculty psychology. But no one questions what it means; selectivity in perception, limitation of perception in the sense of amounts of "data" which can be processed, and "focal points" (**10**) in stimulus arrays have been referred to in the preceding pages. These phrases all imply what is meant by attention. A program devoted to clarification of its meaning and bringing together relevant developmental facts would be of value.

BIBLIOGRAPHY

1. ATTNEAVE, F. "Transfer of Experience with a Class-Schema to Identification Learning of Patterns and Shapes," *J. Exp. Psychol.*, LIV (1957), 81–88.

2. Botha, Elize. "A Study of the Effect of Preference on the Perception of Size," *South African J. Soc. Res.*, VIII (1957), 49–57.
3. ———. "Effect of Preference on Perception of Size," *Percept. Mot. Skills*, IX (1959), 325 (Abstract).
4. Caviness, J. A., and Gibson, J. J. "The Equivalence of Visual and Tactual Stimulation for the Perception of Solid Forms." Paper read at meeting of Eastern Psychological Association, April, 1962.
5. Denis-Prinzhorn, Marianne. "Perceptions des Distances et Constance des Grandeurs (Étude Génétique)," *Archives de Psychol.*, XXXVII (1960), 181–309.
6. Dukes, W. F., and Bevan, W. "Accentuation and Response Variability in the Perception of Personally Related Objects," *J. Pers.*, XX (1952), 457–65.
7. Fantz, R. L. "The Origin of Form Perception," *Sci. American*, CCIV (1961), 66–72.
8. Fraisse, P., and MacMurray, G. "Étude Génétique du Seuil Visuel de Perception pour Quatre Catégories de Stimuli," *Année Psychol.*, LX (1960), 1–10.
9. Ghent, Lila. "Recognition by Children of Realistic Figures Presented in Various Orientations," *Canad. J. Psychol.*, XIV (1960), 249–56.
10. ———. "Form and Its Orientation: A Child's Eye View," *Amer. J. Psychol.*, LXXIV (1961), 177–90.
11. Ghent, Lila, and Bernstein, Lilly. "The Influence of Orientation of Geometric Forms on Their Recognition by Children," *Percept. Mot. Skills*, XII (1961), 95–101.
12. Gibson, Eleanor J.; Gibson, J. J.; Smith, O. W.; and Flock, H., "Motion Parallax as a Determinent of Perceived Depth," *J. Exp. Psychol.*, LVIII (1959), 40–51.
13. Gibson, Eleanor J., and Walk, R. D. "The Visual Cliff," *Sci. American*, CCII (1960), 64–71.
14. Gibson, Eleanor J., and Olum, Vivian. "Experimental Methods of Studying Perception in Children," in *Handbook of Research Methods in Child Development*, pp. 311–73. Edited by P. H. Mussen. New York: John Wiley & Sons, 1960.
15. Gibson, Eleanor J.; Pick, Anne D.; Osser, H.; and Hammond, Marcia. "The Role of Grapheme-Phoneme Correspondence in the Perception of Words," *Amer. J. Psychol.* (in press).
16. Gibson, Eleanor J.; Gibson, J. J.; Pick, Anne D.; and Osser, H. "A Developmental Study of the Discrimination of Letter-like Forms," *J. Comp. Physiol. Psychol.* (in press).
17. Gibson, J. J. *The Perception of the Visual World.* Boston: Houghton Mifflin Co., 1950.
18. ———. "A Theory of Pictorial Perception," *Audio-Visual Communication Review*, I (1954), 3–23.
19. ———. "Ecological Optics," *Vision Res.*, I (1961), 253–62.
20. Gibson, J. J., and Gibson, Eleanor J. "Perceptual Learning: Differentiation or Enrichment?" *Psychol. Rev.*, LXII (1955), 32–41.
21. Graham, Frances K.; Berman, Phyllis W.; and Ernhart, Claire B. "Development in Preschool Children of the Ability To Copy Forms," *Child Develpm.*, XXXI (1960), 339–59.

22. HARLOW, H. F. "Studies in Discrimination Learning by Monkeys: III. Factors Influencing the Facility of Solution of Discrimination Problems by Rhesus Monkeys," *J. Genet. Psychol.*, XXXII (1945), 213–27.

23. HERMELIN, BEATE, and O'CONNOR, B. "Recognition of Shapes by Normal and Subnormal Children," *Brit. J. Psychol.*, LII (1961), 281–84.

24. HOCHBERG, J., and BROOKS, VIRGINIA. "Pictorial Recognition as an Unlearned Ability: A Study of One Child's Performance," *Amer. J. Psychol.* (in press).

25. HOCKETT, CHARLES. "An Analysis of English Spelling. Part I: Analysis of Graphic Monosyllables" (mimeographed).

26. HUDSON, W. "Pictorial Depth Perception in Sub-Cultural Groups in Africa," *J. Soc. Psychol.*, LII (1960), 183–208.

27. JAKOBSEN, R., and HALLE, M. *Fundamentals of Language.* The Hague: Mouton & Co., 1956.

28. JENKIN, N., and FEALLOCK, SALLY M., "Developmental and Intellectual Processess in Size-Distance Judgment," *Amer. J. Psychol.*, LXXIII (1960), 268–73.

29. KOFFKA, K. *Principles of Gestalt Psychology.* New York: Harcourt, Brace & Co., 1935.

30. LEIBOWITZ, H. "Apparent Visual Size as a Function of Distance for Mentally Deficient Subjects," *Amer. J. Psychol.*, LXXIV (1961), 98–100.

31. LEIBOWITZ, H.; WASKOW, I.; LOEFFLER, N.; and GLASER, F. "Intelligence Level as a Variable in the Perception of Shape," *Quar. J. Exp. Psychol.*, XI (1959), 108–12.

32. LIEBERT, R. S., and RUDEL, RITA G. "Auditory Localication and Adaptation of Body Tilt: A Developmental Study," *Child Develpm.*, XXX (1959), 81–90.

33. LOCKE, N. M. "Perception and Intelligence: Their Phylogenetic Relation," *Psychol. Rev.*, XLV (1938), 335–45.

34. MILLER, G. A. "The Magical Number Seven, Plus or Minus Two: Some Limits on our Capacity for Processing Information," *Psychol. Rev.*, LXIII (1956), 81–97.

35. PAGE, E. "Haptic Perception: A Consideration of One of the Investigations of Piaget and Inhelder," *Educ. Rev.*, II (1959), 115–24).

36. PIAGET, J., and INHELDER, BÄRBEL. *The Child's Conception of Space.* New York: Humanities Press, 1956.

37. RUDEL, RITA G. "Decrement of the Muller-Lyer Illusion: A Study of Intermodal Transfer." Paper read at meetings of the Eastern Psychological Association, April, 1960.

38. RYAN, T. A., and SCHWARTZ, CAROL. "Speed of Perception as a Function of Mode of Representation," *Amer. J. Psychol.*, LXIX (1956), 60–69.

39. SCHIFF, W.; CAVINESS, J. A.; and GIBSON, J. J. "Persistent Fear Responses in Rhesus Monkeys to the Optical Stimulus of 'Looming,'" *Science*, CXLI (1962), 982–83.

40. SMITH, O. W., and SMITH, PATRICIA C. "Supplementary Report: On Motion Parallax and Perceived Depth," *J. Exp. Psychol.* (in press).

41. SPITZ, R. A., and WOLFE, K. M. "The Smiling Response: A Contribution to the Ontogenesis of Social Relations," *Genet. Psychol. Monogr.*, XXXIV (1946), 57–125.

42. STEVENSON, H. W., and McBEE, G., "The Learning of Object and Pattern Discrimination by Children," *J. Comp. Physiol. Psychol.*, LI (1958), 752–54.
43. VERNON, M. D. "The Relation of Perception to Personality Factors," *Brit. J. Psychol.*, LII (1961), 205–17.
44. VURPILLOT, ELIANE, and BRAULT, HENRIETTE. "Étude Experimentale sur la Formation des Schèmes Empiriques," *Année Psychol.*, LIX (1959), 381–94.
45. WALK, R. D. "A Study of Some Factors Influencing the Depth Perception of Human Infants." Paper read at meetings of the Eastern Psychological Association, April, 1961.
46. WALK, R. D., and GIBSON, ELEANOR J. "A Comparative and Analytical Study of Visual Depth Perception," *Psychol. Monogr.*, LXXV (1961), 44 (Whole No. 519).
47. WAPNER, S., and WERNER, H. *Perceptual Development: An Investigation within the Framework of Sensory-Tonic Field Theory.* Worcester, Massachusetts: Clark University Press, 1957.
48. WERNER, H. *Comparative Psychology of Mental Development.* New York: International Universities Press, 1957 (revised).
49. WOHLWILL, J. F. "Developmental Studies of Perception," *Psychol. Bull.*, LVII (1960), 249–88.
50. ———. "The Perception of Size and Distance Relationships in Perspective Drawings." Paper read at meetings of Eastern Psychological Association, April, 1962.
51. ZINCHENKO, V. P., and LOMOV, B. F. "The Functions of Hand and Eye Movements in the Process of Perception," *Problems of Psychology*, I (1960), 12–26.

CHAPTER V

Learning

SHELDON H. WHITE[1]

Learning, as the psychologist defines it, is a relatively permanent behavior change which is the result of experience. Since learning in childhood and adolescence plays an important part in shaping adult behavior, psychologists have long been intensely interested in the learning process. Their concern has been with learning as process—with the minimal conditions which are necessary for learning to take place, with the surrounding conditions which better or worsen learning, and with the question of what the basic changes which constitute the learning process (or processes) might be.

Though psychological studies of children's learning date back to the beginning of this century, there have been two periods of high-volume activity. The first, during the 1930's, coincided with the rise of the child development movement. If any one question can be said to have dominated the broad, exploratory work of that time, it seems to have been the question of the uniqueness of learning during the childhood period. Studies during that period often sought out types of learning that might have special importance in childhood, or that might determine common developmental sequences—studies of topics such as classical conditioning, motor learning, reminiscence, or the question of learning *vs.* maturation. In time, the weight of evidence seemed to justify a conclusion which, though negative, was quite important: There are no learning processes which are unique in children, as opposed to animals or adults (**119**).

The second wave of activity began in the mid-1950's and is still

1. Preparation of this review was aided by Grant M-3639 of the National Institute of Mental Health, United States Public Health Service. The writer wishes to express his gratitude to Barbara Notkin White, for valuable critical readings, and to Gerald Plum for aid in the literature search preceding this review.

mounting. Given the experience of the past, the new work is more closely tied in with animal and adult work; it draws strength from their methods and findings and shows clear signs that it may establish conceptual bridges between them. Most of the procedures used with children are also under active investigation with other types of subjects—for example, studies of operant behavior, discrimination learning, learning sets, probability learning, and transfer of training.

Today, as in the 1930's, there is no one strategy which completely encompasses the whole panorama of activity. A dominant theme is the careful, exhaustive examination of simple learning situations in the belief that these kinds of situations contain much of the essence of all learning. As principles are gradually identified with these simple types of learning, and these principles become integrated into a comprehensive theory, perhaps many of the larger issues surrounding learning can be better understood (**110, 188**).

The current workers were not initially disposed to look for developmental sequences. There is some feeling that they should be (**56, 57**) and, in fact, developmental sequences are now appearing in the current data (**88**). The experimental backgrounds of most of the current workers initially predisposed them to view learning in stimulus-response terms, terms flavored with the intimation that stimuli stamp associations into a rather uniform, passive child. This viewpoint is beginning to lose ground, as mounting evidence begins to show how factors of attention, strategy, and "cognitive style" within the child help determine his response to the stimuli which are presented to him.

In all, then, the psychological study of children's learning is today in a period of great activity and great change. The first fruits of some eight years of intense research work are just beginning to appear, in the form of new, broader, and deeper conceptions of the learning processes in children. Much credit for these insights must be given to the innumerable small studies, rather unprepossessing and limited-looking when taken alone, which are the backbone of the current research work. Their great virtue is in their speed of execution; when they are used wisely in continuous research programs, the advantages given by their flexibility and self-correcting power appear to outweigh any disadvantages attributable to their limited scope or brevity.

Basic Learning Situations: Analytic and Parametric Studies

Much recent work has concentrated on a few simple learning situations, fairly standard from one laboratory to the next, though there are local variations in procedure and implementation which are sometimes important. The intent of this work is to establish and explore the conditions (or parameters) that affect the child's performance in each type of learning. The following section will consider the situations which are most widely used: (*a*) operant scheduling, (*b*) discrimination learning, (*c*) transposition and discrimination learning set, and (*d*) probability learning. While only brief characterizations of these procedures are given here, more complete descriptions are to be found in a recent review (**164**).

OPERANT SCHEDULES AND OPERANT ANALYSIS

The development of operant procedures for use with children has been thoughtfully discussed in papers by Bijou and his associates, and the considerations weighed in those papers are useful first guides to the tactics of a continuing experimental program with children (**11, 13, 14, 15, 16, 19**).

The basic element of the operant procedure is a simple response or *operant* (more or less rapidly repeated), such as dropping a ball into a hole or tapping a lever. Once the child is set to making such a response, his rate of responding is quite sensitive to the "control" of various reward and stimulus contingencies: for example, delicate variations in the permitted interval between rewards, or in the ratio of rewards to responses. Such simplicity and sensitivity of the basic procedure are highly desirable characteristics. Also attractive is the flexibility of a format which will accommodate wide-ranging explorations of the effects of stimuli and rewards according to their nature, timing, sequence, or combination.

An important factor in operant work is a characteristic strategy of controlling or shaping behavior as a means of understanding it; while other experimenters usually place the child in a standard procedure and record his responses, operant workers often use arbitrary series of approximations to reach a point where some interesting schedule controls the child's behavior. To some extent they are less interested in route than in endpoint.

The experimenter's choice of routes in operant work sometimes becomes a factor in interpreting his results. Long (**105**) was unable to get multiple schedule control of the behavior of 14 out of 32 normal children. Orlando and Bijou (**18, 126**) report fairly good success with retardates in the same venture. While in the latter study it is suggested that this difference in results may be due to the greater motivation of retardates, one can wonder if perhaps one set of experimenters might not have been more sensitive in gauging when subjects were ready for schedule changes.

Now that operant procedures have been established for children, what can be expected of this type of research? Some work may simply explore the comparability of records of children's behavior with the extensive information about animals (**106**). Several authors (**12, 17, 51**) have discussed the use of operant procedures to set up baselines for individual analysis of behavior. Operant procedures can produce an interesting variety of high, low, or cyclic baseline behaviors, against which responses to known stimuli may be superimposed as short-term deflections. Analysis of behavior using a single subject is possible since the effects of first one and then another treatment may be compared in his record. Gewirtz (**51**) suggests as an analogue the lie detector, where truths and lies are separated by different deflections of essentially stable baseline rates of heartrate, breathing, etc. In operant work, such deflections could reveal motivating or interest values of stimuli, or in some circumstances serve as indices of learning.

The emphasis of operant workers on control of behavior, and their faith in the breadth of their method, have encouraged forays into areas such as social co-operation (**5**), group behavior (**4**), childhood autism (**42**), stuttering (**55**), infant smiling (**21**), social reinforcement (**52, 53, 54**) and programmed learning (**154, 155**).

DISCRIMINATION LEARNING

In contrast to operant work, the study of children's discrimination learning is beyond the stage of preliminary exploration. In its simplest form, a child is repeatedly presented with a choice of two stimuli; choice of the correct stimulus yields a reward, and choice of the other stimulus does not. Learning is judged to have occurred when the correct stimulus is consistently chosen.

Like the operant procedure, the discrimination situation is simple, sensitive, and flexible. Changes in one or two variables can cause the problem to resemble a paired-associates, operant multiple schedule, or concept-formation learning procedure, and this fact has led some to hope that an understanding of discrimination learning will have implications for a broad span of cognitive behavior.

It seems unlikely that discrimination learning necessarily teaches a child to detect differences between stimuli which he could not detect beforehand. Often, children in casual play will notice and use the very kinds of stimulus differences which cause them difficulty in the discrimination procedure. Thus, it seems likely that discrimination learning involves making the child sensitive to specific stimulus differences in the experimental situation and teaching him to be guided by those differences in choosing his response.

The sections which follow will consider the variables which affect discrimination learning. Later, after a discussion of the transposition and learning set work, attention will be given to our knowledge of the fundamental processes of discrimination learning.

Method of presentation.—It is conventional to distinguish between a *simultaneous* and a *successive* discrimination. In the simultaneous problem, both stimuli are present on each trial: for example, a black card may be placed above one button and a white card over another. In the successive problem, only the black card or the white card is present on any trial and, depending on which, the right button or the left button is correct. The simultaneous problem may be solved simply by learning to approach a particular stimulus, wherever it is. The successive problem cannot be solved in this way; logically, solution must involve patterning of cues of the form right-button-if-black-cue and left-button-if-white-cue.

These procedural differences have been the basis for the somewhat technical and subtle issue of whether the response in the discrimination situation is determined by an approach or a patterning mechanism. If the child is learning to approach a particular stimulus, then the simultaneous problem is easily solvable, but the successive problem is impossible. If the child deals with the stimulus-response display as a total pattern, then the successive problem should be easier than the simultaneous.

Neither view is completely supported by the data. Usually, the simultaneous problem is solved more quickly than the successive problem—which, however, is solvable (**39, 132**). The simultaneous problem becomes more difficult as the stimuli are located away from the loci of response (**30**). Under this condition, or if the stimuli are quite distinctive, the successive problem is as easy as, or easier than, the simultaneous problem (**102**). Of course, as the stimuli are located away from the loci of response, it becomes less and less possible to use an approach mechanism.

Between the alternatives—approach or patterning—a choice appears indecisive; rather, they have been shown to intermesh with factors of stimulus similarity, stimulus-response locus, and simultaneous-successive presentation. Perhaps the child is able to use both approach-determined or pattern-determined responses, but finds it somewhat easier to use an approach response. Under some circumstances, however, he may even use a patterning mechanism to solve a simultaneous problem (**197**).

Nature of stimuli.—Almost all of the literature on children's learning involves visual stimuli. Two investigations have tried to rank-order ease of learning to various visual dimensions and found that discriminations were established most easily in relation to size differences, followed by differences in orientation, followed by differences in form, brightness, lightness, and color (**31, 32**). How reliable is this order? Probably it depends upon the particular values of size, brightness, form, and so forth, used in these studies. Other investigators, who used other values, might well find a somewhat different order.

Children can learn discriminations between solid objects more readily than between flat shapes or patterns (**74, 180**). Presumably, three-dimensional stimuli are more distinctive. The difficulty of a problem may be manipulated by spacing stimuli closer or farther on their common dimensions—brightness, size, and the like. Where stimuli are closer together, theory holds that the responses assigned to each will "generalize" more readily to the other, thus impeding the learning. Moreover, in preschool children, early failures on initial trials of a difficult discrimination apparently mobilize factors of inattention, disinterest, and frustration which further downgrade the performance (**161**).

Much more needs to be known about the specific sensitivities of the child to his environment, about his sensory capacities, and about the relation of these factors to learning. First, we should know more about learning in relation to auditory and tactual stimuli, which are important guides to everyday behavior. They present their information to the child in ways different from the visual modality. Consider auditory stimuli: They are given once, sequentially, and cannot be reviewed; they can be detected without any specific prior orientation; they are not clearly located in space. These, and other attributes, might be the bases for interesting tests and extensions of our current vision-based notions of discrimination learning.

Second, it seems worthwhile to ask whether all children are equally capable of using the same kinds of stimulus information. The introspectionists held that some people are "auditory-minded" while others are "visual-minded." Within recent years, Roe (**143**) has felt herself forced to make a similar distinction in characterizing the thought processes of various kinds of adult scientists. There are hints of such differences in the children's literature. Hermelin and O'Connor (**64**) have reported that imbeciles are better than normal children at tactual recognition of stimuli, though worse at visual recognition. Older studies suggested that children show developmental shifts between "form dominance" and "color dominance" in the visual modality (e.g., **27**), although recent work has questioned their generality (**68, 81**). Further examination may show that modality and dimensional preferences play a part in children's learning.

A third area worthy of exploration involves the breadth or narrowness of children's use of available cues. Children solving a problem learn the significance of cues other than those which are directly relevant to solution (**173**). What factors determine the range of other cues which they will pick up? Bruner *et al.* (**29**) have suggested that high drive, or overtraining, reduces the learner's ability to pick up incidental cues. Attempts to confirm this with children have not been completely successful (**43**), but the point is important enough to warrant further study.

Finally, there are worthwhile questions about how interest-value, preference, or motivational significance of cues affect their use in learning. We know that children's preferences among objects can be altered by learning (**76, 149**) and that such learned preferences generalize to similar objects (**49, 50**). It is interesting, and puzzling, that experimentally installed value increases the apparent size of an object to a child (**97, 99**). However, there have been no attempts to deal with learning as a function of interest-value of stimuli, or learning toward or against preference. Such studies would add an interesting new dimension to our understanding of learning in a world where so many important cues are not neutral.

Incentive aspects of reward.—The rewards typically used to signal a correct response to children include light flashes, bells, candies, stickers, marbles, money, praise, or toys. The tangible rewards seem to have more than symbolic value. Kendler *et al.* (**89**) found learning of an inferential sequence to be significantly improved if small charms were visible at the terminus of the task. Stevenson *et al.* (**185**) found discrimination learning to be poorer if their children were initially "satiated" with quantities of the colored stickers that were later used as rewards. In fact, tangible rewards can be too good and can distract. Children given money rewards in Miller and Estes' experiment (**117**) were less efficient than others given only knowledge of results, probably because they became preoccupied with "counting, gloating, worrying" over their hoard. Rudel's retardates had difficulty attending to their task when raisins were given as rewards (**145**).

Rewards differ in their effectiveness, depending on the children used. Lower-class children learn better with a tangible reward, such as candy, for a correct response, while middle-class children appear to learn well with a symbolic reward, such as a simple light flash (**189, 190, 191**).

There appear also to be individual differences in reaction to incentives. Before administering a discrimination task, Brackbill and Jack (**23**) allowed children to express their preference for candies, marbles, or trinkets, using for each child his preferred incentive as a reward for correct performance. These children were slightly better in performance, and significantly less variable, than a control group arbitrarily given candy as a reward.

Positive reward values.—We may think of five values—hedonic, secondary reward, social, stimulation, and, finally, mastery—to account for the effectiveness of children's rewards. These five values are invoked only as a general summary; only further experimentation and analysis will suggest whether one, or a hundred, fundamental processes are contained in that summary.

Certain rewards probably have an appeal which is built into the child. Candy is pleasing. Raucous noises are unpleasant. These may be classed as hedonic rewards.

Some stimuli have a value that is not intrinsic, but that derives from their close association with previous rewards. For example, children will perform for light flashes or for tokens which previously have been accompanied by candy (**98, 100, 120, 121**). Such stimuli are usually spoken of as secondary rewards.

Third, we may class under social rewards situations in which the presence of another person somehow supports learning. Perhaps imitation, an effective facilitator of learning in young children (**144, 206**), is a kind of phenomenon associated with social reward. Studies have shown that praise improves performance and reproof worsens it (e.g., **182**). The effects of social reinforcement are enhanced by preceding periods of social deprivation (**53, 54**).

Essentially social rewards may be effective motivators very early in life. The vocalizations of three-month infants may be increased by smiles, sounds, and caresses (**21, 138**); however, this evidence is not conclusive proof for a social reward mechanism at this age until it is shown that nonsocial stimulation fails to produce the same increase in vocalization.

It is possible that the rewarding effect of others is a kind of secondary reward, conditioned by the intimate associations of others with the satisfactions of an infant's life. It is also possible that social rewards are rooted in more fundamental and innate mechanisms of attachment (**60**).

Recently, psychology has paid new attention to motives associated with curiosity, stimulation-seeking, and exploration (**10, 44**). It seems likely that some of the small rewards given to children, such as charms, picture stamps, and toys, are effective for no other reason than that they are "interesting." Relating to this, in a way, Jeffrey (**78**) has shown that children will work to sustain a taped music presentation, and Baer (**7, 8**) has similarly used TV programs. If a lever is placed in a nursery for about an hour a day, children will press the lever for one or two days in exploratory fashion and then virtually cease responding. If, now, a simple event—turning on a light, turning off a light—is made contingent on the lever press, about a week of sustained responding will occur (**4**). Presentation of a brief burst of garbled sound after a lever press will similarly produce four days of responding at an elevated level (**47**).

Apparently, normal children are more quickly stimulated by a series of colorful pictures, and more quickly lose interest in them, than retarded children (**178**). One is here reminded of the fact that bright children begin TV watching younger, and taper off younger, than duller children (**148**).

A fifth reward principle involves the satisfaction which some children obtain from manipulation and mastery of their environment. Terrell (**187**) has shown that the opportunity for fanciful manipulation is an effective reinforcer of children's discrimination learning. Miller and Estes (**117**) found that third- and fourth-graders who are high "need achievers" (as assessed by a high number of achievement themes in stories elicited from them) are better problem-solvers than low need achievers.

Apparently, as children grow older, their acceptance of the challenge of a task grows. Stevenson (**173**) comments on the greater consistency of performance and goal-directedness of his older subjects. Older children, particularly boys, show an increasing tendency to return to a puzzle on which they have failed rather than one on which they have succeeded (**35**). For such older children, objective self-evaluation dilutes the value of praise—the children are not as easily "kidded" about how well they are doing (**111**).

Terrell's finding (**189, 190**), that middle-class children are more apt to perform well with simple knowledge of results than are lower-class children who need tangible rewards, suggests that the rewarding value of mastery may be a product of cultural indoctrination.

The broadest investment in motives of curiosity and mastery has occurred in a recent much-publicized program designed to teach preschool children to read using entirely "autotelic" (self-purposing, playlike) incentives. The program begins by allowing the child to explore the fascinating gadgetry of an electric typewriter. A teacher sounds the letters as the child hits them until the alphabet is learned. Then the child uses his alphabet to reproduce words flashed on a screen until he is able to read and typewrite stories. Although it is claimed that this sequence proceeds entirely by a well-phased capitalization on children's motivation to play, one might wonder if the teacher is only a source of information, and if the population of children initially used is typical in its motivation and readiness to read. Unfortunately, little published information is available about this work beyond a statement of the autotelic principle (**3**) and demonstration films (**118**). A recent small-scale attempt to teach slum children with these techniques was unsuccessful (**83**).

Negative reward values.—The practical limitations of research on children are unusually severe when negative incentives are used, and to date little more has been done than to attempt to set up practical aversive situations for experimental work with children. Thus, two experiments base an avoidance procedure on the annoying quality of loud sounds (**131, 142**). Baer (**7, 8**) used interruptions of TV programs to motivate "escape" and "avoidance." Important practical questions about punishment make such attempts necessary; however, it will be difficult to experiment flexibly in situations that must be virtually guaranteed beforehand to produce no strong effects.

Motivational level of the child.—Undoubtedly, children who are highly motivated learn differently, sometimes better, sometimes worse, than children at low motivational levels. An important tool in the understanding of children's learning has been the "anxiety scale," which separates children of differing motivational levels. The literature is reviewed in chapter xi.

Informational aspects of reward.—In addition to providing incentive, rewards have the function of signaling the correctness or incorrectness of a preceding response. Is it more important to provide a definite signal to a child when he has been right or when he has been wrong? As might be expected, it is usually best to signal both correct responses and errors; signalling only errors seems next best (**25, 115, 130, 196**). Unfortunately the problem is complicated by the fact that doing nothing takes on positive qualities for the child if one is signaling errors, or negative qualities if one is signaling correct responses (**116, 125**).

Delay of reward.—It is of some interest to delay the feedback of information to the child by delaying reward to him. In general, children given a choice prefer a stimulus to which reward is immediate rather than delayed (**103**). If pretrained before discrimination, with one stimulus given an immediate and the other a delayed reward, the children will then be helped in a subsequent two-choice discrimination with the immediate-reward stimulus correct—perhaps because of an acquired preference for the immediate-reward stimulus; perhaps because the differential delay pretraining has established a point of distinctiveness between the two stimuli (**104**).

Suppose now that a discrimination problem is given under conditions of immediate or delayed reward—one stimulus is never rewarded, and reward for the other may be immediate or delayed. Delaying reward interferes with discrimination problems beyond a certain level of difficulty, but it is not clear where the level of difficulty begins. Hockman and Lipsitt (**65**) reported that delaying reward interfered with a three-choice discrimination problem but not with a two-choice problem. Some other investigators, using two-choice problems, have found no effects of delaying reward (**24**, **132**), but others have found such effects (**192**, **194**). The apparent contradictions here are undoubtedly based upon differences in procedures and subjects; they suggest that other factors pertinent to the effects of delay remain to be isolated and controlled.

Informal comments about children's behavior in such delayed-reward procedures suggest that they find the delay intervals unpleasant, that they fidget, gaze around the room, and look bored during the delay interval. Usually, children's responses slow down when reward is delayed (**103**, **104**, **139**, **140**, **192**), although one opposite finding has been reported (**194**). The majority of the findings are in line with a possible mechanism for the deleterious effects of delay. During the interval between response and reward, the children may engage in extraneous behavior, perhaps random, perhaps frustration-induced, which establishes itself as an ongoing, competitive factor in the learning situation.

Under some circumstances, delay of reward can help memory. Given a problem where they named each stimulus as it came, children did not suffer in performance through delay; moreover, delay enhanced retention (**22**, **24**). Brackbill has suggested that the names serve two important functions. First, by representing the stimulus during the delay interval, they carry the stimulus forward in time to the reward and minimize the deleterious effects of delay on acquisition. In turn, the bridging use of names is strengthened by reward at the end of the delay interval, and the names are installed as efficient mechanisms of retention. Buttressing this reasoning is a study by Spiker (**166**), who showed that giving preschool children names for stimuli helps them when the stimuli are used in a delayed-choice experiment.

TRANSPOSITION

In discussing transposition, it is best to begin with a typical situation. Imagine a series of six cubes graded evenly in size, cube number 1 being the smallest, cube number 2 having double the volume of number 1, etc. A child is repeatedly presented with cubes 1 and 2 and trained to always select cube 2. Has he learned the solution in *absolute* terms (always to select cube 2), or in *relative* terms (always to select the larger one)? To check on this, we may present him with cubes 2 and 3 (a "near" test); if he chooses 2, he is said to have made an absolute choice, while if he chooses 3 he is said to have transposed, or to have made a relative choice. The same terminology is used for a "far test," say between cubes 4 and 5. Choice of 4 is said to be an absolute choice; choice of 5, transposition.

Animals will characteristically make relative choices on a near test; as tests move farther out, the percentage of relative choices will diminish to a chance, or 50 per cent, level. An influential theory of transposition (**156**) has accounted for this pattern of results in S-R terms.

A classic study by Kuenne (**94**) suggested that young children who did not possess the concept "larger than" would show transposition much as animals do—making a relational choice on a near test, choosing at chance on a far test. On the other hand, children who seemed to possess the concept chose relationally both on near and far tests. Confirmed soon after by Alberts and Ehrenfreund (**1**), the Kuenne study seemed immensely promising as a first bridge between an essentially associative, S-R realm of animal learning and the cognitive, word-using learning of human adults. Further, it pointed to the late preschool years of children as a possible point of transition from the associative to the cognitive level.

The studies of Kuenne and of Alberts and Ehrenfreund stimulated additional research. Paradoxically, the more general significance of their research appears to be gaining support, while at the same time their particular interpretation of the transposition experiment appears increasingly limited.

At the general level, two independent lines of research support their intimation that a shift to verbal functioning occurs in the late preschool years. One line consists in a comparison of two types of shift in a complex discrimination problem, a reversal and nonreversal shift. In the typical experiment, stimuli varying in two dimensions, such as brightness and size, are used. Children first learn that black stimuli are correct and white stimuli are incorrect. Transfer to a condition where white stimuli are correct would constitute a reversal shift; transfer to a condition where large stimuli are correct would constitute a nonreversal shift.

If learning is proceeding by associative, S-R processes, the nonreversal shift should be easier than the reversal shift; this is true for animals (**85**) and for young children between three and four (**91**). If verbal mediating processes are used, the reversal shift should be easier, and this is true for college students (**86**). Kendler and Kendler (**90**) found that fast learners among a group five to seven years old were superior on a reversal shift, while slow learners did better on a nonreversal shift. Clearly, a transition point is suggested at this age range.

Russian research with children, quite independently and using different approaches and techniques, has apparently led to the same conclusion. For example, Luria (**109**) comments, "But it is interesting that we find a decisive turning point in all our experiments between the ages of 4 and 5 years. Something very important happens in the human being in this period. It is the period when speech is interiorized, when voluntary movements are developed and performed, and I think there must be some very intimate relation to maturation."

Much evidence for a developmental shift from associational to cognitive-verbal function is summarized in recent reviews (**88, 137**).

Regarding Kuenne's demonstration, however, the recent literature has complicated a once simple picture. First, while some studies have found broad transposition to be characteristic of "concept" as opposed to "no-concept" children (**152, 168, 176**), other studies have found relational responses on far tests from children who could not express any concept (**80, 179**) or else have failed to find a difference between "concept" and "no-concept" children (**134, 135, 145, 147**).

Second, several effects have emerged which appear difficult to explain on the basis of any of the current formulations. Rudel (**147**) has reported a peculiar U-shaped transposition function—with relational responses high on near tests, absent on middle tests, and recurring on far tests. In other work, she has reported that normal children are more likely to make absolute responses than are brain-damaged or retarded children (**145**). Johnson and Zara (**80**) trained children on two intermixed size discriminations. Not only did these children learn more rapidly than children faced with a single such discrimination but they transposed on both near and far tests. Finally, it has been found that transposition increases with time lapse between training and test (**146, 179**).

No existing theoretical formulation explicitly takes into account this variety of findings. It is perhaps not surprising—indeed, it is encouraging—that the Spence and Kuenne notions, set forth in 1937 and 1946, fail to cover what is known in 1962. Some attention must be given to integrating what is now known. Perhaps Stevenson and Bitterman's (**175**) "distance-effect" hypothesis is a step in a new integration.

A new formulation will undoubtedly have to take into account some sort of shift from associative to cognitive function at about age five. This shift probably is not simply a function of developing language skills. Brighter and older children do tend to be more verbally guided in their behavior. But, as Wohlwill (**208**) points out, an absolute choice as well as a relational choice can be verbally guided. Perhaps some underlying developmental event simultaneously prepares the child to learn relational words and to show broad transposition. Word usage and choice behavior would not be linked as cause and effect, but as joint, correlated effects. Such a hypothesis would explain why artificially installed concepts do not always have the same apparent effects as naturally acquired concepts (**170, 210**) and in a broader context, why children's verbalization is so often uncorrelated with their problem-solving success (**117, 142**).

DISCRIMINATION LEARNING SET

Learning set gradually manifests itself when children solve series of discrimination problems; each succeeding problem is solved more quickly. The concept of learning sets provides a bridge between trial-and-error learning and insight learning, once conceived as opposed processes. As Harlow (**63**) points out, a monkey solves his first problem in trial and error fashion; some 200 problems later, the same monkey solves a new problem quickly and decisively, in insightful fashion.

Several demonstrations of learning set are to be found with children (**63, 151**), some showing a relation between the speed with which the set forms and mental age (**84, 93**). White and Plum (**201**) photographed children's eye movements during a series of discrimination problems and found that superior discrimination learning was generally associated with more scanning of stimuli. During individual problems, scanning was maximal at the onset of solution. In the development of the learning set there was a suggestion of a similar mechanism, with maximal scanning movements at a point where learning became most efficient.

The most thoroughgoing analysis of children's learning sets is to be found in the work of House and Zeaman (**69–75, 209, 210**). Despite their use of retarded children, much of their work gets at basic mechanisms of discrimination learning and, accordingly, will be discussed in the section immediately following.

THE PROCESS OF DISCRIMINATION LEARNING

Recent work is forcing a new synthesis of associational and other factors to account for discrimination learning. An adequate explanation of discrimination learning must now deal with at least three processes: associations to positive and negative stimuli, attentional shifts, and "error factors."

Associations to positive and negative stimuli.—It has been conventional to view discrimination learning as a process of gradual strengthening of a correct response tendency together with a weakening of incorrect response tendencies. There is some evidence that one may occur without the other (**171**). Which process plays a predominant role in discrimination learning?

Attempts to answer this question have brought forth interesting twists on the standard discrimination problem: designs where either the positive or negative position of a problem is marked by ever changing stimuli while the other side is marked by a constant stimulus (**69, 202**); simultaneously given problems where the positive stimulus of one is the negative stimulus of the other; or situations where a novel positive or negative stimulus is suddenly introduced into an ongoing discrimination (**209**).

While some papers have seemed to suggest that discrimination learning primarily involves associations to a positive stimulus (**69, 129**), their data are only suggestive rather than conclusive on this point—and, recently, Zeaman and House have furnished new data to show that associations to the negative stimulus are involved in discrimination learning (**209**).

This is consistent with other evidence of the importance of nonrewarded trials. Cantor and Spiker (**34**) gave children extra nonreinforced trials to the negative stimulus in a special discrimination arrangement and found that this facilitated the learning. Stevenson *et al.* (**185**) report that discrimination learning is better when a penalty is provided for incorrect responses. Most studies on the informational aspect of rewards, as noted earlier, suggest that signaling errors helps learning more than signaling correct responses.

Considering all the evidence, it is possible that the basic association in discrimination learning lies in a tendency to make a particular response to a stimulus in a given context. Nonrewarded experiences may be highly useful means toward that end, perhaps even more useful than rewarded experiences. Nevertheless, it is at least questionable whether discrimination learning necessarily implies the formation of a kind of aversion to another response or responses. We insist, through our criterion, that all children emerge from their learning with a definite idea of what to do—depending on their route to this point they may or may not have lasting tendencies not to do other things.

Attentional shifts.—Attentional factors have occupied a back-door position in accounts of children's learning—never an explicit part of anyone's learning theory, except Tolman's—often an unofficial guest in discussion sections. Again and again, learning data seem to require appeals to attention, orientation, or observing responses (cf. discussion section comments in **104, 124, 160, 163, 185, 194, 195**).

Recent findings suggest that attention must be given a more formal place in accounts of children's learning. House and Zeaman (**75**), discussing visual discrimination learning in retardates, have supported a two-process view, "one of which requires that [the subjects] direct and maintain attention to the relevant cues of the situation before and after learning." They base this view on their finding that the learning of retardates is typically quite sudden, with the presolution period consisting of a long or short string of responses at a chance level of success. This finding is confirmed in four studies involving normal children—in re-analysis of two published studies (**198**), and in two unpublished investigations (**201, 202**). Taken in conjunction with the fact that visual scanning of stimuli surges at the onset of criterion, the sudden onset of criterion probably betokens a significant attentional shift in association with solution.

At a simpler level, the effects of distraction show the importance of attentional factors in discrimination learning. Holland and White (**67**) gave children a successive discrimination problem under control conditions, "mild distraction" (a taped educational TV discussion of African politics) and "strong distraction" (taped children's songs and stories). Both mild and strong distraction groups took over twice as long as the control group to learn.

Error factors.—Harlow's error factor theory (**62**) views discrimination learning as a suppression of fallacies of approach to the discrimination problem. These error factors—called "hypotheses" in an older, similar theory—are primitive strategies of responses which are guided by irrelevant aspects of the choice situation. The error factor system described by Harlow is based on his research with monkeys, and the attempts made to apply it to children (**70, 101**) have not yet made it clear how well it fits children's presolution behavior.

Nevertheless, anyone who has worked with children in discrimination procedures is familiar with runs of stereotyped, position-guided responding—persistent preference for one position, single alternation between positions, a win-stay, lose-shift choice of positions. House and Zeaman (**71**) tried to establish a delayed-response set in retardates; out of 3,472 errors in the total study, they noted that 92 per cent could be accounted for either by a position habit or by win-stay, lose-shift behavior.

If the presolution period is occupied by testing and suppressing wrong strategies, and if solution occurs suddenly, when are the associations to positive and negative stimuli being learned? Apparently, this associational process runs concurrently during the presolution period.

There is ample evidence to show that animals form associations to cues while ostensibly being guided by a positional strategy (cf., **141, 157**). Sometimes, they will consistently respond faster to the correct stimulus than to the incorrect stimulus. The record of choices may, therefore, show a position habit, but the record of latencies may show stimulus differentiation (**38, 41**).

If we may accept these data from studies with animals as having significance for children, then the complete course of an average discrimination might rest on the following processes. The child begins by choosing in a position-guided fashion; while concurrently the differential reward process strengthens his tendency to approach the positive stimulus. At some point, the position-guided behavior is superseded, and correct, cue-guided responding appears to burst through. This point is marked by a surge of visual scanning of the stimuli (in animals, by characteristic head movements from side to side, a type of behavior which has been called "vicarious trial-and-error").

Position-guided runs of responses are more frequent in younger children, and it is possible that some developmental process makes their inhibition easier. We may note that House and Zeaman (**73**) were unable to establish a cue-guided learning set in imbeciles but were able to establish a position reversal set in these subjects (**72**). McCullers and Stevenson (**111**) had to eliminate 28 per cent of a sample of four-years-olds because of position habits, none of a sample of nine-year-olds. Considering the ubiquity of position-guided responding in animals—its tendency to recur in discrimination reversals, to persist in strong punishment situations, to appear after some cortical ablations—it may be that position-guided response is rather primitive and basic and that more sophisticated (e.g., cue-guided) behavior is built upon inhibition of position-guided response.

Older children are occasionally hindered by what might be

called "inverse error factors"—they assume that the solution of a problem must be trickier than it actually is (**177, 195**).

PROBABILITY LEARNING

In the probability learning paradigm, the child makes a choice between stimuli, but reward is alternated between the stimuli according to some probability schedule fixed by the experimenter. Rather sophisticated statistical models have been built around adult probability learning, and some efforts have recently been made to extend this paradigm to children.

So far as intermittency of reward itself is concerned, it is a rather broad characteristic of behavior that a response intermittently rewarded persists longer after reward is stopped than does a continuously rewarded response. It is true, for example, of children's learning (**40, 120**) and even of infant smiling (**21**).

Another generality, for adults, is the "probability matching law." If an adult is faced with two buttons (one of which yields a reward 60 per cent of the time, and the other 40 per cent of the time), adults will, over the long run, "match probability" by choosing the 60 per cent button 60 per cent of the time. This is not true for young children; they will choose the 60 per cent button almost all of the time. As they grow older children become more persistent in their attempts to find a strategy to beat the game, and their button choices tend toward probability matching (**184**). This increasing search for pattern and order in probability learning as children grow older has also been noted by Crandall *et al.* (**36**). If children's needs for success are enhanced by using a desirable trinket as prize, or if their expectation of success is enhanced by pretraining with a high-success condition, they will similarly show more variability of behavior and hence more probability matching (**184, 186**).

Variability of behavior in probability learning is sometimes clearly a search for a winning strategy, sometimes not. Do children tend to be more variable in their behavior as they get older? Hanlon (**61**) and Hodgden (**66**) have studied this problem using a toy truck and a miniature layout of houses and streets. Children repeatedly "drove" from one point of the layout to another, and variability was measured by the number of different routes they took. Older children, and children of higher mental age, tended to be more variable in their behavior. Using another variability measure, Siegel and Foshee (**153**) have similarly found that retardates are less variable than normal children.

There appears also to be an age progression in children's notions of strategy and understanding of games. Gratch (**58, 59**) has explored this. In his first study, he had children guess whether a square or a diamond would turn up in a set of cards. Younger children tended to alternate guesses, rationalizing this on grounds of "fairness," or "taking turns." In the second study, children played both hider and seeker in "guess which hand the marble is in." Children of ages two and three could not hide and, in choosing, always chose the same hand. From ages three and one-half to five, children tended to show single alternation, both as hider and seeker. (There is an interesting correspondence between this progression and the error factors in discrimination learning prevalent at these ages.) Finally, Gratch's oldest children were variable in their seeking and showed in their hiding that they were able to grasp the idea of the game.

To date, then, the probability learning studies have yielded no mathematical theories of children's behavior, but they have offered an avenue of approach to children's strategies of search.

Transfer of Training

The previous sections have concentrated on parametric studies of children's learning. Such studies are an essential part of any research discipline. They accumulate information which can be drawn upon to settle issues, while at the same time they frequently raise interesting new issues. In psychology, they have provided a versatile and well-understood set of experimental approaches to new problems, and they have helped shape a clearer sense of which questions can and cannot be usefully put to experimental test.

On the other hand, it must be remembered that the ultimate business of research is not just to collect data but to find orderliness in nature. Experiments must be fused into meaningful generalities by logic, speculation, and theory—or else they can degenerate into a kind of "art for art's sake." The encouraging aspect of the recent research with children lies not in its sheer volume but, rather, in the fact that here and there interesting generalities about process and mechanism begin to be hinted at. They range from simple list-making, such as the picture of "mechanisms of reward" discussed above, to our somewhat more incisive notions about discrimination learning and verbal regulation of behavior. This section, and the next two, will discuss mechanisms of transfer of training, age change, and individual differences.

The term "transfer of training" refers to the effects which older learning has in helping or hindering new learning. Because transfer is an omnipresent factor in human learning—in fact, an inseparable part of it—it is of great theoretical and practical interest.

Actually, there are a number of different aspects of first-learning which can transfer to second-learning, each one reflecting some facet of the first performance which is available for future use. We speak, then, of kinds of transfer; the variety of kinds of transfer which can stem from a simple learning task gives some notion of how unsimple that task really is.

The current picture of the various kinds of transfer is the result of extensive research with adults (**112**). The studies with children, by and large, dovetail with that body of research. In the interest of coherence, what follows will be a brief sketch of the known mechanisms of transfer, together with indications of what the relevant children's work has been.

NONSPECIFIC TRANSFER

Nonspecific transfer between Task 1 and Task 2 occurs when there are no identical or similar stimuli or responses in the two tasks, and yet the first affects the second. One type, *warmup*, is a short-term facilitation produced by some opportunity to "settle down" or "get set" in the experimental situation. For example, in a study by White (**198**), children learned a discrimination between a red and red-orange block faster after they spent a few minutes picking up a single gray block to find a marble beneath it. A second type, *learning-to-learn*, is well exemplified by the discrimination learning set studies already discussed.

Possibly, there should be a third category of nonspecific transfer, *emotional carryover*, to take into account factors of emotionality or frustration generated in one situation and carried over to a second (**172, 181**). The experimental demonstrations have so far shown only short-term carryover; if longer carryovers can be found, then such research might well have significance for the understanding of "learning block" problems in education.

SPECIFIC TRANSFER

Specific transfer refers to the influence of Task 1 on Task 2 through some identifiable commonality or similarity between the stimuli or responses of the two tasks. A rather basic kind of specific transfer is *generalization*, the tendency of a response to transfer from one stimulus to another depending on the physical similarity between stimuli. It is considered basic because it occurs in the most elementary known forms of learning, classical and instrumental conditioning, and because it is often used in attempts to explain other sorts of transfer.

Some of the work on generalization with children as subjects has been devoted to establishing a procedure suitable for preschoolers and to exploring it (**160, 165, 199**). Younger children generalize more than older children (**113, 203**). Since adults' generalization is associated with the degree to which they show impulsiveness of response (**200**), perhaps the greater generalization of younger children is similarly a product of impulsiveness.

Associative transfer is a kind of specific transfer from one complex learning to the next on the basis of common elements—common stimuli or responses—in the two tasks; where there are similar elements this term is usually understood to include a generalization process.

The work done with children has concentrated on negative associative transfer of the "A-B, A-C" variety—in which a subject learns response B to stimulus A and then must, instead, learn C to A. Since the first task helps the second task by warmup and learning-to-learn, any demonstration of A-B, A-C interference must have control groups designed to take into account these positive transfers. In general, because there are so many kinds of transfer effects, precise studies of transfer require rather more complex and careful research design than most other psychological studies.

With proper controls it is found that the more first A-B learning, the more interference with second A-C learning (**159**). The interference shows up mainly in errors of omission on the second task

(**169**). Here, too, there is a suggestion that interference errors are associated with impulsiveness on the part of the subject (**204**).

Two types of specific transfer are occasioned simply by experience with the stimuli of a subsequent problem. *Stimulus* predifferentiation refers to the facilitating effect of observing differences between stimuli upon their subsequent associations to responses (**124**) —presumably, stimulus predifferentiation reduces generalization between stimuli. *Perceptual set* is a kind of stimulus pretraining which guides the subject to base his behavior on one aspect of a complex stimulus (**136**); it may help or may interfere, depending upon which aspect of the stimulus the subject is next called upon to use.

Acquired equivalence and distinctiveness refer to the fact that children, given similar names for stimuli, find it harder to learn a discrimination involving those stimuli, while children given different names find it easier. The similar names cause the stimuli to "acquire equivalence," and the different names cause them to "acquire distinctiveness." This type of transfer has been extensively studied with preschool children who characteristically do not begin learning with self-supplied names for stimuli. It has been of considerable interest theoretically, because S-R theory can "handle" this transfer in a way which might offer an avenue for the extension of this theory into significant areas of language and symbolic behavior.

Actually, the S-R model of acquired equivalence and distinctiveness is rather broad and provides for facilitation or interference with discrimination by pretraining procedures other than naming. Similar or different motor responses attached to stimuli influence subsequent learning involving those stimuli (**77, 79: I, 79: II**). So, also, do similar or different paired associations (**9, 123**).

The effects of similar or dissimilar names have been demonstrated with a variety of procedures (**37, 77, 95, 150**). Careful design of research has been necessary to demonstrate that the transfer is due to the names themselves rather than such alternatives as warmup, learning-to-learn, and stimulus predifferentiation, but these alternative transfer processes have been ruled out (**33, 122, 124**).

While it is thus quite clear that distinctive responses to stimuli help in learning a discrimination, and similar responses hinder it, there is, unfortunately, some doubt that these studies substantiate only the S-R model of symbolic behavior. A simpler explanation is that these responses may have their effect by helping or hindering the child to rehearse his task between trials of the transfer problem—the rehearsal providing, in effect, extra training trials (**162, 167**). This alternative explanation would also apply to the studies of the effects of names on learning and retention of delayed-reward problems, already mentioned.

COMMENTS ON TRANSFER MECHANISMS

Unfortunately, the above categories only provide a named pigeonhole for most of the known transfer phenomena. Each of the classifications borders so closely on others that this scheme might best be considered a helpful, temporary expedient. Even at the moment, it seems difficult to classify certain demonstrated transfer effects. Why do transfer effects change with the passage of time between training and transfer (**179, 183**)? Why does varied training increase generalization (**203**)? Why is discrimination learning helped by pretraining with an easier discrimination (**74, 163**)? Should there be a category of "conceptual set" to include transfer of concepts (**136**), inferential transfer (**87, 89**), or transfer of logical forms (**107**)?

Individual Differences

A few individual-difference variables—I.Q., "cognitive style," and test-defined anxiety—affect learning in ways which are recently beginning to be understood. Other variables, such as sex differences and social class differences, also are known to affect learning, but information about them is presently fragmentary.

The relationship between I.Q. and learning has been most extensively examined in comparisons of the learning of retardates and normal children; this large literature is surveyed in a current review (**174**). Two recent studies have provided interesting comparisons of the learning of high-I.Q. and average-I.Q. children. One study (**127**) found that older and brighter children solved concept-attainment problems by rather sudden, insightful leaps to solution, while younger and duller children were apt to learn gradually. Another (**128**) provided an interesting example of a case where a high I.Q. ostensibly interferes with learning. When a concept-attainment problem was given straightforwardly, high-I.Q. children solved it more quickly than average-I.Q. children; however, when the same problem was presented by complex stimuli which offered many false leads, the high-I.Q. children apparently "wasted time" checking on many possibilities and so took longer than average-I.Q. children to solve it. Can one say here that the slower learners were the poorer learners?

A number of lines of research with adults and children have recently converged upon a significant new dimension of individual difference (**48, 82, 92, 96, 207**). While these subject differences are usually spoken of in terms of cognitive styles, or in terms of "leveling" vs. "sharpening," the differences are expressed in perceptual, emotional, cognitive, social, and even simple motor behavior. At root, they appear to be differences in impulsiveness, attentiveness, and the ability to focus closely on the environment.

The breadth of a distinction among subjects which cuts across so many traditional categories is astonishing (**82**). Some time will be needed to explore and understand this dimension, Possibly, anxiety scales are making a similar distinction among subjects (**205**). Possibly, Brackbill and O'Hara's finding, that children who are highly reactive on the GSR are poor discrimination learners, fits into the same picture (**25**).

Learning and Development

The preceding sections have considered a variety of age changes which are associated with superior learning—such as the growing child's increasing variability of behavior, acceptance of the challenge of a task, adoption of search strategies, or use of verbal mediators. The questions which remain to be answered are, first, why these changes occur and, second, whether these changes are sufficient to account for all of the improvement in problem-solving associated with age.

In part, age-changes in children's problem-solving are a product of stored learning. The learning set demonstrations clearly suggest that previous learning experiences leave an accumulating residue of general skills. In effect, as a child grows older, problem-solving is more and more a matter of transfer and less and less of new learning. Another set of stored associations are the words and symbols which, as the acquired equivalence and distinctiveness demonstrations suggest, play a part in learning when they can be used.

In part, age-changes must also involve maturational processes, which can only be sketchily indicated. Unquestionably, maturation in motor ability must play a part in children's learning (**2, 6**) as, also, must age-changes in susceptibility to classical conditioning (**26**).

An interesting hypothesis, which is currently under development, is that cognitive development proceeds by hierarchical overlays of higher processes upon lower processes, the lower processes being inhibited in favor of the higher. Such a hypothesis is implicit in Russian theorizing about children (**133**). It would fit in with an impressive variety of the information summarized above—the notion that discrimination learning proceeds via a shift from a basic position-guided level of choice to a cue-guided level, the fact that associative transfer and generalization errors of a kind that young children are prone to make are associated with impulsive responding, the fact that one of the clearest attributes distinguishing the cognitive styles of leveling and sharpening is the impulsiveness of the levelers *vs.* the restraint of the sharpeners. It is quite interesting in this connection to note that a current "microgenetic" theory of thought (**45, 46**) argues that chronic or temporary mental pathology causes an impulsive expression of primitive modes of thought which normal subjects ordinarily inhibit—in effect, a regression to childlike thinking caused by a mechanism of disinhibition.

Concluding Comments

RELEVANCE TO EDUCATION

Psychologists and educators, both so interested in learning, have long viewed each other cordially but at some distance. The flow of innovations, problems, and ideas between the two groups has been sparse, and such contributions as psychology has made have mostly been peripheral to the core of education—tests, remedial teaching and guidance, some notions about personality development and adjustment. Is it possible for educators and psychologists to interact on questions of the nature of learning and the betterment of education?

The studies which have been reviewed in this paper are not of great immediate relevance to education, although it can be hoped that some may seem stimulating and interesting. One may hope for more meaningful interactions in the future, and one may base this hope on two tangible signs. First is the fact that a group of psychologists have advanced proposals toward teaching machines and programmed learning (**108**). Their proposals are speculative rather than inescapable consequences of psychological research, and more proof is needed of their practicability. But, regardless of their fate, it seems a certainty that some psychologists and some educators are going to spend a large amount of time during the next few years thinking about the others' activities and needs.

A second, broader channel of communication may, perhaps, be opening through the recent efforts of private and public agencies to bring psychologists, among others, to consider the problems of education. Some fruits of these efforts are in recent publications (**28, 114, 158, 193**). Research by psychologists on problems related to education has undoubtedly been increased by grant programs designed to bring this about. After a time, such channels may remain open without effort. The Russians, it seems, have developed a useful system of interchange between experimental pedagogy, much like our experimental child psychology, and the classroom (**20**).

FUTURE WORK

Some lines of psychological research into children's learning have their own logic, agenda, and sense of movement. In the long run, the push toward basic processes will probably lead psychological investigators of learning toward biological accounts of maturation, sensory development, brain function, emotion, and attention. Certainly, there is much material in the study of animal learning and development which is of unmistakable relevance for the kinds of generalizations child psychologists are seeking to establish, and these animal areas, in turn, now have substantial connections with physiology and biochemistry.

In the short run, several developments might speed forward movement: (*a*) more standardization of today's somewhat arbitrary variations in equipment and procedures, leading to less "noise" in the communications among experimenters; (*b*) more use of automated procedures, recording, and data analysis to increase the yield of information per child and help reduce experimenter influence; (*c*) more research on sensory, attentional, and individual difference processes in children, to further the tying-in of these processes to learning; and (*d*) more efforts toward a task taxonomy, a scheme which might help relate the results found in one procedure to those found in others.

Finally, and most important, there is the continuing need for speculation, integration, and theory. The new wave of research into children's learning is young, conducted by young workers. Their impressive volume of activity over the last few years has already led to significant small attempts at integration. It is to be hoped that soon larger conceptual schemes—imaginative, intelligent, disciplined—can be proposed.

BIBLIOGRAPHY

1. Alberts, E., and Ehrenfreund, D. "Transposition in Children as a Function of Age," *J. Exp. Psychol.*, XLI (1951), 30–38.
2. Ammons, R. B.; Alprin, S. I.; and Ammons, C. H. "Rotary Pursuit Performance as Related to Sex and Age of Pre-adult S's," *J. Exp. Psychol.*, XLIX (1955), 127–33.
3. Anderson, A. R., and Moore, O. K. "Autotelic Folk-models," *Sociol. Quar.*, I (1960), 203–16.
4. Antonitis, J. T., and Barnes, G. W. "Group Operant Behavior: An Extension of Individual Research Methodology to a Real-life Situation," *J. Genet. Psychol.*, XCVIII (1961), 95–112.
5. Azrin, N. H., and Lindsley, O. R. "The Reinforcement of Co-operation between Children," *J. Abnorm. Soc. Psychol.*, LII (1956), 100–102.
6. Bachman, J. C. "Motor Learning and Performance as Related to Age and Sex in Two Measures of Balance Co-ordination," *Res. Quart.*, XXXII (1961), 123–37.
7. Baer, D. M. "Effect of Withdrawal of Positive Reinforcement on an Extinguishing Response in Young Children," *Child Develpm.*, III (1961), 67–74.
8. ———. "Escape and Avoidance Response of Preschool Children to Two Schedules of Reinforcement Withdrawal," *J. Exp. Anal. Behav.*, III (1960), 155–59.
9. Berkson, G., and Cantor, G. N. "A Study of Mediation in Mentally Retarded and Normal School Children," *J. Educ. Psychol.*, LI (1960), 82–86.
10. Berlyne, D. E. *Conflict, Arousal, and Curiosity*. New York: McGraw-Hill Book Co., Inc., 1960.
11. Bijou, S. W. "A Child Study Laboratory on Wheels," *Child Develpm.*, XXIX (1958), 425–27.

12. ———. "Discrimination Performance as a Base Line for Individual Analysis of Young Children," *Child Develpm.*, XXXII (1961), 163–70.

13. ———. "Methodology for an Experimental Analysis of Child Behavior," *Psychol. Reports*, III (1957), 243–50.

14. ———. "Operant Extinction after Fixed-Interval Schedules with Young Children," *J. Exp. Anal. Behav.*, I (1958), 25–29.

15. ———. "A Standard 'Candy' for Research with Children," *J. Exp. Anal. Behav.*, I (1958), 314.

16. ———. "A Systematic Approach to an Experimental Analysis of Young Children," *Child Develpm.*, XXVI (1955), 161–68.

17. Bijou, S. W., and Baer, D. M. "The Laboratory-Experimental Study of Child Behavior," in *Handbook of Research Methods in Child Development.* Edited by P. H. Mussen. New York: John Wiley & Sons, 1960.

18. Bijou, S. W., and Orlando, R. "Rapid Development of Multiple-Schedule Performances with Retarded Children," *J. Exp. Anal. Behav.*, IV (1961), 7–16.

19. Bijou, S. W., and Sturges, P. T. "Positive Reinforcers for Experimental Studies with Children—Consumables and Manipulatables," *Child Develpm.*, XXX (1959), 151–70.

20. Brackbill, Y. "Experimental Research with Children in the Soviet Union: Report of a Visit," *Amer. Psychologist*, XV (1960), 226–33.

21. ———. "Extinction of the Smiling Response in Infants as a Function of Reinforcement Schedule," *Child Develpm.*, XXIX (1958), 115–24.

22. Brackbill, Y.; Bravos, A.; and Starr, R. H. "Delay-improved Retention of a Difficult Task." Unpublished manuscript, 1962.

23. Brackbill, Y., and Jack, D. "Discrimination Learning in Children as a Function of Reinforcement Value," *Child Develpm.*, XXIX (1958), 185–90.

24. Brackbill, Y., and Kappy, M. S. "Delay of Reinforcement and Retention," *J. Comp. Physiol. Psychol.*, LV (1962), 14–18.

25. Brackbill, Y., and O'Hara, J. "The Relative Effectiveness of Reward and Punishment for Discrimination Learning in Children," *J. Comp. Physiol. Psychol.*, LI (1957), 747–51.

26. Braun, H. W., and Geiselhart, R. "Age Differences in the Acquisition and Extinction of the Conditioned Eyelid Response," *J. Exp. Psychol.*, LVII (1959), 386–88.

27. Brian, C. R., and Goodenough, F. L. "The Relative Potency of Color and Form Perception at Various Ages," *J. Exp. Psychol.*, XII (1929), 197–213.

28. Bruner, J. S. *The Process of Education.* Cambridge, Massachusetts: Harvard University Press, 1961.

29. Bruner, J. S.; Matter, J.; and Papanek, M. L. "Breadth of Learning as a Function of Drive Level and Mechanization," *Psychol. Rev.*, LXII (1955), 1–10.

30. Calvin, A. D. "Configurational Learning in Children," *J. Educ. Psychol.*, XLVI (1955), 117–20.

31. Calvin, A. D.; Clancy, J. J.; and Fuller, J. B. "A Further Investigation of Various Stimulus-objects in Discriminative Learning by Children," *Amer. J. Psychol.*, LXIX (1956), 647–49.

32. Calvin, A. D., and Clifford, L. T. "The Relative Efficiency of Various

Types of Stimulus Objects in Discriminative Learning by Children," *Amer. J. Psychol.*, LXIX (1956), 103–6.

33. Cantor, G. N. "Effects of Three Types of Pretraining on Discrimination Learning in Preschool Children," *J. Exp. Psychol.*, XLIX (1955), 339–42.

34. Cantor, G. N., and Spiker, C. C. "Effects of Non-reinforced Trials on Discrimination Learning in Preschool Children," *J. Exp. Psychol.*, XLVII (1954), 256–58.

35. Crandall, V. J., and Rabson, A. "Children's Repetition Choices in an Intellectual Achievement Situation Following Success and Failure," *J. Genet. Psychol.*, XCVII (1960), 161–68.

36. Crandall, V. J.; Solomon, D.; and Kellaway, R. A. "A Comparison of the Patterned and Nonpatterned Probability Learning of Adolescent and Early Grade School-Age Children," *J. Genet. Psychol.*, XCIX (1961), 29–30.

37. Dietze, D. "The Facilitating Effect of Words on Discrimination and Generalization," *J. Exp. Psychol.*, L (1955), 255–60.

38. Eninger, M. J. "The Role of Generalized Approach and Avoidance Tendencies in Brightness Discrimination," *J. Comp. Physiol. Psychol.*, XLVI (1953), 398–402.

39. Erickson, M. T., and Lipsitt, L. P. "Effects of Delayed Reward on Simultaneous and Successive Discrimination Learning in Children," *J. Comp. Physiol. Psychol.*, LIII (1960), 256–60.

40. Fattu, N.; Auble, D.; and Mech, E. V. "Partial Reinforcement in a Bar-pressing Situation with Preschool Children." *J. Genet. Psychol.*, XXCVII (1955), 251–55.

41. Feldman, R. S. "The Specificity of the Fixated Response in the Rat," *J. Comp. Physiol. Psychol.*, XLVI (1953), 487–92.

42. Ferster, C. B. "Positive Reinforcement and Behavioral Deficits of Autistic Children," *Child Develpm.*, XXXII (1961), 437–56.

43. Ficke, B. G., and Kausler, D. H. "Incidental Learning in Children under Varying Levels of Incentive-set." Paper read at Midwestern Psychological Association, Chicago, 1961.

44. Fiske, D. W., and Maddi, S. R. *Functions of Varied Experience.* Homewood, Illinois: Dorsey Press, Inc., 1961.

45. Flavell, J. H., and Draguns, J. "A Micro-genetic Approach to Perception and Thought," *Psychol. Bull.*, LIV (1957), 197–217.

46. Flavell, J. H.; Draguns, J.; Feinberg, L. D.; and Budin, W. "A Microgenetic Approach to Word Association," *J. Abnorm. Soc. Psychol.*, XVII (1958), 1–7.

47. Frey, R. B. "The Effects of Verbal Reinforcers on Group Operant Behavior." Unpublished Master's thesis, University of Maine, 1960.

48. Gardner, R. W. "Cognitive Styles in Categorizing Behavior," *J. Pers.*, XXII (1953), 214–33.

49. Gewirtz, H. B. "Displacement of Preference as a Function of Avoidance-Avoidance Conflict," *J. Abnorm. Soc. Psychol.*, LVIII (1959), 395–98.

50. ———. "Generalization of Children's Preferences as a Function of Reinforcement and Task Similarity," *J. Abnorm. Soc. Psychol.*, LVIII (1959), 111–18.

51. Gewirtz, J. L. "Discussion Comments," in *Child Research in Psycho-*

pharmacology, pp. 127–36. Edited by S. Fisher. Springfield, Illinois: Charles C. Thomas, 1959.

52. ———. "A Program of Research on the Dimensions and Antecedents of Emotional Dependence," *Child Develpm.*, XXVII (1956), 205–21.
53. Gewirtz, J. L., and Baer, D. M. "Deprivation and Satiation of Social Reinforcers as Drive Conditions," *J. Abnorm. Soc. Psychol.*, LVII (1958), 165–72.
54. ———. "The Effect of Brief Social Deprivation on Behaviors for a Social Reinforcer," *J. Abnorm. Soc. Psychol.*, LVI (1958), 49–56.
55. Goldiamond, I., and Flanagan, B. "Delayed Feedback in the Control of Stuttering: An Experimental Analysis," *Amer. Psychologist*, XV (1960), 475.
56. Gollin, E. S. "Observations on Method in Child Psychology," *Merrill-Palmer Quar.*, VI (1960), 250–60.
57. ———. "Some Research Problems for Developmental Psychology," *Child Develpm.*, XXVII (1956), 223–35.
58. Gratch, G. "The Development of the Expectation of the Nonindependence of Random Events in Children," *Child Develpm.*, XXX (1959), 217–27.
59. ———. "The Rise and Fall of Response Alternation in Children: A Developmental Study of Orientations to Uncertainty in a Social Guessing Game." Unpublished manuscript, 1962.
60. Gray, P. H. "Theory and Evidence of Imprinting in Human Infants," *J. Psychol.*, XLVI (1958), 155–66.
61. Hanlon, C. "Response Variability in Children as a Function of Age, Pretraining and Incentive Conditions," *J. Comp. Physiol. Psychol.*, LIII (1960), 267–69.
62. Harlow, H. F. "Analysis of Discrimination Learning by Monkeys," *J. Exp. Psychol.*, XL (1950), 26–39.
63. ———. "The Formation of Learning Sets," *Psychol. Rev.*, LVI (1949), 51–65.
64. Hermelin, B., and O'Connor, N. "Recognition of Shapes by Normal and Subnormal Children," *Brit. J. Psychol.*, LII (1961), 281–84.
65. Hockman, C. H., and Lipsitt, L. P. "Delay of Reward Gradients in Discrimination Learning with Children for Two Levels of Difficulty," *J. Comp. Physiol. Psychol.*, LIV (1961), 24–27.
66. Hodgden, L. H. "Variability of Behavior as a Function of Intelligence and Incentive," *J. Pers.*, XXIX (1961), 183–94.
67. Holland, M., and White, S. H. "Effects of Distraction on Learning to Constant and Occasional Stimulus Cues." Unpublished manuscript, 1962.
68. Honkavaara, S. "A Critical Re-evaluation of the Color and Form Reaction and Disproving of the Hypotheses Connected with It," *J. Psychol.*, XLV (1958), 25–36.
69. House, B. J.; Orlando, R.; and Zeaman, D. A. "Role of Positive and Negative Cues in the Discrimination Learning of Mental Defectives," *Percept. Mot. Skills*, VII (1957), 73–79.
70. House, B. J., and Zeaman, D. A. "Comparison of Discrimination Learning in Normal and Mentally Defective Children," *Child Develpm.*, XXIX (1958), 411–16.

71. House, B. J., and Zeaman, D. A. "Effects of Practice on the Delayed Response of Retardates," *J. Comp. Physiol. Psychol.*, LIV (1961), 255–61.
72. ———. "Position Discrimination and Reversals in Low-grade Retardates," *J. Comp. Physiol. Psychol.*, LII (1959), 564–65.
73. ———. "Reward and Nonreward in the Discrimination Learning of Imbeciles," *J. Comp. Physiol. Psychol.*, LI (1958), 614–18.
74. ———. "Transfer of a Discrimination from Objects to Patterns," *J. Exp. Psychol.*, LIX (1960), 298–302.
75. ———. "Visual Discrimination Learning and Intelligence in Defectives of Low Mental Age," *Amer. J. Ment. Defic.*, LXV (1960), 51–58.
76. Hunt, D. E. "Changes in Goal Object Preference as a Function of Expectancy for Social Reinforcement," *J. Abnorm. Soc. Psychol.*, L (1955), 372–77.
77. Jeffrey, W. E. "The Effects of Verbal and Nonverbal Responses in Mediating an Instrumental Act," *J. Exp. Psychol.*, XLV (1953), 327–33.
78. ———. "New Techniques for Motivating and Reinforcing Children," *Science*, CXXI (1955), 371.
79. ———. "Variables in Early Discrimination Learning: I. Motor Responses in the Training of a Left-right Discrimination," *Child Develpm.*, XXIX (1958), 269–75; II. "Mode of Response and Stimulus Difference in the Discrimination of Tonal Frequencies," *Child Develpm.*, XXIX (1958), 531–38; III. "Simultaneous versus Successive Stimulus Presentation," *Child Develpm.*, XXXII (1961), 305–10.
80. Johnson, R. C., and Zara, R. C. "Relational Learning in Young Children," *J. Comp. Physiol. Psychol.*, LIII (1960), 594–97.
81. Kagan, J., and Lemkin, J. "Form, Color, and Size in Children's Conceptual Behavior," *Child Develpm.*, XXXII (1961), 25–28.
82. Kagan, J.; Moss, H. A.; and Sigel, I. "The Psychological Significance of Styles of Conceptualization," in *Basic Cognitive Processes in Children.* Edited by J. C. Wright and J. Kagan. Monograph of the Society for Research in Child Development, 1962.
83. Kallet, A.; Gatchell, M.; and Hamilton, D. "A Pilot Study on Increasing Reading Readiness of Young Children from an Inner-city Area." Unpublished manuscript, 1961.
84. Kaufman, M. E., and Peterson, W. M. "Acquisition of a Learning Set by Normal and Mentally Retarded Children," *J. Comp. Physiol. Psychol.*, LI (1958), 619–21.
85. Kelleher, R. T. "Discrimination Learning as a Function of Reversal and Nonreversal Shifts," *J. Exp. Psychol.*, LI (1956), 379–84.
86. Kendler, H. H., and D'Amato, M. F. "A Comparison of Reversal Shifts and Nonreversal Shifts in Human Concept Formation Behavior," *J. Exp. Psychol.*, XLIX (1955), 165–74.
87. Kendler, H. H., and Kendler, T. S. "Inferential Behavior in Preschool Children," *J. Exp. Psychol.*, LI (1956), 311–14.
88. ———. "Vertical and Horizontal Processes in Problem-solving," *Psychol. Rev.*, LXIX (1962), 1–16.
89. Kendler, H. H.; Kendler, T. S.; Pliskoff, S. S.; and D'Amato, M. F. "Inferential Behavior in Children: I. The Influence of Reinforcement and Incentive Motivation," *J. Exp. Psychol.*, LV (1958), 207–12.

90. KENDLER, T. S., and KENDLER, H. H. "Reversal and Nonreversal Shifts in Kindergarten Children," *J. Exp. Psychol.*, LVIII (1959), 56–60.

91. KENDLER, T. S.; KENDLER, H. H.; and WELLS, D. "Reversal and Nonreversal Shifts in Nursery-school Children," *J. Comp. Physiol. Psychol.*, LIII (1960), 83–88.

92. KLEIN, G. S. "The Personal World through Perception," in *Perception: An Approach to Personality*. Edited by R. R. Blake and G. V. Ramsey. New York: Ronald Press, 1951.

93. KOCH, M. B., and MEYER, D. R. "A Relationship of Mental Age to Learning in the Preschool Child," *J. Comp. Physiol. Psychol.*, LII (1959), 387–89.

94. KUENNE, M. R. "Experimental Investigation of the Relation of Language to Transposition Behavior in Young Children," *J. Exp. Psychol.*, XXXVI (1946), 471–90.

95. LACEY, H. M. "Mediating Verbal Responses and Stimulus Similarity as Factors in Conceptual Naming by School-age Children," *J. Exp. Psychol.*, LXII (1961), 113–21.

96. LACEY, J. I., and LACEY, B. C. "The Relationship of Resting Autonomic Activity to Motor Impulsivity," *Res. Publ. Assn. Nerv. Ment. Dis.*, XXXVI (1958), 144–209.

97. LAMBERT, W. W., and LAMBERT, E. C. "Some Indirect Effects of Reward on Children's Size Estimates," *J. Abnorm. Soc. Psychol.*, XLVIII (1953), 507–10.

98. LAMBERT, W. W.; LAMBERT, E. C.; and WATSON, P. D. "Acquisition and Extinction of an Instrumental Response Sequence in the Token-Reward Situation," *J. Exp. Psychol.*, XLV (1953), 321–26.

99. LAMBERT, W. W.; SOLOMON, R. L.; and WATSON, P. D. "Reinforcement and Extinction as Factors in Size Estimation," *J. Exp. Psychol.*, XXXIX (1949), 637–41.

100. LEIMAN, A. H.; MYERS, J. L.; and MYERS, N. A. "Secondary Reinforcement in a Discrimination Problem with Children," *Child Develpm.*, XXXII (1961), 349–54.

101. LEVINSON, B. "Strategies in Discrimination Learning-set Formation in Preschool Children." Paper read at Eastern Psychological Association, 1962.

102. LIPSITT, L. P. "Simultaneous and Successive Discrimination Learning in Children," *Child Develpm.*, XXXII (1961), 337–48.

103. LIPSITT, L. P., and CASTANEDA, A. "Effects of Delayed Reward on Choice Behavior and Response Speeds in Children," *J. Comp. Physiol. Psychol.*, LI (1958), 65–67.

104. LIPSITT, L. P.; CASTANEDA, A.; and KEMBLE, J. D. "Effects of Delayed Reward Pretraining on Discrimination Learning in Children," *Child Develpm.*, LX (1959), 273–78.

105. LONG, E. R. "Multiple Scheduling in Children." *J. Exp. Anal. Behav.*, II (1959), 268.

106. LONG, E. R.; HAMMACK, J. T.; MAY, F.; and CAMPBELL, B. J. "Intermittent Reinforcement of Operant Behavior in Children," *J. Exp. Anal. Behav.*, I (1958), 315–40.

107. LUCHINS, A. S. "Mechanization in Problem-solving: The Effect of Einstellung," *Psychol. Monogr.*, LIV (1942), Whole No. 248.

108. LUMSDAINE, A. A., and GLASER, R. *Teaching Machines and Programmed*

Learning: A Source Book. Washington: National Education Association, 1960.

109. Luria, A. R. "Verbal Regulation of Behavior," in *The Central Nervous System and Behavior.* Edited by M. A. B. Brazier. Report of the Third Macy Conference. Madison, New Jersey: Macy Foundation, 1960.

110. McCandless, B. R., and Spiker, C. C. "Experimental Research in Child Psychology," *Child Develpm.,* XXVII (1956), 75–80.

111. McCullers, J. C., and Stevenson, H. W. "Effects of Verbal Reinforcement in a Probability Learning Situation," *Psychol. Reports,* VII (1960), 439–45.

112. McGeoch, J. A., and Irion, A. L. *The Psychology of Human Learning.* New York: Longmans, Green & Co., 1952.

113. Mednick, S. A., and Lehtinen, L. E. "Stimulus Generalization as a Function of Age in Children," *J. Exp. Psychol.,* LIII (1957), 180–83.

114. Melton, A. W. "The Science of Learning and the Technology of Educational Methods," *Harvard Educ. Rev.,* XXIX (1959), 84–95.

115. Meyer, W. J., and Offenbach, S. I. "Effectiveness of Reward and Punishment as a Function of Task Complexity," *J. Comp. Physiol. Psychol.,* LV (1962), 532–34.

116. Meyer, W. J., and Seidman, J. B. "Relative Effectiveness of Different Reinforcement Combinations on Concept Learning of Children at Two Developmental Levels," *Child Develpm.,* XXXII (1961), 117–28.

117. Miller, L. B., and Estes, B. W. "Monetary Reward and Motivation in Discrimination Learning," *J. Exp. Psychol.,* LXI (1961), 501–4.

118. Moore, O. K. *Early Reading and Writing* (Three-part motion picture). Guilford, Connecticut: Basic Education, Inc., 1960.

119. Munn, N. L. "Learning in Children," in *Manual of Child Psychology.* Edited by L. Carmichael. New York: John Wiley & Sons, 1954 (second edition).

120. Myers, N. "Extinction Following Partial and Continuous Primary and Secondary Reinforcement," *J. Exp. Psychol.,* LX (1960), 172–79.

121. Myers, N. A.; Craig, G. J.; and Myers, J. L. "Secondary Reinforcement as a Function of the Number of Reinforced Trials," *Child Develpm.,* XXXII (1961), 765–72.

122. Norcross, K. J. "Effects on Discrimination Performance of Similarity of Previously Acquired Stimulus Names," *J. Exp. Psychol.,* LVI (1958), 305–9.

123. Norcross, K. J., and Spiker, C. C. "Effects of Mediated Association on Transfer in Paired Associate Learning," *J. Exp. Psychol.,* LV (1958), 129–34.

124. ———. "The Effects of Type of Stimulus Pretraining on Discrimination Performance in Preschool Children," *Child Develpm.,* XXVIII (1957), 79–84.

125. Offenbach, S. I., and Meyer, W. J. "Reinforcer Acquisition in Discrimination Learning." Unpublished manuscript, 1962.

126. Orlando, R., and Bijou, S. W. "Single and Multiple Schedules of Reinforcement in Developmentally Retarded Children," *J. Exp. Anal. Behav.,* IV (1960), 339–48.

127. Osler, S. F., and Fivel, M. W. "Concept Attainment: I. The Role of Age

and Intelligence in Concept Attainment by Induction," *J. Exp. Psychol.*, LXII (1961), 1–8.

128. Osler, J. F., and Trautman, G. E. "Concept Attainment: II. Effect of Stimulus Complexity upon Concept Attainment at Two Levels of Intelligence," *J. Exp. Psychol.*, XLII (1961), 9–13.

129. Penney, R. K., and Croskery, J. M. "Excitatory *vs.* Inhibitory Tendencies in Children's Discrimination Learning." Unpublished manuscript, 1962.

130. Penney, R. K., and Lupton, A. A. "Children's Discrimination Learning as a Function of Reward and Punishment," *J. Comp. Physiol. Psychol.*, LIV (1961), 449–51.

131. Penney, R. K., and McCann, B. "The Instrumental Escape Conditioning of Anxious and Nonanxious Children," *J. Abn. Soc. Psychol.*, (in press).

132. Perkins, M. J.; Banks, H. P.; and Calvin, A. D. "The Effect of Delay on Simultaneous and Successive Discriminations in Children," *J. Exp. Psychol.*, XLVIII (1954), 416–18.

133. Razran, G. "The Observable Unconscious and the Inferable Conscious in Current Soviet Psychophysiology: Interoceptive Conditioning, Semantic Conditioning and the Orienting Reflex," *Psychol. Rev.*, LXVIII (1961), 81–147.

134. Reese, H. W. "Transposition in the Intermediate-size Problem by Preschool Children," *Child Develpm.*, XXXII (1961), 311–14.

135. ———. "The Distance Effect in Transposition in the Intermediate-size Problem," *J. Comp. Physiol. Psychol.*, LV (1962), 528–31.

136. ———. " 'Perceptual Set' in Young Children," *Child Develpm.* (in press).

137. ———. "Verbal Mediation as a Function of Age Level," *Psychol. Bull.* (in press).

138. Rheingold, H. L.; Gewirtz, J. L.; and Ross, H. W. "Social Conditioning of Vocalization in the Infant," *J. Comp. Physiol. Psychol.*, LII (1959), 68–73.

139. Rieber, M. "The Effect of CS Presence during Delay of Reward on the Speed of an Instrumental Response," *J. Exp. Psychol.*, LXI (1961), 290–94.

140. ———. "Shifts in Response-Reward Interval and Its Effect upon Response Speed," *Psychol. Rep.*, IX (1961), 393–98.

141. Ritchie, B. F.; Ebeling, E.; and Roth, W. "Evidence for Continuity in the Discrimination of Vertical and Horizontal Patterns," *J. Comp. Physiol. Psychol.*, XLIII (1950), 427–49.

142. Robinson, N. M., and Robinson, H. B. "A Method for the Study of Instrumental Avoidance Conditioning in Young Children," *J. Comp. Physiol. Psychol.*, LIV (1961), 20–23.

143. Roe, A. *The Making of a Scientist.* New York: Dodd, Mead & Co., 1953.

144. Rosenblith, J. F. "Learning by Imitation in Kindergarten Children," *Child Develpm.*, XXX (1959), 69–80.

145. Rudel, R. G. "The Transposition of Intermediate Size by Brain-damaged and Mongoloid Children," *J. Comp. Physiol. Psychol.*, LIII (1960), 89–94.

146. ———. "Transposition of Response by Children Trained in Intermediate-size Problems," *J. Comp. Physiol. Psychol.*, L (1957), 292–95.

147. ———. "Transposition of Response to Size in Children," *J. Comp. Physiol. Psychol.*, LI (1958), 386–90.

148. SCHRAMM, W. "Television in the Life of the Child–Implications for the School," in *New Teaching Aids for the American Classroom.* Stanford: Institute for Communication Research, 1960.

149. SCHRODER, H. M. "Development and Maintenance of the Preference Value of an Object," *J. Exp. Psychol.*, LI (1956), 139–41.

150. SHEPARD, W. O. "The Effect of Verbal Training on Initial Generalization Tendencies," *Child Develpm.*, XXVII (1956), 311–16.

151. ———. "Learning Set in Preschool Children," *J. Comp. Physiol. Psychol.*, L (1957), 15–17.

152. SHEPHARD, W. O., and SCHAEFFER, M. E. "The Effect of Concept Knowledge on Discrimination Learning," *Child Develpm.*, XXVII (1956), 173–78.

153. SIEGEL, P. S., and FOSHEE, J. G. "Molar Variability in the Mentally Defective," *J. Abnorm. Soc. Psychol.*, LXI (1960), 141–43.

154. SKINNER, B. F. "The Science of Learning and the Art of Teaching," *Harvard Educ. Rev.*, XXIV (1954), 86–97.

155. ———. "Teaching Machines," *Science*, CXXVIII (1958), 969–77.

156. SPENCE, K. W. "The Differential Response in Animals to Stimuli Varying within a Single Dimension," *Psychol. Rev.*, XLIV (1937), 430–44.

157. ———. "An Experimental Test of the Continuity and Noncontinuity Theories of Discrimination Learning," *J. Exp. Psychol.*, XXXV (1945), 253–66.

158. ———. "The Relation of Learning Theory to the Technology of Education," *Harvard Educ. Rev.*, XXIX (1959), 84–95.

159. SPIKER, C. C. "Associative Transfer in Verbal Paired Associate Learning," *Child Develpm.*, XXXI (1960), 73–88.

160. ———. "The Effects of Number of Reinforcements on the Strength of a Generalized Instrumental Response," *Child Develpm.*, XXVII (1956), 37–44.

161. ———. "Effects of Stimulus Similarity on Discrimination Learning," *J. Exp. Psychol.*, LI (1956), 393–95.

162. ———. "Experiments with Children on the Hypothesis of Acquired Distinctiveness and Equivalence of Cues." *Child Develpm.*, XXVII (1956), 253–63.

163. ———. "Performance on a Difficult Discrimination Following Pretraining with Distinctive Stimuli," *Child Develpm.*, XXX (1959), 513–21.

164. ———. "Research Methods in Children's Learning," in *Handbook of Research Methods in Child Development.* Edited by P. H. Mussen. New York: John Wiley & Sons, 1960.

165. ———. "The Stimulus Generalization Gradient as a Function of the Intensity of Stimulus Lights," *Child Develpm.*, XXVII (1956), 85–98.

166. ———. "Stimulus Pretraining and Subsequent Performance on the Delayed Reaction Experiment," *J. Exp. Psychol.*, LII (1956), 107–11.

167. ———. "Verbal Factors in the Discrimination Learning of Children," in *Basic Cognitive Processes in Children.* Edited by J. C. Wright and J. Kagan. Monograph of the Society for Research in Child Development (in press).

168. SPIKER, C. C.; GERJUOY, J. R.; and SHEPARD, W. O. "Children's Concept of Middle Sizedness and Performance on the Intermediate-size Problem," *J. Comp. Physiol. Psychol.*, XLIX (1956), 416–19.

169. Spiker, C. C., and Holton, R. B. "Associative Transfer in Motor Paired Associate Learning as a Function of Amount of First Task Practice," *J. Exp. Psychol.*, LVI (1958), 123–32.

170. Spiker, C. C., and Terrell, G. J. "Factors Associated with Transposition Behavior of Preschool Children," *J. Genet. Psychol.*, XXCVI (1955), 143–58.

171. Spiker, C. C., and White, S. H. "Differential Conditioning by Children as a Function of Effort Required in the Task," *Child Develpm.*, XXX (1959), 1–7.

172. Steigman, M. J., and Stevenson, H. W. "The Effect of Pretraining Reinforcement Schedules on Children's Learning," *Child Develpm.*, XXXI (1960), 53–58.

173. Stevenson, H. W. "Latent Learning in Children," *J. Exp. Psychol.*, XLVII (1954), 17–21.

174. ———. "Discrimination Learning," in *Handbook of Research in Mental Retardation.* Edited by N. R. Ellis. New York: McGraw-Hill Book Co., 1962.

175. Stevenson, H. W., and Bitterman, M. E. "The Distance-effect in the Transposition of Intermediate Size by Children," *Amer. J. Psychol.*, LXVIII (1955), 274–79.

176. Stevenson, H. W., and Iscoe, I. "Overtraining and Transposition in Children," *J. Exp. Psychol.*, XLVII (1954), 251–55.

177. Stevenson, H. W.; Iscoe, I.; and McConnell, C. "A Developmental Study of Transposition," *J. Exp. Psychol.*, XLIX (1955), 278–80.

178. Stevenson, H. W., and Knights, R. M. "Effect of Visual Reinforcement on the Performance of Normal and Retarded Children," *Percept. Mot. Skills*, XIII (1961), 119–26.

179. Stevenson, H. W., and Langford, T. "Time as a Variable in Transposition by Children," *Child Develpm.*, XXVIII (1957), 365–70.

180. Stevenson, H. W., and McBee, G. "The Learning of Object and Pattern Discriminations by Children," *J. Comp. Physiol. Psychol.*, LI (1958), 752–54.

181. Stevenson, H. W., and Pirojnikoff, L. H. "Discrimination Learning as a Function of Pretraining Reinforcement Schedules," *J. Exp. Psychol.*, LVI (1958), 41–44.

182. Stevenson, H. W., and Snyder, L. C. "Performance as a Function of the Interaction of Incentive Conditions," *J. Pers.*, XXVIII (1960), 1–11.

183. Stevenson, H. W., and Weir, M. W. "Response Shift as a Function of Overtraining and Delay," *J. Comp. Physiol. Psychol.*, LII (1959), 327–29.

184. ———. "Variables Affecting Children's Performance in a Probability Learning Task," *J. Exp. Psychol.*, LVII (1959), 403–12.

185. Stevenson, H. W.; Weir, M. W.; and Zigler, E. F. "Discrimination Learning in Children as a Function of Motive-Incentive Conditions," *Psychol. Reports*, V (1959), 95–98.

186. Stevenson, H. W., and Zigler, E. F. "Probability Learning in Children," *J. Exp. Psychol.*, LVI (1958), 185–92.

187. Terrell, G. "Manipulatory Motivation in Children," *J. Comp. Physiol. Psychol.*, LII (1959), 705–9.

188. TERRELL, G. "The Need for Simplicity in Research in Child Psychology," *Child Develpm.*, XXIX (1958), 303–10.

189. ———. "The Role of Incentive in Discrimination Learning in Children," *Child Develpm.*, XXIX (1958), 231–36.

190. TERRELL, G.; DURKIN, K.; and WIESLEY, M. "Social Class and the Nature of the Incentive in Discrimination Learning," *J. Abnorm. Soc. Psychol.*, LIX (1959), 270–72.

191. TERRELL, G., and KENNEDY, W. A. "Discrimination Learning and Transposition in Children as a Function of the Nature of the Reward," *J. Exp. Psychol.*, LIII (1957), 257–60.

192. TERRELL, G., and WARE, R. "Role of Delay of Reward in Speed and Size of Form Discrimination Learning in Childhood," *Child Develpm.*, XXXII (1961), 409–15.

193. UNDERWOOD, B. J. "Verbal Learning in the Educative Process." *Harvard Educ. Rev.*, XXIX (1959), 107–17.

194. WARE, R., and TERRELL, G. "Effects of Delayed Reinforcement on Associative and Incentive Factors." *Child Develpm.*, XXXII (1961), 789–93.

195. WEIR, M. W., and STEVENSON, H. W. "The Effect of Verbalization in Children's Learning as a Function of Chronological Age," *Child Develpm.*, XXX (1959), 143–49.

196. WHITE, B. N. "Reward, Punishment, and Reward-Punishment in Children's Discrimination Learning." Unpublished manuscript, 1962.

197. WHITE, B. N., and SPIKER, C. C. "The Effect of Stimulus Similarity on Amount of Cue-position Patterning in Discrimination Problems," *J. Exp. Psychol.*, LIX (1960), 131–36.

198. WHITE, S. H. "Effects of Pretraining with Varied Stimuli on Children's Discrimination Learning," *Child Develpm.*, XXXII (1961), 745–53.

199. ———. "Generalization of an Instrumental Response with Variation in Two Attributes of the CS," *J. Exp. Psychol.*, LVI (1958), 339–43.

200. WHITE, S. H., and GRIM, P. F. "Investigations of a Voluntary Generalization Paradigm," *Amer. Psychologist*, XVII (1962), 378.

201. WHITE, S. H., and PLUM, G. "Children's Eye Movements during a Discrimination Series," *Amer. Psychologist*, XVII (1962), 367.

202. ———. "Children's Eye Movements during Discrimination Learning with Varying Stimuli." Unpublished manuscript (1962).

203. WHITE, S. H., and SPIKER, C. C. "The Effect of a Variable Conditioned Stimulus upon the Generalization of an Instrumental Response," *Child Develpm.*, XXXI (1960), 313–20.

204. WHITE, S. H.; SPIKER, C. C.; and HOLTON, R. B. "Associative Transfer as Shown by Response Speeds in Motor Paired Associate Learning," *Child Develpm.*, XXXI (1960), 609–16.

205. WILSON, J. W. D., and DYKMAN, R. A. "Background Autonomic Activity in Medical Students," *J. Comp. Physiol. Psychol.*, LIII (1960), 405–11.

206. WILSON, W. C. "Imitation and the Learning of Incidental Cues by Preschool Children," *Child Develpm.*, XXIX (1958), 393–97.

207. WITKIN, H. A., *et al. Personality through Perception.* New York: Harper & Bros., 1954.

208. Wohlwill, J. F. "Absolute *vs.* Relational Discrimination on the Dimension of Number," *J. Genet. Psychol.*, XCVI (1960), 353–63.

209. Zeaman, D. A., and House, B. J. "Approach and Avoidance in the Discrimination Learning of Retardates," *Child Develpm.*, XXXIII (1962), 355–72.

210. Zeaman, D. A.; House, B. J.; and Orlando, R. "Use of Special Training Conditions in Visual Discrimination Learning by Imbeciles," *Amer. J. Ment. Def.*, LXIII (1958), 453–59.

CHAPTER VI

Research on Children's Thinking

MICHAEL A. WALLACH

Introduction

This chapter is concerned with current research on the development of children's thinking, concentrating on the work of the last two decades.[1] Within this period a new tradition of research, that of Piaget and his Geneva collaborators, has made its appearance and has contributed extensively to knowledge in this area. The importance of this contribution to the description of developmental aspects of children's thinking has yet to penetrate the United States. Here, with few exceptions, amazingly little secondary source material is available on anything other than Piaget's earliest books, translated in the late 1920's and early 1930's (e.g., **63, 64**). The Geneva group's major work, however, consists of the studies that have been conducted since then. While many of these are now translated, the empirical content of such books as *Le Développement des Quantités chez l'Enfant*, *Les Notions de Mouvement et de Vitesse chez l'Enfant*, *Play, Dreams, and Imitation in Childhood*, *The Child's Conception of Number*, *The Origins of Intelligence in Children*, *The Construction of Reality in the Child*, *The Growth of Logical Thinking from Childhood to Adolescence*, *La Genèse des Structures Logiques Élémentaires: Classifications et Sériations*, *The Child's Conception of Geometry*, and of the many further studies growing out of them, has been all but ignored by American psychologists and educators.

The sources of this neglect are not difficult to find. The studies by the Geneva group contain a close blending of empirical description with theoretical speculation. The speculation is of dispropor-

1. The preparation of this chapter was supported through the Co-operative Research Program of the Office of Education, U.S. Department of Health, Education, and Welfare.

tionate length and is couched in complex logico-mathematical terminology. It is possible, however, to disentangle empirical description from speculative theory and, when one does, there emerges an awareness that Piaget and others who have been doing related work —most notably, Inhelder—have made an unparalleled contribution to the task of observing and describing the development of thinking from birth through adolescence. The major purpose of this chapter is to try to present the descriptive information that emerges from this research.

Our emphasis, therefore, will be upon the main kinds of observations and descriptions of the development of thinking that have been gathered by the Geneva workers and others who have been pursuing similar lines. In addition, recent psychometric studies in the area of intelligence testing that bear on questions raised by the former work also will be reviewed.

Thinking as Continuous with Simpler Forms of Psychological Functioning

Ironically, a philosophically oriented European psychologist has located data that support the early statements of Watson and Skinner to the effect that thinking involves internalized behavior. Piaget's observations of infants suggest that thinking does not emerge suddenly at a particular point in ontogenesis but, rather, that it can be traced to the progressive impact of experience upon sensorimotor functioning. For example, the use of implements as aids in solving problems seems to arise only after the prior occurrence of widespread behavior involving those implements, and development of the ability to represent external events may depend on a gradual reduction in the extensiveness of the responses which those events call forth. This view stands in striking contrast to the traditional separation found in developmental psychology textbooks between the consideration of sensorimotor skills and of intellect. The view shows a most interesting congruence, on the other hand, with recent attempts by learning theorists to conceptualize cognitive activities in terms of fractional anticipatory response mechanisms (**9, 37, 60**). Theories of meaning and of representation which interpret concepts or categories as dispositions to respond in certain ways (e.g., **60, 61**) find a source of corroboration in Piaget's data concerning the newborn's increasing commerce with the environment. These descriptions, to which we now turn, suggest that development results in an increasing internalization of actions originally performed on objects in the world. The internalization at first constitutes a literal simulacrum of these actions, a covert copy of actions just performed or about to be performed; but later gains in complexity, since covert simulacra can combine in ways not available to the original actions.

Development from Birth to Approximately the Second Year

REPRESENTATIONAL PROCESSES: MOTOR RECOGNITION AND IMITATION

The earliest behaviors of the infant consist of reflex-like activities, such as sucking, swallowing, and crying. Learning quickly leads to modifications in such reflexes. Through discrimination, for example, the child differentiates the particular stimulus conditions to which a response such as sucking is attached. A hungry baby will reject from his mouth an adult's finger or a blanket offered to him. Generalization also occurs, for there are conditions under which an ever widening array of stimuli becomes adequate to elicit a particular response. Thus, while the hungry infant's sucking soon comes to show selectivity, the sated infant may suck its blanket, pillow, or a proferred adult's finger (**70**). Such generalization seems to be other than a failure to discriminate (**46**), since it does not decrease but, rather, proliferates with further improvement in discrimination.

With increasing age, other responses also undergo both broadening of the range of stimuli that become invested with the power to elicit them and refinement of their relationship to particular stimuli. The latter type of change includes a shaping of the response to the nature of the stimulus, such as more accurate grasping of differently shaped objects, and a selectiveness of response depending on motivational conditions.

By the age of three or four months, a sated infant applies each of the responses in his repertoire to an object offered him: he shakes it, rubs it against hard surfaces such as the wicker of his bassinet, strikes with it, puts it in his mouth. As new responses are developed, these are applied to whatever objects fit them. Thus, by eight to ten months, an unfamiliar object offered to the infant may be thrown down and picked up, caused to slide, squeezed, scratched, patted, swung about, or splashed in the bath (**70, 73**).

Further observations suggest that the response families applied to each particular object by the infant constitute or are part of the object's "meaning." When an otherwise occupied infant catches sight of an object to which he customarily makes certain responses, he interrupts his other activity only long enough to carry out an abridged, perfunctory performance of the customary responses and then resumes the activity from which he was distracted. Thus, for example, at almost six and one-half months, one of Piaget's daughters notices two celluloid parrots which sometimes had been attached to the hood of her bassinet but which now have been attached to a chandelier beyond reach. When they were attached to her bassinet, she had been accustomed to shaking her legs at them. She clearly but very briefly shakes her legs in the same fashion now. In subsequent days, if, from a distance, she glimpses her dolls, which she is accustomed to swinging with her hand when they are within reach, she limits herself to outlining the movement of swinging them with her hand. About a month later, the same sight elicits an even more abortive and effortless opening and closing of her hand. These and similar observations suggest a progressive ability to internalize reactions to the perception of objects and suggests that these fractional responses constitute or are part of the recognition of the objects in question (see **70, 73, 98**).

These fractional responses soon gain greater freedom, in that they no longer consist only in simulacral reconstitutions of earlier behavior to the object in question. The representation or imitation becomes more schematic. The beginnings of this transition appear in the change from a full outline of a handswing to a mere opening and closing of the hand. These schematic representations soon become useful in problem-solving. Consider, for example, the following observation at almost one and a half years. One of Piaget's daughters already has had practice with turning over a matchbox in order to shake out a desired chain when the drawer of the box is rather fully pulled out and with poking in her index finger and extracting the chain when the drawer of the box is only partly pulled out. Now Piaget returns the chain to the matchbox and closes the drawer even farther. The child first tries to insert her finger into the slit, to no avail. She then interrupts this activity, observes the slit with great attention, and, a number of times in succession, gradually opens her mouth from a narrow to a wide aperture. Following several repetitions of this graduated opening of her mouth, she returns to the box and, without hesitation, pulls the drawer open farther and extracts the chain. Each time the problem is repeated, the child immediately pulls the drawer out before trying to grasp the chain. It appears that gradually widening the aperture of her mouth served to represent the "pullable" property of the drawer, and this representational response, in turn, functioned as a tool of discovery, since the drawer had never been pulled before.

Another kind of freedom that makes its appearance in imitative or representational behavior by the age of approximately one and a half years concerns the ability to defer the behavior to a time when the referent is not perceptually present. Thus, for example, one of Piaget's daughters at this age was visited by a boy who displayed a temper tantrum, stamping his feet violently and screaming as he tried to push his playpen backwards and to escape from it. This scene was viewed by the daughter with amazement, as she had probably never witnessed such an occurrence before. The next day she went through a schematic behavior sequence containing fractional elements of the scene she had observed, but without the previously attendant intense effect shown by the boy. When in her playpen, she cried and tried to push it while stamping her foot lightly a few times—the whole sequence being more controlled, less violent, than its model (see **1, 29, 38, 68, 70, 73, 106**). Representational behavior thus makes its first appearance well in advance of language.

MEANS-ENDS BEHAVIOR: PROBLEM-SOLVING

It is no accident that the use of means to secure goals becomes observable at approximately eight months, for it is around this time that the child becomes adept at categorizing both familiar and new objects in terms of their response-defined uses. This period devoted to learning the properties of environmental manipulanda appears to have a similar function for the child as the utilization of sticks by chimpanzees in Birch's (**10**) and Jackson's (**42**) demonstration that "insightful" problem-solution involving the raking in of a lure depends on prior experience with the uses of stick-like objects. The child has begun to develop the potentiality for efficient utilization of means-objects in problem-solution.

Prior to this age any associative linkage between a response and some environmental effect is sufficient to lead the child to repeat the response in the apparent expectation of repeating the effect, regardless of consideration of spatial proximity. For example, Piaget's son at about three and a half months had been swinging a chain which was attached to a rattle hooked to the hood of his bassinet, thereby causing movement and noise in the rattle. When the chain subsequently dropped from his hand, the infant continued nevertheless to swing his fist for five minutes while watching the rattle. Subsequently, the same reaction was made in an apparent attempt to induce similar effects in other objects—for instance, to induce continued movement of a book or of a bottle which had been swung for a while by an adult at a distance.

From about eight or nine months there appears to be some understanding of the spatial relations necessary to achieve effects with means-objects. "Magical" behaviors of the sort just described drop out in favor of applications of means-objects which respect the properties that they actually possess, such as the need for spatial contact between hand and means-object in order to produce effects. The observations suggest that this transition results from further experience with the use of such objects. For example, prior to the skilful utilization of sticks as rakes there occurs a gradual addition of rake-like properties to the child's behavior with sticks. Thus, Piaget's daughter had an elongated rattle in her hand when she saw a doll and tried to touch it with the hand holding the rattle. Because the hand was filled, the rattle, and not her hand, touched the doll. Once touched in this manner, she repeated the action a number of times. Another daughter, while striking at a pail with a stick, accidentally moved the pail by means of the stick's blows, noticed this, and kept repeating the action. By such chance occurrences as these, stick-like objects come to be regarded as extensions of the hand. And following sufficient experiences of this kind, the child uses sticks proficiently as means for pushing desired goals within grasping range. Generalization also rapidly ensues to any object that can serve the appropriate function: A banana or book will be used if a stick is not handy. The importance of such developmental observations (**70**) in demonstrating the role of past experience in "insightful" problem-solution is apparent.

Similar observational sequences also are found with regard to the use of other means-objects. The act of pulling a cushion in order to obtain a watch supported on the cushion's far side, for example, develops only after months of practice at pulling objects and noting the transit of their far side as a function of moving their near side. Once again, after this support function has become a well-learned part of the child's definition of the relevant means-objects, transfer quickly spreads to related situations. The same kinds of results have been reported on the use of a string to obtain an attached lure.

We already have noted that representational behavior with the referent absent from the immediate perceptual field begins to make its appearance during the second year. This ability to represent absent stimuli has implications for the child's comprehension of means-ends relationships, since, given relevant past experience, it permits the hypothesizing of causes from observed effects, and the anticipation of effects from observed causes. As an example of the former, one of Piaget's children, at almost one and a half years, tries in vain to open a gate which is restrained by an armchair on the other side. The chair cannot be seen from the child's position, nor is there any noise since it holds the gate fast. After a period of fruitless attempts to force the gate, the child suddenly stops, runs around the wall to the other side, removes the armchair, and opens the gate with a triumphant expression. As an example of the anticipation of an effect from a given cause, another of his children, at the same age, was interrupted while playing an absorbing game and placed, much against her will, in her playpen. After a period of calling from her playpen to no avail, she clearly expresses a need to visit the lavatory, although such a visit had just occurred within the last few minutes. Once let out of her playpen she runs back to her game! The child's anticipation of the effect that would ensue upon her expressing the need in question was veridical, indeed (see **67, 68, 70, 73**).

CONCEPTUALIZATION OF OBJECTS

In discussing the development of means-ends behavior and representational processes over the first two years, there is an implied resultant of changes in the growing child's conception of the objects and space that surround him. Consider the kinds of information that the Geneva group and others have gathered toward specifying these changes more exactly (**70, 73, 101**).

In general, observations suggest that the spatial organization of properties that define the enduring "thingness" of objects is a laboriously acquired construction. The establishment of co-ordinations between different kinds of sensory information seems to be critically important in this construction: the expectation of being able to suck that which one grasps, to grasp that which one sucks, to see that which one grasps, to grasp that which one sees, and so forth. Such co-ordinations appear with increasing frequency between approximately three and six months and, presumably, result from repeated co-occurrences among the kinds of information in question. The child begins to respond to objects in terms of a family of use-properties that cut across sense modalities: If a rattle is placed within sight, and if his hand is within sight also, then he will try to grasp the rattle, and, once grasped, will try to suck it. Still later, he comes to be able to grasp what he sees even if his hand is not in the same visual field.

Before approximately the eighth or ninth month, the obvious concealment of a desired goal-object fails to elicit any behavior that would suggest an awareness of the object's continued existence in its concealed location. If, for example, a doll that was being examined with great interest by a very young child is taken and covered with a cloth before the child's eyes, the child immediately stops reacting. A toy which one of Piaget's daughters was trying to grasp fell behind a fold in the sheet on which she was lying. Even though she followed the toy's movement with her hand, she stopped paying attention as soon as the toy disappeared. On each of a number of trials in this and related situations, Piaget made the toy reappear after its initial concealment, whereupon the child immediately tried to grasp it. When, however, the toy was quite obviously concealed once more behind the sheet, the child's reactions immediately ceased. Analogous behavior was obtained in various observations where Piaget's hand constituted the means of concealment: When the child was about to grasp some appealing object placed on its lap, Piaget interposed his hand between the object and the child's eyes.

The child would give up immediately, as if the object had ceased to exist.

That such behavior is not merely revealing of insufficient memory capacity becomes evident in the following few months, in which search activity does ensue upon the concealment of an object, but the child still has gross deficiencies in his view of how objects behave. If an object is concealed under screen A, the child at about ten months of age will locate it. But if the same object is then concealed under screen B, the child, even though he has carefully observed all of this, immediately searches for it under A, and then gives up. The child expects to find the hidden object in the place where it was initially hidden and found, regardless of where he subsequently saw it concealed. A month or so later the child can solve the above problem appropriately, but if the object is not found immediately under B (if, for instance, it is placed far behind a cushion so that it is not revealed when the child raises the cushion's edge) then the child reverts forthwith to searching under A. It is as if the object concealed and found under A has not been wholly identified with the same object which was then concealed under B. There is not full conservation of the object in the face of spatial dislocations; it is not yet maintained as invariant across displacements.

Invisible displacements still baffle the child, however, at an age when visible displacements of the foregoing kind are mastered. Thus, at a little over one year of age, the child will find under B an object which first was concealed under A, was found by the child, and then was placed by the adult under B while the child watched. If the adult buries the object deeply under B at this point, the child will search assiduously under B and may finally give up, but will not return to searching under A. When, however, the transit of the object is not visible, the old errors return. If the object is hidden in Piaget's hand when moved to its place of concealment under A, the child of this age will examine Piaget's hand but will tend not to look under A. Somewhat later, he will look under A after examining the adult's hand, but if the object then is once more hidden in the hand and this time concealed under B, the child, after examining the hand, searches not under B but rather looks under A once more.

Finally, between one and a half and two years, the type of problem described above is solved appropriately. Properties concerned with the hypothesized consequences of manipulation have been added to the child's emerging conception of an object. Processes must occur analogous to, but obviously not in the thing-language of, hypotheses such as, "If I lift the hat, then the doll will be observable again since it was last seen being covered by the hat," "If the doll is not in his hand, then it must have been left under the hat and will be observable again if I lift the hat." Complex co-ordinations have been established concerning kinds of information that would be received if conditions were changed in certain ways. The psychological definition of a thing attained by the child is intriguingly reminiscent of the epistemological definition provided by phenomenalist philosophers beginning with Mill's description of an object as "the permanent possibility of sensation" (**4**, **81**). The patterns of impressions that have been cumulating for the child lead him to postulate a world of enduring objects that can be explored through different senses, in substitution for the world of fleeting experiences with which he seemed to begin. Although a modicum of conservation or stability regarding the contents of his psychological environment thus has been achieved, the world still is conceived of as much more malleable, fickle, variable, than it in fact is—or at least than he later will come to believe it is as a result of his further dealings with it.

Since the findings we have been considering are based largely on Piaget's pioneering observations of his own three children, it is evident that further work along these lines is in order. It is appropriate to note, however, that various checks on the internal consistency of the observations were carried out in some of Piaget's studies. The report by White and Castle (**101**) provides an example of the kinds of additional observations needed in these areas. See also Woodward (**107**) for a related study on mental defectives.

In summary of this section, we have considered the developing child's assignment of meaning to objects in terms of their response-defined uses prior to language, the role of experience in his use of means-objects in problem-solving, and his learning of the conservation or invariance of objects across changes in location and in point of view.

Development from Approximately the Third to the Eleventh Years

CONSERVATION OF PROPERTIES ACROSS IRRELEVANT CHANGES: AMOUNT, WEIGHT, VOLUME

The term "conservation" refers to the understanding that no change has occurred regarding one or more aspects of an object or a relationship, despite change in other perceivable features. Just as conservation of the sheer existence of objects is a slow achievement —the notion of their multiple sensory manifestations and their permanence despite spatial dislocations—so also is the conservation, despite irrelevant changes, of other properties in terms of which we describe objects. Among such properties are amount of matter (the quantity of some basic unit that cannot be compressed), weight (the downward force of an object), and volume (the space occupied by an object). It is evident that the possibility of understanding the latter concepts requires prior development of the thing-concept, but it also seems to be the case that possession of the thing-concept is not sufficient. The physical environment to which the young child responds is still a far cry from the one surrounding the adult—it is still highly dependent on moment-to-moment changes in perceptual impressions.

Consider first the child's understanding of continuous quantity. In the basic experiments by Piaget and Inhelder (**76**), the experimenter gives the child a ball of clay and requests him to fashion another one just like it. When the child has done this to his satisfaction, one ball is used as a standard while the other is subjected to various changes in appearance: It may be cut up into small pieces, or rolled into a sausage shape, or flattened into a pancake. Or, the child is given two glasses of identical dimensions containing the same quantities of liquid. Using one glass as the standard, the contents of the other are poured into other kinds of containers: two small glasses, or a glass which is tall and thin, or a low, trough-like container.

As an example of how the child's comparison of the two quantities is obtained regarding amount of matter, the experimenter inquires whether the sausage-shaped piece provides just as much to eat as the ball-shaped piece; or whether someone with the small glasses has just as much to drink as someone with the large glass. In some procedures the child is asked to select the piece of toffee he is willing to pay more for (**50**); conservation is revealed by the child's not having a systematic preference for standard over deformed toffee or vice versa. To compare the weights of the two quantities, the child is asked to predict whether the ball and the sausage, when placed on the opposite pans of a balance scale, will keep the two arms of the scale out straight. Regarding volume, the child is shown that each of two balls of clay displaces the water in a vessel to the same level. Then the form of one of the balls is changed and the interviewer asks if it will still make the water go up to that same new level.

Observations with such materials suggest that before the age of six or seven perceivable changes in form are believed to render the comparison quantity unequal to the standard in regard to weight, volume, or amount of matter. Over the next few years, amount of matter comes to be regarded as invariant across changes in form, while weight and volume still are considered to vary. Then weight comes to be understood as invariant, but volume does not. And in adolescence, finally, volume comes to be regarded as invariant despite shape changes. For further evidence confirming the general transition from nonconservation to conservation for amount, weight, and volume, see Lovell (**47**); Lovell and Ogilvie (**50, 51, 52**).

To be sure, linguistic factors may enter to influence the absolute ages at which these types of conservation first are exhibited. Experimental attempts to minimize effects of language through, for example, a matching-from-sample technique in which the child is rewarded for selecting that one of several comparison stimuli which is the same as the sample in some relevant respect (see, for instance, Braine, **14**; Wohlwill, **104**; Wohlwill and Lowe, **105**) suggest that in this way one or two years often can be cut off the particular age norms noted by Piaget in connection with various cognitive attainments. Similar systematic shifts in age norms also have been found as a function of varying the sociocultural status of the children. But the same general developmental sequences have, on the whole, been obtained by such work. See, in addition to the studies already cited, Elkind (**21, 22, 23**), Hyde (**39**), Pinard (**80**), Smedslund (**85; 87–93**), and Vinh-Bang (**97**), for further results replicating the basic outline of these sequences. Here, as elsewhere in the sections on development from the third to eleventh and the twelfth to fourteenth years, the main outlines of the original Geneva observations have been confirmed in numerous subsequent studies. Furthermore, the more recent Geneva researches (e.g., **78**) seem to have yielded to the Anglo-Saxon custom of specifying the number of subjects on which generalizations are based. We learn that over two thousand children, for example, constitute the sample in the study just cited.

What seem to be the major problems underlying the nonconservations described and the major cognitive changes reflected in their attainment? Regarding amount of matter, for example, the nonconserving child who sees one of the two balls of clay rolled into a sausage reports it to contain more than the other ball because it is longer, *or* to contain less than the other because it is thinner: He observes length or width, but not the relation between the two. If one of the two balls is cut up into several pieces, he reports it to contain more because there are more pieces, or less because they are smaller. He observes the number of pieces or size of pieces, but not the relation between these two attributes. Later, a modicum of conservation appears, but it is found to be only uneasily maintained in the face of perceptual impressions of size differences. If the comparison ball is only somewhat elongated, it will be reported to contain the same amount of clay as the standard; but if elongated beyond a certain degree, then the child lapses once again into nonconservation. The occurrence of such intermediate reactions, by the way, indicates that nonconservation does not simply result from a failure to realize that the whole of the comparison quantity is to be judged. Later still, an age is reached when there are no longer any breakdowns of conservation in the face of extreme shape differences. The child explains that the comparison stimulus contains the same amount of clay as the standard because what the sausage loses in thickness it gains in length; or because, while there are more pieces of clay, they also are smaller; because nothing has been added or taken away but, rather, just moved around; because the sausage or the several pieces can be molded into a ball again. Similar response transitions occur regarding weight and volume.

The cognitive achievements underlying conservation of amount of matter, hence, seem to be (*a*) an ability to take account of the joint effect of change in two perceived aspects of the material rather than being limited to considering only one aspect at a time, with the result that compensatory changes can be noted; (*b*) the development of an "atomic" theory of matter—a conception that matter consists of small particles that simply change their positions with respect to one another when shape transformations occur; and (*c*) an ability to hypothesize that a reverse change of the transformed shape back into the original could be performed.

To examine these interpretations in more detail, Piaget and Inhelder (**76**) conducted an experiment in which several lumps of sugar are dropped into one of two identical glasses previously demonstrated through weighing to contain equal amounts of water. The rise in water level caused by adding the sugar is marked on the glass, its weight increase is noted, and the child is questioned about what is happening to the sugar as he watches it dissolve. In a fashion reminiscent of nonconservation regarding the object concept, the young child believes that the perceived disappearance of the sugar corresponds to its real annihilation: The child expects that, after dissolving is completed, the water level and weight of the glass containing the sugar will drop back to those of the other glass. Some speculate that a trace of sweet taste may hover, ghost-like (without mass, weight, or volume), in the water for a while afterward, but it, too, is expected to vanish presently. The older child, on the other hand, believes that the water level and weight of the glass will remain higher even after the added sugar can no longer be seen, arguing that (*a*) the sugar is being broken up into very small pieces; but the smaller the pieces become, the more of them there are (change in one attribute compensating for change in another); (*b*) when the pieces become small enough, then, one can't see them any more, but they can be seen if we had sharper eyes; (*c*) the very small pieces could be reassembled into the original cube: thus, a child of approximately eleven years says, "If you take all the little pieces, that makes the big lump again."

When first attained, conservation of matter may, in some cases, be tied to specific materials. Lovell and Ogilvie (**50**), for example, found that some children who exhibited nonconservation in the clay experiment nevertheless showed conservation when a rubber band was stretched and they were asked if it contained the same amount of rubber in this condition as before. Analogously, Beard (**7**) and Hyde (**39**) found that some children who showed nonconservation in the clay experiment nevertheless exhibited conservation when the same type of experiment was carried out with liquids. Differential experience with particular kinds of materials, therefore, may be influential in the initial occurrence of matter conservation. Put another way, such conservation does not necessarily emerge full blown immediately but, rather, may at first be limited to certain familiar materials and only later increase its generality.

Why is conservation of weight more difficult to attain than that of matter, and conservation of volume harder still? After invariance of amount of matter across shape changes is achieved, the child still believes that weight must vary with shape because, according to some of Piaget and Inhelder's findings, he seems to define weight in terms of the feeling of greater or less pressure when holding something, and this pressure feeling is stronger when, for instance, the same mass held on the palm is shaped into a column than when it is shaped into a pancake. That volume conservation is even more difficult may, in part, be a result of the type of test–predictions of water displacement–customarily used in its study. As Lunzer (**54**) and Lovell (**47**) point out, comparison of water displacements is a relatively rare happening in the child's experience and also requires the prior recognition that the volume of the displaced water is conserved. But, in addition, the greater difficulty of volume conservation may result in part from the view–frequently found in the child's first atomic-particle conception and certainly understandable in terms of some of his experiences–that each particle of matter will expand or be compressed depending on its spatial location and, hence, on how many other particles are pressing down upon it.

The question of what is learned in the development of conservations such as these will be further clarified if knowledge is gained concerning the effects of various practice conditions. In the literature on practice conditions are, for instance, studies concerning number by Churchill (**18**) and Wohlwill and Lowe (**105**); classification by Morf (**59**); spatial order by Greco (**32**), and substance and weight by Smedslund (**85, 87–94**). Additional work, suggesting that the effects of practice depend on initial developmental level, includes papers by Goustard (**31**), Greco (**33**), Matalon (**57**), and Smedslund (**95**). Smedslund (**89**), for example, compared children who had already exhibited conservation of weight in a pretest with clay objects and children who had failed to show it in the pretest but had subsequently been taught it via training in which the child's predictions about the weights of standard and deformed objects were checked each time on a scale. Such training was continued to the point where the latter group showed conservation with explanations that were indistinguishable from those of the former group. When an attempt was made to extinguish such conservation by comparing the weights of standard and deformed objects after a subterfuge had left the former heavier than the latter, all who had learned conservation during the experimental training lapsed back into nonconservation explanations. On the other hand, about half of those who had shown conservation in the pretest resisted the attempted extinction, searching for conservation-consistent interpretations such as, "We must have lost some clay on the floor." This evidence suggests that, once acquired, the conservation of weight is difficult to extinguish. A superficially similar concept acquired through a controlled but limited training regimen is not equivalent.

Smedslund (**90**) also tried to discourage the use of perceived largeness as a presumedly veridical cue to heaviness by means of training in which, for example, the larger of two objects was demonstrated to be much lighter than the smaller, and objects equal in size and the same in shape were demonstrated to be very much different in weight. Such attempts did not succeed in hastening children's acquisition of weight conservation across shape changes. They still responded without conservation and continued to explain their judgments of weight differences in terms of the view that largeness is a veridical cue to greater weight.

These experiments suggest that it is difficult to facilitate the acquisition of weight conservation with training that demonstrates the irrelevance of shape and size to weight. This does not mean that training can have no effect, but rather that the requisite learning must be extensive and, perhaps, that the effectiveness of a given type or amount of experience is relative to the conceptual attainments already at the child's disposal—a "discontinuity" theory of the effects of experience. Smedslund's work also suggests that conservation of amount of matter tends to precede conservation of weight. Perhaps the former must be attained before experience can lead to acquisition of the latter. We shall examine in the following section some direct evidence supporting the view that the utility of a given amount and type of training in conservation depends on whether or not some rudiments of the concept in question already have appeared.

CONSERVATION OF PROPERTIES ACROSS IRRELEVANT CHANGES: HORIZONTALITY, LENGTH, AREA

A further example of the effects of conservation training involves the concept of an invariant horizontal. Smedslund (**95**), following work by Piaget and Inhelder (**77**), presented each of 27 children aged five to seven with a picture of a bottle half-filled with water and asked the children to notice the position of the water in the bottle. The child was then requested to draw in the water surface on pictures of each of six bottles tilted at various angles and presented one at a time. There followed a period of observation demonstrating the invariance of the water level across changes in angle of the container: the child watched while a flat-sided bottle half-filled with tinted water was rotated slowly around a full 360 degrees, with a stop for a few seconds after each successive 30-degree step. After this experience, the pictures of the six tilted bottles were presented again, and the child once more was requested to draw in the water surfaces.

The drawings were scored by two independent judges for number correct in the preobservation set and number of improvements from pre- to postobservation set. Of the nine children having no correct drawings in the preobservation set, eight showed no improvement, and only one showed one or more improvements in the postobservation set. Of the 16 children having at least one correct drawing in the initial set, only one showed no improvement, while 15 exhibited at least one improvement in the postobservation set. Since there were no overt differences between these groups in their attention to the actual bottle during its rotation, these results suggest that only the children who showed some initial traces of the horizontality concept profited at all from observing this rotation. It appears, therefore, that before a rudimentary reference system has been constructed—as reflected in some initial traces of a horizontality concept—experience with horizontality will not aid the further development of that concept.

Among other spatial invariances whose development has been studied are those of length and area. In one experiment by Piaget, Inhelder, and Szeminska (**79**), for example, two straight sticks, each about 5 cm. in length, are set up parallel to each other with their ends aligned. The child is asked which of the two sticks is longer or whether they are the same length. All children judge them to be the same length. Then one stick is moved forward a centimeter or two, but kept parallel. Children four or five years of age now claim that the stick that was moved has become longer. What is the basis for their claim? Most of the children who make the claim follow the front edge of the moving stick with their eyes, thus ignoring the compensatory change in the rear edge. Their judgment seems to be based on a comparison of the relative positions of the two front edges, as if they cannot readily take joint account of changes in both rear and front edges. Fraisse and Vautrey (**30**) report a study in which beads are moved the same distance along parallel wires from different starting points. They report that some improvement occurs in children's judgments of the distance moved, if the experimenter attempts to make the children remember where the beads start. This observation clearly is related to the finding that the very young child cannot readily watch the trailing as well as the leading edge of the moving stick but tends, rather, to concentrate on the latter, due to its perceptual prominence.

What further events seem to underlie the transition to an adult conception of length? When the sticks have been staggered, the child of five or six sometimes expresses uncertainty as to whether they are still the same length until he is given an opportunity to realign them. As in the case of quantity conservation, it looks as if length conservation may depend in part on an actual and then a hypothetical restoration of the originally perceived equality: On the notion that if the sticks are lined up again, then their equality will once more become perceptually apparent even though not apparent now. The verdict of this "test by reversibility"—i.e., test by retracing one's steps and thereby returning to one's starting point—does not at first necessarily convince the child. A child who may abide by the verdict when the change in alignment is not too great may, nevertheless, be dominated once again by the perceived discrepancy when a more extensive change in alignment is shown. A child of five, for instance, shown two five-centimeter sticks parallel and in alignment, judged them to be the same length. After one stick was advanced one centimeter and the length question was repeated, the child realigned them and said, "Yes, they're still the same size." When the experimenter then slid one of the sticks around so that it was perpendicular to and touching the other, the child denied that they were the same length, judging the perpendicular longer, despite the test by reversibility that he himself performed a moment before. The apparent difference in length now dominated his decision.

Perceptual impressions of inequality no longer influence the judgment of the child of six to seven years of age. The explanation offered (after parallel sticks, when staggered, are judged still to be the same in length) includes a statement that the difference created between the leading edges is compensated for by the opposite difference created between the trailing edges. "There's a little space there [front edges] and there's the same little space there [rear edges]." Other children of this age explain the same judgment by invoking a hypothetical reversal of the displacement, avowing that if a reversal were carried out it would re-establish the original alignment of the sticks. Both types of explanations—that in terms of compensatory changes in two related variables and that in terms of reversibility—also were observed in the development of quantity conservation. Research by Lovell, Healey, and Roland (**49**) has replicated the general findings on length conservation just described.

The conservation of area was studied in an experiment by Piaget, Inhelder, and Szeminska (**79**). The child is shown two identical rectangles of green cardboard which are said to be two meadows. Beside each meadow the experimenter places a toy cow, noting that the cow has the whole meadow's grass to eat. The child is asked to satisfy himself that the two meadows are exactly the same in size, so that the child then asserts that the two cows have the same amount of grass to eat. Next the experimenter informs the child that the farmer who owns one meadow has decided to build a house, and thereupon deposits a model house on one plot. The subject is asked if the two cows have the same amount of grass to eat, and all children answer that the cow in the meadow without the house has more. The other farmer also has decided to build a house, however, so that an identical house is placed in the homologous position on the other meadow. When asked once more if the two cows now have the same amount of grass to eat, all children agree that they do. At this point the experimenter adds another house to each meadow, asking the usual question; but while the second house is situated away from the first in one meadow, it is placed adjacent to the first in the other. Younger children (approximately age five) believe that the area is greater in the plot where the houses are adjacent, or will believe this as soon as a third house is added to each plot in the same way—spaced apart from the others in one meadow but placed adjacent to the others in the second meadow.

With older children, further houses are added, a pair at a time, in the same manner—the successive members of each pair being spaced out in one plot but placed adjacent to one another in the second plot. Some subjects who maintained conservation thus far will now be able to resist the differing perceptual configurations no longer and will decide that the plot with the adjacent houses yields more to eat than the other. Then, by age seven or eight, the child maintains that both cows have the same amount to eat no matter how many pairs of houses have been added to the plots. Work by Lovell, Healey, and Roland (**49**) has confirmed the general developmental sequence found in the above experiment, although these authors report that most of the children in their sample either lost conservation of area early in the series or maintained it across a large number of houses—i.e., few intermediate cases were observed.

The conceptual development just noted suggests once again an increasing ability to withstand the influence of perceptually prominent but irrelevant features—here the cluttered or uncluttered appearance of equal areas—in rendering one's decision about equality of area.

In closing this section, it is of interest to consider the crucial role played by conservation of area in Wertheimer's (**100**) description of how children who "really understand" area find the area of a parallelogram. He discusses children who had been taught how to determine the area of a rectangle and then were asked, although they had never done so before, to find the area of a nonrectangular parallelogram. Those who could solve the problem were the ones who were able to make compensatory changes in spatial positions of parts of the parallelogram such that the area was redistributed into the form of a rectangle: They would adjust for the extension at one end by adding that part to the gap at the other end. This behavior suggests an understanding of the ideas of compensatory differences and/or reversibility, both of which, as we have seen, are invoked by children who possess the various conservations we have discussed.

CONSERVATION OF PROPERTIES ACROSS IRRELEVANT CHANGES: NUMBER, DURATION

Developmental studies on conservation concerning two other aspects of the child's conceptual world—number and duration—will be briefly described. In the case of number, a typical experiment by Piaget (**69**) begins with six egg-cups which are arranged in a row near a pile of eggs. The child is asked to take just enough eggs for the cups—an egg for each cup, no more and no less. After the child puts one egg in each cup—and a child of about four or five readily does so—the experimenter then takes the eggs out and places them in a row parallel to but spaced farther apart than the cups. Now the child maintains that if he put one egg into each cup there would be some eggs left over. When told to go ahead, the child is startled to find that the eggs and cups correspond. At this point the experimenter once more removes the eggs, placing them this time in a row parallel to but spaced closer together than the cups. The child now insists that if he put one egg into each cup there would be some cups left over. Once again, when the child goes ahead, he exhibits surprise—sometimes even appearing quite upset—upon finding that the eggs and cups correspond. Thus, the one-for-one correspondence between eggs and cups demonstrated by the child does not suffice to maintain the child's judgments of equality when perceptual conditions are altered. The kinds of errors just described occur even though the child can count to a number well above the number of cups or eggs being used. The ability to enumerate collections by counting still leaves the child far from an understanding of number conservation. This finding has been reported by Dodwell (**19**), Hyde (**39**), Wohlwill (**104**), and Wohlwill and Lowe (**105**). With increasing age, development toward conservation takes place.

Analogous sequences are found with other experimental materials: for instance, when the one-for-one correspondence is given the form of an exchange of each of four pennies for each of four flowers. Related studies by Beard (**7**), Greco (**34**), and Inhelder and Noelting (**40**), among others, provide further confirmation for these general results.

In sum, the evidence of these various reports strongly points to an early period in which number is responded to purely on a perceptual basis despite the ability to count. Given, for example, Wohlwill's very careful research (**104**) with matching-from-sample techniques supporting this proposition, it is difficult to consider as seriously conflicting the negative results reported by Estes (**28**) in a study open to criticism that Wohlwill (**104**: 368) has discussed.

As in the case of some of the other conservations described, so also in the case of number conservation a start has been made in the study of sociocultural influences (see, e.g., Hyde, **39**; Slater, **84**) and the effects of controlled experience (see, e.g., Churchill, **18**; Wohlwill, **103**; Wohlwill and Lowe, **105**). Concerning the effects of sociocultural factors, variation in absolute age norms has been found but not in over-all developmental sequences. Concerning the effects of controlled experience, Wohlwill and Lowe have found, for example, that repeated demonstration to the child of the irrelevance of perceived arrangement does not necessarily lead to number conservation, just as Smedslund's analogous work demonstrating to the child the irrelevance of shape and size cues to weight did not per se result in weight conservation. Once again, the absence versus the prior existence of supportive conceptual attainments seems to constitute an important moderating influence on the effectiveness of controlled practice. The Wohlwill-Lowe results do demonstrate that the child of five or six is strongly inclined to respond in terms of differences in length when comparing the number of elements in each of two collections, confirming that a failure to differentiate number from irrelevant perceptual cues underlies lack of number conservation. Furthermore, the over-all direction of all of Wohlwill's work on number (**103, 104, 105**) provides some support for the view that practice on addition and subtraction of elements as yielding nonconservation at least partly underlies conservation's development. Practice on the alteration of a set's numerical value through adding or subtracting elements has turned out to be consistently, although nonsignificantly, superior as regards improvement in conservation, to practice on the constancy of a set's numerical value in the face of spatial rearrangements. While not significant in any one experiment, this result has been obtained in the two separate studies (**103, 105**) conducted on the question, and further supportive evidence has appeared in a third (**104**). To this extent number conservation would represent an inference from the observation that nothing has been added or taken away. Wohlwill and Lowe point out that children typically receive a great deal of experience in simple addition and subtraction in the course of the general time period during which number conservation tends to appear.

Regarding the concept of duration, evidence indicates that the impression of one thing's moving farther in the same direction than another is critically involved in the young child's understanding of time. The child's judgments of temporal interval and temporal order do not remain invariant across changes in this irrelevant phenomenon of one thing's "outdistancing" another (**65, 66, 53**). In one experiment, an inverted bottle filled with water is linked to a piece of tubing shaped like an inverted-Y and containing a valve in its stem. The two identical branches of the tubing pour the water into glasses that differ in diameter. The child watches while the valve is opened and the water starts to flow into the glasses. When the narrower glass is filled—and the wider glass hence is only partly filled—the valve is closed. At about age five, the child judges both temporal order and temporal interval to be different for the water flowing from the two tubes. The flow into the narrow glass is reported to have begun at the same time as the other, but to have stopped after the other, and to have taken a longer time than the other. However questioned, the child cannot express the view that both flows stopped together. The critical variable influencing his judgment seems to be the fact that the water line in the narrow glass moves farther in the same direction than the water line in the wide one.

The crucial role apparently possessed by this "outdistancing" phenomenon in these early conceptions of duration was directly evaluated in another experiment. In an analogue of the water-flow situation, two wind-up mechanical dolls that execute different-sized hops begin racing from a common starting line while the child watches. The dolls are started and stopped simultaneously, the one with the larger "gait" traveling farther than the other in the same direction. The child not only observes this race but also hears them start at the same time, make a whirring noise while moving, and make a click when they stop. As in the water-flow experiment, the five-year-old admits that the dolls started at the same time but insists that the doll which walked farther stopped after the other and walked for a longer time than the other. If one runs the same experiment, having the dolls face each other from opposite starting points, hop toward each other, and stop when they meet—the faster doll going farther than the slower but this time in an opposite direction—then the results change. The child of about five tends, under these conditions, to judge that both dolls not only started at the same time but also stopped simultaneously and walked for the same length of time. The young child's erroneous judgments of temporal order and duration appear to be based, therefore, not on distance traversed or velocity, but rather on the impression of one thing's moving farther in the same direction than another, or "outdistancing" it.

ARRANGEMENT OF OBJECTS: CLASSIFICATION

Besides establishing certain properties as invariant in the face of irrelevant changes, and at least partly as a result of establishing such invariances, the child becomes increasingly facile in the arrangements—the groupings and orderings—that he can impose upon the objects in his environment. Having examined instances of the establishment of invariances, we turn now to research on changes in the principles of grouping and ordering which the child seems capable of applying.

In the development of classification, Piaget and Inhelder (**78**) find that when the child of three or four is given a heterogeneous assortment of objects—cut-out pictures of people, of plants, of animals, cut-out geometrical forms—and is told to put those things together which go together, his grouping is without over-all plan, dominated by accidents of momentary perceptual impressions. He may start to put some circles together, for instance, but then go on to add a few squares and never finish adding all the circles; or he may put some of the people together but then add a few geometrical forms and never finish adding all the people. Resemblance may influence the child's decisions at one moment; spatial proximity at another; some thema, such as "to make a farm," at still another. At the age of five or six, however, the sorting will be more systematic in the sense that a single criterion is exhaustively applied to the domain. The child, for instance, when starting to put geometric figures together, will continue until all geometric figures are in one pile and will not include anything but geometric figures in that pile. He then may further subdivide the geometric figures, making a smaller pile of all the squares, another of all the circles, and so on.

While it looks from this behavior as if the five- or six-year-old understands the concepts of inclusion-exclusion or subordinate and superordinate classes, further ingenious experiments done with children of this age indicate that such understanding still eludes them. In work of a general type that now has been replicated many times (see Piaget, **69**, and Piaget and Inhelder, **78**, for the basic experiments; and Elkind, **24**; Hyde, **39**; Lovell, **47**; Morf, **59**; and Pinard, **80**, for examples of further validation studies), the child of five or six is shown, for instance, a set of wooden beads comprising about 20 of brown and 2 of white color. The experimenter asks the child, "If I strung all the brown beads into a necklace, would there be any left?" "Yes," answers the child, "the white ones." "And if," the experimenter continues, "I strung all the wooden beads into a necklace, would there be any left?" "No," replies the child. "Then," asks the experimenter, "which would be longer, a necklace made with all the wooden beads or a necklace made with all the brown beads?" "One made with all the brown beads," the child erroneously answers, "because there are only a few white ones"; or, "because there are more brown than white ones."

Although the correct answers to the preliminary questions serve to minimize this possibility, it still might be the case that the child who answers in the above manner presumes that once the brown beads have been proposed for one necklace, a necklace of all the wooden beads can consist only of the white beads because the brown ones have been "used up" in some sense, even though he has been told that the necklaces would comprise *all* the brown and *all* the wooden beads, respectively. This possibility has been ruled out by a subsequent variation of the experiment which utilizes two identical sets of beads, with each necklace to be made from its own bead supply. The child still insists that, for instance, a necklace made with all the brown beads from one box will be longer than one made with all the wooden beads from the other, because there are only a few white beads. This occurs despite his admitting that if all the wooden beads in one box are strung together there will be none left, while if all the brown beads in the other are strung together the white ones will be left.

The child of this age seems unable to compare one subordinate class with the superordinate class of which the former constitutes a part. The child can compare brown and white beads, or can think of the brown and white beads as all being wooden, but cannot compare brown with wooden or white with wooden beads. The term to which one part inevitably will be compared is the other part, even when the child is instructed to compare the first part to the whole. Other controls strengthen this description of the difficulty. For example, it might be argued that error is made more likely by using the same verbal term, "beads," in labeling the subordinate (brown beads, white beads) and superordinate (wooden beads) classes. Analogous experiments were conducted, therefore, with classes each of which had a specific name: e.g., "poppies" and "bluebells" for the subordinate classes, "flowers" for the superordinate. The same type of result was obtained. It might also be proposed that, thus far, the subordinate classes have been more prominent perceptually than the superordinate, because the former have been defined in terms of colors. In other experiments, therefore, the superordinate class has been a color (blue beads) while the subordinate ones were shapes (round vs. square beads). Again the same type of result was obtained. Further, the size of disparity between the two subordinate classes might be assumed to aggravate the difficulty, hence the experiments have been repeated using, e.g., 20 brown and 15 white instead of 20 brown and 2 white beads. The same type of result once more has been found. Indeed, Morf (**59**) reports that despite extensive attempts to clarify the elements of the situation, the child of five or six cannot readily be made to understand the correct answer in problems of the above type.

The Piaget-Inhelder work (**78**) indicates that classification based on tactile cues shows the same general developmental sequence as classification based on visual cues. Related developmental findings for visual classification have been reported by Kagan, Moss, and Sigel (**43**) and by Annett (**2**). As Donaldson (**20**) points out, an important next step would be to examine the degree of correlation between individual differences in visual and tactile classification skills for children of the same age. The evidence that we have reviewed suggests that such correlation should be substantial, since degree of competence in classification seems to be a general function demonstrable with various kinds of materials. As has been noted, a critical factor defining such competence concerns the child's ability simultaneously to deal with both subordinate and superordinate classes.

ARRANGEMENT OF OBJECTS: SERIATION

In addition to organizing objects into hierarchies of classes, another activity involved in arranging or sorting the objects of one's environment is that of ordering them in terms of increasing values of some attribute, such as length. If materials are amenable to seriation, i.e., to the construction of an asymmetrical series, then the relations in question are transitive. For example, if B is longer than A, and C is longer than B, then C is longer than A. Various studies suggest that the ability to seriate elements tends to emerge somewhere in the period from about five to seven years. In one of the basic Geneva experiments on this topic (**69, 78**) and confirmed by Hyde (**39**), the child receives ten sticks which vary in length and is to arrange them from smallest to largest. When that is done correctly, if necessary with the experimenter's aid, then nine more sticks which the child is told had been forgotten are brought forth. These additional sticks constitute a series of graded lengths intermediate between the lengths of adjacent sticks in the original series. The child is to place each of these forgotten sticks where it belongs among those of the first series. At an age when the original sticks can be arranged correctly only after a process of trial and error, the child exhibits great difficulty in trying to interpolate each of the additional sticks. At an age, however, when the original sticks are placed in the corrct arrangement by some systematic process such as always selecting the smallest stick of those remaining, then the additional sticks are correctly interpolated without difficulty.

The difference between the two forms of behavior just described seems to hinge on whether the child's attempts at seriation rely entirely on piecemeal perceptual comparisons among the elements, or whether the comparisons are guided by an awareness of the transitivity principle, according to which a particular element will be viewed both as longer than those preceding it and shorter than those following it. In work focusing more specifically on the understanding of transitivity and also designed to minimize the need for verbal interchange, Braine (**14**) first trained children to obtain a candy reward by selecting the longer (or, for half the subjects, the shorter) of two uprights obviously different in height. After this learning was well established, and with continuing checks using the initial uprights to insure that it was not forgotten, new pairs of sticks were presented which, while objectively different in height, were not discriminably so to the eye. The experimenter compared each stick in turn with a third rod whose height was intermediate between the other two, thus informing the child which of the other two sticks was longer if and only if the child applied the transitivity principle. Not until approximately age five did as many as 50 per cent of the children choose correctly on groups of trials of the above kind. Control trials without the third rod indicated that under this condition all children showed chance performance, hence insuring that success on trials with the intermediate-height rod resulted specifically from its use and not from a perceptual comparison of the other two sticks. Such work provides quite strong evidence that an understanding of the transitivity principle as applied to length judgments is not present before the child has achieved a certain developmental status.

Related findings concerning transitivity of weight (**76, 94**) and of preference patterns (**86**) also have been reported. In Smedslund's research on transitivity of weight, for instance, a clay ball, sausage, and cube were among the triads of objects used. The ball is heavier than the sausage and the sausage heavier than the cube, but the weight differences are sufficiently small that a balance is necessary in order to detect them. All three objects are equal in volume. The child weighs ball and sausage, then explicitly states that the ball weighs more than the sausage. Next he weighs sausage and cube and explicitly reports that the sausage weighs more than the cube. The experimenter now presents ball and cube, requiring the child to predict which weighs more or whether both weigh the same. Checks on his recollection of the ball-sausage and sausage-cube weight relationships also are included. Using various materials of this sort and reliability-checked content analysis of the child's replies, it was shown that children in their fifth and sixth years do not yet possess a clear understanding of weight transitivity. Similar results were obtained by Smedslund (**86**) in studying transitivity of preferences: Even when cards were left visible showing pictures of a child preferring, say, a green to a red car and a red to a blue car, children of the above ages could not readily conclude that the green car would be preferred to the blue.

Seriation as well as classification, therefore, seem to constitute principles of grouping and ordering that make their appearance in the course of development over the years in question. Moreover, they perform pervasive roles in our adult conceptualizing activities. See, for instance, Bruner, Goodnow, and Austin (**16**), Shepard, Hovland, and Jenkins (**82**), and Wallach (**99**), on the generality of classification processes in adult thinking; Braine (**14**), Flavell (**29**), and Piaget (**71**), on the importance of seriation in adult conceptions of measurement.

Development from Approximately the Twelfth to the Fourteenth Years

Research by Inhelder and Piaget (**41**) has been concerned with delineating the differences between the problem-solving activities of the early adolescent in contrast to those of the child a few years younger. In a typical experiment the child is confronted with five bottles containing identical-looking, colorless, odorless liquids. Four large flasks are labeled "1" through "4," while a fifth, smaller, bottle with a dropper is labeled "g." Two further glasses are shown to the child: Their contents appear the same, but one actually contains liquid *2* while the other contains a mixture of *1* and *3*. The experimenter pours several drops of liquid *g* into each glass, the child observing that the liquid in the former glass remains unchanged while that in the latter turns a yellow color. The child now is asked to reproduce the yellow color, working with the original five bottles in any way he wishes. As noted, the correct solution actually consists in combining *g* (potassium iodide) with liquids *1* and *3* (diluted sulphuric acid and oxygenated water, respectively).

From approximately ages seven to eleven, the child spontaneously combines *g* with the contents of flasks *1* through *4* taken one at a time, but not until the upper ages in this range does he begin spontaneously to combine *g* with two other flasks at the same time. The latter combinations of *g* with *1* through *4* taken two at a time remain haphazard and unsystematic. Throughout this age range the child tends to believe that the color is caused by one of the flasks, rather than by some combination of them. Some of the children believe that one of the flasks contains a hidden "color pellet."

From about age twelve on, the child systematically works his way through all six of the possible combinations of *g* with *1* through *4* taken two at a time, after he fails to produce yellow by combining *g* with *1* through *4* taken one at a time. Further, he is not satisfied just to discover that the combination of *1* and *3* with *g* yields yellow, but continues to try whatever two-at-a-time combinations still remain, in order to determine whether any other solutions are possible. And he tends now to interpret the color as resulting not from one or another of the flasks but from a particular combination of them: "This one [flask *3*], joined to *1* and to *g*, gives the color: *3* all alone does nothing, and *1* alone does nothing either." Around age fourteen, he even goes on to try the various possible three-at-a-time combinations of flasks *1* through *4* with *g*, thus discovering that *2* (water) has no effect on the yellow color produced by joining *1* and *3* with *g*, while *4* (thiosulphate) turns the liquid clear again.

The older child, in contrast to the younger, seems much more oriented to a consideration of hypothetical possibilities and to their systematic analysis. While the younger child is more limited to a one-at-a-time testing of the fluids that perceptually confront him, the older child is able to represent to himself the hypothetical matrix of all possible combinations that can be constructed from the given elements and, therefore, is able to test systematically the relevance of each combination to the production of color. From somewhat different viewpoints, Berlyne (**8**), Bruner (**15**), and Parsons (**62**) all have noted, in examining the above research, that the older child seems to be much clearer than the younger regarding what is involved in verifying a law—i.e., in discovering which variables are responsible for an effect and which are irrelevant. Flavell (**29**), in discussing the same experimentation, suggests a similar point when he notes that the older child's thinking begins with an attempt to formulate all the possible solutions to a problem and then proceeds to determine which of these possible solutions obtain in reality. This characteristic makes itself apparent not only from the quality of systematic testing evident in nonverbal combinatory behavior but also in the "if-then" nature of the verbal commentary which often accompanies this testing. For example, one adolescent says:

"Combining *2* and *4* makes no color. They are negative. Perhaps you could add *4* to *1* × *3* × *g* to see if it would cancel out the color. [He adds *4* to *1* × *3* × *g*.] Liquid *4* cancels it all. You'd have to see if *2* has the same influence. [He now adds *2* to *1* × *3* × *g*.] No, so *2* and *4* are not alike, for *4* acts on *1* × *3*, and *2* does not" (**41:** 117).

The subject hence is proposing: If *2* and *4* are alike, then they will have the same effect when added to *1* × *3* × *g*. They do not; hence, they are not alike. Research by Lovell (**48**) provides further confirmatory evidence for the general point under discussion. A study by Ervin (**25**) offers further documentation for the nature of the younger child's difficulties with problems of this type.

For the older child to be clear concerning what is involved in verifying a law, he must be able to formulate propositions about external events and objects and make various kinds of logical linkages, such as implication, disjunction, etc., among these propositions. Such linkages represent possible relationships—relationships which may or may not obtain in reality. The younger child's major cognitive attainments concern his increasing skill in dealing with external events and objects—maintaining the constancy of their properties across irrelevant changes, classifying them, seriating them. The older child, obviously with the aid of his increasing linguistic competence, proceeds to describe the results of these dealings in propositions and then to relate the propositions in various ways. These kinds of considerations led the Geneva group (e.g., **41, 75**) to describe the adolescent's thought as "interpropositional," as involving "operations upon propositions," in contrast to the younger child's direct operations upon external objects and events. For example, suppose a child of eight years and one of twelve both find that liquid *2* is present in a mixture which has become yellow. The eight-year-old, from this information, may well decide forthwith that the yellow occurs if liquid *2* is present. The twelve-year-old, on the other hand, is more likely to be aware that two other possibilities yet remain to be tested concerning the relationship of liquid *2* to yellowness in this particular mixture: When *2* is left out, does the mixture stay yellow or lose its yellowness? He tries, finds that it stays yellow, and hence concludes that *2* is irrelevant to the production of yellowness (see also **3, 72**).

Why the problem-solving of the adolescent takes hypothetical possibilities into account more systematically than the problem-solving of the younger child is far from clear at this point. Language obviously plays a role; so also may increasing societal pressure to deal with the world unassisted by one's elders (**15**); as may overlearning of the skills involved in dealing with concrete objects and events per se. Concerning this third possibility, Mandler (**55**) has discussed the role of such overlearning in permitting more facile representation of relationships in the external world. Overlearning of this kind may constitute the key to understanding what Piaget (e.g., **74, 75**) means by "equilibration," that is, achievement of an integrated, steady state in a psychological process.

Evidence concerning Structural Changes in Cognitive Development from Correlational Studies

Implicit in the findings described in the preceding sections is the generalization that structural or "qualitative" changes in thinking occur during its development. The thinking of the ten-year-old, for instance, seems to involve different modes of analysis than that of the four-year-old rather than quantitatively "more" of the "same" modes of analysis. It is of interest to consider whether recent longitudinal studies using standard intelligence-test indices provide any information relevant to evaluating this generalization. As Braine (**14**) has noted, serious changes in the relative orderings of individuals on intellectual measures administered at different ages would provide some evidence for qualitative alterations across cognitive development. Such changes would suggest that different factors or abilities are involved in passing intelligence-test items at different age levels. On the other hand, constancy in such orderings would not necessarily constitute evidence against qualitative alterations, since these might occur even if constancy is preserved. Thus, while constancy in the orderings would be uninformative regarding the issue at hand, nonconstancy would suggest qualitative changes.

Nonconstancy seems, in fact, to be the most pervasive finding. Most of the studies concerning infancy and early or middle childhood have yielded very low correlations. Comparisons have been made between, for instance, California first-year mental-scale scores at 6 months and California preschool-scale scores at 3 years; scores on the former at 13 months and on the latter at 3 years (**5, 6**); indices of early vocalization at 6–18 months and the Stanford-Binet at 36–54 months (**17**); Gesell Developmental Quotient scores at approximately 1–8 months and the Wechsler Intelligence Scale for Children (WISC) at 6–9 years; Cattell I.Q. scores at 1–8 months and the WISC at 6–9 years (**27**); California preschool-scale scores at 21 months and at 5 years (**36**); Gesell scores at 40 weeks and at 3 years; Gesell scores at 40 weeks and Stanford-Binet scores at 3–4 years (**44, 45**); Kuhlmann-Binet scale scores at 13–21 months and Stanford-Binet scale scores at 5–8 years (computed by Braine, **14**, from data published by Skodak and Skeels, **83**); and Gesell scores at 3–14 months and Stanford-Binet scores at 4–9 years (**102**). Whether global clinical appraisals at infancy can predict more successfully, as Escalona (**26**) and Escalona and Moriarty (**27**) suggest, is open to serious question (see **102**).

Among the studies concerning infancy and later childhood, in turn, have been comparisons between California first-year mental-scale scores at 6 months and Wechsler-Bellevue scores at 18 years; scores on the former at 13 months and on the latter at 18 years (**5, 6**); California preschool-scale scores at 21 months and Wechsler-Bellevue scores at 18 years (**36**); and Kuhlmann-Binet scores at 13–21 months and Stanford-Binet scores at 11–16 years (computed by Braine, **14**, from data published by Skodak and Skeels, **83**). Again the correlations have been very low, if positive at all. Comparisons between middle and later childhood have yielded higher and usually statistically significant correlations, ranging to approximately .6 or .7 (see, for instance, **5, 6, 11, 12, 13, 36**).

The general picture that emerges indicates that prediction is poor from infancy to either early, middle, or later childhood, but is somewhat better from middle to later childhood (see **14**). Attempts to improve prediction from infancy by using later intelligence-test results as criteria by which to select the best infant-test items have been quite discouraging (see, for instance, **6, 12, 58**).

Hofstaetter (**35**) has performed a factor analysis of intelligence-test scores obtained from the same individuals at each of a number of ages ranging from 2 months to 17½ years. Some of the data involved in this analysis have been mentioned in the preceding paragraphs. Hofstaetter's results confirm and extend the picture just sketched in showing that three major and different relative orderings of individuals appear across this age range. The first ordering is found most strongly in tests that were given at 5, 8, 11, and 14 months of age; the second, in tests that were given at 21, 32, and 48 months; and the third, in tests given at 72 months and after. These findings support the generalization that whatever is being assessed by "intelligence" tests is structurally or qualitatively different in infancy, early childhood, and middle childhood.

In sum, Hofstaetter's results are consistent with the evidence reviewed in the previous sections of this chapter in suggesting that structural changes in the nature of adaptation to the environment occur in the course of development—with at least one major transition in the relative ordering of individuals occurring between about 5 and 8 years; i.e., the age period during which conservations of many properties across irrelevant changes, classification skills, and seriation abilities all have been found to develop. The transition in relative ordering of individuals appearing at approximately 1½ years, in turn, shows an interesting correspondence with the general age at which evidence has been found for the development of primitive representational activities, an awareness of means-ends relationships, and the object concept. Finally, the absence of a change in relative ordering of individuals in the range of 12, 13, or 14 years does not contradict the view, suggested by evidence which we have sampled, that further structural changes in thinking occur during that period; although, of course, it doesn't specifically support this view either.

As noted earlier, such structural changes may occur even though relative orderings remain constant.

Final Comments

In our examination of current research on the development of children's thinking, we obviously have concentrated on the child's knowledge of the physical world–i.e., on the traditional definition of thinking as reasoning, problem-solving, and understanding, concerning the nonsocial environment (**96**). The extent to which thinking about the social environment follows similar or different ontogenetic patterns must remain an open question at this point. Smedslund's work (**86**) showing nontransivity regarding inferences about the choice behavior of other persons at ages where nontransitivity also is found regarding the ordering of physical objects provides one example of the extensive comparative studies that are needed.

While the present chapter mainly has been concerned with Piaget, his Geneva collaborators, and those elsewhere who have carried on related work, this does not exhaust the recent literature on children's thinking. It does, however, span most of the major areas of this topic that have been subjected to extensive recent study from a developmental point of view, and it was specifically to developmental studies of children's thinking that this chapter addressed itself. Psychometric work on intelligence tests where developmental change or constancy was studied also has been given a brief review.

Two directions of research where developmental work recently has been appearing, but which have not been covered in this chapter, are children's conception or understanding of phenomena concerning chance and probability and children's conceptualization of stimuli in discrimination problems. These are discussed in the chapter on children's learning. It is apparent, therefore, that the point of boundary between "thinking" and "learning" is, to at least some extent, an arbitrary one.

Several other research directions may be mentioned, all concerning aspects of thinking which have yet to be extensively examined from a developmental point of view. These include fantasy and curiosity in cognitive activities; the related topic of originality, inventiveness, or creativity in thinking; and variation in aspects of thinking as related to factors of personality and motivation, to parental attitudes, and to sex of the child. The first and third of these topics have, however, recently been receiving increased attention from the viewpoint of individual differences.

Perhaps the most striking general conclusion to be drawn from the developmental information we have reviewed in this chapter is that the human's basic cognitive categories for analyzing physical reality are a product of slow and laborious construction.

BIBLIOGRAPHY

1. Aebli, H. *The Development of Intelligence in the Child.* Minneapolis: Institute of Child Development, University of Minnesota, 1950.
2. Annett, M. "The Classification of Instances of Four Common Class Concepts by Children and Adults," *Brit. J. Educ. Psychol.*, XXIX (1959), 223–36.
3. Apostel, L. "Logique et Apprentissage," *Études d'Épistémol. Génét.*, VIII (1959), 1–138.
4. Ayer, A. J. *The Foundations of Empirical Knowledge.* New York: Macmillan Co., 1951.
5. Bayley, N. "Consistency and Variability in the Growth of Intelligence from Birth to Eighteen Years," *J. Genet. Psychol.*, LXXV (1949), 165–96.
6. ———. "On the Growth of Intelligence," *Amer. Psychol.*, X (1955), 805–18.
7. Beard, R. "An Investigation of Concept Formation among Infant School Children." Unpublished Doctor's dissertation, University of London, 1957.
8. Berlyne, D. E. "The Teen-ager as Logician," *Contemp. Psychol.*, IV (1959), 54–56.
9. ———. *Conflict, Arousal, and Curiosity.* New York: McGraw-Hill Book Co., Inc., 1960.
10. Birch, H. G. "The Relation of Previous Experience to Insightful Problem-solving," *J. Comp. Psychol.*, XXXVIII (1945), 367–83.
11. Bradway, K. P. "I.Q. Constancy in the Revised Stanford-Binet from the Preschool to the Junior High School Level," *J. Genet. Psychol.*, LXV (1944), 197–217.
12. ———. "Predictive Value of Stanford-Binet Preschool Items," *J. Educ. Psychol.*, XXXVI (1945), 1–16.
13. Bradway, K. P., and Thompson, C. W. "Intelligence at Adulthood: A Twenty-five Year Follow-up," *J. Educ. Psychol.*, LIII (1962), 1–14.
14. Braine, M. D. S. "The Ontogeny of Certain Logical Operations: Piaget's Formulation Examined by Nonverbal Methods," *Psychol. Monogr.*, LXXV (1959), No. 5 (Whole No. 475).
15. Bruner, J. S. "Inhelder and Piaget's *The Growth of Logical Thinking:* I, A Psychologist's Viewpoint," *Brit. J. Psychol.*, L (1959), 363–70.
16. Bruner, J. S.; Goodnow, J. J.; and Austin, G. A. *A Study of Thinking.* New York: John Wiley and Sons, 1956.
17. Catalano, F. L., and McCarthy, D. "Infant Speech as a Possible Predictor of Later Intelligence," *J. Psychol.*, XXXVIII (1954), 203–9.

18. CHURCHILL, E. M. "The Number Concepts of the Young Child," *Leeds Univer. Res. & Stud.*, (1958), No. 17, 34–49, and No. 18, 28–46.

19. DODWELL, P. C. "Children's Understanding of Number and Related Concepts," *Canad. J. Psychol.*, XIV (1960), 191–203.

20. DONALDSON, M. "Review of J. Piaget and B. Inhelder, *La Genèse des Structures Logiques Élémentaires: Classifications et Sériations*," *Brit. J. Psychol.*, LI (1960), 181–84.

21. ELKIND, D. "The Development of Quantitative Thinking: A Systematic Replication of Piaget's Studies," *J. Genet. Psychol.*, XCVIII (1961), 37–46.

22. ———. "Quantity Conceptions in Junior and Senior High School Students," *Child Develpm.*, XXXII (1961), 551–60.

23. ———. "Children's Discovery of the Conservation of Mass, Weight and Volume: Piaget Replication Study II," *J. Genet. Psychol.*, XCVIII (1961), 219–27.

24. ———. "The Development of the Additive Composition of Classes in the Child: Piaget Replication Study III," *J. Genet. Psychol.*, XCIX (1961), 51–57.

25. ERVIN, S. M. "Experimental Procedures of Children," *Child Develpm.*, XXXI (1960), 703–19.

26. ESCALONA, S. "The Use of Infant Tests for Predictive Purposes," *Bull. Menninger Clin.*, XIV (1950), 117–28.

27. ESCALONA, S., and MORIARTY, A. "Prediction of School-age Intelligence from Infant Tests," *Child Develpm.*, XXXII (1961), 597–605.

28. ESTES, B. W. "Some Mathematical and Logical Concepts in Children," *J. Genet. Psychol.*, LXXXVIII (1956), 219–222.

29. FLAVELL, J. *The Developmental Psychology of Jean Piaget.* (Volume in preparation.)

30. FRAISSE, P., and VAUTREY, P. "La Perception de l'Espace, de la Vitesse, et du Temps chez l'Enfant de Cinq Ans: I, L'Espace et la Vitesse," *Enfance*, V (1952), 1–20.

31. GOUSTARD, M. "Étude Psychogénétique de la Résolution d'un Problème (Labyrinthe en T)," *Études d'Épistémol. Génét.*, X (1959), 83–112.

32. GRECO, P. "L'Apprentissage dans une Situation à Structure Opératoire Concrète: Les Inversions Successives de l'Ordre Lineaire par des Rotations de 180°," *Études d'Épistémol. Génét.*, VII (1959), 68–182.

33. ———. "Induction, Déduction et Apprentissage," *Études d'Épistémol. Génét.*, X (1959), 3–59.

34. ———. "Quotité et Quantité," in *Structures Numériques Élémentaires.* Edited by J. Piaget. Paris: Presses Universitaires de France (in press).

35. HOFSTAETTER, P. R. "The Changing Composition of 'Intelligence': A Study in T-Technique," *J. Genet. Psychol.*, LXXXV (1954), 159–64.

36. HONZIK, M. P.; MACFARLANE, J. W.; and ALLEN, L. "The Stability of Mental Test Performance between Two and Eighteen Years," *J. Exp. Educ.*, XVII (1948), 309–24.

37. HULL, C. L. *Principles of Behavior.* New York: Appleton-Century-Crofts, 1943.

38. HUNT, J. MCV. *Intelligence and Experience.* New York: Ronald Press, 1961.

39. HYDE, D. M. "An Investigation of Piaget's Theories of the Development

of the Concept of Number." Unpublished Doctor's dissertation, University of London, 1959.

40. INHELDER, B., and NOELTING, G. "A Pilot Study of Cognitive Functions," in *Perspectives in Personality Research*, pp. 251–54. Edited by H. P. David and J. C. Brengelmann. New York: Springer Pub. Co., Inc., 1960.

41. INHELDER, B., and PIAGET, J. *The Growth of Logical Thinking from Childhood to Adolescence*. New York: Basic Books, 1958.

42. JACKSON, T. A. "Use of the Stick as a Tool by Young Chimpanzees," *J. Comp. Psychol.*, XXXIV (1942), 223–35.

43. KAGAN, J.; MOSS, H. A.; and SIGEL, I. "The Psychological Significance of Styles of Conceptualization." Paper read at conference sponsored by the Social Science Research Council, Minneapolis, April, 1961. (In *Basic Cognitive Processes*. Edited by J. C. Wright and J. Kagan. Monograph of the Society for Research in Child Development, 1963.)

44. KNOBLOCH, H., and PASAMANICK, B. "The Distribution of Intellectual Potential in an Infant Population," in *The Epidemiology of Mental Disorder*, pp. 249–72. Washington: American Association for the Advancement of Science, 1959 (Publication No. 60).

45. ———. "An Evaluation of the Consistency and Predictive Value of the 40-Week Gesell Developmental Schedule," in *Child Development and Child Psychiatry*, pp. 10–31. Edited by C. Shagass and B. Pasamanick. Washington: Psychiatric Research Reports of the American Psychiatric Association, No. 13, 1960.

46. LASHLEY, K. S., and WADE, M. "The Pavlovian Theory of Generalization," *Psychol. Rev.*, LIII (1946), 72–87.

47. LOVELL, K. *The Growth of Basic Mathematical and Scientific Concepts in Children*. London: University of London Press, 1961.

48. ———. "A Follow-Up Study of Inhelder and Piaget's *The Growth of Logical Thinking*," *Brit. J. Psychol.*, LII (1961), 143–54.

49. LOVELL, K.; HEALEY, D.; and ROLAND, A. D. "The Growth of Some Geometrical Concepts," *Child Develpm.* (in press).

50. LOVELL, K., and OGLIVIE, E. "A Study of the Conservation of Substance in the Junior School Child," *Brit. J. Educ. Psychol.*, XXX (1960), 109–18.

51. ———. "A Study of the Conservation of Weight in the Junior School Child," *Brit. J. Educ. Psychol.*, XXXI (1961), 138–44.

52. ———. "The Growth of the Concept of Volume in Junior School Children," *J. Child Psychol. and Psychiat.*, II (1961), 118–26.

53. LOVELL, K., and SLATER, A. "The Growth of the Concept of Time: A Comparative Study," *J. Child Psychol. and Psychiat.*, I (1960), 179–90.

54. LUNZER, E. R. "Some Points of Piagetian Theory in the Light of Experimental Criticism," *J. Child Psychol. and Psychiat.*, I (1960), 191–202.

55. MANDLER, G. "Transfer of Training as a Function of Degree of Response Overlearning," *J. Exp. Psychol.*, XLVII (1954), 411–17.

56. *Manual of Child Psychology*. Edited by L. Carmichael. New York: John Wiley & Sons, 1954 (second edition).

57. MATALON, B. "Apprentissages en Situations Aléatoires et Systematiques," *Études d' Épistémol. Génét.*, X (1959), 61–91.

58. MAURER, K. M. *Intellectual Status at Maturity as a Criterion for Selecting Items in Preschool Tests*. Minneapolis: University of Minnesota Press, 1946.

59. Morf, A. "Apprentissage d'une Structure Logique Concrète (Inclusion). Effets et Limites," *Études d'Épistémol. Génét.*, IX (1959), 15–83.

60. Osgood, C. E. *Method and Theory in Experimental Psychology*. New York: Oxford University Press, 1953.

61. Osgood, C. E.; Suci, G. J.; and Tannenbaum, P. H. *The Measurement of Meaning*. Urbana: University of Illinois Press, 1957.

62. Parsons, C. "Inhelder and Piaget's *The Growth of Logical Thinking*. II. A Logician's Viewpoint," *Brit. J. Psychol.*, LI (1960), 75–84.

63. Piaget, J. *The Child's Conception of the World*. London: Routledge & Kegan Paul, 1929.

64. ———. *The Child's Conception of Physical Causality*. London: Routledge & Kegan Paul, 1930.

65. ———. *Le Développement de la Notion du Temps chez l'Enfant*. Paris: Presses Universitaires de France, 1946.

66. ———. *Les Notions de Mouvement et de Vitesse chez l'Enfant*. Paris: Presses Universitaires de France, 1946.

67. ———. *The Psychology of Intelligence*. New York: Harcourt, Brace, & Co., 1950.

68. ———. *Play, Dreams, and Imitation*. London: William Heinemann, Ltd., 1951.

69. ———. *The Child's Conception of Number*. London: Routledge & Kegan Paul, 1952.

70. ———. *The Origins of Intelligence in Children*. New York: International Universities Press, 1952.

71. ———. "How Children Form Mathematical Concepts," *Scientific Amer.*, CLXXXIX (1953), 74–79.

72. ———. *Logic and Psychology*. Manchester: Manchester University Press, 1953.

73. ———. *The Construction of Reality in the Child*. New York: Basic Books, 1954.

74. ———. "Logique et Équilibre dans les Comportements du Sujet," *Études d'Épistémol. Génét.*, II (1957), 27–117.

75. ———. "The Genetic Approach to the Psychology of Thought," *J. Educ. Psychol.*, LII (1961), 275–81.

76. Piaget, J., and Inhelder, B. *Le Développment des Quantités chez l'Enfant*. Neuchâtel: Delachaux and Niestlé, 1941.

77. ———. *The Child's Conception of Space*. London: Routledge & Kegan Paul, 1956.

78. ———. *La Genèse des Structures Logiques Élémentaires: Classifications et Sériations*. Neuchârel: Delachaux & Niestlé, 1959.

79. Piaget, J.; Inhelder, B.; and Szeminska, A. *The Child's Conception of Geometry*. New York: Basic Books, 1960.

80. Pinard, A. "An Experimental Study of Mental Development Based on Piaget's Theory." Paper read at Yale University, New Haven, December, 1959.

81. Price, H. H. *Perception*. London: Methuen & Co., Ltd., 1950 (second edition).

82. Shepard, R. N.; Hovland, C. I.; and Jenkins, H. M. "Learning and Memo-

rization of Classifications," *Psychol. Monogr.*, LXXV (1961), No. 13 (Whole No. 517).

83. SKODAK, M., and SKEELS, H. M. "A Final Follow-up of One Hundred Adopted Children," *J. Genet. Psychol.*, LXXV (1949), 85–125.
84. SLATER, G. W. "A Study of the Influence Which Environment Plays in Determining the Rate at Which a Child Attains Piaget's 'Operational' Level in His Early Number Concepts." Unpublished Doctor's dissertation, Birmingham University, 1958.
85. SMEDSLUND, J. "Apprentissage des Notions de la Conservation et de la Transitivité du Poids," *Études d'Épistémol. Génét.*, IX (1959), 85–124.
86. ———. "Transitivity of Preference Patterns as Seen by Pre-School Children," *Scand. J. Psychol.*, I (1960), 49–54.
87. ———. "The Acquisition of Conservation of Substance and Weight in Children: I, Introduction," *Scand. J. Psychol.*, II (1961), 11–20.
88. ———. "The Acquisition of Conservation of Substance and Weight in Children: II, External Reinforcement of Conservation of Weight and of the Operations of Addition and Subtraction," *Scand. J. Psychol.*, II (1961), 71–84.
89. ———. "The Acquisition of Conservation of Substance and Weight in Children: III, Extinction of Conservation of Weight Acquired 'Normally' and by Means of Empirical Controls on a Balance," *Scand. J. Psychol.*, II (1961), 85–87.
90. ———. "The Acquisition of Conservation of Substance and Weight in Children: IV, Attempt at Extinction of the Visual Components of the Weight Concept," *Scand. J. Psychol.*, II (1961), 153–55.
91. ———. "The Acquisition of Conservation of Substance and Weight in Children: V, Practice in Conflict Situations without External Reinforcement," *Scand. J. Psychol.*, II (1961), 156–60.
92. ———. "The Acquisition of Conservation of Substance and Weight in Children: VI, Practice on Continuous vs. Discontinuous Material in Problem Situations without External Reinforcement," *Scand. J. Psychol.*, II (1961), 203–10.
93. ———. "The Acquisition of Conservation of Substance and Weight in Children: VII, Conservation of Discontinuous Quantity and the Operations of Adding and Taking Away," *Scand. J. Psychol.*, III (1962), 69–77.
94. ———. "The Acquisition of Transitivity of Weight in Children," *J. Genet. Psychol.* (in press).
95. ———. "The Effect of Observation on Children's Representation of the Spatial Orientation of a Water Surface," *J. Genet. Psychol.* (in press).
96. THOMSON, R. *The Psychology of Thinking.* Baltimore: Penguin Books, 1959.
97. VINH-BANG. "Évolution des Conduites et Apprentissage," *Études d'Épistémol. Génét.*, IX (1959), 3–13.
98. WALLACH, L., and WALLACH, M. A. "On the Conditions of Acquired Stimulus Equivalence" (submitted for publication).
99. WALLACH, M. A. "The Influence of Classification Requirements on Gradients of Response," *Psychol. Monogr.*, LXXIII (1959), No. 8 (Whole No. 478).

100. WERTHEIMER, M. *Productive Thinking.* New York: Basic Books, 1959 (second edition).

101. WHITE, B. L., and CASTLE, P. W. "Observations on the Development of Prehension in Infants." Paper read at meeting of the Eastern Psychological Association, Atlantic City, New Jersey, April, 1962.

102. WITTENBORN, J. R. "A Study of Adoptive Children: I, Interviews as a Source of Scores for Children and Their Homes. II, The Predictive Validity of the Yale Developmental Examination of Infant Behavior. III, Relationships between Some Aspects of Development and Some Aspects of Environment for Adoptive Children," *Psychol. Monogr.*, LXX (1956), Nos. 1–3 (Whole Nos. 408–10).

103. WOHLWILL, J. F. "Un Essai d'Apprentissage dans le Domaine de la Conservation du Nombre," *Études d'Épistémol. Génét.*, IX (1959), 125–35.

104. ———. "A Study of the Development of the Number Concept by Scalogram Analysis," *J. Genet. Psychol.*, XCVII (1960), 345–77.

105. WOHLWILL, J. F., and LOWE, R. C. "An Experimental Analysis of the Development of Conservation of Number," *Child Develpm.*, XXXIII (1962), 153–67.

106. WOLFF, P. H. "The Developmental Psychologies of Jean Piaget and Psychoanalysis," *Psychol. Issues*, II (1960), No. 1 (Monograph 5).

107. WOODWARD, M. "The Behavior of Idiots Interpreted by Piaget's Theory of Sensori-Motor Development," *Brit. J. Educ. Psychol.*, XXIX (1959), 60–71.

CHAPTER VII

Moral Development and Identification

LAWRENCE KOHLBERG

Introduction—Concepts of Morality and of Moral Development

Freud (**53**), Durkheim (**36**), G. Mead (**102**), T. Parsons (**112**) and others found it necessary to use the concept of a moral attitude as the basic building block for social psychology theory. There has long been reason, therefore, to agree with McDougall (**99**) that "the fundamental problem of social psychology is the moralization of the individual by the society."

In spite of this tradition of theoretical interest in children's morality, early research in the area was dominated by obvious, practical concerns about good behavior in children. Only in the last twenty years has research focused upon basic theoretical problems in the development of morality. The present chapter reviews the results of recent research as these results clarify the psychological nature of moral development and the psychological processes leading to such development.

Drawing from traditions inspired by Freud and Durkheim, current investigators consider morality or conscience to be the set of cultural rules of social action which have been internalized by the individual. Rules are said to be internalized if they are conformed to in the absence of situational incentives or sanctions, i.e., if conformity is intrinsically motivated. In spite of loose agreement on the notion of internalized rule, there have been important differences of emphasis in researchers' conceptions of morality.

The criterion of *intrinsically motivated conformity* is implicit in the common-sense notion of "moral character" which formed the basis of the earlier American research on morality (**82**). In this tradition, Hartshorne and May defined character as a set of culturally defined virtues (honesty, service, self-control) which were translated into measurable habits or traits through the use of temptation situations.

A second criterion of the existence of internalized standards is that of *guilt,* i.e., of self-punitive and self-critical reactions after transgression of cultural standards. This focus has been associated with psychoanalytically inspired concepts of moral development as a process of identification with parental authority, i.e., of the conflict-inspired wish to be like the parents.

In addition to conforming and self-punishing behavior, the notion of an internalized standard implies an understanding and positive valuing of that standard by the child. A moral act is conceived by philosophers to be the result of a decision made in terms of conscious reference to a moral standard or value. According to this more "introspective" or judgmental view, "to become morally adult is to learn to make decisions of principle; it is to learn to use 'ought' sentences verified by reference to a standard or set of principles which we have by our own decision accepted and made our own" (**62**: 77–78). This *judgmental* side of moral development has been the focus of the work of Piaget (**117**) and other developmental theorists.

It is apparent that "conformity-learning," "identification-guilt," and "development of judgment" approaches are relevant to the central problem: How does the amoral infant become capable of morality, of functioning in terms of internalized social standards? The results of the first two approaches will be considered together in the next section on "superego strength," since research studies have tended to combine or relate both points of view. The developmentalist approach will then be considered and the relation of moral judgments to moral behavior examined in order to indicate points of possible integration of the various approaches.

Child-rearing Antecedents of Strength of Conscience

RESEARCH STUDIES OF SUPEREGO STRENGTH

Recent research on children's morality has focused largely upon family antecedents of differences in conscience strength. This research has looked both to the Hullian learning theory and to psychoanalysis for theoretical concepts. Learning theory has stimulated a conceptualization of child-rearing antecedents in terms of conditions of reinforcement, while psychoanalysis has stimulated conceptualizations of child-rearing antecedents in terms of mechanisms of identification. Both theories suggest a focus upon "anxiety" or "guilt" as the basic moral motive and upon the inhibition of impulses (sex, aggression, and others) as the basic expression of morality. Many studies of social and family antecedents of morality are conceived in such "superego strength" terms (**4, 10, 19, 24, 28, 30, 46, 59, 60, 61, 71, 79, 93, 96, 100, 108–10, 120, 121, 129, 131, 141**).

In all these studies, measures of child-rearing variables were based on ratings of tape-recorded interviews (e.g., see **129**) of the mother (in some studies, fathers were also interviewed). Subjects' tendencies to cheat in experimental situations in which they thought themselves unobserved have been noted (**30, 61, 119**). Except for four studies (**59, 61, 93, 129**), all employed measures of "guilt" based on unpleasant consequences described by children in completing stories involving moral deviations.

LEARNING-THEORY CONCEPTS OF THE ACQUISITION OF MORALITY

Americans have long been prone to think of moral development as a matter of training in "good habits" through example, tuition, and reward or as a matter of preventing "bad habits" from being practiced or rewarded. This way of thinking, most sensitively formulated by William James, has dominated American philanthropic practice which has assumed that moral tuition in character-education classes, in Sunday school, or in the Boy Scouts, would improve a child's character. It has also dominated the earlier American research on "character" (**82**), best exemplified by the work of Hartshorne and May (**66**).

The results obtained by Hartshorne and May and others appeared to indicate clearly the inadequacies of such a common-sense concept of moral learning. Hartshorne and May found no relationship between honesty or "service" behavior tests and exposure to moral training in Sunday school, Boy Scouts, or character-education classes. Other results also suggested the inadequacy of viewing moral behavior as the result of general good habits. Hartshorne and

May's recommendations were that morality should be studied in terms of specific situational responses related to specific situational reinforcements.

The learning-theory concepts which have actually been influential in recent research on morality have been the Hullian and neo-Pavlovian theories of conditioned fear or anxiety. These theories lead to the expectation that certain conditions of parental punishment should bring about feelings of anxiety and inhibition of deviant responses, regardless of current situational punishments or rewards. Thus, these theories come closer than situational reinforcement theories to morality as "conscience" or "internalized standards," as something carried *into* situations.

The basic assumption used in applying Hullian-Pavlovian theory to morality research has been the assumption of habit generalization. This assumption leads to the expectation that avoidance, anxiety, or inhibition learned in the home should generalize to an unsupervised situation outside the home. The factors in home conditions which a Hullian-Pavlovian analysis would suggest as leading to association of strong anxiety with a deviant response, or to inhibition of the response, may be outlined as follows:

1. Strength of reinforcement
    - *a*) Frequency and intensity of physical punishment after deviation
    - *b*) Frequency and intensity of deprivation of privileges or goods after deviation
    - *c*) Frequency and intensity of reward for conformity
    - *d*) Immediacy of reinforcement after action
2. Severity, height, or extent of parental standards or expectations
    - *a*) Number of acts defined as deviant
    - *b*) Amount of effort made to prevent deviance
    - *c*) Earliness at which act is considered deviant
3. Cognitive clarity of moral training and conditions promoting discrimination of good and bad acts
    - *a*) Verbal labeling and reasoning
    - *b*) Consistency of standards and reinforcement
    - *c*) Providing or defining behavioral models of good and bad acts
4. Level of drive punished by parents

Another antecedent of learning of moral anxiety, proposed by Eysenck (**45**) and others, is that of hereditary differences in conditionability.

LEARNING-THEORY CONCEPTS APPLIED TO FINDINGS ON CHILD-REARING ANTECEDENTS OF RESISTANCE TO TEMPTATION

The research findings relevant to child-rearing antecedents are presented in Table 1. The results do not indicate any general simple relationship between learning conditions and indices of conscience. A first very crude assessment of a general relationship may be based on a general hypothesis that all the learning antecedents should positively correlate with all behavioral inhibition or direct anxiety indicators of conscience. Of the 94 possible associations relevant to this hypothesis, only 19 are positive.

A more refined analysis might begin with a consideration of the relations of amount and method of punishment and reward to various types of conscience indicators. The findings of the two delinquency studies (**19, 59**) are relatively consistent, indicating the use of more punitive, inconsistent, and unreasoning modes of discipline by parents of delinquents. The measures of rated confession in the third column tend to parallel the findings for delinquency in their relationship to more "enlightened" modes of discipline, e.g., consistency, reasoning, use of positive reinforcement, and avoidance of physical punishment (**89**). Similar results are not found, however, in studies using experimental measures of resistance to temptation. Grinder (**61**) and Rau (**119**) found no relationship to modes of discipline while Burton's data (**30**) suggest a relationship between resistance and punitive, nonreasoning discipline.

The findings on height of parental standards are fairly consistent with findings on amount and clarity of reinforcement. Both suggest relationships between a pattern of enlightened, child-oriented techniques and social conformity (nondelinquency and approval-oriented confession). The findings suggest that the "techniques" do not affect moral behavior directly, as would be expected by learning theory, but indirectly as expected by theories of the parent-child relationship discussed later.

Learning theory would more directly predict specific correlations between strength of parental demands for a specific habit and strength of that habit. The evidence with regard to obedience and cheating demands does not, however, indicate any simple, consistent relationship between measures of amount of parental demands or

TABLE 1

Relations between Parental Training Practices and Morality*

Antecedent Conditions of Moral Learning	Morality Variables Investigated		
	Resistance to Temptation	Guilt	Nondelinquency
1. Amount of Reinforcement			
a) Physical punishment	2, + : 30, 93[d] 2, 0 : 61, 119	5, 0 : 79, 93[d], 96, 119[e], 131[c] 3, − : 30[d], 71[c], 129	2, − : 19[c], 59[c]
b) Deprivation of rewards	3, 0 : 30, 61, 119	4, 0 : 71[c], 119[e], 129[d], 131[c]	2, 0 : 19[c], 59[c]
c) Use of praise	4, 0 : 4[c], 30, 61, 119	3, + : 30[d], 71[c], 129[c] 3, 0 : 4[c], 119[e], 131[c]	1, 0 : 19[c]
2. Clarity of Training			
a) Consistency of parental agreement on discipline	2, 0 : 30, 119	2, + : 71[c], 131[c] 2, 0 : 119[e], 129[d]	2, + : 19[c], 59[c]
b) Use of reasoning	2, + : 4[c], 119[a] 1, 0 : 119[b] 2, − : 30, 93[d]	3, + : 30[d], 93[d], 129[d] 3, 0 : 71[c], 131[c], 119[e]	2, + : 19[c], 59[c]
3. Height or Severity of Demands			
a) General moral demandingness	2, + : 28, 119[bd] 2, 0 : 30, 119[a]	2, + : 119[b], 131[c] 1, 0 : 129[d]	1, 0 : 19[c]
b) Assigning chores responsibilities	2, 0 : 63[d], 119	1, + : 131[c] 1, 0 : 129[d] 1, − : 119[ae]	1, 0 : 19[c]
c) Obedience	4, 0 : 4[c], 30, 61, 119	4, 0 : 4[e], 131[c], 119[e], 129[d]	1, + : 19[c]
d) Achievement	1, + : 119[a] 3, 0 : 30, 61, 119[b]	2, 0 : 119[e], 129[d]	1, + : 19[c]
e) Weaning: Severity	1, + : 4[c] 3, 0 : 30[a], 61, 119 1, − : 119	1, + : 71[c] 2, 0 : 79, 119[c]	
Earliness	3, 0 : 4[c], 30, 119	1, − : 4[c]	1, − : 6
f) Neatness	1, + : 61[b] 3, 0 : 30[a], 61[a], 119 1, − : 30	1, 0 : 119[b] 1, − : 119[ae]	
g) Toilet training: Earliness of completion	1, + : 61[a] 4, 0 : 4[c], 30[a], 61[b], 119 1, − : 30[b]	1, 0 : 119 1, − : 4[c]	1, 0 : 19[c]
h) Aggression: Prohibition outside home	3, 0 : 30, 61, 119[b] 1, − : 119[a]	1, + : 79 4, 0 : 46, 119[e], 129[d], 131[c]	1, + : 19[c]
Against parents	3, 0 : 30, 61, 119	4, 0 : 46, 119[e], 129[d], 131[cc]	1, 0 : 19
i) Sex prohibitions	3, 0 : 30, 61, 119	1, + : 119[be] 2, 0 : 79, 131[c] 1, − : 119[ae]	1, + : 19[c] 1, 0 : 19[c]

* The first column in this table lists each of the antecedent conditions of moral learning previously summarized. The second column presents the number of studies finding the given learning condition positively associated with resistance to temptation, the number of studies finding it to be negatively associated with resistance, and the number of studies finding no association ($p < .05$) between the two variables. (The studies listed in the second column of the table used experimental measures of resistance to temptation, except as indicated in the table footnotes.) The third column lists in similar fashion the studies in which measures of "guilt" were correlated with the given learning condition. Unless otherwise specified, all the studies reported in the third column used measures of guilt based on various weightings of unpleasant consequences described by the child in completing stories involving transgressions. The fourth column presents differential use of the various learning conditions by parents of matched delinquent and nondelinquent boys of middle-class and lower-class status.

a) The association was found among girls but not boys.

b) The association was found among girls but not boys.

c) The study was limited to boys.

d) The measure of conscience used was based on a general rating by the mother or teacher. Ratings in the "guilt" column were ratings of tendencies to confess.

e) The measure of conscience was a rating of emotional upset in an experimental transgression situation.

reinforcement and measures of amount of conformity to these standards outside the home in experimental situations tapping tendencies to cheat (**30**) or disobey (**119**).

It is apparent that these results pose a serious challenge to avoidance-learning explanations of moral development. Some of these difficulties are undoubtedly due to weakness in interview measures of child-rearing practices. Some are due to the necessity of studying parental training in terms of relatively gross variables on which interview material can be gathered, rather than in terms of more refined analysis of schedules of training and reinforcement.

EMPIRICAL EVIDENCE ON THE CONCEPT OF CONSCIENCE AS BEHAVIORAL CONFORMITY

The confusing results just discussed also suggest the need to revise the working assumption of the learning-theory approach that moral responses are generalized habits of inhibition. The three following kinds of generalizations are implied by this apparently simple assumption: (*a*) the assumption that habits of moral inhibition are generalized across situations inside or outside the home; (*b*) the assumption that inhibitions learned at home with parents will generalize to situations outside the home; (*c*) the assumption that inhibition habits learned in situations where a punishing agent has been present will be generalized to situations where a punishing agent is not present. The issues raised by these assumptions are not only problems in methods of measuring morality but are fundamental to any application of learning concepts to moral development.

Hartshorne and May (**66**) concluded that there was little consistency of moral behavior from one situation to another. They found relatively low correlations among experimental situations measuring honesty (resistance to cheating), service (expending effort or goods on a group or charitable goal), or self-control (task persistence).[1] Rau (**119**) obtained somewhat similarly low correla-

1. Some qualification of Hartshorne and May's "specificity" conclusion is required, however, in light of a recent factor analysis of the Hartshorne and May data performed by Burton, Carlsmith, and Beswick (**29**), and factor analyses by other workers summarized in the Burton paper. When honesty tests of low retest reliability (less than .70) are eliminated, factor analysis of intercorrelations of the six remaining tests indicates a moderate first general factor indicating some degree of consistency of honesty across tasks. For various reasons discussed by Burton *et al.*, these data cannot be used to infer the exist-

tions between four moral-obedience situations, administered to younger children. Hartshorne and May (**66**) also found little correlation between cheating at home and at school, and Rau (**119**) reports little relation between tendency to confess after deviation in the two situations. Grinder (**61**), however, found tendency to confess at home at age five related to school resistance to temptation at age twelve.

The Hartshorne and May data suggest that realistic punishment in the immediate situation is the most important variable in eliciting cheating or honesty. They found children to be normally distributed on frequency of cheating in experimental situations rather than being bimodally divided into cheating and noncheating groups. Almost all of the children cheated, but they varied in how much risk and effort they would take to cheat.

This evidence of situational specificity suggests that the kind of punishment and reward important for resistance behavior is the punishment and reward in the test situation or in one very similar to it. In so far as home discipline conditions affect resistance, it is probably because of peculiar similarities of the test situation to home learning situations, rather than because of the intervention of generalized avoidance or "conscience."

We are able to say little regarding the generalization of moral inhibition from punished to nonpunished situations. The Hartshorne and May data suggest that even the nonpunished situations are reacted to in terms of more or less realistic punishment concerns. Studies in other areas, such as aggression, suggest that home parental punishment may lead to inhibition in situations of possible punishment but not in permissive situations (**130**). Disobedience and dishonesty may also be inhibited by home punishment, but such inhibition may not generalize much to "permissive" resistance to temptation situations or to the unsupervised situations outside the home in which delinquencies are committed.

Hartshorne and May report other evidence inconsistent with the notion that moral responses are generalized or internalized avoid-

---

ence of a situation-free tendency to be honest or to inhibit cheating. It indicates rather that situations which are very similar will elicit similar tendencies to cheat, and that situations can be ordered on dimensions of similarity to one another.

ance-habits defined by standards brought *into* situations. They found little stability over time in resistance to cheating in the same situation, and great variations with situational "group morale" factors.

The data considered so far, then, do not support the notion that internalized moral conformity or conscience consists of "conditioned anxiety responses" or general avoidance-habits produced by parental discipline. They suggest, rather, the importance of specific situational factors in resistance to temptation.

The resistance-to-temptation data raise a more basic issue than that of adequacy of avoidance-learning theory to account for the development of "conscience" as ordinarily conceived. The data raise the question as to whether there are any psychological dispositions which can be usefully conceived as "conscience" or "internalized standards." On the one hand, no single occurrence of conforming behavior can be used to indicate the existence of an internalized standard, as opposed to indicating the existence of situational wishes and fears. On the other hand, the empirically observed consistency of conformity behavior is not high enough to indicate the existence of internalized standards from a series of behavior observations. If there is little consistency from situation to situation involving the same standard, we cannot assume that conforming behavior is determined by the standard and not by situational forces.

There are two possible conclusions which may be drawn. One is that "morality" is an evaluative and not an explanatory concept, of no more use in explaining human behavior than in explaining the behavior of a rat. An alternative conclusion is that an adequate concept of morality must go beyond a formulation in terms of behavioral conformity, a conclusion leading us to examine next the guilt concept.

LEARNING-THEORY CONCEPTS AND FINDINGS ON "GUILT" REACTIONS TO TRANSGRESSION

Besides behavioral conformity, an often-used criterion of the presence of an internalized standard is that of the occurrence of guilt reactions after real or fantasied transgressions. The definition of conscience in terms of the guilt reaction is close to ordinary language usage (**86**) as well as to psychoanalytic usage.

A conception of morality as guilt seems to avoid the difficulties raised for the behavior-conformity approach, for it is possible to yield to temptation and yet hold an internal standard expressed in the guilt reaction. It would seem possible to infer the existence of such a standard from a single guilt response.

This approach, however, depends on the assumption that some observable responses to transgression are *expressive* of guilt or remorse, i.e., that self-blame reactions genuinely inflict psychic pain upon the self rather than being instrumental responses to a situation. This assumption has been called into question by recent learning-theory analyses of the responses to transgression.

In one such analysis, Aronfreed (**9**) examined children's completions of transgression stories as expressions of guilt reactions. He points out that the core meaning of "guilt" is the tendency to make self-critical, self-blaming verbal responses. Such responses were not universal or even very frequent reactions to transgression stories among Aronfreed's sixth-grade subjects. Self-blame responses also did not appear to be "master reactions" determining a whole series of other frequent transgression reactions, such as confession, restitution, punishment, and the like. Thus, direct "guilt" did not appear to be a major aspect of children's awareness and response to wrongdoing.

Aronfreed goes on to conclude that self-blaming responses, confession, restitution, and other reactions to transgression are anxiety-reducing instrumental responses, rather than pain-inducing "expressions of guilt." He considers the affective component of any internalized reaction to transgression to be essentially anxiety, learned after punishment for transgression in accordance with the laws of learning "secondary drives."

Aronfreed has performed a series of experiments (**7, 10, 11**) designed to demonstrate the role of the reduction of punishment-induced anxiety in the learning of self-critical and other responses. His most basic experiment (**10**) was designed to test the hypothesis that children would learn self-critical responses when the position of adult criticism in the course of punishment was such that its cue components would become secondary reinforcers through their association with anxiety termination. The child would then presumably imitate the critical labels following subsequent transgression because of their anxiety-reducing value. An experimental analogue of the learning of self-criticism was developed through telling children that a "transgression" in the use of an elaborate machine was a "blue" act. The experimenter (E) punished the act with strong verbal disapproval and deprivation of candy already given to the child. In one experimental condition, the child was told by E that he had acted in a "blue" way at the very onset of punishment and at the sounding of a buzzer which served to signal the occurrence of transgression. In a second condition, the child was told he had been "blue" at the very termination of punishment and at the turning off of the buzzer. A third control condition differed from the others in that no punishment was associated with performing a "blue" act. After a number of training trials, test trials were used in which E withheld punishment and asked the children "what had happened" (with the buzzer sounding). Only the group of children who had been trained with the blue label at termination of punishment and buzzer were found to imitate E's labeling to any substantial extent.

Hill (**74**) has also analyzed *confession* as an instrumental response learned if parents reduce punishment ("contingent punishment") to reward it. Levine (**93**) found association between the mother's reported use of contingent punishment and her report of the child's tendency to confess. Confession responses in children's stories are associated with responses indicating expectations that the parents will repair the damage and forgive the child (**119, 141**). The associations suggest the role of confession as an instrumental response to obtain forgiveness. Aronfreed (**9, 7**) has made parallel analyses of confession and restitution responses.

In spite of this evidence of the role of instrumental anxiety-reducing factors in self-criticism and in other internalized responses, Aronfreed (**7**) points out that self-criticism is something more than an instrumental response and that its place in the phenomena of guilt and moral development depends on its cognitive and evaluative precursors. The view that naturally occurring self-blame after transgression is more than an instrumental response is strongly supported by observed relations between self-blame tendencies and other aspects of morality. Self-blame in both projective and self-report material is positively associated with both resistance to temptation and to nondelinquency. All of the six studies which related behavioral conformity indicators to self-criticism responses found a positive relationship between the two variables.[2] If self-criticism were simply an instrumental anxiety-reducing response, there is no reason why it would be inconsistent with high transgression. Aronfreed (**7**) and Kohlberg (**88**) have interpreted the noninstrumental components of self-blame as matters of cognitive-evaluative development. It is also possible, however, that the associations of self-blame with resistance to temptation represent guilt as psychoanalytically conceived, i.e., as tendencies of children to inflict psychic and physical pain upon themselves after transgression in defiance of the "pleasure principle." These conflicting interpretations will be considered in relation to findings related to the psychoanalytic theory of childhood guilt.

The current evidence, then, does not warrant the notion that guilt reactions are nothing but instrumental techniques for reducing anxiety aroused by punishment and blame. It does, however, suggest extreme caution in treating "guilt-expressive" responses as indications of guilt or conscience.

PSYCHOANALYTIC CONCEPTS OF GUILT AND STUDIES OF TRANSGRESSION REACTIONS

The guilt concept has received its most systematic and elaborate treatment in psychoanalytic theory. Three of the basic conceptions of guilt in psychoanalytic theory grow out of common-sense notions:

1. Guilt reactions are conceived as a product of identification, i.e., of an equation of the self with the blaming responses of another.
2. Guilt is viewed as basically self-punishment (rather than as self-criticism or as a reaction of remorse for harm to others and a need to compensate for that harm). This view is, in turn, related to the view that guilt is the inward turning of aggressive drives.
3. Conscience or the guilt-system (superego) is a unitary system relatively distinct from the rest of the personality.

Three additional hypotheses about guilt, diverging further from common-sense notions, are made by psychoanalytic theory:

4. Considerable amounts of guilt are to be found among almost all children and adults (except perhaps "psychopaths").

2. These studies will be listed in Table 2.

5. Guilt may be unconscious, "defended against," and indirectly expressed.
6. Strong guilt may exist in an individual even though the guilt is ineffective in preventing repeated transgression.

Recent researches on children's "projective" responses to incomplete stories of transgression allow an empirical consideration of these hypotheses.

The psychoanalytic interpretation, elaborated by Allinsmith (**4**), and others, views all responses to transgression (except hiding) as possible expressions of guilt, since all involve painful or effortful consequences of transgression which may satisfy the need for punishment and self-blame. This interpretation coincides with common sense with regard to manifest expressions of guilt, such as self-criticism, remorse, and confession. The remaining painful consequences of transgression are seen as indirect forms of guilt resulting from the intervention of defenses against the direct painful remorse experience. The most frequent such response is the portrayal of external punishment and blame.[3] Following A. Freud (**50**), this response is seen as the result of externalizing defense mechanisms somewhat analogous to the paranoid's perception of his own self-accusations as the unjustified derogations of others. Since the punishment described by the child is not a logical outcome to transgression stories in which risk of detection has been ruled out, there is some plausibility in viewing the response as a need-determined defensive distortion.

It is difficult to test directly this psychoanalytic interpretation since it does not discriminate one individual or one kind of response from another. Once the concept of "defense against guilt" is introduced, any response to a transgression situation except escape and enjoyment may be interpreted as a form of guilt. In this regard, the psychoanalytic view (every transgression response represents guilt) is similar to the instrumental-learning view (no transgression response represents guilt) in that it fails to formulate any definite relations between types of transgression response and other aspects of conscience.

The types of response which have been found to be frequently

3. A somewhat similar consequence, accidental or physical harm, is viewed by Maccoby and Whiting (**96**) as a measure of self-punitive tendencies since it is even more distant from realistic concern about punishment by others.

elicited by transgression stories are listed in the first column of Table 2. The results summarized in Table 2 suggest some definite relationships between certain types of transgression reactions which are not only not predicted by the psychoanalytic interpretation but which are actually inconsistent with the interpretation.

TABLE 2

RELATIONS BETWEEN TRANSGRESSION REACTIONS AND OTHER MORAL RESPONSE VARIABLES

Types of Transgression Reaction	Resistance to Temptation	Relations to Confession	Non-delinquency	Age, I.Q., Sex, Class Differences
1. Self-critical reactions, self-report of guilt, remorse	3, + : **4**[ce], **71**[ce], **98**	1, + : **96**	2, + : **19**[c], **97**	Age increase: **8, 96** No I.Q. difference: **8, 97** Middle-class high: **8**
2. Overt anxiety	1, + : **119**[b]			Girls high: **119**
3. Confession	4, + : **61**[d], **93, 119, 121** 2, 0 : **30, 119** 1, − : **30**[d]		1, 0 : **19**[c]	Age increase: **141** No I.Q. difference: **8** Girls high: **121**
4. Fixing by child	1, + : **119**[a] 1, 0 : **30** 1, − : **119**[b]	2, − : **96**[b], **119**[b]	1, 0 : **19**	Age increase: **141** No I.Q. difference: **8** Boys high: **141**
5. Hiding	1, 0 : **119**	1, 0 : **119**	1, 0 : **19**	
6. Punishment	1, + : **119**[b] 2, 0 : **30, 119**[a] 1, − : **4**	3, − : **96**[b], **119**,[b] **139**	1, 0 : **19**	Age decrease: **141** No I.Q. difference: **8** Boys high: **119**
7. Accidental harm	1, 0 : **30**	1, + : **96**	1, 0 : **19**	Age decline: **141**
8. Moralizing		1, + : **141**	1, + : **19**	
9. Total consequences	1, 0 : **4**[ce]			

a) The association was found among girls but not boys.
b) The association was found among boys but not girls.
c) The study was limited to boys.
d) The confession measure was a parent rating.
e) The resistance measure was a parent or teacher rating or a verbal measure.

As was noted earlier, self-criticism and confession (to some extent) are both positively related to behavior conformity. Both, then, have some claim to represent internalized standards. Such conscious "guilt" responses do not seem, however, to indicate deep superego structures. If these responses corresponded to usual notions of guilt, we would expect them to increase after transgression. Rebelsky

(**121**) found no significant increase in projective confession responses after transgression. The responses of noncheaters, who had nothing to feel guilty about, increased slightly more than those of cheaters, who did have something to feel guilty about. Aronfreed (**8**) also failed to find an increase of story completion evidencing direct guilt (self-criticism, remorse, and confession) among college students who were made to believe they had carelessly broken a machine. It is not clear whether these findings indicate defects in usual conceptions of guilt or in the assumptions about the arousal situations and about guilt projection into stories.

The negative experimental evidence of the Rebelsky and Aronfreed studies is especially plausible with regard to the confession response. Evidence for considering it as an instrumental or pain-avoiding response to obtain forgiveness was considered earlier. There is, however, ample evidence that extreme use of confession is a technique of children with a genuinely high need for forgiveness, i.e., a high concern for maintaining an approving and nurturant attitude on the part of parents and others.[4] As discussed later, confession responses are correlated with the child's dependency, with the mother's warmth, and with the mother's manipulation of the dependency relationship in discipline (**129**). Confession is favored by preadolescent girls as compared with boys (**121**), and they are also more approval-oriented in making verbal moral decisions than are boys (**89**). The approval orientation of high confessors seems to lead to resistance to temptation, though the variations in these associations reported in Table 2 suggest that such resistance may be dependent on the high confessor's relationship to the authority person in the temptation situation.

The confession-apology-restitution-conformity complex of responses can be viewed as characteristic expressions of moral identification in the limited sense of a tendency to anticipate and role-take parental disapproval reactions, but not in the sense of internally initiated and maintained self-critical and self-punitive responses.

In conjunction with the experimental evidence, then, the data suggest that the confession response represents a technique of dealing with transgression related to concern about approval. It seems to

4. The restitution or fixing response appears to be almost purely an instrumental punishment-avoiding response, on the other hand.

increase with age in middle childhood, as children become more capable of anticipating disapproval reactions.

For logical reasons and because of apparently closer relations to resistance to temptation, self-criticism has more claim than confession to being an internalized self-reaction. It seems to be largely a product of social-cognitive maturity factors. Self-criticism responses are almost never made by 4–6-year-olds (**96, 141**), but are made by 75 per cent of 12-year-olds (**9**). Similar but weaker age trends are found for confession.

Punishment is first defined as "good" at about age eight. "Disinterested" moral judgments of others, "moral indignation," and the development of a self-concept as someone who wants to be a morally good person, develop in the same preadolescent period in which self-critical responses become frequent (**88**). Hoffman (**76**) found "internal guilt" on story completions associated with internal, developmentally mature types of moral judgment on Piaget-type questions, holding age constant. In light of relations of "story" self-criticism to both behavioral conformity and to development of moral judgment, it seems appropriate, therefore, to view self-criticism as a product of general social development rather than as a product of self-punishing needs or as an anxiety-reducing technique.

We may conclude that manifest expressions of guilt on projective tests, such as self-criticism and confession, reflect socialized concerns about good and bad rather than the deep self-punitive trends implied by the superego concept. Direct expressions of superego or self-punishment responses are also very rare in this material. These conclusions do not coincide with the second and fourth of the listed psychoanalytic assumptions about guilt. However, these assumptions are not meant to hold primarily for direct forms of guilt, but rather for the various disguised forms of guilt which might be indicated by the remaining types of response to transgression.

The evidence from Table 2 fails to support the psychoanalytic interpretation of these responses as representing guilt, however. Neither "punishment" reactions (6) nor "total guilt" measures (9) seem to be positively related to measures of behavioral conformity or internalized standards. Such lack of positive relationship does not support the "defense against guilt" interpretation, although it is not inconsistent with it. Allinsmith (**4**) interpreted negative associations between "externalized guilt" (punishment reactions and physical harm) and verbal resistance to temptation as suggesting that unconscious defensive guilt does not function to prevent deviation as does conscious guilt (an interpretation in line with psychoanalytic theories of unconscious guilt as a cause of delinquency).

Further negative findings are inconsistent, however, with this unconscious guilt. Burton (**30**) found that punishment or impersonal harm responses to deviation doll-play stories administered before an experimental test of cheating did not discriminate preschool cheaters from noncheaters. He did find, however, that noncheaters significantly increased in fantasy punishment in doll play administered *after* temptation, compared to their level before "temptation," and compared to the level of cheaters after temptation. This finding, like the finding on arousal and confession, is quite inconsistent with the notion that fantasy punishment represents guilt in this age group.

Burton's findings are consistent, however, with the notion that increase of fantasy punishment reduces cognitive dissonance (**48**), i.e., it justifies a choice which renounces the rewards of transgression. Mills (**104**) attempted to test Festinger's theory in a situation similar to Burton's, using groups of twelve-year-olds. Mills found that after exposure to temptation to cheat, noncheaters increased in the severity of punishment they said should be inflicted for cheating, while cheaters did not.[5] Like Burton, Mills also failed to find any relations between results on tests of punishment attitudes administered before temptation and of resistance to cheat, suggesting that the results were not a function of personality differences between cheaters and noncheaters, but of situational pressures toward dissonance reduction.

The findings summarized in Table 2, and other findings, also fail to support the fifth assumption about punishment as defensive guilt, e.g., that it should correlate with direct guilt responses in a way which would be expected if it were a substitute for direct guilt reactions.

The evidence, then, does not provide much support for the

5. Neither Burton, Mills, nor Aronfreed (**8**) found significant decrease in punishment among transgressors, suggesting the dissonance interpretation of these situations is oversimplified.

fourth, fifth, and sixth of the tested psychoanalytic assumptions which state that most children have pervasive, unconscious, self-punishing tendencies (guilt) expressed in disguised fashions. The data suggest that the "guilt" concept has a real meaning in terms of the conscious, developmentally advanced, self-critical (and self-controlling) response, but that it loses meaning as one moves away from this response into psychoanalytically conceived self-punitive reactions.

Some qualification of the conclusions derived from Table 2 is required in light of the nature of the story-completion method used. In the first place, the method is not fully "projective" in the usual sense, since the transgression stimulus is well defined. Accordingly, it taps conventional moralistic reactions rather than free-floating guilt. In contrast, "guilt" responses to an unstructured stimulus like the Thematic Apperception Test (TAT) would be based on the subject's intrusion of transgression punishment or remorse into a neutral picture and might illuminate a more "superego-like" concept of guilt. This may be particularly true for the neurotic cases on which psychoanalytic guilt theory has focused.

Closely related to the assumptions of superego theory which were considered in terms of the results presented in Table 2 is the second listed assumption, i.e., guilt is the inward turning of aggression. There is little direct research support for this assumption. The "inward turning of aggression" hypothesis suggests that parental severity and frustrativeness, particularly with regard to restricting aggression, is correlated with guilt. The results presented in Table 1 failed to support this hypothesis. The hypothesis would also suggest that high inhibition of overt aggressive behavior by the children themselves would be associated with high guilt, an implication also not supported, with one exception (**71**), by the various studies.

Unfortunately, the studies of displacement of aggression under experimental arousal have not dealt in detail with the hypothesis that guilt is a form of displacement of aggression (upon the self). MacKinnon's study (**100**) did show that noncheaters in a frustrating task engaged in considerable self-criticism as compared with controls. In light of other results already discussed, however, this result may simply indicate the finding already discussed, i.e., that people capable of self-criticism when they fail or deviate also resist temptation more.

The relationships between aggression-inhibition and morality, which have been rather consistently obtained, involve resistance to temptation rather than guilt. Rau (**119**) found high negative correlations between family doll-play measures of aggressive fantasy and resistance-to-temptation behavior in the experimental situations. Bach (**13**) reported similar relations between fantasy aggression in doll play and teachers' ratings of compliance. Several projective test studies have indicated higher fantasy aggression in delinquent boys than in matched controls.

These relations of conscience to fantasy aggression are probably not simply the reflections of a general tendency to inhibit deviant behavior, since ratings of aggressive behavior did not relate negatively to resistance to temptation in the Rau study. Nevertheless, the correlations do not support the "inward turning of aggression" view of conscience, since resistance to temptation cannot be looked upon as a direct expression of intrapunitiveness. The findings do support another related psychoanalytic hypothesis—the hypothesis that moral transgression is essentially a matter of disguised aggression against family authorities.[6] The fact that transgression against rules in a school situation seems to be related to fantasy family aggression, but not to general aggressive behavior in school, lends support to this hypothesis.

We have considered the Freudian theory of the nature of guilt in detail, not only because of its vast influence upon psychotherapy, literature, and the general culture, but because it is the only systematic theory recognizing the distinctive features of guilt embodied in adult experience. It is perhaps tragicomic to evaluate the theory in terms of children's verbal responses to little stories of transgression, but there is hardly any other systematic evidence concerning children's guilt. We may tentatively conclude, however, that psychoanalytic theory is inadequate to account for the social-developmental research observations on guilt and allied responses.

Some of the neo-Freudian theories (**12, 44, 80, 118, 134**) of

6. It would be interesting to know whether the projective aggression is in any way family specific. Unfortunately, doll-play studies have almost all been restricted to the use of family dolls and situations.

ego-related moral emotions seem more fitting in regard to these findings. Unlike the Freudian view of moral emotion as the product of an internal, unconscious structure, the neo-Freudians have seen moral emotions of guilt, shame, and anxiety as types of reaction of a social self concerned about maintaining self-esteem in the eyes of significant others, in cultures which vary in their concern about internal states of good and evil.

ROLE-LEARNING THEORIES OF IDENTIFICATION AND MORALITY

In the preceding section, we did not directly deal with the most influential concept of Freudian superego theory, that of identification. The root meaning of identification is a tendency to model one's own behavior after another's. Identification is distinguished from imitation (**41, 60, 83, 120, 128**) in that:

1. It is a motivated disposition rather than an instrumental response, i.e., it is maintained without obvious extrinsic or situational rewards. In some sense, the fact of perceived similarity to the model is intrinsically rewarding.
2. Similarity to the model is maintained in the absence of the model.
3. Modeling is relatively global, i.e., many aspects of the model's behavior are reproduced.

Many measures of parental identification have been based on an index of global similarity between the child's responses in a "projective test" situation and his perceptions of the responses which his parents would make in the same situation. The use of global similarity indices in a projective situation where the parent is not present, and where the responses do not serve an instrumental goal, seems to conform to the definition just presented.

This core meaning of the identification concept is shared by both psychoanalytic identification theory, which we consider later, and by the learning theorists (**94, 128, 139**), sociologists (**25**), and social psychologists interested in attitude change (**85**), who might be said to hold role-learning theories of identification. These role-learning theories conceive of identification as a normal type of global social learning of the role-responses of significant others based upon the positive value to the child of making such responses. The value of these responses in turn arises from the child's continuing relation of dependency upon socializing agents, whether this dependency is conceived of as a love relationship (**106**) or as a power relationship (**138**). In this view, the identification type of imitative response-learning differs from other imitative learning in being a learning of a total role and in being based upon a strong emotional tie to the model. In this usage, identification has often been used as an unobservable variable designed to account for correlations between aspects of the parent-child relationship and the child's moral responses.

Role-learning identification theories postulate that conscience is the product of pretransgression imitation of parental prohibiting responses and of posttransgression parental critical and punitive responses. In research applications, it has been assumed that the basic aspect of identification relevant to conscience-formation is the quantitative "strength" of both, i.e., "strong identification leads to strong conscience."

Within role-learning views of identification, two types of theory have emerged: developmental identification theory (**106, 129**) and social-power identification theory (**25, 83, 138**). The two types have differed chiefly in their hypotheses about the aspects of the parent-child relationship which cause identification. According to developmental theory, the antecedents of high identification and conscience include the following:

1. The parent's warmth and nurturance and the child's dependency.
2. The physical presence or absence of the parents and the extent of their interaction with the child.
3. The degree of the parent's manipulation of the love relationship in order to secure conformity, e.g., the use of "love withdrawal" discipline techniques.
4. The clarity and consistency of the parent's role-modeling, including both the strength of parental expectations that the child will be similar to the self or the spouse and the parent's acceptance of his own role.

Social-power theory accepts most of the preceding antecedents of high identification and conscience and adds the following:

5. The parent's power with regard to desired resources which are not consumed by the child, including both the parent's power over his spouse's behavior or the prestige or love awarded him by his spouse and the parent's power and prestige in the outside community.
6. The extent to which the same-sex parent is more powerful.

7. The parent's power over the child and his control over the child's resources. In addition to control over love resources, this includes control over the child's physical gratifications and control over deprivation and pain experienced by the child, e.g., punitiveness.

DEVELOPMENTAL IDENTIFICATION THEORY AND RELATED FINDINGS

Developmental identification theory hypothesizes that the more the child values the presence and responsiveness of the parent, the more the child will value imitative responses he can make which are like the parent's. This result is believed to occur because of processes of secondary drive conditioning and stimulus generalization postulated by the Hullian learning theory.

Some experimental support for this notion has been found. Investigators (**15, 43**) have reported that preschool children imitate a nurturant and responsive adult experimenter more than a passive ignoring experimenter. Their results are also in part supported by the observed correlations between measures of parental attitudes and measures of conscience or identification. These correlations are summarized in Table 3.

Table 3 suggests a relationship between both maternal and paternal nurturance and conscience, such as the developmental identification theory would require. There are a number of qualifications which must be made, however, in considering the fit of developmental identification theory to these results. The evidence for a correlation between maternal nurturance and behavior conformity (resistance to temptation and delinquency) is largely limited to boys. Parental nurturance seems to relate to measures of children's conformity to moral conventions rather than directly to guilt indicators of conscience-identification. The "guilt" response related to parental nurturance is the confession response which we saw was more a measure of approval-sensitive conformity than of identification-based guilt. The relations of nurturance to direct measures of identification tend to be positive but tend to be positive under different conditions from those holding for the conscience relationships.

Many explanations may be advanced for relationships between parental nurturance and conscience. Two explanations of nurturance-conscience relationships which do not involve identification in

TABLE 3

ASSOCIATIONS OF PARENTAL AFFECTION AND POWER WITH IDENTIFICATION AND CONSCIENCE

	IDENTIFICATION	RESISTANCE TO TEMPTATION	GUILT	NONDELINQUENCY
1. a) Maternal warmth and nurturance	3, + : 46[fg], 96[bg], 110[ag] 2, 0 : 110[ag], 131[af]	3, + : 28, 30[b], 93[d] 2, 0 : 61, 119 1, − : 30[a] 3, 0 : 30, 61, 119	3, + : 28[d], 93[d], 129[d] 4, 0 : 71[c], 79, 131[c], 119 1, − : 119 1, 0 : 119	2, + : 19[c], 59[c]
b) Child's dependency or affection for the mother	1, + : 96[ag]			3, + : 6[c], 19, 59[c]
c) Father's warmth and nurturance	3, + : 108[cf] 1, 0 : 131[cf]	1, + : 119[b] 1, 0 : 61 1, − : 119[a] 1, 0 : 119	1, + : 119[a] 2, 0 : 71[c], 119[b]	2, + : 19[c], 59[c]
d) Child's dependency or affection for the father			1, + : 119	3, + : 6[c], 19[c], 59[c]
2. a) Physical presence of mother				1, + : 24
b) Physical presence of father (unbroken home)	2, + : 127[cg]			1, + : 59[c]
3. Predominance of love-withdrawal over direct punishment	1, + : 46[f] 1, − : 46[g]	1, + : 100 4, 0 : 30, 61, 93[d], 119	7, + : 5[c], 8, 46, 79, 93[d], 100[c], 129 4, 0 : 4[c], 71[c], 131[c], 119	1, 0 : 19
4. a) Parental reinforcement for being like self or spouse (if child is of opposite sex)	1, + : 72[gc] 1, 0 : 109	1, 0 : 119	1, 0 : 119	
b) Parental identification with own roles	1, 0 : 108	1, 0 : 119	1, 0 : 119	
c) Maternal self-esteem	1, + : 60[f]		2, + : 60, 131	
5. a) Maternal power over the girl	3, 0 : 75, 96[bg], 108[g]	3, 0 : 30, 61, 119	1, 0 : 119	
b) General maternal authority and prestige in the family (*re:* girl's identification)	1, + : 46[g] 1, 0 : 60 1, − : 75	1, 0 : 119	1, + : 131 1, 0 : 119	
c) Paternal power over the boy (father agent of discipline)	3, 0 : 75[f], 96, 108[g]	1, + : 28[d] 3, 0 : 30, 61, 119	1, + : 119 2, − : 71, 73	1, + : 6 1, − : 59[c]
d) General paternal authority and prestige (*re:* boy's identification)	2, + : 46[g], 75[f] 1, 0 : 60	1, 0 : 119	1, + : 71 2, 0 : 119, 131	1, 0 : 59[c]

a) The association was found among girls but not boys.

b) The association was found among boys but not girls.

c) The study was limited to boys.

d) The measure of conscience used was based on a general rating by the mother or teacher. Ratings in the fourth "guilt" column were ratings of tendencies to confess.

e) The measure of conscience was a rating of emotional upset in an experimental transgression situation.

f) The measure was of personal identification (perceived similarity).

g) The measure was of positional identification (adult or same-sex role).

a strict sense have been advanced by Bowlby (**24**) and Bandura and Walters (**19**). Bowlby sees the "maternal deprivation" he found in the histories of 44 juvenile thieves as causing an emotional flatness and lack of empathy which lead to a general indifference to the effects of action upon other people. Bowlby's explanation ignores the fact that delinquent boys are more clearly "paternally deprived" than "maternally deprived." Bandura and Walters, taking account of this fact, see delinquent rejection of (paternal) authority and consequent misbehavior as the result of a strong conflict about dependency upon both parents.

This explanation of nurturance-delinquency relations does not seem, however, to account for relationships between normal variations of nurturance and conscience among nondelinquent children. A simple explanation of these relationships would be based on the common-sense and cognitive theory notion (**48**) that, if an individual likes an authority, he will conform to the rules taught by that authority, an explanation that does not assume the intervention of imitative responses. It should also be noted that parental nurturance seems to be part of the class-differentiating "enlightened" child-rearing attitudes. It is possible, therefore, that the observed correlations are part of a global "good-parent, good-child" pattern having little relation to identification or parental affection as causal factors.

Although these correlations between conscience and general parental nurturance are important facts, they suggest too many plausible explanations to be useful in supporting identification theories. More interesting hypotheses have been derived from a second implication of the theory that identification-conscience is a substitute response for parental nurturance. The theory implies that while parental presence and loving care would lead to a *learning* to value imitative responses, it would not lead to the *performance* of such responses while the parent is available. If the parent were absent or unresponsive, however, the child would be expected to perform imitative responses as substitutes for the parental responses. Mowrer (**106**) illustrates this point by the results of experiments in which talking birds only learned imitatively to "talk" if the experimenter gave them affectionate care, but only performed the talking responses while the experimenter was out of the room.

Experiments by Hartup (**67**) and Rosenblith (**123**) were designed to test the hypothesis that verbal nurturance followed by withdrawal of nurturance would lead to maximum imitation of an adult experimenter by kindergarten children. Both studies obtained some results supporting this hypothesis, although these results were complicated and depended on the sex of the child and of the experimenter.

The nurturance-withdrawal hypothesis has been applied to moral learning (**129, 140**). It was hypothesized that discipline techniques involving the parent's withdrawal of love after the child's transgression would maximize the child's performance of identificatory guilt response; that "love-withdrawal" discipline techniques of ignoring, isolation, and emotional rejection would increase the need for parental response and stimulate the child's imitation to these responses. In contrast, it was hypothesized that physical punishment and scolding would maximize the unpleasantness of parental responses and so reduce tendencies to imitate the parent after deviation.

Sears, Maccoby, and Levin (**129**) also hypothesized that the effectiveness of love withdrawal would depend on the existence of general strong emotional tie between mother and child. They found that in families with "warm" mothers, high use of love-withdrawal techniques was associated with high reported confession, but this was not true for families with "cold" mothers. Table 3 indicates that this association between love withdrawal and indicators of "guilt" (mainly confession) has been reported in several other studies as well.

It should be noted, however, that love withdrawal does not seem to relate to moral behavior and probably does not relate to transgression responses other than the responses associated with confession (**9**). Thus, the effect of love withdrawal does not appear to be that expected if it caused high general moral identification and guilt.

These negative aspects of the love withdrawal–morality correlations might be taken to suggest the earlier mentioned Hill (**74**) interpretation of the love withdrawal–confession relationship, as based on simple reinforcement. In support of Hill's interpretation, Levine (**93**) found maternal use of contingent discipline (easing punishment as a reward for confession) related to both child's confession and maternal use of love-withdrawal techniques. Further findings, however, did not support the reinforcement interpretation. Levine found love withdrawal significantly correlated with confession, even with use of contingent techniques controlled.

The findings on love withdrawal reinforce our earlier conclusions that love withdrawal in a context of general parental nurturance tends to induce a high need for parental forgiveness and restoration of a positive relationship after transgression.

This interpretation of the love withdrawal–morality correlation is reinforced if consideration is given to a theoretical weakness in the developmental identification theory of conscience. This theory views identification as a substitute for positively valued responses of the parent. Guilt (identification with criticism and punishment responses), however, involves imitation of painful, negatively valued responses. No matter how attached a child is to the parent or how much love withdrawal occurs after deviation, there is no reason why critical and punishing responses should become positively valued by the child, and hence imitated. Identification on a purely positive basis would lead a child who had transgressed to imitate positive responses of the parent on occasions when she had said, "Good boy," rather than to imitate the parent when she had said, "Bad boy."

Aronfreed raises this problem in analyzing the results of two experiments described earlier (**10, 11**). In addition to the variables discussed earlier, his experiments included a condition in which the experimenter was verbally nurturant and a condition in which he was not. No differences in amount of self-critical imitation were found between responses under nurturant and neutral conditions. This lack of effect of nurturance upon imitation of negative response contrasts with its effect upon imitation of neutral responses (**15, 43**).

The findings on love withdrawal, along with findings on nurturance and on enlightened discipline techniques, suggest that moral behavior is related to affectional ties to the parents which cannot be reduced to schedules of punishment and reward. The findings do not provide evidence, however, for an explanation of the affection-morality relationship as based on mechanisms of identification and of intrapunitive guilt.

SOCIAL POWER IDENTIFICATION THEORY AND RELATED FINDINGS

In his early elaboration of developmental identification theory, Mowrer (**106**) recognized the difficulties just mentioned in a theory conjuring pain-causing guilt out of a positive-dependency hat. In part, he turned to A. Freud's (**50**) conception of "identification with the aggressor" or "defensive identification" to account for the learning of the guilt response. This conception is based on the hypothesis that it is less painful for the self to perform a negative response than to have another person perform it. The conception implies a mastery drive in the child, a need to control the environment.

The most directly relevant data to this "defensive identification" hypothesis are those on punitiveness, presented in Table 1. The results indicated no consistent positive relationship between conscience and parental punitiveness. There is indeed evidence that punitive aggression by the parent leads to aggression by the child, but no evidence that it leads to moral learning.

There is no convincing evidence that parental punitiveness or restrictiveness leads to general identification with the parent. While highly masculine boys see their fathers as punitive (**108**) and highly "responsible" boys see their fathers as controlling, later evidence (**109, 110, 119**) indicates that these represent the boys' stereotypes rather than their fathers' behavior. Two studies (**46, 131**) found a negative relationship between punitiveness and perceived similarity to parents, while one study (**68**) found a positive relationship between maternal controllingness and girls' imitation of the mothers.

Mowrer's theory "anticipates" these results and views "identification with the aggressor" as leading to morality only if the aggressor or punisher is loved by the child. The conflict aroused through punishment by a loved person would lead to a need to minimize the correction by the punishment-loved person by taking over the punitive function and also by inhibiting deviation. The Mowrer view would lead to an expectation of high conscience in children who were both highly nurtured and highly punished. While this hypothesis has not been directly tested, it does not seem supported by the results summarized in Table 3.

Besides Mowrer's usage, the identification-with-the-aggressor concept has also recently been generalized into a concept of identification with possessors of any sort of social power or control of resources. According to Kagan (**83**) and Whiting (**138**), the more the child envies the other's control over resources and gratification, the more he will identify with the other. The results of experiments on imitation by Bandura and co-workers (**17, 18**) support this general hypothesis.

In spite of the experimental and naturalistic evidence of imitation based on power and prestige, there is almost no evidence that variations in parental power influence strength of conscience or strength of identification with parents. Table 3 indicates little relationship between relative power of a parent and identification with that parent.[7] There is also little research evidence of a relationship between sex of the dominant parent and measures of conscience.

We may conclude that present research gives little support for either defensive or power concepts of parental identification and conscience, in spite of the occurrence of power-based modeling in extra-familial spheres. It may be that all parents are so powerful relative to children that variations among families in parental power have little importance in basic identification or conscience-formation.

RELATIONSHIPS BETWEEN DIRECT MEASURES OF IDENTIFICATION AND CONSCIENCE: PERSONAL AND POSITIONAL IDENTIFICATION

We saw that several "developmental" antecedents related to morality, but the concept of an identification response was not required to explain these relations. We will now consider whether studies using direct measures of identification and conscience provide more definite validation of the role of identification in moral learning than is provided by studies of child-rearing attitudes.

While role-learning theories have led to conceptual consideration of types of antecedent, they have not led to systematic consideration of *types* of identification responses. Nevertheless, some obvious distinctions suggest themselves. Slater (**132**) discusses the distinction between *personal identification* with parents as individuals, and *positional identification* with the role of the parent. On logical grounds, personal identification would seem more relevant to con-

7. The only positive relationship was L. Hoffman's finding (**75**) of an association between the father's general authority and boy's desired similarity to the father. This suggests an identification based on admiration, consistent with the findings on nurturance, rather than a defensive or envious identification.

science development than positional identification. Positional identification, the desire to play the adult role, need not imply a desire to conform to the parents or their values.

Another distinction in types of identification may be made. There may be identification with the adult's *qualities* rather than with his *expectations*, only the latter being directly relevant to moral learning. A child who identifies with the parent's punitive role behavior, rather than with the parent's expectations, would be punitive toward others but not necessarily morally conforming.

While role-learning studies have not distinguished types of identification, they have been concerned with the sex of the *object* of identification. Hypotheses about relations between object of identification and conscience have been derived from the basic assumption of strong identification leading to strong conscience. Some natural or cultural pressures toward identification with the same-sex role and parent are assumed. Accordingly, a stronger and less conflicted over-all identification with parents as moral authorities is believed to result from a preferential identification with the same-sex parent. Given a strong or clear identification with the same-sex parent, identification with the opposite-sex parent should further contribute to conscience strength.

Results of the scattered studies of direct measures of identification and of conscience are summarized in Table 4. Unless otherwise noted, all measures of identification and conscience are based on projective tests or projective interviews (with the exception of Rau's use of direct observation measures). Studies using the various types of personal identification measures (perceived, desired, and behavioral similarity to parents as individuals) have been combined in Table 4. Seven of the twelve associations between *personal* identification and conscience are significantly positive. The remaining associations between personal identification and conscience were based on parental ratings of the child's similarity to themselves, ratings of quite doubtful meaning or validity.

In contrast to personal identification measures, there is no clear pattern of positive associations between *positional* measures of identification (adult and same-sex role identification) and conscience. Only one out of the ten observed associations was positive.

A positional identification measure which one might clearly expect to be associated with morality was Maccoby's (**95**) measure of rule-enforcing attitudes. Maccoby found the measures associated with some identification-relevant child-rearing antecedents. Nevertheless, there seemed to be little relationship between rule-enforcing attitudes and actual conformity to rules in one's own behavior. This suggests that identification with the parents' *behavior* as a controlling authority and identification with the parents' *expectations* for morally conforming behavior positively are relatively independent processes.

TABLE 4

RELATIONS BETWEEN MEASURES OF IDENTIFICATION AND MORALITY

TYPE OF IDENTIFICATION MEASURE	RESISTANCE TO TEMPTATION	GUILT	NONDELINQUENCY
1–4. Personal Identification			
a) with both parents	1, 0 : **119**[ae] 1, − : **119**[be]	2, + : **76**[b], **131**[c] 1, 0 : **129**[de]	1, + : **19**[c]
b) with same-sex parent	1, 0 : **87**	2, + : **20**[bf], **71**[c] 1, − : **119**[be]	2, + : **59**[c], **87**[c]
5. Adult Role	2, 0 : **96, 119**	2, 0 : **60, 119**	
6. Sex Role	2, 0 : **87, 119**	1, + : **109**[cd] 2, 0 : **71**[c], **119** 1, − : **8**[fc]	1, 0 : **135**[fc]

a) The association was found among girls but not boys.

b) The association was found among boys but not girls.

c) The study was limited to boys.

d) The measure of conscience was based on a rating by parent or teacher. In the third column (guilt), these ratings were of confession.

e) The measure of identification was based on a rating by parents.

f) The study used college-age or adult subjects.

While the results presented in Table 4 are suggestive with regard to *types* of identification, they do not indicate any clear relationship between *object* of identification and conscience. In part, this is due to the absence of relationship between "positional" sex-role measures and conscience. It should also be noted, however, that the studies which show personal identification with the same-sex parent to be related to conscience tend also to show personal identification with the opposite-sex parent to be related to conscience.

The results of studies of direct measures of identification and conscience tend to reinforce our conclusions drawn from studies of parent antecedents. Like the findings on nurturance and love withdrawal, the positive associations between measures of personal (as opposed to a positional) identification and conscience offer some support for a developmental identification theory of conscience. The apparent tendency for identification with parent measures to be associated with conscience, regardless of sex of child and sex of parent, is also more consistent with a developmental theory of identification than with a power theory. Like the findings on childhood antecedents, these findings are readily explainable without the identification concept. Children who consciously like and depend upon their parents would be expected both to accept nonmoral parental stereotypes and ways of doing things ("identification") if asked about such things and to try to conform to moral parental expectation (conscience).

PSYCHOANALYTIC CONCEPTS OF SUPEREGO-IDENTIFICATION AND RELATED EVIDENCE

While role-learning theory conceives of identification as a general disposition to imitate the parent, psychoanalytic theory conceives of identification as a total "introjection" or "incorporation" of the parent into the personality as an "internal object." Furthermore, psychoanalysis views identification as a radically substitutive defense mechanism, i.e., as functioning to end a relationship of dependency and subordination to a real external object under conditions where such dependency is impossible to maintain (death, separation) or is extremely conflictful or painful. Identification ends the relationship to the external object by turning object-directed love and hate inward upon the self, and thus provides instinctual energy for self-punishing guilt reactions. This incorporative-substitutive concept of identification leads to a view of conscience formation as relatively sudden, total, and conflict-focused. Freud (**52, 55**) believed superego-identification to be a mode of dealing with the Oedipal conflict.

There is little research evidence which bears directly upon these points. While the data on the guilt response are ambiguous, other data (discussed in a later section of this chapter) suggest that "conscience" first begins to appear in the years five to eight, the period in which psychoanalysis claims the Oedipus complex is being resolved. However, there is a multitude of plausible reasons for conscience formation first occurring in this period.

Research study of relations between conscience and sexual attitudes of children has been restricted to consideration of ratings of the mother and father's restrictiveness of children's early sex play and of parental anxiety about such play. There appears to be no relationship between parental restrictions of children's sex play and measures of (nonsexual) morality. There does seem to be some evidence that mother's sex anxiety is positively associated with resistance to temptation in boys (**119**) and with projective "guilt" (**60**). The evidence then suggests that there are no relationships between children's morality and parental restrictions on children's sexual behavior, but there may be a relationship between children's morality and parental sexual *attitudes* ("sex anxiety"). The relations between "Oedipal" channeling of aggression have not been the object of research study. The data on family doll-play aggression and conscience discussed previously (**13, 119**) have not been analyzed in relation to "Oedipal" aggression against the same-sex parent, but some correlations involved suggest that morality is not specifically related to particular family targets of aggression.

IDENTIFICATION THEORIES AND THE EFFECTS OF THE PARENT'S SEX ROLE AND THE CHILD'S SEX ROLE UPON CONSCIENCE DEVELOPMENT

Research results do bear upon two beliefs closely associated with Freudian "Oedipal" theory. The first (**55**) is that the father, rather than the mother, is the principal moral authority in the family and, accordingly, the principal object of moral identification for both boys and girls. The second (**56**) is that "for women the level of what is ethically normal is different from what it is in men. Their superego is never so inexorable, so impersonal, so independent of its emotional origins as we require it to be in men."

In regard to the first belief, developmental identification theory tends to postulate the mother rather than the father as the major object of moral identification, because the mother is a more basic object of dependency and a more recurrent source of daily reinforcement and discipline. The developmental identification view implies that variations in maternal nurturance and discipline would be more important for conscience development than variations in the paternal role. The data, however, suggest that paternal variations in these variables are equally or more relevant for conscience than are maternal variations.

Supporters of social power theories of identification (**31**) have given more stress to variations in the father role, since social power variables are less related to direct dependency. Paradoxically, the research results suggest that the father's variations on role dimensions considered paternal specialties, e.g., power and discipline, are of less relevance to conscience than his variation on role dimensions considered maternal specialties, e.g., nurturance.

These rather paradoxical results can be explained by a hypothesis consistent with the psychoanalytic (Freud), social system (**113**), and developmental assumption (**87**) that there are natural tendencies for the child to perceive the father as the dominant authority in almost all societies, regardless of the child's individual family role-pattern. American preschool and kindergarten children perceive the father as more powerful, punitive, controlling, and aggressive than the mother, as indicated by doll-play usage of mother and father dolls (**41, 109**) or by structured questions (**42, 84**). These perceptions do not correspond to actual family variations in authority role as reported in parent interviews (**42, 109**). They seem to correspond, rather, to preschool children's awareness of greater male bodily size and strength and of extra-familial masculine authority roles (**87**). As they become slightly older, children also award power and prestige to the father as owner of family resources (**87**). Thus, a universal trend seems to exist for children to perceive the father as a more dangerous person to transgress against and as a representative of societal norms. Because of these natural tendencies for the father to be perceived as an authority figure, he seems to become as important as the mother in the moral development of the child.

It is also likely that, because of the natural tendency of the father to be perceived as an authority, regardless of his actual social power relative to the mother, variations on social power are relatively unimportant for the child's moral development. The actual variations in the father's role which are important for morality seem to be variations in his affection. Presumably such affection is necessary if the father's "natural" authority role is to be emotionally accepted by the child. While the evidence on the differential impact of the mother's and father's roles upon children's morality is not inconsistent with Freudian theory, it can also be readily explained in sociological-developmental terms.

Freud's second relevant belief, that the superego is weaker in females than in males, is also in part related to the belief that the father is the basic authority and object of moral identification, both for boys and girls. Freud's belief was also based on the assumption that girls remain more fixated in an Oedipal attachment than do boys. Because boys are motivated by fear of castration, they make a stronger renunciation of the Oedipal complex and a stronger superego identification. Girls are believed to be motivated more by fear of loss of love, which is thought to be a less effective motive for moral identification than is fear of castration.

In contrast, developmental identification theory leads to an expectation that girls should tend to have stronger consciences than boys. It is assumed that there is some natural tendency for children to identify with the same-sex parent. Same-sex identification should coincide with the deepest moral identification (with the mother) in girls while it should conflict in boys.[8] In addition, parents tend to treat girls more nurturantly than boys and to use more love-withdrawal discipline with them (**28, 129**), leading to an expectation of stronger conscience in girls.

The observed sex differences relevant to the issue are as follows:

1. *Girls are more conforming to rules and authority than boys.* Terman and Tyler's review (**136**) of sex differences in behavior indicates that girls have a lower rate of delinquency, have fewer school and home behavior problems leading to clinic referral, and are rated higher by peers and teachers for various moral traits.

2. *There are no substantial general differences between boys and girls in conformity to internalized moral standards.* Few sex differences in resistance to temptation have been found. Where differences in honesty appear, they tend to favor the boys; where differences appear in "service" they tend to favor the girls (**66**). Other studies of cheating have found no sex differences (**30, 61, 119**).

8. Actually, this implies that same-sex or mother-identified girls should have the strongest conscience; that opposite-sex identified girls should have the weakest conscience; with boys intermediate between these groups. Some preliminary data analyses do not support this expectation (**89**).

3. *There are no clear differences in strength of tendencies to feel guilt after deviation.* Sex differences in projective responses to transgression were summarized in Table 2. Girls do appear to be more interpersonally oriented (confession, apology) in reactions to transgression, but there is no reason to view them as having more or less guilt reactions than boys.

4. *No clear-cut, consistent differences have been found between boys and girls in measure of total identification with the same-sex parent or with both parents.* There may, however, be some tendency for boys to identify with the same-sex parent or with the same-sex role more than girls (**41, 90**), and for girls to identify more with both parents together or with the adult role (**41**).

These results do not seem to support either the Freudian or the developmental notions of identification-conscience. While girls conform to authority more than boys, they cannot be said either to have a stronger conscience or to have a stronger identification with the same-sex parent.

While sex differences in measure of *quantitative* strength of conscience have not been found, some interesting sex differences have been found in qualitative aspects of moral attitudes. These differences may be summarized in regard to one aspect of Freud's belief in the relative weakness of women's superegos, e.g., his belief that women have less of a sense of justice than men. While a more refined analysis of sense of justice is offered in a later section of this chapter, for present purposes we may define a strong sense of justice as a tendency to praise, sympathize and help, or to blame and punish, other persons in terms of general rules which are consistently applied to all persons, including the self, regardless of personal relationships to the persons judged or helped.

The observed sex differences in conscience related to the sense of justice are the following:

5. *Boys are more rules- or justice-oriented in their expressions of indignation and sympathy.* Terman and Miles found that girls' indignation was directed more toward trivial forms of deviance which personally irritated them, while boys' indignation was directed more toward major offenses against moral rules. They also found that the "sympathy of the female appears personal rather than abstract, less a principled humanitarianism than an active sympathy for palpable

misfortune" (**135**). Maccoby (**95**) found prosocial aggression (blaming on punitive reactions) related to rule-enforcing attitudes in boys but not in girls. This suggests that punitive attitudes are less rule-oriented in girls than in boys. Kohlberg (**89**) has found 13-year-old boys more justice-oriented than girls in verbal moral choices, using a number of criteria of justice.

6. *Boys are more willing to accept rules for their own behavior if they enforce these rules upon others.* Girls tend more to blame and coerce others for the same faults or violations in which they themselves indulge. Boys tend to be high on rule-enforcing attitudes if they also express acceptance of rules and if they actually conform to rules. In girls, tendencies to enforce rules are uncorrelated with acceptance of rules (**95**).

It seems likely that these sex differences in both moral behavior and sense of justice are the results of the "naturally-sociologically" determined perceptions of sex roles which also seemed to determine differential reactions to the mother and father as moral authorities. Girls are expected to be, and expect themselves to be, more obedient, more fearful, more affectionate, and more dependent (**89**). Boys are expected to be more physically aggressive and more independent. These differences are similar to the differences in children's perception of mother and father already mentioned. These differences in self-perceptions of role would be expected to lead to great compliance to authority by girls, regardless of general degree of internalization of moral rules.

These and other differential aspects of sex-role stereotypes would also be expected to lead to a greater sense of justice in boys. Adult male roles involve legitimate, role-enforcing aggression; adult female roles do not. Parents of boys more clearly differentiate rule-oriented aggression, "sticking up" for one's rights, than do parents of girls (**129**). These differences would lead us to expect a more rule-oriented orientation of aggression in boys than girls. It is also clear that male occupational roles involve more universalistic, role-oriented norms, while the housewife-mother role involves more particularistic person-oriented norms. In conjunction with the predominance of males in authority roles, this would lead a boy identified with the male role to a greater general concern about maintaining rules than would be expected in girls.

In summary, the impact of the parent and the child's sex-roles upon moral development appears to be due to certain natural and cultural stereotypes acquired by children largely independent of actual differential child-rearing patterns used by the mother as opposed to the father, or used with boys as opposed to girls, in any particular family. These role stereotypes, in turn, determine the "meaning" of various child-rearing practices to the child. In Rau's study (**119**), about 50 child-rearing measures correlated significantly with the two conscience measures for boys, and about 50 measures correlated with the two measures for girls. Not a single one of these correlations overlapped, i.e., involved the same variable operating in the same direction in both boys and girls. There was a similar lack of overlap between aspects of the mother's child-rearing attitudes and of the father's attitudes relating to children's conscience.

As we saw, Freudian and developmental identification concepts seemed inadequate to explain moral differences related to parent and child's sex-role. It may be that systematic theoretical discrimination of qualitative types of identification and of conscience will be more successful in uncovering fruitful sex-differences in morality.

The Developmental Approach

While a number of moral theories (**12, 14, 52, 58, 102, 115**) may be characterized as "developmental," the bulk of developmental research has derived from Piaget's theories and observations (**117**).

In contrast to the "superego strength" view of moral learning as a matter of increased strength of conscience responses, the developmental approach views moral learning in terms of age-related sequences of changes by which moral attitudes emerge from qualitatively different premoral attitudes and concepts. These differences in *description* of moral learning are associated with differences in conception of the *process* of moral learning. The developmentalist does not accept the "superego strength" view of the role of the social environment as "stamping into" the child given cultural rules which persist as internal moral structures throughout life. The environment is seen rather as a social world which includes rules and which the child understands through conceptually organized role-taking. The mere process of role-taking the attitudes of others in organized social interaction is believed to transform concepts of rules from external things to internal principles. Variations in social environment are viewed as stimulating or retarding role-taking and, hence, as stimulating or retarding sequential development, rather than as variations in effectiveness of stamping in rules through reinforcement or identification.

MORALITY AS RESPECT FOR RULES AND SENSE OF JUSTICE: PIAGET'S CONCEPTION OF THE TWO MORALITIES OF THE CHILD

According to Piaget, the young (4–8-year-old) child's unilateral respect for adults inspires a *heteronomous* attitude toward adult rules as sacred, unchangeable things. This heteronomous emotional attitude is supported by two cognitive defects of the young child. One defect, egocentrism—the confusion of one's own perspective with that of others—leads to an inability to see moral value as relative to various persons or ends. The other defect, realism—the confusion of subjective phenomena with objective things—leads to a view of moral rules as fixed eternal things rather than as psychosocial expectations. The moral ideology resulting from the interaction of heteronomous respect and cognitive realism is described as "moral realism."

Moral realism is represented by the following observable aspects of young children's definitions of right and wrong:

1. *Objective responsibility* (as opposed to intentionalism). Objective responsibility is seen by Piaget as a kind of literalistic evaluation of an act in terms of its exact conformity to the rule rather than in terms of its intent. It is indicated by a judgment of the act in terms of physical consequences rather than in terms of intentions.

2. *Unchangeability of the rules* (as opposed to flexibility). This is interpreted as fixity of rules regardless of changed requirements of the situation to which the rule is to be applied.

3. *Absolutism of value* (as opposed to relativism). According to Piaget, the judgment of an act as either right or wrong is believed by the child to be shared by everyone, since only one perspective is taken toward the act. In cases of clear conflict in judgments of the same act, the adult's view is believed always to be right.

4. *Moral wrongness defined by sanctions* (as opposed to moral judgments made independently of sanctions). According to Piaget,

the young child's definition of an act as wrong is based on the fact that the child is punished.

5. *Duty defined as obedience to authority* (as opposed to duty being defined in terms of conformity expectations of peers or equals). "Any act showing obedience to a rule or even to an adult is right."

Piaget believes that the development of mutual respect toward other individuals leads to an "autonomous" regard for the rules as products of group agreement and as instruments of co-operative purposes. "Mutual respect" is believed to be associated with the cognitive capacity to differentiate one's own perspective from that of others (decline of egocentrism) and both are believed to arise largely through peer-group interaction. Each of the five listed characteristics of moral realism is replaced by its corresponding "morally subjective" opposite. Empirically, this was represented by a tendency of older children to favor the mature alternatives when asked to compare two actions.

Piaget's concept of morality as respect and obligation toward rules (sense of duty) is linked logically to a criterion of morality as justice (sense of rights). Study of the sense of justice is especially useful for indicating internalized standards because justice involves active maintenance of moral norms rather than passive conformity to them.

In addition to the moral realism attributes previously listed, the heteronomous stage is characterized by the following attributes of the sense of justice:

6. *Ignoral of reciprocity in defining obligations* (as opposed to defining obligations in terms of the rights of contract and exchange).

7. *Expiative justice* (as opposed to restitutive justice). Belief in severe, painful punishment rather than in restoration to the victim.

8. *Immanent justice* (as opposed to naturalistic causality). Belief that deviance will lead nature or physical things to injure the culprit.

9. *Belief in collective responsibility* (as opposed to individual responsibility).

10. *Punishment by authority* (rather than retaliative reciprocity by victim).

11. *Favoritism by authority in distributing goods* (rather than impartiality, equality, distributive justice).

According to Piaget (**117**), a sense of justice as reciprocity between individuals is an expression of the autonomous stage of mutual respect for other individuals. As the child moves toward mutual respect, the beliefs just listed as representing heteronomous justice are replaced by their corresponding opposites.

Perhaps less important than Piaget's distinction between two types of moral respect is the distinction between an *arbitrary* morality, representing the stamping in of arbitrary cultural or parental rules through sanctions and authority, and a "*natural*" morality. Norms of reciprocity are believed to develop spontaneously from the child's experience of participation in organized social relations with others, rather than from learning through tuition and sanctions. Piaget says, "The conclusion which we shall finally reach is that the sense of justice, though capable of being reinforced by the precepts and example of the adult, is largely independent of these influences and requires nothing more for its development than the mutual respect and solidarity among children" (**117:** 196). Norms of justice, like the norms of logic, are believed to grow out of the self-organizing developmental regulation of social schemata or concepts. "In contrast to a given rule imposed upon the child from outside, the rule of justice is an immanent condition of social relationships or a law governing their equilibrium."

Piaget, then, believes that restitutive or reciprocal justice develops almost purely out of peer-group interaction on the one hand, and out of a logical capacity for nonegocentric, reciprocal or "reversible" thought on the other. According to Piaget, it is possible that individuals in some primitive societies never reach a mature sense of reciprocal justice because of the intense unilateral constraint operating in these societies. Thus, Piaget believes in universal dimensions of moral maturity and views the failure to display mature moral judgment as the result of developmental retardation or arrest.

RESEARCH FINDINGS CONCERNING PIAGET'S THEORY

A fairly large body of research on Piaget "stages" of moral judgment has been carried on by other workers. Unlike Piaget's study, subsequent researchers have used standardized questions and settings, subject groups with known or representative social background conditions, and statistical analyses. However, most of the studies have relied on the original Piaget verbal-choice techniques, whose defects have been discussed (**33, 86**).[9] The findings of these various studies as to age, I.Q., and social background trends in the Piaget dimensions are presented in Table 5. The percentage of children at ages 6–7, 9–10, and 12–13 giving mature responses on various Piaget dimensions is presented in the second column of Table 5. The studies of Caruso (**33**), in Belgium, and MacRae (**101**) and Lerner (**91**), in America, involved enough subjects and questions to warrant such presentation.

The age trends for several of the Piaget dimensions are consistent enough to warrant the conclusion that they are genuine developmental dimensions in both American (**23, 81, 86, 91, 101**) and in French-speaking (**33, 92, 117**) cultures. These dimensions include (1) objective responsibility, (2) fixity of rules, (3) absolutism of value, (4) definition of wrong by punishment, (7) expiative rather than restitutive justice, and (8) immanent justice.

By a genuine developmental dimension of moral judgment is meant a dimension of response which increases regularly with age, regardless of the particular cultural rules or situations which children are questioned about, regardless of the child's cultural milieu, and in which a substantial portion of other favorable social factors which influence the response are expected to influence it in the same way age does, i.e., by stimulating an increase on the dimension.

Findings on individual differences on these dimensions other than age differences are consistent with the notion that these dimensions are developmental dimensions relatively independent of specific cultural patterns. Both psychometric intelligence and social class are positively related to maturity on these dimensions. Class differences seem to reflect rate of maturity rather than differences in cultural values, since all class groups move in the same direction with age (**86**).

9. The limitations of these techniques are important if their results are used to conclude that young children in a certain age range are (or are not) aware of a given concept, e.g., of the intentions criterion of moral judgment. This has been shown by Caruso's careful study (**33**) of objective responsibility and immanent justice in Belgian parochial school children, a study in which question procedure was systematically varied. Caruso found that some methods elicited use of mature criteria of moral judgment at a considerably younger age than did the Piaget method. The limitations of the Piaget method are not as important, however, if we wish only to validate the Piaget dimensions as general trends in age development rather than to characterize particular age periods in terms of the dimensions.

TABLE 5

RELATIONS OF PIAGET DIMENSIONS TO AGE, INTELLIGENCE, AND SOCIAL VARIABLES

PIAGET'S DIMENSIONS	PERCENTAGE OF CHILDREN OF VARIOUS AGES GIVING MATURE RESPONSES				AGE	INTELLIGENCE	SOCIAL CLASS	PARENTAL PERMISSIVENESS
	6–7	9–10	12–13	Study No.				
Moral Realism								
1. Objective responsibility	46	63	72	: 99	5, + : 83, 98, 35, 91, 22	4, + : 1, 22, 81, 101	4, + : 22, 81, 91, 101	2, 0 : 81, 101
	40	87	86	: 33				
2. Fixity of rules					1, + : 21	1, + : 21		
3. Absolutism of value	58	68	93	: 91	2, + : 91, 98		1, + : 101	
	30	65	65	: 99				
4. Wrong as the punished					1, + : 88		1, + : 86	1, + : 87
5. Right as obeying authority	35	25	50	: 99	3, [*] : 23, 98, 88	3, 0 : 22, 86, 101	3, 0 : 22, 86, 101	1, + : 101
	50	42	71	: 23				
Justice								
6. Reciprocity ignoral					2, 0 : 86, 105	1, 0 : 86	1, 0 : 86	1, 0 : 86
7. Expiative justice					2, + : 65, 81	1, + : 81	2, + : 65, 81	1, 0 : 81
8. Immanent justice	40	45	62	: 99	5, + : 83, 98, 35, 91, 22	2, + : 1, 81	3, + : 81, 91, 101	1, 0 : 101
	38	71	88	: 33				1, + : 81
9. Collective responsibility					1, + : 81	1, 0 : 81	1, 0 : 81	1, − : 81
10. Retaliation by victim					1, [*] : 36	1, 0 : 36	1, 0 : 36	

* These age relationships were curvilinear, the dimension increased in middle childhood (ages 7–10) and decreased thereafter.

Havighurst and Neugarten (**70**) have studied age trends for immanent justice and fixity of rules in several Southwest Indian cultures. In some of these cultures immanent justice decreased with age, in others it remained the same, in still others it increased with age. In light of the known prevalence of "animistic" causal thinking among adults in some of these cultures, this finding is not inconsistent with Piaget's views (**117**) of differential development in primitive, traditionalistic societies.[10]

There is a fairly clear-cut contrast between the dimensions just discussed, which qualify as developmental dimensions, and the remaining Piaget dimensions. The dimensions discussed involve either a greater differentiation of subjective and objective aspects of value including a differentiation of rules and things (Dimensions 1, 2, 3, 4, and 8), or they involve a growing ability to define morality independently of punishment (Dimensions 4 and 7). In either case the Piaget dimensions which hold up as developmental dimensions seem to involve cognitive sophistication in perception of moral value, as the relations to I.Q. suggest.

In contrast, the less cognitive dimensions of reciprocity and peer orientation (Dimensions 5, 6, and 10), which positively characterize Piaget's autonomous stage of morality, do not appear to be "genuine" developmental dimensions. Reciprocity (Dimensions 6 and 10) appears to increase in the years from six to nine but, thereafter, either to stay the same or to decline. Conformity toward peers, as opposed to authorities, fails to increase regularly with age. Intelligence and social class do not relate to these dimensions in a regular way. Studies of the correlations of the various moral-judgment dimensions with one another (**23, 81, 101**) suggest the distinctions just made and lend no support to Piaget's implicit expectation that his dimensions should cluster to define two global stages of development or two basic attitudes toward moral rules and authority.

Direct studies of the relations of the moral-judgment dimensions to social pressures on the child, and to his attitude toward authority, also provide no support for Piaget's theory. His theory leads us to

10. Unlike the data on immanent justice, Havighurst and Taba's data (**69**) on age trends in belief in fixity of rules in various cultures indicate the belief is not a function of the "primitiveness" of the individual or of the society. The degree to which children perceive rules as unchangeable is a function of specific cultural attitudes toward specific cultural rules.

expect the parent's constraint and the child's respect for adult authority to be associated with moral realism, i.e., with objective responsibility, absolutism of value, definition in terms of punishment, and the like. With the possible exception of Dimension 4, the other moral-realism dimensions are related neither to child- or parent-interview measure of parental controllingness (**81, 101**) nor to ratings of children's behavior and attitudes in terms of respect for adult authority (**86**).

Piaget's theory leads us to expect a positive relationship between peer-group participation and an orientation to reciprocity. A trend in the reverse direction (i.e., for sociometric isolates to make more use of reciprocity) was found by Kohlberg (**86**). A morality of reciprocity and equality was found by Kohlberg to be associated with lack of respect for adult authority, but not with peer-group participation. Judgments in terms of reciprocity, relativism, and equality were found to differentiate delinquents from working-class controls.

Piaget's theory is to summarize the research results, validated only in its description of the young child's morality as oriented to obedience and to punishment and as ignoring subjective ends and values, and in its assumption that these features of child morality decline with age and development in various cultural settings.

STUDIES OF AGE-DEVELOPMENT IN MORAL JUDGMENT OUTSIDE THE PIAGET TRADITION

In addition to Piaget's approach, two other types of study of the development of moral ideas have been carried on—the study of "moral knowledge" and the study of types of moral ideology and character.

Considerable research has been directed to creating age scales of moral knowledge based on multiple-choice items involving "correct" and "incorrect" moral clichés, labels, and rules (**66**). While relationships between moral-knowledge tests and morally conforming behavior were found, the tests seemed to reflect the child's intelligence and his cultural-verbal background rather than basic development in moral concepts or attitudes.

In contrast typological approaches have attempted to define types of "world view" and motives underlying moral conformity. Such types have been defined on the basis of character reputation data (**69**), of projective test data (**115**), and of responses to hypothetical moral dilemmas (**77, 87, 98**). Most of these typologies have implied some notions of a developmental ordering of the types, based on theoretical or common-sense conceptions of maturity.

Among the various research studies of moral types, only Kohlberg's (**87**) has been an explicitly developmental study. Six "stages" of moral thinking were defined on the basis of lengthy free interviews with one hundred boys aged 7 to 17 concerning ten hypothetical moral-conflict situations. Both age data and analyses of intercorrelations suggested that the stages did define a genuine sequence in individual development.

Kohlberg's conclusion (**88**), that moral internalization relates closely to the cognitive development of moral concepts, contrasts markedly with prevailing theories in the area. Learning theorists interested in overt behavior, psychoanalysts interested in fantasy, and Piaget, interested in moral judgment, have all assumed that the basic features of adult conscience have developed by early childhood (ages 5–8). This assumption as to the age of appearance of conscience is required if morality is to be derived from an intense unilateral relationship of identification with the parent. It is also required if the "categorical imperative," the objective nonego-oriented aspects of conscience or the sense of obligation are to be seen as survivals of infantile experience rather than as reactions to more adult experiences of the world.

Moral judgment data, however, suggest that anything clearly like "conscience" develops quite late.[11] Kohlberg and Brener (**87**) studied the development of children's capacity to judge action in terms of moral standards as opposed to sanctions by asking them to evaluate deviant acts which they were told were followed by reward and conforming acts which they were told were followed by punishment. Four-year-olds tended to judge the act as good or bad in terms of its reinforcement rather than in terms of the rule. By age five to

11. Piaget interprets his moral judgment data as indicating the existence in young children of a "sense of duty," "sacredness of the rules," etc. There is little empirical evidence supporting his interpretation of his own data, and much that contradicts it. As was discussed earlier, the features of moral judgment interpreted by Piaget as expressing the "sacredness of the rules" were found to be related to cognitive naïveté but not to independent measures of respect for rules and authority.

seven, the children evaluated the act in terms of its moral label rather than in terms of its reinforcement in the story. These older children continued to give the possibility of punishment as reasons for an act being bad, however, so that the distinction between badness and situational reinforcement was in terms of long-range as opposed to short-range reinforcement. By preadolescence, a majority of children made "disinterested" moral judgments and formulated some concept of a morally good self.[12] This steady age increase in internality of moral judgments is correlated with various cognitive features of the development of moral judgment, even with age effects controlled.

These relations between cognitive development of morality and its internalization are not matters of simple cognitive learning of cultural norms. Such simple cognitive learning fails to take account of the sequential qualitative transformations through which moral thinking procedes, as indicated by the Kohlberg data on sequence. Furthermore, the cognitive development involved does not seem to be a simple matter of mental age as defined by I.Q. tests. Level of development on the Kohlberg stages was found to be related to I.Q. ($r = .31$) but to be even more related to chronological age or age-linked experience (r of .59 with chronological age, with mental age controlled). In addition to age, peer-group participation and social class were found to be contributors to development, independent of I.Q. The social class relations cannot be explained as due to middle-class bias in the measure itself and probably indicate the effects of general social participation or experience upon moral development.

The Kohlberg study provides clear support for the general developmental view of morality underlying the specific theories of Baldwin, Mead, and Piaget. The development of moral judgment cannot be explained by "nondevelopmental" view of moral learning as simply the internalization of cultural rules through verbal learning, reinforcement, or identification. The findings, however, are not consistent with Piaget's specific theory. As opposed to Piaget's view, the

12. At this same age, projective methods indicate that the majority of children express direct guilt responses, as was discussed in the section on guilt. The relationships of this slow development of "conscience" or internalized standards in the moral judgment materials to findings on moral behavior data are considered in the next subsection.

data suggest that the "natural" aspects of moral development are continuous and a reaction to the whole social world rather than a product of a certain stage, a certain concept (reciprocity), or a certain type of social relations (peer relations). The development of a morality of identification with authority is dependent upon "natural" social role-taking and the development of concepts of reciprocity, justice, and group welfare in the years from four to twelve.

AGE-DEVELOPMENT OF MORAL CONDUCT AND ITS RELATIONSHIP TO THE DEVELOPMENT OF MORAL JUDGMENT AND TO MENTAL AGE

The research on moral judgment was said to indicate the slow development over time of something like conscience or internalized moral judgments, a development related to general cognitive and social experience. This view implies that the development of moral judgment is related to the development of moral conduct, a relationship implying both parallel age trends for the two aspects of morality and correlations between the two variables within age groups.

Systematic observation of children's moral behavior has been largely restricted to efforts to measure strength of tendencies to violate rules.[13] It seems obvious that age-development of moral conduct cannot be adequately described as a straight-line increase in measurable conformity of "resistance to temptation." The findings (**66, 119**) show no relationship of resistance-to-temptation measures to age,[14] perhaps because age changes in definition of the temptation situations muddy whatever "internalized standard" components exist in such behavior.

Although the behavior studies allow us to say little about age-de-

13. A few studies of "altruistic behavior," such as Lois Murphy's study of sympathy in preschool children (*Social Behavior and Child Personality*. New York: Columbia University Press, 1937), have been carried on. These studies do not provide any over-all view of development of moral conduct, however.

14. The lack of relationships between age and resistance to temptation in the middle school years should not be taken as indicating that conscience or moral character is formed and set in very early childhood. The very limited longitudinal evidence suggests little stability over time of moral traits in middle childhood. (See study by J. MacFarlane, L. Allen, and M. Honzik, "A Developmental Study of the Behavior Problems of Normal Childen between 21 Months and 14 Years," published by University of California Press, 1954.) There appears to be greater stability of moral conduct throughout preadolescence and adolescence. (See, also, **115**.)

velopment of moral conduct and its relationship to developmental trends in moral judgment, they do allow us to draw some tentative conclusions as to the relations between moral judgment and moral behavior within age groups. The Hartshorne and May data (**66**) are directly relevant to the related question, "Is knowledge of conventional norms associated with nonsanctioned conformity to those norms?" A relationship was found between the two among their 11–12-year-old subjects, which was substantial, considering the low reliability of behavior measures. With I.Q. controlled, Hartshorne and May found a correlation of .34 between total moral-knowledge score and total score on experimental measures of character, and a correlation of .43 between moral knowledge and total score on ratings of good character by teachers and peers.

The only efforts to directly relate developmental level of moral judgment to moral conduct have been made by the present writer. With mental age controlled, correlations between moral-judgment level and teacher ratings were .31 for "conscience" and .51 for fairness with peers (**88**). An experimental measure of cheating significantly discriminated those high and low in moral judgment. Delinquents were significantly lower in moral judgment than working-class controls.

A careful analysis of the moral internalization concept implies that fully internalized moral norms should determine behavior, not only when they conflict with impulse or ego-interest but also when they conflict with external authority. This would be expected for the most advanced levels of moral ideology focused upon "principles" rather than upon rules and authority. Kohlberg (**88**) found moderate correlations between level of moral judgment and behavioral measures of resistance to various types of adult and peer pressures to change or violate moral beliefs.

The Hartshorne and May as well as the Kohlberg data provide some support for the view that development of moral conduct depends on the fairly subtle development of moral concepts and of moral judgmental capacities. This conclusion is strengthened by the findings of substantial correlations of moral conduct with intelligence (**66, 115, 126**). Both these correlations and correlations with "ego-strength" ratings suggest a view of overt adolescent moral conduct as a product of the development of broad social-cognitive capacities and values rather than of a "superego" or of "introjection of parental standards."

The actual integration of these developmentalist concepts and findings concerning conscience with the fantasy and pathology data which have suggested superego concepts remains a task for the future.

BIBLIOGRAPHY

1. ABEL, T. M. "Moral Judgments among Subnormals," *J. Abnorm. Soc. Psychol.*, XXXVI (1941), 378–92.
2. ADORNO, T. W.; FRENKEL-BRUNSWICK, E.; LEVINSON, D. J.; and SANFORD, R. N. *The Authoritarian Personality*. New York: Harper & Bros., 1950.
3. ALBERT, E., and KLUCKHOHN C. *Selected Bibliography on Values, Ethics, and Esthetics in the Behavioral Sciences and Philosophy, 1920–58*. Glencoe, Illinois: Free Press, 1959.
4. ALLINSMITH, W. "Moral Standards: II. The Learning of Moral Standards," in *Inner Conflict and Defense*, pp. 141–76. Edited by D. R. Miller and G. E. Swanson. New York: Henry Holt & Co., 1960.
5. ALLINSMITH, W., and GREENING, T. C. "Guilt over Anger as Predicted from Parental Discipline: A Study of Superego Development," *Amer. Psychol.*, X (1955), 320 (Abstract).
6. ANDRY, R. G. *Delinquency and Parental Pathology*. London: Methuen & Co., Ltd., 1960.
7. ARONFREED, J. "The Effect of Experimental Socialization Paradigms upon Two Moral Responses to Transgression." (To be published in *J. Abnorm. Soc. Psychol.*, 1963.)
8. ———. "Moral Behavior and Sex Identity," in *Inner Conflict and Defense*, pp. 177–93. Edited by D. R. Miller and G. E. Swanson. New York: Henry Holt & Co., 1960.
9. ———. "The Nature, Variety, and Social Patterning of Moral Responses to Transgression," *J. Abnorm. Soc. Psychol.*, LXIII (1961), 223–41.
10. ———. "The Origins of Self-Criticism." Unpublished paper (1962).
11. ARONFREED, J.; CUTICK, R.; and FAGEN, S. "Cognitive Structure, Punishment, and Nurturance in the Experimental Induction of Self-Criticism." (To be published in *J. Abnorm. Soc. Psychol.* in 1963.)
12. AUSUBEL, D. *Ego Development and the Personality Disorders*. New York: Grune & Stratton, Inc., 1952.
13. BACH, G. R. "Young Children's Play Fantasies," *Psychol. Monogr.*, LIX (1945), No. 2.
14. BALDWIN, J. M. *Social and Ethical Interpretations in Mental Development*. New York: Macmillan Co., 1906.
15. BANDURA, A., and HUSTON, A. C. "Identification as a Process of Incidental Learning," *J. Abnorm. Soc. Psychol.*, LXIII (1961), 311–19.

16. BANDURA, A., and MCDONALD, F. "The Influence of Social Reinforcement and the Behavior of Modes in Shaping Children's Moral Judgments," *J. Abnorm. Soc. Psychol.*, LXV (1963), in press.

17. BANDURA, A., and ROSS, D.; and ROSS, S. A. "A Test of the Status Envy, Social Power, and Secondary Reinforcement Theories of Identificatory Learning," *J. Abnorm. Soc. Psychol.*, LXV (1963), in press.

18. ———. "Vicarious Reinforcement and Imitation." Unpublished manuscript, Stanford University, 1962.

19. BANDURA, A., and WALTERS, R. H. *Adolescent Aggression.* New York: Ronald Press, 1959.

20. BIERI, J., and LOBECK, R. "Acceptance of Authority and Parental Identification," *J. of Pers.*, XXVIII (1959), 74–86.

21. BOBROFF, A. "The Stages of Maturation in Socialized Thinking and in the Ego Development of Two Groups of Children," *Child Develpm.*, XXXI (1960), 321–38.

22. BOEHM, L. "The Development of Independence: A Comparative Study," *Child Develpm.*, XXVIII (1957), 85–92.

23. BOEHM, L., and NASS, M. L. "Social Class Differences in Conscience Development," *Child Develpm.*, XXXIII (1962), 565–75.

24. BOWLBY, J. *Forty-four Juvenile Thieves: Their Characters and Home Life.* London: Baldiere, Tindall & Cox, 1947.

25. BRIM, O. "Family Structure and Sex Role Learning by Children," *Sociometry*, XXI (1958), 1–16.

26. BRONFENBRENNER, U. "Freudian Theories of Identification and Their Derivatives," *Child Develpm.*, XXXI (1960), 15–40.

27. ———. "Socialization and Social Class through Time and Space," in *Readings in Social Psychology*, pp. 400–25. Edited by E. E. Maccoby, T. M. Newcomb, and E. L. Hartley. New York: Henry Holt & Co., 1958.

28. ———. "Some Familial Antecedents of Responsibility and Leadership in Adolescents," in *Leadership and Interpersonal Behavior*, pp. 239–71. Edited by Bass and Petrullo. New York: Holt, Rinehart & Winston, 1961.

29. BURTON, R. V.; CARLSMITH, J.; and BESWICH, D. "The Generality of Honesty Reconsidered." Mimeographed unpublished paper, National Institute of Mental Health, 1962.

30. BURTON, R. V.; MACCOBY, ELEANOR E.; and ALLINSMITH, W. "Antecedents of Resistance to Temptation in Four-year-old Children," *Child Develpm.*, XXXII (1961), 689–710.

31. BURTON, R. V., and WHITING, J. W. M. "The Absent Father and Cross-sex Identity," *Merrill Palmer Quar.*, VII (1961), 85–97.

32. CARROLL, J., and LEVIN, H. "A Method for Determining the Polarity of Behavior Items," *Child Develpm.*, XXVII (1956), 427–38.

33. CARUSO, I. H. "La Notion de Responsabilité et du Justice Immanente Chez L'Enfant," *Arch. de Psychologie*, XXIX (1943), Entire No. 114.

34. COHEN, A. *Delinquent Boys.* Glencoe, Illinois: Free Press, 1955.

Note:

(For article by ALLISON DAVIS, see Ref. 111.)

35. DUKES, W. "Psychological Studies of Values," *Psychol. Bull.*, LII (1955), 24–50.

36. Durkheim, E. *Sociology and Philosophy*. Glencoe, Illinois: Free Press, 1953. (Originally published, 1906.)
37. Durkin, D. "Children's Acceptance of Reciprocity as a Justice Principle," *Child Develpm.*, XXX (1959), 289–96.
38. ———. "Children's Concepts of Justice: A Comparison with the Piaget Data," *Child Develpm.*, XXX (1959), 59–67.
39. ———. "Children's Concepts of Justice: A Further Comparison with the Piaget Data," *J. Educ. Research*, LII (1959), 252–57.
40. ———. "Sex Differences in Children's Concepts of Justice," *Child Develpm.*, XXXI (1960), 361–68.
41. Emmerich, W. "Parental Identification in Young Children," *Genet. Psychol. Monogr.*, LX (1959), 257–308.
42. ———. "Young Children's Discrimination of Parent and Child Roles," *Child Develpm.*, XXX (1959), 405–19.
43. Emmerich, W., and Kohlberg, L. "Imitation and Attention-seeking in Young Children under Conditions of Nurturance, Frustration, and Conflict." Mimeographed unpublished paper, University of Chicago, 1953.
44. Erikson, E. H. *Childhood and Society*. New York: John Norton & Son, 1950.
45. Eysenck, H. J. "The Development of Moral Values in Children: The Contribution of Learning Theory," *Brit. J. of Educ. Psychol.*, XXX (1960), 11–22.
46. Faigin, H. "Child Rearing in the Rimrock Community with Special Reference to the Development of Guilt." Unpublished doctoral dissertation, Harvard University, 1953.
47. Fenichel, O. "Identification," in *Collected Papers*, Vol. I. New York: W. W. Norton & Co., 1953.
48. Festinger, L. *A Theory of Cognitive Dissonance*. Evanston: Row, Peterson & Co., 1957.
49. Flugel, J. C. *Man, Morals, and Society: A Psycho-analytical Study*. New York: International Universities Press, 1955.
50. Freud, A. *The Ego and the Mechanics of Defense*. London: Hogarth Press, Ltd., 1937.
51. Freud, S. *Civilization and Its Discontents*. London: Hogarth Press, Ltd., 1955. (Originally published, 1930.)
52. ———. *The Ego and the Id*. London: Hogarth Press, Ltd., 1950. (Originally published, 1923.)
53. ———. *Group Psychology and the Analysis of the Ego*. New York: Liveright Pub. Corp., 1949. (Originally published, 1922.)
54. ———. "On Narcissism: An Introduction," *Collected Papers*, Vol. IV. London: Hogarth Press, Ltd., 1946. (Originally published, 1914.)
55. ———. *New Introductory Lectures in Psycholanalysis*. New York: W. W. Norton & Co., 1932.
56. ———. "Some Psychological Consequences of the Anatomical Distinctions between the Sexes," *Collected Papers*, Vol. V. London: Hogarth Press, Ltd., 1950. (Originally published, 1925.)
57. Fromm, E. *Man for Himself*. New York: Rinehart & Co., 1955.
58. Gesell, A., *et al. Youth: The Years from Ten to Sixteen*. New York: Harper & Bros., 1956.

59. GLUECK, S., and GLUECK, E. *Unravelling Juvenile Delinquency.* New York: Commonwealth Fund, 1950.

60. GOETHALS, G. W. "A Study of the Relationships between Family Esteem Patterns and Identification, the Internalization of Values, and Aggression of a Group of Four-year-old Children." Unpublished doctoral dissertation, Harvard University, 1955.

61. GRINDER, R. "Parental Antecedents of Resistance to Temptation," *Child Develpm.* (to appear in 1962 or 1963).

62. HARE, R. M. *The Language of Morals.* New York: Oxford University Press, 1952.

63. HARRIS, D. B.; ROSE, A. M.; CLARK, K. E.; and VALASEK, F. "Personality Differences between Responsible and Less Responsible Children," *J. Genet. Psychol.*, LXXXVII (1955), 103–9.

64. ———. "The Relationship of Home Duties to an Attitude of Responsibility," *Child Devepm.*, XXV (1954), 29–33.

65. HARROWER, M. E. "Social Status and Moral Development," *Brit. J. Educ. Psychol.*, IV (1934), 75–95.

66. HARTSHORNE, H., and MAY, M. A. *Studies in the Nature of Character:* Vol. I, *Studies in Deceit;* Vol. II, *Studies in Self-Control;* Vol. III, *Studies in the Organization of Character.* New York: Macmillan Co., 1928–30.

67. HARTUP, W. "Nurturance and Nurturance-withdrawal in Relation to the Dependency Behavior of School Children," *Child Develpm.*, XXIX (1958), 191–201.

68. ———. "Some Correlates of Parental Imitation in Young Children," *Child Develpm.*, XXXIII (1962), 85–97.

69. HAVIGHURST, R., and TABA, H. *Adolescent Character and Personality.* New York: John Wiley & Sons, 1949.

70. HAVIGHURST, R., and NEUGARTEN, B. *American Indian and White Children.* Chicago: University of Chicago Press, 1955.

71. HEINECKE, C. M. "Some Antecedents and Correlates of Guilt and Fear in Young Boys." Unpublished doctoral dissertation, Harvard University, 1953.

72. HELPER, M. M. "Learning Theory and the Self Concept," *J. Abnorm. Soc. Psychol.*, LI (1955), 184–94.

73. HENRY, A. F. "Family Role Structure and Self-Blame," *Social Forces*, XXXV (1956), 34–38.

74. HILL, W. F. "Learning Theory and the Acquisition of Values," *Psychol. Rev.*, LXVII (1960), 317–32.

75. HOFFMAN, L. W. "The Father's Role in the Family and the Child's Peer-group Adjustment," *Merrill-Palmer Quar.*, VII (1961), 97–107.

76. HOFFMAN, M. L. "Child-rearing Antecedents of Moral Development," *Child Develpm.*, XXXIV (1963), in press.

77. ———. "Progress Report: Techniques and Processes in Moral Development." Detroit: Merrill-Palmer Institute, 1961 (mimeographed).

78. HOFFMAN, M. L., and SALTZSTEIN, H. D. "Parent Practices and the Child's Moral Orientation." Interim research report presented at American Psychological Association, Chicago, September, 1960.

79. HOLLENBERG, ELEANOR. "Child Training among the Zeepi with Special Reference to the Internalization of Moral Values." Unpublished doctoral dissertation, Harvard University, 1952.

80. HORNEY, K. *The Neurotic Personality of Our Time*. New York: W. W. Norton & Co., 1937.

81. JOHNSON, R. "A Study of Children's Moral Judgments," *Child Develpm.*, XXXIII (1962), 327–54.

82. JONES, V. "Character Development in Children: An Objective Approach," in *Manual of Child Psychology*, 781–832. Edited by L. Carmichael. New York: John Wiley & Sons, 1954.

83. KAGAN, J. "The Concept of Identification," *Psychol. Rev.*, LXV (1958), 296–305.

84. KAGAN, J., and LEMKIN, J. "The Child's Differential Perception of Parental Attributes," *J. Abnorm. Soc. Psychol.*, LIII (1956), 257–58.

85. KELMAN, H. "Compliance, Identification, and Internalization." Mimeographed monograph, Harvard University, 1956.

86. KOHLBERG, L. "The Development of Modes of Moral Thinking and Choice in the Years Ten to Sixteen." Unpublished doctoral dissertation, University of Chicago, 1958.

87. ———. "The Development of Children's Orientations toward a Moral Order: I. Sequence in the Development of Moral Thought," *Vita Humana*, (1963), in press.

88. ———. "The Development of Children's Orientations toward a Moral Order: II. Social Experience, Social Conduct, and the Development of Moral Thought," *Vita Humana*, (1963), in press.

89. ———. "Sex Differences in Morality," in "Sex Role Development." Edited by E. Maccoby. New York: Social Science Research Council, 1962 (mimeographed).

90. KOHLBERG, L., and ZIGLER, E. "The Impact of Cognitive Maturity upon the Development of Sex Role Attitudes in the Years Four to Eight," *Monogr. Soc. Res. Child Develpm.* (1963), in press.

91. LERNER, E. *Constraint Areas and the Moral Judgment of Children*. Menasha, Wisconsin: George Banta Pub. Co., 1937.

92. ———. "Perspectives in Moral Reasoning," *Amer. J. Sociology*, XLIII (1937).

93. LEVINE, B. "Child-rearing Antecedents of Conscience." Unpublished doctoral dissertation, Northwestern University, 1961.

94. MACCOBY, E. E. "Role-taking in Childhood and Its Consequences for Social Learning," *Child Develpm.*, XXX (1959), 239–52.

95. ———. "The Taking of Adult Roles in Middle Childhood," *J. Abnorm. Soc. Psychol.*, LXIII (1961), 493–504.

96. MACCOBY, E. E., and WHITING, J. W. "Some Child-rearing Correlates of Young Children's Responses to Deviation Stories." Mimeographed unpublished paper, Stanford University, 1960.

97. MCCORD, W., and MCCORD, J. *Psychopathy and Delinquency*. New York: Grune & Stratton, Inc., 1956.

98. ———. "A Tentative Theory of the Structure of Conscience," in *Decisions, Values, and Groups*. Edited by D. Wellner. New York: Pergamon Press, Inc., 1960.

99. MCDOUGALL, W. *An Introduction to Social Psychology*. London: Methuen & Co., Ltd., 1908.

100. MACKINNON, D. W. "Violation of Prohibitions," *Explorations in Person-*

ality, pp. 491–501. Edited by H. W. Murray. New York: Oxford University Press, 1938.

101. MacRae, D., Jr. "A Test of Piaget's Theories of Moral Development," *J. Abnorm. Soc. Psychol.*, XLIX (1954), 14–18.

102. Mead, G. H. *Mind, Self, and Society*. Chicago: University of Chicago Press, 1934.

103. Medinnus, G. R. "Immanent Justice in Children: A Review of the Literature and Additional Data," *J. of Genet. Psychol.*, XC (1959), 253–62.

104. Mills, J. "Temptation and Changes in Moral Attitudes." Unpublished doctoral dissertation, Stanford University, 1958.

105. Morris, J. F. "The Development of Moral Values in Children," *Brit. J. Educ. Psychol.* XXVIII (1958), 1–14.

106. Mowrer, O. H. "Identification: A Link between Learning Theory and Psychotherapy," *Learning Theory and Personality Dynamics*, pp. 573—616. New York: Ronald Press, 1950.

107. Mussen, P. "Some Antecedents and Consequents of Masculine Sex-typing in Adolescent Boys," *Psychol. Monogr.*, LXXV (1961), Whole No. 506.

108. Mussen, P., and Distler, L. "Masculinity, Identification, and Father-Son Relationships," *J. Abnorm. Soc. Psychol.*, LIX (1959), 350–56.

109. ———. "Child-rearing Antecedents of Masculine Identification in Kindergarten Boys," *Child Develpm.*, XXXI (1960), 89–100.

110. Mussen, P., and Rutherford, E. "Parent-Child Relations and Parental Personality in Relation to Young Children's Sex Role Preferences," *J. Abnorm. Soc. Psychol.* (To be published in 1963.)

111. Davis, A. "Child Training and Social Class," in *Child Behavior and Development*. Edited by Barker, Kounin, and Wright. New York: McGraw-Hill Book Co., 1943.

112. Parsons, T. "The Superego and the Theory of Social Systems," in *A Modern Introduction to the Family*. Edited by N. Bell and E. Vogel. Glencoe, Illinois: Free Press, 1960.

113. Parsons, T., and Bales, R. R. *Family, Socialization, and Interaction Process*. Glencoe, Illinois: Free Press, 1955.

114. Payne, D. E., and Mussen, P. "Parent-Child Relations and Father Identification among Adolescent Boys," *J. Abnorm. Soc. Psychol.*, LII (1956), 358–62.

115. Peck, R. F., and Havighurst, R. J. *The Psychology of Character Development*. New York: John Wiley & Sons, 1960.

116. Peel, E. A. "Experimental Examination of Some of Piaget's Schemata concerning Children's Perception and Thinking, and a Discussion of Their Educational Significance," *Brit. J. Educ. Psychol.*, XXIX (1959), 89–103.

117. Piaget, J. *The Moral Judgment of the Child*. Glencoe, Illinois: Free Press, 1948. (Originally published, 1932.)

118. Piers, G., and Singer, M. *Shame and Guilt: A Psychoanalytic and a Cultural Study*. Springfield, Illinois: Charles C Thomas, Publisher, 1953.

119. Rau, L. "Conscience and Identification," in *Identification in Children*. Edited by Sears, Alpert, and Rau. (To be published, 1963.)

120. ———. "Parental Antecedents of Identification," *Merrill-Palmer Quar.*, VI (1959), 77–82.

121. Rebelsky, F.; Allinsmith, W.; and Grinder, R. "Sex Differences in

Children's Use of Fantasy Confession and Their Relation to Temptation," *Child Develpm.* (to appear in 1962 or 1963).

122. ROBACK, A. A. *The Psychology of Character.* New York: Harcourt Brace & Co., 1927.

123. ROSENBLITH, J. "Learning by Imitation in Kindergarten Children," *Child Develpm.*, XXX (1959), 69–81.

124. SANDLER, J. "On the Concept of Superego," in *Psychoanalytic Study of the Child*, Vol. XV. New York: International Universities Press, 1960.

125. SANFORD, N. "The Approach of the Authoritarian Personality," in *Psychology of Personality.* Edited by J. McCary. New York: Evergreen Books (Grove Press), 1959.

126. SANFORD, N.; ADKINS, M.; COBB, E.; and MILLER, B. *Physique, Personality, and Scholarship.* Monograph of the Society for Research in Child Development, VIII (1943), 1–705. (Summarized in *Child Behavior and Development*, pp. 567–89. Edited by Barker, Kounin, and Wright. New York: McGraw-Hill Book Co., 1943.)

127. SEARS, PAULINE. "Child-rearing Factors Related to the Playing of Sex-typed Roles," *Amer. Psychologist*, VIII (1953), 431 (abstract).

128. SEARS, R. R. "Identification as a Form of Behavior Development," in *The Concept of Development*, pp. 149–61. Edited by D. B. Harris. Minneapolis: University of Minnesota Press, 1957.

129. SEARS, R. R.; MACCOBY, E. E.; and LEVIN, H. *Patterns of Child-rearing.* Evanston, Illinois: Row, Peterson & Co., 1957.

130. SEARS, R. R.; WHITING, J. W. M.; NOWLIS, V.; and SEARS, P. S. "Some Child-rearing Antecedents of Aggression and Dependency in Young Children," *Genet. Psychol. Monogr.*, XLVII (1953), 135–203.

131. SHAPLIN, J. T. "Child Training and the Identification of Preadolescent Boys with Their Parents." Unpublished doctoral dissertation, Harvard University, 1954.

132. SLATER, P. "Toward a Dualistic Theory of Identification," *Merrill-Palmer Quar.*, VII (1961), 113–26.

133. SMITH, A. "The Theory of Moral Sentiments," in *Adam Smith's Moral and Political Philosophy.* Edited by H. Schneider. New York: Hafner Pub. Co., 1948.

134. SULLIVAN, H. S. *An Interpersonal Theory of Psychiatry.* New York: W. W. Norton & Co., 1953.

135. TERMAN, L. M., and MILES, C. C. *Sex and Personality.* New York: McGraw-Hill Book Co., 1936.

136. TERMAN, L. M., and TYLER, L. E. "Psychological Sex Differences," in *Manual of Child Psychology*, pp. 1064–1114. Edited by L. Carmichael. New York: John Wiley & Sons, 1946.

137. WHITING, J. W. M. "Fourth Presentation," in *Discussions on Child Development*, Vol. II. Edited by J. M. Tanner and Barbel Inhelder. London: Tavistock Publications, 1954.

138. ———. "Resource Mediation and Learning by Identification," in *Personality Development in Children*, pp. 112–26. Edited by I. Iscoe and H. W. Stevenson. Austin: University of Texas Press, 1960.

139. ———. "Sorcery, Sin, and the Superego: A Cross-cultural Study of Some Mechanisms of Social Control," in *Nebraska Symposium on Motivation*,

pp. 174–95. Edited by M. R. Jones. Lincoln: University of Nebraska Press, 1959.

140. Whiting, J. W. M., and Child, I. L. *Child Training and Personality: A Cross-cultural Study*. New Haven, Connecticut: Yale University Press, 1953.

141. Wright, J.; Hill, J.; and Alpert, R. "The Development and Expression of Conscience in Fantasy by School Children." Paper read at 1961 meetings of the Society for Research in Child Development, Pennsylvania State University.

CHAPTER VIII

Dependence and Independence

WILLARD W. HARTUP

Whenever the individual gives evidence that people, as people, are satisfying and rewarding, it may be said that the individual is behaving dependently. Since dependency always refers to actions of one person vis-à-vis some other person, it is a form of social behavior. For example, the very young child is concerned with securing the presence and affection of his mother; later, approval from peers seems paramount; still later, a spouse or one's children become sources of nurturance.

Dependency emerges very early in life. By six months of age, most babies respond in a primitive way to the presence and attention of their mothers. The parent's presence may be calming and gratifying; her absence may elicit crying and agitation. Following these first diffuse responses, more direct modes of seeking nurturance are acquired. The older baby elicits contact and cuddling by holding up his arms and smiling; he may creep or walk, following his mother from place to place and clinging to her skirts. Another child may cry and whine. Throughout infancy and childhood manifestations of dependency such as these are tried out, practiced for a while, and subsequently given up. At the age of four or five, the child may use intellectual or physical accomplishment to obtain parental praise or attention. Still other transformations occur on into adulthood. Thus, dependency does not refer to a small group of specific action tendencies. Rather, the term covers a wide variety of behaviors, all of which are directed toward the satisfactions derived from contact with or nurturance from other people.

Frequently, the term *independence* denotes simply the absence of dependence. Such usage places dependence and independence at opposite poles on a single behavioral continuum. High dependency is automatically low independence and vice versa. Some writers (**3**,

30), however, argue that dependence and independence should be conceived separately. Independence, it is suggested, should refer to behavior which is self-reliant but also self-assertive. From this standpoint, a child is independent only to the extent that: (*a*) he seeks nurturance from other people relatively infrequently, and (*b*) he manifests initiative and achievement-striving. This conceptualization of independence does not, of course, remove all overlap with the concept of dependence; independence is simply defined as something more than lack of dependence.

This chapter will place greater emphasis upon dependent than upon independent behavior because the literature relating to the development of the latter is not extensive. The large majority of systematic studies of dependency and independence have been completed since 1946. Occasional findings relevant to dependence may be found in the earlier literature, but for the most part such results are by-products of investigations whose main emphases lay on child-rearing practices, disciplinary techniques, and the like.

Conceptual Issues

Dependency behavior and dependency drive.—The term *dependence* has been employed in two major ways. First, it has been used to denote a group of response tendencies which are instrumental in obtaining social reinforcement (or nurturance). Used in this way, dependency is a *behavioral construct*—it is a category or rubric which may be applied to many different kinds of activity, such as affection-seeking, help-seeking, and bids for attention.

A second use of the term is as a *motivational construct;* dependency frequently refers to a unitary, discriminable *drive.* Virtually all writers who conceptualize dependency in this way assume that the dependency drive is a secondary, rather than a primary, drive. Thus, Sears *et al.* (**48**) speak of an "acquired drive of dependence" which emerges from the interactions of child and caretaker during infancy and early childhood. Beller (**3**) refers to a "general dependence drive." Similarly, Heathers (**30**) employs the term *emotional dependence* to indicate "needs for reassurance and affection," and Bandura and Walters (**2**) refer to the "dependency motive."

The justification for postulating separate drives of dependence, independence, aggression, and the like, has frequently been questioned. Brown (**9**), for example, has suggested that the motivating component of many of the so-called acquired drives is anxiety. Walters and Karal (**57**) and Hartup (**28**) have taken the position that the term *dependency* should refer to behavior rather than to motive. They suggest that such behavior may be acquired in childhood as a means of reducing some generalized, emotion-produced, drive-state, such as anxiety.

Unidimensional vs. multidimensional hypotheses.—As already indicated, dependency is a molar concept, and almost any sequence of actions may be considered dependent so long as it is directed toward obtaining social reinforcement. In children, dependency commonly refers to such behaviors as seeking attention, seeking reassurance, seeking physical contact, and the like. But each one of these goals (attention, for example) may be sought in numerous ways. One child may shout to the teacher, "See me!" Another child may silently force his way to the front row in order to be directly under the eyes of the teacher. A third may smear his neighbor's drawing and then make sure this comes to the teacher's attention. Because there are so many ways to stimulate nurturing behavior in other people, there is considerable question as to whether dependency should be employed as a unitary concept.

Beller has addressed several studies to the problem of generality in the dependency behavior of young children. These investigations have focused on the interrelations among five measures, all presumed to be components of a general dependency drive: *seeking help, seeking physical contact, seeking proximity, seeking attention,* and *seeking recognition* (praise and approval). In the earliest study in this series (**3**), a group of nursery-school teachers were asked to rate (on seven-point scales) each of 43 children on the five components. An analysis of variance of these ratings showed the between-subjects variance to be significant, indicating that most of the children differed consistently from one another in their five scores. Beller concluded that such consistency indicates a general dependency drive in the children studied.

Evidence concerning the generality of independent behavior is also provided in Beller's study. The teachers rated the children on the following components: *taking initiative, overcoming obstacles, persistence, satisfaction from work,* and *wanting to do things by one's self*. The analysis of variance based on these ratings indicated consistency across the five independence components for individual children, suggesting to Beller that independence may also be considered as a general acquired drive.

In the second study, Beller (**4**) focused on dependency and independence in 51 children who attended nursery school at a child guidance clinic. Intercorrelations among the teacher ratings of the five dependency components ranged between .48 and .83, indicating a considerable degree of covariation among the five scales. Most of the components of independence were also quite highly interrelated, although the correlations ranged from a low of .21 to .90. In a third study of 74 clinic subjects (**5**), the range of correlations among the dependency components was from .41 to .79.

These findings give impressive support for a unidimensional theory of dependency. It appears that children who seek contact and nurturance in one way tend to manifest other forms of dependency as well. There is one methodological question, however, which needs to be considered in evaluating Beller's results. When teachers are asked to rate a group of children on several different scales, there is likely to be "haloing" in the resultant scores, i.e., the rating given a particular child on one scale may influence the ratings given him by the teacher on subsequent scales. Beller indicates he has taken considerable precaution against haloing (e.g., irrelevant ratings are interpolated between ratings on the dependency components), but the possibility remains that the reported intercorrelations are somewhat inflated. It seems prudent, therefore, to regard Beller's evidence as only tentative support for the hypothesis that dependency and independence are unitary dimensions.

Mann (**40**) used observations, rather than ratings, to study a group of dependency components. The subjects were 41 children observed during free play periods in a nursery school. Fifty-five two-minute observations were completed on each child. Frequencies of the following kinds of behavior were obtained: *seeking physical contact*, *seeking to be near*, *seeking reassurance*, *seeking positive attention*, *seeking help*, and *seeking negative attention* (seeking attention by means of socially disapproved behavior). Only one of the fifteen intercorrelations among these components was significant; hence the unidimensional hypothesis was not supported. It should be pointed out that Mann employed observational categories which were "mutually exclusive"; that is, a particular act on the part of a child could not be scored under more than one category. Consequently, there is some possibility that Mann's technique worked *against* the hypothesis of unidimensionality, just as Beller's techniques may have worked for such an hypothesis. Heathers (**31**) also employed observations of nursery-school children and found that frequencies of *affection-seeking* and *approval-seeking* were unrelated.

A somewhat different approach to the dimensional problem was employed in a study of attention-seeking by Gewirtz (**20**). Fifty-six four- and five-year-olds were brought individually to a laboratory room where they could paint at an easel in the presence of an adult experimenter. Nine observational measures of attention-seeking were obtained and then factor-analyzed. Two fairly distinct dimensions of attention-seeking were revealed by this analysis. One factor appeared to involve active, direct, verbal attempts to gain or maintain the attention of the adult. The second factor incorporated nonverbal, passive actions probably used by children in conflict concerning more direct means of gaining attention. Gewirtz's findings suggest that even one dependency component (attention-seeking) may be at least two-dimensional.

Over-all, then, the evidence concerning generality in dependency and independence is equivocal. Neither those data which support the unidimensional hypothesis nor the findings which support multidimensionality are entirely free of methodological weaknesses. The generality problem is often ignored and dependency is used repeatedly as a label for a single, unitary dimension in personality. There is, however, a distinct possibility that this label has been used to subsume a multiplicity of factors.

The relation of dependence to independence.—As mentioned previously, independence has sometimes been equated with lack of dependence. On the other hand, behavioral characteristics such as assertiveness and achievement-striving also have been subsumed under the independence concept. Beller (**3**), for example, believes that conditions of learning in early childhood frequently favor increase of *both* dependence and independence. Parents do not always parallel independence demands with the punishment of dependency; indeed, parents frequently use praise and approval (dependency rewards) to encourage the child to care for himself and to accomplish difficult tasks independently and persistently. Beller postulates that if dependence and independence are defined separately, the relationship between measures of the two characteristics should be only moderately negative, or even zero.

In Beller's investigation of 43 normal nursery-school children, the correlation between composite ratings of dependency and independence was — .53 (**3**). For the 51 clinic children studied subsequently, this correlation was — .01 (**4**), and in the study of 74 children the average correlation between ratings of dependence and independence components was — .17 (**5**). Thus, when independence is conceived in terms of both self-reliance and achievement-striving, it is not the opposite of dependence. It is true that the significant negative correlation obtained in Beller's first study indicates some degree of bipolarity. However, the later ratings were probably better, more stable measures, since they were based on repeated evaluations of the children by the teacher over a period of 2½ years. (Single ratings were employed in the earlier study.)

The relation between dependence and independence has also been examined by Heathers (**31**), who defined dependence in terms of *affection-* and *attention-seeking*, and independence in terms of *resisting distractions, self-assertion in determining play activities*, and *resisting interference during nursery-school play*. Frequencies were obtained from observational records of 41 children. The correlations between components of dependency and components of independence ranged between + .64 and — .67, but 85 per cent were not significant. The frequency of self-assertion tended to be negatively related to frequency of affection-seeking, but otherwise these results suggest that dependency and independence may be regarded as separate personality dimensions.

Although the empirical evidence suggests that dependence and independence are orthogonal factors, this evidence may be, in one sense, artifactual. That is, dependency and independence may or may not be overlapping concepts, depending upon how definitions are formulated and measures constructed. It so happens that when independence is defined in terms of both self-reliance and achievement-striving it is not strongly related to dependency. The main issue is whether defining the two concepts separately increases the investigator's capacity to predict either or both forms of behavior.

Methodology

The most commonly used methods for obtaining data on children's dependence and independence are: (*a*) direct observation of the child's interactions with other people; (*b*) ratings, or other types of judgment, made by persons who have had contact with the child; and (*c*) projective techniques. The first two procedures have been most frequently applied to subjects of preschool age in naturalistic situations. Projective techniques, on the other hand, have been used most extensively with older subjects. It is questionable whether such varied techniques yield comparable or equivalent measures. Several studies provide information pertinent to this question, and they will be described in the following paragraphs.

Direct observations.—The usual observational procedure involves trained judges and a time-sampling strategy which will permit some generalizing from the data about the child's day-to-day behavior. Following are some selected examples of observational techniques as they have been applied to the study of dependency behavior:

1. *Naturalistic observations by running account:* This technique involves securing narrative records of the child's behavior covering a specified number of time periods. The written protocols are then analyzed according to a classification scheme selected by the investigator. For example, Heathers (**31**) employed two observers who made running-account records of three-minute samples of each child's behavior in the nursery school. Subsequently, raters scored the records in terms of the following: (*a*) *emotional dependence*—clings to or seeks affection from teacher, clings to or seeks affection from child, seeks attention or approval from teachers, seeks attention or approval from child; (*b*) *emotional independence*—ignores stimuli from teacher, ignores stimuli from child, plays alone intently, structures other children's play, interferes with the play of other children, resists interference from other children.

Running-account records have also been employed by Marshall and McCandless (**42**), who defined dependence on adults in terms of *association* (mutual awareness of common activity or interest), *friendly approach*, and *conversation*. This technique has been used by Marshall (**41**) to study the role of language in play interactions among nursery-school children and also by McCandless, Bilous, and Bennett (**37**). Other examples of running-account methods may be found in the work of Siegel *et al.* (**49**), who studied dependency and independence in children of working mothers, and Osborn (**44**), who observed the child in the home.

2. *Naturalistic observation with direct classification:* An increasingly common observational technique involves the immediate tabulation of behavior frequencies by the person doing the observing. The procedure used by Sears *et al.* (**48**) illustrates this approach. Sixteen 15-minute observations were made on each child, and the frequency with which the children displayed the following five categories was noted: *touching or holding; being near; securing positive attention* (seeking praise, inviting co-operation, asking questions, etc.); *securing reassurance, comfort or consolation;* and *securing negative attention.* Dependency-category scores consisted of the total frequencies observed during the 16 periods. A total dependency score was obtained by summing the five category scores.

Mann (**40**) employed dependency categories similar to those used by Sears *et al.*, but developed a sampling strategy which involved 55 two-minute observations of each subject. Walters *et al.* (**55**) tabulated instances of physical and verbal affection during 40 one-minute behavior samples. The results of all these studies indicate that, with training, dependency categories can be directly applied during observations of young children with satisfactorily high reliability.

3. *Observation in seminaturalistic settings:* Two examples will suggest the potential to be found in standardized, seminaturalistic settings for observation of dependence in young children. Smith's technique (**50**) centers on observation of nursery-school children interacting with their mothers. Subjects were observed in a laboratory room containing toys for the child and reading matter for the mothers. During the final 15 minutes of the 45-minute session, the mothers were asked to fill out a questionnaire in order that they could not give full attention to the child. Direct-scoring categories included: *evoking attention or affection, asking for verbal help, asking for material help,* and *asking for reward* (praise). Frequency of dependency behavior was tabulated for each of the individual categories by a concealed observer.

Gewirtz (**22**) also observed nursery-school children in a laboratory room—in this instance the room was equipped with an easel and material for painting. The child determined for himself how long he remained in the room. A concealed observer recorded and classified all instances of attention-seeking directed toward the adult experimenter. Observation categories included: *attention-seeking* (urgent responses for notice from the adult), *comments* (casual remarks requiring no response from the adult), *glances* at the adult, *number of paintings completed,* and *time* the child remained in the session. These observations furnished the data for the factor analysis mentioned previously. Other examples of observational methods applied in structured laboratory situations may be found in Carl (**13**), Hartup (**28**), Antonovsky (**1**), and Beller and Haeberle (**7**).

Ratings.—By using rating or ranking methods it is possible to summarize a greater number of observations of the child than is ordinarily feasible with direct procedures. Most rating methods are based on relatively uncontrolled observations by persons not entirely "disinterested" in the children (e.g., teachers). Such techniques have, however, proved useful in a large number of studies of dependence and independence.

The rating scales developed by Beller (**3**) are particularly appropriate for use by nursery-school teachers in assessing dependence and independence in preschool-age children. The rater employs a seven-point graphic scale to estimate the frequency and persistence with which the subject manifests each form of dependence or independence during his time at nursery school. The subjects may be rated once on each scale (as has been done in some studies) or several times over an extended period. When repeated ratings are obtained, the final dependency score is either the average rating or the sum of all ratings made. The Beller scales, either in the original form or slightly modified, have been employed in several studies of preschool-age children by Sears *et al.* (**48**), and Hartup (**28**) and in studies with older children and adolescents by Walters (**56**) and Bandura and Walters (**2**).

Finney (**18**) has developed a series of ten five-point scales which can be applied by teachers to children of a wide variety of ages. The scales cover such behaviors as *asking other people to do things* and *crying when hurt.* A Likert-type dependency scale consisting of 37 items has also been worked out by Finney for use by clinical workers.

An unusual feature of Stendler's teacher-ratings (**53**) is their focus on the teacher's observations of the child's behavior toward his mother. For example, teachers are asked to rate the child's need for the presence of the mother outside the school and the tendency of the mother to overprotect her child as well as to rate the child's dependency in the classroom. It should be noted that Stendler developed these scales in an effort to distinguish the so-called *over-dependent* child.

Other judgmental methods differ from the procedures described in the degree to which the rater's judgment is "removed" from the actual behavior of the child and in the manner in which the behavior is categorized. A checklist for nursery-school teachers was used by Livson and Mussen (**36**) to record instances of: *seeking physical contact, asking for help, seeking attention and approval, needing a security object, wanting to go home, revealing hurt feelings, helpless crying*, and the like. Mothers' reports of their children's behavior served as the basis for ratings of dependency by Sears, Maccoby, and Levin (**47**). These ratings included: *how much attention the child wants from his mother, how much he clings and follows his mother about*, and *how he reacts when separated from his mother*. It is important to understand that it was the *mother's report* of the child's behavior that was rated in this study; the relationship between the way a mother describes her child's behavior to an interviewer and the way the child actually behaves is not known. Dependency ratings were applied to summary reports by home visitors, interviewers, observers at nursery school, day camp, and elementary school in a study by Kagan and Moss (**33**).

Paired-comparisons have been employed in at least one study of dependence in preschool-age children. Endsley (**17**) paired each child in a nursery-school group with every other child and asked the teachers to decide, for each of the possible pairings, which child sought praise more frequently. A total praise-seeking score was obtained for each subject by counting the number of comparisons in which the subject was judged to seek praise more frequently than the other child in the pair.

Self-report techniques.—At least two paper-and-pencil inventories contain measures of dependency. Both of these inventories have been more frequently employed with adults than with children. There is little reason, however, why these two instruments could not be employed with preadolescent or adolescent subjects, although both would be completely inappropriate for use with younger children.

The Edwards' *Personal Preference Schedule* (**16**) is a personality inventory patterned after Murray's system of manifest needs. Cairns and Lewis (**12**), among others, have employed this instrument to measure the strength of dependency in a sample of college Freshmen. A dependency index may also be extracted from the Leary *Interpersonal Checklist* (**34**), a personality inventory consisting of self-referent adjectives and phrases. Cairns and Kaufman (**11**) used this instrument and obtained a measure of dependence by computing the algebraic difference between scores on "Octant VI" (docile-dependent) and "Octant I" (autonomous-dictatorial).

Projective techniques.—The projective device most commonly used for the assessment of dependency motivation has been the *Thematic Apperception Test*. The *TAT* has been used to measure dependence in young adults by Mussen and Kagan (**43**), Zuckerman and Grosz (**62**), Fitzgerald (**19**), and Cairns and Kaufman (**11**), but has rarely been employed with children or adolescents. There are at least three studies, however, in which picture-interpretation methods have been employed with younger subjects. Sontag *et al.* (**51**), used the *TAT* to study the resolution of infantile-dependency needs in a group of subjects between 13 and 18 years of age. Beller and Haeberle (**6**) employed three cards from the *Children's Apperception Test* to study the relation between dependency motivation and the responses of young children under mild stress. Finally, Townsend (**54**) used ambiguous pictures to elicit verbal responses which were then scored in terms of dependency themes. In these studies the tendency has been to use pictures which the investigator believes will frequently elicit dependency themes in the stories told by the subject. Usually, the stories obtained are subjectively rated as to whether dependency content is present or absent.

Other projective devices which have been used to study dependence and independence include: the *Incomplete Sentence Blank* (**19**), story completions (**10**), the *Holtzman Inkblot Test* (**45**), responses to cartoons depicting dependency situations (**32**), and standardized doll play (**46, 26**).

Other techniques.—Two other methods, both developed for studies of adults but both having possibilities for older children and adolescents, are a tachistoscopic task and a situational technique. Kagan and Moss (**33**) presented a series of dependency pictures tachistoscopically and obtained recognition thresholds for various component parts of the pictures. The investigators assumed that these thresholds vary positively with strength of dependency conflict. The *Behavioral Dependency Task,* developed by Cairns and Lewis (**12**), involves presenting the subject with an almost insoluble puzzle and recording the time elapsing until he asks for help. In this situation, dependency is presumed to vary negatively with the time spent before seeking help.

Relations among measures of dependency.—A variety of procedures for studying dependency has been described in this section. Some methods, such as the projective devices, are sometimes presumed to measure the motivational strength of dependence. Methods focusing on behavior in naturalistic settings, as indicated previously, have sometimes been interpreted as measures of dependency drive and sometimes as measures of response strength. The published evidence, although it is not extensive, suggests that measures of dependency derived by these methods are not highly related to each other.

For example, the correlations reported by Sears *et al.* (**48**), between teachers' ratings and direct observations of dependence in preschool children are not significantly greater than zero. Hartup (**28**) also reported zero-order correlations between teachers' ratings and observations of children in nursery school, although he did report a significant correlation of .40 between a composite teacher-rating of dependence and a dependency score derived from observation of the child in the laboratory.

The relation between projective measures of dependence and scores obtained by means of other techniques has been more thoroughly examined with adults than with children. Fitzgerald (**19**) studied the relations among dependency measures obtained from the *TAT, Incomplete Sentence Blank,* interview ratings, and sociometric methods. The intercorrelations were not significantly greater than zero, except those between the *ISB* and the interview and sociometric scores. Even those correlations, however, were extremely low (.28 and .25, respectively). Cairns and Kaufmann (**11**) also report a low correlation (.43) between dependency scores on the *TAT* and the *Interpersonal Check List.*

The work of Beller and Haeberle (**6**) with children shows that the relation between projective and observational measures of dependence is not a simple one. They report that preschool-age children scoring high on teacher-ratings of dependence tend to include more dependency elements in both structured doll play and responses to selected cards from the *CAT*. This relationship holds, however, only when an experience which induces "dependency stress" occurs immediately before the presentation of the projective test.

The investigator who wishes to study dependence in children finds himself in an area of considerable methodological confusion. Traditional practice has been to adopt phantasy measures if one wishes to measure strength of dependency motivation while focusing on observational methods if one is interested in measuring response strength. These conventions are by no means universally accepted. The investigator may wish to use a variety of techniques until such time as the relations between projective measures, observational measures, ratings, and rankings are more completely understood.

Theoretical Considerations

A detailed treatment in this chapter of all the theoretical issues pertinent to the study of dependency and independence in children is impossible. A summary will be presented of those approaches which have most heavily influenced recent research on these problems—psychoanalysis, on the one hand, and social learning theories, on the other.

The concept of *object relations*, usually meaning the relationship of the individual to other persons, is a central one in psychoanalysis. It is by means of such relationships that the young child obtains those gratifications needed to maintain life, but it is also postulated that the socialization of the child cannot proceed effectively in the absence of emotional bonds between the child and other persons. For example, some psychoanalytic views suggest that the internalizing of controls (i.e., the development of the superego or conscience) is contingent on the early development of a strong relationship between the child and his parents. Presumably internalization (frequently called identification) is motivated by the threat to the child posed by loss of parental love.

In addition to stressing the significance of dependency in the socialization of the child, psychoanalysis also furnishes certain hypotheses concerning the determinants of dependence. The events of infancy are believed to be paramount, primarily because the baby is so completely and necessarily dependent. It is assumed that experiences with the mother during feeding are of crucial significance and that strong manifestations of dependency in later life are traceable to oral deprivations during this period. The personality pattern called the "oral character," which is marked by excessive dependence, passivity, and depression, is presumed to be a consequence of fixations at the oral stage of development. According to the psychoanalytic view, healthy dependence in young children requires warm, affectionate, indulgent care by the mother during early infancy. The frustrations of later childhood, while they may contribute to dependency conflict and possibly increase dependence, are not presumed to be as crucial as earlier events.

Most social-learning orientations to the problem of dependence also stress the importance of early childhood. The processes which lead to the development of dependence are viewed somewhat differently from the psychoanalytic view. The following account is based on the work of Sears and his collaborators (**47, 48**), who have developed one of the more complete social-learning formulations.

Early in infancy the child acquires certain primitive techniques for obtaining help from others. These behaviors (e.g., clutching the mother, smiling at her, turning toward her) are assumed to be reinforced by the primary gratifications supplied by the mother. Most normal mothers respond nurturantly when their babies cry or behave in ways such as those mentioned; consequently, infantile supplications become part of almost every baby's response repertoire. Heathers (**30**) has called these early help-seeking responses *instrumental dependence*. At this time, the baby does not seek his mother as an end in herself but only as a means for obtaining some basic form of gratification.

If the mother continues to be present at times when primary needs are reduced (e.g., at feeding, changing, and the like), secondary reinforcement properties are acquired by stimuli such as the sheer presence of the mother, her smile, or her voice. The child may cease to cry when the mother walks into view; the maternal smile or voice may also bring about reduction in agitation. It is assumed that a variety of stimuli associated with the mother's presence became secondary reinforcers for the child simply by repeated association with reductions in primary drives.

It is sometimes suggested that this acquisition of secondary reinforcing properties by stimuli connected with the mother's presence is the essential determinant of the dependency drive. It is postulated that, once this has occurred, the child will undergo tension when deprived of social reinforcers and will show satisfaction when they are present. Sears *et al.* (**48**) suggest, however, that a dependency drive emerges only after the mother has occasionally failed to reward, or has even punished, dependent overtures in the child. According to this view, dependency acquires motivational properties as a result of a conflict induced by the mother's nonreward or punishment, a conflict between the previously acquired expectation of reward and the new-found expectation of nonreward. The events in the child's life most relevant to the development of dependence would be the nurturance of the mother (i.e., the frequency with which the mother is a source of gratification) and the frustration or punitiveness of the mother (i.e., the frequency with which she threatens the dependency relationship with the child or actually fails to reinforce it).

As mentioned earlier, Walters (**58**) takes the view that anxiety is the motivational state relevant to much dependency behavior. It is suggested that dependency habits can be learned in connection with many drives—first in response to hunger, thirst, and pain, later in response to the anxiety aroused when the child's relationship with adults is threatened. In any case, reinforcements for dependency behavior center primarily in the nurturant actions of the mother. Relevant variables suggested by this theoretical approach do not differ markedly from those suggested by Sears—maternal nurturance is relevant as a factor leading to the establishment of the mother as a secondary reinforcer; maternal separation or frustration of the child is relevant as a source of anxiety; maternal reinforcement, the degree to which the mother specifically reinforces dependency responses in the child is also significant.

Somewhat different social learning approaches to the study of dependency are described in publications by Beller (**3**), Gewirtz (**22**), Heathers (**30**), and Bandura and Walters (**2**).

Empirical Studies

Developmental studies.—As Sears, Maccoby, and Levin (**47**) suggest, dependency is a form of behavior which society regards as "changeworthy." As they grow older, children are expected to alter the mode used for obtaining nurturance from others. The child is expected to give up infantile clinging and following about in favor of more "mature" forms of attention- and approval-seeking. The child also repeatedly changes the objects of his dependence. Dependence may initially be directed toward the mother, but subsequently the child directs his overtures toward other adults and peers. It is also possible that the strength of the motivation underlying dependency behavior changes over time, although most personality theories assume some continuity between the strength of dependency motivation in early childhood and in adulthood.

Three studies of preschool children demonstrate some of the changes which occur over time in mode and object of dependence. Heathers (**31**) observed the frequency of two forms of dependence, *affection-seeking* and *approval-seeking* in groups of two-year-old and four-year-old children in a nursery school. The observers' records indicated whether the dependence was directed toward teachers or toward other children. It was found that dependency on teachers was significantly more frequent in the group of two-year-olds while dependency on peers was more frequent among the four-year-olds. Similarly, Marshall (**41**) reports that the number of friendly contacts with nursery teachers decreases from age 2½ to 6½. Results such as these reflect at least one of the transfers made by young children in the object of their dependence.

Heathers also found that dependency is manifested in different ways by two-year-olds and four-year-olds. The older children showed less clinging and affection-seeking, relative to attention- or approval-seeking than the younger children. Age differences are also reported in a study of preschoolers by Gewirtz (**21**). Five-year-olds sought both reassurance and positive attention more frequently than four-year-olds. The results of these two studies imply that attention- and approval-seeking are more "mature" forms of dependence than direct bids for affection made by clinging, lap-sitting, and the like.

The only longitudinal study of dependence in the literature is by Kagan and Moss (**33**). These investigators obtained ratings of passivity and dependence from observational data assembled when the subjects were between the ages of six and ten. Further ratings of dependence were based on interviews conducted when the subjects were between the ages of twenty and thirty. For females, those who were dependent as children tended also to be dependent as young adults. No such continuity was found, however, for males. Kagan and Moss suggest that this sex difference may be a reflection of a cultural "double standard." That is, dependency in girls and women is generally acceptable in United States culture, whereas dependency in boys is increasingly punished following the infancy and preschool period.

Effects of child-rearing practices: Infancy.—As indicated in the foregoing paragraphs, it has been assumed that dependency behavior arises in infancy, the period when the child is utterly helpless and dependent on others for gratification of his needs. According to the theories outlined previously, two main aspects of the mother's handling of the infant should be related to later dependence. First, if frequent gratification and nurturance are supplied by the mother, secondary reinforcing properties should become invested in the mother's presence and actions. In other words, the amount of early maternal nurturance should be positively related to later dependence. Second, assuming that instrumental habits of dependence are acquired by almost every baby, rejection or punishment of the child's dependence should lead to increased efforts to obtain dependency satisfactions.

Investigators have not been able to establish the nature of the relation between maternal nurturance in infancy and dependence in later childhood. The studies of Goldfarb (**25**), Spitz (**52**), and Bowlby (**8**) report that children who were institutionalized during infancy and who did not experience consistent "mothering" became apathetic, socially unresponsive, and nondependent. Such results imply that dependency fails to develop unless the child experiences relatively consistent gratification from some person. It is not clear, however, whether the institutionalized children studied *failed* to develop dependency or whether some degree of dependency was established during the first few months of infancy and then was extinguished by lack of consistent nurturance during subsequent months. As Casler (**14**) has recently pointed out, the children studied by these investigators were not all institutionalized from birth; on the contrary, many of them were placed in institutions at six months of age or later.

Sears *et al.* (**48**) attempted to study the relation between early nurturance by the mother and dependency shown when the child was of preschool age. Information concerning the mother's behavior was obtained by means of an interview with special emphasis being given to the mother's feeding, weaning, and toilet-training practices. The dependency of the child was assessed by preschool teachers' ratings and also by observations at preschool. No clear relation between early nurturance and later dependency was found. There were some methodological difficulties in this portion of the Sears study, i.e., the ratings of nurturance from the mothers' interviews were confounded with frustration—low nurturance was equivalent to high frustration. Even so, the investigators suggest that there may be no direct relation between the amount of maternal nurturance experienced by the infant and later dependency. It is possible that all the children who were studied received sufficient nurturance during the early months to establish the basis for a dependency motive. The authors suggest that individual differences in amount of dependency at the preschool ages may not be a function of amount of nurturance in infancy but of some other child-rearing differences, e.g., amount of punishment and frustration.

Turning to such variables, Sears *et al.* found that dependent behavior in their preschool subjects was positively correlated with the severity of the mother's weaning practices; also, the rigidity with which the mother held to a feeding schedule was related to dependency in girls but not in boys. Interestingly, Smith (**50**) reports a positive relation between rigidity of feeding schedules and later dependence in boys but not in girls. Although there is some inconsistency across sexes in the results of these two studies, the findings generally suggest that frustrations experienced during infancy are associated with later dependency manifestations.

Subsequent to the preceding investigation, Sears, Maccoby, and Levin (**47**) assessed (in a new group of subjects) the degree of maternal frustration of the infant and the level of the child's dependency. Both of these measures were obtained by means of an interview with the mother. The previous findings were not replicated; however, the data concerning the child's dependence were acquired by quite different methods in the two Sears studies. The use of the mother's reports about the child's behavior by Sears, Maccoby, and Levin is particularly questionable since the ratings of the child's dependence may be distorted in some unknown degree by the attitudes, either positive or negative, of the mothers toward their children.

In summary, the relevance of infancy experience to the development of dependence has not been clearly established by research. Further work, perhaps focused on direct observation of infant-mother interactions, is needed to clarify the role of early experience in developing this form of social behavior.

Childhood experiences.—The childhood experiences appearing to influence dependency behavior most heavily are parental frustration and punishment of dependence. Sears *et al.* (**48**) found that when the mother is relatively punitive toward her preschool-age child and fails to respond nurturantly to the child's overtures, the frequency of dependency observed in boys is *greater*, and the incidence of dependency observed in young girls is *less*, than when amount of punishment is low. The authors employed two assumptions in interpreting this sex difference in their findings. First, they suggest that the relation between maternal punitiveness and the child's dependence is curvilinear rather than linear; that is, high dependence is associated with moderate amounts of maternal punishment while low dependence is associated with either high or low amounts of maternal punishment. Second, the authors assume that girls, being more completely "identified" with the mother, experience more severe punishment than boys. Although the maternal interviews showed that boys and girls in the sample did not differ in actual amount of punishment by the mother, the authors suggest that the mother's punishment has a greater impact on girls (due to the girl's greater identification with the mother). It is postulated, then, that all the girls in this study were relatively high on a continuum of severity of maternal punishment, at a level where less dependence would be expected with increasing amounts of punishment. On the other hand, it is postulated that boys in this sample were all relatively low on the punishment continuum, at a level where more dependence would be expected with increasing punishment.

Some additional evidence supports the hypothesis that parental frustration and punishment during childhood are associated with the frequency of dependency behavior. There is not, however, further support for the hypothesis that the relation between maternal punishment and children's dependence is curvilinear. Marshall (**41**) found that parental *suppression of the child* and *interpersonal distance*, as measured by a parental attitude inventory, were positively related to number of teacher-contacts made by girls in a nursery school. Also, Whiting and Child (**59**) report that greater dependency-anxiety characterizes adults in cultures where dependency is severely treated in childhood than in cultures where dependency is not severely socialized. These authors also report that anxiety about dependency was less in cultures where parents heavily indulge dependency in early childhood than where parents do not supply this form of indulgence.

Several attempts have been made to relate maternal overprotection or possessiveness to dependency in the child. Levy (**35**), analyzing a group of clinical case histories, found that children of extremely indulgent mothers tended to be aggressive and negative in their attempts to insure contact with the mother. On the other hand, the children of dominant overpossessive mothers tended to be passively and submissively dependent. Smith (**50**) found a relation between overprotection, rated on the basis of the maternal interviews, and dependence in the child (also assessed from the mothers' reports). These data are, of course, contaminated to some extent since information about both the mother and the child was derived from the same source—the interview. Marshall (**41**) also reports a positive relation between overprotection and number of contacts made by the child with his nursery-school teacher. This relation is statistically reliable, however, only for boys.

In attempting to understand the impact of overprotection on the child, some investigators have equated this pattern of maternal behavior with excessive indulgence. On the other hand, it is possible that overprotection may be frustrating to the child, particularly when maternal domination and restrictiveness are involved, and in this way contribute to the development of dependency. Also, the overprotective mother may provide relatively frequent reinforcement to the child for infantile dependency behavior. A study by Finney (**18**) suggests that selective reinforcement of dependence may play an important role in developing such behavior. He reports a low, but significant, correlation (.40) between the mother's tendency to reinforce selectively the dependency and the dependency level of the child. In any case, the literature tentatively indicates that maternal overprotection is relevant to the development of dependence in children.

Maternal rejection has also been studied as an antecedent of dependence. Sears, Maccoby, and Levin (**47**), Smith (**50**), and Wittenborn (**61**) all report that rejection is positively related to dependency. The Wittenborn results are probably the most substantial since the other two studies used maternal interviews to obtain information about the behavior of both mother and child. Wittenborn reports a correlation of only .30 between expressions of rejection in adoptive mothers and a cluster of children's responses assumed to denote dependence. This correlation is quite low, but is statistically significant.

Relatively little empirical work has been done on the child-rearing antecedents of independence. Winterbottom (**60**) reports that the mothers of high-achievement-oriented children make earlier achievement demands, more frequently reward achievement responses, and are less restrictive of independence activity than mothers of low-achievement-oriented children. McClelland (**38**) reports inconsistent results concerning the influence of parental affection and rejection on the achievement motivation of young adults (rejection appeared to be associated with high achievement in one study, with low achievement in another). Crandall *et al.* (**15**), who used observations to assess maternal affection and preschool children's achievement efforts, found no relation between these two variables. These investigators report, however, that direct reward for achievement and direct reward for approval-seeking were positively related to incidence of achievement efforts in nursery-school free play. Thus, there is some indication that specific training for independence increases such efforts.

Experimental studies.—Experimental methods have also been used in the search for determinants of dependency behavior in children. In most instances, the independent variable has consisted of some aspect of the experimenter's behavior toward the child (such as amount of attention or approval). Criterion measures have consisted of changes in the child's dependency behavior or changes in task-performance under social reinforcement.

In an early study, Carl (**13**) observed the frequency with which preschool children made dependent overtures to an experimenter who behaved "nurturantly" and "nonnurturantly" in alternate sessions. "Nurturance" consisted of being near, smiling at, and attending to the child. Differences were not found from session to session in rate of occurrence of the usual kinds of emotional dependency, although "positive social interaction" (friendly conversation) was more frequent during nurturance sessions. The attention of the experimenter apparently reinforced, and thus increased casual, conversational interaction but did not affect other dependent responses.

Gewirtz (**21**) used a technique similar in many ways to Carl's. The form of dependency recorded during the experimental session was attention-seeking. Preschool subjects were employed, some in a session during which attention and other social reinforcers from the experimenter were readily available (i.e., the experimenter sat near and attended to the child), others in a condition of low availability of reinforcers (i.e., the experimenter was "busy" at his own work and did not sit near the child). The results showed that the children in the low-availability condition more frequently sought the adult's attention than the children in the high-availability condition. Regardless of experimental condition, children tended to seek attention from experimenters of the opposite sex more frequently than from experimenters of the same sex.

Gewirtz and Baer (**24**) hypothesized that a period during which the child is deprived of social reinforcers would affect behavior in a manner similar to deprivation of primary reinforcers (i.e., such deprivation was expected to increase a drive for social rewards). Preschool subjects were left alone in an experimental room for twenty minutes, following which they performed a simple task and were reinforced with social approval for correct responses. Frequency of correct responses was greater following isolation than in another session which did not involve a period of being alone. A second study of social isolation effects (**23**) was conducted in which first-

and second-graders were either isolated, satiated (supplied with frequent attention and approval for twenty minutes prior to the performance task), or nondeprived. The reinforcing effectiveness of the adult's approval was found to be greatest after isolation, intermediate after nondeprivation, and least after satiation.

Hartup (**28**) employed somewhat different experimental conditions in still another study of preschool children's performance under social reinforcement. One group of subjects experienced ten minutes of consistent attention and approval from the experimenter, followed by a socially reinforced task. A second group experienced five minutes of attention and approval, followed by five minutes in which the experimenter neither attended to nor approved the child. The results indicated, primarily for girls, that performance in the socially reinforced task was better following inconsistent treatment than following consistent attention and approval. The author suggests that the results may be interpreted as indication that inconsistent nurturance is frustrating or anxiety-evoking to the child. Walters (**56, 58**) has also suggested that the effects of social isolation or deprivation may be related to anxiety. This investigator has found that when anxiety is assessed or manipulated independently, social isolation does not, by itself, account for a significant portion of the variance in performance on socially reinforced tasks. Further evidence that frustration is a determinant of dependency behavior is supplied in an experiment conducted with preschool children by Beller and Haeberle (**7**).

In general, the results of experimental studies of dependency are consistent with the results of the correlational studies described earlier. Specifically, frustration and inconsistency in the behavior of adults toward children appear to elicit greater dependence than consistent attention and approval. At least temporarily, children strive most strongly to obtain social reinforcers when they have been deprived (or frustrated) in their efforts to obtain them.

Behavioral Correlates of Dependency and Independence

Dependency appears to hold a position of pervasive importance in human personality dynamics. This is demonstrated by a large number of studies, from which some of the more significant have been selected for review in the following section.

Responsiveness to social reinforcement.—The results of three studies suggest that emotional dependency is related to more general manifestations of responsiveness to social reinforcement. Using two groups of four-year-olds, Endsley (**17**) found that those children who frequently sought praise from their nursery-school teachers performed at a higher level on a socially reinforced laboratory task than low-praise-seeking children. Cairns and Lewis (**12**) measured the responsiveness of male college Freshmen to the glance of an experimenter and a murmured "mm-hmm" in a conditioning situation. Highly dependent subjects (as measured by the Edwards' *Personal Preference Schedule* and the *Interpersonal Check List*) showed a significantly higher level of conditioning to these social reinforcers than the low-dependent subjects. The results showed, however, a decline in the frequency of the socially reinforced responses manifested by the low-dependency group over the 149 conditioning trials. In other words, the findings did not directly indicate that social reinforcers were more effective (or even effective at all) in producing conditioning in the highly dependent subjects.

Cairns (**10**) has also studied the relation between dependency *inhibition* and responsiveness to social reinforcement. Dependency inhibition was defined in terms of reluctance to accept help from other people and was assessed by means of a five-point rating scale. The experimenter verbally reinforced "confiding" (dependency) responses during four short interview sessions with each subject (adolescent juvenile offenders). It was found that subjects who were rated low on dependency inhibition evidenced significantly more confiding responses (by the fourth interview) than subjects with high-dependency inhibition. Cairns also studied the performance of these subjects in a paired-associates task in which correct responses were reinforced socially. The effectiveness of the social reinforcers decreased over trials for subjects with high-dependency inhibition, but the investigator did not find increasing effectiveness of social rewards for subjects with low-dependency inhibition.

Susceptibility to social influence.—Various investigators have suggested that the highly dependent child should be imitative, should be open to suggestions, and should conform to group norms more readily than children who are relatively nondependent. The basis for these hypotheses is the assumption that suggestibility, conformity, and certain other kinds of susceptibility to social influence are interpretable as forms of dependency behavior. There are comparatively few studies in this general area, but it appears that at least conformity and suggestibility may be interpreted in terms of dependency. Jakubezak and Walters (**32**), for example, found that highly dependent nine-year-old boys (as measured by a semiprojective test) were significantly more suggestible in the autokinetic situation than relatively nondependent subjects. Also, Cairns and Kaufman (**11**) report a moderate correlation (.40) between dependency in college students (as measured by the *TAT*) and suggestibility evidenced in a "postural sway" test. Mussen and Kagan (**43**), who also studied adults, found a significant relation between a projective measure of dependency and a measure of group conformity.

The relation between dependency and imitative tendencies in children has not been well explored. In one study (**39**) of preschool children, the relation between an observational measure of dependency and a laboratory measure of imitation proved to be nonsignificant.

Nurturance.—The relation between dependency and nurturance (giving sympathy and help to others) was explored by Hartup and Keller (**29**). Observations of children's free play in the nursery school indicated that frequency of nurturant behavior is positively associated with the dependency components of seeking help and seeking physical affection (relatively active expressions of dependency) but negatively associated with being near (relatively passive, indirect attention-seeking). These results suggest some commonality in underlying motivation for both dependency and its seeming opposite, nurturance.

Sociometric status.—The relation of dependency to children's popularity with their peers has been examined in several studies with nursery-school children. Using a picture sociometric technique and employing white, upper-middle-class children as subjects, Marshall and McCandless (**42**) found consistently negative correlations between their measure of popularity and their measures of dependence. That is, high dependency tended to be associated with low popularity with peers. This finding was supported by a later investigation by McCandless *et al.* (**37**) which was conducted with children in a racially mixed nursery school. There is some evidence (**27**) which suggests that emotional dependence interferes generally with children's initial adjustment to the nursery school.

Aggression.—The relation between dependency and aggression has been most thoroughly explored by Bandura and Walters (**2**) in a study of delinquent adolescent boys. These investigators postulated that one of the antecedents of aggressive delinquency is frequent frustration of dependency during childhood. Using data drawn from interviews and objective tests, the investigators found that, as compared with a group of nonaggressive subjects, the aggressive delinquents showed: (*a*) less overt emotional dependency, and (*b*) greater dependency-anxiety in the form of resistance to accepting help, spending little time in the company of others, and reluctance to confiding in other people. In combination, these results indicate that conflict concerning dependency appears to be a correlate of adolescent aggression. Bandura and Walters also found from parental interviews that the delinquents had been less consistently reinforced for dependency as children, had experienced less "warmth" in their relationships with their parents, and were more frequently rejected by their parents than the control subjects.

The relation between dependency frustration and aggression in nursery-school children has been studied by Beller (**7**). When an experimenter frustrated the child's dependency overtures by refusing to help obtain a toy, an increase in inhibition of aggression occurred, particularly among children who ordinarily were highly dependent in their interactions in the nursery school. At first glance, these results are inconsistent with the findings of Bandura and Walters; it must be remembered, however, that Beller measured the child's aggressive tendencies in the presence of the person who had frustrated the child's dependence. On the other hand, Bandura and Walters defined aggression in terms of antisocial, delinquent forms of aggression, not in terms of behavior directed toward parents (presumably the persons who originally frustrated the child). It would appear from these studies that the effects of frustration of dependency on aggression in children are relatively complex and probably involve some such process as displacement.

Orality.—As mentioned previously, psychoanalytic theory postulates a direct relation between oral frustration and dependency behavior. Presumably, indices of oral fixation and amount of emotional dependence shown by the child should be positively related. Beller (**4**), correlating teachers' ratings of both dependency and independence with frequency of oral behaviors as mentioned in teachers' routine reports, found a low relation ($r = .30$) between dependence and orality in 49 subjects. This correlation rose to .51 when 16 emotionally disturbed children were eliminated from the total sample. Incidence of anal behavior (lack of bowel control, smearing, etc.) did not relate to dependence but was significantly correlated with the independence rating ($r = -.30$).

Anxiety and defensiveness.—Ruebush and Waite (**45**) report that highly anxious boys (as determined by Sarason's *Test Anxiety Scale*) produce more *direct* oral dependency themes on the *Holtzman Inkblot Test* than low-anxious boys. This finding held only for male subjects who are relatively nondefensive; it did not hold for female subjects. These investigators also found that when anxiety is low, defensiveness is positively associated with incidence of indirect dependence in boys, but negatively associated with indirect dependency in girls. While the basis for this difference between sexes is not clear from the data of this study, the results indicate that dependency needs play a prominent role in the personality dynamics of both highly anxious and highly defensive children.

Concluding Comment

As indicated by the preceding review, recent research on dependency and independence in children has been extensive. This concentrated research effort has furthered both understanding of how dependency develops and how this form of behavior relates to personality functioning. In spite of this effort, however, much remains to be done. Most of the empirical findings presented in this chapter must be regarded as highly tentative since investigations in this area have been too infrequently replicated. Also, a variety of conceptual, theoretical, and methodological questions are pressing for solution.

It is not known how long such molar constructs as dependence and independence will continue to be useful to scientists in their attempts to control and predict interpersonal behavior. These concepts are, at the moment, firmly entrenched in the vocabulary used to describe personality and social behavior in children. New empirical approaches are needed. The early (infant) phases of dependency acquisition require particular attention, and the potential of the laboratory has scarcely begun to be realized in the search for the determinants of social responsiveness in children. Also, direct focus needs to be placed on the development of independence—on its relation to early exploratory and curiosity behavior and on its relation to parent-child interaction. Only the foundations for research on dependency and independence have been laid; definitive study of these personality dimensions lies in the future.

BIBLIOGRAPHY

1. Antonovsky, H. F. "A Contribution to Research in the Area of Mother-Child Relationships," *Child Develpm.*, XXX (1959), 37–51.
2. Bandura, A., and Walters, R. H. *Adolescent Aggression.* New York: Ronald Press, 1960.
3. Beller, E. K. "Dependency and Independence in Young Children," *J. Genet. Psychol.*, XXCVII (1955), 23–25.
4. ———. "Dependency and Autonomous Achievement-striving Related to Orality and Anality in Early Childhood," *Child Develpm.*, XXIX (1957), 287–315.
5. ———. "Effects of Conflict and Stress on Relationships between Motivation and Perception." Unpublished manuscript.
6. Beller, E. K., and Haeberle, A. W. "Motivation and Conflict in Relation to Phantasy Responses of Young Children." Paper read at meetings of Society for Research in Child Development, 1959.
7. ———. "Dependency and the Frustration-Aggression Hypothesis." Paper read at Eastern Psychological Association meetings, 1959.
8. Bowlby, J. "Some Pathological Processes Set in Train by Early Mother-Child Separation," *J. Ment. Sci.*, XCIX (1953), 265–72.
9. Brown, J. S. "Problems Presented by the Concept of Acquired Drives," in *Current Theory and Research in Motivation: A Symposium.* Edited by M. R. Jones. Lincoln: University of Nebraska Press, 1953.
10. Cairns, R. B. "The Influence of Dependency Inhibition on the Effectiveness of Social Reinforcement," *J. Pers.*, XXIX (1961), 466–88.
11. Cairns, R. B., and Kaufman, H. "Prestige Suggestibility and Dependency Inhibition." Unpublished manuscript.
12. Cairns, R. B., and Lewis, M. "Dependency and the Reinforcement Value of a Verbal Stimulus," *J. Consult. Psychol.* (in press).
13. Carl, J. "An Experimental Study of the Effect of Nurturance on Preschool Children." Unpublished Doctor's dissertation, State University of Iowa, 1949.
14. Casler, L. *Maternal Deprivation: A Critical Review of the Literature.* Monograph of the Society for Research in Child Development, XXVI (1961), No. 2 (Serial No. 80).
15. Crandall, V. J.; Preston, A.; and Rabson, A. "Maternal Reactions and the Development of Independence and Achievement Behavior in Young Children," *Child Develpm.*, XXXI (1960), 243–51.
16. Edwards, A. L. *Personal Preference Schedule.* New York: Psychological Corp., 1954.
17. Endsley, R. C. "Dependency and Performance by Preschool Children on

a Socially-reinforced Task." Unpublished Master's thesis, State University of Iowa, 1960.

18. FINNEY, J. C. "Some Maternal Influences on Children's Personality and Character," *Genet. Psychol. Monogr.*, LXIII (1961), 199–278.

19. FITZGERALD, B. J. "Some Relationships among Projective Test, Interview, and Sociometric Measures of Dependent Behavior," *J. Abnorm. Soc. Psychol.*, LVI (1958), 199–203.

20. GEWIRTZ, J. L. "A Factor Analysis of Some Attention-seeking Behaviors in Young Children," *Child Develpm.*, XXVII (1956), 17–36.

21. ———. "Succorance in Young Children." Unpublished Doctor's dissertation, State University of Iowa, 1948.

22. ———. *Three Determinants of Attention-seeking in Young Children.* Monograph of the Society for Research in Child Development, XIX (1954), No. 2 (Serial No. 59).

23. GEWIRTZ, J. L., and BAER, D. M. "Deprivation and Satiation of Social Reinforcers as Drive Conditions," *J. Abnorm. Soc. Psychol.*, LVII (1958), 165–72.

24. ———. "The Effects of Brief Social Deprivation on Behaviors for a Social Reinforcer," *J. Abnorm. Soc. Psychol.*, LVI (1958), 49–56.

25. GOLDFARB, W. "Psychological Deprivation in Infancy and Subsequent Adjustment," *Amer. J. Orthopsych.*, XV (1945), 247–55.

26. GREENBERG, H. M. "The Expectations of Preschool Children for Maternal Dependency-satisfaction and Authority as Related to Their Interaction with Teachers." Unpublished Doctor's thesis, University of Chicago, 1953.

27. HARTUP, W. W. "An Evaluation of the Highberger Early-Adjustment-to-School Scale," *Child Develpm.*, XXX (1959), 421–32.

28. ———. "Nurturance and Nurturance-withdrawal in Relation to the Dependency Behavior of Young Children," *Child Develpm.*, XXIX (1958), 191–201.

29. HARTUP, W. W., and KELLER, E. D. "Nurturance in Preschool Children and Its Relation to Dependency," *Child Develpm.*, XXXI (1960), 681–89.

30. HEATHERS, G. "Acquiring Dependence and Independence: A Theoretical Orientation," *J. Genet. Psychol.*, XXCVII (1955), 277–91.

31. ———. "Emotional Dependence and Independence in Nursery-School Play," *J. Genet. Psychol.*, XXCVII (1955), 37–58.

32. JAKUBEZAK, L. F., and WALTERS, R. H. "Suggestibility as Dependency Behavior," *J. Abnorm. Soc. Psychol.*, LIX (1959), 102–7.

33. KAGAN, J., and MOSS, H. A. "The Stability of Passive and Dependent Behavior from Childhood through Adulthood," *Child Develpm.*, XXXI (1960), 577–91.

34. LEARY, T. *Interpersonal Diagnosis of Personality.* New York: Ronald Press, 1957.

35. LEVY, D. *Maternal Overprotection.* New York: Columbia University Press, 1943.

36. LIVSON, N., and MUSSEN, P. H. "The Relation of Ego Control to Overt Aggression and Dependency," *J. Abnorm. Soc. Psychol.*, LV (1957), 66–71.

37. MCCANDLESS, B. R.; BILOUS, C. B.; and BENNETT, H. L. "Peer Popularity and Dependence on Adults in Preschool-age Socialization," *Child Develpm.*, XXXII (1961), 511–18.

38. McClelland, D. C.; Atkinson, J. W.; Clark, R. A.; and Lowell, E. L. *The Achievement Motive*. New York: Appleton-Century-Crofts, 1953.

39. McDavid, J. W. "Imitative Behavior in Preschool Children," *Psychol. Monogr.*, LXXIII (1959), (Whole No. 486).

40. Mann, N. "Dependency in Relation to Maternal Attitudes." Unpublished Master's thesis, State University of Iowa, 1959.

41. Marshall, H. R. "Relations between Home Experiences and Children's Use of Language in Play Interactions with Peers," *Psychol. Monogr.*, LXXV (1961), (Whole No. 509).

42. Marshall, H. R., and McCandless, B. R. "Relationships between Dependence on Adults and Social Acceptance by Peers," *Child Develpm.*, XXVIII (1957), 413–19.

43. Mussen, P. H., and Kagan, J. "Dependency Themes on the TAT and Group Conformity," *J. Consult. Psychol.*, XX (1956), 29–32.

44. Osborn, D. K. "Dependency in Young Children in Relation to Two Maternal Variables: A Methodological Study." Unpublished Master's thesis, State University of Iowa, 1952.

45. Ruebush, B. K., and Waite, R. R. "Oral Dependency in Anxious and Defensive Children," *Merrill-Palmer Quar.*, VII (1961), 181–90.

46. Sears, P. S. "Measurement of Dependency and Aggression in Doll Play," *Amer. Psychologist*, III (1948), 263 (abstract).

47. Sears, R. R.; Maccoby, E. E.; and Levin, H. *Patterns of Child-rearing*. Evanston: Row, Peterson & Co., 1957.

48. Sears, R. R.; Whiting, J. W. M.; Nowlis, V.; and Sears, P. S. "Some Child-rearing Antecedents of Dependency and Aggression in Young Children," *Genet. Psychol. Monogr.*, XLVII (1953), 135–234.

49. Siegel, A. E.; Stolz, L. M.; Hitchcock, E. A.; and Adamson, J. "Dependence and Independence in the Children of Working Mothers," *Child Develpm.*, XXX (1959), 533–46.

50. Smith, H. T. "A Comparison of Interview and Observation Measures of Mother Behavior," *J. Abnorm. Soc. Psychol.*, LVII (1958), 278–82.

51. Sontag, L. W.; Crandall, V.; and Lacey, J. I. "Dynamics of Personality: Resolution of the Infantile Dependent Need," *Amer. J. Orthopsychiat.*, XXII (1952), 524–41.

52. Spitz, R. A. "Hospitalism: An Inquiry into the Genesis of Psychiatric Conditions in Early Childhood," *Psychoanal. Stud. Child*, I (1945), 53–74.

53. Stendler, C. B. "Possible Causes of Overdependency in Young Children," *Child Develpm.*, XXV (1954), 125–46.

54. Townsend, A. H. "The Relationship between Parental Commitment and Certain Forms of Dependent Behavior." Unpublished Doctor's thesis, University of Michigan, 1959.

55. Walters, J.; Pearce, D.; and Dahms, L. "Affectional and Aggressive Behaviors of Preschool Children," *Child Develpm.*, XXVIII (1957), 15–26.

56. Walters, R. H. "Anxiety and Social Reinforcement." Paper read at American Psychological Association meetings, 1961.

57. Walters, R. H., and Karal, P. "Social Deprivation and Verbal Behavior," *J. Pers.*, XXVIII (1960), 89–107.

58. Walters, R. H., and Ray, E. "Anxiety, Social Isolation, and Reinforcer Effectiveness," *J. Pers.*, XXVIII (1960), 354–67.

59. WHITING, J. W. M., and CHILD, I. *Child Training and Personality*. New Haven: Yale University Press, 1953.

60. WINTERBOTTOM, M. R. "The Relation of Childhood-training in Independence to Achievement Motivation." Unpublished Doctor's thesis, University of Michigan, 1953.

61. WITTENBORN, J. R. "A Study of Adoptive Children: III, Relationship between Some Aspects of Development and Some Aspects of Environment for Adoptive Children," *Psychol. Monogr.*, LXX (1956), No. 410.

62. ZUCKERMAN, M., and GROSS, H. J. "Suggestibility and Dependency," *J. Consult. Psychol.*, XXII (1958), 328.

CHAPTER IX

Aggression

ALBERT BANDURA and RICHARD H. WALTERS

Some Problems of Theory and Definition

THE FRUSTRATION-AGGRESSION HYPOTHESIS

For the past thirty years, the psychology of aggression has been dominated by the hypothesis of Dollard, Doob, Miller, Mowrer, and Sears (**42**), according to which, as it was originally propounded, aggression is a natural and inevitable consequence of frustration. In later modifications of the hypothesis (**43, 104**), aggression was regarded as a natural, though not inevitable, consequence of frustration, since nonaggressive responses to frustration could be learned. Nevertheless, *aggression* was still considered the *naturally dominant* response to frustration, while nonaggressive responses were likely to occur only if aggressive responses had previously met with nonreward or punishment. While some members of the Yale group were willing to discard the notion that aggression is the only unlearned reaction to frustration (e.g., see **141, 168**), *frustration* continued to be regarded as an *inevitable antecedent* of aggression; in other words, whenever an aggressive act occurred, it was assumed that it was instigated by frustration.

In spite of the emphasis on the role of instigators in the frustration-aggression hypothesis, relatively little research has been done on the effects of the three factors that were considered to be responsible for the amount of frustration, i.e., the strength of instigation to the frustrated response, the degree of interference with the frustrated response, and the number of frustrated response-sequences. Instead, as the review by Berkowitz (**22**) indicates, research has been concentrated on inhibition, object-displacement, and response-displacement and on the occurrence of catharsis. The crucial problems of how aggressive responses are originally learned, what form the aggressive responses initially take, and the role of factors other than interference with an ongoing response-sequence involved in the shaping and maintaining of aggressive behavior were largely ignored.

Criticism of the frustration-aggression hypothesis focused at first on the nature of responses to frustration. Bateson (**18**) pointed out that in some cultures, such as that of the Balinese, aggression was by no means a typical response to frustration. Barker, Dembo, and Lewin (**17**) and Wright (**171, 172**) demonstrated that nursery-school children may regress when frustrated, a reaction that was observed also in rats in an ingenious experiment by Mowrer (**111**). A number of critics have argued that some kinds of frustration evoke an aggressive response and that other kinds do not. Maslow (**102**), Rosenzweig (**134**), and, more recently, Buss (**31**) have noted that attack or threat is more likely to elicit aggressive reactions than the blocking of ongoing response-sequences. Pastore (**122**) emphasized the role of the arbitrariness of the frustration in determining whether or not an aggressive response will occur and suggested that arbitrary frustration involved interference with the attainment of an expected goal. Obviously, one of the major sources of controversy is the ambiguity in the definition of frustration, a problem that will be considered later in this section. A search for antecedents of aggression other than ones that have been categorized as frustration has only recently begun. For the most part, the results appear to question further the frustration-aggression hypothesis and to suggest that the time is ripe for a new approach to the problem of aggression.

DEFINITION OF AGGRESSION

In the development of a social learning theory of aggression, the first requirement is a definition of what constitutes an aggressive response. The authors of *Frustration and Aggression* define aggression as a sequence of behavior "the goal-response to which is the injury of the person toward whom it is directed" (**43**: 9). With few exceptions, subsequent theory and research have adopted *intentionality* as an essential aspect in the definition of aggression (e.g., see **15, 145**). The main problem with such definitions is that intentionality is not a property of behavior, but refers to antecedent conditions which frequently have to be inferred from the behavior of which they are supposedly an essential ingredient.

There are, in fact, two possible approaches to the problem of defining and studying aggression. One may define aggression solely by reference to observable characteristics and effects of responses and without reference to goals which the responses supposedly mediate; for example, aggression may be defined as the class of pain-producing or damage-producing responses or as "responses that *could* injure or damage *if* aimed at a vulnerable object." Since the consequences of a single response may depend on circumstances that are irrelevant to the understanding of the development of a habit, the latter definition seems preferable. Children learn derogation partly through imitating the use of derogatory epithets and statements which are uttered in their presence by parents or other adults (**1**); these responses are aggressive, according to the definition in terms of the potential effects of the response, though during acquisition they may not produce injury or damage.

Alternately, references to complex stimulus events, e.g., the social context of the act or the recent or more remote past of the agent, may be included in the definition of aggression. In such a case, intent may be inferred, though not solely on the basis of response variables.

If the first alternative is selected, it is possible to study the manner in which aggressive responses are acquired, strengthened, maintained, extinguished, and inhibited and the conditions under which generalization and discrimination occur. This approach avoids the subjectivity and value judgments involved in studies of aggression in which the intent of the responses is taken into consideration. At the same time, it can generate conceptual confusion because the responses under study are often displayed under circumstances in which they would not be socially judged as aggressive.

Introducing the concept of intentionality, on the other hand, fosters an approach to socially significant problems and facilitates communication among students of social behavior. An investigator who uses the intentionality criterion may study the antecedents of vandalism but will not study the manner in which a lumberjack learns to chop down a tree. In defining his variable, however, this investigator must realize that he is basing his definition on stimulus events and social values, not solely on the characteristics of the responses he is studying.

DEFINING FRUSTRATION

The task of establishing a serviceable definition of frustration is, if anything, more complex than that of defining aggression. A multitude of experimental operations have been employed in "inducing" the condition of "frustration." These consist of simple nonreward (delay of reinforcement), withdrawing or withholding positive reinforcements, or introducing negative reinforcers. Research involving both human and animal subjects reveals that these operations have very diverse effects ranging from the elimination to the intensification of the behavior, the interference with which, according to the frustration-aggression theory, should result in aggression. Moreover, the term "frustration" has been used both for the experimental operations themselves, and for internal responses of the organism which supposedly result from operations of these kinds (**101**). In this chapter, all operations or conditions that prevent or delay reinforcement are regarded as frustrative. Since prevention or omission of reinforcement is equivalent to prolonged or infinite delay, frustration may be defined simply as delay of reinforcement. However, in presenting certain points of view, for the sake of brevity, "frustration" will also be used for hypothetical or inferred states or responses of the organism, which are in other instances more consistently regarded as "frustration-induced."

Delay of reinforcement may arise from the existence or creation of environmental barriers, physical or social; for example, famine, isolation, laws restricting sexual behavior, or conditions under which an excessive amount of work is required for obtaining the necessities of life. Personal limitations, physiological or psychological, genetic or learned, are other potential sources of frustration. Fears and conflicts, which may result from attack or punishment, fall into this category. Thus, the presentation of noxious stimuli may, but need not, result in frustration.

Many of the operations designed to induce frustration have in common the likelihood that they will elicit responses of high magnitude. It should be noted that responses of high magnitude (for example, the vigorous chopping of a tree or the punching or kicking of an object) are frequently learned under conditions that are in no way frustrative. Once learned, these responses can be elicited under frustrative conditions and presumably will be, if the appropriate stimuli are present—stimuli which may include instruments of injury or destruction and the presence of the agent thought responsible for the frustration. A boy who has learned how to use a switch-blade knife through solitary play or through seeing the knife used to produce injury, either in real life or in movies or TV shows, is more likely to injure another child with a switch-blade knife than if he had never learned to use a knife or had never observed a knife being used as an injurious weapon. Given the appropriate stimulus conditions, including one of the forms of frustration, this child is likely to utilize his past learning to perform an act which would undoubtedly be labeled as aggression.

DISCRIMINATION-LEARNING

Let us now consider a father who devotes some of his time to playing punchball with his young son. He punches the ball himself and then, with or without verbal encouragement, elicits a similar response in the boy. He responds to the boy's punching with approval. The boy punches harder and is again reinforced. Indeed, a competition in prowess is likely to develop. In the course of the play, the father both provides the model for the hitting response and reinforces the response when it is made. Once the intense hitting response has been established, it can be elicited in various situations, some frustrative and some nonfrustrative.

In the course of development, then, a child is provided with many opportunities to acquire responses of high magnitude in nonfrustrative situations; these responses may remain relatively high in his response hierarchies and can thus be readily mobilized to cope with the various situations that have been classed as frustrative. While the fact that these responses are not elicited more frequently may be in part due to expectations of punishment, it is probably due no less to good discrimination-learning, which results from differential reinforcement and requires more than simple inhibition.

The same learning principles that account for the development of other social responses can account for the learning of aggressive behavior, as this has been defined by Bandura and Walters (**16**). Social training may proceed by various means. One important way in which novel responses may be elicited is through learning by imitation. It is an empirical fact that exposure to cues produced by the behavior of others is an effective means of eliciting responses for which the original probability of occurrence is low or zero (**9, 12, 13**). Once responses are elicited, they can be strengthened by direct reinforcement until they become relatively dominant in the habit hierarchies which are elicited by cues similar to those present during acquisition. Reinforcement of every response is not necessary for establishment or maintenance of a habit. In fact, responses that have been intermittently reinforced are, generally speaking, more stable and more resistant to extinction than responses that have been reinforced on a continuous schedule, i.e., every time they were made (**152**). Under real-life conditions, intermittent reinforcement is the rule, not the exception, and this perhaps accounts in part for the persistence of many social responses, including those regarded as aggressive once they have been established.

Discrimination-learning involves the concurrent reward of some responses and the nonreward or punishment of others. The effects of nonreward are dependent on the prior experiences of the subject (e.g., nonreward following reward appears to have an energizing effect) and upon its duration. The effects of punishment are very poorly understood, though the bulk of available evidence suggests that noxious stimulation suppresses, at least temporarily, a response with which it is paired (**46, 112**).

Because of their importance in the learning of aggression, the influence of aggressive-role models and of reinforcement patterns are considered in the next two sections of the chapter. The role of frustration is then discussed. The remainder of the chapter is concerned with phenomena, e.g., displacement and catharsis, which can occur only if aggressive response patterns have been both acquired and suppressed or modified through negative reinforcement. The review of the literature is largely confined to studies of children, many of which have been carried out in nursery-school settings, though brief references to studies of adults and animals have sometimes been included.

The Modeling Process

INFLUENCE OF AGGRESSIVE MODELS

Societies that provide approved aggressive models are likely to produce aggressive children. The importance of models in the cultural transmission of aggressive behavior patterns is reflected in

Bateson's account (**19**) of the Iatmul society and in Whiting's description (**166**) of child-training practices among the Kwoma. Among the Kwoma, the form and degree of aggression that is permitted is related to the agent's social status; the adult male is expected to fight and to express hostility freely toward nonrelatives, and the male child is prepared, largely through direct reinforcement, for the aggressive adult role.

The influence of models is also apparent in descriptions of subcultures in which the "delinquent" youth conform to dominant hostile-aggressive patterns of the subgroup. Within his own social group, the subcultural delinquent is well socialized (**72**); only within the context of the larger social group can his behavior be regarded as nonconforming. The prevalence of aggressive models in delinquent subcultures has been noted by a number of sociologists, for example, Whyte (**169**) and Cohen (**36**); in fact, in high-delinquency areas, such as those described by Shaw and McKay (**148**), the crucial psychological process in the development of aggressive antisocial patterns may, in many cases, be identification with an aggressive prototype rather than a hostile reaction to emotional deprivation.

McCord and McCord (**100**), in a reanalysis of data obtained in the Cambridge-Somerville study of delinquency prevention (**128**), examined the effects of parental-role model on criminality. They found that children imitated their father's criminality when the mother was also socially deviant, when parental discipline was erratic, or when the parents were rejecting. Erratic discipline and rejection may, in some families, include the provision of examples of hostile-aggressive behavior. Consequently, the relative importance of aggressive models in the genesis of criminality may be even greater than the McCords' analysis suggests.

Imitation of dissocial aspects of parent behavior among middle-class children has been noted by Bandura and Walters (**15**) and Johnson and Szurek (**74**). The latter authors suggest that some middle-class parents vicariously act out their own antisocial impulses through subtly encouraging their children's misdemeanors. Their observations, like those made in anthropological and sociological studies, indicate how influential adults may both provide aggressive-role models and reinforce aggressive behavior when it occurs.

Bandura and Walters (**16**) found that fathers of aggressive grade-school boys were more aggressively punitive and less emotionally inhibited than fathers of withdrawn boys. Moreover, stories given by the boys to cards depicting social situations indicated that the aggressive boys had adopted dissocial values to a greater extent than had the withdrawn boys; for example, they described deviating characters as responding with self-rewarding behavior following the successful commission of a deviant act.

Several interview studies have provided data concerning the relationship of parental punitiveness to children's aggressive behavior inside and outside the home. Glueck and Glueck (**60**), in a comparison of 500 delinquent and 500 nondelinquent boys, reported that the parents of the delinquents used physical punishment more frequently, and reasoning less frequently, than the parents of nondelinquents. Bandura and Walters obtained similar findings in comparisons of aggressive and nonaggressive adolescents (**15**) and of aggressive and withdrawn preadolescents (**16**). Sears, Maccoby, and Levin (**145**) report a significant correlation between maternal use of physical punishment, in cases in which children were severely punished for aggression, and the incidence of aggressive behavior in children. A parent who is severely punitive, especially if the punishment is physical, provides an aggressive model, the influence of which may more than counteract the inhibitory effects of punishment on the punished behavior.

Buss (**31**) has pointed out that attack in the form of verbal abuse elicits more aggression from subjects in laboratory experiments than does the blocking of ongoing response-sequences. An abusive experimenter or confederate provides an aggressive model, whose influence, like that of a punitive parent, may outweigh the usual inhibitory effects of punishment.

Thus, while impersonally administered punishment for aggression may reduce, at least temporarily, the incidence or amplitude of aggressive behavior, punishment administered by a punitive-aggressive model may, unless the punishment is very severe, increase the incidence or amplitude of aggressive responses.

During recent years, a number of investigators have conducted laboratory-experimental studies in which subjects have been exposed to aggressive real-life or fantasy models. These have differed considerably in the choice of stimulus conditions and of the dependent variables which have served as indices of aggression. The studies suggest that observation of the behavior of models has two rather different effects, both of which may be reflected in an increase in the number or intensity of the observer's aggressive responses. In the first place, the observer may acquire new responses that did not previously exist in his repertory. In order to demonstrate this *modeling* effect experimentally, the model must exhibit highly novel responses, and the observer must reproduce these responses in a substantially identical form. Secondly, observation of aggressive models may weaken inhibitory responses; this *disinhibitory effect* is apparent in studies in which the elicited aggressive responses already exist in the subject's repertory. These responses may, of course, be nonimitative in character. It is possible that observation of an aggressive model sometimes elicits previously learned imitative or nonimitative responses in the observer simply because the perceiving of acts of a certain kind serves as a "releaser" for responses of that same class. This effect could be distinguished from disinhibition only if we knew the past history of our subjects. However, since the classification of a response as *aggressive* implies social censure, and since children are generally taught not to make socially censured responses, it is probably safe to assume that the eliciting of previously learned aggressive responses through exposure to an aggressive model usually, if not always, reflects a disinhibitory process.

Modeling effects have been demonstrated in a series of studies by Bandura and his associates. Bandura and Huston (**10**) observed the incidental imitative responses of preschool children. An adult model made functionless incidental responses, including aggressive acts, while performing a discrimination task, which the children were also required to perform. With the experimental subjects, the model aggressed against dolls located on the discrimination boxes; with the controls the model behaved in a nonaggressive fashion. Ninety per cent of the children in the experimental group behaved in an aggressive manner, whereas none of the control children displayed aggressive behavior. Half the experimental subjects had experienced two periods of rewarding interaction with the adult model before carrying out the discrimination task; the remaining subjects had spent two periods of comparable length with the model, but without interacting with her. Subjects in the reward condition imitated the model's nonaggressive responses to a greater extent than subjects in the nonreward group; both groups, however, displayed a high incidence of imitative aggressive responses. As the authors point out, this study suggests that the mere observation of aggressive models, regardless of the nature of the model-child relationship, is sufficient to produce imitative aggression in children. The hypothesis is thus brought in question that much imitative learning of aggression is a form of "identification with the aggressor" (**52**) or "defensive identification" (**113**), i.e., a process whereby the child transforms himself from the object to the agent of aggression by adopting the characteristics of the aggressive-role model.

In the Bandura and Huston study, imitative aggressive responses were elicited in the presence of the model. A subsequent study by Bandura, Ross, and Ross (**13**) demonstrated the generalization of imitative response patterns to settings in which the model is absent. Forty-eight nursery-school children, 24 boys and 24 girls, observed aggressive and nonaggressive models of either the same sex or the opposite sex to themselves. The control group consisted of 24 children who were not exposed to adult models. Experimental subjects spent ten minutes in a room where they could observe the responses of the model, who either behaved in a distinctive aggressive manner toward an inflated Bobo doll or nonaggressively assembled tinker toys. All children were subjected to a mildly frustrating experience before being tested for delayed imitation of the behavior of the model. They then spent 20 minutes in a room containing a variety of toys, some of which were likely to elicit aggressive behavior. Children who had been exposed to aggressive models showed significantly more imitative physical and verbal aggression than did children exposed to nonaggressive models or children in the control group. Nonimitative aggression also occurred more frequently in the aggressive-model group than in the other two groups. Moreover, boys exposed to a nonaggressive model showed significantly less imitative and nonimitative aggression on a variety of measures than did boys in the control group.

Bandura, Ross, and Ross (**12**) extended their investigations to film-mediated aggressive models in a comparative study of the effects of real-life models, human film-aggression, and cartoon film-aggression on the aggressive behavior of preschool children. Following the exposure treatment, subjects were mildly frustrated and tested for amount of imitative and nonimitative aggression in a different experimental setting. All three groups showed a significantly greater amount of aggression than a control group of children who had not been exposed to an aggressive model. Subjects who observed real-life aggressive models showed more imitative aggression than subjects who had observed the cartoon models, but the real-life and human film-aggression groups did not differ in this respect. Overall findings, based on a variety of measures of imitative and nonimitative aggression, in fact, indicated that exposure to human subjects portraying aggression in movies was the most influential method of eliciting and shaping aggressive behavior.

This latter study also demonstrates that the behavior of models is influential in shaping children's subsequent responses to frustration. Children who observed aggressive models displayed significantly more aggression (both imitative and nonimitative) when subsequently frustrated than did children who were equally frustrated but who had had no prior exposure to models exhibiting aggression. In contrast, children who observed nonaggressive models gave more nonaggressive responses to frustration than did subjects in aggressive-model groups. In addition, they displayed significantly fewer aggressive responses than did control children who were exposed neither to a nonaggressive nor to an aggressive model.

In order to determine whether imitative learning of aggression is partly a function of response-consequences to the model, Bandura, Ross, and Ross (**14**) conducted a study in which one group of nursery-school children viewed a televised aggressive model who amassed considerable rewards through his aggressive behavior; a second group observed the same model receive punishment following the display of aggression, while children in a control group had no exposure to the film-mediated model. The children were then tested for amount of imitative and nonimitative aggression in an experimental room containing a variety of toys, some of which could be used for aggressive purposes. Children who had observed the rewarded model showed significantly more aggression than the other two groups of children, who did not differ in this respect. These findings, however, seemed to reflect primarily a difference in performance and not in learning. Children who had seen aggression punished demonstrated in a subsequent interview that they had learned the cognitive equivalents of the model's behavior although they had not translated them into their motoric forms.

Walters, Leat, and Mezei (**160**) prohibited kindergarten boys from playing with some attractive toys and then left them alone with the toys for a 15-minute period. Immediately before the "temptation" period two groups of boys saw movies in which a child of approximately their own age played with toys which they had previously been forbidden to touch. One group saw the boy rebuked by his mother for playing with the toys, while the other group saw the mother play in a warm, affectionate manner with the child on re-entering the scene. The boys who had seen the child rewarded for deviation showed significantly less resistance to temptation than did the boys who had seen the child punished. A control group of boys, who saw no movie, resisted temptation more than the model-rewarded group but less than the model-punished group.

This study, together with that by Bandura, Ross, and Ross (**14**), lends support to theories of imitation that take into account the consequences to the model of his deviant (or conforming) acts, e.g., Mowrer's theory of empathetic learning (**113**). Evidence that rewarding consequences to the model facilitate the imitative learning of nonaggressive, nondeviant responses is provided by Gelfand (**57**), Kanareff and Lanzetta (**78**), Lanzetta and Kanareff (**84**), Mausner (**103**), and Rosenbaum and Tucker (**133**).

The studies already reviewed indicate that the observation of cues provided by socially deviant models is an effective means of transmitting new patterns of deviant responses; in most cases, the deviant behavior could be categorized as aggressive. Other studies which have involved exposure to aggressive models have not been specifically designed to demonstrate the occurrence of imitative learning. The results of these studies suggest that the presentation of aggressive models either weakens inhibitory responses or serves as an instigation for nonimitative aggression.

Siegel (**149**) obtained ratings of the aggression of like-sexed pairs of preschool children in two free-play sessions. Before one of the sessions the children watched a highly aggressive cartoon; before the other, they watched a nonaggressive cartoon. Contrary to the catharsis hypothesis, which was being tested in this study, more aggression occurred in sessions which followed presentation of the aggressive cartoon than in those which followed presentation of the nonaggressive cartoon. This difference, however, failed to reach an acceptable level of significance.

More recently, Lövaas (**97**) and Mussen and Rutherford (**117**) have confirmed the hypothesis that exposure of children to film-mediated aggression will *increase* the incidence of subsequent aggressive behavior. In Lövaas' study, the subjects, who were children from a day-care center, could depress either of two levers, one of which operated a hitting doll, the other a ball in a cage. Ten subjects were shown an aggressive cartoon film; the remaining ten were shown a nonaggressive cartoon film. Immediately after watching the film, each child was left with the two lever-operated toys for a four-minute period. Children who had watched the aggressive film depressed the lever which operated the hitting-doll toy more frequently than did children who had watched the nonaggressive film.

In the study by Mussen and Rutherford, 18 first-grade pupils were first frustrated by being made to perform the boring repetitive task of copying numbers while their teacher criticized their performance. One-third of the children was then shown an aggressive animated cartoon, one-third was shown a nonaggressive cartoon, while the remainder saw no cartoon. Another eighteen children, who were not frustrated, were assigned in equal numbers to the three cartoon conditions. As a test of aggressive tendencies, the children were asked eight questions concerning their desire to "pop" an inflated balloon held by the experimenter. Subjects who watched the aggressive cartoon expressed more aggressive impulses than those who saw the nonaggressive cartoon or no cartoon at all. Frustrated and nonfrustrated children did not significantly differ in the extent to which they gave aggressive responses in the balloon test.

Walters and collaborators (**161, 162**) used hospital attendants, high-school boys, and young women from a hostel for working girls in studies of the influence of human film-aggression on a non-imitative aggressive response, involving the infliction of pain by means of an electric shock on another person. In comparison to control groups, who watched a nonaggressive film scene, subjects exposed to aggressive movie content showed a significant pretest-to-post-test increment in aggression. In contrast to most other investigators, Walters *et al.* did not frustrate their subjects before obtaining the post-tests measure. Although adolescents tended to use a higher level of shock and to administer shock for longer periods of time than other subjects, those adolescents who were exposed to the aggressive models were no more influenced by the model than were experimental subjects in the other two groups. This finding is especially surprising in view of the fact that the aggressive models were themselves male adolescents. Responses of the male adults to the four aggression scales of the Buss-Durkee (**33**) inventory, which consists of self-descriptive statements, were also influenced by the experimental procedure and suggested that, after viewing aggressive models, subjects perceive themselves as more aggressive.

Two studies by Schachter and his associates, although aimed at clarifying theoretical issues different from those dealt with in this chapter, deserve some notice. Schachter and Singer (**136**) gave college students one of three treatments before placing them in a room with a confederate of the experimenter who behaved in an aggressive manner. In comparison to a placebo group, subjects who were injected with epinephrine, and who were not informed of its physiological side-effects, showed a considerable amount of aggressive behavior, whereas subjects who were injected with epinephrine, and who were informed of its physiological side-effects, showed very little imitative aggression. These results suggest that the influence of models may be most potent when the observers are emotionally aroused and cannot rationally attribute their feelings to stimuli other than the model's behavior. The aggressive behavior of a punitive parent may produce precisely this stimulus condition for the children in his family.

Schachter and Wheeler (**137**) compared the responses of three groups of subjects to a slapstick-comedy film. Before watching the movie, one group was injected with epinephrine, a second group was injected with chlorpromazine, and the third with a placebo. Epinephrine-injected subjects showed a greater amount of amusement, assessed both by self-reports and by observations of behavior, than did placebo subjects. Chlorpromazine-injected subjects were least affected by the slapstick movie. This study again suggests that the social influence exerted by models (film-mediated, as well as real-life) is a function of the degree of emotional arousal of the subjects.

SEX DIFFERENCES IN AGGRESSION

Sex differences in aggressive behavior have been noted by a large number of observers and, for the most part, may be regarded as the joint outcome of social reinforcement and modeling processes. Goodenough (**62**) reported increases in anger outbursts in children of both sexes up to the age of about eighteen months. From then on, the frequency declined sharply for both boys and girls, with sex differences becoming quite marked during the third year of life. By this time, parental and social pressures for sex-appropriate behavior have modified behavior in the direction of socially approved norms, and although anger outbursts continue to diminish in both sexes, boys consistently show more outbursts of this kind than girls.

Doll-play studies, with a few exceptions (e.g., **67, 83**) have shown that boys are more aggressive than girls in doll-play as well as in real-life situations. Sex differences in doll-play aggression appear to increase over the three-year to five-year age range (**139**) and then to decrease in the later childhood years (**35, 75**). Johnson (**75**) found that girls showed more "prosocial" aggression than boys, e.g., more verbal rebukes and reprimands, and less "contrasocial," i.e., physical aggression. This finding is not surprising for children brought up in a society in which aggression is much more tolerated in boys and in which the socially approved physically aggressive models, e.g., sports and film idols, are males.

The influence which the presence in the home of an aggressive masculine model has on the development of aggression has been shown in studies by Bach (**8**) and Sears (**139**). Bach found that both six- and ten-year-old boys and girls whose fathers were absent from home showed less doll-play aggression than those whose fathers were present. On the other hand, Sears found that while the presence or absence of the father influenced the doll-play aggression of boys of nursery-school age, this variable had no influence on the doll-play aggression of nursery-school girls. In both the above studies, the fathers were absent from the home during the period that observations of the children were made. Absence of the father during the first two years of a child's life appears to have no influence on doll-play aggression at the nursery-school stage, provided the father has returned to the home in the meantime (**154**).

Levin and Sears (**88**) used ratings of mother interviews to obtain measures of the punitiveness of parents and of the degree of identification with the same-sex parent shown by their preschool children. Strongly identified boys showed significantly more aggression than weakly identified boys, especially when their fathers were the agents of punishment. Differences between strongly and weakly identified girls occurred only if the mothers were severely punitive, whereas the severity of the father's punishment had little influence on the boys' aggression. The authors suggest that, by the age of five, girls have attained a stable identification with their mothers, who are usually relatively nonaggressive. Consequently, the extent to which they show aggression is little influenced by the extent of their identification. On the other hand, boys have not yet reached a stable identification with their fathers, who usually provide the aggressive models, and the extent of their aggression is therefore highly dependent on the degree of completion of the identification process.

In studies to which reference has been made earlier, Bandura, Ross, and Ross (**12, 13**) examined the influence of the sex of the model and the sex of the child on the imitation of aggression. Boys showed significantly more imitative aggression than girls, but the sexes did not differ in the extent to which they reproduced the model's verbally aggressive responses. These findings are consistent with the doll-play sex differences reported by Johnson (**75**). Bandura, Ross, and Ross found that the male model was a more potent influence on male subjects than was the female model. Male subjects exposed to an aggressive male model exhibited significantly more physical and verbal imitative aggression, more nonimitative aggression, and more aggressive gun play than did female subjects exposed to the male model. Moreover, while subjects exposed to a nonaggressive female model did not differ from control subjects on any measure of aggression, those exposed to a nonaggressive male model performed significantly less imitative and nonimitative physical and verbal aggression than subjects in the control group. In the second study by Bandura, Ross, and Ross (**14**), boys again displayed significantly more imitative and nonimitative aggression than girls, and an aggressive male model was a more powerful stimulus for aggression than an aggressive female model.

The relative potency of male and female models for eliciting imitative responses may be a function of the extent to which the behavior in question is sex-typed. As doll-play and real-life observations indicate, physical aggression is a characteristically masculine response for which sex differences are established within the first three years of life. This kind of behavior thus appears to be more easily elicited by observation of models for whom it is sex-appropriate than by observation of models for whom it is not sex-appropriate. Obviously, appropriateness could be a function of variables other than sex, for example, the occupation of the aggressor. The influence of the sex, social status, and other characteristics of the model, in relation to similar or dissimilar characteristics in the imitator, deserves detailed attention in future studies of the modeling process.

Reinforcement Patterns

POSITIVE REINFORCEMENT

Training in interpersonal aggression has, for ethical and practical reasons, rarely been attempted in a controlled laboratory setting. There is considerable evidence, however, from cross-cultural and field studies that aggressive habits are acquired largely through the direct reinforcement of aggressive responses. In the culture of the head-hunting Iatmul (**19**) the scalping of enemies is reinforced not only by the prestige that accrues to the possessor of the scalp but also, more immediately and tangibly, by the dances and celebrations that follow the decapitation. The success of the hero-killer is, however, only a climax in a series of experiences of inflicting and receiving pain and humiliation in situations in which the agent of injury is acclaimed for his acts. During their own initiation ceremonies, the adolescents of this society suffer bullying and humiliation, then later, as young adults, inflict socially approved suffering on fresh batches of novices. Bateson regards the aggression of the Iatmul male as a form of overcompensation; a more obvious and parsimonious explanation is that the child and adolescent in this society are constantly surrounded by aggressive models and that when the occasion comes for them to reproduce the aggressive behavior of the adult models, their imitative responses are socially approved while failure to behave aggressively is negatively reinforced.

In contrast, among the Hutterites, who stress pacificism as a style of life, aggressive behavior goes consistently unrewarded (**45**). Despite the fact that children in this society are subjected to relatively severe and presumably frustrating socialization pressures, they show virtually no interpersonal aggression.

Social class and ethnic differences in amount of overt aggression appear to be, at least in part, a function of the extent to which members of a particular social group tolerate and show approval of aggressive actions. Lower-class parents were reported by Davis and Havighurst to encourage and reward aggression to a greater extent than middle-class parents and at the same time to impose fewer frustrations on their children's impulses (**39, 40**). While these two findings are not independent, since aggression is one of the impulses under consideration, together they suggest that reward of aggression, and not frustration of impulses, was the more potent determinant of the relatively high degree of aggression found among the lower-class children.

During the past fifteen years there has been a number of investigations of the home backgrounds and experiences of aggressive and nonaggressive children. Bandura and Walters (**15**), in a comparison of the child-training backgrounds of 26 aggressive and 26 nonaggressive boys, found that the parents of the aggressive boys were more inclined to encourage actively and to condone aggression than were the parents of the nonaggressive boys. The difference between the two groups of fathers was particularly marked.

In a second study (**16**) these authors compared the child-training backgrounds of 30 boys who had been identified as aggressive on the basis of school and playground observations with those of 30 nonaggressive boys. Mothers and fathers of these boys were subsequently interviewed in lengthy semistructured interviews by carefully trained and experienced interviewers, and the recorded interview material was then independently coded by pairs of raters. Compared with the mothers of nonaggressive boys, the mothers of the aggressive boys were found to be more permissive of aggression and to give a considerable amount of encouragement and reward for aggression which occurred outside the home. Evidence that parental patterns of reward and punishment of aggression were important determinants of the boys' hierarchies of frustration responses was also provided by the boys' thematic-interview data. In response to stimulus situations depicting parental frustration of dependency behavior, the nonaggressive boys reported significantly more independent and withdrawal behavior than did the boys in the aggressive group. Similarly, instigation to aggression toward the father evoked significantly more withdrawal responses from the nonaggressive boys. The aggressive boys, in contrast, responded to dependency frustration with aggressively dependent behavior, indirect aggression, and, when strongly instigated to aggression toward the parents, with physical aggression directed toward persons outside the home.

An experienced study by Davitz (**41**) demonstrates both the inadequacy of the frustration-aggression hypothesis and the importance of direct training in the development of aggressive modes of response. He first observed ten groups of four children between the ages of seven and nine in a free-play situation and recorded their responses on film. Half the groups were then given seven 10-minute training sessions in which they were rewarded by praise and approval for making aggressive responses, while the remaining children were encouraged and rewarded for engaging in constructive activities. In the final phase of the experiment, the children were led to believe that they would be shown a series of movies. After the first reel, the experimenter handed each child a bar of candy. Frustration was induced by interrupting the second reel just as the movie approached its climax and, at the same time, taking away the candy. Immediately after this interruption, the groups of children were filmed for a second time in a free-play situation. Children who had been trained to behave aggressively in competitive games responded more aggressively to frustration than the groups trained in constructive activities. Moreover, children who had received training in constructiveness responded more constructively to frustration than did the children who had been trained in aggression. This study provides a neat demonstration that most "frustration" situations are simply stressful stimuli that will elicit, according to character of the stimuli that are present, the response pattern that is currently dominant in the subjects' response hierarchy. In the Davitz experiment, one may suspect that the presence of other children with whom they had been trained was the stimulus complex which determined the nature of the responses that were elicited in the stress situation.

Additional evidence for the influence of direct training in shaping frustration-reactions is provided by Updegraff and Keister (**156**), who demonstrated that positive reinforcement of independent task-oriented behavior to failure-induced frustration significantly decreased the occurrence of maladaptive aggressive, dependent, and withdrawal reactions when the children were subsequently frustrated.

Davitz appears to be the only experimenter who has trained children to respond with aggression in interpersonal situations. Other investigators have restricted themselves to training children to respond aggressively to life-sized clowns or to dolls. Cowan and Walters (**37**) studied the responses of institutionalized and noninstitutionalized children to a Bobo toy under three reinforcement conditions: continuous reinforcement, reinforcement on a fixed-ratio 1:3 schedule, and reinforcement on a fixed-ratio 1:6 schedule. Following a baseline period, the experimenter dispensed marbles according to the predetermined schedules until 18 responses had been elicited. The subject was now permitted to continue responding, but no further reinforcements were given. During the reinforcement period rates of response increased for the total group of children, but there were no systematic differences among the group of subjects. In contrast, institutionalized children took longer to "extinguish" than noninstitutionalized children, a finding which the authors attribute to the greater emotionality of the institutionalized children which presumably enhanced the effectiveness of the previously dispensed reinforcers. Moreover, there were significant effects attributable to scheduling, with regularly reinforced subjects giving the smallest number of responses before extinction and subjects reinforced on a fixed-ratio 1:6 schedule giving the largest number.

Patterson, Ludwig, and Sonoda (**124**) studied the effects of verbal reinforcement on the incidence of children's aggressive responses to a life-sized rubber clown. During the first few minutes of play children in the reinforcement group showed an increase in rate of responding which was not found in a nonreinforced control group.

The persistence of reinforcement effects was demonstrated in a second session with the same children. Those children whose aggressive responses had been previously reinforced showed an initially high rate of response, whereas children whose responses had not been reinforced showed an initially low rate of response.

In both these reinforcement studies, the life-size clown was the only stimulus presented to the child. Consequently, general activity level, a fairly stable behavioral characteristic of young children, probably determined to a large extent the incidence of aggressive responses (**66**). In studies of this nature, it may be advisable to present other stimulus objects, in addition to the clown, and to attempt to demonstrate a *relative* increase in incidence of aggressive responses as a result of social and nonsocial reinforcement.

Lövaas (**98**) avoided some of the problems encountered in the Bobo-clown studies by allowing nursery-school children to play with either of two pieces of equipment. One of these consisted of a pair of "striking dolls"; the subject was regarded as making an aggressive response if he depressed a lever which made one doll strike the other on the head. The subject could, instead, make a nonaggressive response, i.e., depressing a lever which flipped a ball up and down inside a cage-like structure. After an initial three-minute period of free play with either toy, the children were placed in front of a "talk box" on which were seated a dirty "bad" doll and a clean "good" doll. Seven subjects were reinforced with trinkets for emitting verbally aggressive responses to the dolls, e.g., "bad doll," "dirty doll"; the remaining seven received trinkets for nonaggressive verbal responses. Following this training period, the children were given a further four-minute period of play with the striking dolls and the ball-toy. During the training session, subjects who were reinforced for verbally aggressive responses showed a marked increase in verbal aggression, in comparison to the subjects reinforced for nonaggressive responses. Moreover, in the subsequent play period, subjects who had been reinforced for verbal aggression showed a significantly greater amount of nonverbal aggression than subjects who had been reinforced for nonaggressive verbal responses. The importance of this study lies in its demonstration that reinforcement of verbal aggression in one play setting has effects that are manifested in nonverbal aggression in a different play setting. In other words, both stimulus and response generalization seemed to have occurred.

Generalization of intermittently reinforced aggressive responses from a noninterpersonal situation to an interpersonal situation has recently been demonstrated by Walters and Brown (**158**). Two groups of seven-year-old boys received two training sessions in which they were reinforced with marbles for hitting, with at least moderate intensity, an automated Bobo doll. One of the experimental groups was reinforced on a fixed-ratio 1:6 schedule, the other on a continuous schedule. Two control groups were included in the study; one of these was given two play sessions with the Bobo doll but was not reinforced, while the other group was given no experience with the doll. In the testing session each child was matched against another child (drawn at random from classmates who were not included in the experimental or control groups) in competitive games similar to those used by Davitz (**41**) and in a free-play session. Half the boys in each of the four groups under study were frustrated immediately before testing by the interruption of a movie they were watching and the loss of an ice cream cone or lollipop which they had been given at the start of the movie. The remaining subjects saw the movie through and were allowed to finish their candy. Children reinforced on the fixed-ratio 1:6 schedule gave significantly more aggressive responses in the testing situation than did children in the other three groups, among which there were no reliable differences. The frustration variable had no significant influence on results.

Except for the study by Lövaas (**97**), investigations of the effects of positive reinforcement of hostile verbal responses have been carried out with adult subjects. In a number of these (**24**, **32**, **174**), operant conditioning methods have been employed to increase the frequency with which subjects emit hostile statements or expressions. Reinforcers have typically consisted of verbal tokens of approval, e.g., "Good," "Hm-hmm." In addition, analysis of response-reinforcement contingencies, as they occur naturally in psychotherapeutic interactions, reveals that positive reinforcement by the therapist of patients' hostile verbal responses greatly increases the probability of occurrence of responses of this class, whereas negative reinforcement substantially decreases the incidence of verbal aggression (**11, 61**). A later study by Simkins (**151**) has shown that material reinforcers (points and pennies) are more effective than verbal reinforcers in increasing the expression of hostile verbalizations. There is every reason to suppose that children could be similarly conditioned to produce hostile verbalizations and that nonverbal reinforcers would be as effective for this purpose as the social reinforcers which are currently more favored by experimental child psychologists.

PUNISHMENT, INHIBITION, AND ANXIETY

Much theorizing concerning aggression has leaned heavily on the assumption that the relatively severe socialization of aggression in North American society leads to an early and fairly generalized inhibition and attenuation of aggressive responses (**167**). Developmental studies of the incidence of aggression in the home (**62**), in nursery school (e.g., **6, 118, 157**), and in doll play (e.g., **139**) do not entirely support this belief. The assumption is, however, so firmly rooted that increases in aggression are frequently explained in terms of decreases of inhibition. It is, therefore, somewhat surprising to find that there has been only one study with children in which punishments have been dispensed for aggressive behavior and the effects of this procedure systematically recorded.

Hollenberg and Sperry (**67**) gave four sessions of doll play to two groups of nursery-school children. Children in the experimental group were verbally rebuked for aggressive behavior during the second of the four sessions. In all other sessions with both experimental and control subjects, the experimenter adopted the customary permissive role. For the control group, aggressive responses steadily increased from session to session—a typical finding and one that is usually interpreted in terms of weakening of inhibitions. The experimental group, in contrast, showed no increase in aggressive responses from the first to the second session and a fairly marked decrease in aggression during the third session. The effect of verbal punishment was, however, only temporary, since differences between the experimental and control groups had largely disappeared by the fourth session.

Sears and his collaborators (**142, 145, 146**) have attempted to establish relationships between parental punishment for aggression and aggressive responses in preschool and grade-school children. In the first of these studies (**146**), the investigators found a positive correlation between maternal punitiveness for aggression and the incidence of boys' aggressive behavior in nursery school, and a negative relationship between the same parent variable and the preschool aggression of girls. Although there was no difference between boys and girls in the amount of punishment they had received, Sears *et al.* made the assumption that the psychological impact of the punishment was greater for the girls because of their more complete identification with the agent of punishment. Thus, they concluded that the relationship between maternal punishment for aggressive behavior and children's aggression in school is a curvilinear one, with children who received a moderate amount of punishment demonstrating the greatest amount of aggression. Interpretation of these results is complicated by the fact that Sears and his collaborators regarded punishment (presentation of a negative reinforcer) as a form of frustration and, consequently, as having partially analogous effects to the blocking of, or interference with, an ongoing response-sequence. They state:

> An hypothesis was suggested that punishment serves as a form of frustration and hence increases the total instigation to aggression, but that when punishment becomes sufficiently severe, it inhibits the specific actions punished; in such cases, the increased aggressive instigation would be manifested only in forms of aggressive activity different enough from those punished not to suffer from inhibition by means of stimulus or response generalization (**142**: 475).

Sears, Maccoby, and Levin (**145**) found a positive relationship between maternal punishment for aggression and children's aggression in the home. In a follow-up study, using 160 of the original 379 families, Sears (**142**) reported that high punishment for aggression in the first five years of a child's life tended to reduce antisocial aggression and to increase prosocial aggression by age 12. However, the correlations on which these conclusions were based were small and mostly nonsignificant.

In discussing the process of socialization many psychologists regard punishment as a source of chronic anxiety or guilt (**44**, **167**).

Psychological literature is replete with speculation, but relatively empty of empirical findings, concerning the antecedents and consequences of guilt and anxiety about aggression.

Bandura and Walters (**15**) obtained ratings of the extent to which parents punished aggression toward themselves, siblings, peers, and other adults and also to which they employed various disciplinary measures. Correlations between parent ratings and ratings of the boys' anxiety and guilt concerning aggression yielded no evidence for the assumption that punitive handling of aggression aroused aggression anxiety; in contrast, parents who employed reasoning as a method of discipline tended to have children who were anxious and guilty about aggressive behavior.

Sears (**142**) obtained a significant positive correlation between severity of parental punitiveness for aggression during early childhood and the degree of anxiety about aggression shown by girls in middle childhood, but no such relationship was apparent in the case of boys. Jegard and Walters (**71**) found little difference in aggression between children whose responses to drawings depicting aggressive behavior suggested high guilt concerning aggression and those whose responses suggested low guilt; while there was a tendency for high-guilt boys to inhibit aggression, high-guilt and low-guilt girls did not differ in this respect.

On the other hand, Mussen and Naylor (**116**) found that the overt aggression of institutionalized boys could be better predicted from Thematic Apperception Test (TAT) stories when both aggressive and anticipation-of-punishment themes were used as predictors than when the incidence of aggressive themes served as the only predictor. Patterson (**123**), who used a nonverbal cartoon technique for assessing boys' reactions to frustration, reports a similar finding. A combination of two test scores, uncontrolled counteraggression (*UCA*) and punishment (Pn), was the most efficient predictor of current overt aggression for both normal grade-school boys and disturbed children. Like Mussen and Naylor, Patterson regards the occurrence of punishment themes as indicating a tendency to inhibit aggression.

Whiting and Child (**168**) report a highly significant relationship between severity of socialization for aggression and adult anxiety about aggression. However, the adequacy of their index of anxiety, the presence in cultures of explanations of illness as due to aggressive activities or objects associated with aggression, is even more questionable than that of reports of interviewees or responses to drawings depicting social situations.

Failure to distinguish guilt from anxiety may obscure any relationships that exist between parental disciplinary practices and inhibition of aggression. Perhaps, as Mowrer (**114**) suggests, the timing of punishment is an important determinant of the nature of its effects. Studies of dogs by Black, Solomon, and Whiting (see **114**), and of children by Walters and Demkow (**159**), suggest that punishment which occurs before a consummatory response is successfully achieved inhibits deviant responses. In contrast, punishment which occurs after the commission of a deviant act may succeed in developing guilt or other self-punitive responses (emotional reactions to deviation) but not in forestalling the punished behavior (**7**).

Moreover, the nature of the punishment which is given for aggression may largely determine its consequences. Harsh, punitive disciplinary measures, which are erratically administered (i.e., not consistently paired with the response which it is desired to inhibit), appear to be antecedents not of aggression inhibition but of aggressive orientations (**15, 16, 60, 145**).

It is obvious that no firm statements can be made concerning the relationship of punishment and aggression, unless the agent of punishment, the recipient of aggression, and the nature of both the punitive and aggressive responses are taken into account. In general, effects of punishment appear to be far more complex than those of reward and, as recent discussions of the literature by Mowrer (**112**) and Hall (**63**) indicate, much less well understood.

Theorizing and experimentation on the inhibition of aggression have focused exclusively on the inhibitory influence of anxiety or guilt, on the assumption that response inhibition is necessarily a consequence of pairing responses with some form of aversive stimulation. The development of aggression inhibition through the strengthening of incompatible positive responses, on the other hand, has been entirely ignored, despite the fact that the social control of aggression is probably achieved to a greater extent on this basis than by means of aversive stimulation.

The effectiveness of positive control over aggression is neatly demonstrated in an infrequently quoted study by Wright (**172**). Preschool children participated in pairs in a frustration experiment in which each pair played freely with a set of highly attractive toys. In a subsequent session, the children were cut off from access to the toys by a screen, a frustration procedure similar to that employed by Barker *et al.* (**17**). The criterion measures were the changes in the children's social behavior toward each other and toward the experimenter from the free play to the frustration sessions.

Eighteen of the pairs of children selected for study were designated as "strong friends," while 21 pairs were "weak friends." The strength of friendship was found to be highly influential in determining the children's reactions to frustration. Strong friends *increased* co-operativeness and *decreased* conflict behavior toward each other under frustration. The behavioral changes of weak friends, while in the same direction, were not of statistically significant magnitude. In addition, intergroup comparisons revealed that, although the two groups of children did not differ in their behavior during the free-play session, the strong friends exhibited significantly more co-operative behavior and less conflict under frustration than did the weak friends. Not only did frustration elicit affiliative peer behavior in the strong friends but the resulting mutual support counteracted the inhibition over aggression toward the adult experimenter who was the agent of frustration. Thus, the strong friends displayed considerably more aggression than the weak friends toward the adult, the difference being particularly marked in the expression of physical aggression.

Wright's study is, of course, pertinent to the problem of the role of frustration, which is discussed later in this chapter. It indicates very clearly the manner in which responses to frustration may be modified by the social context in which they occur.

PERMISSIVENESS

The effects of maternal permissiveness for aggression have received a good deal of attention in the studies by Sears and his collaborators (**145, 146**). A mother who expects and accepts aggressive behavior is providing opportunities for aggression to occur and consequently to be positively or negatively reinforced. Positive correlations between maternal permissiveness for aggression during the child's first five years of life and the amount of aggression the child displayed in the home were reported for both boys and girls (**145**). However, the correlations were small and, for the follow-up sample, Sears (**142**) failed to find significant relationships between earlier maternal permissiveness and the amount of antisocial aggression shown by the children at age 12.

Bandura and Walters (**15**) found that mothers of aggressive boys were somewhat more permissive for aggression directed toward themselves than were mothers of nonaggressive boys. These mothers did not, however, differ in respect to permissiveness for aggression toward other adults, siblings, or peers, nor were there any differences between the two groups of fathers. In their comparison of parents of aggressive and withdrawn boys, the same authors (**16**) found no differences in the extent to which the parents permitted aggression to be shown toward themselves. However, there was more aggression permitted *in the homes* of aggressive boys, since their mothers permitted more aggression toward siblings. In addition, the mothers of aggressive boys permitted more aggression toward peers.

The effects of parental permissiveness are not independent of the consequences which follow the performance of the permitted act. Presumably, parents who permit and reward aggression will develop aggressive habits in their children. On the other hand, parents who both permit and punish aggression appear also to produce highly aggressive children (**15, 16, 145**). This aggression may, however, as a result of discrimination-learning, be mainly directed at persons other than the punitive agents.

The effects of permissiveness have also been noted in studies of doll-play aggression. With a permissive adult present, children's doll-play aggression has been shown to increase from the first half to the second half of a single ten-minute session (**65**) and over two to four consecutive sessions when the experimenter and the experimental setting have remained the same (**8, 67, 139**). Buss (**31**) argues that the presence of a significant permissive adult may serve as a positive reinforcer for aggression. It is difficult, however, to see why aggressive, as opposed to other, responses should be reinforced by the presence of a permissive adult unless it is assumed that the adult responds differentially to aggressive and nonaggressive acts, for example, by unintentional signs of encouragement or approval of the former.

In a study of the influence of antecedent frustration on doll-play behavior, Yarrow (**173**) compared the aggression of preschool children in two 30-minute sessions of permissive doll-play. Immediately preceding the second play session, one group of children experienced task-induced failure, a second group performed a long monotonous motor task, while a control group of children was provided with a pleasant nonfrustrating experience. All three groups increased in frequency of aggressive responses and decreased in latency of aggressive behavior in the second play session, while frustrated and control groups did not differ significantly from each other in these respects. Boys exhibited greater changes in aggressive behavior under the permissive conditions than did girls. In this study, nonaggressive, as well as aggressive, responses increased in frequency in the second session, a finding that suggests that adult permissiveness is a general reinforcer for doll-play activities and not specifically a reinforcer for aggression.

Levin and Turgeon (**89**) reported an increase in aggression when a child's mother and the experimenter were both present in the second of two sessions, but no increase in the second session when an adult stranger accompanied the experimenter. Levin and Turgeon explained their results, which were contrary to an experimental hypothesis developed on the basis of Miller's displacement model (**106**), by assuming that the child had abdicated responsibility in the presence of the mother and had trusted her to inhibit behavior of which she disapproved. This interpretation is highly questionable, especially in view of the fact that increases in aggression from a first to a second session ordinarily occur when the experimenter only is present. The absence of an increase in aggression in the stranger-present group perhaps reflects the inhibitory effect which a strange adult often has on the play activities of children.

In a study by Siegel and Kohn (**150**), pairs of children played with various materials, including balloons, rubber daggers, and a toy clown. One group of children participated in two experimental sessions with a permissive adult experimenter present; the adult experimenter was not present with the other group. Aggression increased from the first to the second session among members of the adult-present group but not among the adult-absent group. Siegel and Kohn provide an interpretation similar to that given by Levin and Turgeon. Again, however, an "abdication of responsibility" interpretation is open to question. For children in the adult-absent group, the consequences of aggression were relatively uncontrolled because these children depended largely on the responses of other children with whom they had been paired. In contrast, consequences to the children in the adult-present group were in part determined by the consistently permissive attitude of the experimenter, whose tacit approval may have provided some reinforcement for all doll-play activities, including aggressive ones. This latter interpretation is supported by Pintler's finding (**127**) that a high degree of experimenter-child interaction results in more doll-play aggression than a low degree of experimenter-child interaction, if one assumes that increased interaction makes somewhat more explicit the tacit approval of the experimenter.

Nonpermissiveness for aggression in the form of early intervention when an aggressive act is anticipated (**145**) involves the blocking of an instrumental act and presumably is frustrative. Thus, nonpermissiveness should, according to the frustration-aggression hypothesis, increase the incidence of aggressive activities. However, there is no evidence that nonpermissiveness consistently influences performance in this manner.

One of the major problems in investigations of child-training antecedents of aggression is that the parents, although perhaps the most important, are not the only socializing agents. Nonpermissiveness for aggression in schools may increase aggression in children whose parents have permitted aggressive habits to be established. On the other hand, consistent nonpermissiveness in the home may prevent aggressive habits from developing.

Role of Frustration

In order to understand the role of frustration, it is necessary to take account of studies in which aggression has not been the dependent variable. In these studies, of which one by Miller and Stevenson (**110**) appears to have been the forerunner, frustration has generally consisted of withholding rewards previously dispensed for a response, removing some of the stimulus objects essential for the performance of the instrumental act, or the eliciting of responses incompatible with the response to be frustrated.

The frustration-drive hypothesis, which has developed from and has guided the majority of these studies, has been recently stated by Brown (**29**) in the following manner: "When stimuli normally capable of eliciting a response are present, but the response is prevented from running its usual course, behavior may be affected as though a motivational variable had been introduced" (**29**: 195). The basic assumption, which is also crucial for the conflict-drive theory of both Whiting (**167**) and Sears *et al.* (**146**) is that frustration, or conflict between expectancy of reward and nonreward, increases the motivational level of the organism, through the addition of conflict-produced, frustration-produced, or "irrelevant" drive (**2, 3, 4, 30, 51, 85**).

A study by Haner and Brown (**64**) is frequently regarded as supporting a frustration-drive theory. The authors set out to test the hypothesis that strength of an aggressive response varies with strength of frustration, the latter being defined in terms of the point in the response-sequence at which blocking occurred. Grade-school children were assigned the task of inserting 36 marbles in holes in a board and were promised a prize if they were successful on four trials. At the end of each trial, the experimenter sounded a buzzer which the subjects turned off by depressing a plunger. On different trials, subjects were failed at varying distances from the goal, and a record was obtained of the amount of pressure they exerted on the plunger. The nearer the subjects were to completing the task when blocked, the greater the pressure they exerted on the plunger. Berkowitz (**22**) and Buss (**31**) have both queried the legitimacy of regarding plunger-pushing as an aggressive response. Nevertheless, if (as was suggested earlier in this chapter) the intensity of a response is an important criterion of aggression, this study is highly relevant to the frustration-aggression problem.

In a somewhat similar study, Holton (**68**) presented preschool children with two identical stimulus panels. Whenever the subject pressed the "correct" panel, a marble was dispensed as a reward. The children had been previously informed that they would receive toys if they could earn enough marbles to fill all the holes in a board.

Two groups of subjects were given 26 reinforced trials before nonrewarded trials were introduced, but one group was nearer to completing the task than the other. For a third group of subjects reward was omitted after 13 reinforced trials, which had already brought these children near to completing the task. On each trial, the strength with which the subject pressed the panel was recorded. All three groups of subjects increased the vigor of their responses on the first four of seven consecutive nonreinforced trials. Subjects who had received 26 reinforced trials and who were blocked near to their goal showed the greatest increase in intensity of response. Holton's findings, like those of Haner and Brown, seem to indicate that the intensity of response to frustration is a function of the strength of the frustrated response.

Haner and Brown showed that blocking may result in the intensification of a response which is not a component of, but immediately succeeds, the frustrated response-sequence. Confirmation of this finding is provided by Penney (**125**), who used with children an experimental paradigm first developed for animal studies by Amsel and Roussel (**5**). The children were trained to manipulate a lever to receive a marble, then to manipulate a second lever and receive another marble. For the experimental groups the first reward was omitted on two-thirds of the test trials. Speed of moving the second lever increased when the first lever-moving response was not rewarded, provided that this latter response had acquired sufficient habit strength from previously dispensed rewards.

Holton's study, in contrast to those by Haner and Brown and Penney, demonstrated an increase in vigor of the frustrated instrumental response following the introduction of nonrewarded trials. Parallel increases in the strength of children's instrumental responses at the commencement of extinction procedures have been noted by Screven (**138**) and Longstreth (**96**).

The vigor of instrumental responses may be increased by delay as well as by omission of reward, which may, in fact, be conceptualized as infinite or indefinite delay. Olds (**119, 120**) carried out a series of experiments with children in which the subject's task was to crank a token machine for poker chips, which were then exchangeable for toys. All children were first habituated to crank the machine at three turns of the crank per chip. Delay of reward was now increased 4 times (16 cranks per chip) for one group of children and 2.5 times for a second group. The force children exerted on the crank increased with increasing delay of reward and decreased with decreasing delay.

While frustration in the form of omission or delay of a reward appears to bring at least a temporary increase in intensity of response, it does not necessarily increase quality of performance. For example, Seashore and Bavelas (**147**) found that children's performance on the Goodenough "Draw-a-Person Test" declined when the children were told that they must perform better on each successive trial. Moreover, it is well established that learning is less efficient when reward is delayed than when reward is immediate (**94**, **95**). Prolonged omission or delay of reward, of course, results in the weakening of a response, a phenomenon which, in social psychology, is reflected in the observation that prolonged "frustration" may lead to apathy (**86**).

The relationship between frustration and aggression can now be conceptualized as follows. Frustration may produce a temporary increase in drive and thus lead to more vigorous responding. The dominant response to stimuli present before frustration may be one that when mild is not classed as aggressive, but when strong is so categorized. Frustration also changes the stimulus situation and consequently changes in the kind, as well as the intensity, of responses that may be expected. Interference with a response-sequence may be a stimulus for eliciting response-hierarchies in which, because of past learning, pain-producing responses tend to be dominant. Modification of the associative strength of responses through stimulus change can thus, independently of changes in the drive level of the subject, lead to the occurrence of aggressive behavior. Prior experiences of frustrated subjects, and particularly their "personality characteristics," i.e., response-patterns that are dominant in many of their response-hierarchies, should consequently determine to a large extent the nature of their responses to frustration.

The studies by Davitz (**41**), Bandura (**9**), and Walters and Brown (**158**), to which reference has already been made, indicate that past experience in the form of prior reinforcement for aggressive responses and exposure to aggressive models make more probable the occurrence of aggressive responses to frustration. Other investigators have compared the responses to frustration of children who differ in "personality characteristics." Otis and McCandless (**121**) "played a game" with preschool children in which the experimenter and subject pushed toy cars along a road, starting from opposite ends. When the cars met in the middle, the child could exhibit "dominant-aggressive" behavior by insisting that his car could pass, or "submissive-complaisant" behavior by yielding to the experimenter. Otis and McCandless reported more dominant-aggressive behavior in children with a dominant "need for power" than in children with a dominant "need for love affection." The authors also reported an increase in dominant-aggressive behavior over eight trials, a finding that, in view of the experimenter's yielding at the child's insistence, is parallel to the increase in aggression found in successive periods of permissive doll-play.

Block and Martin (**26**) compared children previously rated as "overcontrollers" and "undercontrollers" in a frustration situation similar to that used by Barker, Dembo, and Lewin (**17**), i.e., the children were debarred from access to attractive toys. Undercontrollers gave predominantly aggressive responses but overcontrollers played constructively with the less attractive toys to which they still had access.

Several investigators have failed to find differences in aggression between frustrated and nonfrustrated children. Jegard and Walters (**71**) deprived nursery-school children of a preferred reward, then left them in a room with an inflated Bobo clown and a toy dog. Frustrated children showed no more aggression toward these objects than did children who received the reward of their choice, though anticipated sex differences in aggression were clearly apparent. Mussen and Rutherford (**117**) found no differences in aggressiveness between frustrated and nonfrustrated children in the same experimental design which yielded differences attributable to prior exposure or nonexposure to aggressive models. Moreover, in Yarrow's study (**173**) there were no greater session-to-session increases in doll-play aggression for frustrated than for nonfrustrated children. These negative findings, occurring in studies which yielded confirmation of other hypotheses, cast further doubt on the validity of the frustration-aggression hypothesis.

As Buss has stated: "The frustration-aggression hypothesis may have been a useful working hypothesis 20 years ago, but it has limited utility today. . . . Frustration is only one antecedent of aggression, and it is not the most potent one" (**31:** 28).

Displacement and Projection

The frustration-aggression hypothesis was inspired by Freud's belief, reflected in his earlier writings (**55, 56**), that aggression was a "primordial reaction" to the thwarting of pleasure-seeking and pain-avoiding responses. It is, therefore, not surprising that much of *Frustration and Aggression* consisted of attempts to fit psychoanalytic concepts such as displacement, projection, and catharsis within the framework of Hull's drive-reduction theory (**70**).

In cases of "object displacement," it is supposed that the general form of an inhibited response remains the same, but the object changes. The boy who is harshly punished by his parents and fears to retaliate vents his anger in antisocial activities (**15**); frustrated by the weather and angry at the gods, the irate Southerner engages in lynching (**69**). These kinds of phenomena have been interpreted by Miller (**105, 106**) as the outcome of a conflict between an inhibitory (fear or anxiety) response and the response with which it competes, both of which generalize to stimulus situations similar to that in which they were originally learned. Miller assumed that the generalization gradient for an inhibitory response was steeper than that of the response that was inhibited and that, consequently, at some point on the stimulus-similarity continuum the approach tendency became the stronger and was therefore manifested in overt activity. A series of studies with animals (**28, 79, 108, 109, 115**) which supported Miller's basic assumptions has given wide acceptance to the conflict paradigm.

Attempts to use this paradigm to explain the displacement of aggression in humans have been far from satisfactory, partly because of extremely arbitrary, and usually *post hoc*, ordering and locating of targets of aggression on the similarity continuum, and partly because the paradigm does not take into account a number of highly relevant social learning variables. For example, in applications of Miller's conflict-model to social behavior (**15, 146, 168**), it has been assumed that both aggressive responses and aggression-anxiety responses are learned through interactions with parents or other socialization agents and that the conflicting responses generalize to such situations as the school and playground and to stimuli that elicit fantasies. While it is true that more open displays of aggression are, generally speaking, less frequently expressed toward parents than toward teachers or peers, there are children who are tyrants at home but mild-mannered and nonaggressive in school (**90**). Good discrimination-learning may account for the behavior of both typical and atypical children, since interview studies with parents (**15, 16**) clearly indicate that in most families aggression in the home, particularly toward parents, is more strongly disapproved, reprimanded, and punished than is aggression displayed in other situations. A reversal of the usual patterning of aggression may be found in children whose aggressive responses are unsuccessful outside the home but whose parents are relatively permissive and yielding when aggression is displayed in their presence.

Sears (**143, 144**) compared the overt and doll-play aggression of 40 preschool children whose mothers varied in punitiveness. There was a close correspondence between amount of socially directed aggression in school and doll-play aggression for children whose mothers were low or moderate in punitiveness. In contrast, children whose mothers were highly punitive showed much doll-play aggression and little aggression in everyday school activities.

Sears' findings were interpreted in terms of Miller's conflict-producing displacement model (**146**). However, the assumption that a doll-play kit containing parent and child dolls and a house with furniture has *fewer* elements in common with the child's home than has the regular school setting is open to question. Moreover, the complexity of findings concerning the relationships of doll-play aggression to parental-training practices (**88**), to the effects of presence or absence of the mother during doll-play sessions (**89**), and to variations in doll-play material (e.g., **126, 127, 130**) cast doubt on the value of attempts to locate the doll-play situation on a stimulus-dissimilarity continuum.

Lesser (**87**) presented ten pictures, depicting interactions between two boys, to 44 boys whose overt aggression was assessed through a sociometric device. There was no relationship between the measure of fantasy aggression (the number of aggressive acts in stories told to the pictures) and the boys' overt aggression. However, when the boys were divided into two groups on the basis of the mothers' handling of aggression, assessed by means of a questionnaire, Lesser found a significant positive correlation between overt and fantasy aggression for those boys whose mothers encouraged and supported aggression and a significant negative relationship between overt and fantasy aggression for those boys whose mothers discouraged aggression. The significant negative correlation appears at first sight to support a traditional displacement interpretation. However, a considerable number of the boys whose mothers discouraged aggression displayed *high-overt* and *low-fantasy* scores. Lesser suggests that these boys assigned a prohibitory role to the adult experimenter and consequently suppressed aggressive fantasy responses but were, in contrast, aggressive toward their peers. Interpretation of the data in terms of discrimination-learning is therefore indicated.

Lippitt (**93**) and Lewin, Lippitt, and White (**91**) recorded the responses of "clubs" of five ten-year-old boys to authoritarian, democratic, and laissez-faire leadership. Under autocratic leadership the boys "developed a pattern of aggressive domination toward one another," a good example of modeling behavior, and on occasions four of the group members made a concerted attack on the fifth (the "scapegoat"). In a second study, four out of five groups of boys showed generally apathetic, nonaggressive behavior under authoritarian leadership, but became markedly more aggressive when the leader was absent or the atmosphere became more relaxed. Aggression also occurred in the form of expressed dislike for the autocratic leader and of club "wars."

The scapegoats in this study were "the two leaders in the group," certainly not the least fear-provoking members. Perhaps these boys were less conforming to the authoritarian leader and therefore the most deviant members of the group. Since deviant group members elicit aggression and eventual rejection (**135**), the attacks by the other group members may not, in fact, reflect the displacement of repressed aggression toward the leader. Another alternative to a simple displacement interpretation has recently been suggested by White and Lippitt (**164**), who argue that the boys attacked strong rather than weak members of the group in order to regain status and self-esteem which had been lost in their interaction with the authoritarian leader.

The hypothesis that, when a frustrating agent is feared, aggression will be displaced to a less-feared scapegoat has been used to account for the occurrence of hostility and aggression toward minorities or to members of "out-groups" that are identifiably different from the social groups to which the aggressor belongs. Evidence for the scapegoat theory of prejudice is, at best, equivocal (e.g., **20, 21, 38, 92, 107, 153, 164**). Prejudices, like other "aggressive" responses, are acquired through imitation and direct training and make their appearance relatively early in a child's life (**129**). Once a prejudice has been learned, hostile-aggressive responses are, by definition, high in the response-hierarchies that are elicited by the target of prejudice. The "scapegoating" of out-group members can, therefore, be regarded as the outcome of discrimination-learning in which a strong associative bond has been developed between the sight or sound of individuals belonging to certain ethnic or religious groups (**1**), or known to hold certain beliefs (**131**), and hostile-aggressive responses. Since the aggressor is said to select for attack an individual or group who is *unlike* the frustrating agent, the kind of stimulus generalization assumed in the Miller displacement model seems to play little or no part in determining its occurrence.

One reason for the inadequacy of Miller's displacement model is that it adopts a basically nonsocial approach to a problem in social learning. According to this model, the objects and strength of displaced responses can be predicted from knowledge of three variables only—the strength of instigation, i.e., of approach tendencies to the frustrating agent; the severity of punishment of these responses; and a stimulus-similarity dimension. The approach thus ignores the influence of the original agents of frustration and punishment in determining responses toward stimulus objects other than themselves. In fact, parents often through precept, example, and control of reinforcement contingencies determine rather precisely the kind of displaced responses that a child will or will not display. Displaced aggression is further modified by the responses it elicits from other socializing agents and from the objects of the aggression themselves. Miller's generalization gradients thus become relatively meaningless for a human learning situation in which the patterns of reward-punishment contingencies displayed by parents and other agents of socialization have no consistent relationship to the similarity to the parents of possible objects of aggression.

In the area of aggression, social training consists largely in teaching a child to be aggressive only *in certain ways.* For example, he may be taught to "defend his principles" (or his parents) but not to attack his opponent physically. The substitution of more socially acceptable responses for less acceptable ones has been referred to as "response displacement" (**15**). This, however, is again a case of discrimination-learning, and no new principles are required to explain its occurrence. Johnson's demonstration that older children display more prosocial, and less antisocial, aggression in doll play than do younger children reflects this learning process (**75**).

In some cases the "displaced" response is not necessarily a socially commended one. A child who masturbates when frustrated by his parents is not manifesting the results of deliberate social training. The occurrence of responses of this kind can, however, be explained in terms of familiar motivational or learning concepts. It has already been pointed out that one of the effects of frustration is to increase the subject's motivational, drive, or arousal level. What the child does under this condition of heightened emotionality will depend on the nature of the stimulus situation and what responses to the situation have been rewarding in the past. Self-stimulation of some kind may well occur if there are present no salient external stimuli to which some responses in the child's repertory have already been associated. On the other hand, if some stimulus complex to which he has learned to give aggressive responses exists in his environment, the behavior he manifests may be "displaced" aggression. An essentially similar account of displacement has been offered by Bindra (**25**).

Children's responses following brief social isolation, interpreted by Hartup and Himeno (**65**) as a frustrating condition, illustrate this principle. Placed in a learning situation with verbal approval as the reinforcer, children learn a discrimination task more readily following social isolation than following friendly play with an adult or customary school activities (**58, 59, 163**). In contrast, when placed in a doll-play situation, previously isolated children show more aggression, a response dominant in the response-hierarchies of many children in this situation, than do children not previously isolated (**65**).

Studies of response displacement have frequently employed projective methods on the assumption that repressed aggression will be reflected in fantasy. Although projection and displacement were quite different "mechanisms of defense" in Freudian theory (**52**), in studies of fantasy aggression their roles are usually confounded. In doll-play and other studies employing ambiguous stimuli, attempts have been made to define projection in terms of the agent of the fantasy act and displacement in terms of its object (**140, 146, 170**). Since most aggressive fantasy acts have both an agent and an object, the problem of confounding has not in this way been solved. Moreover, use of a doll-agent has also been regarded as an index of identification, a convention that further complicates the status of doll-play "projection."

Projective techniques, other than doll-play, have had wide use in studies of relationships between overt and fantasy aggression in children and adolescents (e.g., **73, 76, 87, 116**). When stimuli are highly ambiguous, they can elicit an infinite range of responses, many of which are certain to be irrelevant to the hypotheses being tested. Consequently, consistent relationships between overt and fantasy aggression should not be expected in studies in which projective stimuli such as the Rorschach and standard *TAT* cards are used. However, if pictorial stimuli are representative of those encountered in real-life social situations, a positive relationship between overt and fantasy aggression should be found. Kagan's studies of fantasy aggression (**76, 77**), for which cards were specially designed to facilitate the production of stories with themes of aggression, bear out this expectation.

One should probably reserve the term "displaced aggression" for cases in which frustration is known to have occurred and aggression is displayed against an object in the absence of provocation. An adequate social learning model for the prediction of aggression of this kind must take into account a number of variables which are ignored in Miller's displacement paradigm. Knowledge of the extent of frustration and of the punitiveness of the primary socializing agents for aggression toward themselves is, of course, needed. In addition, however, crucial for prediction are such variables as the hierarchy of frustration-reactions which the potential aggressor has acquired; the modeling (through overt behavior and attitudes) of responses to potential displacement objects by parents and other socialization agents and the reward-punishment contingencies adopted by these agents in respect both to aggression toward themselves and aggression toward other classes of persons.

Catharsis

As used by Aristotle, the Greek word *katharsis* referred to the purging of the passions or sufferings of the spectators through *vicarious* participation in the suffering of a tragic hero as this is portrayed on the stage (**34**). Consequently, any test of such a cathartic effect should involve the presentation of emotional behavior in some representational art form.

Studies in which children or adolescents have been exposed to film-mediated aggressive models (**12, 14, 97, 117, 149, 161**) have uniformly indicated that vicarious participation in aggressive activity increases, rather than decreases, the frequency and intensity of aggressive responses and thus afford no support to the Aristotelian catharsis hypothesis.

In psychoanalytic writings (**27, 47, 56**), catharsis referred to the "liberation of affect" through the re-experiencing of blocked or inhibited emotions, which is supposedly an essential phase in the solution of unconscious conflicts. In applying this psychoanalytic principle to aggressive behavior, Dollard *et al.* (**42**) stated that "the occurrence of any act of aggression is assumed to reduce the instigation to aggression" (**42:** 50). So stated, the catharsis hypothesis is not essentially different from the displacement and projection hypotheses, since all three imply that in some way one aggressive response can serve as a substitute for another in reducing an instinct, urge, or drive of aggression. Whereas the Aristotelian principle of catharsis must be tested through presenting aggressive (or other) models, the Freudian (and neo-Hullian) hypothesis is more appropriately tested by permitting subjects *themselves* to express aggression in fantasy, play, or real life and then to test them for aggression in the same or a different stimulus situation. This kind of paradigm has been employed in a number of studies of adult subjects but in very few studies of children.

Kenny (**80**) hypothesized that participation in doll-play sessions of the "release-therapy" type would lead to a reduction of aggression. The aggressive responses of children in Grade I to the first half of Korner's *Incomplete Stories Test* formed the pretest measure (**82**). Two "therapy" sessions, in which physical and verbal aggression were fostered, provided the 15 children in the experimental group with opportunities for catharsis. Control children were, instead, given two sessions of nonaggressive play with jigsaw puzzles and swings. Following the play sessions, the second half of Korner's test, which supplied the post-test measure of aggression, was administered to both experimental and control subjects. The control group in the study showed a significantly greater *decrease* in aggression than the experimental group, a finding that provides no support at all for the catharsis hypothesis.

Feshbach (**48**) identified 31 high-aggressive and 30 low-aggressive children on the basis of teachers' ratings. High-aggressive and low-aggressive children were then assigned to one of three groups: aggressive-toy group, neutral-toy group, or control group. Children in the aggressive-toy group were given four 50-minute sessions in which they listened to a record and a story with aggressive themes and spent 21 minutes playing freely with objects designed to stimulate the expression of aggression, e.g., guns. The neutral-toy group listened to nonaggressive themes and played with objects which were more likely to elicit nonaggressive responses, e.g., trains. A third (control) group of children followed their regular classroom-schedule. Contrary to the catharsis hypothesis, children in the aggressive-toy group gave more *nonthematic* aggressive responses during the free-play sessions than did children in the neutral-toy group. After completion of the play sessions, experimental and control children were rerated for aggression in the school situation. Children in the aggressive-toy and neutral-toy play groups did not significantly differ in pretest-to-post-test changes in rated aggression, and they were consequently combined for comparison with the controls. Decreased aggression was no more frequent among initially high-aggressive play-group subjects than among initially high-aggressive control subjects and was less frequent among initially low-aggressive play-group subjects than among initially low-aggressive control sub jects. This study, like Kenny's, therefore, fails to support the drive-reduction catharsis hypothesis.

Bach (**8**) compared doll-play responses of three groups of children, one group rated as high in destructive aggression in nursery school, one group rated as low, and a third group rated as "normal." On the basis of the version of the catharsis hypothesis presented in *Frustration and Aggression*, Bach predicted that by the end of four doll-play sessions highly destructive children would have less instigation to aggression than weakly destructive children. While weakly destructive children showed a slightly greater increase in percentage of aggressive fantasies over the four sessions than did the strongly destructive children, the two groups quite evidently did not differ on the final session. It is difficult to understand why Bach regards his results as supporting, if not substantiating, the hypothesis under investigation. The data are, in any case, inadequate for a test of this hypothesis, since Bach failed to include a measure of pretest-to-post-test change in destructive aggression outside the doll-play setting.

If conclusions were to be based on studies of children alone, the catharsis hypothesis, in all its forms, would have to be discarded. Findings from studies with adult subjects are much less clear cut. Generally speaking, participation, direct or vicarious, in aggressive activities seems to increase the incidence of subsequent aggression, both in the same and different stimulus situations, for most groups of nonangered adult subjects (**31, 162**). For angered subjects, participation has, under some experimental manipulations, resulted in a decrease in subsequent aggression (**49, 50, 132, 155**), but in no case can this reduction be certainly attributed to catharsis.

The discrepancy between findings yielded by child and by adult studies and the conflicting results from experiments based on adult subjects may be partly attributable to variations in criterion measures. The child studies have, without exception, employed measures of overt aggression. In contrast, the adult studies have generally relied on questionnaire responses, self-ratings, and ambiguous measures obtained from ratings of the experiment and the experimenter, all of which are subject to response sets which may seriously affect results.

The "drainage" hypothesis has been severely criticized by McClelland (**99**), Allport (**1**), and others. Its persistence, in spite of criticism and largely negative experimental findings, reflects the resilience of the hydraulic model of personality popularized through psychoanalytic writings. On the basis of present knowledge, it seems reasonable to conclude that there is no more evidence for cathartic reduction of aggression than there is for sublimation of sex (**81**).

BIBLIOGRAPHY

1. Allport, G. W. *The Nature of Prejudice*. Cambridge, Massachusetts: Addison-Wesley, 1954.
2. Amsel, A. "Frustrative Nonreward in Partial Reinforcement and Discrimination Learning: Some Recent History and a Theoretical Extension," *Psychol. Rev.*, LXIX (1962), 306–28.
3. ———. "The Role of Frustrative Nonreward in Noncontinuous Reward Situations," *Psychol. Bull.*, LV (1958), 102–19.
4. ———. "A Three-factor Theory of Inhibition: An Addition to Hull's Two-factor Theory," *Am. Psychologist*, VI (1951), 487 (abstract).
5. Amsel, A. and Roussel, J. "Motivational Properties of Frustration: Effect on a Running Response of the Addition of Frustration to the Motivational Complex," *J. of Exp. Psychol.*, XLIII (1952), 363–68.
6. Appel, M. H. "Aggressive Behavior of Nursery-School Children and Adult Procedures in Dealing with Such Behavior," *J. of Exp. Educ.*, XI (1942), 185–99.
7. Aronfreed, J. "The Origins of Self-criticism." Unpublished Manuscript, University of Pennsylvania, 1962.
8. Bach, G. R. "Young Children's Play Fantasies," *Psychol. Monogr.*, LIX (1945), No. 2 (Whole No. 272).
9. Bandura, A. "Social Learning through Imitation," in *Nebraska Symposium on Motivation*. Edited by M. R. Jones. Lincoln: University of Nebraska Press, 1962.
10. Bandura, A., and Huston, Aletha. "Identification as a Process of Incidental Learning," *J. Abnorm. Soc. Psychol.*, LXIII (1961), 311–18.
11. Bandura, A.; Lipsher, D.; and Miller, Paula E. "Psychotherapists' Approach-Avoidance Reactions to Patients' Expressions of Hostility," *J. Consult. Psychol.*, XXIV (1960), 1–8.
12. Bandura, A.; Ross, Dorothea; and Ross, Sheila A. "Imitation of Film-mediated Aggressive Models," *J. Abnorm. Soc. Psychol.*, (1962) in press.
13. ———. "Transmission of Aggression through Imitation of Aggressive Models," *J. Abnorm. Soc. Psychol.*, LXIII (1961), 575–82.
14. ———. " 'Vicarious' Reinforcement and Imitation," *J. Abnorm. Soc. Psychol.* (1963), in press.
15. Bandura, A., and Walters, R. H. *Adolescent Aggression*. New York: Ronald Press, 1959.
16. ———. *The Social Learning of Deviant Behavior: A Behavioristic Approach to Socialization*. New York: Holt, Rinehart & Winston, 1963 (in press).
17. Barker, R. G.; Dembo, Tamara; and Lewin, K. "Frustration and Regression: An Experiment with Young Children," *Univer. Iowa Stud. Child Welf.*, XVIII (1941), 1–314.

18. Bateson, G. "The Frustration-Aggression Hypothesis and Culture," *Psychol. Rev.*, XLVIII (1941), 350–55.
19. ———. *The Naven.* Stanford: Stanford University Press, 1936.
20. Berkowitz, L. *Aggression: A Social Psychological Analysis.* New York: McGraw-Hill Book Co., Inc., 1962.
21. ———. "Anti-Semitism and the Displacement of Aggression," *J. Abnorm. Soc. Psychol.*, LIX (1959), 182–87.
22. ———. "The Expression and Reduction of Hostility," *Psychol. Bull.*, LV (1958), 257–83.
23. ———. "Some Factors Affecting the Reduction of Hostility," *J. Abnorm. Soc. Psychol.*, LX (1960), 14–21.
24. Binder, A.; McConnell, D.; and Sjoholm, Nancy A. "Verbal Conditioning as a Function of Experimenter Characteristics," *J. Abnorm. Soc. Psychol.*, LV (1957), 309–14.
25. Bindra, D. *Motivation: A Systematic Reinterpretation.* New York: Ronald Press, 1959.
26. Block, Jeanne, and Martin, B. "Predicting the Behavior of Children under Frustration," *J. Abnorm. Soc. Psychol.*, LI (1955), 281–85.
27. Breuer, J., and Freud, S. "Studies on Hysteria," in *Standard Edition of Freud's Complete Psychological Works*, Vol. II. (Translated from German under general editorship of James Strachey.) London: Hogarth Press, 1955. (First German edition, 1895).
28. Brown, J. S. "Gradients of Approach and Avoidance Responses and Their Relation to Level of Motivation," *J. Comp. Physiol. Psychol.*, XLI (1948), 450–65.
29. ———. *The Motivation of Behavior.* New York: McGraw-Hill Book Co., Inc., 1961.
30. Brown, J. S., and Farber, I. E., "Emotions Conceptualized as Intervening Variables with Suggestions toward a Theory of Frustration," *Psychol. Bull.*, XLVIII (1951), 465–95.
31. Buss, A. H. *The Psychology of Aggression.* New York: John Wiley & Sons, 1961.
32. Buss, A. H., and Durkee, Ann. "Conditioning of Hostile Verbalizations in a Situation Resembling a Clinical Interview," *J. Consult. Psychol.*, XXII (1958), 415–18.
33. ———. "An Inventory for Assessing Different Kinds of Hostility," *J. Consult. Psychol.*, XXI (1957), 343–48.
34. Bywater, I. (Trans.) *Aristotle's "On the Art of Poetry."* Oxford: Clarendon Press, 1920.
35. Caron, A. J., and Gewirtz, J. L. "An Investigation of the Effects of Sex Category of the Interacting Adult, Chronological Age (6, 8, and 10), and Sex of Doll on Aggressive (Hostile) Behavior in Doll Play," *Amer. Psychologist*, VI (1951), 307 (abstract).
36. Cohen, A. K. *Delinquent Boys: The Culture of the Gang.* Glencoe, Illinois: Free Press, 1955.
37. Cowan, P. A., and Walters, R. H. "Studies of Reinforcement of Aggression: I. Effects of Scheduling," *Child Developm.* (1963), in press.
38. Cowen, E. L.; Landes, J.; and Schaet, O. E. "The Effects of Mild Frustra-

tion on the Expression of Prejudiced Attitudes," *J. Abnorm. Soc. Psychol.*, LVIII (1959), 33–38.

39. Davis, A. "Child Training and Social Class," in *Child Behavior and Development.* Edited by R. G. Barker, J. Kounin, and H. F. Wright. New York: McGraw-Hill Book Co., Inc., 1943.
40. Davis, A., and Havighurst, R. J. *The Father of the Man.* Boston: Houghton Mifflin Co., 1947.
41. Davitz, J. L. "The Effects of Previous Training on Postfrustration Behavior," *J. Abnorm. Soc. Psychol.*, XLVII (1952), 309–15.
42. Dollard, J.; Doob, L. W.; Miller, N. E.; Mowrer, O. H.; and Sears, R. R. *Frustration and Aggression.* New Haven, Connecticut: Yale University Press, 1939.
43. ———. *Frustration and Aggression.* London: Kegan Paul, 1944.
44. Dollard, J., and Miller, N. E. *Personality and Psychotherapy.* New York: McGraw-Hill Book Co., Inc., 1950.
45. Eaton, J. W., and Weil, R. J. *Culture and Mental Disorders.* Glencoe, Illinois: Free Press, 1955.
46. Estes, W. K. "An Experimental Study of Punishment," *Psychol. Monogr.* LVII (1944), No. 3 (Whole No. 363).
47. Fenichel, O. *The Psychoanalytic Theory of Neurosis.* New York: W. W. Norton & Co., 1945.
48. Feshbach, S. "The Cartharsis Hypothesis and Some Consequences of Interaction with Aggressive and Neutral Play Objects," *J. Pers.*, XXIV (1956), 449–62.
49. ———. "The Drive-reducing Function of Fantasy Behavior," *J. Abnorm. Soc. Psychol.*, L (1955), 3–11.
50. ———. "The Stimulating *versus* Cathartic Effects of a Vicarious Aggressive Activity," *J. Abnorm. Soc. Psychol.*, LXIII (1961), 381–85.
51. Festinger, L. "The Psychological Effects of Insufficient Rewards," *Amer. Psychologist*, XVI (1961), 1–11.
52. Freud, Anna. *The Ego and the Mechanisms of Defense.* New York: International Universities Press, 1946.
53. Freud, S. "On the History of the Psycho-analytic Movement," in *Collected Papers,* Vol. I. Edited by E. Jones. London: Hogarth Press, 1956. (First published in the *Jahrbuch der Psychoanalyse*, Bd. VI, 1914.)
54. ———. *Inhibitions, Symptoms, and Anxiety.* London: Hogarth Press, 1936. (First German edition, 1926.)
55. ———. "Mourning and Melancholia," in *Collected Papers,* Vol. IV. Edited by E. Jones. London: Hogarth Press, 1956. (First published in *Zeitschrift*, Bd. IV, 1917).
56. ———. "A Note on the Prehistory of the Technique of Analysis," in *Collected Papers,* Vol. V. Edited by E. Jones. London: Hogarth Press, 1956. (First published in *Int. Z. Psychoanal.*, Bd. VI, 1920.)
57. Gelfand, Donna. "The Influence of Response-defined and Experimentally Manipulated Self-esteem on Children's Responsiveness to Social Influence." Unpublished Doctor's dissertation, Stanford University, 1961.
58. Gewirtz, J. L., and Baer, D. M. "Deprivation and Satiation as Drive Conditions," *J. Abnorm. Soc. Psychol.*, LVII (1958), 165–72.
59. ———. "The Effects of Brief Social Deprivation on Behaviors for a Social Reinforcer," *J. Abnorm. Soc. Psychol.*, LVI (1958), 49–56.

60. Glueck, S., and Glueck, Eleanor. *Unraveling Juvenile Delinquency.* Cambridge: Harvard University Press, 1950.

61. Goldman, Jeri R. "The Relation of Certain Therapist Variables to the Handling of Psychotherapeutic Events." Unpublished Doctor's dissertation, Stanford University, 1961.

62. Goodenough, Florence L. *Anger in Young Children.* Inst. Child Welf. Monogr. Ser., No. 9. Minneapolis: University of Minnesota Press, 1931.

63. Hall, J. F. *Psychology of Motivation.* Chicago: J. B. Lippincott Co., 1961.

64. Haner, C. F., and Brown, Patricia A. "Clarification of the Instigation to Action Concept in the Frustration-Aggression Hypothesis," *J. Abnorm. Soc. Psychol.*, LI (1955), 204–6.

65. Hartup, W. W., and Himeno, Yayoi. "Social Isolation *vs.* Interaction with Adults in Relation to Aggression in Preschool Children," *J. Abnorm. Soc. Psychol.*, LIX (1959), 17–22.

66. Hinsey, C.; Patterson, G. R.; and Sonoda, Beverly. "Validation of a Procedure for Conditioning Aggression in Children." Unpublished manuscript, University of Oregon, 1961.

67. Hollenberg, Eleanor, and Sperry, Margaret. "Some Antecedents of Aggression and Effects of Frustration in Doll Play," *Personality*, I (1951), 32–43.

68. Holton, Ruth B. "Amplitude of an Instrumental Response Following the Withholding of Reward," *Child Developm.*, XXXII (1961), 107–16.

69. Hovland, C. I., and Sears, R. R. "Minor Studies of Aggression: IV. Correlation of Lynchings with Economic Indices," *J. Psychol.*, IX (1940), 301–10.

70. Hull, C. L. *Principles of Behavior.* New York: Appleton-Century-Crofts, 1943.

71. Jegard, Suzanne F., and Walters, R. H. "A Study of Some Determinants of Aggression in Young Children," *Child Develpm.*, XXXI (1960), 739–48.

72. Jenkins, R. L., and Hewitt, L. E. "Types of Personality Structure Encountered in Child Guidance Clinics," *Amer. J. Orthopsychiat.*, XIV (1944), 89–95.

73. Jensen, A. R. "Aggression in Fantasy and Overt Behavior," *Psychol. Monogr.*, LXXI (1957), Whole No. 445.

74. Johnson, Adelaide M., and Szurek, S. A. "The Genesis of Antisocial Acting Out in Children and Adults," *Psychoanal. Quar.*, XXI (1952), 323–43.

75. Johnson, Elizabeth Z. "Attitudes of Children toward Authority as Projected in Their Doll Play at Two Age Levels." Unpublished Doctor's dissertation, Harvard University, 1951.

76. Kagan, J. "The Measurement of Overt Aggression from Fantasy," *J. Abnorm. Soc. Psychol.*, LII (1956), 390–93.

77. ———. "The Stability of *TAT* Fantasy and Stimulus Ambiguity," *J. Consult. Psychol.*, XXIII (1959), 266–71.

78. Kanareff, Vera T., and Lanzetta, J. T. "The Acquisition of Imitative and Opposition Responses under Two Conditions of Instruction-induced Set," *J. Exp. Psychol.*, LVI (1958), 516–28.

79. Kaufman, E. L., and Miller, N. E. "Effect of Number of Reinforcements

on Strength of Approach in an Approach-avoidance Conflict," *J. Comp. Physiol. Psychol.*, XLII (1949), 65–74.

80. KENNY, D. T. "An Experimental Test of the Catharsis Theory of Aggression." Unpublished Doctor's dissertation, University of Washington, 1952.
81. KINSEY, A. C.; POMEROY, W. B.; and MARTIN, C. E. *Sexual Behavior in the Human Male.* Philadelphia: W. B. Saunders & Co., 1948.
82. KORNER, ANNELIESE F. *Some Aspects of Hostility in Young Children.* New York: Grune & Stratton, 1949.
83. KRALL, VITA. "Personality Factors in Accident-prone and Accident-free Children." Unpublished Doctor's dissertation, University of Rochester, 1951.
84. LANZETTA, J. T., and KANAREFF, VERA T. "The Effects of a Monetary Reward on the Acquisition of an Imitative Response," *J. Abnorm. Soc. Psychol.*, LIX (1959), 120–27.
85. LAWSON, R., and MARX, M. H. "Frustration: Theory and Experiment," *Genet. Psychol. Monogr.*, LVII (1958), 393–464.
86. LAZARSFELD, M., and ZEISL, H. "Die Arbeitslosen von Marienthal," *Psychol. Monographen,* V (1933), 1–123.
87. LESSER, G. S. "The Relationship between Overt and Fantasy Aggression as a Function of Maternal Response to Aggression," *J. Abnorm. Soc. Psychol.*, LV (1957), 218–21.
88. LEVIN, H., and SEARS, R. R. "Identification with Parents as a Determinant of Doll-play Aggression," *Child Develpm.*, XXVII (1956), 135–53.
89. LEVIN, H., and TURGEON, VALERIE. "The Influence of the Mother's Pressures on Children's Doll-play Aggression," *J. Abnorm. Soc. Psychol.*, LV (1957), 304–8.
90. LEVY, D. M. *Maternal Overprotection.* New York: Columbia University Press, 1943.
91. LEWIN, K.; LIPPITT, R.; and WHITE, R. K. "Patterns of Aggressive Behavior in Experimentally Created 'Social Climates,'" *J. Soc. Psychol.*, X (1939), 271–99.
92. LINDZEY, G. "An Experimental Investigation of the Scapegoat Theory of Prejudice," *J. Abnorm. Soc. Psychol.*, XLV (1950), 296–309.
93. LIPPITT, R. "An Experimental Study of the Effect of Democratic and Authoritarian Group Atmospheres," *Univ. Iowa Stud. Child Welf.*, XVI (1939), 43–195.
94. LIPSITT, L. P., and CASTANEDA, A. "Effects of Delayed Reward on Choice Behavior and Response Speeds in Children," *J. Comp. Physiol. Psychol.*, LI (1958), 65–67.
95. LIPSITT, L. P.; CASTANEDA, A.; and KEMBLE, J. D. "Effects of Delayed Reward Pretraining on Discrimination Learning in Children," *Child Developm.*, XXX (1959), 273–78.
96. LONGSTRETH, L. E. "The Relationship between Expectations and Frustration in Children." *Child Develpm.*, XXXI (1960), 667–71.
97. LÖVAAS, O. I. "Effect of Exposure to Symbolic Aggression on Aggressive Behavior," *Child Develpm.*, XXXII (1961), 37–44.
98. ———. "Interaction between Verbal and Nonverbal Behavior," *Child Develpm.*, XXXII (1961), 329–36.

99. McClelland, D. C. *Personality*. New York: William Sloane Assoc., 1951.
100. McCord, Joan, and McCord, W. "The Effects of Parental Role Models on Criminality," *J. Soc. Issues,* XIV (1958), 66–75.
101. Marx, M. H. "Some Relations between Frustration and Drive," in *Nebraska Symposium on Motivation.* Edited by M. R. Jones. Lincoln, Nebraska: University of Nebraska Press, 1956.
102. Maslow, A. H. "Deprivation, Threat, and Frustration," *Psychol. Rev.*, XLVIII (1941), 364–66.
103. Mausner, B. "The Effect of Prior Reinforcement on the Interaction of Observer Pairs," *J. Abnorm. Soc. Psychol.*, XLIX (1954), 65–68.
104. Miller, N. E. "The Frustration-Aggression Hypothesis," *Psychol. Rev.*, XLVIII (1941), 337–42.
105. ———. "Liberalization of Basic S-R Concepts: Extension to Conflict Behavior, Motivation, and Social Learning," in *Psychology: A Study of a Science,* Vol. II. Edited by S. Koch. New York: McGraw-Hill Book Co., Inc., 1959.
106. ———. "Theory and Experiment Relating Psychoanalytic Displacement to Stimulus-Response Generalization," *J. Abnorm. Soc. Psychol.*, XLIII (1948), 155–78.
107. Miller, N. E., and Bugelski, R. "Minor Studies of Aggression: II. The Influence of Frustrations by the In-group on Attitudes Expressed toward Out-groups," *J. Psychol.*, XXV (1948), 437–42.
108. Miller, N. E., and Kraeling, Doris. "Displacement: Greater Generalization of Approach than Avoidance in a Generalized Approach-avoidance Conflict," *J. Exp. Psychol.*, XLIII (1952), 217–21.
109. Miller, N. E., and Murray, E. J. "Displacement and Conflict: Learnable Drive as a Basis for the Steeper Gradient of Avoidance than of Approach," *J. Exp. Psychol.*, LIII (1952), 227–31.
110. Miller, N. E., and Stevenson, S. S. "Agitated Behavior of Rats during Experimental Extinction and a Curve of Spontaneous Recovery," *J. Comp. Psychol.*, XXI (1936), 205–31.
111. Mowrer, O. H., "An Experimental Analogue of 'Regression' with Incidental Observations on 'Reaction Formation,'" *J. Abnorm. Soc. Psychol.*, XXXV (1940), 56–87.
112. ———. *Learning Theory and Behavior.* New York: John Wiley & Sons, 1960.
113. ———. *Learning Theory and Personality Dynamics.* New York: Ronald Press, 1950.
114. ———. *Learning Theory and the Symbolic Processes.* New York: John Wiley & Sons, 1960.
115. Murray, E. J., and Berkun, M. M. "Displacement as a Function of Conflict," *J. Abnorm. Soc. Psychol.*, LI (1955), 47–56.
116. Mussen, P. H., and Naylor, H. K. "The Relationships between Overt and Fantasy Aggression," *J. Abnorm. Soc. Psychol.*, XLIX (1954), 235–40.
117. Mussen, P. H., and Rutherford, E. "Effects of Aggressive Cartoons on Children's Aggressive Play," *J. Abnorm. Soc. Psychol.*, LXII (1961), 461–65.
118. Muste, M. J., and Sharp, D. F. "Some Influential Factors in the Determination of Aggressive Behavior in Preschool Children," *Child Develpm.*, XVIII (1947), 11–28.

119. OLDS, J. *The Growth and Structure of Motives.* Glencoe, Illinois: Free Press, 1956.
120. ———. "The Influence of Practice on the Strength of Approach Drives," *J. Exp. Psychol.*, XLVI (1953), 232–36.
121. OTIS, NANCY B., and MCCANDLESS, B. "Responses to Repeated Frustrations of Young Children Differentiated According to Need Area," *J. Abnorm. Soc. Psychol.*, L (1955), 349–53.
122. PASTORE, N. "The Role of Arbitrariness in the Frustration-Aggression Hypothesis," *J. Abnorm. Soc. Psychol.*, XLVII (1952), 728–31.
123. PATTERSON, G. R. "A Nonverbal Technique for the Assessment of Aggression in Children," *Child Develpm.*, XXXI (1960), 643–53.
124. PATTERSON, G. R.; LUDWIG, M.; and SONODA, BEVERLY, "Reinforcement of Aggression in Children." Unpublished manuscript, University of Oregon, 1961.
125. PENNEY, R. K. "The Effects of Nonreinforcement of Response Strength as a Function of Number of Previous Reinforcements," *Canad. J. Psychol.*, XIV (1960), 206–15.
126. PHILLIPS, RUTH. "Doll Play as a Function of the Realism of the Materials and the Length of the Experimental Session," *Child Develpm.*, XVI (1945), 123–43.
127. PINTLER, MARGARET H. "Doll Play as a Function of Experimenter-Child Interaction and Initial Organization of Materials," *Child Develpm.*, XVI (1945), 145–66.
128. POWERS, E., and WITMER, HELEN. *An Experiment in the Prevention of Delinquency.* New York: Columbia University Press, 1951.
129. RADKE-YARROW, MARION; TRAGER, HELEN G.; and MILLER, JEAN. "The Role of Parents in the Development of Children's Ethnic Attitudes," *Child Develpm.*, XXIII (1952), 13–54.
130. ROBINSON, ELIZABETH F. "Doll Play as a Function of the Doll Family Constellation," *Child Develpm.*, XVII (1946), 99–119.
131. ROKEACH, M. *The Open and the Closed Mind.* New York: Basic Books, 1960.
132. ROSENBAUM, M. E., and DE CHARMS, R. "Direct and Vicarious Reduction of Hostility," *J. Abnorm. Soc. Psychol.*, LX (1960), 105–11.
133. ROSENBAUM, M. E., and TUCKER, I. F. "The Competence of the Model and the Learning of Imitation and Nonimitation," *J. Exp. Psychol.*, LXIII (1962), 183–90.
134. ROSENZWEIG, S. "An Outline of Frustration Theory," in *Personality and the Behavior Disorders.* Edited by J. McV. Hunt. New York: Ronald Press, 1944.
135. SCHACHTER, S. "Deviation, Rejection, and Communication," *J. Abnorm. Soc. Psychol.*, XLVI (1951), 190–207.
136. SCHACHTER, S., and SINGER, J. E. "Cognitive, Social, and Physiological Determinants of Emotional State," *Psychol. Rev.*, LXIX (1962), 379–99.
137. SCHACHTER, S., and WHEELER, L. "Epinephrine, Chlorpromazine, and Amusement," *J. Abnorm. Soc. Psychol.*, LXV (1962), 121–28.
138. SCREVEN, C. G. "The Effects of Interference on Response Strength," *J. Comp. Physiol. Psychol.*, XLVII (1954), 140–44.
139. SEARS, PAULINE S. "Doll-play Aggression in Normal Young Children: Influ-

ence of Sex, Age, Sibling Status, Father's Absence," *Psychol. Monogr.*, LXV (1951), No. 6 (Whole No. 323).

140. SEARS, PAULINE S., and STAFF OF THE LABORATORY OF HUMAN DEVELOPMENT, HARVARD UNIVERSITY. "Child-rearing Factors Related to Playing of Sex-typed Roles." *Amer. Psychologist*, VIII (1953), 431.

141. SEARS, R. R. "Nonaggressive Reactions to Frustration," *Psychol. Rev.*, XLVIII (1941), 343–46.

142. ———. "Relation of Early Socialization Experiences to Aggression in Middle Childhood," *J. Abnorm. Soc. Psychol.*, LXIII (1961), 466–92.

143. ———. "Relation of Fantasy Aggression to Interpersonal Aggression," *Child Develpm.*, XXI (1950), 5–6.

144. ———. "Social Behavior and Personality Development," in *Toward a General Theory of Action.* Edited by T. Parsons and E. A. Shils. Cambridge: Harvard University Press, 1951.

145. SEARS, R. R.; MACCOBY, ELEANOR E.; and LEVIN, H. *Patterns of Child Rearing.* Evanston, Illinois: Row, Peterson & Co., 1957.

146. SEARS, R. R.; WHITING, J. W. M.; NOWLIS, V.; and SEARS, PAULINE S. "Some Child-rearing Antecedents of Aggression and Dependency in Young Children," *Genet. Psychol. Monogr.*, XLVII (1953), 135–234.

147. SEASHORE, H. E., and BAVELAS, A. "A Study of Frustration in Children," *J. Genet. Psychol.*, LXI (1942), 279–314.

148. SHAW, C. R., and MCKAY, H. *Juvenile Delinquency and Urban Areas.* Chicago: University of Chicago Press, 1942.

149. SIEGEL, ALBERTA E. "Film-mediated Fantasy Aggression and Strength of Aggressive Drive," *Child Develpm.*, XXVII (1956), 365–78.

150. SIEGEL, ALBERTA E., and KOHN, LYNNETT G. "Permissiveness, Permission, and Aggression: The Effect of Adult Presence or Absence on Aggression in Children's Play," *Child Develpm.*, XXX (1959), 131–41.

151. SIMKINS, L. "Effects of Examiner Attitudes and Type of Reinforcement on the Conditioning of Hostile Verbs," *J. Pers.*, XXIX (1961), 380–95.

152. SKINNER, B. F. *Science and Human Behavior.* New York: Macmillan Co., 1953.

153. STAGNER, R., and CONGDON, C. S. "Another Failure to Demonstrate Displacement of Aggression," *J. Abnorm. Soc. Psychol.*, LI (1955), 695–96.

154. STOLZ, LOIS MEEK, and COLLABORATORS. *Father Relations of War-born Children.* Stanford: Stanford University Press, 1954.

155. THIBAUT, J. H., and COULES, J. "The Role of Communication in the Reduction of Interpersonal Hostility," *J. Abnorm. Soc. Psychol.*, XLVII (1952), 770–78.

156. UPDEGRAFF, RUTH L., and KEISTER, MARY E. "A Study of Children's Reactions to Failure and an Experimental Attempt to Modify Them," *Child Develpm.*, VIII (1937), 241–48.

157. WALTERS, J. C.; PEARCE, DORIS; and DAHMS, LUCILLE. "Affectional and Aggressive Behavior of Preschool Children," *Child Develpm.*, XXVIII (1957), 15–26.

158. WALTERS, R. H., and BROWN, M. "Studies of Reinforcement of Aggression: III, Transfer of Responses to an Interpersonal Situation," *Child Develpm.* (1963), in press.

159. WALTERS, R. H., and DEMKOW, LILLIAN F. "Timing of Punishment as a Determinant of Response Inhibition," *Child Develpm.* (1962) in press.
160. WALTERS, R. H.; LEAT, MARIAN; and MEZEI, L. "Inhibition and Disinhibition of Responses through Empathetic Learning." *Canad. J. Psychol.* (1963), in press.
161. WALTERS, R. H., and LLEWELLYN THOMAS, E. "Enhancement of Punitive Behavior by Visual and Audio-visual Displays." Unpublished manuscript, Ontario Hospital, New Toronto, 1962.
162. WALTERS, R. H.; LLEWELLYN THOMAS, E.; and ACKER, C. W. "Enhancement of Punitive Behavior by Audio-visual Displays," *Science*, CXXXVI (1962), 872–73.
163. WALTERS, R. H., and RAY, E. "Anxiety, Social Isolation, and Reinforcer Effectiveness," *J. Pers.*, XXVIII (1960), 358–67.
164. WEATHERLEY, D. "Anti-Semitism and the Expression of Fantasy Aggression," *J. Abnorm. Soc. Psychol.*, LXII (1961), 454–57.
165. WHITE, R. K., and LIPPITT, R. *Autocracy and Democracy: An Experimental Inquiry*. New York: Harper & Bros., 1960.
166. WHITING, J. W. M. *Becoming a Kwoma*. New Haven, Connecticut: Yale University Press, 1941.
167. ———. "The Frustration Complex in Kwoma Society," *Man*, XLIV (1944), 140–44.
168. WHITING, J. W. M., and CHILD, I. L. *Child Training and Personality*. New Haven, Connecticut: Yale University Press, 1953.
169. WHYTE, W. F. *Street-corner Society*. Chicago: University of Chicago Press, 1943.
170. WRIGHT, G. O. "Projection and Displacement: A Cross-cultural Study of Folk-tale Aggression," *J. Abnorm. Soc. Psychol.*, XLIX (1954), 523–28.
171. WRIGHT, M. E. "Constructiveness of Play as Affected by Group Organization and Frustration," *Char. and Pers.*, XI (1942), 40–49.
172. ———. "The Influence of Frustration upon the Social Relations of Young Children," *Char. and Pers.* XII (1943), 111–12.
173. YARROW, L. J. "The Effects of Antecedent Frustration on Projective Play," *Psychol. Monogr.*, LXII (1948), No. 6 (Whole No. 293).
174. ZEDEK, MEIRA E. "The Conditioning of Verbal Behavior with Negative Cultural Connotations," *J. Pers.*, XXVII (1959), 477–86.

CHAPTER X

Achievement

VAUGHN J. CRANDALL

General Introduction[1]

The desire to perform competently in achievement situations is a basic and pervasive motive in human experience. The ubiquity of this need is evident, not only in the towering intellectual products of a Spinoza or an Einstein, but also in the first faltering efforts of a toddler to walk unaided or of a preschool child to print his own name. To most humans—philosopher or carpenter, child or adult—the attainment of desired achievement goals, and the attendant approval (whether from self or others) accruing to such attainments, are important sources of personal satisfaction and security. This chapter summarizes research concerned with factors influencing the development of children's achievement propensities and actions, and the role children's achievement motivations play in determining their achievement performances.

The Conceptualization of Achievement

CURRENT DEFINITIONS OF ACHIEVEMENT

Whenever a person observes a child's behavior and subsequently labels the child as aggressive, dependent, or achievement-oriented, that observer invariably assumes that the behaviors or referents on which he based his judgment are those which other persons would also agree upon as "aggressive," "dependent," or "achievement-oriented." Yet this assumption may often be an erroneous one. The same behaviors of a child may lead to quite different labels or abstractions from various observers. For example, the behavior of a

1. The writer of this chapter would like to express appreciation for assistance in the preparation of the chapter to the following members of his staff: Barbara Abrams, Virginia Crandall, Sue Good, Jean Lindholm, Carol Sinkeldam, Nancy Teepen, Elinor Waters, Margaret Wilson, and Shelley Wing. The work was partially supported by USPH Grant M-2238.

child who disrupts a class in school may be regarded by the teacher as "aggressive behavior," while it may be categorized by the school psychologist as a "dependent behavior employing a negative attention-getting device," and later described by the child's parents as an expression of a simple need to dissipate unexpended physical energy. The problem of categorizing social behaviors is especially important for psychologists. Unless some set of behaviors can be agreed upon as being motivated by the same need, the research findings of one study can have little potential comparability with those of a second.

Two of the definitions employed by current achievement researchers follow. One defines achievement motivation; the other, achievement behavior. Both attempt to distinguish achievement from other need or behavioral systems.

McClelland, the originator of achievement-motivation research, provides the following discussion of what he considers the unique characteristics of achievement motivation.

> Now what about achievement? What . . . expectations distinguish this motive from others? Clearly the expectations are built out of universal experiences with problem solving—with learning to walk, talk, hunt or read, write, sew, perform chores, and so forth. The expectations also involve standards of excellence with respect to such tasks. The tasks can be done quickly and efficiently or clumsily and slowly. . . . The child must begin to *perceive performance in terms of standards of excellence* so that discrepancies of various sorts from this perceptual frame of reference . . . can produce positive or negative affect. The surest sign of such a frame of reference is *evaluation* of a performance . . . e.g., "the boy has done a *good* job." . . . What then becomes crucial . . . for achievement motivation is detecting *affect in connection with evaluation* (**82**).

More recently, the writer and his associates reported their views of achievement *behavior* in a symposium on research in child development as follows:

> In our research, three criteria were decided on which, in combination, seemed to distinguish achievement behaviors from other goal-directed behaviors. These criteria were: (*a*) the inferred goal of the behavior, (*b*) the unique characteristic of the behavior involved which might be reinforced, and (*c*) the nature of the situations in which that behavior occurred. The goal of achievement behavior was, as we saw it, the *attainment of approval and the avoidance of disapproval.* Such approval or disapproval could be internal or could come from other persons. But

nevertheless, achievement behavior is directed toward a distinct kind of reinforcement, i.e., approval or disapproval, or symbols representing these. Such approval can be verbal, or expressed symbolically by prizes or rewards. And similarly, disapproval can take the form of direct verbal criticism or be expressed through indirect means such as the withdrawal of privileges or the withholding of prizes. The second defining characteristic of achievement behavior was, we thought, the unique attribute of the behavior itself which elicits the approval or disapproval, i.e., *competence of performance.* Finally, the major requisite of achievement situations, it seemed, was that they entailed tasks or activities in which the individual applies some *standard of excellence* to the competence of his behavior. This analysis suggested the following definition of achievement behavior: Achievement behavior is any behavior directed toward the attainment of approval or the avoidance of disapproval (the goal) for competence of performance (characteristic of the behavior reinforced) in situations where standards of excellence are applied (nature of the situation) (**22**).

It was concluded that all three criteria must be met before a designation of "achievement behavior" was appropriate.

Both of the above positions reflect and illustrate several basic commonalities found in most current definitions of achievement. For example, most definitions agree that the kinds of situations which characteristically evoke achievement motivation, and in which achievement behaviors will ensue, are those in which competence of performance is the focal issue. The aim of achievement behavior, in contradistinction to those of other behavioral systems such as aggression, dependency, and the like, is to obtain positive reinforcement for demonstrated competence. This suggests, also, that when the kinds of situations pertaining to achievement are delineated from other social situations, achievement situations invariably contain cues pertaining to some "standard of excellence" which will define degrees of competence or incompetence.

OTHER CONCEPTS OVERLAPPING THE ACHIEVEMENT CONCEPT

Achievement behaviors may be also subsumed under a different rubric, however, by other investigators. Current examples of this include such concepts as curiosity, creativity, originality, competence motivation, the exploratory drive, and the recently formulated neo-Freudian construct of "the instinct to master." Limitations of space make it impossible to present an extensive discussion of these concepts and their relation to current conceptualizations of achievement. The reader who is especially interested in this problem will find the recent review articles by Maltzman (**85**) and by White (**121**) both comprehensive and provocative.

THE STATUS ACCORDED NEED ACHIEVEMENT IN PERSONALITY THEORIES

As far as child psychology is concerned, the personality theory which undoubtedly has had the most insistent and pervasive influence has been classical psychoanalytic theory. The importance which this theory places on the socialization of id impulses has been especially influential in generating research concerned with dependency, aggression, and identification (cf. chaps. vii, viii, and ix). As a result, few researchers in child psychology have, until very recently, focused their attentions and efforts on such ego functions as achievement motivation.

Alfred Adler, however, has suggested that the gratification of achievement needs may be one of the most important goals of human behavior. His concepts of "inferiority complex," "masculine protest," and "striving for superiority" all point to achievement accomplishments as basic and necessary for feelings of satisfaction and security in human experience (**1**). Kurt Lewin (**75, 76**) has also emphasized the importance of achievement motivation in human experience, although his conceptualizations grew out of Gestalt psychology rather than psychoanalytic theory. He and his students were the first to investigate experimentally the properties of human achievement aspirations and behaviors. Lewin was one of the first psychologists to study systematically the "upward striving" nature of human achievement aspirations and behaviors. Lewin noted that successful goal attainment by humans often produces renewed and increased, rather than decreased, goal striving. Recent research has indicated that such may be the case in children's achievement behavior, and these findings will be discussed in a later section. Another contribution of Lewin was his "level of aspiration" paradigm (**77**). This methodological orientation acknowledged the influence of cognitive functions such as anticipations, expectations, and standards on achievement behavior. The most recent personality theorist, aside from McClelland, to accord a central role to achievement motivation in human experience is Rotter. In his social learning theory of personality (**100**) he, like Lewin, emphasizes the upward striving nature of achievement behavior, as well as the importance and utility of studying anticipatory cognitive "expectancies" as these enter into, and determine, achievement propensities.

The Measurement of Achievement Motivation

Most measures of achievement motivation can be assigned to two broad classes of assessment techniques, projective methods and subjective report measures. Examples of each of these will be briefly described, and the comparability of data resulting from these methods of assessment will be discussed.

PROJECTIVE TECHNIQUES

Four projective techniques have been employed in most studies of achievement motivation: the *Thematic Apperception Test* (*TAT*) or *TAT*-like stimuli, the *French Test of Insight*, the incomplete stories method, and experimental doll-play situations. By far, the projective technique which has been most often used in achievement motivation research is that originally devised by McClelland *et al.*—or some minor variation thereof—in which *TAT*-like stimuli are presented to the subjects (Ss). The stories which Ss tell about these pictures are scored in respect to a large number of empirically-validated indices of achievement motivation. These include, among others, the number of occasions when the S's stories contain a major achievement theme, the S's willingness to impute achievement motivation to the central characters of his stories, and the frequency with which he describes instrumental achievement acts, tools, goals, and the like in his stories (see chapter iv in *The Achievement Motive*, **82**). A second projective technique, the *French Test of Insight* (**42**), presents the S with a number of verbal statements regarding the actions of hypothetical persons. The S is then required to give the most likely reason, in his estimation, why a person might do what the hypothetical person has done. A third projective assessment method is the incomplete-stories technique. An example of its utility can be found in Winterbottom's investigation of the relations between independence training and children's need for achievement (*n* achievement) which will be discussed later (**122**). A fourth projective method is the doll-play technique. Here the experimenter gives the child dolls representing various persons in his daily life (e.g., himself, his siblings, peers, parents, teachers). Then a situation is described to the child, which he uses as the "springboard" for his doll-play drama. Observers rate relevant behavioral indices for whatever motivational system is under consideration.

SUBJECTIVE REPORT MEASURES

Subjective, as well as projective, measures of *n* achievement have been used in achievement motivation research. Standard questionnaires containing subscales which pertain to achievement include the Edwards' *Personal Preference Scale* (*PPS*) (**37**) and the *California Psychological Inventory* (*CPI*) (**50**). Both have been found useful for research on achievement with adults, college students, and adolescents, but neither has been adapted for use with children under twelve years of age.

RELATIONS BETWEEN PROJECTIVE AND SUBJECTIVE RESPONSES

Several recent studies have evaluated relations between *n* achievement as reflected in projective-test responses and similar preoccupations as assessed by questionnaire methods. With one exception, in which a small but significant positive correlation was found (**32**), relations between data obtained with these two kinds of assessments of achievement motivation have been negligible (e.g., **7, 38, 80, 86**). Projective and subjective assessments of achievement propensities are apparently measuring somewhat different components of achievement. However, too few studies have been done to date to clearly ascertain either the relative or combined predictive utility of these two kinds of assessment.

The remainder of this chapter will cover the substantive findings of studies concerned with antecedents of, and relations between, children's achievement motivation and their achievement behaviors. A notational system will be used to designate the sample employed and assessment procedures used in each study. Regarding sample designation, the following symbols will be employed: nursery-school-age children from three through five years of age (NS), elementary-school-age children from six through eleven years of age (ES), and adolescents twelve through eighteen years of age (A).

On some occasions research using college students (designated C) will be included when these studies are concerned with important issues in achievement research not yet studied in children. When both boys and girls are subjects of a study, no symbol will be used; otherwise, "boys only" or "girls only" will follow the age designation. The assessment-technique designation will then follow the sample designation. For example, a total designation (ES-boys only, *TAT*) would indicate that, in this particular study, *TAT* stimuli were presented to elementary-school-age boys.

Antecedents of Achievement Motivation and Behavior

Three classes of antecedent factors influencing achievement will be discussed. These include cultural and social factors, parental influences, and school experiences.

CULTURAL AND SOCIAL FACTORS

At least three broad cultural and social influences have been found to affect the development of children's achievement motivations and behaviors. These are the general cultural milieu (e.g., competitive *vs.* less competitive societies) into which a child is born; his racial, religious and ethnic background; and the socioeconomic class to which his family belongs.

Several comparative studies have evaluated the achievement orientations of preliterate and semiliterate cultures. Usually, these investigations have correlated a culture's prevailing attitudes toward achievement, as revealed in its folktales, with its characteristic child-rearing practices, at least those presumed to be relevant to children's achievement development. The folktales are analyzed for *n* achievement in a fashion similar to that employed in analyzing the *n* achievement of individuals in their projective test responses. In one of the earliest studies of this kind, McClelland and Friedman (**83**) examined one folktale common to several North American Indian tribes and found that the *n* achievement in the tribes' tales was significantly related to both the earliness with which the independence training of children was initiated and the strength of the positive and negative sanctions which were used to bring this about. Tribes whose folktales indicated strong *n* achievement initiated independence training earlier, and both rewarded self-reliant activities and punished the lack of such efforts to a greater degree than did those tribes who were less concerned with achievement. On the other hand, a more recent study by Child, Storm, and Veroff, comparing 46 preliterate cultures throughout the world, found few significant associations between cultural *n* achievement as evidenced in common folktales and the cultures' prevailing child-rearing practices (**14**).

In both the forementioned studies, no distinction was made between the training of boys and of girls in the various cultures studied. However, one large-scale investigation (**5**) using the Yale Cross-Cultural Survey Files to compare child-rearing practices in several societies, found that boys received more achievement training in most of these cultures, while girls were given more obedience and responsibility training. This finding is congruent with those of several investigations of child-rearing within the United States, such as that by Sears, Maccoby, and Levin (**104**). These latter studies have consistently found that achievement is more often stressed in the training of American boys than in that of American girls.

Within a given culture or society, certain subcultural and social influences are also operative on children's achievement development. In the United States, for example, both children's achievement motivations and their achievement performances have been found to be significantly associated with their racial, religious, and ethnic backgrounds. Two recent sociological studies are relevant. Strodtbeck compared third-generation Italian and Jewish adolescent boys and their parents (**110**). It was found that Jewish parents (parents, questionnaire) usually held higher occupational and educational aspirations for their sons than did Italian parents. They also expressed greater preferences for individual rather than collective credit for work done, and more often espoused the belief that an individual can and should make specific plans to control his own future. In spite of the differences in Jewish and Italian parental values, no significant differences were found in their boys' *n* achievement (A-boys only, *TAT*).

An investigation by Rosen (**97**) also compared achievement attitudes of different subcultural groups. Over four hundred mothers and their sons were studied in four of the New England states. They included French Canadians, Italians, Greeks, Jews, Negroes, and

White Protestants. Assessments of the mothers' values and aspirations for their sons' educational and vocational achievement were obtained from interviews. Data on the sons' *n* achievement (ES and A-boys only, *TAT*) were also gathered. The general thesis of the study was that racial and ethnic groups in America differ markedly in their achievement orientations, and that this may be one factor operative in their upward social mobility. The prediction was that Jewish, Protestant, and Greek mothers would place a higher premium on educational achievement for their sons than French-Canadian, Italian, and Negro mothers. With the exception of Negro mothers, this was found to be so. The vocational aspirations held by the mothers for their sons were also evaluated. In descending order of aspiration, were Jews, Greeks, Protestants, Italians, French Canadians, and Negroes. In this respect, while social-class status was also found to be associated with these maternal aspirations, it was not as highly related as was ethnicity per se. This study also evaluated differences in independence training. Jewish mothers expected the earliest evidence of self-reliance from their boys, followed by Protestants, Negroes, Greeks, French Canadians, and Italians. Finally, the boys' needs for achievement were also compared. It was predicted that achievement motivation would be relatively high among Jews, Greeks, and Protestants, and lower for the Italian, French Canadian, and Negro boys. This prediction was generally supported, but in this case social class accounted for more of the variance than did ethnicity.

Turning now to social class influences on children's achievement development, it is commonplace to note that our American class system is primarily defined by achievement performances. In fact, two of the most frequently used indices of a family's social class status, the father's education and occupational position, are both based on the adequacy (or inadequacy) of American fathers' achievement efforts. What factors contribute to differential achievement attainments representing social class status, and how do these influence children's achievement orientations and strivings? First, intellectual ability is often a necessary—though not sufficient—prerequisite for the attainment of symbols representing social status, such as education, vocational success, and the acquisition of prestigeful material possessions. In this respect, surveys of relations between intelligence and occupational status of American men entering the Armed Services during the Second World War report that general intelligence is positively correlated with the prestige of the civilian jobs the men had held (**109**). Moreover, the intellectual levels of fathers and mothers have consistently been found to be positively correlated with those of their offspring (**17**). Thus, while many other factors may contribute to children's achievement proclivities, the fact remains that children of families of higher socioeconomic status are usually intellectually superior to peers coming from families occupying lower social class positions. This intellectual difference gives the former children an initial built-in advantage irrespective of their motivation in many achievement situations including, of course, those pertaining to educational achievement.

A second variable associated with, and helping to define, social class is the vocational status of fathers. This factor, by itself (probably through indirect influences), may also be predictive of children's achievement performances. For example, one study assessing social factors associated with the academic achievements of over one thousand boys in the Boston area reports ". . . fathers' occupations did not affect school performance in the earlier grades, but it began to take effect in the fourth grade, and by the time of junior high school, was slightly more important than the child's I.Q. in predicting children's academic performance" (**66**: 284).

Several recent studies have concerned themselves with social class differences in achievement aspirations, expectations, and standards. In general, these studies suggest (e.g., see **66**), that parents and other adults, such as teachers, usually expect upper- and middle-class children to do well in elementary school and high school, to go on to college, and ultimately to attain high-status vocations; whereas children of lower-class families are more likely to develop achievement expectations (often based on their parents' aspirations and expectations for them) of such nature that competent academic performance is less important for them, that college training is viewed as "not for them," and that any steady job is to be desired regardless of its social prestige. Such class-linked attitudes, values, and expectations are bound to influence children's achievement motivations and performances.

There is some evidence that differences in achievement motivation in both adults and children may be associated with social class membership. For example, a recent large-scale survey found *n* achievement (adults, *TAT*) significantly correlated with both occupational status and education (**115**). Adult males who obtained high *n* achievement scores had higher occupational status than other adult males whose projective responses reflected less achievement preoccupation. Similarly, a significant positive relation was found between *n* achievement and level of education attained by both men and women. The relation between social class membership and achievement motivation, however, may not be a linear one. Sociologists have asserted that middle-class families value achievement as a way of maintaining or increasing social position, while both lower-class and upper-class families place a lesser premium on achievement as a pathway to desired goals. In the case of lower-class families, the attainment of social status through achievement is often seen as an insurmountable obstacle, while upper-class orientations may more often be concerned with the continuation of the *status quo* and the protection of status symbols than in the acquisition of new achievement goals. Results of research suggest that middle-class Ss may have stronger *n* achievement than either upper- or lower-class persons. One study, comparing middle-class with upper-class achievement motivations (C-*TAT*), found those of middle-class Ss stronger than those of upper-class Ss (**78**). Another study, investigating the total range of social class (A-boys only, *TAT*), reports that middle-class Ss evidenced more achievement preoccupation in their fantasy responses than either upper- or lower-class adolescents (**96**).

PARENTAL INFLUENCES

A child's parents are usually considered the major socializing agents influencing and molding his attitudes and behaviors, at least until he enters elementary school. And even later, while other persons such as his teachers and schoolmates may increasingly affect his development, his parents still maintain a focal position in many of his daily experiences. In what ways do parents shape the development of their children's achievement values, standards, expectations, and behaviors?

First, a parent's own personality often determines his attitudes and reactions to his child's behaviors. Both a parent's general attitudes and his own personal needs have been found to be predictive of his child-rearing practices (**11, 25, 53, 68, 125**). Regarding the specific area of achievement development, one recent study reports that parents' orientations toward their own achievements may influence their behaviors with their children in everyday achievement experiences (**69**). For example, the greater the value the fathers placed on their being intellectually competent themselves, the more likely they were to participate with their elementary-school-age children in intellectual pursuits, to instigate their children toward intellectual achievement activities and accomplishments, and to react strongly to their children's achievement efforts. Similar relations were found for mothers, except these were more frequently expressed in interactions with their daughters than with their sons. Also, the parents' own achievement orientations often found expression in their actions with their offspring consistent with prevailing cultural stereotypes of appropriate sex-role behaviors.

Results of research to date concerned with parental influences on children's achievement motivation are somewhat contradictory. Two of the earliest studies in this area, both by McClelland and his colleagues (**82**), report significant associations between parental affection or rejection and their offspring's *n* achievement. In both studies the assessment of the Ss' achievement motivation was based on their responses to *TAT*-like stimuli, and data regarding parental behavior were obtained from the Ss' ratings of their parents. College males with high *n* achievement rated their fathers and mothers as more rejectant than did college males who were less preoccupied with achievement. In contrast, high-school boys with strong achievement motivation rated their fathers as less rejectant (mothers were not rated) than did their low *n* achievement peers.

Two investigations have assessed the effect of independence training on children's achievement motivation. Winterbottom's pioneering study reported the following findings (**122**): Children with strong *n* achievement (ES-boys only, incomplete stories) had mothers who expected earlier evidence of self-reliant behavior from their sons, gave more frequent and intense rewards when their sons were successful in these attempts, and placed fewer restrictions on the spontaneous efforts of their offspring toward independence (mothers, questionnaire). A follow-up study by Feld some six years later found the maternal independence training reported by the mothers at the time of the first study was still predictive of the boys' achievement motivations in adolescence (**40**). However, while this early independence training was positively associated with these adolescent boys' *n* achievement, the mothers' reactions to the boys' independence efforts during adolescence were inversely associated with their sons' achievement motivation. This was in spite of the fact that the boys' *n* achievement scores were found to be relatively stable over the six-year interim between the two studies.

Rosen and D'Andrade assessed parent behaviors in semiexperimental situations (**98**). Forty boys with extremely high and low *n* achievement scores were selected from an original sample of 140 Ss (ES-boys only, *TAT*). The experimenters took several achievement tasks into the homes of these children and required the boys to perform these while their parents were present, and the parents' behaviors during these testing sessions were observed and rated. Parents of the high *n* achievement boys held both higher aspirations and expectations for their sons' performances than did parents of boys with lesser achievement motivation. The former parents also set higher standards for their sons' achievement performances. Mothers of boys with strong *n* achievement were more concerned with their sons' performances and acted accordingly, giving approval when performance was good and readily criticizing incompetent efforts. In respect to this, the investigators state, ". . . although these mothers are likely to give their sons more option as to exactly what to do, they give less option about doing something and doing it well" (**98**).

Studies concerned with parental influences on children's achievement behaviors, while still infrequent, are more numerous than those pertaining to the development of children's achievement motivation. One investigation has reported that maternal behaviors may influence children's achievement efforts as early as nursery-school age (**26**). Among the results of this study were these: Mothers who usually rewarded their children's achievement efforts in the home were found to be less nurturant, but no more or less affectionate, than mothers who were less prone to give such rewards (mothers, behavior ratings). Neither maternal affection nor maternal nurturance was predictive of the children's achievement efforts in nursery-school free play (NS-behavior ratings). However, the mothers' direct reactions to their children's achievement behaviors were related to their children's efforts outside the home. Mothers who characteristically responded positively when their children sought approval for their achievements had children who exhibited more achievement efforts in nursery-school free play than did mothers who less often responded in this fashion. Moreover, the mothers who usually spontaneously praised and rewarded their children's achievement efforts even when the children did not seek approval had children who displayed especially strong and frequent achievement efforts outside the home.

In a second study (**24**), children's achievement behaviors were observed and rated in respect to four achievement areas: intellectual, physical skills or athletics, artistic-creative, and manual-mechanical. Two aspects of the children's achievement behaviors in these areas were rated during their participation in free play in a day-camp setting (ES-behavior ratings): the amount of time each child spent in an achievement area and the intensity of his achievement striving while participating. Parents' reactions to these children's achievement behaviors in everyday situations in the four achievement areas under investigation were also evaluated (parents, interviews). Significant associations between parental reactions and the children's achievement behaviors were found to vary by sex of parent and child, as well as the achievement area under consideration. For example, in respect to intellectual achievement, girls who preferred to spend their time in intellectual-achievement activities during free play had fathers who often encouraged and instigated them toward intellectual pursuits and who also frequently spent time with them in everyday intellectual activities. Moreover, the girls who exhibited intense achievement striving while working on intellectual tasks in the day camp were those whose mothers characteristically pushed them toward intellectual pursuits and whose fathers were especially prone to participate with them in intellectual activities. This did not obtain for the boys. On the other hand, when the children's athletic-achievement activities were assessed, significant relations were found for *both* boys and girls and primarily along same-sex, parent-child lines. The more a parent participated with a same-sex child, the more likely it was that the child would exhibit intense striving in his (or her) athletic endeavors outside the home.

Recently, several studies have evaluated the influence of parents' attitudes and actions on children's intellectual performances. This research suggests that these parents' attitudes and behaviors may be associated with their children's performances on standard intelligence tests. One longitudinal investigation compared children whose I.Q.'s increased during preschool and elementary-school years with those whose I.Q.'s decreased during these periods (**108**). The children with increasing I.Q.'s were more emotionally independent of their parents (parents, children, behavioral observations, and interviews). In addition, during the elementary-school years, parental emphasis on school achievement was positively associated with I.Q. increases. An incidental finding was that almost twice as many boys as girls belonged to the group whose I.Q.'s increased. Another investigation related the degree that mothers attempted to accelerate their children's achievement development (mothers only, behavioral ratings) with the level of children's I.Q. in two separate samples of children (**90**). In both samples, maternal acceleration was positively associated with height of I.Q. during nursery-school but not at grade-school ages and was significant for boys only. It has also been found that highly intelligent grade-school-age children are more apt to come from homes which could be characterized either as "acceptant-democratic" or "acceptant-democratic-indulgent" (mothers only, behavioral ratings) while the homes of less-intelligent children were more often "autocratic" or "rejectant" (**3**). Finally, a more recent study reports that mothers of intelligent junior high school children expressed more acceptant and less dominating child-rearing attitudes (mothers, questionnaires) than mothers of less-intelligent offspring (**57**).

There still remains the important question of the impact of parent behaviors on children's academic achievement performances. In this respect, a number of older studies have suggested that *positive* parent-child relations (such as closeness to the child, high interest, understanding and/or approval of him, etc.) are conducive to competent academic achievement (**16, 61, 71, 95, 114, 118**). Unfortunately, these and other studies of a similar vintage have usually been based on either qualitative evaluations or quantitative assessments with serious methodological flaws (e.g., contamination between parent and child data, inappropriate statistical analyses, and unwarranted generalizations).

Three recent studies have obtained results which are contradictory to the reports of the earlier research in this area; these latter investigations suggest that high academic achievement may be associated with *negative* parental behaviors, such as rejection, coerciveness and/or overprotection. For example, Drews and Teahan find that mothers of high-achieving junior high school students (mothers, interviews), in contrast with mothers of children who are performing less adequately, express "more punitive attitudes toward child disobedience" and are more rejectant of their offspring. These researchers add:

> If these results reflect the typical attitudes which characterize the parents of high achievers it is not surprising that Gough discovered his successful high school children to be conforming, orderly, docile and conventional (**35**).

A second investigation in this area (**21**) assessed relations between the attitudes and behaviors of parents of young elementary-school children (parents, interviews) and the children's academic performances (ES-academic achievement tests). The investigators state:

> Girls who were especially competent readers had both less affectionate and less nurturant mothers than did girls who demonstrated less proficiency in this academic area. . . . In addition, girls who performed better on the arithmetic achievement test had mothers who were also relatively low on nurturance (**21**).

This result, however, did not obtain for the fathers' relations with their children, nor for mothers' relations with their sons. In fact, few significant relations were found in this study between parents' attitudes and/or actions and their boys' academic achievement, although several additional significant findings were reported for the girls. High-achieving girls, for example, had mothers who set high standards for their general intellectual performances and fathers who frequently praised, and infrequently criticized, their intellectual and academic efforts. The authors of this study present additional data to support their thesis that academic-achievement motivations of young boys and girls may be different, with those of the girls more often oriented toward reactions from others (and therefore more susceptible to parental influence), while those of boys may be more autonomously determined by their own internal standards for achievement.

Another recent study of parental behavior and children's academic achievements is in essential agreement with the two preceding investigations in that it also found significant associations between negatively valued parental child-rearing practices and children's academic competence. This investigation assessed, among other things, relations between parental coerciveness (ES-boys only, their ratings of their parents) and these boys' academic proficiencies (teachers' ratings). Boys who perceived their parents as coercive performed more competently in the classroom than those who rated their parents as more lenient (**54**). Finally, another recent study assessed the influence of independence training on children's academic competence (**13**). Early independence training (mothers, interviews) was found to be negatively associated with children's academic competence (GS-standard achievement tests). Mothers who accepted and fostered dependence rather than the development of independence and self-reliance had offspring who were especially competent on elementary-school achievement tests.

SCHOOL EXPERIENCES

Outside of the family, the school is probably the most important social institution shaping children's achievement motivations and behaviors. Here, a child's achievement orientations and actions are influenced by two broad classes of factors: his interactions with his teachers and classmates, and the formal structure of his particular school system.

Taba suggests that participation with classmates in extracurricular activities may increase children's academic achievement motivation. She conducted a survey of student activities in seven junior and senior high schools and found that many children who did not participate in extracurricular school activities had "a lack of a sense of belonging affecting their self-expectations and motivation regarding academic success, and therefore also academic achievement, because integration of individuals in school groups seems to enhance motivation for learning, while disintegration, cleavage and isolation lessen effort and motivation" (**112**). However, the results of several other studies indicate that such a generalization may not be applicable for many school environments. These investigations point up the fact that peer affiliations and pressures can either reward *or* punish academic-achievement motivation and performance dependent on the values held by various peer groups. It is not uncommon that a child who is intellectually superior and/or academically competent may experience ridicule and ostracism from his classmates in some American schools. Tannenbaum, investigating peer attitudes toward academically superior high-school students (A-peer ratings), found that the exceptionally intelligent or studious child was ranked lowest of all by his peers on social popularity (**113**). Coleman reports that of the criteria employed by high-school students for acceptance into prestigeful social groups, academic proficiency ranked sixth out of the eight criteria used. Coleman summarizes his findings with the following statement:

> The variation among the schools was not nearly as striking in this research as the fact that, in all of them, academic achievement did not count for as much as other activities. In every school the boy named as the best athlete and the boy named as most popular with the girls was far more often mentioned by a member of a leading crowd as someone to "be liked" than was the boy named as the best student (**15**).

The effect of teachers' personalities and behaviors on their students' academic achievements has not been studied in any great detail. Solomon summarizes as follows the results of a preliminary investigation with college teachers in which teacher behaviors and academic progress of students were assessed:

> It seems reasonable that the teacher who stimulates the students and makes the subject interesting to them by being dramatic or energetic can thereby encourage them to go beyond the facts of a topic, to think about it, and perhaps become adept at the type of reasoning which the topic requires for adequate comprehension. Perhaps this is because the teacher himself is treating the topic, not as a collection of facts to be learned, but as something of intrinsic interest and excitement (**107**).

The formal educational policies of a school system may also be a relevant influence on children's achievement development. Any or all of the following educational procedures and methods can conceivably affect a child's achievement motivation and performance:

ability groupings, acceleration, enrichment programs, special guidance and therapy facilities, and specific teaching methods (e.g., lecture *vs.* discussion, independent study, "inquiry training," the use of teaching machines). This general problem has been discussed by Goldberg, although her review is mainly concerned with gifted children (**48**).

It is also likely that there can be an *interactive* effect of these educational procedures and children's personalities on the development of motivation and on performance. That is, some children, because of their unique motivational propensities, may thrive in an independent study program, for instance, while others may not only be less productive in such a situation but may also feel threatened by the lack of structure inherent in this kind of learning experience. Several recent studies have found that children's academic-achievement performances are often the product of both the kinds of formal learning experiences they undergo and the motivational propensities which children bring to these learning situations. An example of this has been reported by Suchman and his associates who are currently conducting a series of "inquiry-training" programs in several school systems throughout the United States. Their general aim is to teach children the orientations and skills needed for independent problem-solving in new academic-achievement situations rather than, as is usual in many schools, to rely solely on teachers for "facts and answers" (**111**). Suchman notes that most children are originally resistant and anxious in such a novel educational experience and, also, that marked individual differences are subsequently apparent in children's willingness to rely on their own problem-solving capacities.

It has been reported by several other educational researchers that the personality predispositions of students may "filter" the effect of various teaching innovations (**6, 84, 106, 123, 124**). Such personal propensities as general anxiety, sociability, compulsivity, and the desire for "structure" and "autonomy" have all been observed to be operative in students' reactions to various learning experiences. In this respect, a recent investigation by Grimes and Allinsmith (**51**) studied the dual role of anxiety and compulsivity in children's academic performances in structured and unstructured academic-learning environments. Here, the children's anxiety (ES-questionnaires) and compulsivity (parent reports) were evaluated in respect to their academic performances (standardized reading and intelligence tests) following experiences in structured and unstructured classrooms. Compulsive children scored higher on reading-achievement tests when they were in structured, rather than unstructured, learning environments. Within the structured classroom situations, the compulsive children also performed more adequately than their less-compulsive peers. Highly anxious children did as well in structured environments but performed less adequately than their less-anxious peers after unstructured classroom experiences. Thus, in general, anxious and/or compulsive children were more "at home" in structured academic achievement situations and performed accordingly, while their less-anxious and compulsive fellows were less threatened by, and were more productive in, learning situations where less structure was imposed on their academic learning.

Personality Predictors and Correlates of Achievement

We turn now to studies evaluating those children's personality characteristics which are associated with their achievement behaviors. Two kinds of personality factors are relevant here: those intrinsic to achievement per se and those which are not but, nevertheless, have been found to differentiate achieving from nonachieving children. For heuristic purposes, the former attributes have been labeled "predictors," since these are personality variables *within* the achievement rubric which are, or may be, predictive of children's achievement performances. These include individual differences in children's achievement motivations, preferences, test-taking anxieties, personal achievement standards, expectations of success or failure in achievement situations, and the like. The second class of personality characteristics which will be discussed have been designated as "correlates," since these are either propensities which are operative, not only in achievement situations but in other experiences as well (e.g., general anxiety and compulsivity), or are personality characteristics usually associated with other dispositional systems (e.g., conformity, dependence or independence, and dominance).

PREDICTOR VARIABLES

The one predictor of achievement performances, aside from ability, which has been most often employed in achievement research to date has been achievement motivation or *n* achievement. Well over two hundred studies, mostly with college students, have been reported during the last decade assessing the influence of achievement motivation on achievement performances in a variety of situations. For example, *n* achievement has been found to be related to such diverse behaviors as "level-of-aspiration" expectations and performances (**70**), risk-taking (**79**), perceptual-field dependence (**120**), autokinetic movement (**41**), problem-solving effectiveness (**44**), preferences for active *vs.* static images (**56**), creativity (**93**), verbal learning (**10**), maze learning (**60**), stimulus generalization (**88**), recall of interrupted and completed tasks (**2**), fluency of speech (**117**), academic achievement (**119**), vocational choice (**34**), choice of work partners (**43**), and one's general self concept (**87**).

In contrast, research on *children's* achievement motivation is still quite meager and scattered. Two recent studies, however, are especially pertinent. Winterbottom compared children's achievement motivation (ES-boys only, incomplete stories) with teacher ratings of performances in the school (**122**). High *n* achievement boys, in contrast to their low *n* achievement peers, were rated as displaying stronger achievement motivation in general as well as specifically in sports and schoolwork. They were also more independent in their problem-solving attempts and evidenced greater pleasure when successful in achievement efforts. In another study, Rosen and D'Andrade selected twenty high and twenty low *n* achievement boys (ES-boys only, *TAT*-like stimuli) from a larger group of Ss. The final sample was matched with respect to age, race, I.Q., and social class. Several achievement tasks were administered each boy in his own home while his parents were present. The high *n* achievement boys were found to be more proficient on the tasks, asked for less aid from their parents, were more competitive, and displayed greater self-reliance in general (**98**).

The second most frequently used personality predictor in achievement research has been anxiety. Numerous studies have assessed the effect of anxiety on achievement performances in a variety of conditions. These are discussed in chapter xi.

Other variables have also been found to influence children's intellectual achievement behaviors in diverse achievement situations (**23**). The influence of these variables, as well as *n* achievement and anxiety, on children's achievement performances was assessed in this study in respect to the following achievement behaviors: the amount of time elementary-school-age children chose to spend in intellectual activities in a free-play Day Camp environment, the intensity of their striving on intellectual tasks in this setting, and the competence of their performances on a standard intelligence test and on academic achievement tests. Among others, the following results were obtained: First, neither *n* achievement nor anxiety was significantly related to any of these young children's achievement behaviors. Second, several other personality variables did predict individual differences in the children's intellectual-achievement performances, but these operated very differently for the boys than for the girls. The only personality variable which was significantly correlated with the girls' intellectual achievement efforts was their desire for intellectual competence. The greater the value the girls placed on intellectual proficiency, the more time they spent in intellectual activities in the day camp and the more intense were their achievement strivings in these activities. In contrast, the achievement orientations of the boys which were associated with their achievement performances were very different from those of the girls. The one variable which was predictive for the girls, achievement value, was not related to performance for the boys. However, most of the other variables under consideration in the study were related to their behaviors. For example, the boys who felt they were intellectually competent (i.e., expected to be successful in intellectual pursuits) spent more time in intellectual activities in free play and exhibited more intense achievement-striving than did less-confident boys. Moreover, boys who set high standards for their intellectual performances were also likely to spend more time and strive harder in intellectual pursuits. The boys who were especially proficient on intelligence and achievement tests were those who characteristically expressed confidence in their intellectual abilities, set high standards for their intellectual performances, and usually believed that they, rather than others, were responsible for the reinforcements which followed their achievement attempts. The differences found in this study in the achievement orientations affecting boys' and girls' achievement performances suggests that the motivations for achievement of young males and young females may be quite different.

Many other studies of achievement have reported that relations between the achievement orientations (especially *n* achievement) and performances of males and females in our American culture often differ. While *n* achievement appears to be an important determinant of men's achievement behaviors in many achievement situations, this has seldom been found to be true for women. In fact, in recent years—perhaps because of this—most achievement-motivation research has exclusively employed males as Ss. While such a research procedure is legitimate, it avoids the important question of the unique motivational components of the achievement behaviors of females, whether they are children or adults. Two investigators have recently addressed their research specifically to this question. French and Lesser are currently studying the achievement motivations of females in several colleges throughout the country, as well as those of younger adolescents. While most of this research is still in progress, a study of high-school girls has recently been reported which suggests that sex-role identity must be assessed, as well as *n* achievement per se, if the motivational determinants of adolescent girls' academic-achievement performances are to be clearly understood (**73**). More specifically, this investigation found that the girls' *n* achievement (A-girls only, *TAT*-like stimuli) was predictive of their academic competence (standard achievement tests) only when the sex of the protagonist of their stories was taken into account. In the study, half of the *TAT* stimuli presented the Ss contained male figures and half portrayed female figures. Academically proficient girls were more prone to tell achievement themes to stimuli-containing female characters, while the opposite was true for girls who displayed less academic competence. The experimenters suggest that the achievement motivation of high-school girls may more often enter into, and influence, their academic-achievement behaviors when girls of this age perceive achievement as an appropriate sex-role activity than when they do not.

The reasons for achievement striving may also vary for males and females. For example, approval and affection from others may more often be the ultimate goals of girls' achievement efforts, while achievement *qua* achievement appears to be the more characteristic aim of boys' achievement behaviors. In other words, girls' achievement activities and striving seem to be "other-directed," while those of boys are more autonomously determined by their own internal achievement standards and their need of self-approval. For instance, the writer and his colleagues have found that the approval-seeking of elementary-school-age girls is positively correlated with the amount of achievement efforts they display in free play while that of boys is not (**21**). A similar relation has also been found in the preoccupations of adolescent children with achievement as this is reflected in the achievement themes of the stories they tell to *TAT* stimuli (**72**). Here, when girls gave achievement themes, they were also likely to mention the possibility of approval or disapproval from other persons following the achievement efforts of the central character of the story. In contrast, boys' achievement themes focused on competence per se rather than on the reactions of others.

In respect to such sex differences in motivations for academic achievement, Pauline Sears and her associates have recently reported that needs other than *n* achievement can be operative in young girls' achievement behaviors while this may not be so for boys (**103**). These investigators assessed elementary-school children's needs for achievement and for affection. The boys' preoccupations with achievement were found to be predictive of their performances on standard academic achievement tests; the more *n* achievement they displayed about school situations, the more proficient were their performances on standard academic achievement tests. This did not hold for the girls. The *n* achievement found in the girls' projective responses was essentially unrelated to their academic competence. On the other hand, their concern with obtaining affection from others (*n* affiliation) was predictive; the more this need was evident, the more proficient were these girls' academic-achievement performances. Thus, the satisfaction of needs other than achievement seems, often, to be the final goal of girls' achievement efforts.

A final study relevant to the present discussion reports that girls' needs for achievement, moreover, may be expressed in areas other than the conventional ones of intellectual or academic achievement. This investigation related achievement motivation (ES-doll play) to a social reputation questionnaire. Significant positive correlations between both the boys' and the girls' *n* achievement and their academic work habits were found. However, the girls' *n* achievement, but not that of the boys, was also associated with the adequacy of their social relations. The investigator suggests that the general results of his study present a picture "translated into adult terms, which might describe a successful woman, but not necessarily a woman whose success is in the world of books. The high *n* achievement girls work and are seen as enjoying school subjects, but they also enjoy the more recreational side of the classrom while this does not appear to be a significant factor in the personality structures of the high need achievement boys" (**39**).

Finally, there is also some indication from recent research that not only may the achievement motivations of boys and girls differ but also that the motivations which are conducive to successful achievement endeavors at one age may not be so at later ages. For example, the research of Gough and his associates on the *California Personality Inventory* suggests that successful academic achievement may be contingent on different personality variables in high school and in college (**49**). These investigators report that achievement via conformity (A-questionnaire) is associated with academic achievement during the high-school years, while achievement via independence (C-questionnaire) is more often characteristic of scholastic achievement in college.

It is possible that the achievement motivations of children may also be associated with their intelligence-test performances. At the moment, however, there is little evidence to suggest that intelligence and achievement motivation are necessarily correlated. Jordan and de Charms, for example, compared the *n* achievement (A-incomplete stories) of normal and mentally retarded children and found no significant differences (**62**). Other studies of normal children have also reported insignificant relations between achievement motivation and intelligence. On the other hand, achievement motivation has been found to be related to I.Q. *changes*. One longitudinal investigation periodically administered standard intelligence tests to a group of the same children over a span of years. Extreme groups were then selected from this sample—groups whose I.Q. increased and decreased most during the elementary-school years. Children with I.Q. increases during this period displayed more achievement imagery in their stories to standard *TAT* pictures than did those whose I.Q.'s decreased (**65**).

Research with adults mentioned earlier has usually found that *n* achievement is a contributing factor to the efficiency of Ss' learning in experimental situations. The one study of this nature using children as Ss did not find as clear-cut results (**67**). Achievement motivation of high-school Freshmen (A-*TAT*) was positively associated with amount of incidental learning but was not significantly related to the direct learning of the subject material in the experiment.

Several recent investigations have assessed relations between children's achievement orientations and their performances on less-standard kinds of achievement tasks as well as those which are not usually considered as achievement situations. One of these studies, concerned with risk-taking propensities, reports that relations between *n* achievement and risk-taking behaviors may be similar for children and adults (**81**). Children with high *n* achievement, like adults in other similar studies, were more likely to take moderate risks while their less-achievement-oriented peers preferred either very safe or very speculative ventures and commitments. Another study assessed factors influencing children's perceptual responses (**28**). The general orientation of this investigation was based on previous reports by Witkin *et al.* that perceptual-field dependence of adults (i.e., inability to extract figures from backgrounds in which they were imbedded) was associated with their social dependence. However, this relationship was not found with children, but the children's achievement orientations (ES-free play behavior ratings) were predictive of their perceptual performances. Children who were achievement-oriented were especially proficient in the perceptual testing situation; they readily differentiated figure from ground. The investigators suggest that even experiments which deal with perceptual stimuli may be seen by children as testing situations and thereby may elicit differential achievement motivations which can affect children's perceptual performances. Finally, children's *n* achievement has also been found to be a determinant of their willingness to delay immediate gratification in favor of less-immediate goals and rewards (**89**). This study by Mischel reports that children's *n* achievement (ES-*TAT*) was positively related to their choices for delayed gratification.

BEHAVIORAL CORRELATES

Studies evaluating relations between children's achievement behaviors and their behaviors in respect to other needs have recently reported associations between children's achievement behaviors in free play and their dependent behaviors in these situations. One investigation (NS-behavior observations) reported that preschool children who spent most of their time and effort in achievement activities were less dependent on adults than were peers whose free-play behaviors were less often achievement kinds of activity (**26**). The former group of children sought less instrumental help and emotional support from the nursery-school staff than did the latter. Similar results were also obtained with older children (**28**). During free play in a summer day camp, elementary-school-age children who displayed more achievement efforts and who were rated as task persistent were less likely to seek assistance from the staff. On the other hand, no significant relations were found between the children's achievement behaviors and their affection-seeking or approval-seeking—two behaviors which have usually also been included under the rubric of dependency.

Behavioral correlates of children's academic competence have also been investigated. Perhaps the single most intensive study of this kind has been that conducted by Haggard and his colleagues and students. In a report covering the first phase of their seven-year research project on this problem, these investigators present their findings on the third-grade children in the University of Chicago Laboratory School. These Ss were gifted children; the median child of the sample fell above the 90th percentile on national norms of standard intelligence and academic achievement tests. In the study, these children were administered academic achievement tests and projective personality tests. Behavioral observations and ratings were also made in respect to their in-school behaviors. Finally, information on parental values and pressures was obtained from teacher interviews with parents, parent questionnaires, and interviews with the children. Behavior correlates which were found to be significantly associated with superior academic achievement were these: the more proficient children were less dependent on their teachers, were more competitive with their peers, were more task persistent, expressed less warmth toward their siblings, and had more guilt feelings. The investigators summarized their findings as follows:

> The personality picture of the achievers obtained in the present study is, on the whole, in harmony with the trends reported elsewhere, which suggest a picture of children who have responded to cultural pressures and have made strides in internalizing adult values. The achiever's ac-

ceptance of these values is reflected in his academic interests; for example, his conscious effort to achieve in school and such related traits as compliance with authority, perseverance and emotional control. It would seem that the achiever's acceptance of such upper middle-class values has been accomplished at the cost of a certain degree of anxiety, strain, and loss of freedom in emotional expression (**33**).

Haggard has subsequently noted that some of these characteristics change as children mature. In a preliminary report of assessments of the same children four years later, the following summary comment is made:

> Although they continued to respond to the socialization pressures of adults and to strive toward adult standards of behavior, they had developed strong antagonistic attitudes toward adults and often pictured adults as being inadequate and ineffective. . . . At the same time they showed a marked increase in the level of their anxiety and a corresponding decrease in intellectual originality and creativity. . . . The high achievers were able, however, to control and channel their anxiety in various ways, for example, through the intellectualization of their experiences or the mastering of new knowledges and intellectual skills. They also became more aggressive, persistent, hard driving, and competitive, and they showed signs of willingness to be aggressive and destructive in order to defeat and win over other persons (**52**).

In respect to aggression and achievement, Shaw and Grubb (**105**) also found that overachieving students expressed more hostility (A-questionnaires) than did underachievers.

In summary, the limited research findings at the moment suggest that academic achievers tend to conform to and to incorporate adult values and prescriptions. On the other hand, academically proficient children appear to be self-reliant (nondependent), assertive, competitive, and even aggressive in their everyday academic experiences.

The Consistency of Achievement

How consistent are children's achievement orientations and behaviors at a given time as well as at different ages? For example, is the child who displays intense achievement-striving in the classroom also likely to do so on the playing field? And, if he does so this year, will he do so five years from now? These, and other similar questions, require research evaluating the consistency of children's behavior in various kinds of achievement situations as well as the stability of their motivations and performances as they grow older.

CONSISTENCY ACROSS SITUATIONS

There is some evidence that children's achievement behaviors are somewhat similar from one locus to another, even by nursery-school age (**26**). Moderate but significant associations have been found between such behaviors in the home and in nursery school (NS-behavioral ratings). Children who displayed frequent self-initiated achievement efforts at home were found in this study to do so in free play at nursery school as well. Moreover, those children who often sought approval from their mothers for their achievements were likely to behave similarly with their nursery-school teachers.

Children's achievement attitudes and actions may not only generalize across loci of activity (home, school, and other interests) and persons (mothers, teachers, and peers) but may also evidence generality or specificity dependent on the areas of achievement under consideration. To what degree do children's achievement orientations and performances become specific to particular kinds of achievement activities as they mature? Apparently there is no simple answer to this question. For example, one recent investigation reports that certain aspects of children's orientations toward achievement were highly generalized, while many of their achievement behaviors were more specific to achievement areas (**20**). This study found that early-grade-school children's achievement orientations were consistent across the four areas investigated; i.e., intellectual, athletic, artistic, and mechanical. A child at this age, who was confident of his ability to perform capably in one achievement area, was also likely to expect that his efforts would be successful in other areas. And this was also true of his standards; the child who was satisfied only when his performance was quite exceptional in a given achievement area held similarly high standards for his achievement efforts in other kinds of achievement endeavors. On the other hand, the children's actual achievement behaviors (e.g., intensity of striving) in each of the four areas were much more specifically tied to the achievement activities under consideration.

A second study covering the same questions with slightly older Ss (ES-behavior ratings) reports that the degree of children's intellectual striving at this age is highly associated with their mechanical striving, but that neither of these is necessarily related to how intensely a child will strive in athletic pursuits (**91**).

CONSISTENCY OVER TIME

In order to examine the stability (or lack of stability) of children's motivations and behaviors as they mature, longitudinal research is necessary. One large-scale project of this nature, the Fels Research Institute's longitudinal study, has followed the same children from birth to eighteen years of age and has also reassessed these Ss as young adults (**64**). In respect to children's *n* achievement, moderate but significant positive correlations were found between the number of achievement themes the children gave to *TAT* pictures at eight years of age, and those given by the same Ss when they were eleven and fourteen years of age (**63**).

A recent study by Feld is also germane (**40**). This follow-up study of the sample of children originally used in the Winterbottom investigation was discussed earlier in this chapter (**122**). Winterbottom assessed the children's *n* achievement (boys only-incomplete stories) when they were eight, nine, or ten years of age. Feld retested these same Ss six years later, and a correlaion of .38 was obtained.

A second report of the Fels Institute's longitudinal study covered the stability of children's actual achievement behaviors over time (**91**). This investigation related children's achievement striving (behavioral ratings) at various age periods, as well as the achievement striving of these Ss as young adults (interviews). Major findings, among others, were these: (*a*) children's achievement behaviors during the first three years of life were essentially unrelated to their later achievement performances; (*b*) achievement efforts during nursery-school age were significantly associated with those displayed at the elementary-school age; (*c*) similar relations between elementary-school age and early adolescence were obtained, though these were more evident for intellectual achievement than for athletic or mechanical achievement; and (*d*) childhood achievement behaviors were sometimes, though not always, predictive of adult achievement performances. That is, girls' achievement strivings during nursery-school age were significantly related to their adult achievement striving, while those of nursery-school boys were not. However, by early elementary-school age, both girls' and boys' achievement behaviors were predictive of their adult behavior. At ages ten through fourteen, only intellectual achievement striving was associated with adult achievement efforts, while athletic and mechanical achievement striving were not.

Changes in Achievement Orientations and Behaviors Following Experimentally Manipulated Reinforcements

Experimental studies determining how children's achievement values, expectations, standards, and performances can be changed under controlled laboratory conditions are necessary in order to understand better the relevant forces which are operative *in situ* in children's achievement development. This section reports studies of this nature. These have been grouped under three general headings: changes in preferences for achievement activities, changes in expectations of success or failure, and changes in achievement performances.

CHANGES IN PREFERENCES FOR ACHIEVEMENT ACTIVITIES

Recent research has shown that the preferences persons have for various achievement tasks can be experimentally changed. The two pioneering investigations concerned with this problem employed college women as Ss rather than children (**45, 46**). Several other studies have used children as Ss. Schroder had second-, third-, and fourth-grade girls rate their preferences for twenty charms (**102**). The Ss were then required to place a token in a vending machine which might or might not give out a charm. Some of the girls received a charm each time they put a token in the machine; others obtained a charm only half of the times they inserted a token. Then, the Ss were again asked to state their preferences for the twenty charms. The preference for the specific charm the girls had obtained from the machine was greater for the girls who had received it each time they had put in a token than it was for the girls who had received one only half of the time. Frequency of attainment increased preference value.

Two studies involving elementary-school boys, one by Dunlap (**36**) and the other by Hunt (**55**), both found that verbal approval for performing a task increased that task's preference value, and verbal criticism decreased its value, with the amount of approval or criticism given determining the amount of change in preference value for the achievement tasks. In respect to this latter point, however, an investigation by Jessor (**59**) reports that successive statements of verbal approval over a long period of time can become decreasingly effective.

Several studies have investigated children's preferences for achievement tasks after they have been experimentally failed on one but allowed to succeed on another. The standard technique used in these studies is one originally developed by Rosenzweig (**99**) in which an S is administered two puzzles and told he has a specified amount of time to complete each. Actually, no time limit is really used, and the S is allowed to complete one of the puzzles but is told his time is up before he finishes the other puzzle. He thus succeeds on one and fails on the other. He is then asked which of the two puzzles he would like to do again. This repetition choice is the basic data for these studies. Rosenzweig reported that the desire to repeat a failed task in an attempt to master it increased significantly with age. Crandall and Rabson (**27**), comparing the repetition choices of nursery-school children with those of elementary-school children, found the same relation, but only for boys. While there were no differences for the girls of the two age groups, the older boys much more frequently preferred to attempt to master the failed task than did the younger boys. In addition, elementary-school-age boys were less dependent on adults and peers for help than were girls, and boys were less ready to withdraw from threatening situations, although these sex differences were not apparent at the earlier nursery-school age. In other words, it appears that by elementary-school age, boys may have developed stronger needs to independently master threatening situations or those in which they have previously experienced failure than have girls of that age.

Studies by Bialer (**8**) and by Bialer and Cromwell (**9**), both using mentally-retarded children as Ss, have also found that chronological age is positively associated with repetition choices for failed tasks. In addition, both studies report that mental ages of children are similarly associated with their repetition choices; brighter children in these studies preferred to return to, and attempt to master, failed tasks more often than less-intelligent children. In fact, in

Bialer's study, mental age was a better predictor than chronological age.

Using a slightly different technique, Gewirtz conducted a study of the gradients of preference children developed for several achievement tasks following experimentally manipulated success or failure on one of the tasks (**47**). Elementary-school children were shown five puzzles whose outlines represented different points along a dimension of shape running from a square diamond to an elongated diamond. They then experienced success (successful completion of puzzle and praise from the examiner) or failure (stopped before puzzle was complete and criticized) on a puzzle at one extreme of this shape dimension. Failure almost invariably produced steep avoidance gradients of preferences. That is, the children preferred repeating puzzles which were increasingly dissimilar in shape to the one on which they had failed. Success, on the other hand, resulted in approach gradients for some children and avoidance gradients for others. The children who had avoidance gradients (i.e., wanted to perform tasks dissimilar from the one on which they had succeeded) had higher I.Q.'s and characteristically gave explanations that they made these choices because they wanted harder, more challenging tasks. Thus, following success on a puzzle, some children seem to prefer tasks of a similar (presumably easy) nature, while other children exhibit "upward-striving" achievement orientations, i.e., they now wanted to tackle more difficult problems. In line with Gewirtz's findings Rychlak (**101**) reports that elementary-school boys who had high expectations of success preferred difficult intellectual tasks, while boys who were less confident of their ability chose easier ones. Coopersmith (**18**) found that children's *n* achievement is also associated with their repetition choices following success and failure. His Ss were fifth- and sixth-grade children. Children with strong achievement motivation more often preferred to return to tasks on which they had failed than did children with lesser achievement concerns.

CHANGES OF EXPECTATIONS OF SUCCESS AND FAILURE

Children's expectations of success in achievement situations have also been shown to be amenable to experimental change. Rao and Russell (**94**) manipulated success and failure on the Rotter "level-of-aspiration board" with a novel adaptation of this technique which allowed the experimenters to control the performance scores the children obtained. Significant results, among others, were that failure experiences rapidly decreased the Ss' expectations of success during initial failure trials, but the rate of decrease slackened as the failure series progressed. When failure was discontinued, the Ss' expectations of success increased rapidly, then leveled off again. However, the more failure trials the boys had experienced, the longer it took them to readjust their expectations of success upward after the experimentally induced failure had ceased.

Two recent studies have assessed the impact of an adult's positive and negative reactions and nonreaction (silence) on changes of junior high school boys' expectations of success (**29, 30**). As might be expected, positive adult reactions during these brief experimental sessions significantly increased the boys' expectations of success, and negative reactions decreased such expectations. However, negative adult reactions produced significantly greater decreases in the boys' expectancies of success than positive adult reactions increased them. Finally, the adult's nonreactions (her silence following either positive or negative reactions) had demonstrated active reinforcing properties. When the adult's silences were preceded by positive reactions, the boys (apparently) perceived her nonreaction, by contrast with her previous behaviors, as indicating unexpressed criticism, and they accordingly decreased their expectations of success when this occurred. The opposite was true when nonreaction followed negative adult reactions. Here, silence produced increased expectations of success. The possible implications of the fact that an adult's silence may sometimes actively reinforce children's achievement orientations and performances are intriguing. This would seem to imply that the teacher, school psychologist, or child-development researcher who automatically assumes that his silent observation of children's achievement performances has no effect on the children may be in error in many teaching, testing, or experimental situations.

A study by Davids and White (**31**) compared the achievement expectations of a group of normal and emotionally-disturbed elementary-school boys in a "level-of-aspiration" experiment. The disturbed boys' expectations of success increased following successful performances, but not as much as those of their better-adjusted peers. In contrast, the disturbed boys, following failure experience, decreased their expectations of success more than did the "normal" Ss. This study suggests that the maladajusted children may be less ready to believe that they were actually successful and more likely to accept the fact that they had failed, at least as far as changes in their expectations of achievement success were concerned.

So far in this subsection, research has been reported on factors producing changes in children's expectations of success for the specific achievement tasks on which they had previously experienced success or failure, praise or criticism, and the like. An additional basic question remains. Do these social reinforcements given for specific achievement behaviors affect expectations for success in other achievement or nonachievement situations? Do such experiences produce increased or reduced expectancy of success in, for example, affiliative situations? So far, research addressed to this question has been conducted only with college students (**12, 19, 58**). To date, findings have suggested the generalization here is predictably related to the "need-relevance" of the behaviors under consideration; i.e., that expectancies will be changed most for those needs most similar to that engaged in during the reinforcement experience.

CHANGES IN ACHIEVEMENT PERFORMANCES

Experimental conditions may also change children's achievement performances. One recent study found that the presence or absence of an audience can affect the achievement performances of children (**74**). Ten-to-twelve-year-old children told "make-up" stories either to an examiner alone or to an audience of several adults. The children produced longer stories when alone with the experimenter in all instances. A questionnaire was given the children to assess their exhibitionism and their self-consciousness. The length of stories told by exhibitionistic children was less influenced by the presence of an audience than were the stories of the self-conscious children. Both highly exhibitionistic and highly self-conscious children made the most speech errors when an audience was present.

Experimentally induced success and failure experiences can affect elementary-school-age children's performances on a repetitive motor task (**4**). In one experiment, the Ss were required to cancel all letter *a*'s appearing in a continuous story they read. After failure was arbitrarily introduced by the experimenter (E), the Ss cancelled more *a*'s but also made more errors; i.e., omitted more *a*'s. Following experimentally manipulated success, the opposite effect occurred; the children worked less rapidly and made fewer errors. Experimental reinforcements have also been shown to influence children's performances in a standard reaction-time experiment (**92**). Elementary-school-age children were first given a series of visual choices and their reaction times were noted. Then they were randomly assigned to one of three groups: a control group which was simply told they were going to do the experiment again, a group to whom urging and critical instructions were given before the experiment was resumed, and a third group which obtained relaxing and reasurring instructions at that point. The control group's reaction times during the second part of the experiment decreased, those of the group receiving the relaxing and reassuring instructions remained the same, while the reaction times of the children who experienced urging and critical instructions were faster.

In a complex but well-controlled study, Vogel and Lazarus (**116**) investigated the effect of need characteristics (intrinsic motivation for achievement or for affiliation), expectations of success for efforts related to these two needs, and experienced stress (measured by physiological reactions) on prep-school boys' achievement performances with two kinds of achievement tasks—a sensory-motor task and a conceptual task. Extreme groups of Ss were preselected according to their motivations and expectations of success for the two needs under investigation. The results of this study were many; those especially pertinent to the topic under discussion were these: Boys with high-achievement motivation displayed intense autonomic reactivity in the achievement conditions of the experiment but milder autonomic reactions in the affiliation situation. The opposite was true for the Ss with strong affiliation needs. Second, the boys' performances were more proficient when the task they performed was relevant to the need which was especially important to them or when they were high autonomic reactors in that experimental situation. Finally, when the task was relevant to the S's more important need, *and* when this task produced high autonomic activity, his performance was especially competent.

Concluding Remarks

This chapter has summarized recent research pertaining to children's achievement development. Research in child psychology concerning this dispositional or behavior system, in contrast to many of the other areas covered in this yearbook, is still in its infancy. While research pertaining to children's achievement *abilities* has been an integral part of research in child psychology from its inception, inquiries into the motivational components of children's achievement behaviors—and the antecedents of these—are just beginning. Nevertheless, several studies were cited which indicated that a variety of naturally occurring influences from society, school, and parents can, and do, shape and mold children's achievement attitudes and actions. Studies dealing with the motivational determinants and personality correlates of children's achievement performances were also discussed. From the limited findings to date, these propensities seem to differ for boys and girls, and at various ages, yet do so in a predictable and understandable fashion. Other research focusing on the stability (or consistency) of children's achievement motivations and behaviors was mentioned. In general, these investigations have found moderate but statistically significant consistencies across situations at a given period of time as well as over the years as children mature. Finally, research was summarized in which brief experimentally induced reinforcements (e.g., praise, criticism, and success and failure experiences) have been used in controlled experimental situations to better understand how children's achievement preferences, expectations, and performances may be susceptible to change.

BIBLIOGRAPHY

1. Adler, A. *The Practice and Theory of Individual Psychology*. New York: Harcourt, Brace & Co., 1927.
2. Atkinson, J. "The Achievement Motive and Recall of Interrupted and Completed Tasks," *J. Exp. Psychol.*, XLVI (1953), 381–90.
3. Baldwin, A.; Kalhorn, Joan; and Breese, Faye. "Patterns of Parent Behavior," *Psychol. Monogr.*, LVIII (1945), No. 3 (Whole No. 268).
4. Baldwin, A., and Levin, H. "Effects of Public and Private Success or Failure on Children's Repetitive Motor Behavior," *Child Develpm.*, XXIX (1958), 363–72.
5. Barry, H.; Bacon, M.; and Child, I. "A Cross-Cultural Survey of Some Sex Differences in Socialization," *J. Abnorm. Soc. Psychol.*, LV (1957), 327–32.

6. Beach, L. "Sociability and Academic Achievement in Various Types of Learning Situations," *J. Educ. Psychol.*, LI (1960), 208–12.
7. Bendig, A. "Manifest Anxiety and Projective and Objective Measures of Need Achievement," *J. Consult. Psychol.*, XXI (1957), 354.
8. Bialer, I. "Conceptualization of Success and Failure in Mentally Retarded and Normal Children," *J. Pers.*, XXIX (1961), 303–20.
9. Bialer, I., and Cromwell, R. "Task Repetition in Mental Defectives as a Function of Chronological and Mental Age," *Amer. J. Ment. Defic.*, LXV (1960), 265–68.
10. Birney, R. "The Achievement Motive and Task Performance: A Replication," *J. Abnorm. Soc. Psychol.*, LVI (1958), 133–35.
11. Block, J. "Personality Characteristics Associated with Fathers' Attitudes toward Child-rearing," *Child Develpm.*, XXVI (1955), 41–48.
12. Chance, June E. "Generalization of Expectancies among Functionally Related Behaviors," *J. Pers.*, XXVII (1959), 228–38.
13. ———. "Independence Training and First Graders' Achievement," *J. Consult. Psychol.*, XXV (1961), 149–54.
14. Child, I.; Storm, T.; and Veroff, J. "Achievement Themes in Folk Tales Related to Socialization Practice," in *Motives in Fantasy, Action, and Society*, pp. 479–92. Edited by J. W. Atkinson. Princeton: D. Van Nostrand Co., Inc., 1958.
15. Coleman, J. "The Adolescent Subculture and Academic Achievement," *Amer. J. Sociology*, LXV (1960), 344.
16. Conklin, A. *Failures of Highly Intelligent Pupils.* Teachers College Contributions to Education, No. 792. New York: Teachers College, Columbia University, 1940.
17. Conrad, H., and Jones, H. "A Second Study of Familial Resemblances in Intelligence: Environmental and Genetic Implications of Parent-Child and Sibling Correlations in the Total Sample," *Intelligence: Its Nature and Nurture*, pp. 97–141. Thirty-ninth Yearbook of the National Society for the Study of Education, Part II. Chicago: Distributed by University of Chicago Press, 1940.
18. Coopersmith, S. "Self-Esteem and Need Achievement as Determinants of Selective Recall and Repetition," *J. Abnorm. Soc. Psychol.*, LX (1960), 310–17.
19. Crandall, V. "An Investigation of the Specificity of Reinforcement of Induced Frustration," *J. Soc. Psychol.*, XLI (1955), 311–18.
20. ———. "Parents as Identification Models and Reinforcers of Children's Achievement Behavior." Progress report, NIMH Grant M-2238, January, 1961 (mimeographed).
21. Crandall, V.; Dewey, Rachel; Katkovsky, W.; and Preston, Anne. "Parents' Attitudes and Behaviors and Grade School Children's Academic Achievements," *J. Genet. Psychol.* (in press).
22. Crandall, V.; Katkovsky, W.; and Preston, Anne. "A Conceptual Formulation of Some Research on Children's Achievement Development," *Child Develpm.*, XXXI (1960), 787–97.
23. ———. "Motivational and Ability Determinants of Young Children's Intellectual Achievement Behaviors," *Child Develpm.*, XXXIII (1962) 643–61.

24. Crandall, V.; Katkovsky, W.; and Preston, Anne. "Parent Behavior and Children's Achievement Development." Paper read at meeting of American Psychological Association, Chicago, 1960.

25. Crandall, V., and Preston, Anne. "Verbally Expressed Needs and Overt Maternal Behaviors," *Child Developm.*, XXXII (1961), 261–70.

26. Crandall, V.; Preston, Anne; and Rabson, Alice. "Maternal Reactions and the Development of Independence and Achievement Behavior in Young Children," *Child Develpm.*, XXXI (1960), 243–51.

27. Crandall, V., and Rabson, Alice. "Children's Repetition Choices in an Intellectual Achievement Situation following Success and Failure," *J. Genet. Psychol.*, XCVII (1960), 161–68.

28. Crandall, V., and Sinkeldam, Carol. "Children's Dependent and Achievement Behaviors in Social Situations and Their Perceptual Field Dependence," *J. Pers.* (in press).

29. Crandall, Virginia. "The Reinforcing Effects of Adult Reactions and Non-Reactions on Children's Achievement Expectations," *Child Develpm.* (in press).

30. Crandall, Virginia; Good, Sue; and Crandall, V. "The Reinforcing Effect of Adult Reactions and Non-Reactions on Children's Achievement Expectations: A Replication Study," *J. Abnorm. Soc. Psychol.* (in press).

31. Davids, A. and White, A. "Effects of Success, Failure, and Social Facilitation on Level of Aspiration in Emotionally Disturbed and Normal Children," *J. Pers.*, XXVI (1958), 77–93.

32. de Charms, R.; Morrison, H.; Reitman, W.; and McClelland, D. "Behavioral Correlates of Directly and Indirectly Measured Achievement Motivation," in *Studies in Motivation*, p. 414. Edited by D. C. McClelland. New York: Appleton-Century-Crofts, 1955.

33. D'Heurle, A.; Mellinger, Jeanne; and Haggard, E. "Personality, Intellectual, and Achievement Patterns in Gifted Children," *Psychol. Monogr.*, LXXIII (1959), Whole No. 483.

34. Douvan, Elizabeth, and Adelson, J. "The Psychodynamics of Social Mobility in Adolescent Boys," *J. Abnorm. Soc. Psychol.*, LVI (1958), 31–44.

35. Drews, Elizabeth, and Teahan, J. "Parental Attitudes and Academic Achievement," *J. Clin. Psychol.*, XIII (1957), 328–32.

36. Dunlap, R. "Some Effects of Social Reinforcement on Changes in Attractiveness of Children's Goal Objects," *Amer. Psychologist*, VII (1953), 344.

37. Edwards, A. *Manual for Edwards' Personal Preference Schedule.* New York: Psychological Corporation, 1954.

38. Eschenbach, A., and Carp, A. "Interrelationships among Three Measures of Need Achievement," *J. Consult. Psychol.*, XXII (1958), 451–52.

39. Fadiman, J. "Motivation in Children: An Exploratory Study." Honors essay, Stanford University, April, 1960.

40. Feld, Shiela. "Need Achievement and Test Anxiety in Children and Maternal Attitudes and Behaviors toward Independent Accomplishments: A Longitudinal Study." Paper read at the Meeting of American Psychological Association, Cincinnati, 1959.

41. Fisher, S. "Achievement Themes and Directionality of Autokinetic Movements," *J. Abnorm. Soc. Psychol.*, LXIII (1961), 64–68.

42. French, Elizabeth. *Development of a Measure of Complex Motivation.*

USAF Personnel Training and Research Center, Research Report, No. AFPTRCTN-56-48, 1956.

43. ———. *Motivation as a Variable in Work-Partner Selection.* USAF Personnel Training Research Center, Research Report, No. 7704, 1955.

44. French, Elizabeth, and Thomas, F. "The Relation of Achievement Motivation to Problem-solving Effectiveness," *J. Abnorm. Soc. Psychol.*, LVI (1958), 45–48.

45. Gebhard, Mildred. "The Effect of Success and Failure upon the Attractiveness of Activities as a Function of Experience, Expectation, and Need," *J. Exp. Psychol.*, XXXVIII (1948), 371–88.

46. ———. "Permanence of Experimentally Induced Changes in the Attractiveness of Activities," *J. Exp. Psychol.*, XXXIX (1949), 708–13.

47. Gewirtz, Hava. "Generalization of Children's Preferences as a Function of Reinforcement and Task Similarity," *J. Abnorm. Soc. Psychol.*, LVIII (1959), 111–18.

48. Goldberg, Miriam. "Recent Research on the Talented," *Teachers College Record*, LX (1958), 150–63.

49. Gough, H. "What Determines the Academic Achievement of High School Students," *J. Educ. Res.*, XLVI (1953), 321–31.

50. ———. *Manual for the California Psychological Inventory*. Palo Alto: Consulting Psychologists Press, Inc., 1957.

51. Grimes, Jessie W., and Allinsmith, W. "Compulsivity, Anxiety, and School Achievement," *Merrill-Palmer Quar. of Beh. Develpm.*, VII (1961), 247–71.

52. Haggard, E. "Socialization, Personality, and Academic Achievement in Gifted Children," *School Review*, LXV (1957), 388–414.

53. Hart, I. "Maternal Child-rearing Practices and Authoritarian Ideology," *J. Abnorm. Soc. Psychol.*, LV (1957), 232–37.

54. Hoffman, Lois; Rosen, S.; and Lippett, R. "Parental Coerciveness, Child Autonomy, and Child's Role at School." Study reported at meeting of American Psychological Association, 1958.

55. Hunt, D. "Changes in Goal-Object Preference as a Function of Expectancy for Social Reinforcement," *J. Abnorm. Soc. Psychol.*, L (1955), 372–77.

56. Hurley, J. "Achievement Imagery and Motivational Instructions as Determinants of Verbal Learning," *J. Pers.*, XXV (1957), 274–82.

57. ———. "Maternal Attitudes and Children's Intelligence," *J. Clin. Psychol.*, XV (1959), 291–92.

58. Jessor, R. "The Generalization of Expectancies," *J. Abnorm. Soc. Psychol.*, XLIX (1954), 196–200.

59. Jessor, Shirley. "The Effects of Reinforcement and Distribution of Practice on Psychological Satiation." Unpublished Doctor's dissertation, Ohio State University, 1951.

60. Johnston, R. "The Effects of Achievement Imagery on Maze-learning Performance," *J. Pers.*, XXIV (1955), 145–52.

61. Jones, E. "The Probation Student: What He Is Like and What Can Be Done about It," *J. Educ. Res.*, XLIX (1955), 93–102.

62. Jordan, T., and de Charms, R. "The Achievement Motive in Normal and Mentally Retarded Children." Unpublished manuscript.

63. KAGAN, J., and MOSS, H. "Stability and Validity of Achievement Fantasy," *J. Abnorm. Soc. Psychol.*, LVIII (1959), 357–64.

64. ———. *Birth to Maturity: A Study in Psychological Development.* New York: John Wiley & Sons, 1962.

65. KAGAN, J.; SONTAG, L.; BAKER, C.; and NELSON, VIRGINIA. "Personality and I.Q. Change," *J. Abnorm. Soc. Psychol.*, LVI (1958), 261–66.

66. KAHL, J. *The American Class Structure.* New York: Rinehart & Co., 1957.

67. KAROLCHUCK, PATRICIA, and WORELL, L. "Achievement Motivation and Learning," *J. Abnorm. Soc. Psychol.*, LIII (1956), 255–57.

68. KATES, S., and DIAB, L. "Authoritarian Ideology and Attitudes on Parent-Child Relationships," *J. Abnorm. Soc. Psychol.*, LI (1955), 13–16.

69. KATKOVSKY, W.; Crandall, V.; and Preston, Anne. "Parent Attitudes toward their Personal Achievements and toward the Achievement Behaviors of Their Children," *J. Genet. Psychol.* (in press).

70. KAUSLER, D., and TRAPP, E. "Achievement Motivation and Goal-setting Behavior on a Learning Task," *J. Exp. Psychol.*, LV (1958), 575–78.

71. KIMBALL, B. "Case Studies in Educational Failure during Adolescence," *Amer. J. Orthopsychiat.*, XXIII (1953), 406–15.

72. LANSKY, L.; CRANDALL, V.; KAGAN, J.; and BAKER, C. "Sex Differences in Aggression and Its Correlates in Middle-Class Adolescents," *Child Develpm.*, XXXII (1961), 45–58.

73. LESSER, G.; KRAWITS, ROTA; and PACKARD, RITA. "Experimental Arousal of Achievement Motivation in Adolescent Girls," *J. Abnorm. Soc. Psychol.* (in press).

74. LEVIN, H.; BALDWIN, A.; GALLWAY, MARY; and PAIVIO, A. "Audience Stress, Personality, and Speech," *J. Abnorm. Soc. Psychol.*, LXI (1960), 469–73.

75. LEWIN, K. *A Dynamic Theory of Personality.* New York: McGraw-Hill Book Co., 1935.

76. ———. *Principles of Topological Psychology.* New York: McGraw-Hill Book Co., 1936.

77. LEWIN, K.; DEMBO, TAMARA; FESTINGER, L.; and SEARS, PAULINE. "Level of Aspiration," in *Personality and the Behavior Disorders,* pp. 333–78. Edited by J. McV. Hunt. New York: Ronald Press, 1944.

78. MCARTHUR, C. "Personality Differences between Middle and Upper Classes," *J. Abnorm. Soc. Psychol.*, L (1955), 247–54.

79. MCCLELLAND, D. *Interest in Risky Occupations among Subjects with High Achievement Motivation.* Technical Report, Need Analysis Research Project #NR 172–363, Office of Naval Research, 1956.

80. ———. "Methods of Measuring Human Motivation," in *Motives in Fantasy, Action, and Society,* pp. 7–42. Edited by J. Atkinson. Princeton: D. Van Nostrand Co., Inc., 1958.

81. ———. "Risk Taking in Children with High and Low Need for Achievement," in *Motives in Fantasy, Action, and Society,* pp. 306–21. Edited by J. Atkinson. Princeton: D. Van Nostrand Co., Inc., 1958.

82. MCCLELLAND, D.; ATKINSON, J.; CLARK, R.; and LOWELL, E. *The Achievement Motive.* New York: Appleton-Century-Crofts, 1953.

83. MCCLELLAND, D., and FRIEDMAN, G. "A Cross-cultural Study of the Relationship between Child-training Practices and Achievement Motivations

Appearing in Folk Tales," in *Readings in Social Psychology*. Edited by G. Swanson, T. Newcomb, and E. Hartley. New York: Henry Holt & Co., 1952.

84. McKeachie, W. "Students, Groups, and Teaching Methods," *Amer. Psychologist,* XIII (1958), 580–84.
85. Maltzman, I. "On the Training of Originality," *Psychol. Rev.* LXVII (1960), 229–42.
86. Marlowe, D. "Relationships among Direct and Indirect Measures of the Achievement Motive and Overt Behavior," *J. Consult. Psychol.,* XXIII (1959), 329–32.
87. Martire, J. "Relationships between the Self Concept and Differences in the Strength and Generality of Achievement Motivation," *J. Pers.,* XXIV (1956), 364–75.
88. Mednick, S. "Stimulus Generalization as a Function of Level of Achievement Imagery," *Psychol. Reports,* IV (1958), 651–54.
89. Mischel, W. "Delay of Gratification, Need for Achievement, and Acquiescence in Another Culture," *J. Abnorm. Soc. Psychol.,* LXII (1961), 543–52.
90. Moss, H., and Kagan, J. "Maternal Influences on Early I.Q. Scores," *Psychol. Reports,* IV (1958), 655–61.
91. ———. "Stability of Achievement and Recognition Seeking Behaviors from Early Childhood through Adulthood," *J. Abnorm. Soc. Psychol.,* LXII (1961), 504–13.
92. Owen, W. "Effects of Motivating Instructions on Reaction Time in Grade School Children," *Child Develpm.,* XXX (1959), 261–67.
93. Pine, F. "Thematic Drive Content and Creativity," *J. Pers.,* XXVII (1959), 136–51.
94. Rao, K., and Russell, R. "Effects of Stress on Goal Setting Behavior," *J. Abnorm. Soc. Psychol.,* LXI (1960), 380–88.
95. Rickard, G. "The Relationship between Parental Behavior and Children's Achievement Behavior." Unpublished Doctor's dissertation, Harvard University, 1954.
96. Rosen, B. "The Achievement Syndrome: A Psychocultural Dimension of Social Stratification," *Amer. Sociological Rev.,* XXI (1956), 203–11.
97. ———. "Race, Ethnicity, and the Achievement Syndrome," *Amer. Sociological Rev.,* XXIV (1959), 47–60.
98. Rosen, B., and D'Andrade, R. "The Psychosocial Origins of Achievement Motivation," *Sociometry,* XXII (1959), 185–218.
99. Rosenzweig, S. "Further Comparative Data on Repetition-Choice after Success and Failure as Related to Frustration Tolerance," *J. Genet. Psychol.,* LXVI (1945), 75–81.
100. Rotter, J. *Social Learning and Clinical Psychology.* New York: Prentice-Hall, Inc., 1954.
101. Rychlak, J. "Self-Confidence, Ability, and the Interest-Value of Tasks," *J. Genet. Psychol.,* XCIV (1959), 153–59.
102. Schroder, H. "Development and Maintenance of the Preference Value of an Object," *J. Exp. Psychol.,* LI (1956), 139–41.
103. Sears, Pauline S. "Correlates of Need Achievement and Need Affiliation

and Classroom Management, Self-Concept, Achievement and Creativity." Unpublished manuscript, Laboratory of Human Development, Stanford University, 1962.

104. SEARS, R.; MACCOBY, ELEANOR; and LEVIN, H. *Patterns of Child Rearing*. Evanston: Row, Peterson & Co., 1957.

105. SHAW, M., and GRUBB, J. "Hostility and Able High School Underachievers," *J. Counsel. Psychol., V* (1958), 263–66.

106. SMITH, D.; WOOD, R.; DOWNER, J.; and RAYGOR, A. "Reading Improvement as a Function of Student Personality and Teaching Method," *J. Educ. Psychol.*, XLVII (1956), 47–59.

107. SOLOMON, D. "Teaching Styles and Student Achievement." Paper read at meeting of American Educational Research Association, Atlantic City, 1962.

108. SONTAG, L.; BAKER, C.; and NELSON, VIRGINIA. *Mental Growth and Personality Development: A Longitudinal Study*. Monograph of the Society for Research in Child Development, XXIII (1958), No. 2 (Whole No. 68).

109. STEWART, NAOMI. "AGCT Scores of Army Personnel Grouped by Occupation," *Occupations*, XXVI (1947), 5–41.

110. STRODTBECK, F. "Family Interaction, Values, and Achievement," in *Talent and Society*, pp. 186–89. Edited by D. McClelland, A. Baldwin, U. Bronfenbrenner, and F. Strodtbeck. Princeton: D. Van Nostrand Co., Inc., 1958.

111. SUCHMAN, R. Personal communication. May, 1962.

112. TABA, HILDA. *School Culture: Studies of Participation and Leadership*, p. 115. Washington: American Council on Education, 1955.

113. TANNENBAUM, A. "Adolescents' Attitudes toward Brilliance." Unpublished Doctor's dissertation, New York University, 1960. Cited in *Adolescent Society*, p. 310. Edited by J. Coleman. New York: Free Press, 1961.

114. TIBBETS, J. "The Role of Parent-Child Relationships in the Achievement of High School Pupils," *Dissert. Abstr.*, XV (1955), 232.

115. VEROFF, J.; ATKINSON, J.; FELD, SHIELA; and GURIN, G. "The Use of Thematic Apperception to Assess Motivation in a Nationwide Interview Study," *Psychol. Monogr.*, LXXIV (1960), Whole No. 499.

116. VOGEL, W.; RAYMOND, SUSAN; and LAZARUS, R. "Intrinsic Motivation and Psychological Stress," *J. Abnorm. Soc. Psychol.*, LVIII (1959), 225–33.

117. WAGNER, R., and WILLIAMS, J. "An Analysis of Speech Behavior in Groups Differing in Achievement Imagery and Defensiveness," *J. Pers.*, XXIX (1961), 1–9.

118. WALSH, A. *Self-concepts of Bright Boys with Learning Difficulties*. New York: Teachers College, Columbia University, 1956.

119. WEISS, P.; WERTHEIMER, M.; and GROESBECK, B. "Achievement Motivation, Academic Aptitude, and College Grades," *Educ. Psychol. Measmt.*, XIX (1959), 663–66.

120. WERTHEIM, J., and MEDNICK, S. "The Achievement Motive and Field Independence," *J. Consult. Psychol.*, XXII (1958), 38.

121. WHITE, R. "Motivation Reconsidered: The Concept of Competence," *Psychol. Rev.*, LXVI (1959), 297–333.

122. WINTERBOTTOM, MARIAN. "The Relation of Need for Achievement in Learning Experiences in Independence and Mastery," in *Motives in Fan-*

tasy, Action and Society, pp. 453–78. Edited by J. Atkinson. Princeton: D. Van Nostrand Co., Inc., 1958.

123. Wispe, L. "Evaluating Section Teaching in the Introductory Course," *J. Educ. Res.*, XLV (1951), 161–87.

124. ———. "Teaching Methods Research," *Amer. Psychologist*, VIII (1953), 147–50.

125. Zuckerman, M., and Oltean, M. "Some Relationships between Maternal Attitude Factors and Authoritarianism, Personality Needs, Psychopathology and Self-acceptance," *Child Develpm.*, XXX (1959), 27–36.

CHAPTER XI

Anxiety

BRITTON K. RUEBUSH

In recent years there has been a metamorphosis in the study of anxiety in children. Once a concept primarily of clinical interest and of central scientific importance only within psychoanalytic theory, anxiety has become a concept of ubiquitous theoretical relevance and the focus of considerable systematic research with normal children. While the causes of this transformation are diverse, two factors seem especially implicated. These are the increasing interest of methodologically sophisticated researchers in testing psychoanalytic hypotheses concerning the interrelationships between affective and other behavior systems and the meteoric rise to prominence of anxiety as a drive or drive-related construct in learning theory. The resulting application of experimental methods and design in the study of anxiety and the development of reliable measures of anxiety in children served as further spurs to research activity in this area.[1]

Although there is a vast clinical literature concerning anxiety in children (**19, 60, 72, 73, 89, 127, 194, 228**), this chapter is limited primarily to a discussion of research with normal children. Three aspects of this research are emphasized. First, an attempt is made to delineate some of the major conceptual problems which affect the generality and comparability of research findings. Second, salient theoretical contributions are briefly discussed. Third, considerable emphasis is placed on methodological and measurement problems in anxiety research with children. In addition, although a comprehensive discussion of all studies of behavioral correlates of anxiety in children is not within the scope of this chapter, an attempt is made to review briefly the findings from the research literature concerning

1. Levy (**135**) has presented interesting but circumstantial evidence that the development of reliable measures of anxiety were the causal antecedents of the increase in research activity.

the intellectual, personality, social, and physical correlates of anxiety. The aim is to summarize the current state of knowledge concerning the relationship between anxiety and these behavioral correlates without focusing specifically on any particular theory of anxiety.

Conceptual Issues

Anxiety is one of the terms in most frequent current use by researchers in child psychology. It is also a term whose definition varies considerably among authors. Anxiety is an important construct in theories of behavior, ranging from psychoanalysis to learning theory, and most authors tend to use a theoretically derived definition, although some use empirically derived definitions. The comparability of findings from different studies is not only complicated by differences in theoretical definitions but also by differences in operational criteria from study to study within the same theoretical framework. A meaningful comparison of findings from different studies, and particularly across theoretical frameworks, is contingent on a careful analysis of each author's assumptions and definitions. It becomes more difficult to compare the findings of studies using different theoretical and operational measures of anxiety as the number of unique components characterizing these definitions increases. This is not to say that the various definitions do not share a common core of meaning which remains constant from study to study. Almost everyone agrees that anxiety is an unpleasant-feeling state, clearly distinguishable from other emotional states and having physiological concomitants (**124**). In addition to this common core of meaning, however, the term takes on other nuances and shadings of meaning, depending on the particular theoretical orientation and operational criteria employed by individual researchers.

CONCEPTIONS OF ANXIETY

Anxiety and fear.—Anxiety is generally assumed to differ from fear in its lack of objective focus, the two affective states differing mainly in the extent to which the principal antecedents have an objecive or subjective basis (**74**, **124**). As Erikson (**64**) has pointed out, however, in children the more immature the intellectual and personality processes which differentiate between inner and outer, real and imagined dangers, the more difficult it becomes to maintain a distinction between fear and anxiety. Further, the experiential components of anxiety and fear do not seem reliably different (**91**). In general, the distinction between anxiety and fear is consistently maintained only within psychoanalytic theory; the terms tend to be used interchangeably in studies conducted within other frameworks. For example, in studies testing learning-theory hypotheses, measures of subjective anxiety (such as an anxiety questionnaire) and manipulations of anxiety (fear) through use of objective threats by the experimenter are often considered alternate and equally valid methods of studying the effects of anxiety on performance.

Anxiety as an empirical construct.—Used as an empirical construct, anxiety is a descriptive label for a class of related responses or operations, the constituents of which are physiological responses, statements concerning unpleasant feelings, and the like. The empirical "discovery" of an anxiety factor by the factor analysts (**37**) is illustrative of this approach, but some authors using other methods have also taken a largely empirical point of view in which little attempt is made systematically to specify antecedents or to predict consequents. Anxiety is sometimes used as both an empirical construct and as an intervening variable. Used in these ways, the term may refer to either a set of correlated behaviors or to the *relationship* between a specified class of stimuli and responses. For example, anxiety is used as an empirical intervening variable in studies in which scores on an anxiety questionnaire are found to be functionally connected with a preceding variable (e.g., experimenter behavior) and a following variable (e.g., problem-solving performance), but the term is not assumed to have meanings other than as a convenient label for scores on the questionnaire.

Anxiety as a hypothetical construct.—Assuming the theoretical framework is reasonably well stipulated, meanings of the term and research results are more easily assessed and compared with those of other studies when anxiety is used as a hypothetical or theoretical construct. Used in this way, anxiety is assumed to be an entity or process that actually exists (but is not at present fully observable) and which gives rise to measurable phenomena, including phenomena other than the observables that led to hypothesizing the construct. Thus anxiety, inferred from one aspect of the child's behavior (e.g., stating his feelings on a questionnaire) is conceived of having certain other, predictable consequences (e.g., interference with performance on a complex learning task), which follow from the role of the construct in its theoretical framework.

When used as a hypothetical construct, anxiety may be used as either a hypothetical-state variable or as a hypothetical-process variable (**212, 216**). It is important to read each author's use of the term carefully as valid understanding and comparability of findings and fair assessment of their relevance to a particular theory are, in part, dependent on whether anxiety is defined as a state or process variable.

Anxiety as a state variable.—As a state variable, anxiety is assumed to be an enduring condition of the child that is hypothesized to have resulted from and is defined by a past interaction of the child and his environment. Studies of anxiety in children have employed the term as a state variable in two different ways. Some authors view anxiety as a chronic emotional state (general trait) of the child; the anxious child's anxiety is almost always with him, and he is expected to behave differently from his low-anxious counterpart more or less independently of variations in the current situation. Others view anxiety as a predispositional state variable; the anxious child is not thought to be chronically anxious in all situations but to have a predisposition to become anxious in certain situations specified by the theory. Thus, anxiety may refer to a secondary drive acquired by the child, the operation for which is an avoidant response to a particular stimulus or situation (**55**). The child is assumed to become anxious if, and only if, such an avoidant response is stimulated. Or anxiety may be expected to be aroused reliably in some but not all children if, and only if, they are exposed to a situation with evaluative components (**194**). Whether anxiety is studied as a chronic emotional state or as a predispositional state variable, it is usually assumed to be correlated with stable cognitive and/or action systems of behavior, the manifestations of which are predictable from the theoretical framework of the study.

Anxiety as a process variable.—The term *anxiety* is used as a hypothetical process variable when it refers to an actual, but presently unobservable, inferred activity or process that is conceived to have properties and/or effects other than those leading to its being inferred, and the arousal of which depends upon the presence of an experimental condition which has at least consensual validity as being generally threatening for most children. Thus, the arousal of anxiety in a particular situation may be inferred from the presence of a common "stressor" and/or some physiological response such as galvanic skin response; anxiety inferred in this way is then expected to affect performance in the situation in a systematic manner (e.g., facilitate the acquisition of a simple conditioned response). When anxiety is studied as a hypothetical process variable, individual differences in state are assumed to be randomly distributed within the experimental and control groups. Further, in such studies, anxiety is sometimes assumed to be a transitory phenomenon, equally manipulable in all subjects regardless of prior state.

Anxiety as a behavioral construct and anxiety as a drive.—The term *anxiety* is sometimes used as a behavioral construct to denote a group of responses or response tendencies, some of which are largely instrumental in removing the child from a threatening situation (e.g., adreno-sympathetic arousal), and some of which are "stimulus-producing" sensory effects serving as danger cues or signals to trigger off associative tendencies or habits (**105, 157**) or defenses (**74**). In psychoanalytic theory, the danger signaled by anxiety is a psychic danger, deriving from the intensification of a particular drive (**74**). Aiken (**3**), in a discussion of anxiety questionnaires, stresses the importance of defining anxiety strictly in terms of response clusters, thus rendering the question of "what stimuli are reliably and contiguously precedent to those responses" a subject of empirical research.

A second major use of the term is as a motivational construct; anxiety in this context usually refers to a unitary, discriminable drive or drive-related state. It is sometimes conceived as a generalized energizer of behavior, which combines indiscriminately and multiplicatively with all habits present (**212**); in this case, the investigator is usually interested in anxiety only in so far as it is an operation for Spence's drive-related (D) emotional responsiveness construct, r_e. The theoretical rationale for this relationship is discussed in a later section. Other investigators view anxiety as a learned drive which is differentially associated with certain (avoidant) patterns of behavior and the operation for which is the observation of avoidance responses (**55**). Anxiety used in this way is a hypothetical construct, which mediates between certain situational stimuli and various learned and unlearned responses. Brown (**24**) has suggested that anxiety is the motivating component of many of the so-called acquired drives, and it has been suggested that behaviors, such as dependency (**9, 93**) and responses to such conditions as social isolation (**233**), can be more parsimoniously explained as due to the mediating effects of anxiety. Brown (**23**) has recently suggested that, within learning theory, increased conceptual clarity would result from referring to anxiety as a hypothetical variable with *both* a drive (motivating) function and sensory effects which combine with associative tendencies to direct behavior in specific situations.

General anxiety and specific situational anxieties.—Some investigators conceptualize anxiety as a generalized phenomenon and have developed measures of general anxiety (**31, 194**), while other researchers (**56, 194**) have focused on specific situational anxieties, such as test or arithmetic anxiety. It has been pointed out (**3**) that use of these terms can be misleading in so far as they denote qualitative differences in kinds of anxiety in different situations rather than differences in *sources* of anxiety. Although definitions of anxiety may differ, it would be difficult to demonstrate qualitative differences in anxiety, defined in a given manner, which are a function of situational variations. Apparently, the only logical differences between general and situational anxieties are in the numbers and types of situations which elicit anxiety reactions in the child. Whether a child becomes anxious in a given situation and how anxious he becomes depends upon the perceived significance of that situation for that child. Individual differences in such perception are a function of constitutional factors, previous experiences, and the degree of similarity of the situation to anxiety-arousing situations previously experienced.

The number of children who become anxious in a given situation and the extent to which anxiety in one situation is correlated with anxiety in others are functions of factors, such as the role of the situation in the culture and the number and degree of similarity of the potentially anxiety-arousing components they contain.

Anxiety as a multidimensional versus unidimensional construct.—The question of whether anxiety is a multidimensional or unidimensional concept has important implications for the design of anxiety research. The findings of several investigations of anxiety in adults tend to indicate that anxiety is a multidimensional concept (**108**, **178**), but relatively little evidence directly relevant to this question is available from research with children. As noted below, however, the various available measures of anxiety in children tend to be relatively homogeneous in item content but generally not very highly interrelated. While this may indicate that the instruments are operational measures of different theoretical constructs, it may also indicate that the manifestations of a particular anxiety construct are multidimensional rather than unitary and that these different dimensions are relatively uncorrelated. Research in progress in Cattell's laboratory also tends to support the view that anxiety is a second-order multidimensional factor in children (**37**). To the extent that a particular anxiety construct is multidimensional, obtaining a valid operational measure of the construct may be contingent upon the use of several homogeneous measures in each study or the construction of new multidimensional measures. This may be particularly true where a measure of generalized anxiety is required (**108**).

Major Theoretical Approaches

The term *anxiety* first attained status as a central theoretical construct in psychoanalytic theory (**74**), although it has now become an important concept in almost every theory of personality and behavior. While studies of anxiety and variables similar to anxiety (e.g., stress) in children have been conducted within a wide variety of theoretical frameworks, including those of Lewin (**134**), Festinger (**7**), Rotter (**176**), and McReynolds (**154**), the majority of recent theory-based studies have used concepts or attempted to test hypotheses derived from some version of psychoanalysis or S-R learning theory. Consequently, this section is limited to a discussion of these two general theoretical approaches to the study of anxiety in children.

PSYCHOANALYTIC THEORY

In the major psychoanalytic work on anxiety (**74**), Freud states that the three attributes which define anxiety are: "(*a*) a specific quality of unpleasure, (*b*) acts of discharge, and (*c*) perceptions of those acts." Thus, anxiety is an unpleasant emotional state (with physiological and motor concomitants), which is consciously experienced by the child. Freud defines anxiety as strictly an experiential phenomenon, although in an earlier work (**75**) he uses the term *unconscious anxiety;* however, it is clear that, in referring to unconscious anxiety, he is referring to a "potential disposition" rather than to anxiety itself: "In every instance where repression has succeeded in inhibiting the development of an affect, we apply the term 'unconscious' to those affects that are restored when we undo the work of repression" (**75**). The term *unconscious anxiety* is thus a label which Freud reserves for that complex, dynamic personality state which includes all of the following: drives capable of arousing anxiety, conflicts, and the like; strong defenses; and the *absence* of anxiety. Others (**182, 185**) have labeled this personality state "defensiveness." Such highly defensive children are thought to experience anxiety only in unusually stressful circumstances; at such times, dangerous drives, conflicts, memories, and the like, may approach conscious awareness and precipitate the experience of anxiety, due to an increase in their strength and/or to a breakdown in the defenses.

As stated earlier, the characteristic which distinguishes anxiety from fear in psychoanalytic theory is its lack of objective focus (**74**). The disproportionate characteristic of anxiety also suggests that the descriptive criteria of the reaction are "indicators of a complex set of relationships between internal and external events. The . . . anxious child can relate his affective experience to certain external objects and events, i.e., he can 'explain' his anxious reaction, but he is unaware that his reaction signifies the concurrent strength of certain unconscious ideas, motivations, and anticipations" (**194**).

This definition is largely descriptive and does not specify the origin or functions of anxiety. Freud considers the pattern of sensory and physiological stimuli to which the fetus is exposed at birth to be traumatic; the "automatic" anxiety reaction to this traumatic state of helplessness is the prototype of all later anxiety reactions (**74**). Some writers have stressed the contributing role of intra-uterine and constitutional factors in determining variations in the intensity of these early reactions to danger (**16, 54, 83**). Kessen and Mandler (**118**) have presented an important new theoretical formulation which supplements Freud's theory of the traumatic origin of anxiety. They suggest that the periodic cycles of distress observed in the human newborn may occur in the absence of any specifiable antecedent trauma and consequently serve as an alternate or additional source of later anxiety and learned modes of reducing or inhibiting anxiety. Whatever the nature of the original anxiety evoker, the central function of anxiety in psychoanalytic theory is to precipitate defensive (avoidant) behaviors. The early paradigm (traumatic experience—anxiety—avoidant behavior—reduction of danger—reduction of anxiety) is gradually supplanted in normal development by a different model in which anxiety gradually acquires a signaling function. This enables the child to take defensive action *before* actually experiencing the trauma; the change is adaptive, in that the intensity of the anxiety is controlled, and the child does not experience the full impact of an anxious reaction to trauma. In addition, Kessen and Mandler (**118**) maintain that "anxiety may be controlled not only by flight from trauma and its signals but may be reduced by the action of specific inhibitors . . . [which] may be responses of the organism (for example, the sucking response of the newborn) or external environmental events (for example, Harlow's experimental 'mother')." The authors also suggest that events associated with these inhibitors may take on learned inhibitory characteristics.

According to psychoanalytic theory, then, the major functions of anxiety in the normal child are: (*a*) to signal the presence of psychic danger, and (*b*) to signal the withdrawal of an inhibitory response. It is important to note that psychoanalytic theory postulates different aspects of a given situation, or different situations trigger the danger signal for different children; prediction in this area requires knowledge of the individual history of the child. The theory specifies a number of situations, however, which are likely to elicit anxiety in many children (**74**). Children also differ not only in the number of stimuli or stimulus configurations capable of eliciting anxiety but also in the strength and number of unconscious processes and in the number, strength, and flexibility of their defenses. Children who rarely experience anxiety may be characterized as having defense systems which are highly effective in protecting the child from experiencing his unconscious drives. These defense systems, while effective in this limited sense, may be efficient or inefficient in the role they play in the over-all personality functioning of the child. A child whose defense system is rigid and inflexible may use defenses which interfere with other behavioral processes, whereas the child who has acquired a variety of defenses may "match" the defense to the danger and the over-all situation so as to maximize protection from danger and, at the same time, minimize interference with other aspects of intellectual and personality functioning.

Some authors, working within the psychoanalytic framework (**198**), take a different position in defining anxiety, primarily in terms of the vicissitudes of the child's defenses and only secondarily in terms of the experiential phenomena mentioned above. Rosenwald (**182**), in a recent paper concerning the assessment of anxiety in psychological experimentation, has summarized this point of view:

> . . . anxiety is the psychological mechanism whereby the current intensification of a dangerous drive results in the elicitation of defenses. . . . Anxiety is therefore a theoretical construct which is anchored on the antecedent side to the intensification of a dangerous drive and on the consequent side to the rise of defensive behavior. . . . This definition of anxiety makes no phenomenological references to feelings of distress.

Rosenwald also states that the secondary experiential and physiological features of anxiety appear only "if the defense mechanism does not sufficiently block or distort the dangerous drive, and the drive grows in intensity." This definition of anxiety approaches what Freud defined separately as unconscious anxiety. The contrasting implications of these two definitions for the development of measures of anxiety are discussed in the section on methodology.

The theoretical and clinical literature of psychoanalysis is rich in hypotheses concerning the effects of anxiety on the behavior of the child (**64, 71, 73, 74, 155**). In addition, although some behaviors are not thought to be mediated by anxiety (**92**), these hypotheses comprehensively encompass the full range of intellectual and personality development and functioning. Unfortunately, however, these hypotheses are not generally available in the rigorously logical and testable form of learning theory, although there is considerable current interest in tightening the logical structure of the theory (**15, 41, 77, 99, 177**). Consequently, individual investigators conducting research within the psychoanalytic framework have usually found it necessary to interpret the theory and to derive their own predictions regarding the specific variables being studied. For example, Ruebush (**184**), starting with the psychoanalytic proposition that the effect of anxiety upon performance is mediated primarily by defensive reactions to the anxiety, outlined a simple theoretical network which provides a rationale for predicting whether anxiety will facilitate or interfere with performance. The model states that (*a*) defensive reactions are strongly overlearned "automatic" responses to the anxiety triggered off by various stimuli in the task situation; (*b*) the effects of anxiety upon performance in these situations are mediated by these defensive reactions to the anxiety; (*c*) in problem-solving situations where such defensive reactions are highly similar to those required for successful solution of the task, anxiety has a facilitating effect upon performance; and (*d*) in problem-solving situations where such defensive reactions interfere with or are counter to the responses or operations required for successful solution of the task, anxiety has an interfering effect upon performance.

The summary of research recently reported by Sarason *et al.* (**194**) is an example of one recent effort to develop a systematic and, at the same time, comprehensive program of research within the psychoanalytic framework. These investigators have formulated a series of hypotheses and predictions concerning the unconscious significances and behavioral correlates of anxiety in a specific situation (i.e., evaluative test situations) and their genesis in the previous experiences of the child in school and family life.

LEARNING THEORY

In an attempt to synthesize the concepts of psychoanalytic theory with those of Hullian learning theory, one group of theorists, including Mowrer (**157**) and Dollard and Miller (**55**), accord anxiety (fear) a central place in the socialization of the child. This position, sometimes referred to as social learning theory, and psychoanalytic theory differ little in their basic definitions of anxiety and in their conceptions of its origin as an unconditioned response to traumatic stimulation in early infancy. As in psychoanalytic theory, it is postulated that previously neutral stimuli may, through learning, easily acquire anxiety-evoking properties. Both theories also postulate that the learned response of anxiety ". . . brings with it a number of reactions that are either parts of the innate pattern of fear or high in the innate hierarchy of responses to it," and ". . . it serves as a cue to elicit responses that have previously been learned in other frightening situations" (**55**).

Both social learning theory and psychoanalysis emphasize the cue (signaling) function of anxiety and the reinforcing effects of responses which reduce or prevent the experience of this unpleasant affect. In fact, some learning theorists (**24**, **55**) have either stated or implied that anxiety-reduction is the central motivational factor involved in the socialization of the child; and more recently it has been suggested that a wide variety of specific behaviors, including dependency (**93**) and aggression (**231**), may be learned because they reduce or prevent the child from experiencing anxiety. Similarly, it has been argued that a number of stimulus variables, such as social isolation (**233**) and stimulus complexity (**188**), may affect behavior through the mediating effects of anxiety. The study by Walters and Ray (**233**) appears to be the only published study, using children as subjects, which was designed specifically as a test of this hypothesis.

In general, although anxiety has played a central theoretical role in social learning theory in explaining the personality development of the child, it has rarely been studied as an independent or dependent variable in research with children conducted within this particular framework. Several investigators (**148**), however, have conducted studies within this framework on the effects of anxiety on the learning performance of college students. These authors have focused on the directive function and signaling properties of the responses, both learned and unlearned, which define or are highly correlated with the anxious response (**38**). These responses are thought to serve as cues which elicit the various defensive (task-irrelevant) responses, which in the past have been reinforced by reduction of anxiety. These avoidant habits are thought to conflict with the correct habit or response required for successful performance in the learning situation. Thus, an increase in anxiety is thought always to interfere with performance in these kinds of tasks.

Much of the research on anxiety in children which utilized learning theory concepts, on the other hand, has been designed to test a number of hypotheses advanced by Spence (**212**), and Taylor (**216**), which emphasize the nondirective energizing function of anxiety in relatively simple learning situations.

Anxiety is of major interest in these studies, due largely to its motivational rather than its cue properties; consequently, it is assumed in these investigations that measures of anxiety are operational measures of Hull's concept of drive level (D). It should be noted that some investigators working within this framework mistakenly refer to anxiety as an actual equivalent of drive level, but Taylor (**216**) more cautiously suggests that anxiety is "in some manner related to emotional responsiveness, which, in turn, contributes to drive level." A more formal theoretical rationale for the assumed relationship between anxiety and level of drive has been presented recently by Spence (**213**).

Spence begins with Hull's basic assumption that several hypothetical constructs mediate between the stimulus and the response in any learning situation. These constructs include habit (H), drive (D), and excitatory potential (E). In simple learning situations, such as classical conditioning, the frequency of the conditioned response (level of performance) is "some positive monotonic function of E." In addition, drive level (D) combines multiplicatively with the strength of the habit to perform the response (H) to determine the level of E; i.e., $E = (H \times D)$. Further, in more complex situations where more than one habit is associated with the task stimuli, drive level combines *indiscriminately* with all of these habits.

To provide a rationale for the relationship between the constructs of anxiety and drive level in simple learning situations, Spence introduces an additional hypothetical construct, *a persisting internal emotional response* (r_e), which is assumed to mediate between drive level and operational measures of anxiety or aversive stimulation. For example, ". . . aversive, stressful stimulation is assumed to arouse activity under the control of the autonomic nervous system which . . . may act as an energizer of cortical mechanisms. . . ." (**213**). Theoretically, there are several possible operational measures of this hypothetical emotional response mechanism, including the presence of noxious stimulation, physiological responses, and scores on anxiety scales. In addition, r_e possesses a number of important properties. First, r_e behaves so that D varies directly and positively with the level of intensity of the aversive stimulus (e.g., an unconditioned stimulus such as electric shock). Second, r_e tends to adapt to repeated aversive stimulation with the consequence that drive level is reduced and performance is impaired. Third, where the intensity of the aversive stimulation is held constant, there are characteristic individual differences in the magnitude of r_e, individuals with high levels of r_e showing higher levels of drive (and performance) in situations such as classical defense conditioning than individuals with low r_e. Thus, performance in simple conditioning situations is a function of (*a*) the intensity of the stressful stimulation or other operational measure of r_e; (*b*) the amount of adaptation which has occurred in r_e; and (*c*) characteristic individual differences in r_e.

Complex learning situations, on the other hand, introduce two main complications for the theory. The first of these complications concerns the issue raised earlier regarding the predispositional versus chronic nature of the high anxiety level of the anxious child. In terms of the theory under discussion, the two alternatives are: (*a*) the child, whose high level of anxiety is determined by one of the operational measures of r_e, is anxious (emotional) in a chronic manner in all situations, even those containing no obviously stressful components; or (*b*) in contrast with the low-anxious child, the anxious child is predisposed to become anxious in situations containing some degree of stress, due to a lower threshold of r_e and/or to a predisposition to respond with a more intense emotional response. As Spence points out (**213**), it is not yet clear which of these hypotheses is valid, although it does make a difference in terms of predicting performance in complex learning situations. On the basis of the first hypothesis, it would be predicted that nonstressful situations would still produce a differential level of drive in children scoring high on an anxiety scale; whereas, if one assumed the validity of the emotional reactivity hypotheses, no difference would be predicted between high- and low-anxious children in such a situation.

The second complication arises because, in complex learning situations with children, there are almost always a number of different habits (competing responses) aroused by the situation. The effects of drive on performance in these complex situations depends on the strength of the habit which is "correct" in the situation relative to many other "incorrect" responses elicited in the situation. Much of the research on anxiety in children conducted in this theoretical network has been designed to test two predictions deriving from this aspect of the theory: (*a*) In situations where the strength of one or more of the competing incorrect responses elicited by some aspect of the situation is greater relative to the strength of the correct response, an increase in the drive factor will interfere with the child's performance; and (*b*) if the correct response or habit is dominant in the hierarchy of responses which the child brings to the situation, i.e., if its strength is greater than other incorrect habits aroused by the task, the child's performance will be facilitated by an increase in drive. In other words, the degree of interference or facilitation of performance in complex learning situations is a function of the relative strength or probability of occurrence of the correct response or habit at the time of the increase in drive level.

In summary, although these two applications of learning theory differ in their focus on the drive and cue properties of anxiety, respectively, they demonstrate how the construct of anxiety may be useful in the systematic analysis and prediction of children's behavior in learning and problem-solving situations.

Methodology

Considering the prominence of anxiety as a theoretical construct in most theories of behavior, it is somewhat surprising that objective methods of assessing anxiety in normal children for research purposes have, for the most part, been developed only recently. The lag between theory and methodology is due, partly, to conceptual problems discussed earlier in this chapter; partly, to certain measurement and technical problems. The purposes of this section are to review briefly the various measures of children's anxiety which have been developed, focusing on the rationale for the measure, evidence of reliability and validity, available normative data, and some of the major methodological problems involved in their use. The measures are divided into the two categories noted earlier: (*a*) questionnaires, projective tests, and other measures which view anxiety primarily as a state variable; and (*b*) physiological and other measures of transitory anxiety, and the various kinds of experimental manipulations which have been used to arouse anxiety as a process variable.

MEASURES OF ANXIETY AS A STATE VARIABLE

Questionnaires.—The questionnaire method of obtaining an operational measure of anxiety has been used most often in studies of anxiety in normal children. Some investigators have devised "special-purpose" anxiety scales for use in one particular study (**6, 14, 90, 110, 111, 145, 161, 232**). The great majority of these studies, however, have used one or more of the following scales: the *Children's Manifest Anxiety Scale*, the *General Anxiety Scale for Children*, or the *Test Anxiety Scale for Children.* An additional scale, the *Questionnaire Measurement of Trait Anxiety in Children*, is being developed in Cattell's laboratory at the University of Illinois (**34, 37, 172**).

a) The *Children's Manifest Anxiety Scale* (CMAS). The CMAS was adapted through modification in wording, format, and instructions for use with groups of children by Castaneda, McCandless, and Palermo (**31**) from the *Manifest Anxiety Scale* developed by Taylor (**215**). The CMAS, administered by classroom teachers, contains 42 items from the Taylor scale judged to be most appropriate for children; e.g., "It is hard for me to keep my mind on anything. . . . I get angry easily. . . . My hands feel sweaty. . . . My feelings get hurt easily." The test items were selected originally from a group of MMPI items judged by a group of clinical psychologists to be indicative of manifest anxiety according to Cameron's clinical definition of the chronic anxiety reaction (**27**). This definition characterizes anxiety as a diffuse and chronic condition of psychological and somatic tension, restlessness, distractibility, fatigue, irritability, predisposition to anxiety attacks on slight provocation, and the like. *By definition*, therefore, the CMAS is a measure of the child's tendency to experience a general and chronic state of anxiety, rather than of a tendency to experience anxiety only in specific situations or as a process or transitory phenomenon; it is also assumed to be an operational measure of Spence's hypothetical emotional response construct, r_e, which is related to drive level, D, according to certain rules noted above in the discussion of Spence's theoretical network.

The CMAS has been found to be internally consistent (**121**) and reliable (**31, 102, 163**). Item analyses of the scale indicate that, while most items differentiate significantly between the extreme quartiles in the expected direction (**87, 160**), some of the items—including most of the physiological complaint items—do not discriminate between the upper quartile and the remainder of the distribution (**87**). A separate adaptation of the original Taylor scale has been developed by Lyle and Smock (**144**) for use with high-school-age populations. A short form of the CMAS has been developed (**136**); and "verbal" and "somatic" subscales have been proposed (**179**). Investigators using high-school students have tended to use the *Taylor Manifest Anxiety Scale* (**2, 29, 117, 205**).

(1) *Normative data.* Extensive normative data are available for the CMAS (**31, 102, 114, 132, 160, 163**). The scale has been used with elementary-school children at all grade levels above the second grade. Some studies (**29, 114**) report no grade differences in CMAS scores, but other studies have found an inverse relationship between grade level and CMAS scores (**156, 163**). High-school subjects, on the other hand, obtain higher anxiety scores than elementary-school children on a scale similar to the CMAS (**144, 205**). Evidence concerning sex differences is equivocal with some studies reporting that girls obtain significantly higher scores than boys (**31, 163, 181**), whereas other studies find no sex difference in CMAS scores (**80, 102, 125, 156, 160**). One recent study (**114**) found that junior high school girls obtained higher scores than boys, whereas there was no sex difference at the elementary-school level. In addition, Negro children obtain higher scores than white children (**163**), and rural children obtain higher scores than those with an urban residence (**86, 102, 103, 132**). Scores have also been found to vary with type of school (**90, 102**) and with geographic region (**102**). These normative findings indicate the need to consider population variables in the design of studies using the CMAS. Some of the inconsistencies in these normative data may be due to variables contributing to unreliability in the scale (e.g., test-taking attitudes, reading ability), but it seems likely that they may be due largely to other relatively unexplored variables (including characteristics of Ss and Es) and instructional variables, which may confound with anxiety measures, such as the CMAS (**188**).

(2) *Lie scale.* The CMAS contains 11 items (Lie Scale) selected on an a priori basis to measure the child's tendency consciously to censor or to falsify his responses to the anxiety items. These items do not contain anxiety or anxiety-relevant content. Reliability coefficients for the L scale are adequate. A few studies (**28**) have excluded children with high L scores, but, other than this, relatively little use has been made of the scale.

(3) *Clinical validity*. The CMAS has been used as a measure of anxiety, primarily, in studies of personality and clinical variables. While this is somewhat paradoxical, in view of the original aim to develop a measure of anxiety which could be used to predict drive level in learning studies, it is also understandable in view of the use of a clinical definition of anxiety in the construction of the scale and of the face validity of the items as indicators of clinical anxiety. The research evidence concerning the validity of the CMAS as a measure of clinical anxiety, however, is somewhat contradictory.

On the positive side, school children with behavior (adjustment) problems obtain significantly higher CMAS scores than a control group (**121**); and high-grade retarded children, particularly those who have been diagnosed as emotionally disturbed, also obtain higher CMAS scores than samples of normal children (**140, 181**). CMAS scores have been found to be highly related to scores on another general anxiety scale (**80**). In addition, other relevant studies have reported positive relationships between CMAS scores and self-disparagement (**142**), emotional instability (**90**), insecurity (**159**), use of fantasy, (**197**), unpopularity with peers (**151, 220**), some areas of psychosexual conflict (**221**), and inaccurate perception of one's own but not others' social status (**222**). CMAS scores have also been found to be highly loaded on a personality factor defined by such variables as dissatisfaction with self and others, social inadequacy, lack of personal adjustment, and family tensions (**170**).

Negative evidence concerning the validity of CMAS scores as measures of clinical anxiety includes the finding of no relationship between CMAS scores and anxiety as rated by teachers or as rated by a psychologist after diagnostic study, nor between scores of children referred to a clinic and those of a control group (**239**). Grams, Hafner, and Quast (**80**) found no relationship between CMAS scores and teacher-ratings of adjustment, although they did find that mothers—in contrast with fathers—were able to predict their child's CMAS score. Hospitalization for surgery produces no increase in scores (**113**); and scores of emotionally disturbed, high-grade retarded children do not decrease after treatment with either tranquilizing medication or placebos (**181**). Levitt (**131**) found that CMAS scores were not related to a number of alleged Rorschach indexes of anxiety in a group of emotionally disturbed children (**131**). L'Abate (**125**) presents evidence supporting the contention that relationships between CMAS and the concept of anxiety, as used in the clinic, may be confounded by sex differences in defending against anxiety. It seems likely that failure to take into account individual and group differences in coping with anxiety (defensiveness) may be one of the factors responsible for the negative findings reported in the literature. Other factors involved in the inconsistent findings in this area probably include differences in definitions of clinical anxiety and in diagnostic instruments and methods of interpretation from study to study, as well as in the population variables discussed above.

(4) *CMAS as a measure of* r_e. The studies of most direct relevance to the validity of the CMAS as an operational measure of the drive-related construct, r_e, are those designed to investigate the effects of drive level upon simple and complex learning in children. As in the case of the evidence for the validity of the scale as a measure of anxiety, the evidence from these learning studies is also equivocal. A study conducted by Castaneda (**28**) is an example of a typical validity study which provides positive evidence. Castaneda, in line with Spence's theoretical network, predicted that anxiety would facilitate learning performance when the dominant response was compatible with the to-be-learned response, whereas it would interfere with performance when it was incompatible. The criterion task involved learning a number of light-button combinations; one condition was designed so that the dominant response was correct (i.e., the correct button was always directly under the light), whereas the other condition was designed so that the dominant response was incorrect. The subjects consisted of fifth-grade boys and girls who were high- and low-anxious on the CMAS. The results were generally consistent with theoretical expectations concerning the role of drive in learning situations more complex than simple classical and instrumental conditioning. In the condition where the dominant response was correct, anxiety facilitated performance, whereas anxiety appeared to impair performance in the condition where the dominant tendency was incorrect.

Other positive evidence includes the finding that the performance of high-anxious children compared with that of low-anxious children is impaired on difficult but not on easy items in a relatively complex motor-learning task (**32**), and in a verbal concept-formation task (**141**). Supporting evidence is also available from studies of response amplitude in an auditory-conditioning experiment (**30**), and performance on a nonverbal paired-associates learning task (**217**). The latter study used high-, medium-, and low-anxiety groups and found that performance was a nonmonotonic function of anxiety. The authors suggest that this means there may be different optimal levels of anxiety in learning nonverbal materials of differing complexity. Also of some relevance here are the consistent findings of low, but statistically significant, relationships between CMAS scores and performance on very complex tests, such as intelligence tests (**66, 85, 86, 150, 170**), and achievement tests (**66, 90, 150, 156, 179**). It appears, however, that CMAS scores of highly intelligent children may not be related to their performance in these complex situations (**66**), or that the relationship may be quite complicated (**117**).

Several studies have reported evidence which fails to support the validity of the CMAS as a measure of drive level. For example, Rowley and Keller (**183**), in a study of the operant conditioning of verbal behavior, found that anxiety did not facilitate or interfere with the rate of acquisition of simple verbal responses to two types of social reinforcement. Other studies have found no significant relationship between anxiety and digit-span performance in high-grade retarded children (**115**); between anxiety and performance on group psychometric tests varying in complexity (**171**); or between anxiety and reaction or movement time in a simple reaction-time task (**164**). As the authors themselves often point out, however, these negative findings tend to be inconclusive, due to various problems and deficiencies of research design and execution; these include a lack of systematic analysis of task-complexity and organization of response hierarchies, failure to anticipate the role of instructional and other experimenter variables, as well as failure to control for certain confounding subject and population variables.

b) The *General Anxiety Scale for Children* (GASC) was developed by a group of investigators at Yale University (**194**) primarily as a measure of general anxiety, which could be used to investigate the relationship between anxiety in a specific situation (tests) and anxiety in a variety of other situations. The test is identical in format and method of administration to the *Test Anxiety Scale for Chil-*

dren. Designed as a measure of general anxiety to be used in research within the psychoanalytic framework, the items were selected to be consistent with Freud's definition of anxiety. The GASC contains 34 items concerning anxiety about a number of different situations; e.g., "If you were to climb a ladder, would you worry about falling off it?" "Do you get a funny feeling when you see blood?" "When your mother is away from home, do you worry about whether she is going to come back?"

The GASC has been found to be internally consistent with a high level of homogeneity of item content (**46**) and to have adequate test-retest reliability coefficients for periods up to nine months (**46, 194**). Mean scores on a second administration of the scale tend to be lower; the effect of this serial position is, in part, a function of length of interval between testings and sex of the child (**139, 194**). Variances are not affected by serial position or time interval (**194**).

(1) *Normative data.* These data are available for American (**194**), English (**194, 195**), and Australian (**44, 45, 46**) school children. The scale has been used with elementary-school children of second- through fifth-grade levels; GASC scores do not appear to be reliably related to grade (**45, 194**), although Sarnoff *et al.* (**195**) found a tendency for scores to increase with grade level in English children. Girls consistently obtain significantly higher scores than boys (**45, 46, 194**).

(2) *Lie scale.* The GASC contains a lie scale consisting of 11 items highly homogeneous in item content according to a factor analysis (**194**). Unlike the items of the CMAS L scale, however, which measure the tendency to lie generally, GASC lie items concern the detection of a tendency to be defensive about anxiety and anxiety-related experiences specifically; e.g., "Have you ever been afraid of getting hurt?" and "Do you ever worry?" In addition, there is a much larger negative relationship between GASC lie score and both GASC and CMAS anxiety scores than between these anxiety scores and CMAS lie score (**194**). Although there is a small but significant positive relationship between performances on the two lie scales, they apparently measure different aspects of defensiveness. Also opposite to findings with the CMAS lie scale, girls consistently obtain lower scores than boys on the GASC lie scale (**194**). Although children with high lie scores have been excluded from several studies,

relatively little direct evidence is available concerning the validity of the scale as a measure of defensiveness about the admission of anxiety. Partly because of the very high negative correlation of the lie scale with test anxiety, it has been replaced as a measure of defensiveness in most recent investigations by a new scale, the *Defensiveness Scale for Children.*

(3) *Validity studies.* In general, the GASC has not been employed in research studies as extensively as either the CMAS or the *Test Anxiety Scale for Children.* The GASC was constructed within a psychoanalytic framework to measure general anxiety in a variety of situations to test the hypothesis that the child who is anxious in testing situations also tends to experience anxiety in other situations. Consistent with this prediction, moderately strong positive relationships have been obtained between GASC scores and test anxiety at elementary-grade levels (**45, 194**). Compared with the CMAS, there is less direct evidence available concerning the validity of the GASC as a measure of general anxiety, although it has been found to be highly related to the CMAS (**80**) and is apparently relatively independent of specific situational factors (**45**). GASC scores have also been found to be related significantly and positively to the number of errors on the *Bender-Gestalt Visual Motor* test (**238**), to show a curvilinear relationship with school grades (**44**); and to correlate positively with mothers' estimates of their children's anxiety (**80**).

Sarason and his co-workers have reported the results of a series of studies in which their high- and low-anxiety subjects were selected from the upper and lower quartiles of both the GASC and TASC distributions. While the results of these studies have generally supported hypotheses derived from psychoanalytic theory concerning the relationship between anxiety and learning (**226**), personality variables (**69, 191**), classroom behavior (**192**), and a number of parental and socioeconomic variables (**48, 50**), it is not possible to evaluate the degree to which these findings contribute to the validity of the two scales as separate measures of general and test anxiety. Recent studies by these investigators have used only test-anxiety and defensiveness scales in the selection of subjects. One exception, however, is Waite's study (**225**), in which groups were selected who were high and low on each of three anxiety scales (test anxiety,

GASC, and CMAS). Unfortunately, the results of the study were confounded to some extent by certain task and I.Q. differences.

c) Cattell's *Questionnaire Measurement of Trait Anxiety in Children* must be assembled from the *High School Personality Questionnaire* (**37**). The latter, appropriate for children from 11–18 years of age, is available in two equivalent forms (**34**) and yields scores on 14 first-order personality factors (e.g., excitability, dominance) and on several second-order factors, one of which is defined as clinical anxiety. The QMTAC is a specific measure of this second-order anxiety factor in children. It consists of a battery of 50 items, covering several anxiety-related primary factors. The *Child Personality Questionnaire* (**172**) for school-age children also yields scores on primary personality factors and the second-order anxiety, but a separate anxiety questionnaire for this age group is not yet available.

d) The *Test Anxiety Scale for Children* (TASC) was developed to measure anxiety concerning test-like situations; it differs from the general anxiety scales discussed above in that it is a measure of physiological concomitants and subjective experiences of anxiety in a specific class of situations rather than in a variety of different situations (**191, 194**). The items were selected to be consistent with Freud's definition of anxiety, but all of the 30 test items concern reactions to a variety of evaluative and test-like situations; e.g., "Do you worry when the teacher says that she is going to ask you questions to find how much you know?" "When the teacher says she is going to find out how much you have learned, does your heart begin to beat faster?" "Are you afraid of school tests?"

The TASC is internally consistent (**46, 191**) and has satisfactory test-retest reliability (**191, 194**). The reliability coefficients decrease markedly after an 18-month interval (**46**) but the decrease may reflect meaningful changes in anxiety status (**190**). Mean scores on a second administration of the scale tend to be lower although variances are not affected by serial position (**194**); the position effect on TASC means is less than on GASC means, is larger when the scale is administered by teachers, and in part is a function of length of interval between testings and sex of the child (**139, 194**).

Doris (**56**) devised a limited-purpose version of the test-anxiety scale to measure anxiety concerning arithmetic tests. Some studies (**2, 144, 189**) have used the college form of the scale (**148**) successfully with high-school populations, but Cowen (**43**) has adapted the scale for use with high-school children.

(1) *Normative data.* Normative data means and variances are available for American (**122, 191, 194**), English (**194, 195**), Australian (**44, 45, 46**), and Norwegian (**175**) elementary-school children; and for a high-school version of the scale (**147**). Test-anxiety scores have been found to increase linearly with grade (**45, 191, 194, 195**). Girls consistently obtain significantly higher scores than boys (**46, 122, 191, 194, 195**), although there is evidence that the difference is smaller among retarded children (**122**). Small, but significant, negative relationships have been obtained between test anxiety and father's occupational level (**1, 2, 191**). TASC scores may be partly a function of an interaction between area of residence (industrial or suburban) and teaching methods (**45**). There is little other evidence, however, that test anxiety is related to social class variables (**194**).

(2) *Validity studies.* There are several types of direct evidence concerning the validity of the TASC as a specific measure of anxiety in test-like situations. For example, a small but systematic positive relationship between TASC scores and teacher ratings of anxiety has been obtained (**191**); that this relationship is not a strong one is probably due more to lack of reliability in the teacher ratings than to lack of validity of the TASC (**49**). In view of the tendency for more tests to be administered as grade level increases, it is relevant that TASC scores increase significantly with grade (**194**). In England, where results of the so-called "11+" examinations play a crucial role in determining children's educational futures, TASC scores are significantly higher than in America, whereas general anxiety (GASC) scores in the two countries are similar (**195**). Other directly supporting evidence has been obtained from father (but not mother) ratings (**48, 50**), and from observations that high test-anxious children display more negative affect in the evaluative (test-like) condition of a recorded interview (**11, 241**). High test-anxious compared with low test-anxious children also rate school concepts more negatively in a semantic differential task (**10**), and show a decrease in reaction time to emotional but not to neutral words in a word association test (**57**). To the writer's knowledge, however, evidence concerning the relationship between TASC scores and

other indexes of anxiety in test situations (e.g., physiological responses) has not been published. There are also relatively few data concerning the validity of the TASC as a measure of "clinical" or general anxiety, although moderate but consistent positive relationships have been obtained between TASC and GASC scores (**194**), and Knights (**122**) obtained significantly higher TASC scores in institutionalized than in noninstitutionalized children. Ruebush (**184**), however, obtained no relationships between TASC scores and anxiety scores on the *Holtzman Inkblot Test*.

The construct validity of the TASC as a measure of psychoanalytic anxiety in test-like situations is supported by the over-all pattern of generally confirmatory results of a number of studies designed to test several psychoanalytic hypotheses concerning the role of test anxiety in intellectual and personality functioning (**194**). Early investigations of TASC construct validity were concerned with the relationship between TASC scores and a number of group administered tests. For example, moderate but consistently significant negative relationships have been obtained between TASC scores and group intelligence and achievement tests (**43, 189, 194**). Evidence that TASC scores and not I.Q. scores are the causative factor in this relationship includes: (*a*) the size of the relationship varies systematically with certain characteristics of the intelligence test, such as its test-like or game-like quality, and cultural familiarity of item content (**138, 204, 242**); and (*b*) children equated in group intelligence test scores vary in their performance on other tasks according to their anxiety level (**194**). This includes the performance of boys, but not girls, on individually administered intelligence tests (**184**). In addition, TASC scores predict intelligence and achievement test scores significantly better than do GASC scores (**194, 238**). Compared with children high in test anxiety, low-anxious children (boys) obtain higher grades in social behavior, language, social studies, science, music, and work habits (**48**), and significant relationships have been obtained between test anxiety and teacher variables and ability grouping (**44, 45, 49**).

The results of studies of children with high and low TASC scores in individual test situations indicate that test anxiety may interfere with performance or may facilitate it depending upon certain predictable task and situational variables, such as the degree to which the child's dependency needs are satisfied, the extent to which learned modes of coping with anxiety are compatible with required methods of problem solution, and the test-like or game-like nature of the task (**194**). In addition, compared with children scoring low on the TASC, high test-anxious children are significantly more concerned with bodily integrity, and are more conflicted about aggression and dependency behaviors (**194**). Finally, test anxiety in adolescents is negatively related to the reported absence of early parental expectations of independent accomplishments (**65**), and children with high TASC scores are reported to have experienced more unfavorable experiences and relationships during their earlier years than children with low scores (**194**).

While the number and pattern of these findings rather strongly support the validity of the TASC as a measure of a stable predisposition to experience anxiety in evaluative situations, the results of some investigations provide evidence which is either negative or inconclusive. For example, Broen (**22**) found that, with I.Q. level controlled, TASC scores did not predict current achievement test performance or changes in achievement test scores during the school year in fifth-grade boys. Abelson (**1**) found that, with I.Q. controlled, the habitual mode of responding to achievement situations, as reflected in grade records of fifth-grade boys, was a better predictor of new learning than TASC scores. Abelson's study also demonstrated, however, that some high test-anxious boys use adaptive coping responses in learning situations, whereas others use interfering ego-defensive modes of response. It is increasingly apparent that the predictive validity of TASC scores is increased when habitual modes of response [as well as task and situational factors (**194**)] and defensiveness (**49, 100, 185, 186**) are taken into account. There is evidence (**57**) that even apparently minor variations in such variables (e.g., instructions) may be responsible for conflicting results.

A major question concerning the validity of the TASC involves the problem of sex differences. Although significant findings have been obtained with girls in some studies, the general pattern of findings for boys which has emerged is much clearer and more consistent (**100, 184, 194**). Further, a number of studies (**49, 100, 184, 192**) report that high test-anxious girls present a more favorable impression than low test-anxious girls. High test-anxious girls manifest higher need-achievement in the classroom (**48, 192**) and are more outgoing and forceful in their verbalizations than boys (**11**). These results support Davidson's speculation (**48**) that the TASC may measure a combination of drive and anxiety-related interfering responses in the case of girls whereas for boys it may be a measure of anxiety-related interfering responses.

Sarason *et al.* (**194**) contend that sex differences in defensiveness may play a major role in these inconsistent findings with girls. They assume that admitting test-anxiety is not inconsistent with the feminine role, and that the content of the TASC items may not tap areas of as much concern to girls as to boys. Thus, in addition to being more numerous, high test-anxious girls should be psychologically less deviant, more heterogeneous, and behaviorally more inconsistent, as a group, than their male counterparts. There is evidence that the emotional behavior of girls may be more affected by variations in teacher behavior than that of boys (**49**); and it would seem useful to investigate learned modes of response within anxiety and sex groups controlling for teacher variables. A number of recent investigations, using the *Defensiveness Scale for Children* as a measure of defensiveness, have obtained evidence that the girl who is highly defensive about the admission of negative affect is psychologically and behaviorally more deviant among girls than is the high test-anxious girl (**49, 100, 185, 186**). It seems apparent that defensiveness is an important variable in accounting for sex differences in behavior found in studies of anxiety.

e) The *Defensiveness Scale for Children* (DSC) was developed as a measure of defensiveness to be used in conjunction with the TASC (**49, 184, 187, 190**). It is composed of the 11 Lie-Scale items (e.g., "Has anybody ever been able to scare you?"), which were previously embedded within the GASC, plus three items designed to pick up negative-response set (e.g., "Do you like to play in the snow?"), plus 24 items designed to measure the tendency to deny the experience of negative feelings such as anxiety, guilt, hostility, and inadequacy, even when their expression is appropriate. These include questions such as: "Do you feel cross and grouchy sometimes?" "Are there some people that you don't like?" "Are you sorry for some of the things that you have done?" "When someone scolds you, does it make you feel badly?" The split-half reliability of the scale is .82 (**187**). Wallach *et al.* (**229**) have published a shorter unidimensional defensiveness scale somewhat similar in item content to the DSC but developed in a different theoretical context.

(1) *Validity studies.* Although the DSC was developed only recently, initial findings concerning its validity are promising. In addition to the findings concerning sex differences discussed above, there is evidence that defensive and test-anxious children experience similar conflicts (e.g., dependency), but that these conflicts are manifested more indirectly by defensive children (**185, 187**). Impairment in the intellectual functioning of defensive children seems to occur mainly in unstructured and/or unfamiliar situations (**185, 186**), whereas in the case of test-anxious children the impairment seems more pervasive (**185, 194**). There is also evidence that defensiveness (with text anxiety controlled) is negatively related to sociometric status (**100**), and that taking defensiveness into account improves predictions concerning the verbal behavior of low- and high-anxious boys (**241**).

As noted earlier, there are two somewhat different definitions of anxiety within the psychoanalytic framework; one stresses the experiential aspects of anxiety, and the other defines anxiety primarily in terms of defensiveness. Use of the TASC and DSC in recent research with children seems to indicate that these two positions may not be incompatible or mutually exclusive. The TASC may be an operational measure of anxiety as viewed by the former position, whereas the DSC may be a measure of the term as defined by the latter position. In any event, defensiveness has proved to be a crucial variable in investigations of anxiety in children.

f) Methodological problems. The main advantages of the question method of measuring anxiety include ease in selecting items with face validity, convenience and ease of administration and scoring, and quantifiability. Disadvantages are also inherent in the use of anxiety scales with children, however, and an attempt is made here to discuss four of the more important of these methodological problems.

It has been pointed out that anxiety questionnaires probably do not all measure the same thing (**188**). Thus, one of the more important problems in anxiety research is to determine the extent of communality among scales. Three of the scales discussed above, the CMAS, GASC, and QMTAC, appear to be quite similar in that they all apparently measure the child's tendency to experience a general and chronic state of anxiety. There is little research evidence concerning the extent of their similarity, however, except that one study (**80**), using the GASC method of administration, obtained a high positive correlation between the CMAS and the GASC. Despite the apparent similarity of these two scales, however, they are sufficiently different on a number of dimensions to justify further investigations, and there is not sufficient evidence as yet to justify either substitution of the scales for each other or the currently prevalent practice of uncritical comparison of the results obtained in investigations using different instruments.

The second problem concerns the meaning and distance between scores at various points in the total distribution of scores for each scale. Little is known concerning the relationship between frequency of admissions of anxiety in one or a number of different situations and the intensity of the anxiety reaction. A related problem involves the linearity versus curvilinearity of the relationship between anxiety scores and other variables. Most studies, assuming a linear relationship between anxiety scores and dependent variables, have used subjects selected from either extreme of the distribution of anxiety scores or above and below the median so that relatively little is known concerning the behavior of children scoring at the middle of the distribution. The relationship between anxiety scores and performance may be monotonic with some variables (**57, 179**), but nonmonotonic for others (**11, 45**).

A third major problem concerns the general area of response sets, test-taking attitudes, and defensiveness, all of which have been discussed extensively (**188, 194**). These factors may affect scores at any point in the distribution. For example, high scores may be obtained by certain children because of a general tendency to say bad things about themselves, because they are unusually sensitive or perceptive of their feelings, because of a tendency to be acquiescent, and the like; low scores, on the other hand, may be obtained by some children who are consciously or unconsciously defensive about the admission of the experience of negative affects, or who have a general response set to always answer "No." Relatively little research has been reported concerning the effects of most of these factors on responses to children's anxiety scales. One study (**194**), however, failed to find a relationship between scores on a test of acquiescence and CMAS, GASC, or TASC scores. Also, as noted above, some recent studies have attempted to account for defensiveness either through use of scores from a lie scale imbedded within the anxiety questionnaire or through use of a separate defensiveness scale in conjunction with an anxiety scale. It is apparent, however, in view of findings such as the low correlation between the CMAS and GASC lie scores, that children may vary in defensiveness according to the content of the item or situation.

The fourth methodological problem is how to account for extreme changes in anxiety scores over a period of time. It appears they are due to one or more of the following factors: (*a*) measurement errors; (*b*) a change in defensiveness between administrations of the anxiety scales; (*c*) actual changes in the anxiety status of the child. The findings cited earlier concerning the effects of serial position on GASC and TASC scores (**194**) support the second interpretation, whereas findings from Sarason's longitudinal study (**190**) seem to indicate that extreme changes reflect true changes in anxiety status. Assuming that meaningful changes in anxiety status do occur, it would seem crucial to investigate the processes responsible for these changes, particularly some of the teacher-variables discussed earlier; e.g., little is known concerning the psychological effects on the child of the annual change in teachers, one of the more prominent environmental changes experienced by the average child in our culture. It would also seem useful to explore the value of early scores on defensiveness scales in predicting changes in anxiety scores.

Projective techniques.—The *Children's Anxiety Pictures* (**25, 26**) and the *Amen's Anxiety Pictures* (**58, 218**) were constructed as specific measures of anxiety in children and have been used in several studies (**5, 123, 181**). A number of other projective tests yield anxiety scores in children, along with scores on other personality variables, or were developed and used in only one study. Tests which yield scores on anxiety and anxiety-like responses, as well as other personality variables, include: the *Rorschach Test* (**21, 42, 61, 79, 120, 131, 143**); the *Holtzman Inkblot Test* (**57, 104, 187**); the *Thematic Apperception Test* (**129**); the *Blacky Test* (**18, 206**);

the *Rock-a-bye Baby Film* (**94, 95, 96**); and the *Maller Personality Sketches* (**137**). Measures developed primarily for use in a specific study include: a nonstructured drawing test (**62**); a number of sentence- or story-completion tests (**47, 78, 145, 182**); and two word-association tests (**4, 57**).

Objective tests.—An intriguing battery of disguised verbal, performance, and physiological tests—which yield scores loaded on Cattell's anxiety factor—is in the experimental stage of development at the University of Illinois (**37**). The tests are labeled "objective" because deliberate falsification of responses is difficult and because the emphasis is on performance and behavior. Objective test batteries for measuring anxiety in early school children (**37**) and preschool children (**36**) are in preparation, but only the *Objective Test Battery for Measuring Anxiety as a Trait in the Child* (for ages 11 to 17) is available at present (**37**).

Observations, ratings, and interviews.—A variety of other clinical techniques have received limited use as measures of anxiety as a state variable in children. These include: (*a*) observations of classroom behavior by trained observers (**49, 192, 234**); (*b*) ratings by teachers (**35, 53, 58, 107, 154, 192**); (*c*) ratings by parents (**12, 169, 194**); (*d*) interviews with parents (**13, 17, 48, 129, 190, 211**); and (*e*) observations and interviews with children (**20, 21, 51, 63, 81, 88, 166, 199, 223, 236, 239**). There is considerable variability in the level of methodological sophistication of the studies cited. In general, however, the results of investigations which used highly trained observers, interviewers, and raters seem more consistently reliable than the results of studies using parent and teacher ratings. It is possible to obtain reliable measures of children's anxiety from teachers and parents (**12, 13, 35, 48, 107, 169**) but only if rating scales and psychological terms are carefully defined, and if interviewers and judges are well trained in the application of clinical methods. Further, while observations, ratings, and interviews are subject to a host of methodological problems (e.g., construction of reliable rating scales, training of observers and interviewers, defensiveness of parents and teachers), they are potentially less affected by some of the distortions inherent in the questionnaire approach (such as response sets and test-taking attitudes of the child).

Physiological measures.—While most theories of anxiety assume the necessity of physiological involvement—autonomic, adreno-sympathetic, or reticular activation—in the child's experience of anxiety, little direct evidence concerning this assumption is available. In fact, relatively few investigations have even used physiological measures of dispositional anxiety in children. The dearth of evidence in this area is due, in part, to the difficulty in defining physiological involvement independently of the introspective report or other "molar" behavior of the subject and of knowledge of the type of stressor present in the situation; and, partly, to practical and ethical problems in the use of physiological recording apparatus with children. Krause (**124**) has drawn similar conclusions in a review of anxiety research with adults. Martin (**149**), in another review, recently concluded that no ". . . clear-cut pattern of physiological-behavioral responses associated with anxiety arousal, distinguishable from other arousal patterns has been demonstrated." Apparently, according to our present knowledge, either a report of a feeling of anxiety or the observation of a defensive-response sequence must accompany physiological reactivity if we are to be certain that the latter is specifically indicative of a state of anxiety.

Nevertheless, a limited number of investigations have used physiological measures of anxiety or "emotionality" in research with children. These measures include electrical resistance of the skin (**67, 166, 199, 202, 219, 224**) systolic and diastolic blood pressure (**224**), heart rate (**67, 202, 224**), respiratory movements (**202**), and electroencephalogram patterns (**116, 199, 202**). The findings of three of these studies (**116, 199, 202**) are but indirectly relevant, in that they show that one or more of these measures differentiate normal from emotionally disturbed children. The two most recent studies (**166, 224**), however, are more directly relevant as well as more sophisticated in their methodology and design. Their results offer some suggestive leads for further research, although they also emphasize the complexities involved in the use of physiological measures. For example, Patterson *et al.* (**166**) obtained interference with verbal learning in children who fell at either extreme on the skin-conductance measure of anxiety. The authors also report that, among high skin-conductance children, those who inhibited motor activity learned faster than those who expressed motor activity. In addition, Vogel *et al.* (**224**), working with adolescents, found that physiological measures of "stress reactions" are a function of a complex interaction among situational stress, intrinsic motivational states, type of task, and learned modes of coping with stress reactions.

Two important methodological problems which need to be taken into account in the design of studies using physiological measures are: (*a*) the tendency of change scores to correlate with initial level of the physiological response (**149**); and (*b*) the relatively low intercorrelations among physiological measures (**149**) leading to difficulties in combining several measures to provide a single index of physiological reactivity. Regarding the latter problem, research from Lacey's laboratory (**126**) indicates the best technique is either to employ the most reactive physiological channel for each subject across all conditions as an index of physiological reactivity or to use the most reactive measure for each subject in each separate condition. Vogel *et al.* (**224**) found a high positive correlation between these two methods in a group of adolescents.

There is some evidence (**33**) that autonomic reactivity may be even more important as a component of the anxious response in children than in adults. In any event, the central importance of physiological variables in theories of anxiety and the current technical advances in the development of apparatus suggest that physiological measures will be included in the design of an increasing number of investigations of anxiety in children.

Experimental arousal of anxiety.—A few recent studies of anxiety as a state variable in children have included an anxiety-arousing condition. Such investigations typically use scores on one of the anxiety measures discussed above to select matched groups of high- and low-anxious children; half of each group then receives the experimental condition, and the other half receives a nonthreatening control condition. Anxiety-arousing conditions which have been used include evaluative-nonevaluative (**10, 11, 115, 153, 241**), failure-success (**56, 197, 226**), and the presence-absence of the mother (**186**).

One of the assumptions implicit in the design of these studies is that the anxiety tests measure a predisposition to experience anxiety in certain threatening situations rather than chronic highly generalized anxiety. As noted above, however, there is considerable evidence that some of the measures of anxiety as a state variable have validity as measures of chronic anxiety; thus, one would expect that, when subjects are selected on the basis of scores on these measures, high-anxious children are likely to experience more anxiety in the control condition than low-anxious children, due to their tendency to be anxious in many situations. The predisposition assumption seems more tenable when the instrument used in the study is a measure of anxiety in a specific situation (e.g., tests) than when it is a measure of general anxiety. In the two studies known to the writer (**115, 226**) which used a measure of general anxiety (GASC, CMAS) in the selection of high- and low-anxious children, the experimental manipulation apparently was not successful, whereas in the studies using a measure of specific anxiety (TASC), significant interactions generally were obtained between anxiety level and experimental condition (e.g., **11**). None of the latter studies, however, reported significant interactions for all of the dependent variables used in the study. In addition, none of these studies obtained direct measures of the efficacy of the manipulation from the children themselves (e.g., introspective self-reports, physiological reactivity). In view of these factors, plus the very limited number of such studies reported thus far, it may be concluded that at present there remains unresolved the issue of whether measures of anxiety as a state variable tap a predisposition to experience anxiety in certain situations or whether they tap the presence of chronic generalized anxiety.

INVESTIGATIONS OF ANXIETY AS A PROCESS VARIABLE

Most of the systematic research on anxiety in children has focused upon anxiety as a state, rather than process, variable. This is due to several factors, including the emphasis on exploration of the antecedents, correlates, and consequents of anxiety states and the ethical and practical problems involved in the experimental arousal of transitory anxiety in children. The study of transitory anxiety requires either placing the child in a threatening experimental laboratory situation or observing him in a "naturally occurring" crisis situation. In general, although children have been studied in a number of situations which have consensual validity as being potentially anxiety-arousing, only a relatively limited number of such investigations have been explicitly concerned with manipulations of anxiety.

Experimental manipulations of transitory anxiety.—Two types of investigations have used experimental manipulations of transitory anxiety in testing hypotheses concerning the effects of anxiety upon performance or behavior. One of these types (**29, 101, 162, 208, 233**) investigates the effects of a stressor (e.g., pacing, hostile instructions) on a performance variable, such as complex learning. If the hypothesis is confirmed, the findings support the construct validity of the stressor as an anxiety-arouser; if the hypothesis is not confirmed, it is not known whether the hypothesis was wrong or whether the stressor failed to arouse anxiety in some of the subjects. A second type of study (**232**) is similar to the first except that an independent check of the anxiety manipulation (e.g., self-report of anxiety in the anxiety-arousing condition) is included in the design. This feature permits more confident interpretation of negative findings. Finally, a third kind of study simply obtains a measure of the child's anxiety in response to a stressful or anxiety-arousing experimental condition. Clinical observations, checklists of molar behavior, and questionnaires have been used to obtain measures of the level of anxiety aroused in preschool children by experimentally manipulating loss of balance (**70**), by putting them into a strange new social situation (**97**), and, in adolescents, by exposing them to a threatening communication on dental hygiene (**110**). Alexander and Alderstein (**4**) found increased emotional reactivity, as measured by reaction time and changes in skin resistance, to death words in a word-association task.

Anxiety as a result of "natural" crisis.—These studies have generally been of the third type discussed above, in that they obtain measures of the anxiety aroused by a crisis situation. For example, Bloch *et al.* (**17**) used interview and questionnaire methods to obtain measures of anxiety in children who had been in a motion-picture studio struck by a tornado, and Freud and Burlingham (**72**) used clinical techniques with children evacuated from London in World War II in demonstrating that anxiety from separation from parents was greater than the fear of bombing. Many studies have been concerned with the anxiety-arousing properties of hospitalization and surgical experiences for children (**39, 59, 63, 109, 112, 113, 133, 134, 167, 173, 174, 236, 240**). Most of these studies used clinical interviews and observations as measures of anxiety; but Clayton and Hughes (**39**) used a measure of blood-pressure variations, Erickson

(**63**) used structured-play interviews, and Kaplan and Hafner (**113**) used the CMAS. Several studies have investigated the role of school test situations in arousing transitory anxiety in children (**21, 53, 67, 227**). The measures used in these studies include a photopolygraph for measuring physiological variables (**227**); concomitant self-ratings by students (depressing a lever during the test to indicate anxiety) and recordings of pulse and palmar skin resistance (**67**); and clinical techniques (**21**).

Methodological problems.—Investigations of anxiety as a process variable which have attempted to measure the degree of anxiety aroused by an experimental manipulation or other anxiety-arousing condition generally have used introspective self-reports, physiological techniques, or clinical evaluations as measures of transitory anxiety. These techniques are subject to certain methodological problems discussed earlier in this chapter. In view of the relatively short time interval between the arousal of anxiety and its measurement in studies of transitory anxiety, self-report and clinical measures are probably less subject to reliability errors in such studies than in investigations of anxiety as a state variable. For reasons discussed earlier, however, it would seem difficult to obtain changes in transitory anxiety as a function of an anxiety-arousing condition when anxiety is measured with tests designed to measure chronic anxiety. The failure of such studies (e.g., **113**) to obtain significant findings does not allow rejection of the validity of the stressor as an anxiety-arouser or the validity of the test as a measure of anxiety as a state variable. In general, it would seem preferable in investigations of transitory anxiety to use measures which are directly relevant to the particular manipulation or anxiety-arousing condition used in the study.

As Krause (**124**) and others have noted, studies of transitory anxiety are also subject to a number of special methodological problems deriving from the basic requirement of the presence of a stressor or threatening condition. One problem concerns the independence of the criteria used in defining the anxiety-arousing qualities of the experimental manipulation. It is not possible to consider the presence of a stressor (e.g., hospitalization) as a criterion for the validity of the measure of anxiety (e.g., a physiological measure) and *at the same time* to consider the physiological measure to be a criterion of the anxiety-arousing properties of the stressor. Independent evidence of the validity of both the manipulation and the measure should be available.

Once the validity of the experimental manipulation is established, other problems arise, such as how to insure or measure the orientation of the child to the threatening stimulus. Krause (**124**) concludes that when *either* an introspective self-report of anxiety *or* a defensive reaction *and* the simultaneous occurrence of physiological activation are obtained, one cannot be more certain that the subject has attended to the anxiety-arousing condition and is experiencing transitory anxiety. It would also seem desirable to obtain separate analyses of the data from each child because of marked tendency of children to respond differentially to the same anxiety-arousing condition; as has been suggested (**124**), this effect can be minimized by exposing each child to a number of different stressors. This calls for considerable ingenuity on the part of the investigator, however, if the use of such anxiety-arousing conditions is not to violate ethical limitations involved in research with children.

Little is known concerning the effects of differing base rates or initial levels of anxiety in studies of transitory anxiety in children. Evidence is available, however, that base rate is an important factor in transitory anxiety research with adults (**124**), and it seems possible that the "law of initial value" which has been found to govern physiological responses (**126**) may also result in differential responses to anxiety-arousers and anxiety-reducers in children with differing initial levels of anxiety. For example, the child who is anxious to begin with (i.e., in a state of chronic anxiety) may not show much response to an attempted experimental arousal of anxiety due to already being near his anxiety "ceiling," whereas he might respond markedly to an attempt to reduce anxiety due to being far from his basal level of anxiety.

INVESTIGATIONS OF ANXIETY-RELATED VARIABLES

The designs of many studies in the research literature include experimental manipulations of variables not labeled as anxiety-arousers or transitory anxiety but which are considered as such by other investigators, or for which it seems logical to assume that anxiety is aroused and is a mediating variable in the study. These include studies of "stress" (**76, 158, 176, 224**), frustration (**52, 143, 200, 202, 235**), audience stress (**8, 130**), physical threat (**97**), threat of punishment (**7**), and nurturance-withdrawal (**93**). In addition, as the work of Walters *et al.* (**232, 233**) suggests, anxiety may be the principal manipulated or mediating variable in investigations of social isolation, cognitive dissonance, intolerance of ambiguity, success-failure, level of aspiration, and the like.

Behavioral Correlates of Anxiety

This section presents a brief but comprehensive bibliography of available investigations of intellectual, perceptual, personality, social, and physical correlates of anxiety in children. The major aims are to provide a picture of the scope of recent research and a reference useful to investigators interested in designing research in these areas. Space limitations, however, preclude summarizing the specific results of each of the relatively large number of relevant studies. In addition, the conceptual and methodological problems emphasized earlier also severely limit detailed comparison and integration of these investigations. An example of such a problem is the frequent assumption that different measures (e.g., the CMAS and TASC) are equivalent measures of the same variable. More detailed discussions of hypotheses and research in some of these areas appear in other chapters of this volume and in Sarason *et al.* (**194**).

INTELLECTUAL VARIABLES

Intelligence.—Small to moderate negative relationships have generally been obtained between measures of anxiety and scores on conventional intelligence tests (**22, 43, 66, 81, 85, 87, 90, 119, 137, 138, 150, 160, 170, 185, 189, 190, 194, 203, 242**), although a few studies (**121, 125, 146, 220, 239**) failed to find a negative relationship between CMAS scores and intelligence test scores. In addition, these interfering effects appear to be long-range rather than transitory and to increase with grade level (**138, 190, 194**). It also appears that qualitative differences between intelligence tests (e.g., test-like or game-like) affect the relationship between anxiety and intelligence (**190, 194**). Finally, several studies (**66, 117, 184**) obtained evidence of an interaction between anxiety and intelligence test performance.

Learning.—There is some evidence that anxiety facilitates learning in simple nonverbal conditioning tasks (**30, 233**), and that the affects of anxiety on simple conditioning are partly a function of factors such as stimulus intensity (**30**) and adaptation training (**168**). Several studies of learning a complex visual-motor task report an interaction between anxiety and task complexity or difficulty (**28, 29, 32**), and relative strength of correct and incorrect habits (**162, 165**). These investigations tend to report facilitating effects of anxiety on learning where the task is easy or where a dominant habit is correct, and interfering effects where the task is difficult or the dominant response is incorrect. Tecce and Furth (**217**), using a nonverbal paired-associates learning task, also report an interaction between anxiety and task complexity, but they report that the interaction appears to be nonmonotonic. Lipman and Griffith (**141**) report that anxious children make more interfering task-irrelevant responses on a verbal-learning task than low-anxious children, and that this effect is greatest on difficult tasks. However, they failed to find that anxiety has a facilitating effect on easy tasks. Patterson *et al.* (**166**) found that anxiety interferes with the conditioning of complex verbal responses but that this effect is partly a function of the type of measure used. Rowley and Keller (**183**), however, failed to find that anxiety affected verbal conditioning. Other studies of learning report that anxiety interferes with learning on a nonverbal paired-associates task (**226**), a stimulus-recall task (**207**), an intelligence test (**101**), and a digit symbol task (**1**). The latter study also found that the interfering or beneficial effects of anxiety on learning are a function of certain learned modes of coping with anxiety.

Educational indexes.—There is a great deal of evidence of a negative relationship between anxiety and various educational indexes such as achievement test scores (**56, 67, 84, 90, 101, 119, 150, 156, 160, 179, 185, 190, 191, 194, 238, 239**), although a few studies report either no relationship (**22, 115, 196**) or that anxiety and achievement are positively related (**145**). In addition, Davidson (**48**) found that low-anxious boys obtain higher school grades than high-anxious boys, but Cox (**44**) found a curvilinear relationship between anxiety and grades, moderately anxious children obtaining the best grades. Investigations have also shown that the general negative relationship between anxiety and educational indexes is significantly affected by factors such as characteristics of the task (**66, 88, 145, 190, 194, 224**), teaching methods (**67, 84, 90**), sex of the child (**156, 185, 192**), I.Q. level (**66, 115**), need-achievement level (**152, 192**), grade level (**84, 150, 156, 191**), and social class level (**101**). In addition, several studies have shown that past experiences of educational success and failure and learned ways of coping with such experiences play an important role in mediating the effects of anxiety on school achievement (**1, 84, 224**). Finally, evidence from clinical studies (**88, 120, 194, 230**) indicates that anxiety and defensiveness are of central importance in the personality dynamics of both under- and overachieving children.

Other problem-solving processes.—Anxiety has been found to affect children's performance on many verbal problem-solving tasks, including an anagrams test (**182**), semantic differential tests (**10, 117**), a word-fluency test (**51**), word-association tests (**51, 57**), word-completion and artificial language tests (**227**), and the *Stroop Color-naming Test* (**225**). In general, the findings from these studies show that anxiety tends to impair children's performance on verbal tasks. Anxiety also has been found to impair certain speech characteristics, such as voice quality, voice comprehensibility, and the like, as well as the use of abstract concepts (**11, 241**).

The effect of anxiety on nonverbal kinds of problem-solving also has been studied rather extensively, using such tasks as progressive matrices (**51**), the *Witkin Embedded-Figures Test* (**106, 184**), jigsaw puzzle tests (**186, 208**), the *Porteus Maze Test* (**186, 225**), the *Cornell-Coxe Performance Ability Scale* (**81**), a physical causality test (**159**), the *Bender Visual Motor Test* (**238**), and a human figure drawing test (**69**). In general, the findings of these studies show that anxiety has interfering effects on performance, although the findings of several studies indicate that anxiety may facilitate performance on complex tasks under some conditions (**184, 194, 225**). Finally, it appears that in children anxiety is negatively related to scores on tests of creativity (**170, 180, 194**) and object curiosity (**154**).

PERCEPTUAL VARIABLES

Relatively few investigations have been concerned with the relationship between anxiety and perceptual processes in children. It appears that anxiety and defensiveness reduce responsiveness to perceptual cues (**143, 193, 209**), particularly those which are anxiety-arousing (**210**). Smock (**206**), however, reports evidence of increased perceptual sensitivity to stimuli associated with anxiety. There is evidence that anxiety generally interferes with the accurate perception of external reality (**57, 185, 194, 238**), but there is also evidence that anxiety may result in improved perceptual performance under some conditions (**185**). Other studies have shown that anxiety is positively related to perceptual rigidity and negatively related to perceptual closure (**209**), and that anxiety is negatively related to perceptual field dependence in girls (**106**).

BIOLOGICAL VARIABLES

It was pointed out in the methodological section that several studies have used physiological measures of anxiety. Some of these investigations (**33, 39, 67, 156, 166, 199, 202, 224, 240**) were concerned with the relationship between physical variables and other measures of anxiety in children. In addition, Davidson *et al.* (**51**) found a significant relationship between body-type and anxiety, anxious children tending to be ectomorphs. Other studies have shown relationships between anxiety and physical disability (**47**). In general, however, relatively little is known concerning the biological antecedents and correlates of anxiety in children.

PERSONALITY VARIABLES

As emphasized earlier, the concept of anxiety is of central importance in personality theory and research. This section very briefly reviews the general research findings concerning the relationship between children's anxiety and such variables as dependency, aggression, self-concept, and the like.

Dependency.—There is evidence of a positive relationship between anxiety and both active and passive forms of dependency behavior in children (**97, 193, 194, 232, 233**). In addition, anxiety is positively related to reaction time to dependency words in a word-association task (**57**), and to oral dependency content in inkblot responses (**185, 187**). There is some evidence that the relationship between anxiety and dependency is greater for boys than for girls (**192, 193, 214**). It appears that anxiety in boys is related to behavioral indications of dependency toward teachers (**192**), to social inadequacy and insecurity in play (**98**), and to immature game preference (**214**). Relationships have also been obtained between dependency socialization anxiety and severity of dependency socialization (**237**), and between anxiety and certain behaviors theoretically related to dependency needs, such as food aversions (**205**).

Aggression.—In general, anxiety in children is negatively related to the direct expression of aggression toward others (**48, 128, 143, 185, 193, 197**), and positively related to indexes of the presence of underlying conflict concerning aggression (**57, 185**), and to the expression of self-aggression (**56**). It appears, however, that the mode of expression of aggression toward external figures by anxious children is, in part, a function of teacher and parent variables (**194**). The relationship between anxiety and aggression seems to be more reliable for boys than for girls (**185, 194**). Other studies have shown that anxiety concerning aggression is related to severity of socialization (**237**) and to religious affiliation (**129**). In addition, children with strong defenses against the expression of aggression perform less well in a threatening experimental situation than children without such defenses (**182**), and children who are defensive regarding the expression of almost all negative affects show more evidence of underlying conflict concerning aggression than low-defensive children (**185**).

Self-concept and body-image.—Several studies have obtained significant relationships between anxiety and measures which reflect a negative conception of the self or a tendency toward self-disparagement (**56, 142, 170, 230**). Apparently, the anxious child's tendency to derogate himself tends to generalize and to affect his attitudes toward his body as well (**194**). Evidence supporting the relationship between anxiety and a concern with bodily integrity and adequacy is available from children's inkblot responses (**185, 193**), human-figure drawings (**69**), word-association tests (**4, 57**) and WISC performance (**185**). As noted earlier, several studies have obtained relationships between anxiety and surgical interventions, hospitalization, and the like (**47, 112, 133, 236, 240**). Finally, there is some evidence that defensiveness is related to negative self- and body-concepts in children (**185, 230**). Several investigators have noted the need to consider the different types of defensive reaction used by children in coping with threats to bodily integrity (**78, 110**).

Other personality variables.—Most studies have reported positive relationships between anxiety in children and various measures of clinical maladjustment and insecurity (**17, 37, 48, 107, 121, 123, 159, 192**), although there are a few exceptions (**80, 125, 239**). As noted earlier, evaluation and comparison of findings in this area are complicated by differences in the operational measures of anxiety and adjustment used in different studies.

There is considerable research evidence of a positive relationship between anxiety and general behavioral constriction (**48, 68, 69, 143, 210, 223**). Anxious children tend to be indecisive and guarded (**193**), cautious (**185, 225**), and rigid (**121**) in their behavior. It also appears, however, that anxiety in children is positively related to high utilization of fantasy (**197**). Other studies report relationships between anxiety and exhibitionism (**130**), authoritarian attitudes (**203**), jealousy and guilt (**94, 95**), masculinity-femininity (**82, 100, 214**), and level of aspiration (**192, 223**). The relationship between anxiety and these kinds of variables may be affected by differences in age (**210**) and sex (**49**).

Several recent investigations of personality correlates of anxiety in children have shown—directly or indirectly—that there is considerable variability among anxious children in the ways they have learned to defend against, cope with, or respond to anxiety, and that these defensive or coping patterns may have different but predictable effects on performance (**52, 78, 125, 158, 182, 184, 194, 229, 241**).

SOCIAL AND SCHOOL VARIABLES

Reliable relationships have been obtained between anxiety in children and a host of social variables, including conformity, interpersonal relationships, socioeconomic status, and the like. In addition, several studies have investigated the relationships between anxiety and various school variables, such as teaching methods and curriculum differences.

Anxiety is positively related to suggestibility in an autokinetic situation (**232**) and to susceptibility to propaganda (**78, 110**). Compared with low-anxious children, high-anxious children condition faster to social reinforcement under some conditions (**233**), and slower under other conditions (**166**). One study reports no relationship between anxiety and social reinforcement (**183**).

Several studies have reported negative relationships between sociometric status with peers and anxiety (**106, 151, 180**). Gray (**82**) found a positive relationship between anxiety and social acceptance in boys but not in girls. Hill (**100**) found that, whereas anxiety was not related within the same sex to sociometric status, boys favor low-anxious girls, and girls favor high-anxious boys. Hill also reports a reliable negative correlation between defensiveness and sociometric status in girls but not in boys. A negative relationship has been reported between anxiety and accuracy of perception of own sociometric status (**222**). Finally, several studies have reported detailed observations of anxious children in the classroom situation (**49, 192, 194**).

Many studies have reported relationships between anxiety in children and teacher-child relationships (**40, 49, 67, 171, 192, 194, 234**), teaching methods (**44, 49, 67, 84, 194**), and teacher ratings (**12, 21, 35, 36, 49, 53, 58, 80, 100, 107, 119, 125, 191, 194, 239**). In addition, it appears that children's performance is, in part, a function of an interaction between anxiety and differences in school curriculum variables (**21, 45, 49, 84, 88, 90, 111, 121, 159, 195, 196, 199, 223**).

One study (**233**) found no relationship between anxiety and birth order, whereas another (**48**) reported significant relationships between anxiety and sibling order and sex of sibling. A large number of studies have emphasized the importance of the relationship between anxiety in children and parent-child relationships (**2, 12, 13, 17, 48, 50, 72, 94–98, 123, 128, 134, 169, 171, 173, 174, 190, 203, 237**). Sarason *et al.* (**194**) have discussed this relationship in some detail.

In general, negative relationships have been obtained between anxiety and socioeconomic status (**2, 48, 123, 163**), although there is some evidence (**101**) that middle-class children are more anxious about improving their performance than lower-class children. The relationship between anxiety and socioeconomic class may be complicated by differences in type of anxiety (**6**) and teaching methods (**44**). Other studies have reported relationships between anxiety and industrial-residential (**44**) and urban-rural areas of residence (**103, 132**). Several cross-cultural studies of anxiety have also been reported (**195, 196, 237**).

Concluding Comment

The preceding summary of research concerning the behavioral correlates of anxiety in children demonstrates the extensive scope of recent efforts in this area. It is not possible to present a final synthesis of these studies, however, because of their diverse theoretical and methodological bases and the diversity of the findings. Comparison and integration of the results of future studies will be facilitated by systematic attention to problems, such as the underlying rationale and interrelationships between different measures of anxiety. It seems likely that the emphasis of future research designs will shift from studies of general anxiety to studies of the interfering and facilitating effects of anxiety in relatively specific and carefully defined situations. There is also a trend toward applying experimental and laboratory methods in conjunction with clinical methods in the design of research on anxiety in children.

In addition, several areas of investigation seem especially promising. These include the role played by constitutional antecedents and experiences in infancy in the development of anxiety, the characteristic ways in which different children learn to defend against or to cope with anxiety, and the relationships between teacher and parent behavior and the development and reduction of anxiety in children of school age. Finally, despite many conceptual and methodological limitations, the research findings cited in this chapter constitute evidence of the viability and prominence of anxiety as a variable of basic and enduring concern in child psychology.

BIBLIOGRAPHY

1. Abelson, Willa D. "Differential Performance and Personality Patterns among Anxious Children." Unpublished doctoral dissertation, Harvard University, 1961.
2. Adams, Elsie B., and Sarason, I. G. "The Relationship between Anxiety in Children and Their Parents, *Child Develpm.* (in press).
3. Aiken, L. R., Jr. "Paper and Pencil Anxiety," *Psych. Rep.*, X (1962), 107–12.
4. Alexander, I. E., and Adlerstein, A. M. "Affective Responses to the Con-

cept of Death in a Population of Children and Early Adolescents," *J. Genet Psychol.*, XCIII (1958), 167–77.

5. Amen, E. W., and Renison, N. "A Study of the Relationship between Play Patterns and Anxiety in Young Children," *Genet. Psychol. Monogr.*, L (1954), 3–41.

6. Angelino, H.; Dollin, J.; and Mech, E. V. "Trends in the 'Fears and Worries' of School Children as Related to Socioeconomic Status and Age," *J. Genet. Psychol.*, LXXXIX (1956), 263–76.

7. Aronson, E., and Carlsmith, J. M. "The Effect of Severity of Threat on the Devaluation of Forbidden Behavior." Unpublished manuscript, Harvard University, 1961.

8. Baldwin, A. L., and Levin, H. "Effects of Public and Private Success or Failure on Children's Repetitive Motor Behavior," *Child Develpm.*, XXIX (1958), 363–80.

9. Bandura, A., and Walters, R. H. *Adolescent Aggression.* New York: Ronald Press, 1959.

10. Barnard, J. W. "The Effects of Anxiety on Connotative Meaning in Elementary School Children." Unpublished doctoral dissertation, Yale University, 1963.

11. Barnard, J. W.; Zimbardo, D. G.; and Sarason, S. B. "Anxiety and Verbal Behavior in Children." *Child Develpm.*, XXXII (1961), 379–92.

12. Becker, W. C. "The Relationship of Factors in Parental Ratings of Self and Each Other to the Behavior of Kindergarten Children as Rated by Mothers, Fathers, and Teachers," *J. Consult. Psychol.*, XXIV (1960), 507–27.

13. Becker, W. C., *et al.* "Relations of Factors Derived from Parent-Interview Ratings to Behavior Problems of Five-Year-Olds," *Child Develpm.*, XXXIII (1962), 509–35.

14. Bene, E. M. "A Study of Some Aspects of A. Davis's Theory of Socialized Adaptive Anxiety." Unpublished doctoral dissertation, University of London, 1954.

15. Benjamin, J. D. "Methodological Considerations in the Validation and Elaboration of Psychoanalytical Personality Theory," *Amer. J. Orthopsychiat.*, XX (1950), 139–56.

16. Bergman, P., and Escalona, Sybille, K. "Unusual Sensitivities in Very Young Children," *Psychoanalytic Study of the Child*, III/IV (1949), 333–52. New York: International Universities Press, Inc., 1949.

17. Bloch, D. A.; Silber, E.; and Perry, S. E. "Some Factors in the Emotional Reaction of Children to Disaster," *Amer. J. Psychiat.*, CXIII (1956), 416–22.

18. Blum, G. S. *The Blacky Pictures: A Technique for the Explanation of Personality Dynamics.* New York: Psychological Corp., 1950.

19. Bornstein, Berta. "The Analysis of a Phobic Child. Some Problems of Theory and Technique in Child Analysis," *The Psychoanalytic Study of the Child*, III/IV, (1949) 181–226. New York: International Universities Press, Inc., 1949.

20. Boston, M. V. "Some Factors Related to the Expression of Fear in a Group of Average and Superior Children," *Smith Coll. Stud. Soc. Work*, X (1939), 106–7.

21. Bowyer, Ruth. "Individual Differences in Stress at the Eleven Plus Examination," *Brit. J. Educ. Psychol.*, XXXI (1961), 268–80.

22. Broen, W. E., Jr. "Anxiety, Intelligence, and Achievement," *Psychol. Repts.*, V (1959), 701–4.

23. Brown, J. S. *The Motivation of Behavior*. New York: McGraw-Hill Book Co., 1961.

24. ———. "Problems Presented by the Concept of Acquired Drives," in *Current Theory and Research in Motivation: A Symposium*, pp. 1–21. Lincoln: University of Nebraska Press, 1953.

25. Callahan, R. J. "Unrealistic Fears as a Measure of Anxiety in a Group of Sixth-Grade Children." Unpublished doctoral dissertation, Syracuse University, 1955.

26. Callahan, R. J., and Keller, J. E. "Digit Span and Anxiety: An Experimental Group Revisited," *Amer. J. Ment. Deficiency*, LXI (1957), 581–83.

27. Cameron, N. *The Psychology of Behavior Disorders*. Cambridge, Massachusetts: Houghton Mifflin Co., 1947.

28. Castaneda, A. "Differential Position Habits and Anxiety in Children as Determinants of Performance in Learning," *J. Exp. Psychol.*, LXI (1961), 257–58.

29. ———. "Effects of Stress on Complex Learning and Performance," *J. Exp. Psychol.*, LII (1956), 9–12.

30. ———. "Reaction Time and Response Amplitude as a Function of Anxiety and Stimulus Intensity," *J. Abnorm. Soc. Psychol.*, LIII (1956), 225–28.

31. Castaneda, A.; McCandless, B. R.; and Palermo, D. S. "The Children's Form of the Manifest Anxiety Scale," *Child Develpm.*, XXVII (1956), 317–26.

32. Castaneda, A.; Palermo, D. S.; and McCandless, B. R. "Complex Learning and Performance as a Function of Anxiety in Children and Task Difficulty," *Child Develpm.*, XXVII (1956), 327–32.

33. Cattell, R. B. "Anxiety, Extraversion, and Other Second-order Personality Factors in Children," *J. Pers.*, XXVII (1959), 464–76.

34. Cattell, R. B.; Beloff, H.; and Coan, R. W. *Handbook for the IPAT High School Personality Questionnaire* ("*HSPQ*"). Champaign, Illinois: Institute for Personality and Ability Testing, 1958.

35. Cattell, B. R., and Coan, R. W. "Child Personality Structure as Revealed in Teachers' Behavior Ratings," *J. Clin. Psychol.*, XIII (1957), 315–27.

36. Cattell, R. B., and Peterson, D. H. "Personality Structure in Four- and Five-Year-Olds in Terms of Objective Tests," *J. Clin. Psychol.*, XV (1959), 355–69.

37. Cattell, R. B., and Scheier, I. *The Meaning and Measurement of Neuroticism and Anxiety*. New York: Ronald Press, 1961.

38. Child, I. L. "Personality," *Ann. Rev. Psychol.* V (1954), 149–70.

39. Clayton, G. W., and Hughes, J. G. "Variations in Blood Pressure in Hospitalized Children," *J. Pediat.*, XL (1952), 462.

40. Coan, R. W., and Cattell, R. B. "Reproducible Personality Factors in Middle Childhood," *J. Clin. Psychol.*, XIV (1958), 339–45.

41. Colby, K. M. *An Introduction to Psychoanalytic Research*. New York: Basic Books, Inc., 1960.

42. Cowen, E. L., and Thompson, G. C. "Problem-solving Rigidity and Personality Structure," *J. Abnorm. Soc. Psychol.*, XLVI (1951), 165–76.

43. COWEN, JUDITH E. "Test Anxiety in High-School Students and Its Relationship to Performance on Group Tests." Unpublished doctoral dissertation, School of Education, Harvard University, 1957.
44. COX, F. N. "Correlates of General and Test Anxiety in Children," *Australian J. Psychol.*, XII (1960), 169–77.
45. ———. "Educational Streaming and General and Test Anxiety," *Child Develpm.*, XXXIII (1962), 381–90.
46. COX, F. N., and LEAPER, P. M. "General and Test Anxiety Scales for Children," *Australian J. Psychol.*, XI (1959), 70–80.
47. CRUICKSHANK, M. "The Relation of Physical Disability to Fear and Guilt Feelings," *Cerebral Palsy Rev.*, XII (1952), 9–15.
48. DAVIDSON, K. S. "Interviews of Parents of High-anxious and Low-anxious Children," *Child Develpm.*, XXX (1959), 341–51.
49. DAVIDSON, K. S., and SARASON, S. B. "Test Anxiety and Classroom Observations," *Child Develpm.*, XXXII (1961), 199–210.
50. DAVIDSON, K. S., *et al.* "Differences between Mothers' and Fathers' Ratings of Low-anxious and High-anxious Children," *Child Develpm.*, XXIX (1958), 155–60.
51. DAVIDSON, M. A.; MCINNES, R. G.; and PARNELL, B. W. "The Distribution of Personality Traits in Seven-Year-Old Children: A Combined Psychological, Psychiatric, and Somatotype Study," *Brit. J. Educ. Psychol.*, XXVII (1957), 48–61.
52. DAVITZ, J. R. "The Effects of Previous Training on Post-Frustration Behavior," *J. Abnorm. Soc. Psychol.*, XLVII (1952), 309–15.
53. DELONG, A. R. "Emotional Effects of Elementary-School Testing," *Understanding the Child*, XXIV (1955), 103–7.
54. DEUTSCH, HELEN. *The Psychology of Women*, Vol. I. New York: Grune & Stratton, 1944.
55. DOLLARD, J., and MILLER, N. E. *Personality and Psychotherapy: An Analysis in Terms of Learning, Thinking, and Culture.* New York: McGraw-Hill Book Co., 1950.
56. DORIS, J. "Test Anxiety and Blame-Assignment in Grade-School Children," *J. Abnorm. Soc. Psychol.*, LVIII (1959), 181–90.
57. DORIS, J.; SARASON, S. B.; and BERKOWITZ, L. "Test Anxiety and Performance on Projective Tests," *Child Develpm.* (in press).
58. DORKEY, M., and AMEN, E. W. "A Continuation Study of Anxiety Reactions in Young Children by Means of a Projective Technique," *Genet. Psychol. Monogr.*, XXXV (1947), 139–83.
59. ECKENHOFF, J. E. "Relationship of Anesthesia to Postoperative Personality Changes in Children," *Amer. J. Dis. Child.*, LXXXVI (1953), 587–91.
60. EISENBERG, L. "School Phobia: A Study in the Communication of Anxiety," *Amer. J. Psychiat.*, CXIV, No. 8 (1958), 712–18.
61. ELIZUR, A. "Content Analysis of the Rorschach with Regard to Anxiety and Hostility," *J. Proj. Tech.*, XIII (1949), 247–84.
62. ENGLAND, A. O. "Nonstructured Approach to the Study of Children's Fears," *J. Clin. Psychol.*, II (1946), 364–68.
63. ERICKSON, FLORENCE H. "Play Interviews for Four-Year-Old Hospitalized Children," *Monogr. Soc. Res. Child Develpm.*, XXIII (1958), No. 3.
64. ERIKSON, E. H. *Childhood and Society.* New York: W. W. Norton & Co., Inc., 1950.

65. Feld, Sheila. "Personal Communication," in S. B. Sarason *et al.*, *Anxiety in Elementary School Children*, pp. 248 ff. New York: John Wiley & Sons, 1960.

66. Feldhusen, J. F., and Klausmeier, H. J. "Anxiety, Intelligence, and Achievement in Children of Low, Average, and High Intelligence," *Child Develpm.*, XXX (1962), 403–9.

67. Flanders, N. A. "Personal-Social Anxiety as a Factor in Experimental Learning Situations," *J. Educ. Res.*, XLV (1951), 100–110.

68. Fleming, Elyse S. "Behavioral and Attitudinal Rigidity as Related to Socioeconomic Status and Other Factors." Unpublished doctoral dissertation, University of California, Berkeley, 1956.

69. Fox, Cynthia; Davidson, K. S.; Lighthall, F. F.; Waite, R. R.; and Sarason, S. B. "Human Figure Drawings of High- and Low-anxious Children," *Child Develpm.*, XXIX (1958), 297–301.

70. Franus, E. "Fear Reactions of Children," *Psychol. Wych.*, (1961), No. 3, 281–94.

71. Freud, A. *The Ego and the Mechanisms of Defense*. New York: International Universities Press, Inc., 1946.

72. Freud, Anna, and Burlingham, Dorothy T. *War and Children*. New York: International Universities Press, Inc., 1944.

73. Freud, S. "Analysis of a Phobia in a Five-Year-Old Boy," *Collected Papers of Sigmund Freud*, III. London: Hogarth Press, Ltd., 1925.

74. ———. *Inhibitions, Symptoms, and Anxiety*. London: Hogarth Press, Ltd., 1936.

75. ———. "The Unconscious," *Collected Papers of Sigmund Freud*, IV. London: Hogarth Press, Ltd., 1925.

76. Gardner, B. D.; Pease, D.; and Hawkes, G. R. "Responses of Two-Year-Old Children to Controlled Stress Situations," *J. Genet. Psychol.*, XCVIII, (1961), 29–35.

77. Gill, M. "The Present State of Psychoanalytic Theory," *J. Abnorm. Soc. Psychol.*, LVIII (1959), 1–8.

78. Goldstein, M. J. "The Relationship between Coping and Avoiding Behavior and Response to Fear-arousing Propaganda," *J. Abnorm. Soc. Psychol.*, LVIII (1959), 247–52.

79. Gorlow, L.; Zimet, C. N.; and Fine, H. J. "The Validity of Anxiety and Hostility Rorschach Content Scores among Adolescents," *J. Consult. Psychol.*, XVI (1952), 73–75.

80. Grams, A.; Hafner, A. J.; and Quast, W. "Children's Anxiety Compared with Parents' Reports and Teachers' Ratings of Adjustment." Paper read at meeting of American Psychological Association, 1962.

81. Granick, S. "Intellectual Performance as Related to Emotional Instability in Children," *J. Abnorm. Soc. Psychol.*, LI (1955), 653–56.

82. Gray, Susan W. "Masculinity-Femininity in Relation to Anxiety and Social Acceptance," *Child Develpm.*, XXVIII (1957), 203–14.

83. Greenacre, Phyllis. "The Predisposition to Anxiety: I," *Psychoanalytic Quart.*, X (1941), 66–94.

84. Grimes, J. W., and Allinsmith, W. "Compulsivity, Anxiety, and School Achievement," *Merrill-Palmer Quart.*, VII (1961), 247–69.

85. Hafner, A. J.; Pollie, D. M.; and Wapner, Irwin. "The Relationship

between the CMAS and WISC Functioning," *J. Clin. Psychol.*, XVI (July, 1960), 322–23.

86. HAFNER, A. J., and KAPLAN, A. M. "Children's Manifest Anxiety and Intelligence," *Child Develpm.*, XXX (1959), 269–71.
87. ———. "An Item Analysis of the Children's Manifest Anxiety Scale," *Child Develpm.*, XXX (1959), 481–88.
88. HAGGARD, E. A. "Socialization, Personality, and Achievement in Gifted Children," *Sch. Rev.*, LXV (December, 1957), 388–414.
89. HALL, JENNY. "The Analysis of a Case of Night Terror," *The Psychoanalytic Study of the Child*, II. New York: International Universities Press, 1946.
90. HALLWORTH, H. J. "Anxiety in Secondary Modern and Grammar School Children," *Brit. J. Educ. Psychol.*, XXXI (1961), 281–91.
91. HAMBURG, D. A., *et al.* "Classification and Rating of Emotional Experiences," *AMA Arch. Neurol. Psychiat.*, LXXIX (1958), 415–26.
92. HARTMANN, H. *Ego Psychology and the Problem of Adaptation.* New York: International Universities Press, Inc., 1958.
93. HARTUP, W. W. "Nurturance and Nurturance-Withdrawal in Relation to the Dependency Behavior of Preschool Children," *Child Develpm.*, XXIX (1958), 191–210.
94. HAWORTH, MARY R. "Repeat Study with a Projective Film for Children," *J. Consult. Psychol.*, XXV (1961), 78–83.
95. ———. "The Use of a Filmed Puppet Show as a Group Projective Technique for Children," *Genet. Psychol. Monog.*, LVI (1957), 257–96.
96. HAWORTH, MARY R., and WOLTMAN, A. G. *Rock-a-bye Baby: A Group Projective Test for Children* (Manual and Film). University Park, Pennsylvania: Psychological Cinema Register, 1959.
97. HEATHERS, G. "The Adjustment of Two-Year-Olds in a Novel Social Situation," *Child Develpm.*, XXV (1954), 147–58.
98. ———. "Emotional Dependence and Independence in a Physical Threat Situation," *Child Develpm.*, XXIV (1953), 169–79.
99. HILGARD, E. R.; KUBIE, L. S.; and PUMPIAN-MINDLIN, E. *Psychoanalysis as Science.* New York: Basic Books, Inc., 1952.
100. HILL, K. T. "The Relationship of Test Anxiety, Defensiveness, and Intelligence to Sociometric Status," *Child Develpm.* (in press).
101. HOFFMAN, M. L.; MITSOS, S. B.; and PROTZ, R. E. "Achievement-striving, Social Class, and Test Anxiety," *J. Abnorm. Soc. Psychol.*, LVI (1958), 401–3.
102. HOLLOWAY, H. D. "Normative Data on the Children's Manifest Anxiety Scale at the Rural Third-Grade Level," *Child Develpm.*, XXXII (1961), 129–34.
103. ———. "Reliability of the Children's Manifest Anxiety Scale at the Rural Third-Grade Level," *J. Educ. Psychol.*, XLIX (1958), 193–96.
104. HOLTZMAN, W. H., *et al.* *Inkblot Perception and Personality.* Austin, Texas: University of Texas Press, 1961.
105. HULL, C. L. *Principles of Behavior.* New York: Appleton-Century-Crofts, 1943.
106. ISCOE, I., and CARDEN, JOYCE ANN. "Field Dependency, Manifest Anxiety,

and Sociometric Status in Children," *J. Consult. Psychol.*, XXV, No. 2 (1961), 184.

107. Iscoe, I., and Cochran, Irene. "Some Correlates of Manifest Anxiety in Children," *J. Consult. Psychol.*, XXIV (1960), 97.
108. Jackson, D. N., and Bloomberg, R. "Anxiety: Unitas or Multiplex?" *J. Consult. Psychol.*, XXII (1958).
109. Jackson, Edith. "The Treatment of the Young Child in the Hospital," *Amer. J. Orthopsychiat.*, XII (1942), 56–67.
110. Janis, I. L., and Feshbach, S. "Effects of Fear-arousing Communications," *J. Abnorm. Soc. Psychol.*, XLVIII (1953), 78–92.
111. Jersild, A. T.; Goldman, B.; and Loftus, J. J. "A Comparative Study of the Worries of Children in Two School Situations," *J. Exp. Educ.*, IX (1941), 323–26.
112. Jessner, Lucie, and Kaplan, S. "Observations of the Emotional Reactions of Children to Tonsillectomy and Adenoidectomy," in *Problems of Infancy and Childhood. Transaction: Third Conference*, pp. 97–156. New York: Josiah Macy, Jr., Foundation, 1949.
113. Kaplan, A. M., and Hafner, A. Jack. "Manifest Anxiety in Hospitalized Children," *J. Clin. Psychol.*, XV (1959), 301–2.
114. Keller, E. D., and Rowley, V. N. "Junior High School and Additional Elementary-School Normative Data for the Children's Manifest Anxiety Scale," *Child Develpm.*, XXXIII (1962), 675–81.
115. Keller, J. "The Relationship of Auditory Memory Span to Learning Ability in High-grade Mentally Retarded Boys," *Am. J. Ment. Def.*, LXI (1957), 574–80.
116. Kennard, M. A., and Willner, M. D. "Significance of Paroxysmal Patterns in Electroencephalograms of Children without Clinical Epilepsy," *Assn. Res. Nerv. and Ment. Dis., Proc.*, XXVI (1947), 308–27.
117. Kerrick, Jean S. "The Effects of Manifest Anxiety and I.Q. on Discrimination," *J. Abnorm. Soc. Psychol.*, LII (1956), 136–38.
118. Kessen, W., and Mandler, G. "Anxiety, Pain, and Inhibition of Distress," *Psychol. Rev.*, LXVIII (1961), 396–404.
119. Keys, N., and Whiteside, G. H. "The Relation of Nervous-Emotional Stability to Educational Achievement," *J. Educ. Psychol.*, XXI (1930), 429–41.
120. Kimball, Barbara. "Case Studies in Educational Failure during Adolescence," *Amer. J. Orthopsychiat.*, XXIII (1953), 406–15.
121. Kitano, H. H. L. "Validity of the Children's Manifest Anxiety Scale and the Modified Revised California Inventory," *Child Develpm.*, XXXI (1960), 67–72.
122. Knights, R. M. "Test Anxiety and Defensiveness in Institutionalized and Noninstitutionalized Normal and Retarded Children," *Child Develpm.* (in press).
123. Koch, Margaret B. "Anxiety in Preschool Children from Broken Homes," *Merrill-Palmer Quart.*, VII (1961), 225–31.
124. Krause, M. S. "The Measurement of Transitory Anxiety," *Psychol. Rev.*, LXVIII (1961), 178–89.
125. L'Abate, L. "Personality Correlates of Manifest Anxiety in Children," *J. Consult. Psychol.*, XXIV (1960), 342–48.
126. Lacey, J. I. "The Evaluation of Autonomic Responses: Toward a General Solution," *Ann. N.Y. Acad. Sci.*, LXVII (1956), 123–64.

127. Langford, W. "Anxiety Attacks in Children," *Amer. J. Orthopsychiat.*, VII (1937), 210–19.

128. Lesser, G. S. "Population Differences in Construct Validity," *J. Consult. Psychol.*, XXIII (1959), 60–65.

129. ———. "Religion and the Defensive Responses in Children's Fantasy," *J. Proj. Tech.*, XIII (1959), 64–68.

130. Levin, H., *et al.* "Audience Stress, Personality, and Speech," *J. Abnorm. Soc. Psychol.*, LXI (1960), 469–73.

131. Levitt, E. E. "Alleged Rorschach Anxiety Indices in Children," *J. Proj. Tech.*, XXI (1957), 261–64.

132. ———. "Ecological Differences in Performance on the Children's Manifest Anxiety Scale," *Psychol. Rep.*, III (1957), 281–86.

133. Levy, D. M. "Psychic Trauma of Operations in Children," *Amer. J. Dis. Child.*, LXIX (1945), 7–25.

134. Levy, E. "Children's Behavior under Stress and Its Relation to Training by Parents To Respond to Stress Situations," *Child Develpm.*, XXX (1959), 307–24.

135. Levy, L. H. "Anxiety and Behavior Scientists' Behavior," *Amer. Psychol.*, II (1961), 66–68.

136. Levy, Nissim. "A Short Form of the Children's Manifest Anxiety Scale," *Child Develpm.*, XXIX (1958), 153–54.

137. Lightfoot, Georgia. *Personality Characteristics of Bright and Dull Children.* Teachers College Contributions to Education, No. 919. New York: Teachers College, Columbia University, 1951.

138. Lighthall, F. F., *et al.* "Change in Mental Ability as a Function of Test Anxiety and Types of Mental Test," *J. Consult. Psychol.*, XXIII (1959), 34–38.

139. Lighthall, F. F., *et al.* "The Effects of Serial Position and Time Interval on Two Anxiety Questionnaires," *J. Gen. Psychol.*, LXIII (1960), 113–31.

140. Lipman, R. S. "Children's Manifest Anxiety in Retardates and Approximately Equal M.A. Normals," *Amer. J. Ment. Def.*, LXIV (1960), 1027–28.

141. Lipman, R. S., and Griffith, B. C. "Effects of Anxiety Level on Concept Formation: A Test of Drive Theory," *Amer. J. Ment. Def.*, LXV (1960), 342–48.

142. Lipsitt, L. P. "A Self-Concept Scale for Children and Its Relationship to the Children's Form of the Manifest Anxiety Scale," *Child Develpm.*, XXIX (1958), 463–72.

143. Lucas, Winafred B. "The Effects of Frustration on the Rorschach Responses of Nine-Year-Old Children," *J. Proj. Tech.*, XXV (1961), 199–204.

144. Lyle, W. H., and Smock, C. D. "The Relationship between Manifest and Test Anxiety," *Proc. Iowa Acad. Sci.*, LXII (1955), 405–10.

145. Lynn, R. "Temperamental Characteristics Related to Disparity of Attainment in Reading and Arithmetic," *Brit. J. Educ. Psychol.*, XXVII (1957), 62–67.

146. Malpass, L. F.; Mark, Sylvia; and Palermo, D. S. "Responses of Retarded Children to the Children's Manifest Anxiety Scale," *J. Educ. Psychol.*, LI (1960), 305–8.

147. Mandler, G., and Cowen, J. E. "Test Anxiety Questionnaires," *J. Consult. Psychol.*, XXII (1958), 228–29.

148. Mandler, G., and Sarason, S. B. "A Study of Anxiety and Learning," *J. Abnorm. Soc. Psychol.*, XLVII (1952), 166–73.

149. Martin, B. "The Assessment of Anxiety by Physiological Behavioral Measures," *Psychol. Bull.*, LVIII (1961), 234–55.

150. McCandless, B. R., and Castaneda, A. "Anxiety in Children, School Achievement, and Intelligence," *Child Develpm.*, XXVII (1956), 379–82.

151. McCandless, B. R.; Castaneda, A.; and Palermo, D. S. "Anxiety in Children and Social Status," *Child Develpm.*, XXVII (1956), 385–91.

152. McClelland, D. C. *The Achievement Motive.* New York: Appleton-Century-Crofts, 1953.

153. McCoy, Norma. "Performance of Elementary-School Boys as a Function of Test Anxiety and Instructions." Unpublished doctoral dissertation, University of Minnesota, 1962.

154. McReynolds, P.; Acker, Mary; and Pietila, Caryl. "Relation of Object Curiosity to Psychological Adjustment in Children," *Child Develpm.*, XXXII (1961), 393–400.

155. Monroe, Ruth. *Schools of Psychoanalytic Thought.* New York: Dryden Press, Inc., 1955.

156. Morgan, E.; Sutton-Smith, B.; and Rosenberg, B. G. "Age Changes in the Relation between Anxiety and Achievement," *Child Develpm.*, XXXI (1960), 515–19.

157. Mower, Q. H. "A Stimulus-Response Analysis of Anxiety and Its Role as a Reinforcement Agent," *Psychol. Rev.*, XLVI (1939), 553–65.

158. Murphy, Lois B. "Methods of Coping with Stress in the Development of Normal Children: A Research Project," *Bull. Menninger Clinic*, XXIV (1960), 97–154.

159. Muuss, R. E. "The Relationship between 'Causal' Orientation, Anxiety, and Insecurity in Elementary-School Children," *J. Educ. Psychol.*, LI (1960), 122–29.

160. Østby, H. "Forsøk med CMAS," *Pedag. Forsk.*, III (1960), 139–55.

161. Paivio, A.; Baldwin, A. L.; and Berger, S. M. "Measurement of Children's Sensitivity to Audiences," *Child Develpm.*, XXXII (1961), 721–30.

162. Palermo, D. S. "Proactive Interference and Facilitation as a Function of Amount of Training and Stress," *J. Exp. Psychol.*, LIII (1957), 293–96.

163. ———. "Racial Comparisons and Additional Normative Data on the Children's Manifest Anxiety Scale," *Child Develpm.*, XXX (1959), 53–57.

164. ———. "Relation between Anxiety and Two Measures of Speed in a Reaction Time Task," *Child Develpm.*, XXXII (1961), 401–8.

165. Palermo, D. S.; Castaneda, A.; and McCandless, B. R. "The Relationship of Anxiety in Children to Performance in a Complex Learning Task," *Child Develpm.*, XXVII (1956), 333–37.

166. Patterson, G. R.; Helper, M. E.; and Wilcott, R. C. "Anxiety and Verbal Conditioning in Children," *Child Develpm.*, XXXI (1960), 101–8.

167. Pearson, G. H. J. "Effect of Operative Procedures on the Emotional Life of the Child," *Amer. J. Dis. Child.*, LXII (1941), 716–29.

168. Penney, R. K., and McCann, B. "The Instrumental Escape Conditioning of Anxious and Nonanxious Children," *J. Abnorm. Soc. Psychol.* (in press).

169. Peterson, D. R., and Cattell, R. B. "Personality Factors in Nursery-

School Children as Derived from Parent Ratings," *J. Clin. Psychol.*, XIV (1958), 346–55.

170. PHILLIPS, B. N.; HINDSMAN, E.; and JENNINGS, E. "Influence of Intelligence on Anxiety and Perception of Self and Others," *Child Develpm.*, XXXI (1960), 41–46.

171. PHILLIPS, B. N.; KING, F. J.; and MCGUIRE, C. "Studies on Anxiety: I. Anxiety and Performance on Psychometric Tests Varying in Complexity," *Child Develpm.*, XXX (1959), 253–60.

172. PORTER, R. B., and CATTELL, R. B. *Handbook for the IPAT Children's Personality Questionnaire* ("*the CPQ*"). Champaign, Illinois: Institute for Personality and Ability Testing, 1960.

173. PRUGH, D. G. "Investigations Dealing with the Reactions of Children and Families to Hospitalization and Illness: Problems and Potentialities," in *Emotional Problems of Early Childhood*, pp. 307–21. Edited by G. Caplan. New York: Basic Books, 1955.

174. PRUGH, D. G., *et al.* "A Study of the Emotional Reactions of Children and Families to Hospitalization and Illness," *Amer. J. Orthopsychiat.*, XXIII (1953), 70–106.

175. RAND, P. "Anxiety in Connection with School Performance: III. Try-out of a Norwegian Translation of the Test-Anxiety Questionnaire for Children," *Pedag. Forsk.*, IV (1960), 178–99.

176. RAO, K. U., and RUSSELL, R. W. "Effects of Stress on Goal-setting Behavior," *J. Abnorm. Soc. Psychol.*, LXI (1960), 380–88.

177. RAPAPORT, D. "The Structure of Psychoanalytic Theory (a Systematizing Attempt)," in *Psychology: A Study of a Science*, Vol. III, pp. 55–183. Edited by S. Koch. New York: McGraw-Hill Book Co., Inc., 1959.

178. RAPHELSON, A. C. "The Relationships among Imaginative, Direct Verbal, and Physiological Measures of Anxiety in an Achievement Situation," *J. Abnorm. Soc. Psychol.*, LIV (1957), 13–18.

179. REESE, H. W. "Manifest Anxiety and Achievement Test Performance," *J. Educ. Psychol.*, LII (1961), 132–35.

180. REID, J. B.; KING, F. J.; and WICKWIRE, PAT. "Cognitive and Other Personality Characteristics of Creative Children," *Psychol. Rep.*, V (1959), 729–37.

181. ROSENBLUM, S., and CALLAHAN, R. J. "The Performance of High-grade Retarded, Emotionally Disturbed Children on the Children's Manifest Anxiety Scale and Children's Anxiety Pictures," *J. Clin. Psychol.*, XIV (1958), 272–75.

182. ROSENWALD, G. C. "The Assessment of Anxiety in Psychological Experimentation: A Theoretical Reformulation and Test," *J. Abnorm. Soc. Psychol.*, LXII (1961), 666–73.

183. ROWLEY, V., and KELLER, E. D. "Changes in Children's Verbal Behavior as a Function of Social Approval and Manifest Anxiety," *J. Abnorm. Soc. Psychol.*, LXV (1962), 53–57.

184. RUEBUSH, B. K. "Interfering and Facilitating Effects of Test Anxiety," *J. Abnorm. Soc. Psychol.*, LX (1960), 205–12.

185. ———. "Children's Behavior as a Function of Anxiety and Defensiveness." Unpublished doctoral dissertation, Yale University, 1960.

186. RUEBUSH, B. K.; BYRUM, MILDRED; and FARNHAM, LOUISE J. "Problem-

solving as a Function of Children's Defensiveness and Parental Behavior." Unpublished manuscript, University of Minnesota.

187. Ruebush, B. K., and Waite, R. R. "Oral Dependency in Anxious and Defensive Children," *Merrill-Palmer Quart.*, VII (1961), 181–90.

188. Sarason, I. G. "Empirical Findings and Theoretical Problems in the Use of Anxiety Scales," *Psychol. Bull.*, LVII (1960), 403–15.

189. ———. "Test Anxiety and Intellectual Performance," *J. Abnorm. Soc. Psychol.* (in press).

190. Sarason, S. B. "Report on Project USPHA M-712. The Development of Anxiety in Children," 1962 (mimeographed).

191. Sarason, S. B., *et al.* "A Test Anxiety Scale for Children," *Child Develpm.*, XXIX (1958), 105–13.

192. ———. "Classroom Observations of High- and Low-anxious Children," *Child Develpm.*, XXIX (1958), 287–95.

193. ———. "Rorschach Behavior and Performance of High- and Low-anxious Children," *Child Develpm.*, XXIX (1958), 277–85.

194. ———. *Anxiety in Elementary School Children.* New York: John Wiley & Sons, Inc., 1960.

195. Sarnoff, I.; Lighthall, F.; Waite, R.; Davidson, K.; and Sarason, S. "A Cross-cultural Study of Anxiety among American and English School Children," *J. Educ. Psychol.*, XLIX (1958), 129–36.

196. ———. "Test Anxiety and the 'Eleven-Plus' Examination," *Brit. J. Educ. Psychol.*, XXIX (1959), 9–16.

197. Saxton, George H. "Spontaneous Fantasy as a Resource of High-grade Retardates for Coping with a Failure-Stress Frustration," *J. Abnorm. Soc. Psychol.*, LXIV (1962), No. 1, 81–84.

198. Schafer, R. *Psychoanalytic Interpretation in Rorschach Testing.* New York: Grune & Stratton, 1954.

199. Schiff, E.; Dougan, C.; and Welch, L. "The Conditioned PGR and the EEG as Indicators of Anxiety," *J. Abnorm. Soc. Psychol.*, XLIV (1949), 549–52.

200. Sears, R. R. "Symposium on Genetic Psychology: III. Effects of Frustration and Anxiety on Fantasy Aggression," *Amer. J. Orthopsychiat.*, XXI (1951), 498–505.

201. Sells, S. B. "Structured Measurement of Personality and Motivation: A Review of Contributions of Raymond B. Cattell," *J. Clin. Psychol.*, XV (1959), 3–21.

202. Sherman, M., and Jost, H. "Frustration Reactions of Normal and Neurotic Persons," *J. Psychol.*, XIII (1942), 3–19.

203. Siegman, A. W. "Authoritarian Attitudes in Children: I, The Effect of Age, I.Q., Anxiety, and Parental Religious Attitudes," *J. Clin. Psychol.*, XIII (1957), 338–40.

204. Silverstein, A. B. "Test Anxiety and the Primary Mental Abilities," *Psychol. Rep.*, VIII (1961), 415–17.

205. Smith, W.; Powell, Elizabeth K.; and Ross, S. "Manifest Anxiety and Food Aversions," *J. Abnorm. Soc. Psychol.*, L (1955), 101–4.

206. Smock, C. D. "Replication and Comments: 'An Experimental Reunion of Psychoanalytic Theory with Perceptual Vigilance and Defense,'" *J. Abnorm. Soc. Psychol.*, LIII (1956), 68–73.

207. ———. "The Relationship between 'Intolerance of Ambiguity,' Generalization and Speed of Perceptual Closure," *Child Develpm.*, XXVIII (1957), 27–36.

208. ———. "Recall of Interrupted and Noninterrupted Tasks as a Function of Experimentally Induced Anxiety and Motivational Relevance of the Task Stimuli," *J. Pers.*, XXV (1957), 589–99.

209. ———. "Perceptual Rigidity and Closure Phenomenon as a Function of Manifest Anxiety in Children," *Child Develpm.*, XXIX (1958), 237–48.

210. Solley, C. M., and Engel, M. "Perceptual Autism in Children: The Effects of Reward, Punishment, and Neutral Conditions upon Perceptual Learning," *J. Genet. Psychol.*, XCVII (1960), 77–91.

211. Solomon, A. L. "Personality and Behavior Patterns of Children with Functional Defects of Articulation," *Child Develpm.*, XXXII (1961), 731–37.

212. Spence, K. W. *Behavior Theory and Conditioning*. New Haven, Connecticut: Yale University Press, 1956.

213. ———. "A Theory of Emotionally Based Drive (D) and Its Relation to Performance in Simple Learning Situations," *Amer. Psychol.*, XIII (1958), 131–41.

214. Sutton-Smith, B., and Rosenberg, B. G. "Manifest Anxiety and Game Preferences in Children," *Child Develpm.*, XXXI (1960), 307–11.

215. Taylor, Janet A. "A Personality Scale of Manifest Anxiety," *J. Abnorm. Soc. Psychol.*, XLVIII (1953), 285–90.

216. ———. "Drive Theory and Manifest Anxiety," *Psychol. Bull.*, LIII (1956), 303–20.

217. Tecce, J. J., and Furth, H. G. "Nonverbal Paired-Associates Learning as a Function of Children's Anxiety and Response Competition," *Amer. Psychol.*, XVII (1962), 323 (abstract).

218. Temple, R., and Amen, E. W. "A Study of Anxiety Reactions in Young Children by Means of a Projective Technique," *Genet. Psychol. Monogr.*, XXX (1944), 59–113.

219. Terrell, G., and Ware, R. "Emotionality as a Function of Delay of Reward." Unpublished manuscript, University of Colorado, 1962.

220. Trent, R. D. "The Relationship of Anxiety to Popularity and Rejection among Institutionalized Delinquent Boys," *Child Develpm.*, XXVIII (1957), 379–83.

221. ———. "An Exploration of Relationships between Manifest Anxiety and Selected Psychosexual Areas," *J. Proj. Tech.*, XXI (1957), 318–322.

222. ———. "Anxiety and Accuracy of Perception of Sociometric Status among Institutionalized Delinquent Boys," *J. Genet. Psychol.*, XCIV (1959), 85–91.

223. Veness, Thelma. "Goal-setting Behavior, Anxiety, and School Streaming," *Brit. J. Educ. Psychol.*, XXX (1960), 22–29.

224. Vogel, W.; Raymond, Susan; and Lazarus, R. S. "Intrinsic Motivation and Psychological Stress," *J. Abnorm. Soc. Psychol.*, LVIII (1959), 225–33.

225. Waite, R. R. "Test Performance as a Function of Anxiety and Type of Task." Unpublished doctoral dissertation, Yale University, 1959.

226. Waite, R. R., *et al.* "A Study of Anxiety and Learning in Children," *J. Abnorm. Soc. Psychol.*, LVII (1958), 267–70.

227. WAITE, W. H. "The Relationship between Performance on Examinations and Emotional Responses," *J. Exper. Educ.*, XI (1942), 88–96.

228. WALDFOGEL, S. "The Development, Meaning, and Management of School Phobia," *Amer. J. Orthopsychiat.*, XXVII (1957), 754–80.

229. WALLACH, M. A., *et al.* "Contradiction between Overt and Projective Personality Indicators as a Function of Defensiveness," *Psych. Monogr.*, LXXVI (1962), No. 1.

230. WALSH, A. M. *Self-Concepts of Bright Boys with Learning Difficulties.* New York: Bureau of Publications, Teachers College, Columbia University, 1956.

231. WALTERS, R. H. "Anxiety and Social Reinforcement." Paper read at meeting of American Psychological Association, 1961.

232. WALTERS, R. H.; MARSHALL, W. E.; and SHOOTER, J. R. "Anxiety, Isolation, and Susceptibility to Social Influence," *J. Pers.*, XXVIII (1960), 518–29.

233. WALTERS, R. H., and RAY, E. "Anxiety, Social Isolation, and Reinforcer Effectiveness," *J. Pers.*, XXVIII (1960), 358–67.

234. WANDT, E., and OSTREICHER, L. M. "Validity of Samples of Classroom Behavior," *Psychol. Monogr.*, CCCLXXVI (1954), 12.

235. WATERHOUSE, I. K., and CHILD, I. L. "Frustration and the Quality of Performance," *J. Pers.*, XXI (1953), 298–311.

236. WATSON, E. JANE, and JOHNSON, ADELAIDE M. "The Emotional Significance of Acquired Physical Disfigurement in Children," *Amer. J. Orthopsychiat.*, XXVIII (1958), 85–97.

237. WHITING, J. W., and CHILD, I. L. *Child Training and Personality.* New Haven, Connecticut: Yale University Press, 1953.

238. WIENER, G.; CRAWFORD, E. E.; and SNYDER, R. T. "Some Correlates of Overt Anxiety in Mildly Retarded Patients," *Amer. J. Ment. Def.*, LXIV (1960), 735–39.

239. WIRT, R. D., and BROEN, W. E., JR. "The Relation of the Children's MAS to the Concept of Anxiety as Used in the Clinic," *J. Consult. Psychol.*, XX (1956), 482.

240. YLPPO, A.; HALLMAN, N.; LANDTMAN, B.; and PIIPARI, R. "Effect of Short-time Hospitalization on the Behavior and on Some Somatic Functions of Children," *Ann. Paediat. Fenniae,* II (1956), Suppl. 8 (24 pp.).

241. ZIMBARDO, P. G.; BARNARD, J. W.; and BERKOWITZ, L. "The Role of Anxiety and Defensiveness in Children's Verbal Behavior," *J. Pers.* (in press).

242. ZWEIBELSON, I. "Test Anxiety and Intelligence Test Performance," *J. Consult. Psychol.*, XX (1956), 479–81.

CHAPTER XII

Developmental Theory in Transition

URIE BRONFENBRENNER[1]

It is the purpose of this chapter to examine the theoretical conceptions which underlie and animate current research in child psychology. Our concern is with theory, not in the abstract, but in its scientific application. Theory of this kind differs from that ordinarily discussed in systematic treatments of the subject, which deal for the most part with explicitly defined and logically interrelated constructs and hypotheses. The body of theory which actually guides scientific work includes much more than these. Explicit definitions and hypotheses are but the small portion of the iceberg visible above the water; beneath is a mass of often unrecognized assumptions, constructs, and modes of thought which reflect the prevailing scientific ethos about the kinds of research questions that should be asked, how problems are to be formulated, and what strategies are best employed in pursuit of an answer.

In the realm of research, such tacit conceptions have a character and importance akin to those of the "naïve theory," which, as Heider and others have shown, underlies so much of our everyday social behavior. In the scientific, as in the interpersonal sphere, the theory is "naïve," not in the sense of being simple or ineffective (on the contrary, it is both complex and highly functional), but in being unrecognized or, at least, taken for granted.

To determine the nature of such latent theory is especially difficult for one who, like the present author, is himself a "naïve" practitioner. To the extent that the task can be accomplished at all, it requires resort to some device which can make tacit assumptions salient by setting them against a contrasting background.

1. The author acknowledges the valuable assistance of Beth E. Bronfenbrenner in the preparation of the manuscript.

One such device is provided by the perspective of history. Although developmental psychology is still a young science, it is no longer in its infancy. Indeed, there exist reasonably comprehensive records of the status of its growth at two earlier developmental stages. These records are the compendia prepared for the field, the first by Murchison (**9**) in 1931, and the second by Carmichael (**5**) in 1946 (with a subsequent, relatively minor revision in 1954). Both of these volumes had as their aim, to quote from Murchison's original preface, "a proper and systematic presentation of the problems of child psychology, presented as problems experimentally investigated" (**10:** ix). It is our hope that a juxtaposition of these earlier systematic presentations with one from a more recent period will alert us to both continuities and new departures in the "working theories" of developmental psychology.

As a representative of current research activity, we can hardly do better than take the present volume. Although less comprehensive than its predecessors, it was prepared with a similar aim in view. Like the earlier works, it consists of chapters representing the major areas of ongoing scientific endeavor and was written by different authors, each a specialist in his own field.

It is, of course, necessary to keep in mind that the content of all three volumes was determined not only by the nature of the research being carried out at the time but also by the particular scientific biases of the editors, who decided on the organization of the book and selected the authors of individual chapters. For example, the committee that planned the present compendium has chosen to conceptualize the field in a manner rather different from that of its predecessors. Although we shall argue that this shift reflects a general trend, our judgment may be incorrect. Awareness of this possibility, however, must be balanced by the recognition that an editor's selections for an authoritative research compendium, even when unrepresentative of the *status quo*, tend to direct and delimit the course of future scientific work.

We begin our comparative survey of working theories of child psychology with a consideration of what, at first glance, may not seem to be theoretical material at all—namely, chapter topics. Yet these are quite relevant, if we adhere to our initial understanding of theory as encompassing all conceptions and modes of thought which guide the formulation of scientific problems and their investigation. The fact that such conceptions have changed appreciably over the past thirty years is readily apparent from Table 1, in which the chapters from each of the the three volumes are classified, according to content, under one of several headings and subheadings. Chapters are categorized, first of all, on the basis of whether they are concerned principally with the presentation of factual material at a purely descriptive level or whether they give equal if not greater emphasis to more abstract constructs and processes derived from the data. Thus, contributions classified under the first major rubric include those devoted primarily to such matters as description of methods and techniques, anecdotal accounts of behavior, or normative data. Falling under the second heading are analyses of general psychological processes (e.g., learning, perceiving, thinking) or of abstracted behavior variables (e.g., aggression, anxiety, achievement) and their dynamics. Although only chapter titles are listed, the classification was based on the actual content.[2] For example, the chapters on language development in both the Murchison and Carmichael volumes report mainly descriptive studies of changes in language behavior with age; hence, they both appear under the first major heading. A chapter with the same title in the present volume, however, was classified in the second general category, since it goes substantially beyond raw description in its concern with such abstracted phenomena as "system of contrasts" and "rules of substitution."

Turning from method to substance, we observe, first of all, as the most salient feature of Table 1, a shift over the thirty-year period away from sheer description of molecular phenomena toward a concern with more abstract psychological processes and behavior constructs. Indeed, the more detailed results of our comparative analysis turn out to be simply a further specification of this trend. We now turn to an examination of these specifics through a systematic comparison of the two major successive contrasts available to us, namely, a comparison of the research of 1931 with that of 1946, and the work of 1946 with the activity of 1963.

2. Although most chapters fell clearly under one particular heading and subheading, a few required more detailed consideration.

TABLE 1

A COMPARISON OF CHAPTER TOPICS IN THREE SUCCESSIVE COMPENDIA OF RESEARCH IN CHILD PSYCHOLOGY

TOPIC	COMPENDIA		
I. Presentation of Descriptive Material	Murchison (1931)	Carmichael (1946)	Stevenson (1963)
A. Methods	Methods of Child Psychology	Methods of Child Psychology	
B. Content 1. Specific Areas *a*) Particular Behavior	1. Children's Drawings 2. Children's Play, Games and Amusements 3. Children's Dreams 4. Eating, Sleeping, Elimination		
b) Particular Groups of Settings	1. The Gifted Child 2. The Primitive Child 3. Feeblemindedness 4. Special Gifts and Deficiencies 5. Order of Birth 6. The Eidetic Child 7. The Developmental Psychology of Twins	1. Gifted Children 2. Research on Primitive Children 3. The Feeble-minded Child 4. Psychopathology of Childhood 5. Psychological Sex Differences	
2. General Areas *a*) Areas of Activity	1. Physical and Motor Development 2. Language Development 3. Children's Morals 4. Social Behavior of the Child 5. Environment Optimal for Mental Growth	1. Physical Growth 2. Maturation of Behavior 3. Language Development in Children 4. Social Development* 5. Character Development in Children	

		6. Environmental Influences on Mental Development 7. The Measurement of Mental Growth in Childhood 8. Emotional Development	
b) Developmental Stages		1. The Onset and Early Development of Behavior 2. The Neonate 3. Animal Infancy 4. The Ontogenesis of Infant Behavior 5. The Adolescent	
II. Analyses of Constructs and Processes A. General Processes	1. Learning in Children 2. Conditioning of Children's Emotions 3. Children's Philosophies 4. Psychoanalysis of the Child 5. Environmental Forces	1. Learning in Children 2. Behavior and Development as a Function of the Total System 3. The Influence of Topological and Vector Psychology*	1. Biological Correlates of Child Behavior 2. Sociological Correlates of Child Behavior 3. Language Development 4. Perceptual Development 5. Learning 6. Research on Children's Thinking
B. Specific Constructs			1. Moral Development and Identification 2. Dependency and Independence 3. Aggression 4. Achievement 5. Anxiety

* Added in the 1954 edition.

Changing Conceptions of Child Psychology: From 1931 to 1946

As we compare our first two compendia, the movement toward higher levels of conceptualization is reflected both in the number and content of the chapters in each volume. Thus, the greater number of chapters in the Murchison book (22 in all) results primarily from the separate consideration given to such highly specific topics as "biological functions in infancy," "children's drawings," "dreams," "eidetic imagery," and the like. By 1946, such particularized subjects are no longer singled out for extensive treatment. Descriptive material still predominates over conceptual concerns, but it is organized under more comprehensive chapter headings of two types. First, Carmichael employs Murchison's classification of general psychological functions (e.g., physical growth, language development, etc.), but alters and expands it to give greater emphasis and scope to developmental data in the socioemotional sphere. New chapters are added on "Emotional Development" and, in the 1954 edition, on "The Psychopathology of Childhood."

The second organizing focus employed by the Carmichael volume for the presentation of descriptive data is the chronological stage of development. There are chapters on prenatal, neonatal, infant, and adolescent behavior. Here data from all spheres of growth –physical, intellectual, emotional, and social–are brought together as they apply to one or another genetic period.

The fact that only two chapters from Carmichael's 1946 volume could be classified as dealing primarily with concepts and processes rather than with the presentation of descriptive material would seem to suggest a waning of theoretical interest during the fifteen years following publication of the Murchison *Handbook*. Closer examination of the material, however, suggests that such a judgment is warranted only at a limited level, and that, if one examines the role of conceptualization in actual empirical work, there are grounds for drawing the very opposite conclusion.

In what sense, then, did interest in theory decline from the early 1930's to the middle 1940's? For an answer to this question, we have only to look at those topics represented in the 1931 volume which were retained and those which were dropped in 1946. A chapter on

"Learning in Children" appears in both books; likewise, an exposition by Lewin of environmental forces affecting the child's behavior. The 1946 compendium, however, no longer devotes a chapter to psychoanalysis or to the work of Piaget. While naming no names, Carmichael himself makes clear the changed character of the criterion of selection:

> Until comparatively recent years most of those who wrote upon the development of individual mental life elaborated essentially speculative theories. They attempted to describe man's so-called inborn instincts or the allegedly *tabula rasa* character of the mind of the young child. The present book is testimony that today psychologists and other scientists by the use of appropriate techniques have established a large body of important and reliable facts concerning the details of human development. This book is a clear demonstration that the speculative period in child psychology is past (**5**: v).

Especially in a matter such as this, the question arises as to how representative the editor's judgment is of the views prevailing in the field at the time. In the present instance, even the most cursory examination of textbooks and review articles published in the twenties and thirties indicates that Carmichael's position was, indeed, widespread among American research psychologists. Given such an avowed distaste for theoretical speculation, coupled with emphasis on establishing "a large body of important and reliable facts concerning the details of human development," how can we arrive, as we do, at the conclusion that during this same period research in developmental psychology moved away from a preoccupation with descriptive details toward a concern with more generalized constructs and processes?

We have already cited one type of evidence supporting this contrary inference; namely, the disappearance in the 1946 volume of chapters devoted to highly specific forms of behavior. Additional evidence of a positive nature comes from an examination of the actual content of the chapters included. Although most of these, true to the editor's promise, concentrate on offering still more and "harder" facts than were available in Murchison's *Handbook*, they exhibit several other features which reflect greater interest in inferred processes and constructs.

The most salient sign of this differential trend is a change in the types of descriptive statistics most often cited. While frequency distributions predominate in both volumes, in the Carmichael *Manual* they are far more frequently followed by cross-tabulations or correlations relating the behavior in question to a variety of variables, ranging from consanguinity and nutritional factors to family, school, and other sociocultural influences. Such analyses clearly imply an interest in causal influences.

Second, more explicitly and with greater frequency than in the earlier work, an effort is made to evoke some general principle from the arrays of curves and correlations. Thus, Carmichael, in his own chapter on "The Onset and Early Development of Behavior," interrupts an encyclopedic recital of factual findings on nonhuman organisms to call attention to the presence of cephalocaudal and proximo-distal gradients in behavioral development; and the same trends are identified from data on human young in a chapter by Gesell. H. E. Jones grapples with data from a score of studies on mental growth in an effort to extract some general principles regarding the relative contributions of heredity and environment. A similar but less successful attempt is made by V. Jones working with far poorer material on character development. The Andersons invoke the concept of entropy in an effort to integrate the results from studies of domination and submission in children's groups. Perhaps the only exception to this disposition to interpret data at a higher level of generalization occurs in the chapters on learning. The studies reviewed in 1946, with only minor exceptions, maintain the same unelevated theoretical perspective found in the work summarized in 1931. The investigators represented in the later review merely appear to have taken over the preoccupation of their predecessors, with such stolid issues as the differential effect of massed *vs.* distributed practice, material *vs.* verbal rewards, and transfer of training. Theoretical models do not go much beyond classical conditioning and associative learning. (There are only two references in the chapter to instrumental learning—one to Ivanov-Smolensky's work; the other to that of Skinner.)

But, if learning theory has lain fallow during this period, the same cannot be said of other conceptual approaches—least of all those of Piaget and of Freud. Paradoxically, although these theorists were deprived of chapters in their own right in the 1946 manual, their ideas are far from absent in its pages. If anything, they are even more

prevalent. Thus, the total number of references to each of these men actually rises from the 1931 to the 1946 publication.

It is instructive also to observe the different context in which the ideas now appear. In the Murchison volume, the contributions of Piaget and of Freud, especially, were presented essentially as isolated endeavors, almost outside the main stream of scientific work. Such references as were made to their efforts by other psychologists were generally adversely critical. By 1946, the pattern has changed. Although the original work of Piaget and Freud is still criticized, their concepts and hypotheses are continually drawn upon as frames of reference, both for the interpretation of existing data and for the design and execution of new research. Thus, McCarthy, who wrote the chapters on language development in both volumes, in 1931 cites only four studies based on Piaget's work; by 1946, this number has increased almost fourfold. In like manner, Piaget's concepts play a significant role in Jersild's 1946 review of studies of children's thought and feelings and in V. Jones' survey of research on character development.

The impact of Freud's ideas on empirical work during this same period is even more pronounced. Two types of influence may be discerned: one explicit; the other indirect. The first type encompasses a variety of investigations undertaken with the specific aim of testing Freudian hypotheses. Studies of this kind are cited on almost every other page of Jersild's 1946 chapter on emotional development. They include investigations of oral behavior, weaning, feeding, bowel-training, sexual behavior, maternal separation, anxiety, sibling rivalry, parent-child relations, and cultural differences in socialization.

At the same time, the influence of Freudian theory during this period clearly extends beyond the investigations which acknowledge its inspiration. Its imaginative hypotheses, even when they evoked antagonism and rejection, aroused scientific interest in aspects of human behavior, which hitherto had received little attention. From this point of view, the proliferation we have noted in the Carmichael volume of developmental studies in the socioemotional area probably owes its existence, in large part, to this indirect impact of Freudian concepts and suppositions.

But psychoanalytic theory was not alone at this time in giving impetus to a social-psychological approach to developmental phenomena. A second powerful influence was the work of Kurt Lewin. Its effect was, perhaps, less pervasive but more direct, because it interlinked theory construction with empirical investigation. The direction of its development and of its impact is apparent from a comparison of the chapters written by Lewin, fifteen years apart, for each of the two review volumes. The earlier article is far more abstract, both in its treatment of the person and of the situation. In discussing these entities, Lewin has much to say about formal structure but little on substantive content. By 1946, the picture has changed. The person's psychological state is now described by such motivational concepts as "level of aspiration" and "satiation," and the "field" is no longer an abstract schema of forces and barriers but, rather, a group consisting of leaders, allies, and competitors. In short, in the interim, Lewin has become a social psychologist.

To summarize, an examination of the actual content of chapters in the Murchison and Carmichael volumes suggests that the disdain for speculative theorizing and the emphasis on gathering objective facts, which characterized developmental psychology during the late thirties and early forties, were not accompanied by a deterioration in the development of theory. On the contrary, whereas heretofore theory-building and systematic empirical work had been carried out in relative isolation from each other, during the period under discussion this separation began to break down. While theoretical systems lost scientific popularity as systems, their component constructs and hypotheses became diffused more broadly and were applied in empirical work on delimited problems. Particularly influential in this connection were the ideas of Piaget, Lewin, and Freud.

Having discerned this trend toward theoretical differentiation and increased articulation with empirical work, one naturally wonders how it has developed in the period since 1946. Has the tendency progressed, or has there been a leveling-off, perhaps even a reversal in direction? Have the same ideas continued to hold sway, or have others assumed ascendancy? For some evidence on these questions we turn to a comparison of the earlier conceptions of developmental psychology with those of 1963.

Current Theoretical Perspectives

The change in the character of developmental theory over the past fifteen years is dramatically reflected in the shift in placement of topical entries in Table 1 as one moves from the first and second to the third column. First and foremost, the gathering of data for data's sake seems to have lost favor.[3] The major concern in today's developmental research is clearly with inferred processes and constructs. Moreover, as the level of abstraction has risen, the focus of interest has often been sharpened, with the result that entire chapters are now addressed to particular constructs, such as aggression, dependence, and anxiety.

The absence of chapters devoted primarily to description of methods and objective facts does not mean that developmental psychologists no longer occupy themselves extensively with such matters. On the contrary, both the devising of techniques and the accumulation of data continue to flourish. [The reason that no chapter on methods in child psychology appears in the present volume is that an entire tome (**11**) has recently been published on this subject.[4]] Nor is the presentation of methods or descriptive material lacking, but they are closely intertwined with problems of construct validity and hypothesis-testing. In other words, the trend toward closer articula-

3. The one notable exception to this assertion is found in the work of Barker and Wright (**2, 3**), which is not represented in the present volume. These investigators assert that developmental psychology has unwisely by-passed a necessary scientific phase of naturalistic observation and argue for the accumulation of descriptive data on child behavior explicitly, without regard to their possible theoretical relevance. This view, however, has not thus far been widely accepted by other researchers.

4. It is of some interest that the three sections of the Mussen *Handbook* dealing with psychological (as distinguished from physiological) methods have a topical organization which parallels in a number of respects that of the present compendium. Thus, a section on cognitive development includes separate chapters on learning, thinking, and language. Another section is concerned with the child's social behavior and environment, with an entire chapter devoted to the measurement of family variables. The third section focuses on personality development, with the chapter on measurement of personality characteristics singling out for detailed consideration three variables: aggression, anxiety, and achievement. Such parallelism suggests that the differing picture of developmental psychology given in the present volume is not merely an idiosyncratic view of particular editors but reflects a changing scientific *Zeitgeist.*

tion between theory and empirical work has continued. Let us now examine it in greater detail.

We turn, first, to the general topics that have analogues in the earlier compendia and shall begin with Ervin and Miller's chapter on language development, since in some respects current work in this sphere retains the descriptive emphasis characteristic of the earlier periods. As the authors indicate, research on language development has undergone a revolution, brought about through the application of modern structural linguistics to the study of children's utterances. At the present time the major effort is concentrated on investigation of changes in the language behavior of individual children. In the authors' words, "It is necessary, first, to develop techniques and discover units through the study of individual systems before comparisons between individuals, or group studies, are possible."

In view of this state of affairs, how is it that we have chosen to classify Ervin and Miller's chapter as concerned primarily with constructs and processes rather than with gathering of descriptive information? As we have already acknowledged, the judgment can be called into question, but the determining consideration, as this reviewer sees it, is that the major aim of the description discussed by Ervin and Miller is to discover not merely what kinds of sounds the child is making in what combinations but to derive the invariances that characterize the pattern as a whole and to identify the qualitative changes that take place in this pattern over a period of time.

A similar interest in systemic properties and their qualitative alterations over the course of development distinguishes the research on cognitive development reviewed by Wallach. Moreover, we appear here to be recapitulating the past, for, once again, as in the Murchison volume thirty years back, we are presented with an entire chapter dealing with the work of Piaget and his collaborators. A comparison of content of the two chapters is especially instructive, since it reveals the kind of theoretical development that has occurred over the three decades. Gone are diffuse, static concepts, such as the familiar trinity of "realism, animism, and artificialism." In their place, there has emerged a new set of constructs, borrowed and adapted from mathematical set theory and much more precise in their meaning. Mental processes are defined in terms of the child's capacity to

recognize specified types of invariance, such as conservation and transitivity. The constructs are especially powerful since they can, and have been, applied to almost every aspect of the child's activity and experience, including primitive infant movements, preverbal problem-solving, perceptual constancy (first in physical objects and then in abstracted properties, such as horizontality, length, and area), time perception, the learning of number concepts, principles of grouping and ordering, and complex processes of logical deduction and induction. Finally, as Wallach points out, although the application has not yet been made, Piaget's constructs and hypotheses are altogether appropriate for analyzing the child's thinking about his social environment.

Two aspects of this contemporary theoretical achievement are especially significant as departures from modes of thought prevailing at earlier periods. First, Piaget's formulations, together with the experimental data they have generated, indicate a functional continuity between the emergence of sensori-motor skills and the development of concept formation, a view which, as Wallach notes, stands in striking contrast to the traditional separation of these spheres, as manifested in Carmichael's handbook. It is noteworthy that this same linkage, conceptualized in similar but less systematic fashion, is demonstrated in the series of Soviet studies on language development summarized in the chapter by Ervin and Miller.

The second notable theoretical innovation derives from Piaget's emphasis on system properties as against specific isolated behaviors. By and large, the studies presented in the Carmichael volume conceive of development as a series of movements along a monotonic scale. The constructs applied or implied do not permit clear conceptualization of structural or organizational changes, and the data accordingly follow suit. In contrast, the formulations adapted by Piaget from set theory and the theory of groups invite precisely these kinds of qualitative observations of development. Indeed, Wallach reports nonconstancy to be the most pervasive finding, and discerns at least two periods of cognitive reorganization—one at approximately eighteen months of age, and the second, even more clear, between five and eight years.

Wallach might have cited additional evidence from two other contemporary lines of investigation. Both of these are described in

White's chapter on learning. The first body of corroborative material is found, once again, in the work of Soviet psychologists, who likewise employ a conception of hierarchical levels in cognitive functioning. The second line of evidence comes from contemporary American studies of transposition learning (e.g., learning to choose the larger of two blocks rather than simply a particular block). In developmental studies of this phenomenon, a marked shift is observed among children around the age of five. White acknowledges that contemporary concepts in learning theory are inadequate to handle these phenomena but makes no reference to the obviously relevant formulations and findings of Piaget.

This omission highlights a characteristic feature of contemporary work on learning summarized in White's chapter. Here, too, there has been a progression and refinement of theoretical constructs, but, in contrast to the work inspired by Piaget, the new formulations, rather than permitting conceptualization of a broader range of phenomena in children's behavior and development, have led to a kind of theoretical introversion, with much of the research effort being concentrated on investigation of problems generated by and specific to a particular theory. The underlying assumption of this contemporary endeavor is concisely stated by White when he describes as its dominant theme 'the careful, exhaustive examination of simple learning situations in the belief that these kinds of situations contain much of the essence of all learning."

The nature of the "simple" learning situation is not constant but depends on the particular theoretical orientation of the investigator. Thus, students of operant behavior are preoccupied with discovering the schedules of reinforcement which are most efficient in shaping the behavior of the organism, be it animal or child. Workers on discrimination learning are concerned with the differential effects of simultaneous *vs.* successive discrimination. Investigators of transposition learning seek to resolve inconsistencies in response observed on so-called "near," "middle," and "far" tests of the capacity to perceive relative differences. Similar specialized interests characterize the work on learning sets, probability learning, transfer, and other theoretical problems.

As indicated by the preceding array of concepts, contemporary research in learning is no longer dominated by one or two relatively simple conceptual models of classical conditioning or associative learning typical of the earlier period. But, for the reasons already outlined, this theoretical proliferation has reduced rather than enhanced interest in developmental problems. It is no accident that the section in White's chapter devoted to "learning and development" is scarcely a page in length. As he points out, "The experimental backgrounds of most of the current workers initially predisposed them to view learning in stimulus-response terms, terms flavored with the intimation that stimuli stamp associations into a rather uniform passive child." White sees hope for the future in the increasing attention being given by some workers in the field to factors of attention, strategy, and cognitive style, but his optimism remains restrained, for he recognizes that the principal obstacle to scientific progress lies in the limited theoretical perspective of contemporary work. One can only echo his concluding sentiment: "It is to be hoped that soon larger conceptual schemes–imaginative, intelligent, disciplined–can be proposed."

An entirely different theoretical strategy animates the research reviewed in the chapters by Clausen and Williams, Ruebush, and Kohlberg. Here we note, first of all, the continuation and flourishing of a trend already discerned in the preceding period; namely, the influence of Freudian thinking on the selection of phenomena for study and the formulation of hypotheses. Apparent as this influence is in contemporary developmental psychology, Freud himself would probably have a great deal of difficulty in recognizing many of these ideas as originally his own. And understandably so, for in the intervening years psychoanalytic theory, especially as it has been applied in psychological research, has undergone what might well be called a "socialization." The biological and instinctual bases of the theory have been set aside, and the social aspects have been further developed through the infusion of concepts and data from the fields of cultural anthropology and sociology.[5]

The empirical work growing out of this theoretical fusion has yielded two types of findings especially challenging to the develop-

5. This trend is foreshadowed as early as the 1931 compendium in Margaret Mead's chapter on "The Primitive Child." Its steady but still restricted development by 1946 is documented in the subsequent contribution by the same author on this same subject for the Carmichael volume, as well as in the chapter on "Character Development" by Vernon Jones.

ment of theory. First is the repeated observation that patterns of child behavior and familial relationships vary substantially across culture, class, community, and reference group. Second is the complementary finding that the same piece of behavior may have quite different meaning and impact in different social structures.

The "socialization" of Freudian theory and the variation in research results for subjects with different social roles and backgrounds emerge also as dominant features of the type of research characteristic of the present period: the systematic study of particular behavioral variables. Moreover, in this more differentiated context, the specific theoretical implications of these two lines of development are perhaps seen most clearly. Accordingly, we turn to an examination of the theoretical assumptions and modes of thought underlying such behavioral studies.

Theoretical Approaches in Variable-oriented Research

Although we are concerned here with several different classes of behavior, the theoretical assumptions involved in the selection of problems, the formulation of hypotheses, and the interpretation of results are sufficiently similar to permit considerable generalization across variables. One can discern four major common theoretical concerns: (*a*) problems of definition and construct validation; (*b*) conceptualizing processes and effects of parental influence; (*c*) conceptualizing the operation of contemporaneous situational factors; and (*d*) coping with sex, class, and cultural differences. Examples are drawn primarily from the area of socialization in the discussion of these concerns.

Problems of definition and construct validation.—Central to the analysis of every one of the behavioral variables is the distinction between *motive* and *overt response*. Although the distinction is as old as psychology itself, the attention being accorded to it in current research is unprecedented. For an explanation of this special emphasis one needs only to recall the focal importance of analogous distinctions both in psychoanalysis (e.g., latent *vs.* manifest content) and in Lewinian theory (e.g., the psychological *vs.* the physical field). Such theoretical origins are even more explicitly reflected in the prevailing operational definitions of the two types of constructs. Although some motives are still being measured, in part, by questionnaires (viz., anxiety, achievement values), and overt behavior by ratings and time samples in naturalistic settings, these are typically not the methods of choice. The way to assess motivation today is through the analysis of fantasy materials; whereas, to study overt response, one observes subjects in experimentally contrived social situations.

The enthusiastic devotion to these procedures has been somewhat tempered, however, by the research results obtained. First, the correlations between measures of motive and behavior have been disappointingly low. Second, interpretation even of these findings is complicated by the recurrence of reliable but puzzling sex differences. Third, correlations between different measures of what is presumed to be the same motive or the same behavioral variable have typically turned out to be as low as, if not lower than, the relationships across these two domains.

Conceptualizing processes and effects of parental influences.—Formulations in this area may be grouped into three general families of hypotheses. The first family, based principally on psychoanalytic theory, focuses on the general affective quality of the parent-child relationship (e.g., nurturant *vs.* rejecting) as the antecedent condition for the development of a particular form of behavior. Empirical investigations of this type of generalization have produced a series of results which, taken together, argue for a more differentiated theoretical structure and corresponding experimental design than those employed in the earlier researches.

It turns out, for example, that the presence of parental rejection is associated with high levels of dependency, aggressiveness, and (if one is to judge from results of the more recent and rigorous studies of the problem) with high levels of academic achievement. The interpretation of this series of findings is complicated by a number of theoretical questions. First, at the most superficial level, studies based on a theoretical approach which focuses on a single dependent variable at a time leave unanswered the question of whether the above behaviors appear in the same or in different children. Second, it is not clear which of the above outcomes are attributable to the operation of rejection alone or to the occurrence of rejection following a period of nurturance. The few studies that have endeavored to examine the joint effect of both parental variables point to an explanation in terms of social deprivation. But here again, the observed relationships between parental and child behaviors appear to be different for boys and girls (e.g., **13**) and for fathers and mothers (e.g., **12**).

Third, interpretation of the joint effects of nurturance and rejection in terms of social deprivation are complicated by inconsistencies in the use of the latter concept. At times, as in studies of the effect of maternal separation on the development of anxiety or dependency, social deprivation is conceived as something which happens to the child and is not in any way contingent upon his own behavior. In other researches, such as the work of Sears *et al.* (**13**) on dependency and most of the research on antecedents of achievement, social deprivation is linked to particular actions of the child; that is to say, it is treated as a negative reinforcer. It seems entirely possible that the two forms of parental behavior might have rather different consequences as a function of the operation of specific reinforcement in one instance and not in the other.

The second family of hypotheses is concerned with the effects of parental reward and punishment. The conceptual models for most of the investigations derive from the fusion of psychoanalytic and learning theory developed by the Yale group (e.g., Sears, Mowrer, Whiting, Child). Compared to the first family of studies, the results of these researches lead to more straightforward interpretations, at least as far as the effects of positive reinforcement are concerned. While, as might be expected, no studies are reported of parental reward for expressions of anxiety or dependency, the evidence on development of aggression and achievement is quite clear cut: children tend to learn the behaviors approved by their parents. There is, of course, the usual qualification of sex differences.

The findings on the influence of parental punishment are considerably more complex. According to simple reinforcement theory, punishment of a response might be expected to result in its eventual elimination from the behavioral repertoire. Although results in accordance with this expectation are occasionally obtained, the typical finding for such variables as aggressiveness and dependency is that their frequency increases as a positive function of parental punishment for the act in question. Several explanations are offered for this apparent contradiction. First, there is the difficulty, noted by several of the chapter authors, of distinguishing in a retrospective study which behavior is cause and which effect. For example, are children being aggressive because they have been punished, or are they being punished because they have been aggressive? Second, at a more theoretical level, a number of investigators, notably Sears, invoke the frustration-aggression hypothesis to explain the positive relationship between punishment and aggression. In this perspective, aggression is seen as a reaction to the frustration induced by punishment.

The foregoing interpretation is forcefully challenged by Bandura and Walters in their chapter in this volume. They argue that aggression is but one of many possible reactions to frustration. The determining factor is, therefore, not frustration; nor is it positive reinforcement, since aggressiveness is seen to develop in the absence of reward and, what is more, often flourishes under exposure to punishment. The authors assert that the common element underlying all positive instances of the emergence of aggressiveness is exposure to a model whose behavior the child can and does adopt.

This concept of "modeling" constitutes the central focus of the third family of hypotheses on parental influences. With respect to the effects of parental behavior, Bandura and Walters endeavor to show, through a review of existing researches on familial antecedents of aggression, that the weight of the evidence favors their modeling hypothesis. In addition, although this hypothesis is not given explicit consideration in the studies of other behavior variables treated in this volume, the obtained results, especially in the area of achievement, frequently give support to the importance of the parent as a role model for the child.

Conceptualizing the operation of contemporaneous situational factors.—The results from experimental investigations of antecedent-consequent relationships show remarkable theoretical continuity with findings from retrospective studies. In addition, experimental manipulation has made possible the separation and control of independent variables, thus leading to further conceptual clarification. Such continuity and progress are evident with respect to each of the three families of hypotheses discussed in the preceding paragraphs.

With respect to the general quality of the interpersonal relationship, the experimental introduction of nurturance and its subsequent withdrawal has demonstrated clearly that this type of treatment enhances dependent behavior in the child. At the same time, as Hartup and Himeno (**7**) have shown, children exposed to this same sequence of conditions will, if given an opportunity, engage in more aggressive behavior than will nondeprived controls. Finally, the researches of Gewirtz and others (**6**) indicate that this same kind of social deprivation increases the child's susceptibility to verbal reinforcement and accuracy in learning. Clarification of the issue is supplied in an experiment by Walters (**14**), who found that controlling for level of induced anxiety accounts for the significant variance in behavior associated with social deprivation. The entire set of findings lends support to the view that social deprivation acts as a source of frustration which increases the child's general motivational level. What the child does under these circumstances depends on the nature of the available stimuli and the hierarchy of previously learned responses.

Experimental evidence on the effects of reinforcement in the development of particular forms of behavior corroborates the findings from retrospective studies regarding the effectiveness of reward. But the major theoretical advance in this area comes from a series of experiments which examine the separate but interrelated contributions of reinforcement, frustration, and modeling in the learning of behavior.

This development is sufficiently important to merit more detailed consideration. First of all, exposure to a model is in itself a sufficient condition for evoking behavior in the child; the behavior appears in the absence both of frustration and of positive or negative reinforcement (see chap. ix). Indeed, when the factor of exposure to an aggressive model is kept constant, frustrated subjects exhibit no more aggressive behavior than nonfrustrated controls. Positive reinforcement, however, continues to play a significant role, since subjects exposed to a model who had previously been rewarding invariably imitate the model's behavior (whether aggressive or nonaggressive) to a greater extent than do nonrewarded controls. Regrettably, an analogous experiment using a previously punishing model has apparently not yet been carried out.

Finally, as in all research in this general area, experimental studies of modeling have shown substantial sex differences. In general, boys respond with more imitative aggression than girls, and an aggressive male model has a more potent influence than an aggressive female model, especially when the subjects are boys. Bandura and Walters suggest that this pattern is a function of the extent to which the behavior in question is sex-typed, but hasten to add that the appropriateness could be a function of variables other than sex, such as occupation and social status. This reference brings us to the final theoretical concern emerging in current research on the development of particular behavior patterns.

Coping with sex, class, and cultural differences.—If variations by class and culture are cited less frequently than sex differences, it is only because they have not been looked for so often. Wherever the investigator has taken the trouble to collect and examine the necessary data, social-structural differences have almost invariably appeared. These findings inevitably pose theoretical problems, but to date these have typically been dealt with after the fact. This has been especially true for sex differences, where investigators have drawn on psychoanalysis, the only body of theory that addresses itself to the problem, and have come up with interpretations that outdo those of Freud himself in their intricate turnings.

We conclude our examination of theoretical approaches in variable-oriented research by calling attention to two general features of the total endeavor. First, it is apparent in this research context that psychoanalytic theory is not the only one that is undergoing "socialization"; the same can be said of learning theory as well. The picture of learning theory in action that emerges in the discussion of particular variables is markedly different from that portrayed in typical laboratory studies of learning. The major difference, however, lies not in the locale but in the explicitly social definition of the behavior being reinforced, and—perhaps even more importantly—of the agent of reinforcement and his relation to the subject. In the neo-classical learning experiment, as in its classical forebears, the experimenter has no identity; he is devoid of sex, age, occupation, ethnic background, and, above all, of attitudes toward the subject. All of these are viewed as properly irrelevant to the experiment itself. In investigations of "social learning," these same attributes become major parameters of investigation.

And yet, with all their differences, the two approaches share in common a striking feature of omission. Like its "purer" counterpart, research in social learning (though it uses children as subjects and professes to deal with genetic problems) actually has little to say about the development of the *child.* Its concern is with the genesis of *behavior* as a function of forces *outside* the child. In this respect it stands in sharp contrast to the work of Piaget and his colleagues, which focuses on developmental changes in the psychological structure of the child himself.

In our view, it is precisely the convergence of these two theoretical developments which constitutes the major challenge and promise for the future of research in developmental psychology. We turn, therefore, to a more explicit examination of what such a convergence might imply.

Emerging Problems and Prospects for Developmental Theory

Our analysis of change, over a thirty-year period, in the theoretical conceptions underlying research in developmental psychology has revealed a pronounced shift away from a preoccupation with purely descriptive concepts and data toward a concern with more abstract psychological processes and behavior constructs. Within this general progression, we can now discern two major and, by and large, independent streams of theoretical development. The first, stemming almost entirely from the work of Piaget, has been concerned primarily with cognitive function and has sought to conceptualize the qualitative, organizational changes taking place in the growing child's mental processes. The second, centering in the socioemotional sphere, represents a fusion of concepts and hypotheses from psychoanalysis, learning theory, field theory, and theoretical developments in cultural anthropology and sociology. At its present stage, this second line of development has become preoccupied with two types of problems: (*a*) the definition and construct validation of behavioral variables; and (*b*) conceptualizing processes of socialization.

In the course of these efforts certain advances have been made, and certain difficulties encountered. Taken together, these achievements and problems almost inevitably shape the course of future research and theoretical development. Accordingly, by way of a summing up, we shall recall these accomplishments and difficulties and examine their implications.

We shall begin with the aforementioned problems of definition and construct validation. In this connection substantial progress has been made in clarifying the concept of motive and its relation to overt response. At least on first consideration, the trouble appears to be not with the theory but with the data; correlations between measures of the same motive, of the same behavior, or of corresponding motive and response are disappointingly low. But there are grounds for believing that the wrong party is being indicted; if it is theory that has led to the expectation that the correlations should be higher, then it is theory that is at fault—and out of date, in the bargain. This conclusion is indicated on several counts.

First, psychological measures—be they projective, objective, or subjective—are themselves necessarily based on behavior occurring in a situation. One of the major contributions of the research discussed in this volume is the identification and demonstration of the importance of situational factors in the determination of response. One cannot, therefore, expect high correlations for the same person across situations unless these determining factors have been held constant. To argue, as some investigators have done, that the best strategy under present circumstances is to use a combination of several different measures is to violate what little theory we have. One would do better to stick to one measure, for at least then it is possible to be clear about what it is that has been measured. But the broader implication of the current state of affairs points to the importance of investigating the circumstances under which different measures do and do not yield comparable results. One possible consequence of such research is indicated by Lesser's finding (**9**) of a positive correlation between overt and fantasy aggression for boys whose mothers encouraged aggression, and a negative association for those boys whose mothers discouraged such behavior. Results of this kind suggest that an adequate model for predicting relationships between projective and overt responses requires consideration of such prior or contemporaneous situational influences.

Progress in another avenue of investigation calls attention to a second theoretical lag in present-day efforts at construct validation. In research practice, children's responses on projective measures are interpreted almost exclusively in motivational terms. But as the work of Piaget so clearly shows, the telling of stories or the playing of games is markedly influenced by the child's level of cognitive development. Measures requiring different levels of cognitive function can, therefore, not be expected to yield comparable results even though the underlying motives may be the same. To date, almost no attention has been given to influence of such developmental factors or the relation between projective and overt behavior.

The preceding example focuses attention on a major theoretical difference underlying methods of construct validation in the work of Piaget and that of social-learning theorists. The former investigates and utilizes (as a criterion for construct validation) changes in the child's performance at different age levels. Workers in social learning pay very little attention to such differences. They are highly attuned, however, to variations in behavior associated with sex of child, sex of experimenter, social class, and other social-structural variables. These same parameters are scarcely ever given explicit consideration in the researches of Piaget and his colleagues. It would seem that both lines of research and theorizing would profit by adopting the concepts and concerns of the other.

But for both groups of workers, the principal obstacle to the further development of theory lies less in the absence of certain concepts than in the absence of data. Workers in the Piaget tradition typically do not possess or gather information about how thought processes vary (if they do) among children of different sexes and social backgrounds who are examined or taught by adults differing in these same attributes. As a result, these researchers do not become aware of any inadequacies cognitive theory might have in accounting for such social variations as might, in fact, prevail.[6]

The empirical situation of social-learning theorists is even more impoverished. Not only do they lack information about developmental differences in behavior but their actual knowledge of social structural variations is spotty at best. The acquisition of factual information is especially crucial for the further development of socialization theory. We can no longer afford to rely, for example, on Freud's magnificent but largely intuitive speculations about differences in the relationship of each parent with the child of each

6. Some indication of the high prevalence of such variations, and their theoretical implications, is obtained from a comparative analysis of results from Piaget-type studies done in different countries or with children from different social class levels (*vid.* **4**).

sex. The facts of differential interaction need first to be empirically established. The same considerations apply even more forcefully with respect to variations in family behavior in different class and cultural subgroups. Finally, there is the virtual *terra incognita* of socialization influences outside the family setting in the peer group, namely, the school and the community. In short, if socialization theory is to develop, it is first necessary to establish the variances and invariances in both values and behavior that require theoretical explanation.

The process of socialization, however, does not constitute all of developmental psychology. Nor can it be properly understood unless some attention is focused on the internal changes in the psychological organization of the child, which both respond to and are affected by the forces of socialization. Conversely, no conception of such internal development can be adequate if it fails to take into account the operation of these external social influences.

Given this perspective, the further growth of developmental theory appears to call for a convergence between the approach of Piaget and that of social learning, with each incorporating and applying the concepts and concerns of the other. Even at the purely hypothetical level, the idea of such a "cultural and scientific exchange" raises some fascinating questions. For example, what role does social reinforcement or modeling play in furthering or impeding the transition from one stage of cognitive development to the next? Or, conversely, what part does cognitive development have in determining the child's susceptibility to social reinforcement or modeling?

The proposal of convergence between these two major streams of theoretical development is not merely a reviewer's fantasy. It is an extrapolation of existing trends and a prediction of the future. Its signs can already be seen in the current studies of moral development being carried on by such workers as Aronfreed (1) and Hoffman (8).[7] In short, there is reason to believe that developmental theory itself is about to undergo a transition to a new and more mature level of cognitive organization.

7. An analysis of this new theoretical development appears in Bronfenbrenner (4).

BIBLIOGRAPHY

1. Aronfreed, J. "The Nature, Variety and Social Patterning of Moral Responses to Transgression," *J. Abnorm. Soc. Psychol.*, LXIII (1961), 223–41.
2. Barker, R. G., and Wright, H. F. *One Boy's Day.* New York: Harper & Bros., 1951.
3. ———. *Midwest and Its Children: The Psychological Ecology of an American Town.* New York: Row, Peterson & Co., 1955.
4. Bronfenbrenner, U. "The Role of Age, Sex, Class, and Culture in Studies of Moral Development," *Research Supplement, J. of Relig. Educ.*, 1962.
5. Carmichael, L. (Editor). *Manual of Child Psychology.* New York: John Wiley & Sons, 1946 (revised edition, 1954).
6. Gewirtz, J. L., and Baer, D. M. "The Effects of Brief Social Deprivation on Behaviors for a Social Reinforcer," *J. Abnorm. Soc. Psychol.*, LVI (1958), 49–56.
7. Hartup, W. W., and Himeno, Yayoi. "Social Isolation *vs.* Interaction with Adults in Relation to Aggression in Preschool Children," *J. Abnorm. Soc. Psychol.*, LIX (1950), 17–22.
8. Hoffman, M. L. "Child-rearing Antecedents of Moral Development." Unpublished mimeographed paper, Merrill-Palmer Institute, 1961.
9. Lesser, G. S. "The Relationship between Overt and Fantasy Aggression as a Function of Maternal Response to Aggression," *J. Abnorm. Soc. Psychol.*, LV (1957), 218–21.
10. Murchison, C. (Editor). *A Handbook of Child Psychology.* Worcester, Massachusetts: Clark University Press, 1931.
11. Mussen, P. H. (Editor). *Handbook of Research Methods in Child Development.* New York: John Wiley & Sons., 1960.
12. Rosen, B. C., and D'Andrade, R. "The Psychosocial Origins of Achievement Motivation," *Sociometry,* XXII (1959), 185–218.
13. Sears, R. R.; Maccoby, E.; and Levin, H. *Patterns of Child Rearing.* Evanston, Illinois: Row, Peterson & Co., 1957.
14. Walters, R. H., and Ray, E. "Anxiety, Social Isolation, and Reinforcer Effectiveness," *J. Pers.*, XXVIII (1960), 358–67.

Index

INFORMATION CONCERNING THE NATIONAL SOCIETY FOR THE STUDY OF EDUCATION

1. Purpose. The purpose of the National Society is to promote the investigation and discussion of educational questions. To this end it holds an annual meeting and publishes a series of yearbooks.

2. Eligibility to Membership. Any person who is interested in receiving its publications may become a member by sending to the Secretary-Treasurer information concerning name, title, and address, and a check for $8.00 (see Item 5), except that graduate students, on the recommendation of a faculty member, may become members by paying $6.00 for the first year of their membership. Dues for all subsequent years are the same as for other members (see Item 4).

Membership is not transferable; it is limited to individuals, and may not be held by libraries, schools, or other institutions, either directly or indirectly.

3. Period of Membership. Applicants for membership may not date their entrance back of the current calendar year, and all memberships terminate automatically on December 31, unless the dues for the ensuing year are paid as indicated in Item 6.

4. Duties and Privileges of Members. Members pay dues of $7.00 annually, receive a cloth-bound copy of each publication, are entitled to vote, to participate in discussion, and (under certain conditions) to hold office. The names of members are printed in the yearbooks.

Persons who are sixty years of age or above may become life members on payment of fee based on average life-expectancy of their age group. For information, apply to Secretary-Treasurer.

5. Entrance Fee. New members are required the first year to pay, in addition to the dues, an entrance fee of one dollar.

6. Payment of Dues. Statements of dues are rendered in October for the following calendar year. Any member so notified whose dues remain unpaid on January 1, thereby loses his membership and can be reinstated only by paying a reinstatement fee of fifty cents.

School warrants and vouchers from institutions must be accompanied by definite information concerning the name and address of the person for whom membership fee is being paid. Statements of dues are rendered on our own form only. The Secretary's office cannot undertake to fill out special invoice forms of any sort or to affix notary's affidavit to statements or receipts.

Cancelled checks serve as receipts. Members desiring an additional receipt must enclose a stamped and addressed envelope therefor.

7. Distribution of Yearbooks to Members. The yearbooks, ready prior to each February meeting, will be mailed from the office of the distributors, only to members whose dues for that year have been paid. Members who desire yearbooks prior to the current year must purchase them directly from the distributors (see Item 8).

8. Commercial Sales. The distribution of all yearbooks prior to the current year, and also of those of the current year not regularly mailed to members in exchange for their dues, is in the hands of the distributor, not of the Secretary. For such commercial sales, communicate directly with the University of Chicago Press, Chicago 37, Illinois, which will gladly send a price list covering all the publications of this Society. This list is also printed in the yearbook.

9. Yearbooks. The yearbooks are issued about one month before the February meeting. They comprise from 600 to 800 pages annually. Unusual effort has been made to make them, on the one hand, of immediate practical value, and, on the other hand, representative of sound scholarship and scientific investigation.

10. Meetings. The annual meeting, at which the yearbooks are discussed, is held in February at the same time and place as the meeting of the American Association of School Administrators.

Applications for membership will be handled promptly at any time on receipt of name and address, together with check for $8.00 (or $7.50 for reinstatement). Applications entitle the new members to the yearbook slated for discussion during the calendar year the application is made.

Herman G. Richey, *Secretary-Treasurer*

5835 Kimbark Ave.
Chicago 37, Illinois

PUBLICATIONS OF THE NATIONAL SOCIETY FOR THE STUDY OF EDUCATION

NOTICE: Many of the early yearbooks of this series are now **out of print.** In the following list, those titles to which an asterisk is prefixed are not available for purchase.

POSTPAID PRICE

*First Yearbook, 1902, Part I—*Some Principles in the Teaching of History.* Lucy M. Salmon...

*First Yearbook, 1902, Part II—*The Progress of Geography in the Schools.* W. M. Davis and H. M. Wilson........

*Second Yearbook, 1903, Part I—*The Course of Study in History in the Common School.* Isabel Lawrence, C. A. McMurry, Frank McMurry, E. C. Page, and E. J. Rice........

*Second Yearbook, 1903, Part II—*The Relation of Theory to Practice in Education.* M. J. Holmes, J. A. Keith, and Levi Seeley........

*Third Yearbook, 1904, Part I—*The Relation of Theory to Practice in the Education of Teachers.* John Dewey, Sarah C. Brooks, F. M. McMurry, *et al.*........

Third Yearbook, 1904, Part II—*Nature Study.* W. S. Jackman........ $0.85

*Fourth Yearbook, 1905, Part I—*The Education and Training of Secondary Teachers.* E. C. Elliott, E. G. Dexter, M. J. Holmes, *et al.*........

*Fourth Yearbook, 1905, Part II—*The Place of Vocational Subjects in the High-School Curriculum.* J. S. Brown, G. B. Morrison, and Ellen Richards........

*Fifth Yearbook, 1906, Part I—*On the Teaching of English in Elementary and High Schools.* G. P. Brown and Emerson Davis........

Fifth Yearbook, 1906, Part II—*The Certification of Teachers.* E. P. Cubberley........ .64

*Sixth Yearbook, 1907, Part I—*Vocational Studies for College Entrance.* C. A. Herrick, H. W. Holmes, T. deLaguna, V. Prettyman, and W. J. S. Bryan........

*Sixth Yearbook, 1907, Part II—*The Kindergarten and Its Relation to Elementary Education.* Ada Van Stone Harris, E. A. Kirkpatrick, Marie Kraus-Boelté, Patty S. Hill, Harriette M. Mills, and Nina Vandewalker........

*Seventh Yearbook, 1908, Part I—*The Relation of Superintendents and Principals to the Training and Professional Improvement of Their Teachers.* Charles D. Lowry........

*Seventh Yearbook, 1908, Part II—*The Co-ordination of the Kindergarten and the Elementary School.* B. J. Gregory, Jennie B. Merrill, Bertha Payne, and Margaret Giddings........

Eighth Yearbook, 1909, Part I—*Education with Reference to Sex: Pathological, Economic, and Social Aspects.* C. R. Henderson........ .85

*Eighth Yearbook, 1909, Part II—*Education with Reference to Sex: Agencies and Methods.* C. R. Henderson and Helen C. Putnam........

*Ninth Yearbook, 1910, Part I—*Health and Education.* T. D. Wood........

*Ninth Yearbook, 1910, Part II—*The Nurse in Education.* T. D. Wood, *et al.*........

*Tenth Yearbook, 1911, Part I—*The City School as a Community Center.* H. C. Leipziger, Sarah E. Hyre, R. D. Warden, C. Ward Crampton, E. W. Stitt, E. J. Ward, Mrs. E. C. Grice, and C. A. Perry........

*Tenth Yearbook, 1911, Part II—*The Rural School as a Community Center.* B. H. Crocheron, Jessie Field, F. W. Howe, E. C. Bishop, A. B. Graham, O. J. Kern, M. T. Scudder, and B. M. Davis........

*Eleventh Yearbook, 1912, Part I—*Industrial Education: Typical Experiments Described and Interpreted.* J. F. Barker, M. Bloomfield, B. W. Johnson, P. Johnson, L. M. Leavitt, G. A. Mirick, M. W. Murray, C. F. Perry, A. L. Safford, and H. B. Wilson........

*Eleventh Yearbook, 1912, Part II—*Agricultural Education in Secondary Schools.* A. C. Monahan, R. W. Stimson, D. J. Crosby, W. H. French, H. F. Button, F. R. Crane, W. R. Hart, and G. F. Warren........

*Twelfth Yearbook, 1913, Part I—*The Supervision of City Schools.* Franklin Bobbitt, J. W. Hall, and J. D. Wolcott........

*Twelfth Yearbook, 1913, Part II—*The Supervision of Rural Schools.* A. C. Monahan, L. J. Hanifan, J. E. Warren, Wallace Lund, U. J. Hoffman, A. S. Cook, E. M. Rapp, Jackson Davis, and J. D. Wolcott........

*Thirteenth Yearbook, 1914, Part I—*Some Aspects of High-School Instruction and Administration.* H. C. Morrison, E. R. Breslich, W. A. Jessup, and L. D. Coffman........

*Thirteenth Yearbook, 1914, Part II—*Plans for Organizing School Surveys, with a Summary of Typical School Surveys.* Charles H. Judd and Henry L. Smith........

*Fourteenth Yearbook, 1915, Part I—*Minimum Essentials in Elementary School Subjects—Standards and Current Practices.* H. B. Wilson, H. W. Holmes, F. E. Thompson, R. G. Jones, S. A. Courtis, W. S. Gray, F. N. Freeman, H. C. Pryor, J. F. Hosic, W. A. Jessup, and W. C. Bagley

Fourteenth Yearbook, 1915, Part II—*Methods for Measuring Teachers' Efficiency.* Arthur C. Boyce........ .79

*Fifteenth Yearbook, 1916, Part I—*Standards and Tests for the Measurement of the Efficiency of Schools and School Systems.* G. D. Strayer, Bird T. Baldwin, B. R. Buckingham, F. W. Ballou, D. C. Bliss, H. G. Childs, S. A. Courtis, E. P. Cubberley, C. H. Judd, George Melcher, E. E. Oberholtzer, J. B. Sears, Daniel Starch, M. R. Trabue, and G. M. Whipple........

*Fifteenth Yearbook, 1916, Part II—*The Relationship between Persistence in School and Home Conditions.* Charles E. Hollye........

*Fifteenth Yearbook, 1916, Part III—*The Junior High School.* Aubrey A. Douglass........

*Sixteenth Yearbook, 1917, Part I—*Second Report of the Committee on Minimum Essentials in Elementary-School Subjects.* W. C. Bagley, W. W. Charters, F. N. Freeman, W. S. Gray, Ernest Horn, J. H. Hoskinson, W. S. Monroe, C. F. Munson, H. C. Pryor, L. W. Rapeer, G. M Wilson, and H. B. Wilson........

POSTPAID PRICE

*Sixteenth Yearbook, 1917, Part II—*The Efficiency of College Students as Conditioned by Age at Entrance and Size of High School.* B. F. Pittenger....

*Seventeenth Yearbook, 1918, Part I—*Third Report of the Committee on Economy of Time in Education.* W. C. Bagley, B. B. Bassett, M. E. Branom, Alice Camerer, J. E. Dealey, C. A. Ellwood, E. B. Greene, A. B. Hart, J. F. Hosic, E. T. Housh, W. H. Mace, L. R. Marston, H. C. McKown, H. E. Mitchell, W. C. Reavis, D. Snedden, and H. B. Wilson....

*Seventeenth Yearbook, 1918, Part II—*The Measurement of Educational Products.* E. J. Ashbaugh, W. A. Averill, L. P. Ayers, F. W. Ballou, Edna Bryner, B. R. Buckingham, S. A. Courtis, M. E. Haggery, C. H. Judd, George Melcher, W. S. Monroe, E. A. Nifenecker, and E. L. Thorndike....

*Eighteenth Yearbook, 1919, Part I—*The Professional Preparation of High-School Teachers.* G. N. Cade, S. S. Colvin, Charles Fordyce, H. H. Foster, T. S. Gosling, W. S. Gray, L. V. Koos, A. R. Mead, H. L. Miller, F. C. Whitcomb, and Clifford Woody....

Eighteenth Yearbook, 1919, Part II—*Fourth Report of Committee on Economy of Time in Education.* F. C. Ayer, F. N. Freeman, W. S. Gray, Ernest Horn, W. S. Monroe, and C. E. Seashore $1.10

*Nineteenth Yearbook, 1920, Part I—*New Materials of Instruction.* Prepared by the Society's Committee on Materials of Instruction....

*Nineteenth Yearbook, 1920, Part II—*Classroom Problems in the Education of Gifted Children.* T. S. Henry....

*Twentieth Yearbook, 1921, Part I—*New Materials of Instruction.* Second Report by the Society's Committee....

*Twentieth Yearbook, 1921, Part II—*Report of the Society's Committee on Silent Reading.* M. A. Burgess, S. A. Courtis, C. E. Germane, W. S. Gray, H. A. Greene, Regina R. Heller, J. H. Hoover, J. A. O'Brien, J. L. Packer, Daniel Starch, W. W. Theisen, G. A. Yoakam, and representatives of other school systems....

*Twenty-first Yearbook, 1922, Parts I and II—*Intelligence Tests and Their Use.* Part I—*The Nature, History, and General Principles of Intelligence Testing.* E. L. Thorndike, S. S. Colvin, Harold Rugg, G. M. Whipple, Part II—*The Administrative Use of Intelligence Tests,* H. W. Holmes, W. K. Layton, Helen Davis, Agnes L. Rogers, Rudolf Pintner, M. R. Trabue, W. S. Miller, Bessie L. Gambrill, and others. The two parts are bound together....

*Twenty-second Yearbook, 1923, Part I—*English Composition: Its Aims, Methods, and Measurements.* Earl Hudelson....

*Twenty-second Yearbook, 1923, Part II—*The Social Studies in the Elementary and Secondary School.* A. S. Barr, J. J. Coss, Henry Harap, R. W. Hatch, H. C. Hill, Ernest Horn, C. H. Judd, L. C. Marshall, F. M. McMurry, Earle Rugg, H. O. Rugg, Emma Schweppe, Mabel Snedaker, and C. W. Washburne....

*Twenty-third Yearbook, 1924, Part I—*The Education of Gifted Children.* Report of the Society's Committee. Guy M. Whipple, Chairman....

*Twenty-third Yearbook, 1924, Part II—*Vocational Guidance and Vocational Education for Industries.* A. H. Edgerton and Others....

Twenty-fourth Yearbook, 1925, Part I—*Report of the National Committee on Reading.* W. S Gray, Chairman, F. W. Ballou, Rose L. Hardy, Ernest Horn, Francis Jenkins, S. A. Leonard, Estaline Wilson, and Laura Zirbes.... 1.50

*Twenty-fourth Yearbook, 1925, Part II—*Adapting the Schools to Individual Differences.* Report of the Society's Committee. Carleton W. Washburne, Chairman....

*Twenty-fifth Yearbook, 1926, Part I—*The Present Status of Safety Education.* Report of the Society's Committee. Guy M. Whipple, Chairman....

*Twenty-fifth Yearbook, 1926, Part II—*Extra-curricular Activities.* Report of the Society's Committee. Leonard V. Koos, Chairman....

*Twenty-sixth Yearbook, 1927, Part I—*Curriculum-making: Past and Present.* Report of the Society's Committee. Harold O. Rugg, Chairman....

*Twenty-sixth Yearbook, 1927, Part II—*The Foundations of Curriculum-making.* Prepared by individual members of the Society's Committee. Harold O. Rugg, Chairman....

Twenty-seventh Yearbook, 1928, Part I—*Nature and Nurture: Their Influence upon Intelligence.* Prepared by the Society's Committee. Lewis M. Terman, Chairman.... 1.75

Twenty-seventh Yearbook, 1928, Part II—*Nature and Nurture: Their Influence upon Achievement.* Prepared by the Society's Committee. Lewis M. Terman, Chairman.... 1.75

Twenty-eighth Yearbook, 1929, Parts I and II—*Preschool and Parental Education.* Part I—*Organization and Development.* Part II—*Research and Method.* Prepared by the Society's Committee. Lois H. Meek, Chairman. Bound in one volume. Cloth.... 5.00
Paper.... 3.25

Twenty-ninth Yearbook, 1930, Parts I and II—*Report of the Society's Committee on Arithmetic.* Part I—*Some Aspects of Modern Thought on Arithmetic.* Part II—*Research in Arithmetic.* Prepared by the Society's Committee. F. B. Knight, Chairman. Bound in one volume. Cloth 5.00

Thirtieth Yearbook, 1931, Part I—*The Status of Rural Education.* First Report of the Society's Committee on Rural Education. Orville G. Brim, Chairman. Cloth.... 2.50
Paper.... 1.75

Thirtieth Yearbook, 1931, Part II—*The Textbook in American Education.* Report of the Society's Committee on the Textbook. J. B. Edmonson, Chaiman. Cloth.... 2.50

Thirty-first Yearbook, 1932, Part I—*A Program for Teaching Science.* Prepared by the Society's Committee on the Teaching of Science. S. Ralph Powers, Chairman. Paper.... 1.75

Thirty-first Yearbook, 1932, Part II—*Changes and Experiments in Liberal-Arts Education.* Prepared by Kathryn McHale, with numerous collaborators. Cloth.... 2.50
Paper.... 1.75

Thirty-second Yearbook, 1933—*The Teaching of Geography.* Prepared by the Society's Committee on the Teaching of Geography. A. E. Parkins, Chairman. Cloth.... 4.50
Paper.... 3.00

Thirty-third Yearbook, 1934, Part I—*The Planning and Construction of School Buildings.* Prepared by the Society's Committee on School Buildings. N. L. Engelhardt, Chairman. Cloth 2.50

Thirty-third Yearbook, 1934, Part II—*The Activity Movement.* Prepared by the Society's Committee on the Activity Movement. Lois Coffey Mossman, Chairman. Cloth.... 2.50
Paper.... 1.75

	POSTPAID PRICE
Thirty-fourth Yearbook, 1935—*Educational Diagnosis.* Prepared by the Society's Committee on Educational Diagnosis. L. J. Brueckner, Chairman. Cloth	$4.25
Paper	3.00
*Thirty-fifth Yearbook, 1936, Part I—*The Grouping of Pupils.* Prepared by the Society's Committee. W. W. Coxe, Chairman. Cloth	
*Thirty-fifth Yearbook, 1936, Part II—*Music Education.* Prepared by the Society's Committee. W. L. Uhl, Chairman. Cloth	
*Thirty-sixth Yearbook, 1937, Part I—*The Teaching of Reading.* Prepared by the Society's Committee. W. S. Gray, Chairman. Cloth	
Thirty-sixth Yearbook, 1937, Part II—*International Understanding through the Public-School Curriculum.* Prepared by the Society's Committee. I. L. Kandel, Chairman. Cloth	2.50
Paper	1.75
Thirty-seventh Yearbook, 1938, Part I—*Guidance in Educational Institutions.* Prepared by the Society's Committee. G. N. Kefauver, Chairman. Cloth	2.50
Paper	1.75
Thirty-seventh Yearbook, 1938, Part II—*The Scientific Movement in Education.* Prepared by the Society's Committee. F. N. Freeman, Chairman. Paper	3.00
Thirty-eighth Yearbook, 1939, Part I—*Child Development and the Curriculum.* Prepared by the Society's Committee. Carleton Washburne, Chairman. Paper	2.50
Thirty-eighth Yearbook, 1939, Part II—*General Education in the American College.* Prepared by the Society's Committee. Alvin Eurich, Chairman. Cloth	2.75
Paper	2.00
Thirty-ninth Yearbook, 1940, Part I—*Intelligence: Its Nature and Nurture. Comparative and Critical Exposition.* Prepared by the Society's Committee. G. D. Stoddard, Chairman. Paper	2.25
Thirty-ninth Yearbook, 1940, Part II—*Intelligence: Its Nature and Nurture. Original Studies and Experiments.* Prepared by the Society's Committee. G. D. Stoddard, Chairman. Cloth	3.00
Paper	2.25
Fortieth Yearbook, 1941—*Art in American Life and Education.* Prepared by the Society's Committee. Thomas Munro, Chairman. Cloth	4.00
Paper	3.00
Forty-first Yearbook, 1942, Part I—*Philosophies of Education.* Prepared by the Society's Committee. John S. Brubacher, Chairman. Cloth	3.00
Paper	2.25
Forty-first Yearbook, 1942, Part II—*The Psychology of Learning.* Prepared by the Society's Committee. T. R. McConnell, Chairman. Cloth	3.25
Paper	2.50
Forty-second Yearbook, 1943, Part I—*Vocational Education.* Prepared by the Society's Committee. F. J. Keller, Chairman. Cloth	3.25
Paper	2.50
Forty-second Yearbook, 1943, Part II—*The Library in General Education.* Prepared by the Society's Committee. L. R. Wilson, Chairman. Cloth	3.00
Paper	2.25
Forty-third Yearbook, 1944, Part I—*Adolescence.* Prepared by the Society's Committee. Harold E. Jones, Chairman. Cloth	3.00
Paper	2.25
Forty-third Yearbook, 1944, Part II—*Teaching Language in the Elementary School.* Prepared by the Society's Committee. M. R. Trabue, Chairman. Cloth	2.75
Paper	2.00
Forty-fourth Yearbook, 1945, Part I—*American Education in the Postwar Period: Curriculum Reconstruction.* Prepared by the Society's Committee. Ralph W. Tyler, Chairman. Cloth	3.00
Paper	2.25
Forty-fourth Yearbook, 1945, Part II—*American Education in the Postwar Period: Structural Reorganization.* Prepared by the Society's Committee. Bess Goodykoontz, Chairman. Cloth	3.00
Paper	2.25
Forty-fifth Yearbook, 1946, Part I—*The Measurement of Understanding.* Prepared by the Society's Committee. William A. Brownell, Chairman. Cloth	3.00
Paper	2.25
Forty-fifth Yearbook, 1946, Part II—*Changing Conceptions in Educational Administration.* Prepared by the Society's Committee. Alonzo G. Grace, Chairman. Cloth	2.50
Paper	1.75
Forty-sixth Yearbook, 1947, Part I—*Science Education in American Schools.* Prepared by the Society's Committee. Victor H. Noll, Chairman. Paper	3.75
Forty-sixth Yearbook, 1947, Part II—*Early Childhood Education.* Prepared by the Society's Committee. N. Searle Light, Chairman. Cloth	4.50
Paper	3.75
Forty-seventh Yearbook, 1948, Part I—*Juvenile Delinquency and the Schools.* Prepared by the Society's Committee. Ruth Strang. Chairman. Cloth	4.50
Forty-seventh Yearbook, 1948, Part II—*Reading in the High School and College.* Prepared by the Society's Committee. William S. Gray, Chairman. Cloth	4.50
Paper	3.75
Forty-eighth Yearbook, 1949, Part I—*Audio-visual Materials of Instruction.* Prepared by the Society's Committee. Stephen M. Corey, Chairman. Cloth	4.50
Forty-eighth Yearbook, 1949, Part II—*Reading in the Elementary School.* Prepared by the Society's Committee. Arthur I. Gates, Chairman. Cloth	4.50
Paper	3.75
Forty-ninth Yearbook, 1950, Part I—*Learning and Instruction.* Prepared by the Society's Committee. G. Lester Anderson, Chairman. Cloth	4.50
Paper	3.75
Forty-ninth Yearbook, 1950, Part II—*The Education of Exceptional Children.* Prepared by the Society's Committee. Samuel A. Kirk, Chairman. Cloth	4.50
Paper	3.75

POSTPAID PRICE

Fiftieth Yearbook, 1951, Part I—*Graduate Study in Education*. Prepared by the Society's Board of Directors. Ralph W. Tyler, Chairman. Cloth $4.50
Paper 3.75

Fiftieth Yearbook, 1951, Part II—*The Teaching of Arithmetic*. Prepared by the Society's Committee. G. T. Buswell, Chairman. Cloth 4.50
Paper 3.75

Fifty-first Yearbook, 1952, Part I—*General Education*. Prepared by the Society's Committee. T. R. McConnell, Chairman. Cloth 4.50
Paper 3.75

Fifty-first Yearbook, 1952, Part II—*Education in Rural Communities*. Prepared by the Society's Committee. Ruth Strang, Chairman. Cloth 4.50
Paper 3.75

Fifty-second Yearbook, 1953, Part I—*Adapting the Secondary-School Program to the Needs of Youth*. Prepared by the Society's Committee. William G. Brink, Chairman. Cloth 4.50
Paper 3.75

Fifty-second Yearbook, 1953, Part II—*The Community School*. Prepared by the Society's Committee. Maurice F. Seay, Chairman. Cloth 4.50
Paper 3.75

Fifty-third Yearbook, 1954, Part I—*Citizen Co-operation for Better Public Schools*. Prepared by the Society's Committee. Edgar L. Morphet, Chairman. Cloth 4.50
Paper 3.75

Fifty-third Yearbook, 1954, Part II—*Mass Media and Education*. Prepared by the Society's Committee. Edgar Dale, Chairman. Cloth 4.50
Paper 3.75

Fifty-fourth Yearbook, 1955, Part I—*Modern Philosophies and Education*. Prepared by the Society's Committee. John S. Brubacher, Chairman. Cloth 4.50
Paper 3.75

Fifty-fourth Yearbook, 1955, Part II—*Mental Health in Modern Education*. Prepared by the Society's Committee. Paul A. Witty, Chairman. Cloth 4.50
Paper 3.75

Fifty-fifth Yearbook, 1956, Part I—*The Public Junior College*. Prepared by the Society's Committee. B. Lamar Johnson, Chairman. Cloth 4.50
Paper 3.75

Fifty-fifth Yearbook, 1956, Part II—*Adult Reading*. Prepared by the Society's Committee. David H. Clift, Chairman. Cloth 4.50
Paper 3.75

Fifty-sixth Yearbook, 1957, Part I—*In-service Education of Teachers, Supervisors, and Administrators*. Prepared by the Society's Committee. Stephen M. Corey, Chairman. Cloth 4.50
Paper 3.75

Fifty-sixth Yearbook, 1957, Part II—*Social Studies in the Elementary School*. Prepared by the Society's Committee. Ralph C. Preston, Chairman. Cloth 4.50
Paper 3.75

Fifty-seventh Yearbook, 1958, Part I—*Basic Concepts in Music Education*. Prepared by the Society's Committee. Thurber H. Madison, Chairman. Cloth 4.50
Paper 3.75

Fifty-seventh Yearbook, 1958, Part II—*Education for the Gifted*. Prepared by the Society's Committee. Robert J. Havighurst, Chairman. Cloth 4.50
Paper 3.75

Fifty-seventh Yearbook, 1958, Part III—*The Integration of Educational Experiences*. Prepared by the Society's Committee. Paul L. Dressel, Chairman. Cloth 4.50
Paper 3.75

Fifty-eighth Yearbook, 1959, Part I—*Community Education: Principles and Practices from World-wide Experience*. Prepared by the Society's Committee. C. O. Arndt, Chairman. Cloth 4.50
Paper 3.75

Fifty-eighth Yearbook, 1959, Part II—*Personnel Services in Education*. Prepared by the Society's Committee. Melvene D. Hardee, Chairman. Cloth 4.50
Paper 3.75

Fifty-ninth Yearbook, 1960, Part I—*Rethinking Science Education*. Prepared by the Society's Committee. J. Darrell Barnard, Chairman. Cloth 4.50
Paper 3.75

Fifty-ninth Yearbook, 1960, Part II—*The Dynamics of Instructional Groups*. Prepared by the Society's Committee. Gale E. Jensen, Chairman. Cloth 4.50
Paper 3.75

Sixtieth Yearbook, 1961, Part I—*Development in and through Reading*. Prepared by the Society's Committee. Paul A. Witty, Chairman. Cloth 5.00
Paper 4.25

Sixtieth Yearbook, 1961, Part II—*Social Forces Influencing American Education*. Prepared by the Society's Committee. Ralph W. Tyler, Chairman. Cloth 4.50
Paper 3.75

Sixty-first Yearbook, 1962, Part I—*Individualizing Instruction*. Prepared by the Society's Committee. Fred. T. Tyler, Chairman. Cloth 4.50

Sixty-first Yearbook, 1962, Part II—*Education for the Professions*. Prepared by the Society's Committee. G. Lester Anderson, Chairman. Cloth 4.50

Sixty-second Yearbook, 1963, Part I—*Child Psychology*. Prepared by the Society's Committee. Harold W. Stevenson,Editor. Cloth 6.50

Sixty-second Yearbook, 1963, Part II—*The Impact and Improvement of School Testing Programs*. Prepared by the Society's Committee. Warren G. Findley, Editor. Cloth 4.50

Distributed by
THE UNIVERSITY OF CHICAGO PRESS, CHICAGO 37, ILLINOIS
1963